D1531737

Mental Disorders in the Social Environment

FOUNDATIONS OF SOCIAL WORK KNOWLEDGE SERIES

FOUNDATIONS OF SOCIAL WORK KNOWLEDGE SERIES

Frederic G. Reamer, Series Editor

Social work has a unique history, purpose, perspective, and method. The primary purpose of this series is to articulate these distinct qualities and to define and explore the ideas, concepts, and skills that together constitute social work's intellectual foundations and boundaries and its emerging issues and concerns.

To accomplish this goal, the series will publish a cohesive collection of books that address both the core knowledge of the profession and its newly emerging topics. The core is defined by the evolving consensus, as primarily reflected in the Council of Social Work Education's Curriculum Policy Statement, concerning what courses accredited social work education programs must include in their curricula. The series will be characterized by an emphasis on the widely embraced ecological perspective; attention to issues concerning direct and indirect practice; and emphasis on cultural diversity and multiculturalism, social justice, oppression, populations at risk, and social work values and ethics. The series will have a dual focus on practice traditions and emerging issues and concepts.

David G. Gil, *Confronting Injustice and Oppression: Concepts and Strategies for Social Workers*

George Alan Appleby and Jeane W. Anastas, *Not Just a Passing Phase: Social Work with Gay, Lesbian, and Bisexual People*

Frederic G. Reamer, *Social Work Research and Evaluation Skills*

Pallassana R. Balgopal, *Social Work Practice with Immigrants and Refugees*

Dennis Saleeby, *Human Behavior and Social Environments: A Biopsychosocial Approach*

Frederic G. Reamer, *Tangled Relationships: Managing Boundary Issues in the Human Services*

Roger A. Lohmann and Nancy L. Lohmann, *Social Administration*

David M. Austin, *Human Services Management: Organizational Leadership in Social Work Practice*

Joan Shireman, *Critical Issues in Child Welfare*

Mental Disorders

IN THE SOCIAL ENVIRONMENT

Critical Perspectives

Stuart A. Kirk, Editor

COLUMBIA UNIVERSITY PRESS   NEW YORK

Columbia University Press
Publishers Since 1893
New York Chichester, West Sussex

Library of Congress Cataloging-in-Publication Data

Mental disorders in the social environment : critical perspectives /
    Stuart A. Kirk, editor.
        p. cm. — (Foundations of social work knowledge)
        ISBN 0-231-12870-3 (cloth : alk. paper) — ISBN 0-231-12871-1
(pbk. : alk. paper)
        1. Mental illness—Treatment. 2. Social psychiatry. 3. Community
mental health services. I. Kirk, Stuart A., 1945– II. Series.

    RC455.M4425 2004
    362.2—dc22

                                                        2004052790

Columbia University Press books are printed on permanent and
durable acid-free paper.
Printed in the United States of America
c 10 9 8 7 6 5 4 3 2 1
p 10 9 8 7 6 5 4 3 2 1

This book is dedicated to Ben, Colin, and Lucas,
in the hope that they, in due course, develop critical perspectives.

Contents

Acknowledgments

This book is the product of the contributors, who have my heartfelt gratitude for their willingness to work with me on this project. I approached them to contribute because of their expertise and wisdom, as well as their passion for these topics. The book, however, changed character as I collaborated with them and they offered their own ideas about the content. In the end, I am honored to have corralled such an eminent group that includes some of the most respected social work scholars, as well as some bright, younger scholars who are early in their academic careers. While each of them needs to "own" only his or her chapter, I bear responsibility for the overall shape of the volume.

One eminent contributor to this book, William J. Reid, a longtime friend and colleague, died suddenly while this manuscript was being readied for publication. With his passing, the social work profession lost one of its stellar scholars. I, and several generations of social work researchers, will miss him.

The responsibilities of a book editor are not eagerly sought among otherwise active authors. Some who edit a book like this swear that they won't do it again. Other editors complain that it would have been easier writing their own book than getting others to contribute on schedule. As the deadline for all chapters arrived, Rick Reamer, the one who roped me into this task, inquired jokingly if I was at the end of my tether. Not at all, I replied. In fact, with only routine prompting and reminders, the authors were responsive and responsible. I'm in their debt.

I'm also in the debt of others whose general support is always appreciated, if infrequently acknowledged. My colleagues in the Department of Social Welfare at UCLA, especially our recent chair, Ted Benjamin, have provided a supportive social environment, stimulating students, and a much-needed sabbatical to finish this book. Carol Ann Koz not only tolerates me during these book projects but also keeps my life in balance with her grace, her generosity of spirit, and her lighthearted willingness to laugh with me. I couldn't do it without her.

Stuart A. Kirk
Ojai Valley, California

Contributors

John R. Bola is an assistant professor in the School of Social Work at the University of Southern California. He has written about the effectiveness of psychosocial interventions in early-episode psychosis and about identifying treatment-responsive subgroups as a way to begin individualizing treatment, particularly for those individuals who do not require antipsychotic medications. He is coauthor with Loren Mosher of "The Treatment of Acute Psychosis Without Neuroleptics: Two-Year Outcomes from the Soteria Project" in the *Journal of Nervous and Mental Disease* (2003); and "Predicting Drug-Free Treatment Response in Acute Psychosis from the Soteria Project" and "Clashing Ideologies or Scientific Discourse?" both published in *Schizophrenia Bulletin* (2002).

David Cohen is a professor in the School of Social Work at Florida International University. His articles on psychotropic drugs have been published in journals in social work, sociology, psychology, and medicine. His edited or coauthored books include *Challenging the Therapeutic State* (1990) and *Your Drug May Be Your Problem* (1999). In 2003 he received the American Sociological Association's Freidson Award for outstanding publication in medical sociology. E-mail: cohenda@fiu.edu

Julanne Colvin, M.A., M.S.W., is coordinator of child and family services at Liberty Resources, a large human services agency in central New York. She is responsible for the design and development of home-based, school-based, and outpatient treatment programs for children and families involved with the child welfare, probation, or family court systems. She is also a doctoral student at the State University of New York at Albany. E-mail: jburton2@twcny.rr.com

Kevin Corcoran is a professor of social work at Portland State University. He has an M.A. from the University of Colorado, an M.S.W. and a Ph.D. from the University of Pittsburgh, and a J.D. from the University of Houston. He has been involved in research since 1973, and his métiers include psychometrics and methodology. He is currently part of an evaluation of substance abuse prevention among those who are parenting adolescents. He has written many articles and book chapters, as well as eight books, including *Measures for Clinical Practice* (with Joel Fischer) and *Maneuvering the Maze of Managed Care* (with Vikki Vandiver).

Donald T. Dickson is a professor and the director of the doctoral program at the School of Social Work of Rutgers University. He has written about legal issues in the human services, mental health, and social work. His recent books include *HIV, AIDS, and the Law: Legal Issues for Social Work Practice and Policy* (2002) and *Confidentiality and Privacy in Social Work* (1998).

Tonya Edmond is an assistant professor at the George Warren Brown School of Social Work at Washington University in St. Louis. Her research interests include violence against women, trauma, and practice effectiveness. She is currently conducting a national survey to identify the theoretical and intervention preferences of direct service providers working in domestic violence and rape crisis centers.

William M. Epstein teaches social welfare policy at the University of Nevada, Las Vegas. He has published five books and numerous articles covering the politics, economics, and sociology of American social welfare. His books include *The Illusion of Psychotherapy* (1995) and *American Policy Making: Welfare as Ritual* (2002). E-mail: wepstein@ccmail.nevada.edu

Eileen Gambrill is a professor and holds the Hutto Patterson Chair in Child and Family Studies in the School of Social Welfare, University of California at Berkeley. Her areas of interest include professional decision making, ethics, the integration of research and practice, and propaganda in the helping professions. Her books include *Critical Thinking in Clinical Practice* (1990), *Social Work Practice: A Critical Thinker's Guide* (1997), *Critical Thinking for Social Workers: Exercises for the Helping Professions* (with Len Gibbs, 1997), and *Controversial Issues in Social Work Ethics, Values, and Obligations* (with Robert Pruger, 1997). E-mail: gambrill@associate.berkeley.edu

Tomi Gomory is an assistant professor in the School of Social Work at Florida State University. He has written about mental health policy and services, as well as about issues pertaining to the impact of epistemology (principally of the Popperian fallibilist sort) and theory development on social work education, intervention, and policy. His latest research examines the extent to which social work programs offer students the best-tested information available about psychopathology, whether or not these findings conform to conventional and institutional assumptions about mental "disorderliness." E-mail: tgomory@mailer.fsu.edu

Stephen Gorin holds a Ph.D. from Brandeis University and an M.S.W. from the State University of New York at Stony Brook. He is a professor in the Department of Social Work, Plymouth State University. The author of many articles, he serves as editor of the National Health Line for the journal *Health and Social Work*. He is coauthor of *Health and Health Care Policy: A Social Work Perspective*.

Matthew O. Howard is a professor of social work and psychiatry at the University of Michigan in Ann Arbor. He is also the recipient of two grants from the National Institute on Drug Abuse and an author of more than eighty articles in the mental health practice area.

Derek K. Hsieh received his Ph.D. in social welfare from the University of California at Los Angeles and is the clinic coordinator at South Bay Children's Health Center and Child Guidance Clinic in Torrance, California. He is the coauthor of a series of articles on *DSM* that have appeared in *Social Service Review, Social Work Research, Journal of Child Psychology and Psychiatry, American Journal of Orthopsychiatry,* and other journals. E-mail: dkhsieh@yahoo.com

Stuart A. Kirk is a professor and holds the Marjorie Crump Chair in the Department of Social Welfare at the University of California at Los Angeles. He has written extensively about mental health services, research utilization, and psychiatric diagnosis. Among his books are *The Selling of DSM* (1992) and *Making Us Crazy* (1997) (both with Herb Kutchins) and *Science and Social Work: A Critical Appraisal* (2002, with William J. Reid). He received the 2003 award for Significant Lifetime Achievement in Social Work Education from the Council on Social Work Education. E-mail: kirk@ucla.edu

Amy LaPan is a doctoral student in social welfare at the University of California at Los Angeles. She received her M.S.W. from California State University at Sacramento. Her research has focused on the impact of genetic technologies on social work practice and policy. E-mail: alapan@ucla.edu

Mark A. Mattaini is an associate professor and the director of the doctoral program in social work at Jane Addams College of Social Work, University of Illinois at Chicago. His writing and research focus on social work assessment, practice theory, ecobehavioral practice, and violence prevention. He is author/coeditor of eight books, including *Finding Solutions to Social Problems: Behavioral Strategies for Change* (1996), *Clinical Practice with Individuals* (1997), *Clinical Intervention with Families* (1999), *Peace Power for Adolescents: Strategies for a Culture of Nonviolence* (2001), and *Foundations of Social Work Practice: A Graduate Text* (2002).

Cynthia Moniz holds a Ph.D. from Brandeis University and an M.S.W. from the State University of New York at Stony Brook. She is a professor in and chair of the Department of Social Work, Plymouth State University. She is coauthor of *Health and Health Care Policy: A Social Work Perspective.*

Tally Moses is an assistant professor of social work at the University of Wisconsin, Madison. She has worked with children, adolescents, young adults, and families in mental health settings. She is interested in the way individuals form treatment relationships and respond to various forms of treatment. Her current research interests involve the study of the psychosocial impacts of drug treatment. E-mail: tmoses@ucla.edu

The late **Loren R. Mosher, M.D.,** was a psychiatrist and the director of Soteria Associates, a mental health consulting firm in San Diego. He was also a clinical professor of psychiatry at the University of California at San Diego. He researched and published extensively on the psychosocial treatment of schizophrenia. His book *Community Mental Health: A Practical Guide* (with Lorenzo Burti, 1994) has been translated into five languages.

William R. Nugent, Ph.D., is a professor and the director of the doctoral program in the College of Social Work at the University of Tennessee. He has published numerous articles on measurement and assessment issues and is coauthor (with Jackie Sieppert and Walter Hudson) of the recently published *Practice Evaluation for the Twenty-first Century.* He has also published articles on the use of various quantitative approaches to data analysis and on the relationship between participation in victim-offender mediation and subsequent delinquent behavior.

Deborah B. Pitts is a clinical faculty member of the Department of Occupational Science and Occupational Therapy at the University of Southern California. For more than twenty-five years she has practiced and served in leadership positions in community mental health and psychiatric rehabilitation services targeting people diagnosed with psychiatric disabilities. She is responsible for both classroom and fieldwork teaching for entry-level and advanced occupational therapy practitioners. E-mail: pittsd@usc.edu

Tony Platt, a professor of social work at California State University at Sacramento, is a member of the editorial board of *Social Justice* and author of *The Child Savers: The Invention of Delinquency* and *E. Franklin Frazier Reconsidered.* E-mail: amplatt@earthlink.net

Kathleen J. Pottick is a professor in the School of Social Work and a core member of the Institute for Health, Health Care Policy, and Aging Research at Rutgers University. Her research focuses on understanding barriers to the provision of effective mental health services for youth and developing strategies for removing them. She is currently investigating racial and ethnic disparities in service utilization in the United States for youth with serious emotional disorders. E-mail: pottick@rci.rutgers.edu

Frederic G. Reamer is a professor in the graduate program of the School of Social Work at Rhode Island College. He has served as a social worker in mental health, correctional, and housing agencies, as well as in a governor's office. He chaired the committee that wrote the current Code of Ethics of the National Association of Social Workers. His most recent books include *Tangled Relationships: Managing Boundary Issues in the Human Services* (2001), *The Social Work Ethics Audit* (2001), and *Criminal Lessons: Case Studies and Commentary on Crime and Justice* (2003). E-mail: freamer@ric.edu

The late **William J. Reid** was a distinguished professor at the School of Social Welfare of the State University of New York at Albany, where he taught research methods and clinical practice. His most recent books are *Gerontological Social Work: A Task-Centered Approach* (with Matthias Naleppa, 2003), *Educational Supervision in Social Work* (with John Caspi, 2002), and *Science and Social Work: A Critical Appraisal* (with Stuart Kirk, 2002), all published by Columbia University Press.

Stephen M. Rose is a professor of social work at the University of New England and a Fulbright professor in the Department of Social Policy and Social Work at the University of Helsinki. He has focused on and written about empowerment-based practice for some time. His current research addresses the social determinants of health and chronic illness and empowerment in the health sector. E-mail: srose@une.edu

Sarah Rosenfield is an associate professor of sociology and a core member of the Institute for Health, Health Care Policy, and Aging Research at Rutgers University. Her research focuses on gender differences in mental health problems and on how these differences vary by race/ethnicity. She also is interested in empowerment issues among individuals with severe mental illness. E-mail: slrosen@rci.rutgers.edu

Dennis Saleebey is a professor of social welfare in the School of Social Welfare at the University of Kansas. In 2002–2003 he was the Moses Visiting Distinguished Professor at Hunter College School of Social Work. He has written about the epistemology of the professions, the brain and behavior, and the strengths perspective in practice. He is author/editor of *The Strengths Perspective in Social Work Practice,* 3d ed. (2002) and the author of *Human Behavior and Social Environments: A Biopsychosocial Approach* (2001). E-mail: denniss@ku.edu

Steven P. Segal is a professor and the director of the Mental Health and Social Welfare Research Group in the School of Social Welfare, University of California, Berkeley; the director of the Center for Self-Help Research, Public Health Institute; and the codirector and co-principal investigator of the NIMH/NRSA Pre/Post Doctoral Research Training Program in Financing and Service Delivery in Mental Health, School of Public Health and School of Social Welfare, University of California at Berkeley. He has received senior Fulbright research and lecture awards in Australia, the United Kingdom, and Italy, as well as a Distinguished Investigator Award from NARSAD and the Distinguished Career Award for the Society for Social Work and Research. His research interests include long-term community and residential care, civil commitment, the assessment of dangerousness and the quality of psychiatric emergency care in general hospital psychiatric emergency rooms, and consumer roles in the provision of mental health services.

Bruce A. Thyer is the dean of the School of Social Work at Florida State University. Among his recent edited books are *Handbook of Empirical Social Work Practice* (with John S. Wodarski), *International Perspectives on Evidence-based Practice in Social Work* (with Mansoor A. F. Kazi), and *The Philosophical Legacy of Behaviorism.* E-mail: Bthyer@mailer.fsu.edu

Michael G. Vaughn is a fellow of the National Institute on Drug Abuse and a doctoral student at the George Warren Brown School of Social Work at Washington University in St. Louis. His current research interests are in the areas of adolescent and childhood substance abuse, youth violence, syntheses of prevention and intervention research, and conceptual issues in science and social work. E-mail: mvaughn@gwbmail.wustl.edu

Jerome C. Wakefield is a university professor and a professor in the Ehrenkranz School of Social Work at New York University. His writing focuses on conceptual foundations of the mental health professions. He also holds a second doctorate, in philosophy, from the University of California at Berkeley. Recent publications appeared in *Archives of General Psychiatry* (on problems of measurement in psychiatric epidemiology) and *Minds and Machines* (on conceptual foundations of artificial intelligence). E-mail: jw111@nyu.edu

Mental Disorders in the Social Environment

Chapter 1
Introduction: Critical Perspectives

Stuart A. Kirk

The origins of this book are older than a few of its younger contributors. It dates from the 1960s, when I was an undergraduate student at the University of California at Berkeley. While my political education during those years took place in Sproul Plaza and outside classrooms, my professors were no strangers to intellectual controversy. At what was arguably ground zero for a decade of political, social, and cultural turbulence in the United States (Cohen and Zelnik 2002; Rorabaugh 1989), few courses in the social sciences, to which I had gravitated from engineering, could be taught without addressing what was taking place in the local streets. The civil rights movement, community organizing, civil disobedience, nonviolent protest, free speech, and antiwar marches were as much daily activities as abstract concepts. Questioning authority was standard operating procedure. Political radicalism was normative; what passed as received wisdom was critically scrutinized; alternative possibilities, however seemingly improbable, were seriously considered. The ethos of the time and place was to question the underlying assumptions of the dominant paradigms, elucidating their subtle biases and exposing their ruling class functions. Being critical minded was not just a useful attitude for intellectual work on campus; it was a moral obligation of citizenship. That was a long time ago.

In this context—social environment, if you will—I was first exposed to the concept of mental illness from many different academic perspectives. Psychoanalytic perspectives had radically rewritten the understanding of madness and at the time dominated American psychiatry, providing a paradigm for the training of psychiatrists to treat the mentally ill, as well as a framework to reinterpret social and cultural life. The psychoanalytic hegemony, however, was being contested. Academic behavioral psychologists offered views of mental disorder and treatment that didn't rely on suppositions about infant development, frustrated drives, unconscious defense mechanisms, and transference. Sociologists viewed the mental health field and psychoanalysis very skeptically, questioning whether mental illness really existed as anything more than a socially constructed fiction to serve the interests of those in the tinkering trades, as Erving Goffman in *Asylums: Essays on the Social Situation of Mental Patients and Other Inmates* referred to mental health professionals. Feminists, racial minorities, gay activists, and others were also beginning to question the psychiatric establishment (see, for example, Phyllis Chesler, *Women and Madness*; Alexander Thomas and Samuel Sillen, *Racism and Psychiatry*; Ronald Bayer, *Homosexuality and American Psychiatry: The Politics of Diagnosis*; and Seymour Halleck, *The Politics of Therapy*).

These diverse observers had sharply different viewpoints, professional interests, values, and beliefs—and they weren't shy or apologetic about espousing them. Fundamental questions about the nature, causes, and treatment of mental illnesses were being actively debated. Was long-term psychotherapy effective? Did state asylums do more good than harm to patients? Were specific child-rearing practices or family dynamics contributing to mental illnesses in later life? Why were more women than men being treated in mental health clinics? Were the poor discriminated against when they sought help? Psychoanalytic assumptions about the causes and treatment of mental disorders, which had long escaped from the elementary requirements of scientific research, were now being held up to scientific scrutiny. As a young student, I thought that this was an exciting arena.

But what was more exciting, these academic controversies spilled out into the world beyond the university. Mental health practices and policies were in flux. The preeminence of long-term psychoanalytic psychotherapy gave way to multiple new therapeutic approaches from milieu therapy, family and group therapy, to crisis intervention. Social scientists and community-minded mental health professionals pressed for the reform of massive state psychiatric hospitals, which for more than fifty years had provided very little treatment or rehabilitation and had served instead as custodial institutions warehousing the displaced, decrepit, and dysfunctional. Advocates of new psychotropic medications began hailing them as miracle drugs, as keys to the effective treatment of mental disorder. Champions of civil liberties successfully challenged psychiatric authority in the courts and in the process rewrote the guidelines for involuntary commitment to state hospitals. The patients' rights movement confronted professional authority, pushed for the end of coercive treatments, and insisted on honest disclosure and informed consent. The federal government for the first time got actively involved in mental health under President John F. Kennedy. Congress, in fact, passed the historic community mental health centers legislation of 1963. Social workers, if they were not leaders in these developments, were often supportive and involved.

Of course, none of these developments were without shortcomings and unanticipated consequences, and some, like deinstitutionalization, have contributed to enduring problems, like homelessness, that still confound the psychiatric community. The point is that ideas that at other times might have remained confined to seminar discussions appeared to have real-life consequences in the society.

Needing a way to both avoid the military draft for the Vietnam War and find a future job, I thought that the profession of social work was where I could be involved in these psychiatric controversies and policy developments. Although it was a partially naïve decision, since I knew very little about social work, it was a reasonable one. After all, the profession did have a commitment to taking a broad, social-minded view of individual troubles, psychiatric and otherwise, and a commitment to social reform. What I found in social work was that the profession had a less critical view of mental health problems and practices than I expected. To understand this unexpectedly more conservative view required delving into the evolution of social work's ties to psychiatry.

Social Work and Mental Disorders

Social casework, the profession of social work's primary method, took a psychological turn early in the twentieth century. This was consistent with other developments of the time, including the initiation and widespread use of intelligence and other tests of individual cognitive differences, new concerns about the significance of child development, the shift of emphasis from insanity to a more preventive focus on "mental hygiene," and the invention of child guidance clinics (Leiby 1978). Freudian theory was rising in popularity, and the purpose of the casework method of "friendly visiting" was being reconceptualized, shifting from its initial purpose of investigating applicants for assistance to determine whether they were worthy but in need of moral exhortation (Lubove 1969) to a view of casework as a therapeutic relationship. This was buttressed in midcentury by the increasing popularization of social and psychological science that provided the added legitimacy for social workers to view their work as applied science, thereby enhancing their claim to professional status.

The model adopted for this professionalization mimicked medicine—the possession of technical know-how based on science and theory, which guided diagnosis, followed by treatment. The style of psychiatric social work that emerged from the child guidance clinics served as the avenue to enhanced status for the whole profession (Leiby 1978). Thus medicine, particularly psychiatry, became the major orientation with which social work self-consciously strove toward professionalization.

Psychiatry, too, was changing in a compatible direction. Community-minded psychiatrists such as Adolf Meyer attempted to move psychiatry from its isolation in the state asylums and its extreme organically oriented views of behavior into the community, with a greater sensitivity to the social environmental influences on psychopathology (see, for example, the discussion in chapter 3 of Lubove 1969). Social workers found a useful niche within this movement and helped to further it. Social work shared objectives with the changing profession of psychiatry, as both professions were trying to account for behavior in functional, dynamic terms. But the close association also created troublesome problems as social workers tried to differentiate themselves from both psychiatrists and nurses (Lubove 1969:78).

Social workers were never the dominant professionals in the field of mental health in terms of power, influence, or legitimacy. For a century their involvement has been guided by medical authorities, and their roles, while varied, have been viewed as supplementary. As patients were admitted to or discharged from psychiatric facilities, social workers traditionally identified and coordinated community resources, managed referrals, gathered information from members of the family and others to formulate social diagnoses, and assisted families with challenges arising from the hospitalization of patients or their return to the community. The "treatment" of the identified patient was usually reserved for the doctor who had been trained to provide therapy, while the social worker worked with the family and community. But this arrangement was never fully satisfactory, since the mother lode of status came with providing psychotherapy.

The opportunity for social workers to be therapists opened up, and it was irresistible. As outpatient services expanded in the last third of the twentieth century, there was much more demand for psychiatric services than psychiatrists could possibly meet. Psychotherapy, once the tonic for the wealthy, became a type of interpersonal assistance sought increasingly by the middle and working classes. Partly to meet this expanding need, various short-term outpatient services were offered, some of them developed by social workers (Reid and Shyne 1969). These new forms of therapy quickly achieved ascendancy over long-term psychoanalytic-oriented therapy. More important, these new services didn't appear to require special medical training, a situation that opened doors to social workers while making the contributions of psychiatrists in community mental health appear much less distinctive. In fact, many professionals working in mental health—psychologists, rehabilitation specialists, psychiatric nurses, counselors, and social workers—were quick to offer psychotherapeutic treatment services to patients, thereby greatly blurring the roles of all mental health "providers."

Despite these expanding opportunities, the close association of social work with psychiatry has been controversial. As Lubove states: "The emergence of psychiatric social work not only reinforced the quest for skills and technique in casework, but foreshadowed major changes in the entire structure of theory and practice" (1969:79).

> Psychiatry seemed at first like an unmixed blessing which would elevate social work to its cherished professional status. The psychiatric influence, however, created two serious long-range problems. The first was that of defining a satisfactory relation between social work and social reform. The social worker's primary responsibility was service to individuals, but this did not rule out the interest in social, economic, and cultural conditions typical of the Progressive era. In embracing psychiatry, social workers undoubtedly acquired a more sophisticated awareness of the subtleties and ambiguities of personality, but in the process they undermined their capacity to promote institutional change and deal effectively with problems of mass deprivation in an urban society.
> (117)

> The second problem was that the close affiliation with psychiatry

> threatened the professional identity which social workers were so anxious to attain. If psychiatric knowledge and technique were fundamental to social work, then what distinguished the social worker from the psychiatrist, and social casework from psychotherapy, except the social worker's inferior training?
> (117)

As psychiatry became more community-minded in the 1920s, social work's partnership with it appeared to make strategic sense for both professions. Such partnership, or at least a similar mission, was also apparent in the 1960s and 1970s in the heyday of the community mental health movement. Working closely with community psychiatry seemed less problematic for social workers than Lubove feared, because community psychiatrists had gained a measure of stature within psychiatry. These ties became more problematic for social work by the 1990s, as community psychiatrists and their allies fell from grace and psychiatry took a hard turn into biomedicine (Kirk 1999; Luhrmann 2000), leaving the psychodynamic psychiatrists, community psychiatrists, and those interested in the healing power of therapeutic relationships without as much influence.

The relationship of social work to psychiatry produced tensions, apparent for more than half a century, and these strains have periodically expressed themselves in debates in social work. Has social work in its quest for professional status become too closely associated with psychiatry and too medicalized? Has it jeopardized its broad social environmental perspective, becoming too therapeutically oriented (see, for example, the critique by Specht and Courtney [1994])? Has its reliance on the trappings of psychiatric diagnosis and treatment warped its ability to act independently? Has the focus on the therapeutic relationship gutted social work's commitment to social reform? And now, after decades of investment in time and effort to link social work's identity with professional psychiatry, is social work once again marginalized as psychiatry has turned away from a concern with the social environment to a focus increasingly on brain chemistry and the latest pharmaceuticals? These are the kinds of important questions—questions very much in the spirit of intellectual debate that was alive in the Berkeley of my youth—that need continuing examination.

The Shifting Landscape of Mental Disorder

The field of mental health is not a stable domain; it has constantly shifting terrain. In terms of personnel, it has been contested territory, with ministers, social reformers, politicians, and physicians all struggling for jurisdiction (Abbott 1988; Abbott 1995; Rothman 1971; Starr 1982). Jurisdiction among the mental health professions is constantly contested, negotiated, and gerrymandered. Currently, for example, psychologists fight to gain the authority to write prescriptions—long reserved only for physicians. Social workers serve as administrators, psychoanalysts, or forensic experts. Marriage and family counselors do social work and psychotherapy. Nurses assume positions as managers of community mental health programs, and an array of others from pharmacists to special educators claim some special authority over mental disorder. Psychiatric treatment has evolved from custodial care in state insane asylums overseen by politically appointed, non-medically trained superintendents to a medley of services and therapies offered by many different professions. Even M.B.A.'s with an eye trained on efficiency and the bottom line in managed-care organizations now have an important say in who gets treatment and what that treatment will look like.

One reason for the great diversity of professions and therapies is that the concept of mental disorder itself has changed and broadened immensely. Most conditions defined today by the American Psychiatric Association in its *Diagnostic and Statistical Manual of Mental Disorders (DSM)* as mental disorders (e.g., ADHD, anxiety disorders, personality disorders, etc.) were not viewed as mental illnesses until the latter half of the twentieth century, and some only very recently (e.g., social phobia, tobacco dependency). A hundred years ago, mental illnesses were confined to major, serious conditions—overt psychoses—treated or at least managed, if at all, in state institutions. Most of what today are defined as mental disorders have been viewed in other eras as quirks, moral failings, questionable habits, or common personal idiosyncrasies—clearly not the stuff of pathology or the target of doctoring.

By contrast, today there is a vast array of behaviors that are viewed as possible symptoms of mental disorders—common behaviors such as worrying, feeling sad, having trouble at school, drinking a bit too much, and not sleeping well. Mental illness, once seen as a rare problem afflicting only a few unfortunate souls, is now purported to be as ubiquitous as the common cold, affecting nearly everyone in their lifetimes. Despite the fact that the scientific validity of even such bedrock notions as schizophrenia has been seriously questioned (Boyle 2002), the idea of mental disorder has been mainstreamed, transformed by the medical establishment from serious disabling behaviors into pedestrian, less serious "problems in living" (Kutchins and Kirk 1997). Clearly, this remaking of mental disorder has greatly broadened the psychiatric terrain, but at the expense of making the search for causes and remedies much more complicated and controversial.

Ironically, although psychiatry has spearheaded this effort to make more behaviors "pathological" in the eyes of the public, the potential threat exists that such an expansive medicalization of everyday behaviors will eventually undermine medical authority by appearing to covet too much social and cultural space that has been under the purview of others, such as ministers, social workers, educators, and counselors. Already, there are many professions vying for legitimacy and jurisdiction, which one would expect as the nature of disorder changed and the array of mental health services expanded as well.

Services themselves have changed too. Mental health treatment has become more like outpatient physical health treatment. Once psychiatry succeeded in defining problems in living as the result of internal psychopathology, it became logically inconsistent to "treat" the family, just as it would be peculiar to "treat" the parents for a child with pneumonia. Individuals make short visits to a clinic, where they receive an uncertain diagnosis and a prescription. Reimbursement mechanisms make it more difficult to provide extended psychotherapy or to treat couples or families or individuals in groups. The shortest and most impersonal treatments are favored; the fifteen-minute medication check is replacing psychotherapy as a reimbursable service. Encouraged by the changing way our culture views the use of drugs (Breggin and Breggin 1994; Kramer 1993), pills are very big business. Pharmaceutical companies are steadily making progress, not in eradicating mental disorder for which there has been no diminution over the decades (Whitaker

2001) but toward the more profitable goal, rapidly being achieved, of having all children and adults in the United States taking expensive pills for every disappointment or discomfort in life. The drugging of America, once a feared and despised undercurrent of the counterculture youth of Berkeley, is now relentlessly pursued by the corporate establishment, with incredible success.

The psychiatricization of everyday troubles has its benefits. For example, public views of mental illness have changed dramatically, in the direction of more tolerance and acceptance. Not only has insanity been transformed into a gentler conception of mental disorder, but those who are labeled as mentally disordered are no longer locked in the family cellar, made the subject of whispered rumors, or hustled off after dark to a distant asylum. Those with mental disorders are now less stigmatized, less stereotyped, and much more likely to be as close as one's own family or friends. How rapidly this change has come about can be gauged by the contrast in the public reaction to U.S. senator Thomas Eagleton, the Democratic vice presidential nominee in 1972, who was unkindly scratched from the national ticket when it was learned that he had received psychiatric treatment in the past, versus the mild reaction to Republican presidential candidate George W. Bush in 2000 when it was revealed that he had struggled with a drinking problem. In the intervening years, of course, many prominent people have admitted publicly that they have experienced various problems that are comfortably within the purview of *DSM*. As psychiatric difficulties have been "normalized," mental disorders are more quickly recognized, help is sought sooner, and public support for mental health services has increased.

These benefits have created their own problems. Some have argued that medicalizing so many behaviors and misbehaviors has created the opportunity for the inappropriate use of the "sick role" in which "bad" behavior is socially excused and institutional supports for it are provided, in the form of legal protections and disability benefits. Furthermore, as the willingness to seek help and the number of people who do so have increased, access to care has become much more cumbersome. Seeking help requires more than just an individual screwing up the courage to contact a psychotherapist. First, the costs of office visits for therapy can run more than a hundred dollars per hour, which few people can afford. Many help seekers rely on health insurance, but many citizens don't have access to such benefits. Even among those who do, their insurance companies farm out "behavioral health care" to other companies with gatekeeping responsibilities to decide who qualifies for service and for what kind. These companies may have no direct contact with the individual seeking help. Yet they have the task of negotiating with the primary care provider what the problems seem to be, whether those problems can be considered a diagnosable mental disorder, whether there is a medical necessity to treating them, and who will provide what kind of service and for how long. Needless to say, this bureaucratization of reimbursement for mental health care has altered the nature of seeking help and the therapeutic relationship.

Losing Ground

Social workers are often in the middle of this swirl of cultural currents. They are the ground troops in the battle against mental disorder. Social workers provide more services to those defined as mentally disordered than any other professionals, including psychiatrists, clinical psychologists, and psychiatric nurses. In addition to serving as frontline therapists and case managers, social workers are supervisors, clinic directors, and, at times, commissioners of state mental health departments. Their roles have changed with the evolving theories of mental illness, the rise and fall of other professions, the shifts in funding for services, and the popularity of different treatments. Their multiple vantage points should provide them with a perspective on the vast terrain of mental disorders in America, but if it does, it is a view that has remained difficult to identify or decipher.

For example, I can't find a developed social work point of view of what has been a major transformation in psychiatry, namely the narrowing of the approach to understanding mental disorders. Recent years have seen a huge resurgence of the biomedical approach and a corresponding diminution of concerns with the social environment. The new concern about what once was called organicity is clearly evident at the National Institute of Mental Health, in medical schools and departments of psychiatry, where biochemistry, brain imaging, and genetics are the salient focus of research and training and where psychopharmacology is the treatment of choice. The search for the causes of mental disorder and the exploration of possible treatments have increasingly been restricted to consideration of an individual's internal neurobiology. This narrowing of focus is remarkable in the face of our admitted ignorance of the causes of and effective treatment for most mental disorders. There have been no biochemical discoveries of the cause of mental disorders, no biological markers that can be used to identify mental illness—nor has pharmacological treatment conclusively demonstrated effective ways to prevent, cure, or even safely treat most mental disorders.

Thus we have a curious paradox: psychiatry's biochemical view of the etiology and treatment of personal troubles has become much more narrow, now largely subscribing to the biochemical view despite the shakiness of the scientific evidence, while at the same time the concept of mental disorder has expanded to include problems in living. These are incredibly important matters and should be a focus of debate and analysis in social work, but they rarely are, at least not in any critical fashion.

Social work's failure to critically discuss the implications of the new/old biomedical paradigm of mental disorders is all the more surprising because the paradigm directly diminishes the importance of the social environment as both contributing cause and element of treatment—what is usually considered the province of psychiatric social work. Indeed, the social environment is not merely a peripheral concern of social work as a profession; historically it has been the central, primary focus, the raison d'être, not only in mental health but in other fields of practice as well. The biomedical turn in mental health, under the leadership of a biomedical psychiatry, has undermined the role of the traditional practices of social workers. Practices, such as working with families and groups, advocacy on behalf of clients, development of community level programs and interventions, and concerns with how the broad social environment affects people, including the mentally ill, have been marginalized, as they were early in the twentieth century. One might expect that such an assault on the value of their views would have elicited a thoughtful but critical examination by social workers. Instead, there has been hardly a peep. Clinical psychologists, on the other hand, with some similar concerns have been much more vociferous and critical minded about these developments (see, for example, Fisher and Greenberg, eds., *From Placebo to Panacea: Putting Psychiatric Drugs to the Test*; Beutler and Malik, eds., *Rethinking the DSM: A Psychological Perspective*; Valenstein, *Blaming the Brain: The TRUTH About Drugs and Mental Health*).

There may be many explanations for this silence. For one, social workers are remarkably adaptable. Although they have historically championed the powerless and disenfranchised, their advocacy is usually aimed toward influencing powerful institutions. These are the same powerful institutions, i.e., the political and corporate elites, that the profession depends on financially and otherwise for its own survival. Since social workers usually don't enjoy high status or broad popular support, they have learned to adapt to the priorities of others in order to get by. Certainly in mental health, social workers have found ways to fit into changing service priorities, adjust to new state policies, protect their jobs, and maintain a presence, if not a powerful one, in the field. To some critics within social work, this adaptability translates to little more than being co-opted by the establishment.

In addition to being adaptable, social work has limited capacity to participate fully in the scientific debates that have marked changes in professional practices. Social workers are primarily practitioners, not scientists or researchers or scholars. Their training is much less grounded in scientific methods than that of psychiatrists and psychologists. Very few of those with M.S.W.'s ever obtain doctorates. There is no major network of research institutions or any federal agency such as the National Institutes of Health that sponsors the development of knowledge for social work practice. Even among the professorate, the field lacks unified paradigms to guide its research efforts (Kirk and Reid 2002; Labaree 1998; Tucker 1996). Since the bio-medicalization of mental disorder has occurred under a banner of scientific progress, social workers have been institutionally unequipped to be very critical, if there is indeed even a motivation to be so. Whatever critical concerns social workers may have, their voices are seldom heard or their views articulated.

Harry Specht and Mark Courtney, in *Unfaithful Angels: How Social Work Has Abandoned Its Mission,* suggest another possible reason for the silence. They argue that social workers, in their quest for social status, have been lured by the "popular psychotherapies" and pulled from their commitment to the poor and have turned themselves into junior psychiatrists, content with office-based private practice and middle-class clients. By implication, social work would be hesitant to bite the hand that feeds it or to rail against a psychiatric establishment that provides so many with a modicum of status and employment. Indeed, a recent survey of the content of psychopathology courses taught in schools of social work suggests that students are shielded from content that is critical of the psychiatric establishment (Lacasse and Gomory 2003).

Missing Critical Perspectives

This lack of critical perspectives—indeed what at times appears to be an ignorance of controversies in mental health—was not what I expected when I entered social work in the late 1960s. In fact, I expected that social work would be a natural home for critical perspectives. After all, social work was a profession that grew out of social reform efforts, one that generally took a broader social view of established institutional practices and policies, respected the views of individual clients, and worried about their fate in the face of grinding social conditions. I imagined that social work had a less conventional perspective on human problems.

Consequently, I was perplexed and disappointed when I began reading the social work journals and popular textbooks. Rather than reflecting critical thinking about mental health, the books about practice seemed antiquated, and the journal articles contained little cutting edge criticism. To find critical examinations of mental health issues and practices, I needed to read the sociology, psychology, or interdisciplinary mental health journals. Even the mainstream psychiatric journals seemed to have more critical content than the social work journals, as contending schools of psychiatric thought waged intellectual battles over the future of psychiatry and psychiatric practice.

Social work's focus seemed to lag a decade behind current developments. For example, when social work suffered a crisis of casework's effectiveness, it was a decade after the effectiveness of psychotherapy had been called into question. While social work was championing community mental health, others were already criticizing its assumptions and the unintended problems springing from deinstitutionalization. By the time social work was promoting the need for practitioners to be more knowledgeable about the wonders of psychiatric medications, a chorus of critics had already begun to call into question the benefits of the "wonder drugs." As social workers were becoming enthralled with *DSM,* others were skeptical of its central claims and social functions. In social work's insecurity about even being invited to the psychiatric party, it frequently failed to note that there was an earlier fight, the party was over, and the important guests had departed.

If the recent survey of the content of mental health courses in schools of social work is any indication (Lacasse and Gomory 2003), the profession may have become even less skeptical and critical minded about mental disorder than it was three decades ago. This reluctance is not because there are no critical views within social work or in other disciplines; such views do exist, but they simply do not receive much attention in the training of future social workers.

Social workers need to be more skeptical of psychiatric claims and more critical minded about mental health practices. The purpose of this book is to give voice to the concerns of some social work scholars and to offer alternative views to current popular beliefs and practices, along with the accompanying evidence. Questioning current practices isn't a new exercise for me. My first article, which now, thirty years later, seems quaint, was written during my first term as a doctoral student at Berkeley. In it I questioned the dominant conventional psychiatric view of problem behavior. Some might say I haven't changed. And that, too, is why this book has its origins in the 1960s.

Organization of the Book

The impetus for this book began with an inquiry from Frederic (Rick) Reamer, the social work series editor for Columbia University Press, about my interest in working on a book on mental health. I'm not certain what Rick originally had in mind, but I'm pretty sure that what we have here is quite different. To his credit and my good fortune, Rick encouraged that difference as I began thinking about the shape of this volume and sending him my ideas. I proposed assembling a diverse group of contributors to invigorate debate on mental health topics. I benefited from Rick's counsel, which was responsible for launching me into a book project that I hadn't anticipated.

The key to producing a valuable volume, of course, rested entirely on recruiting a competent cadre of contributors. Having been enticed by Rick to do an unexpected book, I now had to entice a group of harried, over-worked authors to produce unexpected chapters. I began making lists of distinguished social work scholars who could articulate views that question conventional practice and beliefs and encourage social work students and practitioners to be constructively skeptical and critical minded. I expected that I would have to ask many more contributors than I needed, as a sub-stantial proportion would undoubtedly decline my invitation for them to do more uncompensated work. As it turned out, virtually no one declined.

In writing to them to invite their participation, I let them know that the book I had in mind was not a conventional book that provides an introduc-tory overview to the field of mental health, such as the useful volumes by Phil Fellin (*Mental Health and Mental Illness* [1996]) and David Mechanic (*Mental Health and Social Policy* [1999]). Nor did I seek chapters that merely summarized the research literature on specific mainstream topics, like Williams and Ell's edited volume, *Advances in Mental Health Research* (1998). Rather, I explained, this book was designed to serve as a provocative sup-plement to such texts, offering different views on conventional topics. I hoped that this one, unlike many edited books, would be noticed and broadly used.

I had no expectation that the book's contributors would promote a sin-gular point of view or would form an integrated thesis. In fact, many of the authors have sharp disagreements with each other. Rather, my objective was to select contributors who would enliven discussions and enlighten the field about important mental health topics. Accordingly, I sought authors who are not shy about taking controversial stands, espousing unpopular view-points, offering uncommon interpretations of common facts, or expressing carefully reasoned contrary opinions. At the same time, I wanted their ar-guments to be firmly grounded in reason and supporting evidence.

I sought contributors who had already written thoughtfully and critically on mental health topics, and I encouraged them to draw on their past con-tributions. Some authors decided to do so more than others. An organizer of such a volume, of course, is never quite certain what will be submitted and so to some extent shaping this book was an inductive task of finding connections among disparate theses. Certainly, I had a rough idea for the organization of the book, which guided the selection of topics and authors, but after the chapters arrived, whole sections of the book were rearranged and renamed, and chapters were reshuffled several times to arrive at the structure represented in the table of contents. Many of the chapters could logically be placed in more than one subsection. Perhaps a word of explanation is in order.

Assessment and Diagnosis

The book begins with a section on assessment and diagnosis. Assessment has always enjoyed a central role in social work, at least since the time of Mary Richmond's 1917 book, *Social Diagnosis*. The purpose of assessment is to gain an accurate picture of the individual, the problem, and his or her social environment. Over the decades, with the emergence of psychiatric social work (now generally referred to as clinical social work), the original social work conception of assessment has inadvertently narrowed into diagnosis, the medical categorization of disease. This evolution has been unfortunate, for reasons covered in the chapters in this section.

Dennis Saleebey in chapter 2 reflects on this "discourse of deficit" and offers an alternative discourse of strengths for social work. Similarly, Mark Mattaini reminds us (chapter 4) that assessment systems are master narratives that have consequences for workers and clients. Some of the many problems with the discourse of deficit, which is epitomized in the American Psychiatric Association's *Diagnostic and Statistical Manual of Mental Disorders (DSM)*, are addressed in the other chapters in this section. The need for a broader, more inclusive consideration of the social environment in diagnosis is discussed in chapter 3 by Derek Hsieh and me; we demonstrate that clinicians take social context into account in arriving at judgments of mental disorder, although *DSM* does not necessarily require them to. Jerome Wakefield in chapter 5 sees the flaws in *DSM* as opportunities for restructuring the relationship between social work and psychiatry. Regardless of the possible uses of diagnoses, if they are inaccurate they have little utility for either clinical work or scientific research. William Nugent, in chapter 6, relying on probability theory and what we know about the accuracy of psychiatric diagnoses, argues that diagnoses are likely to be very inaccurate. In chapter 7, John Bola and Deborah Pitts also rely on scientific reasoning and evidence to critically examine the concept of schizophrenia—the most prominent mental disorder, and conclude that it has significant limitations in both construct and clinical validity.

The Social Context of Intervention

Social work is a practice profession; it rests on doing, not just theorizing. In the doing, the client is at the heart of the enterprise. Regardless of the elegance of the theory or the apparent reasonableness of the intervention, the primary goal—the ultimate benchmark of success—is to help clients. One of the most difficult tasks for any profession is to be critical minded in assessing its own efforts to be helpful. A warm heart and good intentions are not enough. The second section of the book turns a critical eye to intervention efforts. In chapter 8, Amy LaPan and Tony Platt explore a disturbing period in social work and psychiatric history—the involvement in the eugenics movement, a movement where promoting the client's welfare was clearly not the primary goal. This is followed by a critique in chapter 9 of one of the most popular and common contemporary interventions for those with severe mental disorders—assertive community treatment. Tomi Gomory reviews the empirical evidence for the frequent claims of effectiveness of this intervention and arrives at the uncommon conclusion that client interests are not always being served.

Stephen Rose in chapter 10 steps back to take a broad view of the nature of professional-client relationships and to reflect on the principles that would promote human dignity and social justice by guiding practitioners to empower clients. Empowerment is also a theme in Steven Segal's chapter on self-help mental health agencies (chapter 11). In a fundamental way, self-help agencies challenge one of the assumptions of mental health professions, namely that professionals alone have the expert knowledge and authority to structure services and determine what clients need. Empowerment takes on a new meaning when clients control agencies and can reshape their views of themselves and their disabilities. Conceptions of the self are central to chapter 12, in which Sarah Rosenfield and Kathleen Pottick tackle one of the enduring puzzles in psychiatric epidemiology, the gender differences in types and rates of mental disorder. They suggest that these differences are deeply rooted in socialization into gender roles and that social workers have an opportunity to counter these influences.

Evidence-Based Practice

One of the most talked-about developments in social work and medicine in the last decade has been recognition of the need to allow scientific evidence to guide practice. It is easier to find rhetoric promoting this laudable goal than to find material that figures out how to actually do it. This third section of the book consists of three chapters that examine facets of evidence-based practice. In chapter 13, William Reid and Julanne Colvin examine some of the methodological problems, ambiguities, and barriers to making evidence-based practice a reality. In the following chapter, Eileen Gambrill places evidence-based practice in the general framework of critical thinking and reviews some of the many lapses in the mental health field in which claims might be considered as propaganda rather than expressions of science. Finally, Matthew Howard, Tonya Edmond, and Michael Vaughn provide a comprehensive review of the development and uses of practice guidelines and the challenges that lie ahead (chapter 15).

Psychotherapy and Social Work

The fourth section addresses some broad concerns about the practice methods at the heart of clinical social work—those under the umbrella of psychotherapy—and offers some very different perspectives on this matter. Jerome Wakefield (chapter 16) analyzes social work's mission and develops some surprising answers to questions about whether providing psychotherapy and treating mental disorders are legitimate activities within its mission of distributive justice. William Epstein (chapter 17) attempts to explain the endurance and popularity of psychotherapy in social work in the face of psychotherapy's checkered record of effectiveness and the common methodological weaknesses of the scientific studies that undergird its justification. Bruce Thyer (chapter 18) laments an intervention road not taken, at least not yet, by social work—behavioral social work. He attributes part of the neglect to the way behavioral approaches are misrepresented in the social work literature and, in doing so, he raises concerns about how well or adequately the profession borrows and synthesizes knowledge from other professions and disciplines.

Questioning Psychiatric Medications

No invention in the last half century has had more impact on psychiatric thinking or treatment, the structure of service delivery, or popular beliefs about mental disorders than psychiatric drugs. Moreover, no psychiatric treatment has been as commercialized or promoted for profit as have psychoactive medications. The lure of drugs is easy to understand. They symbolically medicalize behavioral problems that have often been popularly viewed as immoral, irresponsible, or deviant. Furthermore, treatment by drugs appears to be efficient, allowing clients to avoid intensive psychotherapy or hospitalization or even the need for a therapist or client to delve at all into the nature and causes of the meaning of aberrant behavior. Finally, the pharmaceutical industry continually proclaims that these medications are much more effective than other treatments and that their side effects are not a problem. In this section, contributors raise questions about such claims.

David Cohen (chapter 19) provides a rigorous critique of the scientific methodologies used in the standard drug trials that form the basis for the ubiquitous claims of effectiveness. John Bola, Loren Mosher, and David

Cohen in the following chapter review Soteria, a psychosocial treatment program for those with schizophrenia, in which less reliance on drugs appears to produce outcomes that are more successful. Unintended and generally neglected potential psychosocial side effects of medication on adolescents are explored in chapter 21 by Tally Moses and me.

Ethics, Laws, and Regulations

Providing services to clients takes place in an institutional context where practice is shaped by professional codes of ethics, agency policy and procedures, complex systems of authorization and reimbursement, and laws governing the conditions under which treatment can be provided. The chapters in this section explore some of these larger institutional contexts. First, in chapter 22, Frederic Reamer provides a broad overview of professional ethics and discusses ethical dilemmas faced by social workers in mental health settings. Examining the new world of managed care, Kevin Corcoran, Stephen Gorin, and Cynthia Moniz (chapter 23) provide a useful overview of the evolving regulations and laws that are increasingly shaping mental health practice. Donald Dickson in chapter 24 illuminates a dark corner of mental health practice, namely involuntary medication of the mentally disordered, particularly those in the criminal justice system, an issue that was the topic of an important U.S. Supreme Court decision as he completed his chapter.

Back to Berkeley

This stimulating array of chapters—from sweeping analyses of the proper mission of social work in the mental health field to detailed critiques of current research—touch on a multitude of diverse topics that have relevance for social workers. Nevertheless, no volume can cover all the worthy issues that need to be addressed, nor was it the intention of this book to do so. A few additional important topics were scheduled to be included, but at the last minute, a variety of unexpected developments made it necessary for the authors to withdraw. Nevertheless, the objective of the book was not to be comprehensive in coverage but rather to selectively raise critical questions, probe neglected topics, and examine mental disorders in their larger social environment.

The purpose of the book is to serve as a counterpoint to conventional wisdom, which is usually all that social workers are exposed to. This purpose is in the best tradition of Berkeley in the 1960s, a tradition that encourages raising questions about established practices, examining fundamental beliefs and assumptions, and proposing alternative views or interpretations. It is a tradition of critical perspectives. Perhaps it should not have surprised me to discover, as I reviewed the table of contents for the completed book, that more than a third of the contributors have Berkeley connections, as graduate students or faculty. That is only fitting.

References

Abbott, A. 1988. *The System of Professions*. Chicago: University of Chicago Press.

———. 1995. Boundaries of social work or social work of boundaries? *Social Service Review* 69:545–562.

Boyle, Mary. 2002. *Schizophrenia: A Scientific Delusion?* East Sussex, UK: Routledge.

Breggin, Peter R. and Ginger Ross Breggin. 1994. *Talking Back to Prozac: What Doctors Aren't Telling You About Today's Most Controversial Drug*. New York: St. Martin's.

Cohen, Robert and Reginald E. Zelnik, eds. 2002. *The Free Speech Movement: Reflections on Berkeley in the 1960s*. Berkeley: Unversity of California Press.

Kirk, S. A. 1999. Instituting Madness: The Evolution of a Federal Agency. In C. S. Aneshensel and J. C. Phelan, eds., *Handbook of the Sociology of Mental Health,* 539–562. New York: Kluiwer Academic/Plenum.

Kirk, Stuart A. and William J. Reid. 2002. *Science and Social Work: A Critical Appraisal*. New York: Columbia University Press.

Kramer, Peter D. 1993. *Listening to Prozac*. New York: Viking.

Kutchins, H. and S. A. Kirk. 1997. *Making Us Crazy: DSM—the Psychiatric Bible and the Creation of Mental Disorders*. New York: Free Press.

Labaree, D. 1998. Education researchers: Living with a lesser form of knowledge. *Educational Researcher* 27:4–12.

Lacasse, J. R. and T. Gomory. 2003. Is graduate social work education promoting a critical approach to mental health practice? *Journal of Social Work Education* 39:383–408.

Leiby, James. 1978. *A History of Social Welfare and Social Work in the United States*. New York: Columbia University Press.

Lubove, R. 1969. *The Professional Altruist: The Emergence of Social Work as a Career, 1880–1930*. New York: Atheneum.

Luhrmann, T. M. 2000. *Of Two Minds: The Growing Disorder in American Psychiatry*. New York: Knopf.

Reid, William J. and A. Shyne. 1969. *Brief and Extended Casework*. New York: Columbia University Press.

Rorabaugh, W. J. 1989. *Berkeley at War: The 1960s*. New York: Oxford University Press.

Rothman, David J. 1971. *The Discovery of the Asylum: Social Order and Disorder in the New Republic*. Boston: Little, Brown.

Specht, Harry and Mark Courtney. 1994. *Unfaithful Angels: How Social Work Has Abandoned Its Mission*. New York: Free Press.

Starr, P. 1982. *The Social Transformation of American Medicine*. New York: Basic Books.

Tucker, D. J. 1996. Eclecticism is not a free good: Barriers to knowledge development in social work. *Social Service Review* 70:400–434.

Whitaker, Robert. 2001. *Mad in America: Bad Science, Bad Medicine, and the Enduring Mistreatment of the Mentally Ill*. Cambridge, Mass.: Perseus.

PART I

ASSESSMENT
AND DIAGNOSIS

Chapter 2

Balancing Act: Assessing Strengths in Mental Health Practice

Dennis Saleebey

The continuing growth of the medical-psychiatric/pharmaceutical/insurance cartel, in terms of the share of the market as well as social and cultural influence, is unprecedented. I call this a cartel advisedly, since it seems to meet the definitional test—a group of institutions that control a particular market or social sector through a melding of their interests and exercising of their social power. The power is not simply a matter of controlling the fate of people who fall under the sway of such an alliance, but it is also conceptual, swallowing up other definitions, conceptions, and ideas about the nature of mental health and illness, human nature and the human condition. It is that concern that I would like to address here. The signal of the influence of this conceptual framework is the ever expanding reach of the *Diagnostic and Statistical Manual of the American Psychiatric Association (DSM)* (2000) and its growing influence in many areas of daily life.

The *DSM* and Social Construction: Whose Truth?

The Discourse of Deficit

As many critics have pointed out, the exercise of putting together a manual to describe the cognitive, emotional, behavioral, motivational, interpersonal, and social tangles and afflictions that dog humanity is ultimately a series of acts, conversations, discourses, and relationships that are fueled by a socially constructed worldview—a paradigm of disharmonies and disorders—that has significant institutionalized hegemony over other discourses about the nature of our miseries and burdens (Kirk and Kutchins 1992; Walker 1997; Gergen 1994; Cutler 1991). We see here not the dispassionate hand of science but the human play of creating a world of ideas, images, mythologies, and ideologies that, when combined with institutional power (the canon that prescribes social policies, laws, the treatment of various groups of people) and the suppression of other views of the same human condition, convert professional and secular consciousness about these matters in a serious way. The propagators of this orientation do this by expending their considerable cultural and institutional capital in the typical venues—journals, conferences, books, consultations, various popular media—of the field and the larger culture and by couching their efforts in the vernacular and methods of science. What has developed, then, is a language, a definitional web, metaphors, and narratives meant to capture human behaviors under a long-standing, culturally supported discourse, an explanatory and descriptive tradition. To critique the language that has developed, the meanings that this idiom reflects, it is important to ferret out not only what kinds of assumptions those meanings are based upon but also what kind of practices they support. And we must ask what other possibilities have been omitted or suppressed as this dominion has expanded. Since all discourses "sustain and support certain ways of doing things and prevent others from emerging" (Gergen 1994:147), it is important to examine both the elements of the canonical discourse and those that may generate other alternatives.

Kenneth Gergen (1994, 2001) makes several interesting observations about the language and resulting acts that permeate mental health, the psychotherapy professions, and psychology in general. For my purposes, one reflection is especially trenchant. Over the years, the mental health professions and institutions—psychiatry, psychology, and medicine—have created an increasingly luxuriant language of deficit, pathology, frailty, and infirmity. This text, of course, frames the terminology and execution of practice and policy. It affects how we think and act. It has personal and social consequences for those who come under its descriptive and indicative jurisdiction. Not the least of these effects is the fact that such designations are hardly limited or circumscribed, as is the case with many physical illnesses. Rather, once applied, they often suffuse deeply in one's identity, becoming part of the package we think of as personality. Furthermore, they prompt others to see the individual carrying this label as essentially that disorder. Frank has schizophrenia, a serious human condition involving practically all of the elements of one's self—biological, psychological, social, and in some cases spiritual. Briefly hospitalized, now on medication and in a community support program, Frank slowly transmutes, in his eyes and the eyes of others, into "a schizophrenic." By the way, Frank is a plumber, a father of two young children, an accordion player, an avid softball player, and a loyal spouse. But he is now Frank the schizophrenic plumber, Frank the schizophrenic father, etc. As his identity metamorphoses to give prominent place to the label, other attributes, skills, resources, and desires may slowly fade, or at least subside in importance. Because the language and labels of deficit and pathology saturate our society, and in part because there is already a vigorous cultural preoccupation with psychological and moral aberrations, addictions, weirdness, psychopathology, and frailties, hundreds of thousands of people experience what Frank is experiencing.

The discourse also hides within it a variety of culturally grounded and professionally supported assumptions about the good and the acceptable and, hence, the unacceptable. These include:

> The definitions and classifications within the diagnostic canon are the products, and reflect the methods and objectivity of science and therefore are true and good. Because of this assumption, they can and do trump other views of the human condition, especially those that are not thought to be scientifically adept. The further presumption is that these depictions and understandings of human suffering and striving have emerged from empirical study and systematic observation, rather than folk psychology, discourse, clinical preferences, political maneuvering, or the exertion of social and moral influence.
>
> By implication, the definitions of mental disorder embodied in the *DSM* paint for us a spare and puritanical picture of what is exciting, interesting, captivating, motivating about human nature and the human condition: restraint and temperance in the use of all kinds of substances; moderation in physical movement (ADHD); moderation in sexual behavior; moderation in conduct of all kinds (see personality disorders); stability of mood and emotion; relationships that are uncomplicated. The leitmotif is that there is a lie to be lived that is restrained and predictable, and that life's problems are mostly a result of how we think, feel, and act—they are not produced by social conditions, fads, cultural requisites, political transformations, economic distress, spiritual revelations, and existential and moral dilemmas.

The conditions and experiences bound between the covers of *DSM* are thought to be, in fact, disorders and diseases that require professional intervention. The supposition also is that these mental disorders mirror physical disorders—they are abnormalities, dysregulations, and lesions with unspecified biochemical and neurobiological substrates. Just as in physical medicine, as the amount of research increases and extends, new illnesses will be "discovered" all the time. This premise drives the nearly manic output of *DSM* editions, accessories, and training.

Others have written well, both critically and instructively, about the evolution of the various iterations of the *DSM* (Andreasen 2001; Kirk and Kutchins 1992; Kutchins and Kirk 1997). In a nutshell, *DSM-III* and all the subsequent editions and revisions were the result of a neo-Kraepelinian revolution in the profession of psychiatry, a shift of power from the psychodynamic/psychoanalytic members of the profession to those who wanted to emulate the precise, descriptive, categorical style of Emil Kraepelin. It was Kraepelin and his minions, many of whom were neuroscientists (Nissl, Brodmann, Alzheimer) who, in Munich at the turn of the nineteenth century, wanted to make the diagnoses of mental diseases as exact and definitive as those applied to physical illnesses. They also sought the underlying neurochemical, neuroanatomical substrates of mental disorders. However, at the end of his distinguished career, Kraepelin did not think they had yet found the neurological smoking gun. Beginning in the 1950s there was a palace revolution and eventually a coup in the realm of clinical diagnostic psychiatry. The appearance of *DSM-III* signaled the triumph of the Kraepelinian point of view over the more psychodynamic views that had prevailed in the first two editions of the *DSM*.

THE EFFECTS OF THE DISCOURSE

The impact and influence of this discourse and its institutionalization occur at several different levels of human experience. As discussed briefly above, for people who fall under the thrall of its dictates, it has the power to transmute one's identity, to refashion the expectations and views of others in the person's life, to suggest limitations on what one could reasonably be expected to do and to be: in a word, for some individuals this is a major existential transformation. The person has become, in a way, the pathology, has been reborn as a case instead of remaining an individual. I have heard professionals, ignoring the reality of the remarkable recovery of many people (Jamison 1995; Deegan 1996; Ralph 1998) who have suffered severe and persistent mental illnesses, declare that the person will never be the same, as competent or as complete, as he or she was before the illness. But those individuals who do recover, or who live remarkably despite the challenges of their physical, emotional, cognitive, and behavioral trials, are those who, with support and/ or sheer determination, must have escaped, in some ways that we do not understand well, the kind of symbolic bondage of the label they bear. It is my belief that labeling is different from assessment. Labeling is the affixing of a "diagnosis" arrived at from a position of power, in a foreign tongue, absent a genuine, thoughtful, collaborative, and thorough assessment of a person's condition, ordeals, and challenges. Labels usually stick. So a person (like Frank above) becomes a schizophrenic or a bipolar or a borderline, a convention common enough that we hardly give it a thought. Other elements of a person's background, character, accomplishments, statuses recede into the background. This is what Howard Becker (1963) calls a "master status." Such a transformation is suffused with pessimism and cynicism, revealing an egregious doubt about a person's ability to rebound, recover, or rehabilitate. Andrew Weil (1995) calls this practice "medical hexing." "I cannot help feeling," he writes, "embarrassed by my profession when I hear the myriad ways in which doctors convey pessimism to patients. I . . . am working to require instruction in medical school about the power of words and the need for physicians to use extreme care in the words they speak to patients" (64).

In terms of the community and the larger society, the language of deficit and pathology, unleavened by talk or recognition of other aspects of the human condition, continues the professionalization of the ordinary, the triumph of staple values over use-values (Illich 1975), the ascendancy of professional intervention over natural and communal caring (McKnight 1995), and the replacement of moral imagination with clinical acumen. None of this is a totality; rather it is a rising crescendo in the clamor of daily life. Consequently, we have become somewhat less able and interested in caring for each other and ourselves (unless, of course, we have to because we are poor or have no insurance or access to services).

From its beginnings as a profession, social work has not been immune to the discourse of deficit, or the scientific/medical model. But there has almost always been a contrapuntal theme, of varying degrees of vigor, about the abilities and assets of the client, family, or community. Mary Richmond, in the classic *Social Diagnosis* (1917), clearly based her model upon the medical disposition, thinking that *diagnosis* was a better word to describe the complete process of investigating, gathering evidence, and coming to a judgment about the social difficulties and personality problems presented by the client. But she also counseled that

> most types [of diagnosis] will have to include, in addition to a general description of the difficulty, a statement of those peculiarities of circumstance and personality which differentiate the case under review from all others. Then should come an enumeration of the causal factors, so far as known, in order of their importance. . . . And last should come the just mentioned *appraisal of assets for reconstruction* [my emphasis] discovered in the course of inquiry—those within our client, within his immediate family, and outside.
> (360)

Bertha Capen Reynolds (1951), although very much a devotee of professional responsibility, believed that the time had come to revise the idea of professional authority. She wrote:

> The aim of the efforts of the social caseworker, then, under this philosophy [of self-determination], is not to make changes in the client's life and point to these as professional achievement, but to give the client something for his own development which he was not able to extract for himself and one which will increase his capacity for living with satisfaction in the social group.
> (35)

In her monograph *Between Client and Community* (1934), she appreciatively includes a quote from one of her students, speaking of the clients: "That's all they need [a chance to grow], not pushing. . . . All I'm doing is opening doors, windows, and . . . painting a picture of how it would feel to them to use this added air, light, and sunshine" (98). I would take this as a statement of the innate possibility of growth. Reynolds was acutely aware of the fact that social conditions can grind anyone down and that without social or community action, little can be done by the individual worker. But more than most early writers and practitioners, she believed in the natural, though sometimes inchoate, capacities of the client. This was most evident in her advocacy of a new kind of practice, genuinely based upon the self-determination of clients. "Shall we be content to give with one hand and withhold with the other, to build up or tear down the strengths of a person's life? Or shall we become conscious of our own part in making a profession which will stand forthrightly for human well-being, including the right to be an active citizen?" (Reynolds 1951:175).

As social work turned toward the psyche in its interests in the 1930s and 1940s, the refrain of problems, pathologies, deficits became louder and more strident. Florence Hollis, among others, admonished social workers (in the three editions of her widely read book on practice, *Casework: A Psychosocial Therapy*) to develop a thorough knowledge of the three forces that cause human misery, problems, and "breakdown": unresolved or unmet infantile needs and drives, life pressures, and faulty ego and superego functioning (1964). It was not uncommon for social work students in this era to supplement their reading of social casework texts with psychiatric ones. When Helen Harris Perlman came out with her text *Social Casework: A Problem-Solving Process* (1957), it caused consternation among the majority of those who were disposed to psychodynamic counsel and instruction. A few other scholars and practitioners were advocating the writings of Alfred Adler, Karen Horney, and Harry Stack Sullivan as better models for social casework because they did attend seriously to the interpersonal and the environmental. As a reaction to this and to Perlman's framework, Hollis (1964) wrote: "Casework will drastically impoverish itself if it follows the lead of Horney and Sullivan in trying to explain human behavior primarily in interpersonal terms, omitting those key intrapsychic phenomena that from the start influence the child's perception of a reaction to his interpersonal experiences" (11). (See Blundo 2001 for an excellent discussion of this point.)

There have been some changes over the years. Newer textbooks on practice give more acknowledgment to the ideas of building on strengths, empowerment, and collaboration with clients, but often see it as simply one of many perspectives, with no particularly groundbreaking contribution to make. Only one basic practice text, however, grounds its assumptive and methodological appreciations on these ideas: *Generalist Social Work Practice: An Empowerment Approach* (2002) by Karla K. Miley, Michael O'Melia, and Brenda DuBois. Of course, two recent books, Charles Rapp's *The Strengths Model of Case Management* (1998) and Saleebey's *The Strengths Perspective in Social Work Practice* (3d ed., 2002) depict the strengths approach as radically different from social casework or social work practice as usual. That is the point to be made here: the strengths perspective, that discourse, requires a fundamental revision of the way that we think, talk, and act as professionals.

The Discourse of Strengths

The strengths perspective has many philosophical and historical kin. Elements of strengths thinking can be traced back to the ideals of democracy, old-fashioned American idealism, the romance of possibility stirred by the American frontier, the social gospel, transcendentalism, and the insistent cadence of positive thinking. The drumbeat of hope, optimism, positive expectations, the promise of the future, the possibility of always revising the self has flourished in one form or another. Even today the shelves of bookstores, libraries, and online booksellers fairly gush with manifestos of self-reinvention, self-development, self-righting, and self-help. The underside of this—the obsession with a world gone wrong, lives wrecked on the shoals of personal tribulations and aberrations, is what Philip Slater (1990) has called the nether side of culture. For example, German culture, which celebrates order, restraint, and precision, has, as a counterpoint, Götterdämmerrung fantasies, and Wagnerian intrigues. So as we paint in this dominant culture a positive picture of what can be, we find ourselves captivated by what went wrong.

While the roots of strengths-based approaches might lie in the lineage of positive thinking, the strengths perspective is far more than that. It is a language, fired by moral acumen, about the possibilities of human character, fueled by a belief in social justice and restoration, that reflects both the realities of the human condition and the promise of the human spirit.

Jane Addams (1902), certainly no peddler of easy panaceas and nostrums, sounded the call early: "We are gradually requiring of the educator that he shall free the powers of each man and connect him with the rest of life. We ask this not merely because it is the man's right to be thus connected but because we have become convinced that the social order cannot afford to get along *without his special contribution* [my emphasis]" (178).

The Strengths Perspective

Not a theory in the modernist sense, the strengths perspective is a generative theory in the social constructionist sense (Gergen 2001). Modernist/scientific theory is dedicated to telling it like it is. Generative theory is telling it like it might become. There are four constituents to generative theory (I have added the last two): (1) Generative theory creates doubt, serious doubt, about the prevailing canon or conventional wisdom in a particular field. It poses questions about the intent, the meaning, the methods, and the truths of the institutionalized convention. (2) It creates promising alternatives to thinking and doing. (3) These alternatives are consistent with the relevant values and principles that guide this subversion (in this case, social work values—particularly those that knit together the concept of social justice). (4) It encourages creative and inventive thinking—imagining the "untested feasibles" (Freire 1994) around a given sphere of social action and reckoning. The strengths perspective obligates social workers (and others who might employ it) to appreciate that however burdened and beaten people, families, or communities are, they have managed to survive. They have learned from their struggle, even developed some new ideas, traits, and perspectives. They have taken steps, summoned up resources, screwed up courage, and tried to cope. We must ask not so much what is wrong with you, what hurts, what is missing, but how did you carry on, where did you find encouragement, what did you draw on, and where do you want to go from here? Many who appear to be resigned to their fate, oppressed by their circumstances, hampered by regrettable decisions, culpable in the inflicting of pain on themselves and others are almost always working on their situation, courting resolve, digging for resources, and flirting with possibility. It is these attributes that we acknowledge, affirm, and act on.

THE STRENGTHS LEXICON

Every dialogue (roughly, democratic, meaning-making conversation) and discourse (descriptions, explanations, metatheories, directives, suppositions, and dialogues) depend on a lexicon of words, images, and symbols and, more broadly, narratives and stories. This is as true of any of the *DSMs* as it is for any other approach, perspective, theory, or method, including, obviously, the strengths perspective. Let us examine some of the vocabulary of strengths-based practice, especially in the field of mental health.

Heroism. Once reserved for acts that truly transcended the usual or expected, *heroism* has become a frequently used and occasionally hackneyed term, especially since the malign catastrophe of 9/11 and the ensuing "war against terror" and the war in Iraq. As far as I know, Duncan and Miller (2002) were the first to apply the term to psychotherapy, the helping relationship, and mental health. While they did not offer an explicit definition, their intent is clear enough: in psychotherapy and counseling, clients do most of the work and they should direct the operation. People who do not become clients usually overcome their hardships and ordeals using the resources within and around them.

Anaïs Nin (cited in Wolin and Wolin 1993), commenting on the tiny, immanent sprit of children, says this: "One discovers that destiny can be directed, that one does not have to remain in bondage to the first wax imprint made on childhood sensibilities. Once the deforming mirror has been smashed, there is the possibility of wholeness. There is the possibility of joy" (65). To value and stimulate the heroic in clients is to assist them in confronting their ordeals, to make an alliance with the strong and unyielding in them, to enliven their dreams and hopes, and to engage their powers in working toward a better day or moment. An old saying among Caucasus mountaineers is that "heroism is endurance for one moment more" (Kennan 1921).

Many of the people that we help have endured situations and conditions that stagger our minds and break our hearts. This is the starting point for connecting to the heroic—we must discover how people have survived, how they have gone on in the face of their trials and disappointments, how they have taken charge of their fate and their future.

Promise, Possibility, and Hope. Every human being is a promise, an organism full of yet-to-be-developed or developing capacities, interests, accomplishments, and involvements. The fantastic blueprint of our DNA is so abundant and complex that, even abiding in the most propitious and luxurious of environments, much of our potential remains unformed. When people suffer or make decisions that cause pain for themselves or others, we do not typically think in terms of the promise of that person. Rather, it is common enough to think in terms of the implausibility of self-righting, the dubious probability of health and wholeness, and the unlikely prospect of overcoming their anguish or mistakes. Diagnoses and other deficit-based designations

32 • *Assessment and Diagnosis*

seduce us into thinking of limitations. Why not think of promise unfulfilled? Beth Blue Swadener and Sally Lubeck (1995), in challenging the discourse of deficit used in describing children who are not doing well or struggling, ask, instead of thinking of these young people as "at-risk" why don't we think or them as "at-promise"? The expectations affixed to one who is at risk are likely to be negative or circumscribed. Someone who is seen as having promise may be the benefactor of more optimistic and constructive expectations. Promise, of course, implies possibility, an eye to what might be, or what one might become. Because promise and possibility are future oriented, they involve the kindling of a dream or vision of a better life. People seemingly beaten down by life circumstances are not inclined to look at the feasible, but it may be that doing so is precisely what helps them take, however hesitatingly and slight, a step toward their dreams. This dynamic is obviously predicated on the awakening of hope. The belief in the possible and hope are central to emancipation of the spirit. Paulo Freire (1994), the great pedagogue of liberation, admitted that he had underestimated the considerable power of hope:

> But the attempt to do without hope, in the struggle to improve the world, as if that struggle could be reduced to calculated acts alone, or a purely scientific approach, is a frivolous illusion. To attempt to do without hope, which is based on the need for truth as an ethical quality of the struggle, is tantamount to denying that struggle as one of its mainstays. . . . Hope, as an ontological need, demands an anchoring in practice. . . . Without a minimum of hope we cannot so much as start the struggle.
> (8–9)

Much of what we do in the name of assessment and treatment is to rob people of hope or to make them mere pawns in the exercise of our interventions. C. S. Snyder and his colleagues (2002) have studied hope for years and have developed a theory of hope. As a preface to that theory, they say simply, "Hopeful thought reflects the belief that one can find pathways to desired goals and become motivated to use those pathways. . . . Hope, so defined, serves to drive the emotions and well-being of people" (257). Hope involves goals and finding pathways to goals. Hope also implies agency. The work that we do based on strengths is often the work of vivifying hope through collaborative projects between client and worker and summoning the internal and external resources to engage in the project of realizing the possible.

Another interesting source of support for these ideas comes from studies of the placebo effect. We have ignored the power of placebo for a long time, possibly because it seems as though it cannot be about real change; it is faux, artificial, and fleeting. Nonetheless, it is common in the case of psychotropic medications being tested clinically for their effects and side effects for the placebo group to have a percentage of improved or positive response among anywhere from 30 percent to 60 percent (occasionally higher, sometimes lower) of subjects. In a recent meta-analysis of Federal Drug Administration (FDA) data, heretofore unavailable to the public, four researchers (Kirsch et al. 2002) used the Freedom of Information Act to obtain the medical and statistical reviews of every clinical trial from 1987 to 1999 that included placebo and antidepressants reported to the FDA for initial approval of the six most widely used antidepressant drugs. The drugs included Prozac, Paxil, Zoloft, Serzone, Effexor, and Celexa (brand names). After careful analyses, one conservative and one less restricted, the researchers came to the conclusion that there is no clinically significant difference between placebos and antidepressant drugs. There could hardly be a stronger statement of the power of hope, belief, and positive expectation. Another of many examples that illustrate the potency of placebos is this: in the 1950s researchers at the University of Kansas Medical Center developed an experimental surgical procedure to relieve chronic angina. Ethical concerns aside, they randomly assigned patients with angina to one of two groups. One group received the actual surgical treatment, the other group merely had some superficial incisions made in their chests and then were sewn up to make it appear as though they had had surgery. The patients were contacted every year for five years. After five years, 70 percent of the men who underwent the genuine procedure reported no symptoms. A good thing. But 100 percent of the men who had the bogus surgery had no complaints of angina (Fisher 2000).

The placebo effect speaks loudly about the "pharmacy within," mobilized by positive expectations, hope, faith in the product or the professional, and the motivation to get better. Why we do not regard this as astonishing is perplexing. Even if the effects are short-lived (we do not know for sure that they are in most cases), the idea that we can mobilize energy and motivation through the appeal to possibility speaks to another side of human nature.

Empowerment. Though the term *empowerment* is becoming trite through excessive and sometimes inappropriate use, it indicates the intent to, and the processes of, helping individuals, families, and communities discover, develop, and employ their resources, assets, and capacities in order to confront and overcome elements in their life that oppress and stifle them, that undermine the use of their knowledge and powers, or that cause them pain and torment. Empowerment is a collaborative endeavor and does not involve giving power to individuals and groups; rather it is the discovery and rediscovery of powers within and around. It might be anything—a blazing spiritual faith, resilience, determination, caring individuals and informal associations in the community, extended family supports. These then become the tools and resources for change. Empowerment also means, as so many have shown (Lee 1994; Freire 1973, 1994), assisting in the development of a critical consciousness—fostering an emergent awareness of the forces, intimate and institutional, that coerce and oppress. This process frequently requires recognition that the oppressor's definitions and views of those who are oppressed have often subverted the native ones of the subjugated.

Health and Wholeness. There is, says Roger Mills (1995), an innate urge to health and wellness in human beings. This inclination is often embryonic or suppressed by the expectations of others. His community empowerment and health realization projects in some of the most devastated and downtrodden communities in the country have produced miraculous results. The approach is based on the idea that many demoralized and distraught people have, underneath their misery and self-doubt or self-inflicted pain, an instinct toward health and wisdom. In an interview with Jack Pransky, Mills observed:

> As soon as people started letting go of their attachment to their negative or alienated beliefs, their natural propensity to function in a healthy way came to the surface. . . . When [people] started to change, their buoyancy, their positive movement toward a higher state of mental health spilled over to other people and the whole community started to rise.
> (1998:265)

Like disease, health and wellness are the artifacts of a complex, reticulate relationship between body, mind, and environment. (The separation of mind and body here is a conceptual convenience, not a reality.) Natural or spontaneous healing is predicated on the mobilization of resources—hormonal, immunological, and neurochemical—within the body, psychological resources and perspectives, and environmental supports and encouragement. Regrettably, the medical/psychiatric establishment has little use for this kind of healing or approach to care. Ivan Illich (1975) in his classic (updated in 1995 and reprinted in 2002) *Limits to Medicine: Medical Nemesis* argues that medicalized health care is a threat to a healthy life in three ways. The first is clinical iatrogenesis, when heteronomous medical management replaces the capacity for innate and organic health. The second is social iatrogenesis, wherein individuals and families are deprived or turned away from those basic supports and conditions in the environment that sustain healing and provide care. The last is cultural iatrogenesis. This is a widespread condition in which the medical enterprise saps the will of people to "suffer their reality. . . . Professionally organized medicine has come to function as a domineering moral enterprise that advertises industrial expansion as a war against all suffering" (127).

To realize health, to encourage spontaneous recovery and regeneration after illness, to achieve new levels of well-being and wholeness, some of the following factors are important:

1. People have the innate capacity for and urge to health and healthy living. The possibility of soundness and wellness lies within (Mills 1995; Pelletier 2000; Weil 1995)
2. Positive beliefs about oneself and one's state—hopefulness—are often a spur to recovery or, at the least, a better quality of life, even if one is chronically ill (Snyder and Feldman 2000; Ornstein and Sobel 1989)
3. Positive emotions are often health promoting and maintaining in that they support and/or elevate elements of the immune system (Restak 1995)
4. The community plays an essential role in health. The connections between people, mutual projects, mentoring, support, respite, healing rituals and tools, common visions and hopes are all potential contributors to the sense of health and capacity for residents. Hope always has a collective element (Snyder and Feldman 2000)

Like the literature on resilience, this view of health asserts that individuals and groups have native, innate capacities for rebound, recovery, and regeneration. "Both suggest that individuals are best served . . . by creating belief and thinking around possibility and health serving values, around accomplishment and renewal, rather than focusing on disease and risk processes" (Saleebey 2002).

Mental Health Revisited: Restoring Balance to an Institution Careening Out of Balance

Over the years the psychiatric/medical establishment has pushed us to accept the fact that we cannot be responsible in any real way for our own health and mental health. Ultimately, this appropriates our responsibility for our health and disables our own individual and collective wisdom about what is right and good for us. In physical medicine (a misnomer, for all medicine has mental, physical, and usually untapped spiritual components) a recent nod has been made to alternative methods of healing and somewhat more attention paid to the promotion of "healthy lifestyles," although the definition of *healthy* rests completely with the physicians. No similar developments have occurred in the field of mental health, except on the fringes by various conceptual and methods rebels, former patients and their families, and social activists.

Those who propose a different way of understanding and acting face a dilemma at the outset. It would be of some benefit to some individuals if the *DSM* could be thoroughly revised, even scrapped, and the process of reconstructing what diagnosis and assessment mean could begin in earnest. But this authority grows antically and wildly. In my state, Kansas, as in many others, in order to get your highest clinical license as a social worker, you must complete a course on "diagnosis." Essentially what that means is that you must have a course on the use of the *DSM*. The licensing examination has many questions that require knowledge of the *DSM*. This means that schools of social work must offer a course that covers this sort of material. I teach such a course. This poses many dilemmas for me, my values, social work values, and humane working conceptions about human nature and the human condition. The best I can do is to teach this material from a critical/radical point of view, to present alternative views of mental health and illness, and to present ideas and tools for infusing one's assessments and actions with ideas that support client wisdom, client strengths, and the innate capacity for self-righting and health. What follows here are some ideas that others and I have developed for restoring balance to this unbalanced equation.

THE DIAGNOSTIC STRENGTHS MANUAL

What if there were a manual, as definitive, categorical, and hefty as the *DSM*, that required us to account for and appraise the assets, capacities, resources, and dreams of an individual, a family, or a community? To ignore the virtues, gifts, talents, and skills of people is to draw only a faint outline of those individuals. As a matter of fact, a diagnosis wrought by consulting the *DSM* confers upon the individual the status of case: one among many with similar afflictions and limitations.

With apologies to skilled ironists, imagine the following:

The Diagnostic Strengths Manual

Code 300: Estimable Personal Qualities

301.00 TRUSTWORTHINESS

A. For at least six months, nearly every day, the individual has exhibited at least three of the following behaviors and qualities:
  • Did what he or she promised
  • Kept at a task that had many snares and difficulties
  • Did not reveal a confidence

- Stuck by a friend, relative, or colleague during a difficult time
- Did more than expected

B. This is not better explained by codependency or a pathological desire to please others

C. Such behavior must have improved the lives of others

D. Rule out the possibility of a self-seeking desire to cash in on these loyalties later

302.00 PATIENCE

A. For at least six months, nearly every day, the individual has exhibited at least three of the following:

- Held her or his own wishes in abeyance while allowing a young child or a dependent to struggle to master a behavior
- Demonstrated forbearance in the face of a serious delay, not of her or his own doing, in achieving an important goal
- Calmly endured serious challenges and stresses in the environment
- Exhibited tolerance and understanding when confronted with a personal situation that defied personal values and standards of taste
- Maintained equilibrium and steadfastness in the midst of a situation of rapid change and transition.

B. This is not better explained by sedative, hypnotic, or anxiolytic abuse

C. Such behaviors have a positive, calming effect on others in stressful situation

D. Such behaviors do not interfere with taking assertive action when required (Saleebey 2001)

Such a classification has many possibilities—from the further detailing of personal virtues and traits (as above), to including family, community, and cultural strengths and assets. The above also has some of the hermeneutic, arbitrary indicators of the *DSM* (Why six months? Why three characteristics? Why tolerance when faced with a challenge to one's beliefs? Etc.). There is a literature about human virtues, admirable attitudes and behaviors, socially productive and morally consequential accomplishments. There is also a literature about the survival of one's humanity under the most stressful of conditions (Antonovsky 1987; Glover 2000; Vaillant 1993).

Gnosis and Diagnosis

Robert Hutchins (1998) has proposed an ingenious way of initiating some balance to the assessment of individuals and their environments. He contrasts the indicators of pathology (diagnosis) with those that elucidate specific and relevant appreciation of the complete person (gnosis—it has many other meanings as well). Hutchins calls both of these *documents of identity,* but the *DSM* fails the test as a representative, respectful, and undiminished regard for the person's gifts and resources. Imagine a clinical evaluation that has two five-axis assessments.

Let us just contrast a couple of axes with a real client.

GNOSIS

Axis I. Frank's dream is to be a pilot (he currently washes dishes in a downtown grill), to have self-respect and the respect of others, and to be responsible for the safety of others (as a pilot).

DIAGNOSIS

Axis I. Schizophrenia chronic undifferentiated type, chronic. Major depressive episode, mild, chronic. (These are from *DSM-III-R* and have never been updated.)

GNOSIS

Axis II. Frank has determination, a vivid vision of what he wants his life to be like, and is a hard and reliable worker. He also quit drinking on his own, yet still meets with his friends who still drink, because they are his buddies and he doesn't want to abandon them, and feels a sense of responsibility for them. Frank takes his medication, even though he still suffers from occasional anticholinergic effects, because, in his words, he has "a kind of brain disease."

DIAGNOSIS

Axis II. Mental retardation, mild.

In the case of gnosis, although she did not use the term, the social worker spent a lot of time with Frank, hearing his story, about his hopes and dreams, and the ordeals he has been through. In fifteen years of passage in and out of hospitals no one had ever recorded his wishes and dreams, or his strengths (e.g., quitting drinking on his own, his urge to self-management and the normalization of his life)—probably because it never occurred to anyone to ask. With regard to the diagnosis, as noted above, Axis I has not been changed since Frank first was hospitalized, and while mental retardation was recorded on Axis II, it has not been reassessed in all this time. By the way, the social worker does not think that Frank shows any signs of retardation.

While both of these strengths assessments, in different ways, appeal to the field to develop some proportion in its understanding (and there are many more strengths-based assessments, some of them in use—see Rapp 1998, McQuaide and Ehrenreich 1997, Cowger and Snively 2002, Benard 2002, Kisthardt 2002, Wolin and Wolin 1993), without a vocabulary, a rationale,

Table 2.1

Gnosis	Diagnosis
Axis I. Life goals and dreams	Axis I. Clinical disorders Other disorders that may be the focus of attention
Axis II. Core gifts and abilities	Axis II. Personality disorders Mental retardation
Axis III. Physical gifts and abilities	Axis III. General medical conditions
Axis IV. Gifts of support: psychosocial and environmental supports	Axis IV. Psychosocial and environmental problems
Axis V. Family, culture, community gifts	Axis V. Global assessment of functioning

and a set of principles, it is unlikely that symmetry will be restored. The language of strengths is ordinary and stems from the broader concepts above (the strengths lexicon): courage, conviction, self-discipline, hope, possibility, resolve, moral imagination, capacity, character, reserves, creativity, resilience, resources (in family, culture, and community), resourcefulness, insight—one could go on for some time. But until we employ such a vocabulary in mental health, we are resigned to speak medico/psychiatric argot and to see what we speak ("I'll see it when I believe it," as the social constructionists say).

The principles of a strengths approach flow from this language and create the beginnings of a discourse. These beliefs and rhetorical standards are many. Three of the most important are

1. Everybody—every individual, family, and community—has strengths. There are no exceptions here. This is difficult. Sometimes people do not appear to have much in the way of resources. Their ordeals have been so consuming and onerous. Or perhaps they have engaged in behavior that the practitioner finds distasteful or at least a sign of a serious and abiding disturbance. But first and foremost the strengths approach obligates the practitioner to seek out, to acknowledge, affirm, appreciate, and act on those resources and abilities. It is these that have the potential for reversing misfortune, countering illness, easing pain, and reaching goals. "In the end, clients want to know that you care about them, that how they fare makes a difference to you, that you will listen to them, that you will respect them no matter what their history, *and that you believe that they can build something of value with the resources within and around them* [my emphasis]." (Saleebey 2002:14)

2. You cannot know the upper limits of an individual's, family's, or community's capacity to grow and develop. We often do not appreciate—because

of appearance, reputation, stereotype, or diagnosis—that people do have an urge to health, an innate capacity for self-righting, and an inherent wisdom about what is right for them (Mills 1995). "Appreciating the inborn urge to growth and change challenges us to harness the motivating power of positive expectations—the healing power that is often the product when the faith, hope, and love conveyed by one person ignites the fire of potential and possibilities for another" (Kisthardt 2002:168). Lest we think that this is a syrupy sentiment worthy of a lugubrious televangelist, Michael Lambert (1992), in his research on the core conditions of change in psychotherapy and counseling (a meta-analysis of studies of positive change in those fields), concludes that two of the four factors in promoting change are (1) the quality of the helping relationship and (2) the existence of positive expectations, hope, and a belief in the possibility of a better life. These two factors obviously go together. All too often we believe that a person with a diagnosis cannot change or cannot pursue the dreams and hopes that many of us take for granted. We would be wrong in most cases.

3. People who confront stress and adversity, acute or chronic, almost always develop ideas, capacities, traits, and motivations as they struggle to meet the challenges of these ordeals or as they resist the oppression of others. We have been much too enterprising in looking for the impediments and injuries, the failures and fractures that people bring on themselves or that are inflicted from the outside. The Wolins (1997) urge us to move away from a damage model, wherein individuals, especially children, are seen as suffering nothing but harm from, say, the abuse or addiction of their parents. Rather we should construct and conceive a challenge model that honors the injuries inflicted on individuals, the risks to them that may remain, but that also seeks out, respects, and acts upon the resiliencies that people, even little children, accrue as they struggle. Unfortunately, we seem to view the ordeals of life only through the lens of despair, damage, and doubt.

> The resiliency paradigm is no match for the risk paradigm. Talking about the human capacity to repair from harm, inner strengths, and protective factors, professionals feel that they have entered alien territory. They grope for words and fear sounding unschooled and naïve when they replace pathology terminology with the more mundane vocabulary of resourcefulness, hope, creativity, competence and the like. . . . We believe that the struggle can be tipped in the other direction by offering a systematic, developmental vocabulary of strengths that can stand up to pathology terminology that is the standard in our field.
> (27)

That, in a word, is our hope and our agenda.

Conclusion

The strengths perspective also struggles against a broad cultural fascination with aberrations, abnormalities, danger, disaster, diseases, and failure. While there is a tie here to American optimism, and the belief in the reinvention of the self, that side of American culture and history has barely laid a hand on the mental health enterprise. Of the strengths approach, Stan Witkin (2002) has written: "Do not be fooled by the simplicity of the strengths perspective; it has transformational potential. Indeed, if all its tenets were adopted and put into practice, we would be living in a different world. . . . The strengths perspective has been quietly fostering a small revolution in which the hegemony of deficit explanations is beginning to weaken, belief in resilience is rebounding, and collaborative practice is growing" (xiv, xv).

Historian Howard Zinn (1999), writing of the rebellions against oppressive powers in this country's history, says: "To recall this [the rebellions] is to remind people of what the Establishment would like them to forget—the enormous capacity of apparently helpless people to resist, of apparently contented people to demand change. To uncover such history is to find a powerful human impulse to assert one's humanity. It is to hold out, even in times of deep pessimism, the possibility of surprise" (648).

I believe that the work that we might do in mental health, however modest in compass, is work that, added up, could be an inspiration to that urge to affirm one's very humanity. And that is the welcome surprise.

References

Addams, Jane. 1902. *Democracy and Social Ethics.* New York: Macmillan.

American Psychiatric Association (APA). 2000. *Diagnostic and Statistical Manual of Mental Disorders (DSM-IV-TR).* Washington, D.C.: APA.

Andreasen, Nancy C. 2001. *Brave New Brain: Conquering Mental Illness in the Era of the Genome.* New York: Oxford University Press.

Antonovsky, Aaron. 1987. *Unraveling the Mystery of Health: How People Manage Stress and Stay Well.* San Francisco: Jossey-Bass.

Becker, Howard. 1963. *Outsiders: Studies in the Sociology of Deviance.* New York: Free Press.

Benard, Bonnie. 2002. Turnaround People and Places: Moving from Risk to Resilience. In D. Saleebey, ed., *The Strengths Perspective in Social Work Practice,* 213–227. 3d ed. Boston: Allyn and Bacon.

Blundo, Robert. 2001. Learning strengths-based practice: Challenging our personal and professional frames. *Families in Society* 82:296–304.

Cowger, Charles D. and Carol A. Snively. 2002. Assessing Client Strengths: Individual, Family, and Community Empowerment. In D. Saleebey, ed., *The Strengths Perspective in Social Work Practice*, 106–123. 3d ed. Boston: Allyn and Bacon.

Cutler, Carol E. 1991. Deconstructing the *DSM-III*. *Social Work* 36:154–157.

Deegan, Pat E. 1996. Recovery as a journey of the heart. *Psychiatric Rehabilitation* 19:91–97.

Duncan, Barry and Scott Miller. 2002. *The Heroic Client*. San Francisco: Jossey-Bass.

Fisher, Michael J. 2000. Better living through the placebo effect. *Atlantic Monthly* 286:16–18.

Freire, P. 1973. *Pedagogy of the Oppressed*. New York: Seabury.

———. 1994. *Pedagogy of Hope: Reliving Pedagogy of the Oppressed*. New York: Continuum.

Gergen, Kenneth. J. 1994. *Realities and Relationships*. Cambridge, Mass.: Harvard University Press.

———. 2001. *Social Construction in Context*. New York: Sage.

Glover, Jonathan. 2000. *Humanity: A Moral History of the Twentieth Century*. New Haven, Conn.: Yale University Press.

Hollis, Florence. 1964. *Casework: A Psychosocial Therapy*. New York: Random House.

Hutchins, Robert L. R. 1998. "Beyond Diagnosis to Gnosis: Diagnosis for Gifts and Abilities, Not Just Deficits and Pathology." Unpublished manuscript, Santa Rosa, California, Narrative Training Associates.

Illich, Ivan. 1975. *Limits to Medicine: Medical Nemesis—The Expropriation of Health*. London: Marion Boyars.

Jamison, Kay Redfield. 1995. *An Unquiet Mind: A Memoir of Moods and Madness*. New York: Vintage.

Kennan, George. 1921. Letter to Henry Munroe Rogers. In *Bartlett's Familiar Quotations*, 554. 16th ed. Boston: Little, Brown.

Kirk, Stuart A. and Herb Kutchins. 1992. *The Selling of DSM: The Rhetoric of Science in Psychiatry*. New York: Aldine de Gruyter.

Kirsch, Irving, Thomas J. Moore, Alan Scoboria, and Sarah S. Nicholls. 2002. The emperor's new drugs: An analysis of antidepressant medication data submitted to the U.S. Food and Drug Administration. *Prevention and Treatment* online at http://journals.apa.org/prevention/volume5/pre0050023a.html.

Kisthardt, Walter E. 2002. The Strengths Perspective in Interpersonal Helping: Purpose, Principles, and Functions. In D. Saleebey, ed., *The Strengths Perspective in Social Work Practice*, 163–185. 3d ed. Boston: Allyn and Bacon.

Kutchins, Herb and Stuart A. Kirk. 1997. *Making Us Crazy: DSM—the Psychiatric Bible and the Creation of Mental Disorders*. New York: Free Press.

Lambert, Michael J. 1992. Implications of Outcome Research for Psychotherapy Integration. In J. C. Norcross and M. R. Goldfried, eds., *Handbook of Psychotherapy Integration*. New York: Basic Books.

Lee, J. A. B. 1994. *The Empowerment Approach to Social Work Practice*. New York: Columbia University Press.

McKnight, John. 1995. *The Careless Society: Community and Its Counterfeits*. New York: Basic Books.

McQuaide, Sharon and John H. Ehrenreich. 1997. Assessing client strengths. *Families in Society* 78:201–212.

Miley, Karla K., Michael O'Melia, and Brenda DuBois. 2001. *Generalist Social Work Practice: An Empowerment Approach.* 3d ed. Boston: Allyn and Bacon.

Mills, Roger. 1995. *Realizing Mental Health.* New York: Sulzburger and Graham.

Ornstein, Robert and David Sobel. 1989. *Healthy Pleasures.* Reading, Mass.: Addison-Wesley.

Pelletier, Kenneth R. 2000. *The Best Alternative Medicine: What Works? What Does Not?* New York: Simon and Schuster.

Perlman, Helen Harris. 1957. *Social Casework: A Problem-Solving Process.* Chicago: University of Chicago Press.

Pransky, J. 1998. *Modello: A Story of Hope for the Inner City and Beyond.* Cabot, Vt.: NEHRI Publications.

Ralph, Ruth O. 1998. "Recovery." Background paper for the Surgeon General's Report on Mental Health. Portland, Maine: Edmund S. Muskie School of Public Service, University of Southern Maine.

Rapp, Charles A. 1998. *The Strengths Model: Case Management of People Suffering from Severe and Persistent Mental Illness.* New York: Oxford University Press.

Restak, Richard M. 1995. *Brainscapes.* New York: Hyperion.

Reynolds, Bertha C. 1934. *Between Client and Community: A Study in Responsibility in Social Work.* NASW Classics Series. Silver Spring, Md.: National Association of Social Workers.

———. 1951. *Social Work and Social Living: Explorations in Philosophy and Practice.* Silver Spring, Md.: National Association of Social Workers.

Richmond, Mary E. 1917. *Social Diagnosis.* New York: Russell Sage.

Saleebey, Dennis. 2001. The Diagnostic Strengths Manual? *Social Work* 46:183–187.

———. 2002. Power in the People. In D. Saleebey, ed., *The Strengths Perspective in Social Work Practice,* 1–22. Boston: Allyn and Bacon.

Slater, Philip. 1990. *The Pursuit of Loneliness.* Boston: Beacon.

Snyder, C. R. and David B. Feldman. 2000. Hope for the Many: An Empowering Social Agenda. In C. R. Snyder, ed., *Handbook of Hope: Theory, Measurement, and Applications,* 389–411. San Diego: Academic Press.

Snyder, C. R., Kevin L. Rand, and David R. Sigmon. 2002. Hope Theory: A Member of the Positive Psychology Family. In C. R. Snyder and S. J. Lopez, eds., *Handbook of Positive Psychology,* 257–276. New York: Oxford University Press.

Swadener, Beth B. 1995. Children and Families "At Promise." In B. B. Swadener and S. Lubeck, eds., *Children and Families "At Promise": Deconstructing the Discourse of Risk.* Albany: State University of New York Press.

Vaillant, George E. 1993. *The Wisdom of the Ego.* Cambridge, Mass.: Harvard University Press.

Walker III, Sydney. 1997. *A Dose of Sanity: Mind, Medicine, and Misdiagnosis.* New York: John Wiley and Sons.

Weil, Andrew. 1995. *Spontaneous Healing.* New York: Knopf.

Witkin, Stan. 2002. Foreword to D. Saleebey, ed., *The Strengths Perspective in Social Work Practice,* xiii–xv. 3d ed. Boston: Allyn and Bacon.

Wolin, Steven and Sybil J. Wolin. 1997. Shifting paradigms: Talking a paradoxical approach. *Resiliency in Action* 2:23–28.

Wolin, Sybil J. and Steven Wolin. 1993. *The Resilient Self: How Survivors of Troubled Families Overcome Adversity.* New York: Villard.

Zinn, Howard. 1999. *A People's History of the United States: 1492 to the Present.* New York: HarperCollins.

Chapter 3

The Limits of Diagnostic Criteria: The Role of Social Context in Clinicians' Judgments of Mental Disorder

Derek K. Hsieh and Stuart A. Kirk

Introduction

In response to criticism that psychiatric diagnosis was inappropriately medicalizing deviant behavior, *DSM-III* (APA 1980) and subsequent editions (APA 1987, 1994, 2000) provide a formal definition of mental disorders that tries to distinguish them from nonpathological problems, such as social deviance or problems in living. In addition, descriptions of each category of disorder are more detailed and offered with information about associated features, age of onset, course, and so on. *DSM-III* (and later versions) are descriptive and attempt to avoid assumptions about the etiology of disorders, which is largely unknown or in dispute. *DSM-III*'s central defining feature in this descriptive approach is the explicit list of diagnostic criteria that it provides for each disorder. By requiring the presence of a number of specific indicators (e.g., symptom counts, duration, impaired functioning) to warrant a particular diagnosis, *DSM* attempts to improve diagnostic agreement and provide guidance to clinicians in distinguishing between mental disorders and other problems in living. This approach also changed the nature of the diagnostic process by minimizing the need for clinicians to make causal inferences about behaviors in order to arrive at a diagnosis.

In this chapter we will present findings from a study that was designed to examine whether the *DSM* diagnostic criteria can be used independent of the symptoms' social context to validly distinguish mental disorder from other problems in living. For this study, vignettes describing behavior that meets the criteria for conduct disorder (CD) are used, but the core issue examined—whether valid psychiatric diagnosis can be achieved by using the diagnostic criteria alone, without consideration of social context—could apply to many other diagnostic categories as well.

Conduct disorder was selected because we believe adolescent antisocial behavior can be a manifestation of psychopathology or of normal and adaptive responses to a problematic environment, as many have suggested (Richters and Cicchetti 1993; Wakefield 1993). Antisocial behavior is also relatively common at different points in normal development (Achenbach et al. 1991), and some amount of adolescent risk-taking behavior may be part of healthy psychosocial development (Peterson 1988; Shedler and Block 1990). However, serious and persistent childhood antisocial behavior is often associated with impaired neuropsychological, cognitive, social, and behavioral functioning (Richters and Cicchetti 1993). Thus it is important to be able to distinguish diagnostically between antisocial behavior that is normal and antisocial behavior that is pathological. We recognize that this distinction between normal and pathological behavior depends on how one defines psychopathology, a question about which there is yet no professional consensus. The conceptual distinction we make in this study is guided by *DSM*'s definition of mental disorder (Wakefield 1992). *DSM-IV* explicitly recognizes this distinction in its text describing conduct disorder:

> Consistent with the DSM-IV definition of mental disorder, the Conduct Disorder diagnosis should be applied only when the behavior in question is symptomatic of an underlying dysfunction within the individual and not simply a reaction to the immediate social context. Moreover, immigrant youth from war-ravaged countries who have a history of aggressive behaviors that may have been necessary for their survival in that context would not necessarily warrant a diagnosis of Conduct Disorder. It may be helpful for the clinician to consider the social and economic context in which the undesirable behaviors have occurred.
> (APA 1994:88)

These general considerations regarding the social context of behavior, however, are not explicitly included in the list of fifteen diagnostic criteria of CD (see figure 3.1). Diagnostic decisions in practice are increasingly based specifically on whether the presenting symptoms meet the explicit diagnostic criteria; by not including an explicit reference to social context, clinicians using the diagnostic criteria could misdiagnose conduct disorder when no mental disorder is actually present (Jensen and Hoagwood 1997).

Some might argue, however, that the *DSM-IV* diagnostic criteria are by themselves sufficient to validly diagnose CD. The diagnostic criteria for CD

Figure 3.1
DSM-IV **Diagnostic Criteria for Conduct Disorder**

A. A repetitive and persistent pattern of behavior in which the basic rights of others or major age-appropriate societal norms or rules are violated, as manifested by the presence of three (or more) of the following criteria in the past 12 months, with at least one criterion present in the past 6 months. . . .

 (1) often bullies, threatens, or intimidates others
 (2) often initiates physical fights
 (3) has used a weapon that can cause serious physical harm to others (e.g., a bat, brick, broken bottle, knife, gun)
 (4) has been physically cruel to people
 (5) has been physically cruel to animals
 (6) has stolen while confronting a victim (e.g., mugging, purse snatching, extortion, armed robbery)
 (7) has forced someone into sexual activity . . .
 (8) has deliberately engaged in fire setting with the intention of causing serious damage
 (9) has deliberately destroyed others' property (other than by fire setting) . . .
 (10) has broken into someone else's house, building, or car
 (11) often lies to obtain goods or favors or to avoid obligations (i.e., "cons" others)
 (12) has stolen items of nontrivial value without confronting a victim (e.g., shoplifting, but without breaking and entering; forgery) . . .
 (13) often stays out at night despite parental prohibitions, beginning before age 13 years
 (14) has run away from home overnight at least twice while living in parental or parental surrogate home (or once without returning for a lengthy period)
 (15) is often truant from school, beginning before age 13 years

B. The disturbance in behavior causes clinically significant impairment in social, academic, or occupational functioning.

C. If the individual is age 18 years or older, criteria are not met for Antisocial Personality Disorder.

Source: APA 1994:90–91.

have been established through field trials (Lahey et al. 1994; Spitzer, Davies, and Barkley 1990). In conducting these field trials, the general approach was to ask expert clinicians to rate clients against a list of diagnostic criteria and to also use their clinical judgment in assigning an appropriate *DSM* diagnosis.

The diagnostic criteria were "validated" to the extent that they corresponded to the clinical diagnoses of the experts. In this way, the development of diagnostic criteria for CD attempted to capture the clinical wisdom of experts and reduce it to a behavioral checklist, requiring a minimum of causal inference. But the expert clinicians who made the clinical diagnoses of CD were encouraged to consider all the available information, presumably including information about the social context and presumably using whatever causal inferences they found helpful in formulating a diagnosis. Can one assume, therefore, that the official diagnostic criteria have captured these contextual considerations and that the application of these criteria is sufficient to produce valid diagnoses?

Others have argued that using diagnostic criteria alone may not always result in valid diagnoses (Jensen and Hoagwood 1997; Jensen and Watanabe 1999; Spitzer and Wakefield 1999; Wakefield, Pottick, and Kirk 2002), because constructs such as "dysfunction" and "disorder" can only be inferred from the relationship between the behaviors and the situations in which they occur. That is why, in the past, a comprehensive psychiatric evaluation has always included the examination of the social and environmental factors that precipitated or contributed to the presenting problems. It may be impossible to distinguish disordered and non–disordered adolescent antisocial behavior solely on the basis of the presence of behavioral symptoms, independent of their context.

Purpose of the Study

This study examines whether meeting the *DSM-IV* diagnostic criteria for conduct disorder is sufficient to validly identify cases of mental disorder and exclude non–disordered problems in living, without considering the social context of adolescent antisocial behavior. Like the *DSM-III-R* and *DSM-IV* field trials for disruptive behavior disorders, which used expert judgments to validate diagnostic criteria, we also rely on expert intuition. If the *DSM-IV* criteria for conduct disorder can adequately capture the concept of mental disorder independent of the situational context in which the symptoms occur, then cases meeting the established *DSM* criteria should be judged by expert clinicians as cases of mental disorder regardless of the context of their occurrence. We hypothesize, however, that experienced clinicians in social work, psychology, and psychiatry will rely on social context in their assessment about the presence of a mental disorder.

Method

This study employed a between–subject experimental design involving the use of experimentally manipulated case vignettes. In each vignette a set of antisocial behaviors was held constant, while the situational context of those behaviors varied. This study parallels an earlier survey of graduate students (Kirk et al. 1999; Wakefield, Pottick, and Kirk 2002), but here we surveyed experienced mental health professionals. Participants received a cover letter, a brief case description of a youth engaging in antisocial behaviors, and a series of questions to answer after reading the case. The questions centered around whether the described youth had a mental disorder, as well as the likely course, etiology, and treatment responsiveness of the youth's problematic behavior. (A copy of the survey instrument can be obtained from the authors.) In this chapter for the first time we examine the responses from three mental health professionals to the critical question about whether they believed that the youth had a mental disorder. Other related reports from this study can be found elsewhere (Hsieh and Kirk 2003; Kirk and Hsieh, 2004).

Sampling Frame

The sampling frame consisted of psychiatrists, psychologists, and social workers in the United States who were most likely to have clinical experience with children or adolescents. This pool of clinicians was derived from the national membership directory of the three respective professional organizations: the American Psychiatric Association, the American Psychological Association, and the National Association of Social Workers. In addition, subgroups most likely to have experience with children and adolescents were specified to ensure an expert sample with regard to the focus of this study: adolescent antisocial behavior. For example, only psychiatrists who indicated an interest in child or adolescent psychiatry were selected. For psychology, only psychologists who are "active practitioners" (i.e., clinicians) and whose specialty or areas of interest relate to children and adolescents (e.g., clinical child psychology, conduct disorder, school psychology, etc.) were selected. For social work, only social workers whose areas of practice are in clinical mental health or school social work were selected. Student members were excluded. From this sampling frame, with the help of the research offices of the three professional organizations, 800 social workers, 1,100 psychologists, and 1,100 psychiatrists were randomly selected, resulting in 3,000 mental health clinicians for the initial sample.

After piloting and revising the survey instrument, we obtained approval from the university's Office for the Protection of Human Subjects. We then mailed a questionnaire to each member selected. The survey was conducted in four waves between January and April of 2000. Three additional waves of follow-up mailings were sent to nonrespondents after intervals of about three weeks (the second wave consisted of a reminder postcard, and the third and fourth waves contained a new cover letter and a complete questionnaire).

Vignette Development

We developed several experimental variations, systematically altering several aspects of the vignette. In this report we will focus only on how two contrasting versions of the social context of the youth's behavior affected judgments of the presence of mental disorder.

In both versions of the vignette, the youth's behavior met the *DSM-IV* criteria for conduct disorder. Each vignette begins with the same one-paragraph summary of symptoms and demographic information of an adolescent who has engaged in behaviors meeting the *DSM-IV* diagnostic criteria for conduct disorder. The behavior depicted in the vignettes resembles the "aggression" subtype of child conduct problems (Frick et al. 1993). The demographic information includes the adolescent's age, gender, ethnicity, and family background, as one might encounter in a brief clinical case summary, without much contextual information and no explanation for the symptoms. The first paragraph of the vignette reads as follows:

> Carlos is a 12-year-old Hispanic youth who lives with his parents and two older brothers in a blue-collar neighborhood in Los Angeles, where the family settled six years ago after moving from Mexico. Because of many disciplinary actions initiated by his teachers, he was referred to the school social worker for an evaluation. In addition to his often being truant, teachers have reported that Carlos often bullies or threatens his classmates and often initiates physical fights, which has seriously limited his social relationships. He was recently caught using a baseball bat as a weapon in a schoolyard fight.

The *DSM* conduct disorder criteria (see figure 3.1) that are met are: often truant, often bullies, often initiates physical fights, has used a weapon that can cause serious physical harm (a baseball bat), and that the behavior causes impaired social functioning (seriously limited his social relationships).

The second paragraph of the vignette was systematically altered to provide two very different contexts for the symptomatic behavior. In what we will call the "Environmental Reaction" vignette, the second paragraph describes the social context in which the youth's behavior occurred, suggesting that his behavior may have been rational, normal, or expected reaction to the given circumstances. It read as follows:

> The school social worker developed the following information through interviews with Carlos and his family. Carlos attends a public

junior high school that has recently gained citywide publicity for the rapid rise in violent juvenile gang activity. When Carlos first arrived at the school, he was terrified by the violence. Eventually, to avoid being preyed on, he and many of his classmates joined one of the rival gangs. Gang fights at the school often involve weapons like bats and bricks on both sides, as in the fight where Carlos was caught with a bat. To not engage in such warfare with one's gang would be seen as cowardly and lead to expulsion from the gang or worse. Carlos learned over time that the most effective defense against trouble-makers, other than staying away from school, was to be highly aggressive and intimidating to others. However, within his gang and outside in the community, he has close relationships and a keen sense of loyalty. Last summer, when Carlos returned to Mexico for his first extended visit with his grandparents, he seemed to be the model child they remembered and he got into no trouble whatsoever. But, once he returned to Los Angeles, his problematic behavior began again.

The other version of the second paragraph we will call the "Internal Dysfunction" vignette, because it was written to suggest that the youth's antisocial behavior was not a rational or normal response but may be the manifestation of a dysfunction of some cognitive, affective, or behavioral mechanisms. To accomplish the first part of this manipulation, the paragraph describes no potent environmental circumstances that would be expected to elicit the youth's antisocial behavior, nor do the behaviors seem to be proportional responses to social circumstances. Further, the paragraph describes the behaviors as directed relatively indiscriminately at others and consistent across settings, suggesting that something about the person, rather than the environment, is the likely cause. It also suggests that the behaviors seem irrational, that the youth lacks empathy, remorse, or concern for consequences, and that the behaviors appear to be impulsive despite punishments. The text of this version read as follows:

> The school social worker developed the following information through interviews with Carlos and his family. Carlos attends a respected public junior high school that has very little violence and provides a secure learning environment. However, Carlos reacts to the slightest perception of provocation with severe anger. Once he gets angry he often remains that way for several hours, and it is very hard to calm him down. He often escalates fights from fists to weapons like bat and bricks even when the other boy wants to stop. Carlos consistently ignores his teachers' requests and discipline seems to only exacerbate his problematic behavior. Even with those he hangs out with,

Carlos is easily irritated and frequently initiates fights. Last summer, when Carlos returned to Mexico for his first extended visit with his grandparents, he got into trouble in their town for the same kinds of problematic behavior he displayed in Los Angeles.

Measures

The primary dependent variable was the clinician's judgment of whether the youth described in the vignette had a mental disorder, as determined by the response to this questionnaire item: "According to my own view, this youth has a mental/psychiatric disorder." Participants responded to a six-point Likert scale ranging from 1 ("strongly disagree") to 6 ("strongly agree"). We report their responses as both mean scores and as dichotomous responses, the latter reflecting what is often required in clinical practice.

Response Rates

After incomplete responses, those deceased, and those without forwarding addresses were eliminated, the response rates were 58.2% from social workers ($N = 454$), 56.7% from psychologists ($N = 603$), and 45.8% from psychiatrists (483), resulting in a 53% overall response rate for the total sample ($N = 1,540$) (Hsieh 2001).

The sample averaged 53.6 years old; 47.8% male; 90% White/Caucasian. Our respondents were highly experienced clinicians. They averaged 21.7 years working in the field of mental health and 20.7 years of experience working with children or adolescents. More than 96% were licensed to practice. They were employed primarily in the following settings: 8.7% in general hospital, 4.7% in psychiatric hospital, 9.9% in outpatient clinic, 41% in private practice, 4.1% in CMHC, 0.6% in HMO, 14.2% in school (preschool–12th grade), 0.8% in criminal justice system, 5.9% in college/university, and 10.1% in others.

Comparisons of our sample with the known characteristics of clinical social workers, psychologists, and psychiatrists in the United States (Gibelman and Schervish 1997; Hsieh 2001; Zarin et al. 1998) indicated that we obtained a fairly representative sample; most known demographic characteristics fall within the 95% confidence interval of our sample's characteristics.

Findings

We hypothesized that mental health professionals would reach different judgments about the presence of mental disorder when an identical set of adolescent antisocial behaviors occurred in different social contexts. This hypothesis was supported (see table 3.1). Using analysis of variance, we compared whether there are differences in the judgment of the presence of a mental disorder (on a six-point agreement scale) between those who read the Environmental Reaction vignette and those who read the Internal Dysfunction vignette. Among social workers, psychologists, and psychiatrists there was significantly greater agreement ($p < .001$) with the view that the youth had a mental/psychiatric disorder when the behavior occurred in a context that suggested internal dysfunction than when the same behavior occurred in the context that suggested that the youth may have been responding to a difficult social environment. Among all three professions, the mean scores were strongly in the direction of agreeing that there was evidence of a mental disorder (means ranged from 4.65 to 5.25 on a six-point scale) when the ID vignette was presented and similarly skewed toward disagreement (means ranged from 2.06 to 3.12) when the ER vignette was presented.

When we dichotomized the responses into agree/disagree, almost all of the clinicians (96% of the psychiatrists, 94% of the psychologists, and 88% of the social workers) reading the Internal Dysfunction vignette agreed that the youth had a mental disorder (see table 3.2). When reading the ER vignette, however, significantly fewer agreed to the presence of a mental disorder (49%, 39%, and 15%, respectively, $p < .001$). Social context had a significant effect on experienced clinicians' judgments of the presence of mental disorder, despite the fact that the behaviors in both vignettes met the *DSM* diagnostic criteria for conduct disorder.

As secondary analysis, we also examined whether differences in judgments of mental disorder exist among the three mental health professions. *DSM* is designed to be used by all mental health professionals, and the purpose of the objective diagnostic criteria was to guide all practitioners to the same clinical judgments regardless of their theoretical orientation or professional background. In table 3.3 we compare the responses of the three groups of mental health professionals when they read the same vignettes. With both the ER and the ID vignettes, the responses of the psychiatrists and psychologists are similar, but in both vignettes social workers are significantly ($p < .05$) less likely than psychologists and psychiatrists to agree that a mental disorder is present. Social workers also seem to be most affected by contextual information. The difference in their mean scores between the two vignettes is 2.59, as compared with 2.13 for psychiatrists and 2.14 for psychologists.

Table 3.1
Context Effect on Judgments of the Presence of Mental Disorder by Profession (ANOVA)

Profession	N	Mean	SD	df	F	Prob
Social Workers						
ER	172	2.06	1.32	1	307.2	<.001
ID	133	4.65	1.22			
Psychologists						
ER	200	2.89	1.48	1	299.9	<.001
ID	206	5.03	.97			
Psychiatrists						
ER	161	3.12	1.58	1	209.2	<.001
ID	159	5.25	.97			

Notes: ER = Environmental Reaction; ID = Internal Dysfunction. Response scale from 1 = strongly disagree to 6 = strongly agree.

Table 3.2
Context Effect on Judgments of the Presence of Mental Disorders by Profession (Percent-Agreement)

Profession	N	Percent Agreeing to Presence of Mental Disorder	Chi-Square	df	Prob
Social Workers			159	1	<.001
ER	172	15.1			
ID	133	88.0			
Psychologists			139	1	<.001
ER	200	39.0			
ID	206	94.2			
Psychiatrists			89	1	<.001
ER	161	49.1			
ID	159	96.2			

Notes: ER = Environmental Reaction; ID = Internal Dysfunction. Response scale from 1 = strongly disagree to 6 = strongly agree. Percent agreeing include those responding 4 (mildly agree), 5 (moderately agree), and 6 (strongly agree).

Discussion

Our findings demonstrate the limitations of *DSM*'s operational criteria in differentiating mental disorders from non–disordered problems in living when they are used without consideration of the broader social context of the symptomatic behavior. We found that experienced mental health clinicians reached very different judgments about the presence of mental disorder when identical sets of adolescent antisocial behaviors, meeting the *DSM-IV*

Table 3.3
Differences Among Professions on Judgments of Presence of Mental Disorder

Context/Profession	N	Mean	SD	df	F	Prob	Scheffe Prob
ER	533			2	24.4	<.001	
Social Workers	172	2.06	1.32				<.05
Psychologists	200	2.89	1.47				
Psychiatrists	161	3.12	1.58				
ID	498			2	11.8	<.001	
Social Workers	133	4.65	1.21				<.05
Psychologists	206	5.03	.97				
Psychiatrists	159	5.25	.97				

diagnostic criteria of conduct disorder, occurred in different situational contexts. This result implies that making a judgment of mental disorder on the basis of symptoms alone may fail to validly distinguish disordered from non-disordered adolescent antisocial behavior. This failure could lead to the over-diagnosis of conduct disorder, since identical behavioral symptoms may indicate internal dysfunctions as well as normal or adaptive responses to a problematic environment, depending on the context of their occurrence, but the behavioral criteria will identify both as cases of mental disorder. This possibility is in line with the concerns of others who have suggested that the *DSM* criteria may contain a bias toward false-positive diagnosis (i.e., diagnosing non-disordered individuals as disordered) (Cantwell and Rutter 1994; Jensen and Hoagwood 1997; Spitzer and Wakefield 1999; Wakefield, Pottick, and Kirk 2002). Coolidge, Merwin, and Hyman (1990), for example, found that 39% of male college students met the *DSM-III-R* conduct disorder criteria, suggesting that the criteria have a tendency to overdiagnose conduct disorders in purportedly normal adults.

This risk of overdiagnosis of conduct disorder is likely to be greatest when the criteria are used in the assessment of youth living in disadvantaged communities, because problematic behaviors, even when associated with significant duration and social impairment, can be normal or adaptive responses to problematic environments. Our Environmental Reaction vignette describes the unfortunate reality of many youth in these communities. For example, in a study of eighth-grade inner-city children, Shakoor and Chalmers (1991) found that 75% of boys and 70% of girls surveyed had seen someone shot, stabbed, robbed, or killed. In another survey of inner-city youth, 42% of the males surveyed reported that their lives had been threatened (Gladstein, Slater-Rusonis, and Heald 1992). Although many children may respond to this increasing danger by staying out of harm's way, for others, guns and gang affiliation become the preferred methods of self-defense. The problematic behaviors of these latter youth may qualify them for a diagnosis of conduct disorder based on the *DSM-IV* diagnostic criteria, but our findings indicated that a majority of the mental health professionals in the United States would disagree that these youth have a mental disorder. These findings raise questions about the validity of the *DSM* diagnostic criteria for CD when used independent of the symptoms' social context.

Although experienced clinicians appear to use social context to make distinctions between adaptive and pathological antisocial behavior, epidemiological studies may not. Epidemiological surveys are often administered by lay interviewers using highly structured questionnaires based on the *DSM* diagnostic criteria. Their primary objective is to identify cases of particular disorders. These common data–gathering methods, however, do not require the interviewer to record social contextual information about the symptoms or to make causal inferences about the possibility that the behavior may be adaptive rather than pathological. Typically, such studies find that conduct disorder is more prevalent among youth from families of low socioeconomic status and neighborhoods characterized by high crime rates and social disorganization (Lahey et al. 1999). While our findings by no means refute the possibility that an adverse environment or poverty may contribute to the higher prevalence of psychiatric disturbance in those communities (Offord 1985), they do suggest an alternative explanation—namely, that epidemiological studies using the *DSM* criteria alone without regard to social context could lead to inflated prevalence rates. This possibility is consistent with the high prevalence rates of mental disorders identified in both the NIMH Epidemiologic Catchment Area (ECA) Study and the National Cormorbidity Survey (NCS), which prompted questions about whether some of the identified cases represent true psychopathologic disorders (Regier et al. 1998; Zarin and Earls 1993).

On the other hand, conduct disorder may not be as overdiagnosed in clinical populations as it is in community populations. First, clinicians may not adhere closely to *DSM* criteria in actual practice (Blashfield and Herkov 1996; Morey and Ochoa 1989). Furthermore, in clinical interviews clinicians tend to consider additional information, such as extenuating circumstances, in forming clinical judgments, and this may correct for the criteria's tendency toward overdiagnosis (Perry et al. 1987). Second, youth often get referred to mental health clinics because their behaviors (or the consequences of their behaviors) are beyond what others around them can tolerate. If a set of behaviors is considered quite normal and adaptive in the youth's particular social environment, and there is little distress on the part of the youth or others around them, the youth may never get referred to a mental health clinic and therefore will never be diagnosed. In this way, the criteria's seemingly dramatic tendency toward false positive diagnosis may be mitigated to some extent by help-seeking processes.

The fact that identical behaviors meeting the *DSM-IV* diagnostic criteria for conduct disorder are judged very differently by experienced clinicians, depending on the social context in which the symptomatic behaviors occur, suggests that some cases meeting the *DSM* diagnostic criteria do not necessarily warrant a diagnosis of conduct disorder. What is apparent from these data is that the *DSM* criteria alone are not always sufficient for validly differentiating mental disorders from non-disordered problems in living. To determine the presence of mental disorders, experienced clinicians make inferences about whether the condition at hand manifests internal dysfunction or normal responses to the environmental circumstances, and they rely on information concerning the social or situational context of the presenting symptoms when making such inferences. These clinical inferences are crucial for valid diagnosis, although currently they are not required by the *DSM* diagnostic criteria.

With regard to professional differences in clinicians' judgments of mental disorder, social workers appear to be more reluctant to judge someone to have a mental disorder than are psychologists and psychiatrists. Although the reasons for this are not entirely clear, we offer some possible explanations. First, compared to other mental health professions, social work tends to espouse the ecological perspective, which emphasizes environmental causes and circular causal transactions between individuals and their environments (Mattaini, chapter 4; Meyer 1983; Germain 1973), as opposed to intrapsychic or biological causes of human behavior. This orientation may predispose social work clinicians to attribute problematic behavior to environmental causes. Given that mental disorder is generally defined as a manifestation of a behavioral, psychological, or biological dysfunction *in the individual* (APA 1994), rather than in the social world, this propensity to attend to environmental causes may decrease the odds of reaching a judgment of mental disorder. Second, the professional culture of social work is averse to labeling an individual as pathological when social stigma might accompany such labeling; instead, it may tend to see problematic behaviors as normal responses by people who are in stressful or oppressive social environments. Third, social workers often work with people in disadvantaged or impoverished environmental settings. Consequently, they may have a higher perceived base rate of the kinds of adolescent antisocial behavior that are depicted in the vignettes and thus be more likely to consider them as normal, whereas psychologists and psychiatrists would not. Last, it is possible that social workers' implicit notion of mental disorder is more context-based. Although our findings show that context affects disorder judgments for all three mental health professions, social workers may be least acculturated to *DSM*'s *operational* definition of disorder as a syndrome or pattern of problematic behavior associated with significant duration and impaired functioning and largely independent of context. This may also explain why social workers' judgments of mental disorder seem to be affected the most by varying contextual information. Nevertheless, the explanations offered here are somewhat speculative. Future studies are needed to further examine the effects of theoretical orientation, causal attribution, and other factors that might underlie such professional differences. This study has limitations. Because our experimental stimuli consist of behaviors that meet the *DSM-IV* diagnostic criteria for conduct disorder, the findings may not be generalizable to other disorder categories in the *DSM*. It is possible that different symptom features vary in their diagnostic value for the construct of "mental disorder." The term *diagnostic value*, borrowed from the literature on social cognition, refers to a behavioral cue's ability to distinguish between different categories (Fiske and Taylor 1991). For example, "frequently initiating fights" may have a low diagnostic value, whereas "auditory hallucinations" may have a high diagnostic value for the concept of mental disorder, because they are associated with a narrower pool of other possible trait categories. Thus, certain symptoms, such as hallucinations, may be less dependent on contextual information to accurately identify the underlying disorder construct, compared to other symptoms, such as criteria for conduct, depressive, or anxiety disorders. It will be valuable for future studies to examine whether social context affects judgments across multiple disorder categories.

Although written case vignettes have been used extensively in studies of clinical decision making (Garb 1998), they do have shortcomings. The information presented lacks the behavioral subtleties that can be observed in personal interviews. Respondents to vignettes have minimal information, less than they would have in actual practice, and are not subjected to real-life externalities, such as clinic constraints, pressure from the patient's family, or reimbursement structures that might otherwise influence their judgments. Also, in the particular vignettes used in this study, the youth's antisocial behaviors were presented in two deliberately unambiguous contexts, suggesting either internal dysfunction or normal adaptation to difficult circumstances. Frequently, antisocial behavior in childhood and adolescence likely involves reciprocal transactions between the child's propensity to antisocial behavior and adverse environmental influences (Lahey, Waldman, and McBurnett 1999). Thus the conceptual distinction of internal dysfunction and environmental reaction delineated in this study and endorsed by the clinicians we surveyed may be less clear-cut in real life than our results appear to suggest.

The current approach to psychiatric diagnosis relies on the use of the *DSM* diagnostic criteria to identify cases of mental disorder. The *DSM* assumes that mental disorders can be identified by the presence of "objective" behavioral indicators, largely independent of the causes of the symptomatic behavior or the social context in which it occurs. At least in the case of conduct disorder, our findings demonstrate the limitations of diagnostic criteria in differentiating mental disorders from non-disordered problems in living when such criteria are used alone, without consideration of the social context of the symptomatic behavior. Consideration of the social context is indispensable in accurately determining the presence of mental disorders.

References

Achenbach, T., C. Howell, H. Quay, and K. Conners. 1991. National survey of problems and competencies among four- to sixteen-year-olds: Parents' reports for normative and clinical samples. *Monographs of the Society for Research in Child Development* 56:1–131.

American Psychiatric Association (APA). 1980. *Diagnostic and Statistical Manual of Mental Disorders (DSM-III).* 3d ed. Washington, D.C.: APA.

———. 1987. *Diagnostic and Statistical Manual of Mental Disorders (DSM-III-R).* 3d ed. rev. Washington, D.C.: APA.

———. 1994. *Diagnostic and Statistical Manual of Mental Disorders (DSM-IV).* 4th ed. Washington, D.C.: APA.

———. 2000. *Diagnostic and Statistical Manual of Mental Disorders (DSM-IV-TR).* Washington, D.C.: APA.

Blashfield, R. K. and M. Herkov. 1996. Investigating clinician adherence to diagnosis by criteria: A replication of Morey and Ochoa (1989). *Journal of Personality Disorders* 10:219–228.

Cantwell, D. and M. Rutter. 1994. Classification: Conceptual Issues and Substantive Findings. In M. Rutter, E. Taylor, and L. Horsov, eds., *Child and Adolescent Psychiatry,* 3–21. London: Blackwell.

Coolidge, F., M. Merwin, and J. Hyman. 1990. Some problems with the diagnostic criteria of the antisocial personality disorder in DSM-III-R: A preliminary study. *Journal of Personality Disorders* 4:407–413.

Fiske, S. and S. E. Taylor. 1991. *Social Cognitions.* 2d ed. New York: McGraw-Hill.

Frick, P., B. Lahey, R. Loeber et al. 1993. Oppositional defiant disorder and conduct disorder: a meta-analytic review of factor analyses and cross-validation in a clinical sample. *Clinical Psychology Review* 13:319–340.

Garb, Howard N. 1998. *Studying the Clinician: Judgment Research and Psychological Assessment.* Washington, D.C.: American Psychological Association.

Germain, C. B. 1973. An ecological perspective in casework practice. *Social Casework* 54:323–330.

Gibelman, M. and P. Schervish. 1997. *Who We Are: A Second Look.* Washington, D.C.: NASW Press.

Gladstein, J., E. J. Slater-Rusonis, and F. P. Heald. 1992. A comparison of inner-city and upper-middle class youths' exposure to violence. *Journal of Adolescent Health* 13:275–280.

Hsieh, Derek K. 2001. Distinguishing mental disorders from problems in living: The effect of social context in judgments of adolescent antisocial behavior. Ph.D. diss., Department of Social Welfare, University of California, Los Angeles.

Hsieh, D. and Stuart A. Kirk. 2003. The effect of social context on psychiatrists' judgments of adolescent antisocial behavior. *Journal of Child Psychology and Psychiatry* 44:877–887.

Jensen, P. S. and K. Y. Hoagwood. 1997. The book of names: DSM-IV in context. *Development and Psychopathology* 9:231–249.

Jensen, P. S. and H. Watanabe. 1999. Sherlock Holmes and child psychopathology assessment approaches: The case of the false-positive. *Journal of the American Academy of Child and Adolescent Psychiatry* 38:138–146.

Kirk, S. A. and D. Hsieh. 2004. Diagnostic consistency in assessing conduct disorder: An experiment of the effect of social context. *American Journal of Orthopsychiatry* 74:43–55.

Kirk, Stuart A., J. C. Wakefield, D. Hsieh, and K. Pottick. 1999. Social context and social workers' judgment of mental disorder. *Social Service Review* 73:82–104.

Lahey, B., B. Applegate, R. Barkley et al. 1994. DSM-IV field trials for oppositional defiant disorder and conduct disorder in children and adolescents. *American Journal of Psychiatry* 151:1163–1171.

Lahey, B., T. Miller, R. Gordon, and A. Riley. 1999. Developmental Epidemiology of the Disruptive Disorders. In A. Hogan, ed., *Handbook of the Disruptive Behavior Disorders,* 23–48. New York: Plenum.

Lahey, B., I. Waldman, and K. McBurnett. 1999. Annotation: The development of antisocial behavior—An integrative causal model. *Journal of Child Psychology and Psychiatry and Allied Disciplines* 40:669—682.

Meyer, C. H. 1983. *Clinical Social Work in an Eco-systems Perspective.* New York: Columbia University Press.

Morey, L. and E. Ochoa. 1989. An investigation of adherence to diagnostic criteria: Clinical diagnosis of the DSM-III personality disorders. *Journal of Personality Disorders* 3:180–192.

Offord, D. 1985. Child psychiatric disorders: Prevalence and perspectives. *Psychiatric Clinics of North America* 8:637–652.

Perry, J., P. Lavori, S. Cooper, L. Hoke, and M. O'Connell. 1987. The diagnostic interview schedule and DSM-III antisocial personality disorder. *Journal of Personality Disorders* 1:121–131.

Peterson, A. 1988. Adolescent development. *Annual Review of Psychology* 38:583–607.

Regier, D., C. Kaelber, D. Rae et al. 1998. Limitations of diagnostic criteria and assessment instruments for mental disorders. *Archives of General Psychiatry* 55:109–115.

Richters, J. and D. Cicchetti. 1993. Mark Twain meets DSM-III-R: Conduct disorder, development, and the concept of harmful dysfunction. *Development and Psychopathology* 5:5–29.

Shakoor, B. and D. Chalmers. 1991. Co-victimization of African-American children who witness violence: Effects on cognitive, emotional, and behavioral development. *Journal of the National Medical Association* 83:233–238.

Shedler, J. and J. Block. 1990. Adolescent drug use and psychological health: A longitudinal inquiry. *American Psychologist* 45:612–630.

Spitzer, R., M. Davies, and R. Barkley. 1990. The DSM-III-R field trial of disruptive behavior disorders. *Journal of the American Academy of Child and Adolescent Psychiatry* 29:690–697.

Spitzer, R. and J. C. Wakefield. 1999. DSM-IV diagnostic criterion for clinical significance: Does it help solve the false positives problem? *American Journal of Psychiatry* 156:1856–1864.

Wakefield, J. C. 1992. The concept of mental disorder: On the boundary between biological facts and social values. *American Psychologist* 47:373–388.

———. 1993. The limits of operationalization: A critique of Spitzer and Endicott's (1978) proposed operational criteria for mental disorder. *Journal of Abnormal Psychology* 102:160–172.

Wakefield, Jerome C., Kathleen Pottick, and Stuart A. Kirk. 2002. Should the DSM-IV diagnostic criteria for conduct disorder consider social context? *American Journal of Psychiatry* 159:380–386.

Zarin, D. and F. Earls. 1993. Diagnostic decision making in psychiatry. *American Journal of Psychiatry* 150:197–206.

Zarin, D., H. Pincus, B. Peterson et al. 1998. Characterizing psychiatry with findings from the 1996 National Survey of Psychiatric Practice. *American Journal of Psychiatry* 155:397–404.

Chapter 4

Mapping Practice: Assessment, Context, and Social Justice

Mark A. Mattaini

The approach taken to assessment in social work practice has critical social justice implications. Social work, including mental health social work, can be a major factor in determining whether clients/consumers, families, and communities remain mired in misery or achieve statuses consistent with human dignity and human rights. The choice of assessment models is therefore not simply a matter of convenience, preference, or practicality. How the worker—and the client—see and understand the situation largely determines what can and will be done (Meyer 1993).

Professional practice is necessarily driven by a recognized or unrecognized *master narrative* (Follette, Houts, and Hayes 1992:325), an overall epistemic understanding of the phenomena of interest. This narrative determines not only how things are seen but also what is seen. Krasner (1992) uses Kuhn's (1970) construct of the *disciplinary matrix* to describe such an epistemic perspective, which includes "symbolic generalizations, beliefs in models, shared values . . . and *exemplars* or recognized puzzle solutions" (Krasner 1992:309). While selections among possible master narratives are often shaped by historical chance, pragmatic effects of the choices are critical. For example, the most common system of assessment in contemporary mental health social work, and increasingly in other fields of practice as well, is psychiatric diagnosis structured by the *Diagnostic and Statistical Manual of Mental Disorders (DSM)* (APA 1952, 1968, 1980, 1987, 1994, 2000). A *DSM* diagnosis justifies intervention in the life of a person who may be disturbing the social order, provides entrée into service systems, offers an explanation to patient and family for a confusing and frightening set of behaviors and feelings, may exempt an individual from punitive consequences for actions, provides clarity to the confused practitioner, enables the practitioner to be paid, and sim-plifies research, among other consequences (Follette, Houts, and Hayes 1992). Given these effects, it is not surprising that *DSM* diagnosis has become a well-established cultural practice in most helping professions, in some cases after some years of resistance.

Note, however, that the effects of diagnosis listed above are largely short term. In agency settings, as in the contemporary business world, short-term effects tend to drive institutional practice, but there are often longer-range consequences that may be much less advantageous. *DSM* diagnosis fits a corporate model of services driven by financial and status considerations and provides a tool for a major contemporary industry. Optimal individual and collective long-term outcomes may not be heavily weighted within such a corporate paradigm. Alternative systems for assessment may therefore be more consistent with social work's historic mission, and with client/consumer and community well-being.

The choice of a master narrative requires clarity regarding the purpose of the work to be done. "The purpose of social work is to enhance adaptations among clients ('clients' may include individuals, families, communities, and other cultural entities) and the systems within which those clients are em-bedded, consistent with social justice" (Mattaini, Lowery, and Meyer 2002:x). The purpose of social work, at its core, is dynamic and transactional. The purpose of social work is not to cure mental illness (although social work practice may contribute to that outcome). The purpose of social work is to assist in moving from a present life configuration to a more personally and collectively satisfying and just configuration. In addition, "social work" ought always to be, on some level . . . *social*. The selection of adequate as-sessment systems emerges from this professional purpose and identity.

Professional assessment involves collaboratively achieving an understand-ing of *what is happening* in the client's transactional world, *why* what is hap-pening may be happening, what the client and others *want to construct,* and *what resources* are available for that work. Conceptual frameworks—disciplinary matrices—are necessary for determining what to look at (since time is always limited), for answering the "why?" question in parsimonious ways, and for determining how to do the constructional work required. Some approaches to assessment provide much more useful conceptual tools for this work than do others. Ethically, decisions among approaches ought to be based on what is the most useful for practice.

One way to discriminate among systems of assessment is to contrast cat-egorical, dimensional, and contextual approaches (Mattaini and Kirk 1991). *Categorical systems* (like *DSM*) separate phenomena into mutually exclusive classes. Some of the distinguishing features of *DSM,* for example, are an emphasis on differential diagnosis (e.g., "Is this patient suffering from borderline personality disorder or from histrionic personality disorder?") and criteria—as clear as possible—for determining whether a person does, or does not, "have" a disorder. All categorical systems discard information, since only some factors are examined—and those often in binary (yes | no) ways. This simplification can be viewed as both advantageous and disadvantageous. Simple organizing categories that encompass many cases may facilitate communication and statistical recording, but the information discarded includes the details that make each case unique and that are often critical for case planning.

Dimensional systems (Rapid Assessment Instruments [RAIs] are examples) focus on answering the question "how much" of a problem, like depression, is present, although they also often include clinical cutting scores, which can be used to assess categorically whether a significant problem is or is not present. The advantages of dimensional systems are probably apparent; being able to track whether problems are getting better or worse is central to much of professional practice. Interestingly, *DSM* increasingly includes dimensional measures, acknowledging that it is important to recognize degrees of certain problems.

Contextual systems begin with the assumption that most cases that come to the attention of social workers involve multiple dimensions, multiple persons, and multiple systems in transaction. For example, a woman may present who meets the criteria for dysthymic disorder, but it may be much more important to discover that she is being battered (a violation of the Universal Declaration of Human Rights, 1948), that her extended family and neighbors know this but have not taken action (a reflection of larger societal justice issues), and that she has two children that she does not believe she can support if she leaves the batterer than it is to determine whether her mood has been depressed for most of the day for a full two years or whether she meets at least two of six possible associated features, as called for in *DSM*. Contextual approaches to assessment may include categorical ("Is there a significant problem in the client's marriage?") and dimensional ("What is this patient's global level of functioning?") components, but their essence is a holistic, transactional view.

Categorical Systems

The two most commonly discussed categorical systems for social work in mental health settings, and increasingly in other settings, like family services (where "family service" agencies have often become "child and family mental health" agencies as the result of shifts in funding streams), are *DSM* and the Person-in-Environment (PIE) system (Karls and Wandrei 1994a). PIE is a social work–developed adjunct to *DSM* that includes attention to categories of role functioning and environmental problems. Because it is not closely tied to funding, however, and has inherent limitations (Karls et al. 1997), PIE does not appear to have penetrated the field very deeply. Other categorical systems are available as well, some of which are discussed below. Still, *DSM* is clearly the major categorical player in contemporary practice, and it is emphasized in the material that follows.

In part, the hegemony of *DSM* is the result of a decision by the psychiatric community to encourage social workers and psychologists to use psychiatry's diagnostic system, which now underpins payment in nearly all mental health programs. As a result, a medical perspective that sees the work to be done as treatment of specific disorders, and views clients as carriers of personal pathology, has become a nearly universal disciplinary matrix in mental health practice across professions. An undercurrent of criticism of this disease-oriented framework has been present in the medical community for decades (e.g., Laing 1967; Peele 1995; Szasz 1960), but such critiques have largely been marginalized.

There are a number of advantages to categorical systems of diagnoses or problems. There are also a number of problems related to the use of such systems, some of them quite serious; these will be briefly sketched in the material that follows. Alternate taxonomies that distinguish classes of goal-states or targets have also been proposed. These share some but not all of the advantages and disadvantages of problem-focused diagnostic systems, and are discussed separately.

Advantages of Categorical Systems for Problem Assessment

Clearly, some level of categorization is necessary for communication. In fact, discarding all categorization would require giving up language altogether, since language relies on classes of objects, events, conditions, and actions (Hayes and Follette 1992). At the same time, categorization must usually be seen as a useful fiction. For example, one chair or one event labeled a hallucination is not the same as another; it is just similar on some dimensions. For some purposes, like billing, statistical records, and some research, rough taxonomies may have significant utility.

In situations where a "first-generation" disease is present (one in which the physical cause, e.g., a bacillus or a tumor, can be specifically traced [Peele 1995]), identifying who has and who does not have that disorder can be extremely important for intervention planning. There are a few examples of such disorders in *DSM*—but very few. Most *DSM* disorders are "second-generation" problems known only from "what the sufferers say and do" (Peele 1995:5) in transaction with others, essentially social constructions. The validity of such diagnoses is a significant issue, and it will be discussed later in this chapter.

One potential advantage of categorical systems is their fit with some forms of evidence-based practice and with practice guidelines, which are increasingly regarded as important for practice (*Research on Social Work Practice* 1999). Current efforts to develop evidence-based practice in many cases begin by identifying a categorical problem, although subsequent steps move into more-contextual analyses (Gambrill 1999). Similarly, most efforts to develop practice guidelines begin with a diagnosis or class of problems and provide guidance for dealing with that issue on the basis of current best-supported interventive options. Note, for example, that a key developer of task-centered practice has recently published the Task Planner (Reid 2000), essentially an index of target problems listing empirically supported tasks that might be used to address each. (A certain amount of dimensional and contextual material is often included in such efforts.)

Limitations of Categorical Systems for Problem Assessment

There are at least four important issues related to the use of categorical systems like *DSM* or PIE for problem assessment. First, the existing systems almost universally apply the diagnosis or problem label to the individual, rather than to the case, considerably limiting attention to issues of family and other collective processes within which considerations of social justice and oppression are likely to be embedded. Second, existing categorical systems and treatment arrangements are deeply culture-bound and may inadvertently support cultural colonialism (Bolling 2002). Third, the evidence so far suggests that it is difficult to achieve adequate reliability in categorical diagnosis. Finally, the validity of current systems has not been established, and in many cases probably cannot be, because of the very nature of those systems.

INDIVIDUAL FOCUS

Current taxonomies focus on the individual client/consumer, asking the central question "What is her problem?" Asking the question in this way precludes a primary focus on collective processes or oppressive environments and institutions. It might be possible to develop a categorical system that includes different classifications based on the multiple actors and systems that have an impact on the case, but such a system would come at the cost of overwhelming complexity. A staggering number of categories capturing most of life's realities as embedded in multiple interlocking systems would be required.

As a result, current taxonomies focus primarily on mapping a class of problem or a diagnosis to an individual, even when doing so may badly distort the realities. Consider, for example, the PIE system, in which a "woman who defers to her husband because she fears beatings" is seen as having a "spouse role problem, victimization type" (Karls and Wandrei 1994b:21). Victimization is defined in the same section as "turning . . . fear [of anticipated harm] into a behavioral pattern in which a person *gives in to fears, giving up his or her power* to deal with the intimidator or victimizer" (Karls and Wandrei 1994b:21, emphasis added). The need to assign an individual category in this example results in suggesting that the problem lies in the "behavioral pattern" of the client who "gives in" and "gives up . . . power," rather than seeing her as the victim of a serious human rights violation. The real problem in this case, of course, lies elsewhere.

In some cases, like recent versions of *DSM,* efforts have been made to include a separate axis that lists environmental issues. These axes are usually not actually used in agency settings, however, and at best can begin to capture only a small part of the dynamics of a case. Studies indicate that unless assessment is specifically structured to direct attention to environmental issues, social workers tend to attend primarily to intrapersonal problems (Lindsey 1998; Mattaini 1993; Rosen and Livne 1992). Although some suggest that the core assessment issue is clarification of the client's problem (e.g., Wakefield 1996), social work assessment that is consistent with professional purpose and social justice is, rather, about "what new reality should be constructed, how this differs from the present reality, and what resources are needed to move from the latter to the former" (Mattaini and Meyer 2002:19).

CULTURAL ISSUES

DSM is designed to focus on individual pathology, consistent with European worldviews and medical epistemology. The assumption that a single classification system, developed within a particular cultural and disciplinary matrix, can be universally applicable reflects a frightening level of cultural arrogance. A classification developed by white, middle-class Americans (and a few members of other groups whom they have trained) is unlikely to be universally reliable or valid even in the United States, much less internationally (for extensive examples, refer to Castillo 1997 and Castillo 1998). Diverse cultural groups define human problems and normative development in ways that are often incompatible with a Euro-American medical narrative (e.g., Alemán et al. 2000; Canino and Spurlock 2002; Murguia, Peterson, and Zea 2003). Mainstream professionals sometimes indicate that some groups are not adequately "psychologically minded" and tend to "somaticize." An Asian helping professional, however, might just as validly suggest that persons in Western culture are not adequately "somatically minded" and tend to "psychologize" (Fabrega 1989).

A study of depression and problem drinking on the Flathead reservation in Montana (O'Nell 1993) provides an example. The results suggest that behavior and emotions may appear similar across groups but may differ dramatically at their cultural core. Among the Flathead people studied, "to be sad is to be aware of human interdependence and the gravity of historical, tribal, familial and personal loss. To be depressed, and that includes tearfulness and sleep and appetite disturbances, is to demonstrate maturity and connectedness to the Indian world. A carefree attitude is often thought of as indicative of immaturity" (218). Clearly, *DSM* criteria are inadequate for capturing such realities, and would in fact suggest that culturally normative behavior is a reflection of mental illness. If even such a clearly defined problem as depression does not hold well cross-culturally, imagine the potential issues with diagnoses like personality disorders.

Something like schizophrenia appears around the world—but with significantly different manifestations, prevalence, course, and outcome. The World Health Organization supported cross-national studies of a core schizophrenic syndrome that was identified by one or more Schneiderian symptoms (Castillo 1997). That syndrome was often manifested in culturally specific symptomatology, but other important differences also emerged. In industrialized societies, the prevalence of the syndrome appeared to be higher, the course longer, and the typical outcome substantially worse than in "less developed" nations. In part this may be because of the stresses present in modern societies, as suggested by the stress-diathesis model for understanding schizophrenia. The differential results are also apparently related to differences between sociocentric societies (those in which the primary unit of attention is the group) and egocentric societies (those in which the central cultural construct is the individual) (Castillo 1997). In sociocentric societies, problems are likely to be conceptualized primarily in terms of "What do we need to do?" rather than in terms of "What is wrong with the person, and how can it be cured?" As a result, the levels of expressed emotion (Brown et al. 1962) and patterns of coercive transactions in family and community (Halford 1991) may be lower than in egocentric societies, leading to improved course and outcome.

DSM now includes an appendix outlining certain culturally specific disorders, some of which may be subsumed under standard *DSM* categories. While useful, this addition does not address the larger issues, which, within a particular cultural group, include:

- What is happening here—is there a "mental illness" or something else?
- Is the pattern we are seeing outside the norm? If so, is it a problem?
- If the pattern is a problem, where do the roots of the problem lie?

- Is this a personal problem or a collective problem?
- Is intervention necessary? If so, what will help?

Given that culture is additive and augmentative, particularly in the modern world, particular individuals and groups may be influenced by multiple and often conflicting cultural meanings, values, and experiences. Constructing and validating a single taxonomy that can encompass all of these factors is a challenge with which no current categorical system has begun to grapple.

RELIABILITY

The reliability of categorical diagnosis has so far proven to be quite weak. *DSM* is the only categorical system for which extensive reliability testing has been conducted, and the results have been disappointing (Kirk and Kutchins 1992; Kutchins and Kirk 1986). Reliability testing of recent revisions has not been conducted, probably in part because there is little reason to expect improvements from the results obtained for *DSM-III*. To briefly summarize the problem, interrater reliability for most Axis I diagnoses did not reach a kappa level of .70 (the developer's standard for good agreement). Except for specific development disorders, no Axis II diagnoses reached this level (Kirk and Kutchins 1992).

This issue is discussed more extensively by Nugent (chapter 6) and will not be further considered here. The roots of the problem, however, merit mention. Those of us who have had considerable practice experience in mental health settings know that people's problems often do not fall neatly into a single diagnostic category. A client/consumer may manifest features of delusional, psychotic, personality, and mood disorders, for example. Many cases are not a good fit in any single category, and reliability and related problems are only compounded if one simply begins to list multiple diagnoses. In addition, the contingencies surrounding reimbursement result in high levels of underdiagnosis and overdiagnosis, which further distort the process and raise critical legal and ethical problems (Kirk and Kutchins 1988).

VALIDITY

The validity of taxonomies of "mental disorders" is among the most serious issues. Are diagnoses "real" or are they fictions that distort the practice process in ways that raise additional practical, ethical, and even moral problems? The implications of assigning labels that indicate that clients carry pathology, even, for personality disorders, "pathologies of the entire person" (Davis and Millon 1994) are profound. The social construction of mental illness stigmatizes and often fosters internalized oppression (Lundin 1998). Some disorders probably are illnesses in the classic sense; they emerge from biological abnormalities, although environmental transactions clearly shape their manifestation and course. Many of the problems included in existing taxonomies, however, appear at their core to involve learning processes and fit poorly into a medical matrix (Mattaini 1994). The continuing expansion of what is considered a mental illness may also trivialize those disorders that really are illnesses.

The heart of the validity problem is the effort to construct a classification system that has no connection with an understanding of the roots of the problem, a decision that was made for *DSM-III* and subsequent editions in order to escape the psychodynamic roots of *DSM-I* and *DSM-II*. This atheoretical course is not consistent with a scientific approach. Scientific advance does not come from developing increasingly detailed and ultimately unwieldy descriptive taxonomies but rather from increased understanding of the roots of differences found. Follette, Houts, and Hayes (1992) indicate that biology moved to a new scientific level when "taxonomies no longer did the job of explaining, but instead became the thing to be explained" resulting in "a reduction of categories by theory" (328). The ultimate taxonomy unconstrained by an explanatory framework would include one or more unique diagnoses for each case—because each case is genuinely different from others. Scientific understanding, by contrast, focuses on determining what "really goes together" in a single class.

In addition, contemporary work in biology, physics, and other scientific disciplines increasingly suggests that the most parsimonious and powerful way to explain complex phenomena is to begin with an epistemological assumption that relationships, rather than entities, provide the primary structure of reality (Capra 1996). The world is best understood from this perspective as an inseparable web of transactions, rather than an aggregate of individual, autonomous, discrete entities. This epistemic view is consistent with contextual approaches to understanding cases, but it is very hard to capture categorically.

Target/Goal-Focused Taxonomies

While in many service systems a client must have a "problem" as a ticket into services, there is increasing interest in social work in categorical systems that are structured around "targets" or "goal-states" rather than disorders or problems (Kanfer and Schefft 1988; Mattaini 2003; Rosen, Proctor, and Staudt 2003). Such proposals are, however, controversial (Kirk and Reid 2002). Many of the issues discussed earlier with regard to problem-focused taxonomies are equally challenging in target-focused systems, including reliability and some validity questions. Some target-focused approaches, however, have taken the important step of attempting to construct a classification system that emerges from scientific understandings of human behavior in context, a major advance over merely descriptive systems (e.g., functional analysis, Hayes and Follette 1992; behavior analysis, Kanfer and Schefft 1988).

This said, the problems of individual focus and cultural challenges are present in many target-based approaches as well. While such systems could target behaviors not just of client/consumers but also of system actors, such a wider focus is not found in the existing categorical literature to any substantial extent. It appears to be much easier to expand the worker's perspective using contextual systems like those discussed later. Focusing on the goal-state to be constructed may be particularly useful in work with cultural groups who do not construe human problems in terms of pathology or mental disorders. Constructional (Goldiamond 2002) practice of this kind may therefore help in expanding the utility of practice with diverse populations, if grounded in a perspective that honors cultural differences. Still, such work is in its infancy, and there are few financial incentives to pursue it.

Dimensional Systems for Assessment

Categorical systems for assessment are based on nominal scales. Dimensional systems involve measurement at higher levels—at least ordinal, though many claim at least interval level. Dimensional systems discard less information than do categorical systems, and at least in the areas of the dimensions considered, can therefore offer a richer assessment. Even *DSM* increasingly uses at least ordinal ratings of problem severity, a genuine advance. Not every assessment system that claims dimensional status actually achieves it, however. For example, the standard model of strengths assessment recommended in the strengths perspective (Cowger and Snively 2002) is sometimes described as multidimensional, involving the intersection of an environmental-client axis and a strengths-deficits axis. The examples provided, however, involve the construction of four lists of categorical factors: a list of social and political strengths (environment), a list of physical/physiological strengths (client), a list of social and political obstacles (environment), and one of psychological obstacles (client). The approach is only a very limited approximation of a dimensional system providing ordinal or higher data.

Dimensional assessment is increasingly popular in mental health practice and research. The use of Rapid Assessment Instruments (e.g., Corcoran and Fischer 2000) is becoming more common in practice, as students in professional schools are taught how to use them in evaluating practice. Clients also often react very positively to measuring and tracking progress over time (see Mattaini 2002b). Once "the problem"—for example, depression—is established, the use of an RAI to track progress over time, sometimes even very short intervals, can provide very useful data to guide intervention. Behavioral observation, which involves counting actual events, is an even more sensitive and often more valid form of dimensional assessment. Rating scales of various kinds are easy to use, and often appear to be genuinely facilitative of practice. Dimensional assessments of various kinds can be useful for demonstrating improvement to funders as well, which is obviously important for program survival in many organizations. Such measures are also the basis of the single-system evaluation designs that are now widely recommended in social work practice.

Issues raised with regard to categorical systems also need to be examined for dimensional systems. There are well-established dimensional systems for assessing family and organizational functioning; an exclusive focus on individual factors is not necessarily characteristic of dimensional assessment. On the other hand, if problems are construed as individual (often because of an initial categorical diagnosis), the clinician is likely to select dimensional measures that focus on the individual. This is a particular issue in organizations in which reimbursement depends on such diagnosis, and especially in those in which reimbursement is available only for work with individuals. (The power of family and systemic intervention is often not harnessed in such settings. There are still many children receiving play therapy, for example, who should be receiving educational and family-based services instead—a serious ethical issue.)

The cultural-fit question is not resolved by the use of dimensional measures, but sometimes it at least begins to be addressed. Observational data regarding the incidence, severity, or duration of either problem behaviors or target behaviors can be useful cross-culturally, but only if behaviors that are culturally important to the case are the ones tracked. In addition, actions on the part of an individual client are commonly easier to observe and track than are those of system actors and larger systems, so the sociocentric/egocentric question remains important. Validation procedures for some RAIs have examined differences across ethnic and racial groups, clearly a valuable step. Still, if the dimension being tracked is culturally dystonic, even if reliable results can be obtained by using a particular measure, they may be irrelevant or may even structure an inadvertent process of imposing another cultural group's understanding of the problems being faced. What is asked, and what is not asked, on the instrument may teach what should be considered during intervention. Clients from some groups are also often concerned about the secrets that may be revealed through "psychological testing" as well, and this issue can threaten validity.

Dimensional measures shine in the reliability area. Not all such measures have been carefully evaluated for reliability, but the processes for doing so are well established (Hudson 1982, 1989), and reliability data are increasingly available to help the practitioner decide whether to use a particular measure and how confident to be about the results. Inter-observer reliability for observational data and test-retest and internal consistency data for paper and pencil measures can be evaluated, and measurement procedures can be improved by doing so. Validity is a more complex question. Observational data are likely to be the most valid. Rating scales, especially individualized scales constructed with the client, often have high social and face validity, although their reliability, and validity of other types, is generally unknown. Measurement approaches that have been validated for some groups usually have not been for many others, so there is still considerable work to be done.

An underlying issue with dimensional systems, however, is which dimension(s) to assess. A prior decision needs to be made; for example, one would ordinarily use a depression measure only if there appears to be depression present. The decision is critical, since practitioner and client are most likely to focus on the factors that they are measuring, to the exclusion of many others. The best single-problem scale is worse than useless if used to track the wrong problem, so how can we be sure we are capturing data on the right one? Walter Hudson, who spent decades developing and validating measures of particular problem dimensions, turned to this problem later in his career. Hudson and McMurtry (1997) note that "social work practice increasingly emphasizes the person-in-environment and ecological systems models, but assessment in this context is rendered more rather than less difficult by the practitioner having to resort to a jumbled array of unidimensional assessment tools" (79). Hudson and McMurtry's Multi-Problem Screening Inventory (MPSI) is an effort to address this problem, collecting information on twenty-seven different dimensions which can be used to develop an intervention plan and guide selection of dimensional measures that relate to the core issues in the case.

More work related to reliability and validity is needed on the MPSI and similar systems before they can be confidently relied on for practice decisions. But the issue they are trying to address is absolutely critical. Both contemporary science and practice experience suggest that networks of interlocking transactions within the ecological context are key for understanding all but the simplest cases, although some social workers remain unconvinced. Wakefield (1996), for example, doubted the "general existence of the . . . circular transactions in social work cases" (11) often described by ecological frameworks for practice. According to the available research, however, the examples Wakefield provided to support his doubt do in fact demonstrate the importance of reciprocal transactions among multiple actors and systems (Mattaini and Meyer 2002). Some form of contextual assessment appears to be essential to practice with most challenging and complex cases, regardless of field of practice.

Contextual Systems for Assessment

By their very nature, contextual systems of assessment address some of the problems that necessarily limit the utility of categorical and dimensional systems. At the same time, they raise other very challenging issues. Contextual assessment begins by trying to make sense of the case, not just the individual. Adequate contextual assessment captures the networks of transactions occurring in the case over time, with the client (of whatever system level) as a critical nexus for determining where to focus. The contextual question is either "What is wrong in this web of transactions?" or, even better, "What changes do we (worker, client, others) want to see in this web?" rather than "What is the client's problem?" (the categorical question) or "How serious is the client's problem?" (the dimensional question). Assessment structured by the contextual question is profoundly different from the process structured by categorical or dimensional questions. It is possible in a contextual assessment to be excessively individually focused, essentially conducting a PERSON-in-environment rather than a person-in-environment process, but such an error is less likely. And not only are multiple dimensions likely to be noticed, but the connections among them can be noticed as well. For example, not only would substance use, quality of a spousal relationship, and work status in a case all be noticed, but so would the interlocks among them.

In the abstract, contextual systems do not ensure that cultural colonialism will be avoided. It is certainly possible to see only some of the transactional processes present in a case and to be blind to others, as guided by one's own cultural training. However, many culturally specific approaches to intervention developed by non-European groups that rely on indigenous practices are, in fact, deeply contextual. Afrocentric practice, for example, often focuses on community transformation, "cultural work," how people see themselves in relationship with others in the community, principles like the Nguzo Saba (Seven Pillars: unity, self-determination, collective work and responsibility, cooperative economics, purpose, creativity, and faith), and the roots of problem behavior in oppressive structures, rather than on diagnosis of individual pathology (O'Donnell and Karanja 2000; Schiele 1996). The teaching of the Five Waves among the Inuit is used metaphorically to explain how multiple factors need to be considered to understand why a person does what he does (Ross 1996). Before venturing out on the water, in Ross's interpretation of the traditional framework, an Inuit needs to understand the confluence of (1) the waves produced by winds that are coming but have not fully arrived; (2) the waves associated with the weather system now fading, whose effects remain; (3) the waves caused by the ocean currents running at the time as they round features of the bay; (4) the waves caused by the Gulf Stream; and (5) the waves associated with the rotation of the earth. All of these, in transaction, explain the current and emerging situation. Remaining with the metaphor, if waves from larger forces like ocean currents are ignored because it is too hard to think about them at the same time one thinks about weather-related conditions, the boat is likely to capsize. If social work reality really is complex, we need ultimately to find ways to capture such complexity in assessment and intervention. Ross describes collective interventive strategies flowing from such understandings of reality that serve as elegant examples of contextual assessment and practice.

The Ecosystems Perspective

The ecological (Germain and Gitterman 1996) or ecosystems (Mattaini and Meyer 2002; Meyer 1983, 1988) perspective has been widely accepted in social work theory and practice, precisely because it was elaborated to capture multiple transactional phenomena constituting a case "all at once." Unfortunately, but perhaps not surprisingly given its abstraction, it has often been misunderstood and oversimplified. Many social work authors claim to be using an ecosystems (or ecological) perspective without demonstrating even a basic understanding of ecological science or classical General Systems Theory, two quite rigorous bodies of thought on which the perspective was originally based. Even less common is familiarity with current and emerging aspects of empirically grounded systems theories, including autopoiesis (roughly, the process of self-organization and "self-making" within dynamic systems) and the primacy of transactions over entities in the construction of reality (Mattaini and Meyer 2002). Some view an ecological understanding of social work cases as strictly a metaphor that can be stretched as desired, but in fact, ecosystemic practice can and should be grounded in rigorous science.

The intent of the application of these science-based ways of examining a case is to ensure that practitioners attend to all major transactional phenomena that are present in the case. Particular models of practice, or attempts to rely on only empirically validated interventions for specific problems, are likely to limit the vision taken of a case, unless counterbalanced by something like a structured ecosystemic method for asking questions of the case. The ecomap was an early and useful attempt to provide such a structure; given the increased bandwidth of visual images, many graphic tools can contribute to capturing complex case realities (Mattaini 1993). Over time, technologies like neural networks may also help to extract and organize important dimensional and contextual patterns from raw case data, but that work lies in the future.

Note that the ecosystems perspective was never intended to somehow integrate incompatible theoretical models of practice—although it has occasionally been described in this way. A weak theoretical model for understanding human and larger-system actions cannot be saved by an ecosystems view. What appears to be necessary is a deeply contextualized, ecologically grounded structure for assessment that draws on the best available scientific understanding of the dynamics of behavior in context, and thereby provides strong guidance for action. An ecosystems perspective by itself cannot do this—and was never meant to—but can provide a critical foundation for organizing practice (Mattaini and Meyer 2002).

Ecobehavioral Assessment and Practice

Many well-explicated practice models can structure the collection and organization of case data with an eye to context. "Contextual analysis" has long been a key feature in task-centered practice, for example (Reid 1985; Reid and Epstein 1972). Some models, however, are much more explicit than others in attending comprehensively to the transactional behavioral ecology present in the case. In ecobehavioral practice (Mattaini 1997, 1999, 2002a), for example, the worker and client elaborate the interlocking webs of transactions present in the case, including those that structure autopoietic networks, in a flexible but orderly process that results in a plan for intervention.

Assessment in this approach begins with a broad ecobehavioral scan of the case, in which the transactional dynamics present are understood in terms of the natural science of behavior. That science provides an organizing framework for understanding interlocking personal and collective behavioral transactions (relying on the most recent research in areas like equivalence relations and cultural analysis, not just simplistic mid-twentieth-century behavior science). From this collaborative examination, key focal points emerge (problems, goals), based on what is most troubling or on the client's deepest hopes. Those focal problems or goal-states are described in terms of behaviors of system actors. Each focus is then analyzed using ecobehavioral theory to understand the dynamics involved, within multidimensional contingency space (see figure 4.1). On the basis of that analysis and methods of evidence-based practice (Gambrill 1999), interventive tasks likely to influence those dynamics are selected. This may all occur very rapidly for a practitioner who knows and understands the underlying science and has strong practice skills, but considerable learning is necessary to reach that point. Professional practice by definition is not simple.

Note that the case assessed may revolve around an individual (Mattaini 1997) or a family (Mattaini 1999), but may also focus on a larger system like

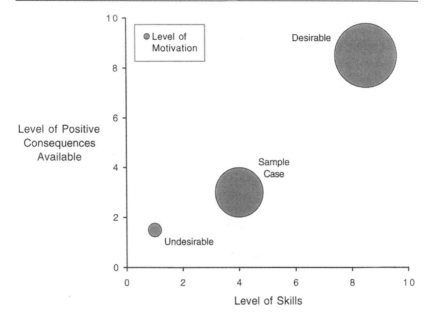

Figure 4.1   A multidimensional understanding of behavior in context. The dimensions included are the extent to which the person has the needed skills in his or her repertoire (*X* axis); the extent to which positive consequences for the desired behavior are available (*Y* axis); and the extent of motivation to obtain those consequences (technically, a matter of establishing operations like deprivation and experience with existing reinforcers), shown here by the diameter of the spheres. (A fourth dimension, the extent to which the person discriminates occasions when action will be reinforced from those when it will not be, can be shown by differential shading of spheres.) In the sample case, a young man has some, but limited, job skills; the availability of employment is very limited; and motivation is high. Skills training (an individual strategy) or increased availability of employment (an environmental strategy) or both may be required.

a school or community, for example with a goal of decreasing aggregate antisocial behavior and building a nurturing community (Mattaini 2001). The science of behavior suggests that a process of shared power in which the client system is an active partner (Lowery and Mattaini 1999) is critical to an accurate assessment as well as to effective intervention of this kind. Within a shared-power process, culturally specific factors are more likely to emerge, and dynamics with social justice dimensions are more likely to be noticed.

The Work That Remains

The development of systems for assessment is advancing. Non-contextualized, atheoretical taxonomies will apparently always have severe limitations, but they have some utility. Human beings cannot think or communicate without relying on categories, although the risk of reification of hypothetical constructs that lack true referents must always be weighed. While the widespread acceptance of *DSM* will present some obstacles, ultimately scientific advances will produce categorical systems that are more firmly grounded in the origins of problems and that recognize diverse realities. The risks of applying oversimplified labels that carry profound implications for services and quality of life will remain a serious issue for some time to come, however. The distorting power of market forces that view services (and mental health) as commodities to be bought and sold to maximize profit also needs to be consistently acknowledged and assertively challenged.

Dimensional systems are advancing rapidly and have proved very valuable for monitoring practice. A number of cultural issues related to dimensional systems remain, however. The development of culturally specific instruments to measure culturally important dimensions (e.g., Shek 2002; Tran, Ngo, and Conway 2003) is a barely emerging area. Most dimensional measures have not yet been validated, and such validation will be expensive, so it is important that priorities for that work are consistent with critical social needs. Approaches for integrating dimensional measures within a broad contextual perspective also require particular attention.

A critical challenge facing mental health practice by all of the professions involved is the development of systems for assessment that do not victimize clients and patients through overly narrow focus on intrapersonal issues while neglecting larger systemic forces. The best of contextual approaches to assessment can help here. But there is an enormous amount to be done in moving from metaphor to science-based systems for contextual assessment, and the number of researchers doing this work is very modest. Categorical and dimensional systems are cognitively simpler to grasp and to validate. Tools for contextual assessment also need to be accessible enough to be used in everyday practice (a major advantage of the ecomap) or, no matter how elegantly developed, they will not be used.

Defining cases and structuring intervention in ways that guide practice toward the best possible individual and collective outcomes, consistent with social justice, is the work of assessment. Intellectual oversimplification, cultural colonialism, market forces, and maintenance of professional privilege, however, pose serious obstacles to the development and application of socially and scientifically valid assessment technologies. Such technologies have the potential for strengthening the web of human life, supporting human rights, and contributing to a more just society; their absence may support current individual and structural inequalities. The extent to which this work will advance in the face of these obstacles remains an open question, the answer to which will depend on the intellectual integrity, and the ethical and moral commitments, of the profession.

References

Alemán, S., T. Fitzpatrick, T. V. Tran, and E. W. Gonzales. 2000. *Therapeutic Interventions with Ethnic Elders*. New York: Haworth.

American Psychiatric Association (APA). 1952. *Diagnostic and Statistical Manual of Mental Disorders (DSM)*. Washington, D.C.: APA.

———. 1968. *Diagnostic and Statistical Manual of Mental Disorders (DSM)*. 2d ed. Washington, D.C.: APA.

———. 1980. *Diagnostic and Statistical Manual of Mental Disorders (DSM-III)*. 3d ed. Washington, D.C.: APA.

———. 1987. *Diagnostic and Statistical Manual of Mental Disorders (DSM-III-R)*. 3d ed. rev. Washington, D.C.: APA.

———. 1994. *Diagnostic and Statistical Manual of Mental Disorders (DSM-IV)*. 4th ed. Washington, D.C.: APA.

———. 2000. *Diagnostic and Statistical Manual of Mental Disorders (DSM-IV-TR)*. 4th ed. text rev. Washington, D.C.: APA.

Bolling, M. Y. 2002. Research and representation: A conundrum for behavior analysts. *Behavior and Social Issues* 12:19–28.

Brown, G. W., E. M. Monck, G. M. Carstairs, and J. K. Wing. 1962. Influence of family life on the course of schizophrenic illness. *British Journal of Prevention and Social Medicine* 16:55–68.

Canino, I. A. and J. Spurlock. 2002. *Culturally Diverse Children and Adolescents: Assessment, Diagnosis, and Treatment*. 2d. ed. New York: Guilford.

Capra, F. 1996. *The Web of Life: A New Scientific Understanding of Living Systems*. New York: Anchor.

Castillo, R. J. 1997. *Culture and Mental Illness: A Client-Centered Approach*. Pacific Grove, Calif.: Brooks/Cole.

———, ed. 1998. *Meanings of Madness*. Pacific Grove, Calif.: Brooks/Cole.

Corcoran, K. J. and J. Fischer. 2000. *Measures for Clinical Practices: A Sourcebook*. 2 vols. 3d ed. New York: Simon and Schuster.

Cowger, C. D. and C. A. Snively. 2002. Assessing Client Strengths: Individual, Family, and Community Empowerment. In D. Saleebey, ed., *The Strengths Perspective in Social Work Practice*, 106–123. 3d ed. Boston: Allyn and Bacon.

Davis, R. D. and T. Millon. 1994. Can Personalities Be Disordered? Yes. In S. A. Kirk and S. D. Einbinder, eds., *Controversial Issues in Mental Health*, 40–47. Boston: Allyn and Bacon.

Fabrega, H. 1989. Cultural relativism and psychiatric illness. *Journal of Nervous and Mental Disease* 177:417–425.

Follette, W. C., A. C. Houts, and S. C. Hayes. 1992. Behavior therapy and the new medical model. *Behavioral Assessment* 14:323–343.

Gambrill, E. 1999. Evidence-based practice: An alternative to authority-based practice. *Families in Society* 80:341–350.

Germain, C. B. and A. Gitterman. 1996. *The Life Model of Social Work Practice.* 2d ed. New York: Columbia University Press.

Goldiamond, I. 2002. Toward a constructional approach to social problems: Ethical and constitutional issues raised by applied behavior analysis. *Behavior and Social Issues* 11:108–197. Originally published in 1974 in *Behaviorism* 2:1–84.

Halford, W. K. 1991. Beyond expressed emotion: Behavioral assessment of family interaction associated with the course of schizophrenia. *Behavioral Assessment* 13:99–123.

Hayes, S. C. and W. C. Follette. 1992. Can functional analysis provide a substitute for syndromal classification? *Behavioral Assessment* 14:345–365.

Hudson, W. W. 1982. *The Clinical Measurement Package.* Homewood, Ill.: Dorsey.

———. 1989. *Computer Assisted Social Services.* Tempe, Ariz.: Walmyr.

Hudson, W. W. and S. L. McMurtry. 1997. Comprehensive assessment in social work practice: The Multi-Problem Screening Inventory. *Research on Social Work Practice* 7:79–98.

Kanfer, F. H. and B. K. Schefft. 1988. *Guiding the Process of Therapeutic Change.* Champaign, Ill.: Research Press.

Karls, J. M., C. T. Lowery, M. A. Mattaini, and K. E. Wandrei. 1997. The use of the PIE (Person-in-Environment) system in social work education (Point/Counterpoint). *Journal of Social Work Education* 33:49–58.

Karls, J. M. and K. E. Wandrei. 1994a. *Person-in-Environment System: The PIE Classification System for Social Functioning Problems.* Washington, D.C.: NASW Press.

———. 1994b. *PIE Manual—Person-in-Environment System: The PIE Classification System for Social Functioning Problems.* Washington, D.C.: NASW Press.

Kirk, S. A. and H. Kutchins. 1988. Deliberate misdiagnosis in mental health practice. *Social Service Review* 62:225–237.

———. 1992. *The Selling of DSM: The Rhetoric of Science in Psychiatry.* New York: Aldine de Gruyter.

Kirk, S. A. and W. J. Reid. 2002. *Science and Social Work: A Critical Appraisal.* New York: Columbia University Press.

Krasner, L. 1992. The concepts of syndrome and functional analysis: Compatible or incompatible? *Behavioral Assessment* 14: 307–321.

Kuhn, T. S. 1970. *The Structure of Scientific Revolutions.* 2d ed. Chicago: University of Chicago Press.

Kutchins, H. and S. A. Kirk. 1986. The reliability of DSM-III: A critical review. *Social Work Research and Abstracts* 22 (4): 3–12.

Laing, R. D. 1967. *The Politics of Experience.* Baltimore: Penguin Books.

Lindsey, E. W. 1998. Service providers' perception of factors that help or hinder homeless families. *Families in Society* 79:160–172.

Lowery, C. T. and M. A. Mattaini. 1999. The science of sharing power: Native American thought and behavior analysis. *Behavior and Social Issues* 9:3–23.

Lundin, R. K. 1998. Living with mental illness: A personal experience. *Cognitive and Behavioral Practice* 5:223–230.

Mattaini, M. A. 1993. *More Than a Thousand Words: Graphics for Clinical Practice.* Washington, D.C.: NASW Press.

———. 1994. Can personalities be disordered? No. In S. A. Kirk and S. D. Einbinder, eds., *Controversial Issues in Mental Health,* 48–56. Boston: Allyn and Bacon.

———. 1997. *Clinical Practice with Individuals.* Washington, D.C.: NASW Press.

———. 1999. *Clinical Intervention with Families.* Washington, D.C.: NASW Press.

———. 2002a. Generalist Practice: People and Programs. In M. A. Mattaini, C. T. Lowery, and C. H. Meyer, eds., *Foundations of Social Work Practice: A Graduate Text,* 291–315. 3d ed. Washington, D.C.: NASW Press.

———. 2002b. Monitoring Social Work Practice. In M. A. Mattaini, C. T. Lowery, and C. H. Meyer, eds., *Foundations of Social Work Practice: A Graduate Text,* 132–148. 3d ed. Washington, D.C.: NASW Press.

———. 2003. Constructing Practice: Diagnoses, Problems, Targets, or Transactions? In A. Rosen and E. Proctor, eds., *Developing Practice Guidelines for Social Work Intervention: Issues, Methods, and Research Agenda,* 156–166. New York: Columbia University Press.

Mattaini, M. A. and S. A. Kirk. 1991. Assessing assessment in social work. *Social Work* 36:260–266.

Mattaini, M. A., C. T. Lowery, and C. H. Meyer. 2002. Introduction to M. A. Mattaini, C. T. Lowery, and C. H. Meyer, eds., *Foundations of Social Work Practice: A Graduate Text,* ix–xxiv. 3d ed. Washington, D.C.: NASW Press.

Mattaini, M. A. and C. H. Meyer. 2002. The ecosystems perspective: Implications for practice. In M. A. Mattaini, C. T. Lowery, and C. H. Meyer, eds., *Foundations of Social Work Practice: A Graduate Text,* 3–24. 3d ed. Washington, D.C.: NASW Press.

———, with the PEACE POWER Working Group. 2001. *Peace Power for Adolescents: Strategies for a Culture of Nonviolence.* Washington, D.C.: NASW Press.

Meyer, C. H. 1988. The eco-systems perspective. In R. A. Dorfman, ed., *Paradigms of Clinical Social Work,* 275–294. New York: Brunner/Mazel.

———. 1993. *Assessment in Social Work Practice.* New York: Columbia University Press.

———, ed. 1983. *Clinical Social Work Practice in an Ecosystems Perspective.* New York: Columbia University Press.

Murguia, A., R. A. Peterson, and M. C. Zea. 2003. Use and implications of ethnomedical health care approaches among Central American immigrants. *Health and Social Work* 28:43–51.

O'Donnell, S. M. and S. T. Karanja. 2000. Transformative community practice: Building a model for developing extremely low income African-American communities. *Journal of Community Practice* 7 (3): 67–84.

O'Nell, T. D. 1993. "Feeling worthless": An ethnographic investigation of depression and problem drinking at the Flathead reservation. *Culture, Medicine, and Psychiatry* 16:447–469.

Peele, S. 1995. *Diseasing of America: How We Allowed Recovery Zealots and the Treatment Industry to Convince Us We Are Out of Control.* San Francisco: Jossey-Bass.

Reid, W. J. 1985. *Family Problem Solving.* New York: Columbia University Press.

———. 2000. *The Task Planner.* New York: Columbia University Press.

Reid, W. J. and L. Epstein. 1972. *Task-Centered Casework*. New York: Columbia University Press. *Research on Social Work Practice*. 1999. Vol. 9. Special Issue: Practice guidelines and clinical social work.

Rosen, A. and S. Livne. 1992. Personal versus environmental emphases in formulations of client problems. *Social Work Research and Abstracts* 29 (4): 12–17.

Rosen, A., E. K. Proctor, and M. Staudt. 2003. Targets of change and interventions in social work: An empirically based prototype for developing practice guidelines. *Research on Social Work Practice* 13:208–233.

Ross, R. 1996. *Returning to the Teachings*. Toronto: Penguin Canada.

Schiele, J. H. 1996. Afrocentricity: An emerging paradigm in social work practice. *Social Work* 41:284–294.

Shek, D. T. L. 2002. Assessment of family functioning in Chinese adolescents: The Chinese version of the Family Assessment Device. *Research on Social Work Practice* 12:502–524.

Szasz, T. S. 1960. The myth of mental illness. *American Psychologist* 15 (February): 113–118.

Tran, T. V., D. Ngo, and K. Conway. 2003. A cross-cultural measure of depressive symptoms among Vietnamese Americans. *Social Work Research* 27:56–64.

Universal Declaration of Human Rights. 1948. New York: United Nations.

Wakefield, J. C. 1996. Does social work need the eco-systems perspective? Part 2: Does the perspective save social work from incoherence? *Social Service Review* 70:183–213.

Chapter 5

Disorders Versus Problems of Living in DSM: Rethinking Social Work's Relationship to Psychiatry

Jerome C. Wakefield

The relationship between social work and psychiatry is already an intimate one, to the point of provoking controversy about whether psychotherapeutic treatment of mental problems is swallowing up the broader social work field (Specht 1990; Specht and Courtney 1994; Wakefield 1992c, 1992d). Nonetheless, I believe that in the future we can expect to see social work and psychiatry enter into an even more integrated relationship than now exists. This further intertwining will occur, I maintain, not primarily for reasons of professional self-interest, turf wars, status, reimbursement incentives, or even cost containment. The reasons go much deeper and concern the very conceptual foundations of the two professions and fundamental flaws in the current approach to psychiatric diagnosis.

The *DSM* and the Mission of Psychiatry

To understand social work's relationship to psychiatry, it is essential first to have a clear view of the nature of psychiatric diagnosis and where it has recently gone wrong. Psychiatry is by definition a medical profession that

This chapter contains a revised version of material that appeared in J. C. Wakefield (1997), Social Work and Psychiatry: Toward a Conceptually Based Partnership, in E. Gambrill and M. Reisch, eds., *Social Work in the Twenty-first Century*, 328–339 (New York: Pine Forge Press).

deals with mental disorders. If psychiatry is to be a viable medical discipline, it must distinguish mental disorders—that is, conditions in which something has gone wrong with how the mind is supposed to work—from the many other problems of living with which human beings must contend. "Disorder," in the medical sense, refers only to those negative conditions caused by an internal dysfunction. A dysfunction occurs when something goes wrong with the functioning of some internal mechanism, so that it is no longer capable of performing its natural function—the function for which it was designed by natural selection (Wakefield 1992a). For example, when the heart cannot adequately pump the blood to oxygenate the cells of the body, that is a dysfunction, because the heart was naturally selected to perform that task; and when the eyes cannot see, that is a dysfunction, because the function of the eyes is to make one capable of seeing. A mental disorder occurs when the dysfunctional mechanism is one of those psychological mechanisms that form the "mind," such as mechanisms concerned with motivation, perception, thinking, emotion, language, learning, socialization, and other basic psychological functions (these mechanisms are still largely unknown, but through observation of human capacities we can infer that they exist). When such a mechanism breaks down and becomes incapable of performing its functions, a mental dysfunction has occurred; if the dysfunction causes harm to the individual, there is a mental disorder. Thus, mental disorders are harmful mental dysfunctions (Wakefield 1992a, 1992b, 1999; Wakefield and First 2003).

The American Psychiatric Association's *Diagnostic and Statistical Manual of Mental Disorders,* 4th edition (APA 1994), is used throughout the mental health professions as the standard for psychiatric diagnosis. In addition to its function of listing and briefly identifying and describing the various categories of mental disorders that clinicians and researchers might confront, the *DSM* has the additional function of operationally defining each disorder in terms of a set of diagnostic criteria that are supposed to constitute the necessary and sufficient criteria for correct diagnosis of the disorder. These criteria are tremendously influential in all areas of the mental health field and in many other settings as well, such as research, epidemiology, eligibility for disability benefits, and law.

The *DSM* specifies that psychiatric disorders must be caused by a dysfunction in some internal mental mechanism; that is, something must have gone wrong with the workings of the individual's mind (Spitzer and Endicott 1978). The *DSM* defines psychiatric disorders in terms of criteria that generally refer to observable symptoms. Symptom-based criteria have been embraced because they are considered the best way to achieve the *DSM*'s twin goals of reliability (i.e., the criteria should lead to the same diagnosis every time, no matter who is using them) and theory neutrality (i.e., the criteria should not be based on concepts that are special to any one unproved theory of etiology).

The *DSM* itself provides a definition of mental disorder that underscores these points. The *DSM* asserts that mental disorders, like all medical disorders, are distresses or disabilities resulting from internal dysfunctions (1994:xxi).

Obviously, there are many ways that internal mental mechanisms can go wrong. For example, the mechanisms that mediate sadness responses can produce deep sadness reactions despite the lack of an appropriate environmental situation that would warrant the sadness, causing depression. The mechanisms that generate appropriate fear and anxiety responses to environmental dangers may fire inappropriately, leading to panic attacks and generalized anxiety (Barlow 1991, 2001). The brain mechanisms responsible for producing rational thought may break down, leading to psychotic conditions. The mechanisms that allow children to be socialized and to internalize moral rules may not function properly, and thus some children may suffer from disorders of conduct. And attentional mechanisms or learning mechanisms may not function properly, yielding attentional disorders and learning disorders, respectively. Just as physical mechanisms sometimes do not function as they were designed to function and thus cause physical disorders, so mental mechanisms may also break down and cause mental disorders.

Note that nothing in the *DSM*'s definition of disorder in terms of internal dysfunction implies that all mental disorders must be physiological disorders. Just as computer software can malfunction even when the underlying hardware is functioning flawlessly, so, in principle, the mind's "programming" might become dysfunctional for reasons other than that there is a malfunction of underlying brain mechanisms. For example, a sequence of experiences ("inputs") that the programming was not designed to handle might occur, leading to dysfunctions in some mental processes, as in post-traumatic stress disorder.

The *DSM*'s definition of mental disorder emphasizes that the distress, disability, or other harm warranting a condition's classification as a disorder must occur as a direct result of a dysfunction and not just because society disapproves of the person's condition or for other reasons originating in interpersonal or social conflict. This last requirement is meant to preclude the misuse of psychodiagnosis for sheer social control purposes. For example, the Soviet Union classified many political dissidents as mentally disordered, incarcerated them in mental institutions, and "treated" them with sedating drugs. Many of these "patients" were clearly not really mentally disordered, even though they were socially deviant and they were in distress and socially impaired in their functioning as a result of their refusal to accept the tyrannical nature of their state. The *DSM*'s definition of mental disorder explains why such cases are not genuine cases of mental disorder. These individuals' problems could not be attributed to a breakdown in the designed functioning of some internal mental mechanism but developed as their normal-range reaction to an unjust and adverse environment. They suffered not from internal dysfunctions but from the consequences of their courage in a repressive situation. The definition of mental disorder is supposed to distinguish true disorders in the medical sense from such problems caused by a normal response to a difficult environment.

An Inconsistency in the *DSM*

There is, however, a basic inconsistency in the *DSM*'s system that limits the effectiveness of its symptomatic diagnostic criteria. The problem is that for many categories of disorder, the diagnostic criteria for identifying specific disorders do not in fact satisfy the general definition of mental disorder presented in the *DSM*'s own introduction. Although the categories themselves are generally perfectly good categories of mental disorder, the criteria used to identify people as having those disorders do not in fact distinguish the genuinely disordered, who, according to *DSM*'s own definition of disorder, must have an internal dysfunction, from the nondisordered, who do not have internal dysfunctions of some psychological mechanism. The source of the inconsistency between the definition and the criteria is what systems theorists call "equifinality"; many different causes can lead to the same effect. In this case, the same symptoms can result from normal reactions to adverse environments and from mental dysfunctions. Thus, the very "symptoms" that would indicate a psychiatric disorder may instead indicate a normal response to an adverse social environment.

For example (see below for more elaborated examples), the same intense sadness that satisfies *DSM* criteria for the diagnosis of major depressive disorder could be indicative of a genuine depressive disorder in which something is wrong with one's sadness-response mechanisms, or it could result from a normal response to a serious loss; the same antisocial conduct that satisfies *DSM* criteria for the diagnosis of conduct disorder or antisocial personality disorder could be indicative of a genuine mental disorder resulting from a dysfunction in, for example, the sense of empathy, or it could be the result of a normal response to adverse, deprived, or otherwise criminogenic environments; and the same intense anxiety that satisfies *DSM* criteria for a diagnosis of generalized anxiety disorder could be indicative of a genuine anxiety disorder that involves inappropriate triggering of anxiety response mechanisms or it could indicate a normal response to overwhelming environmental demands.

In these cases and many more, the "symptoms" of a normal response to an adverse environment, where nothing is wrong with the workings of the internal mechanisms, can satisfy *DSM* diagnostic criteria for the corresponding mental disorder. Yet such normal responses are not true mental disorders in the medical sense that the *DSM* embraces. Thus, *DSM* symptomatic criteria often do not successfully distinguish between true mental disorders (i.e., internal dysfunctions), which are within the domain of psychiatry, and problems in the interaction of persons and environments, which are traditionally within the province of social work.

To achieve the goal of reliable diagnosis that is theory-neutral, *DSM* criteria must be composed of easy-to-assess symptoms and behaviors that do not make reference to unobservable internal etiological processes. Thus *DSM* criteria do not generally say much about how the symptoms were caused. Yet, as noted earlier, the *DSM*'s definition of mental disorder requires not only that there be symptoms but that the symptoms be caused by an internal dysfunction, if the problem is to be viewed as a genuine mental disorder. This is why *DSM* criteria often fail to distinguish symptoms that indicate genuine mental disorders from symptoms that indicate normal reactions to adverse environments or other problems in living (Wakefield 1992a, 1992b, 1993, 1996).

The notion of relying on symptomatic "syndromes" to identify disorders makes some sense in physical medicine, where, on average, symptomatic conditions are very different and clearly delineated from normal functioning and the same symptoms tend to be caused by the same underlying etiology without too much influence of environmental context. But in the mental domain, neither of these generalizations holds true. As the above examples illustrate, the symptoms of many mental disorders often are very much like normal responses to extreme environments, and whether a certain symptom set is best presumed to constitute disorder or normality depends heavily on the environmental context in which the symptoms occur. Thus, within the mental domain, the symptom-syndrome approach to diagnostic criteria does not work as well as in the physical domain.

The result is that *DSM* categories in fact (contrary to their medical intent) go beyond disorders and overlap substantially with nondisordered conditions that have traditionally been seen as falling within social work's distinctive domain of person-in-environment problems, blurring the boundary between the two professions. This flaw in the *DSM* makes greater involvement of social workers in the mental health system inevitable. People with normal responses to adverse environments must be distinguished from people with breakdowns in internal mechanisms, whether or not they are incorrectly labeled as disordered for reimbursement purposes. Effective treatment depends on such a discrimination of causes; the alternative is chronic misdiagnosis and mistreatment of nondisordered clients. Yet psychiatrists are neither motivated nor trained to deal with environmental diagnosis or treatment. As it becomes apparent that the symptoms that determine *DSM* diagnosis do not indicate whether a mental disorder or an interactional problem exists, it will become necessary to routinely involve social workers and psychiatrists in teams that can diagnose and treat both internal dysfunctional causes and interactional, environmental causes of a patient's symptoms.

Examples of Invalid Criteria Sets That Fail to Adequately Discriminate Normal and Disordered Responses

The problems described above occur in categories throughout the *DSM*. Let me offer a few examples:

Separation Anxiety Disorder

This disorder is diagnosed on the basis of symptoms indicating inappropriate and excessive anxiety concerning separation from home or from those to whom the individual is attached, lasting at least four weeks. The symptoms (e.g., excessive distress when separation occurs, worry that some event will lead to separation, refusal to go to school because of fear of separation, reluctance to be alone or without major attachment figure) are just the sorts of things children experience when they have a normal, intense separation anxiety response. The criteria do not distinguish between a true disorder, in which separation responses are triggered inappropriately, and normal responses to perceived threats to the child's primary bond because of an unreliable caregiver or other serious disruptions.

Substance Abuse

Diagnosis of substance abuse requires any one of four criteria: poor role performance at work or home due to substance use; substance use in hazardous circumstances, such as driving under the influence of alcohol; recurrent substance-related legal problems; or social or interpersonal problems due to substance use, such as arguments with family members about substance use. Contrary to the *DSM*'s definition of mental disorder, these criteria allow diagnosis on the basis of conflict between the individual and social institutions such as police or family. Arguments with one's spouse about alcohol or drug use, or between a child and his or her parent, are sufficient for diagnosis, as is being arrested more than once for driving while under the influence of alcohol or for possession of marijuana. These social problems and interpersonal conflicts need not be the result of mental disorders.

Learning Disorders

The sole basis for diagnosis of learning disorders is achievement test results that are "substantially below that expected." However, this criterion does not distinguish true learning disorders, in which some internal mechanism necessary for learning is dysfunctional, from problems of learning that occur because of family problems, lack of motivation, lack of adequate language skills, or other acculturation issues.

Major Depression

Diagnosis of major depression is made on the basis of a set of symptoms indicating an extreme sadness response. The criteria correctly contain an exclusion for uncomplicated bereavement (i.e., one is not diagnosed as disordered if the symptoms are the result of a normal-range response to having recently lost a loved one), but they contain no exclusions for equally normal reactions to other losses, such as a terminal medical diagnosis in oneself or a loved one, separation from one's spouse, or losing one's job.

Antisocial Personality Disorder

The *DSM* criteria for antisocial personality disorder are the following: in addition to having experienced conduct disorder before age fifteen, the adult must meet three or more of the following criteria: either inconsistent work history or failure to honor financial obligations, breaking the law, irritability and aggressiveness, impulsivity, deceitfulness, recklessness, and lack of remorse. These criteria do not adequately distinguish between career criminals and the mentally disordered. The criminal will satisfy the illegal activity criterion and possibly or even probably satisfy the work/finance criterion (criminal activity is not "work" as intended in this criterion), the deceit criterion (by the nature of a criminal career), and one or more of the impulsivity, recklessness, or irritability/aggressiveness criteria (by the nature of criminal activity).

Note that because our society tends to be more generous in reimbursing for medical ailments than for other problems of living that might be equally impairing, there is tremendous pressure on social service agencies to diagnose their clients as having mental disorders, whatever the reason that brings them into the agency. Reimbursement pressure puts a premium on looking at cases through a psychiatric prism, whether or not the condition is in fact a disorder. While pragmatically useful, this strategy raises complex ethical questions. Such pragmatic reimbursement-driven decisions to classify certain patients as having mental disorders do not necessarily reflect the clinician's best judgment that those patients do in fact have mental disorders (Kirk and Kutchins 1988).

Further Reasons for the Blurring of the Psychiatry–Social Work Boundary

There are several more reasons for the breakdown in professional boundaries between social work and psychiatry that warrant brief mention—one of them specific to the *DSM* and the other one more general. First, the authors of the latest edition of the *DSM* did perceive that there was a problem with validity, and they did attempt to deal with it. The main thing they did was to add to almost all the criteria sets a "clinical significance" requirement that the symptoms must cause clinically significant distress or impairment of social, academic, or occupational functioning.

However, that was the wrong medicine for the *DSM*'s ailment (Spitzer and Wakefield 1999). Normal responses to adverse environmental factors can also cause intense distress or impairment (for example, as the *DSM* implicitly acknowledges, normal bereavement can be as distressing and impairing as the disorder of major depression). In all of the above examples, the disorders and the corresponding nondisordered responses cause similar "symptoms." So the central problem with the *DSM*'s validity is not that the criteria do not require enough symptomatic distress or impairment but that such distress or impairment itself often does not tell you whether the condition is a disorder or a normal response. The distress or impairment requirement does, however, have the effect of making explicit a central feature of the *DSM*, which is that the judgment of whether a condition is a disorder often depends largely on assessment of social functioning. There is a *DSM* axis for rating social functioning, but I am referring to something different here; the symptoms in the diagnostic criteria themselves and especially the role-impairment part of the clinical significance criterion reflect issues in social functioning. Thus, the distress or impairment requirement further erodes the distinction between psychiatric disorders and those problems of social functioning that constitute the domain of social work.

Second, there is a more general reason for a breakdown in the distinction between the respective professional domains of psychiatry and social work. Internal mechanisms are designed to operate in certain "expectable" environments. Indeed, that is the heart of evolution; the organism's nature adapts to features of the environment. The concept of disorder is to some degree based on the simple idea that sometimes something goes wrong with an internal mechanism and it can no longer do what it was designed to do. However, there is a hidden presupposition here—namely that the environment stays roughly the same in relevant ways, so that the internal mechanism could perform its functions if nothing was wrong with it.

The problem with this assumption is that humankind is so radically altering the environment that it is becoming less clear when a problem results from a breakdown in a mechanism and when it results from changes in the environment that make it impossible for the mechanism to perform its function. For example, pervasive anxiety may be a disorder in which internal anxiety-generating mechanisms start firing inappropriately, or it may be the response of normal anxiety mechanisms to unprecedented demands of modern life that did not exist when humankind was evolving. These are not exclusive possibilities, of course. However, as the environment changes, it becomes more difficult to tell whether symptoms indicate true disorders or failures of the environment to provide what people need to have in order to function adequately. Again, this means that the traditional roles of psychiatry and social work are becoming conceptually harder to separate.

A final source of confusion is not substantive but semantic. These days, the label "dysfunctional" is commonly used for all manner of negative behavior or mismatches between individual and environment; thus one can have a "dysfunctional marriage" or, if bored and distracted, be "dysfunctional at work." It is easy to confuse "dysfunctional" in this broad sense with "dysfunction" in the sense that warrants attribution of disorder. But this common use of "dysfunctional" does not in fact imply the existence of a dysfunction in the medical sense, which refers to something going wrong with some internal mechanism.

Implications: Toward a New Conceptually Based Partnership

What we see in the examples presented earlier, and in many other criteria sets in the *DSM,* is a breakdown in the basic distinction between psychiatric and social work problems. Not only do the criteria that are now universally used to diagnose mental disorders in fact diagnose either mental disorders or person-in-environment problems, but one cannot tell from the criteria themselves which category applies in a given case.

What are the implications of this fundamental problem for the relationship between psychiatry and social work? Because an understanding of the nature and source of a problem is critical to effective treatment planning, there is no alternative but for patients to be routinely assessed for both internal dysfunctions and person-in-environment problems. This sort of joint assessment requires coordination; if cases are to be properly understood and treated, psychiatrists must routinely work together with social workers.

Ironically, the need for such radical integration of psychiatric and social work efforts is a result of psychiatry's attempt to define itself as a medical discipline, different from social work. To do so, it tried to formulate reliable diagnostic criteria for genuine mental disorders in terms of symptoms. The resulting diagnostic criteria, considered from a medical standpoint, possess flaws (elaborated above) that yield false positives (i.e., they sometimes incorrectly diagnose nondisordered, normal responses as disordered). But these same flaws make *DSM* criteria important to social work because they mean that the *DSM* encompasses a large part of social work's domain.

There are powerful intellectual, historical, and institutional reasons for framing psychiatric diagnostic criteria in the *DSM*'s operationalized, symptom-based way. This practice is unlikely to change. Moreover, the equifinality problem in this area is so great that it is hard to envision any operational criteria that could distinguish true disorders from person-in-environment problems without detailed assessment of both kinds of possible causal factors. Thus, for the foreseeable future, psychiatric diagnostic criteria will continue to encompass social work problems, and psychiatry and social work will be even more deeply connected at a conceptual level than the traditional roles would indicate.

Psychiatrists have neither the training nor the motivation to explore the patient's environmental circumstances adequately enough to distinguish internal from external problem sources or to treat the environment when necessary. Indeed, many psychiatric visits are extremely brief and targeted at prescribing and monitoring medication (Olfson, Marcus, and Pincus 1999). Short of a radical shift in psychiatric training and practice, psychiatrists are not about to routinely do direct assessments of the family and community context of the patient's symptoms or intervene directly in those systems when the person-environment relationship is the source of a client's problem; these are the tasks of social work. Yet, if the above arguments are correct, such assessments are necessary to decide whether a patient meeting *DSM* diagnostic criteria actually has a mental disorder or not, and such environmental interventions may be necessary to deal effectively and appropriately with the client's problem. Thus the future of psychiatric diagnosis and treatment will have to involve teams of psychiatrists and social workers sorting out the social and internal factors that determine the individual's problem and implementing the appropriate psychiatric and social treatment strategies.

Granting that those who meet *DSM* criteria are often not genuinely disordered and are suffering instead from normal reactions to problematic person-in-environment interactions, and granting that psychiatrists are not about to engage in social diagnosis and person-in-environment intervention on the scale required by the flaws in the *DSM,* why can't psychiatrists still just ignore these conceptual points and continue to treat as psychiatric disorders the entire range of disorders and social problems encompassed by *DSM* criteria? The answer is that to do so would be unethical, for informed-consent reasons if for no others. People care greatly about whether a problem is a normal problem of living or a genuine mental disorder; controversies often erupt when medical treatment is provided to those who are not genuinely disordered, in areas ranging from the use of hormone treatments to increase normal children's height to using Prozac to elevate normal patients' moods. It is even more problematic to label and treat normal people as disordered when they are not so. Given that *DSM* diagnostic criteria do not correctly distinguish the normal from the disordered, it will eventually become apparent that a great wrong is being done in summarily dispensing psychotropic medication or psychotherapy without adequate differential diagnosis (including social diagnosis) to ensure that a genuine disorder exists.

To take just one example, drug trials for separation anxiety disorder using *DSM* criteria risk giving drugs to children to suppress a normal separation anxiety response. The use of drugs to treat normal, nondisordered reactions is generally controversial and raises complex value questions, but it is particularly problematic to use drugs to treat normal reactions in children without proper social diagnostic assessment and thus without consideration of alternative environmental interventions. Such inadvertent errors can be prevented only if genuine disorders and normal reactions to environmental problems can be distinguished through the combined efforts of social workers and psychiatrists during the diagnostic phase of treatment. Indeed, it is the professional responsibility of social workers to insist that such errors not be allowed to continue.

Conclusion

A genuine psychiatric disorder exists when symptoms are caused by a breakdown in the functioning of some internal mental mechanism. This is why it is thought that anyone diagnosed with a psychiatric disorder needs intervention into the internal workings of their mental mechanisms, whether through psychotherapy or drug treatment. However, this assumed connection between psychiatric diagnosis and internal dysfunction no longer holds. Psychiatry has embraced symptom-based criteria for mental disorders, for a variety of intellectual and institutional reasons. It turns out that the same "symptoms" (e.g., sadness, anxiety, antisocial behavior) that can be caused by internal dysfunctions can also be caused by normal responses to social problems. Therefore, psychiatry's symptom-based criteria inadvertently and incorrectly classify a large part of social work's domain as medical disorders. Moreover, it is impossible to tell from symptoms alone which apparent disorders are actually genuine disorders that require change of internal functioning and which are normal responses to environmental problems that require social intervention. Thus parallel social and psychiatric assessment is necessary if correct diagnosis and effective and appropriate treatment are to be achieved. It follows that social workers and psychiatrists must work together to respond to presenting symptomatic complaints. Such teamwork is necessary so long as psychiatry remains committed to symptom-based criteria and so long as psychiatrists are not trained or interested in doing what social workers now do, including direct family and community assessment and intervention.

References

American Psychiatric Association (APA). 1994. *Diagnostic and Statistical Manual of Mental Disorders (DSM-IV)*. 4th ed. Washington, D.C.: APA.

Barlow, D. H. 1991. Disorders of emotion. *Psychological Inquiry* 2:58–71.

———. 2001. *Anxiety and Its Disorders: The Nature and Treatment of Anxiety and Panic*. 2d ed. New York: Guilford Press.

Kirk, S. and H. Kutchins. 1988. Deliberate misdiagnosis in mental health practice. *Social Service Review* 62:225–237.

Olfson, M., S. Marcus, and A. Pincus. 1999. Trends in office-based psychiatric practice. *American Journal of Psychiatry* 156:451–457.

Specht, H. 1990. Social work and the popular psychotherapies. *Social Service Review* 64:345–357.

Specht, H. and M. E. Courtney. 1994. *Unfaithful Angels: How Social Work Has Abandoned Its Mission*. New York: Free Press.

Spitzer, R. L. and J. Endicott. 1978. Medical and Mental Disorder: Proposed Definition and Criteria. In R. L. Spitzer and D. F. Klein, eds., *Critical Issues in Psychiatric Diagnosis*, 15–39. New York: Raven Press.

Spitzer, R. L. and J. C. Wakefield. 1999. DSM-IV diagnostic criterion for clinical significance: Does it help solve the false positives problem? *American Journal of Psychiatry* 156:1856–1864.

Wakefield, J. C. 1988a. Psychotherapy, distributive justice, and social work. I. Distributive justice as a conceptual framework for social work. *Social Service Review* 62:187–210.

———. 1988b. Psychotherapy, distributive justice, and social work. II. Psychotherapy and the pursuit of justice. *Social Service Review* 62:353–382.

———. 1992a. The concept of mental disorder: On the boundary between biological facts and social values. *American Psychologist* 47:373–388.

————. 1992b. Disorder as harmful dysfunction: A conceptual critique of DSM-III-R's definition of mental disorder. *Psychological Review* 99:232–247.

————. 1992c. Why psychotherapeutic social work don't get no re-Specht. *Social Service Review* 66:141–151.

————. 1992d. Is Private Practice a Proper Form of Social Work? In E. Gambrill and R. Pruger, eds., *Controversial Issues in Social Work,* 221–230. Boston: Allyn and Bacon.

————. 1993. Limits of operationalization: A critique of Spitzer and Endicott's 1978 proposed operational criteria for mental disorder. *Journal of Abnormal Psychology* 102:160–172.

————. 1996. DSM-IV: Are we making diagnostic progress? *Contemporary Psychology* 41:646–652.

————. 1999. Evolutionary versus prototype analyses of the concept of disorder. *Journal of Abnormal Psychology* 108:374–399.

Wakefield, J. C. and M. First. 2003. Clarifying the Distinction Between Disorder and Non-disorder: Confronting the Overdiagnosis ("False Positives") Problem in DSM-V. In K. A. Phillips, M. B. First, and H. A. Pincus, eds., *Advancing DSM: Dilemmas in Psychiatric Diagnosis,* 23–56. Washington, D.C.: American Psychiatric Press.

Chapter 6

The Probabilistic Nature of Diagnosis: Rolling the Dice in Social Work Practice

William R. Nugent

A number of years ago I was working with a group of practitioners to develop standardized intake procedures for a group of human service agencies. During this work one of the practitioners regaled us with tales about a recent workshop that the practitioner had attended on the subject of multiple personality disorder, or MPD. Our colleague had never seen a case of MPD before attending this workshop. However, after the workshop our colleague had "learned what to look for" and noticed that clients with MPD were "coming out of the woodwork." This practitioner claimed to currently have a caseload with more than a dozen cases of MPD, a rather surprising assertion given the relative rarity of MPD. Multiple personality disorder, or what is now referred to as dissociative identity disorder (DID), is in fact a controversial diagnosis with respect to its nature, etiology, and prevalence (Campbell 1996; Garb 1998; Lilienfeld and Lynn 2003).

This experience led me to investigate the likelihood of a practitioner's having in her or his caseload certain numbers of clients with specific disorders, and consideration of this topic quickly led to consideration of the probability that a client actually has a disorder that he or she has been diagnosed as having. As we will see below, the sensitivity and specificity of an assessment procedure play significant roles in this probability, as does the prevalence of a disorder (Dawes 1996; Garb 1998). Practitioners have been criticized for not taking prevalence rates into account during assessment and diagnosis, since ignoring these rates can lead to biases and errors (see, for example, Arkes 1991; Dawes 1986; Finn 1982).

Gibbs and Gambrill (1999:135) discussed this issue, noting that ignoring prevalence rates can lead, for example, to the erroneous belief that the same assessment procedure will identify individuals with some problem or disorder just as well in a low-prevalence group as in a high-prevalence group. For example, imagine a particular individual named "Joe Schmoe" in two different situations. In the first, Joe is one of five persons in a group in a particular room. In this situation the "prevalence" of Joe Schmoe is one in five, or .20. In the second situation Joe is one of 104,078 persons at Neyland Stadium in Knoxville, Tennessee, watching the University of Tennessee football team play the University of Georgia football team. In this second situation the "prevalence" of Joe Schmoe is one in 104,078, or about .000001. In the first situation, if we were to select one person at random from the group in the room, the probability of correctly picking Joe Schmoe would be .20, while if we used the same procedure to try and correctly pick Joe Schmoe out of the Neyland Stadium crowd, the probability that we would correctly do so would be only about .000001, or one in one million. The "assessment" procedure used to identify Joe in the high-prevalence situation—the first one—is much less likely to identify Joe in the low-prevalence situation—the second one.

In this chapter probability theory is used to explore the effects that prevalence rates and the sensitivity and specificity of an assessment procedure have on the probability that a client actually has a disorder that he or she has been diagnosed as having and on the probability that a client does *not* have a disorder that he or she has been judged *not* to have. When we apply estimates of the prevalence rates of specific disorders, as well as of the sensitivity and specificity of current structured assessment procedures, to the results of our probability considerations, we will find that the probability that a client actually has the disorder that he or she has been diagnosed with may be very low and that the probability a client does *not* have a disorder that he or she has been judged *not* to have may be very low as well, raising the possibility that misdiagnosis may be all too common. Other considerations will suggest that there is more measurement error in inferences made from unstructured assessment approaches than from structured approaches. Next, a proof is invoked that implies that once a practitioner has judged a client to have, or not have, a particular disorder, then efforts to obtain new information *inconsistent* with the practitioner's inference will do more to increase the probability of a correct assessment decision than will efforts to obtain new information *consistent* with the inference. Finally, the implications of these findings for social work practice and education are considered. These implications take on particular saliency given the growing evidence of iatrogenic outcomes for clients in a wide range of human service fields, including health (Kohn, Corrigan, and Donaldson 2000), child welfare (Baker 1998; Caplan and Caplan 2001; Wexler 1990; Wordinsky, Vizcarrondo, and Cruz 1995), and mental health (Lynn et al. 2003), and the role that misdiagnosis may play in these iatrogenic outcomes (see, for example, Boisvert and Faust 2002; Poulin, Dishion, and Burraston 2001; Witztum et al. 1995).

The Probability That a Client Who Has Been Diagnosed with a Disorder Actually Has That Disorder

Let's first review several concepts that are important to our subsequent discussion. The box in figure 6.1 shows both reality and the outcomes of an assessment inference made by a practitioner on the basis of assessment results. The labels above the cells of the box represent reality: a client either has (yes) or does not have (no) a particular disorder. The labels on the side of the box represent the judgments made by a practitioner from the results of some assessment procedure: the practitioner either infers that the client has the particular disorder (yes) or that the client does not have it (no). The terms within the cells of the box describe the inferences made by the practitioner. If the client does not have the disorder, and the practitioner infers that the client does not have the disorder (upper left cell in the box), then this correct inference is referred to as a "true negative." The proportion of persons who do not have a disorder and are correctly inferred to not have the disorder on the basis of the results of some assessment procedure is referred to as the "specificity" of the assessment procedure. If the client does have the disorder, and the practitioner infers that the client does indeed have the disorder (lower right cell), then this correct inference is referred to as a "true positive." The proportion of persons who have a disorder and are correctly inferred to have the disorder on the basis of the results of some assessment procedure is referred to as the "sensitivity" of the assessment procedure.

If the client does not have the disorder, but the practitioner infers that the client does have the disorder (lower left cell), then this erroneous inference is referred to as a "false positive." The proportion of persons who do not have a disorder but are incorrectly inferred to have the disorder on the basis of the results of some assessment procedure is referred to as the "false-positive rate" of the assessment procedure. If the client does indeed have the disorder, but the practitioner infers that the client does not have the disorder, then this incorrect inference is referred to as a "false negative." The proportion of persons who have a disorder and are incorrectly inferred to not have the disorder on the basis of the results of some assessment procedure is referred to as the "false-negative rate" of the assessment procedure.

Now suppose that an assessment or diagnostic procedure produces results that are "positive," leading a practitioner to infer that a client has some disorder, say "disorder X." What is the probability that the client actually has disorder X given that he or she has been diagnosed as having it? This

Reality: Does
Client have disorder?

		no	yes
Inference made from assessment results: Does client have disorder?	no	True negative	False negative
	yes	False positive	True positive

Figure 6.1 A representation of the outcomes of assessment inferences. The columns represent the two possibilities concerning whether a client has or does not have a specific disorder, while the rows represent the two possible outcomes of assessment inferences about whether or not the client has the specific disorder.

probability can be computed using the diagram in figure 6.2 (see Ash 1993:58–61; Mendenhall 1975:80–82), which represents the possible outcomes, shown in figure 6.1, of an assessment procedure. First, the client either has or does not have disorder X. Figure 6.2 represents this state of affairs by showing two paths, A and B. Path A represents the situation in which a person has disorder X, while path B shows the situation in which the person does not have disorder X. A number is placed in parentheses next to the letter A to represent the prevalence of the disorder in a given population or subpopulation. Let's assume the prevalence is .05, so the number .05 is placed in the parentheses in figure 6.2 next to the letter A. A number can also be placed next to the letter B to represent the prevalence of "not having disorder X." This number will be $1 - p$, where p is the prevalence of disorder X, so if the prevalence is .05, then the prevalence of "not having disorder X" will be .95, as shown in figure 6.2.

The path in figure 6.2 marked with the letter C represents the situation in which *a person who has disorder* X *is identified via some assessment procedure as having disorder* X, and a number can be placed next to the letter C to represent the true positive rate, or the sensitivity, of the assessment procedure. *The sensitivity can be interpreted as the probability that a person who has disorder* X *is identified by use of the assessment procedure as having disorder* X. Similarly, the path labeled with the letter D in figure 6.2 shows the situation in which *a person who has disorder* X *is incorrectly inferred, from the assessment, to not have the disorder.* This event is, of course, a false negative, and a number can be placed next to the letter D to represent this rate. The false-negative rate, FNR, which is the proportion of persons who have disorder X who are erroneously inferred as *not* having this disorder, is related to the sensitivity

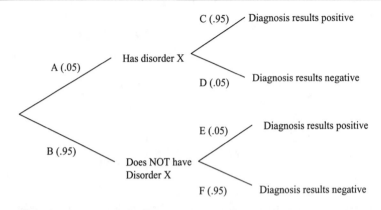

Figure 6.2 A tree diagram representing assessment inferences as a two-stage process. The number in parentheses next to the letter A represents the prevalence of a disorder or problem; the number in the parentheses next to the letter C represents the sensitivity of an assessment method; and the number in parentheses next to the letter F represents the specificity of the assessment method.

by FNR = 1 − sensitivity. For example, since the sensitivity in figure 6.2 is .95, the FNR would be 1 − .95 = .05.

The path labeled *E* in figure 6.2 represents the state of affairs in which *the person does not have disorder* X *but is incorrectly inferred from the results of the assessment procedure to have the disorder.* This situation is a false positive, and a number can be placed next to the letter *E* to represent the false-positive rate, which gives the proportion of persons who do *not* have disorder *X* who are erroneously inferred as having the disorder. Finally, the path labeled *F* represents the situation in which *the person who does not have disorder* X *is correctly determined to not have the disorder.* This is referred to as a true negative, and the number representing the specificity—the proportion of persons who have disorder *X* who are accurately inferred to have the disorder—of the assessment procedure can be placed next to the letter *F* to represent this rate. The false-positive rate, FPR, is related to the specificity by FPR = 1 − specificity. For example, since the specificity in figure 6.2 is .95, the FPR will be 1 − .95 = .05.

Figure 6.2 shows a hypothetical assessment procedure with a sensitivity of .95 (FNR = .05), and a specificity of .95 (FPR = .05), for detecting the presence or absence of disorder *X*. This assessment procedure is being used in the context of a disorder with a prevalence rate of .05. The question thus becomes, "If a client is inferred to have disorder *X* from the results of the assessment procedure, what is the probability that the client does, in fact, have disorder *X*?" Equation (1) discussed in appendix 6.1 (and in Nugent 2003) can be used to compute this probability. As can be seen from equation

(1), this probability depends upon (a) the sensitivity of the assessment procedure for detecting the presence of disorder X (b) the specificity of the assessment procedure for detecting the absence of disorder X, and (c) the prevalence of disorder X. So, assuming that the sensitivity and specificity are both .95, as in figure 6.2, and that the prevalence of disorder X is .05, then the probability that a client actually has disorder X, given that he or she has been diagnosed as having it will be .50. The reason for this perhaps counterintuitive result for the probability that a client has disorder X, given that he or she has been diagnosed as having the disorder through use of the assessment procedure, given the high sensitivity and specificity values for the assessment procedure, is the low prevalence rate. Note that if the sensitivity and specificity both remain at .95, but the prevalence rate of disorder X increases to .50, then equation (1) now shows that the probability that the client has disorder X, given that he or she has been diagnosed with it from the results of the assessment procedure, will be .95. This shows how the same assessment procedure works differently in a high- versus a low-prevalence-rate context.

In a similar vein, the probability that a client does *not* have disorder X, given that the assessment procedure produces results that lead the practitioner to infer that he or she does *not* have the disorder, will be given by equation (2). Therefore, for the situation in figure 6.2, the probability that a client does not have disorder X, given that the assessment results suggest that he or she does not have it, will be .997. Note that in this context, where the prevalence of disorder X is .05, the prevalence of *not* having disorder X is 1 − .05 = .95. This high-prevalence context of *not* having disorder X is why the assessment procedure leads to such a high probability that a client does *not* have disorder X, given that he or she has been inferred to *not* have the disorder from the results of the assessment procedure.

As Ash (1993) points out, what the practitioner would like to know is whether or not the client has disorder X, but this cannot be ascertained without the use of some assessment procedure. In a very real sense, the actual state of affairs at the first stage in figure 6.2—whether or not the client has disorder X—is hidden from the practitioner. The outcome of the second stage—the assessment results—is known. The best that the practitioner can do is to make an inference about the first stage—the presence or absence of the disorder—from the outcome of the second stage, the assessment procedure.

The two probabilities discussed above—the probability that a client has disorder X given that he or she has been diagnosed as having the disorder and the probability that the client does *not* have disorder X given that he or she has been inferred to *not* have the disorder from the results of the assessment procedure—can be viewed as indicators of the accuracy of the inference about the first stage from the outcome of the second stage. For the sake of economy of writing, and for consistency with discussion (but at the risk of creating some distaste on the part of readers who hate to see anything resembling a formula or equation), let's use the symbol $p(X|dX)$ to represent the probability that a client actually has disorder X given that he or she has been diagnosed as having disorder X from the results of an assessment procedure. Similarly, let's use the symbol $p(\sim X|\sim dX)$ to represent the probability that a client does in fact *not* have disorder X, given that the results of the assessment procedure have led to the inference that the client does *not* have disorder X. Then we can define two forms of diagnostic error, error type A (symbolized as Ω_1) and error type B (symbolized as Ω_2). Error type A will be equal to $1 - p(X|dX)$ and can be interpreted as the probability that the client does *not* have disorder X, given that he or she has been diagnosed as having it. As will be seen below, the type A diagnostic error is not the same as the false-positive rate. Similarly, error type B will be equal to $1 - p(\sim X|\sim dX)$ and is interpretable as the probability that the client does have disorder X, given that he or she has been inferred as *not* having it. As will be seen below, the type B diagnostic error is not the same as the false-negative rate.

Some Common Misunderstandings

When asked what the probability is that a client has the disorder that he or she has been diagnosed as having, many of my students have responded by saying that this probability is the same as the sensitivity of the assessment procedure, or, equivalently, the same as the true positive rate. For example, if the sensitivity (true positive rate) is .95, then the probability that a client has disorder X given that he or she has been diagnosed as having the disorder will be .95. However, this is incorrect, as can be seen by closely considering equation (1). Equation (1) can be written in a form in which the numerator gives the number of persons who have disorder X who have been (accurately) inferred as having disorder X by use of the assessment procedure, while the denominator gives the *total number of persons who have been diagnosed as having disorder X*. In contrast, the sensitivity can be written in a form in which the numerator is the number of persons who have disorder X who have been (accurately) inferred as having disorder X by use of the assessment procedure, while the denominator is *the total number of persons who have disorder X in the population*. Thus, $p(X|dX)$ and the sensitivity (the true positive rate) will be equal only when these denominators are equal. A similar line of reasoning leads to the conclusion that $p(\sim X|\sim dX)$ and the specificity (true negative rate) will not be the same except in unusual circumstances (see discussion).

Another error that is commonly made is to assume that the type A error defined and discussed above is the same as the false-positive rate and that the type B error is the same as the false-negative rate. However, the type A error and the false-positive rate are usually not the same, and the type B error and the false-negative rate are most often not the same.

So What Does the Above Imply About the Results of Assessment Inferences in Practice?

The above discussion immediately raises the questions of what the probabilities that clients actually have the disorder with which they have been diagnosed as having, and what the probabilities that clients actually do *not* have the disorders that they have been inferred as *not* having, might be in actual clinical practice. Before we consider these probabilities, we first need to determine the best estimates of the prevalence rates of specific disorders, and of the sensitivities and specificities of commonly used assessment procedures, and then use these in our calculations of $p(X|dX)$ and $p(\sim X|\sim dX)$.

Prevalence Estimates

Estimates of the prevalence of a disorder in a given population can be specified as the proportion (or percentage) of the population that has the disorder at a given point in time, a "point estimate"; over a specific duration of time, a "period estimate"; or over a person's lifetime, a "lifetime estimate" (Banks and Kerns 1996). For example, Eaton, Dryman, and Weissman (1991) reported data from the Epidemiologic Catchment Area (ECA) Study (see below) suggesting that the point prevalence of panic disorder (PD) in the general U.S. population is .0053 (.53%); the one-year prevalence .0091 (.91%); and the lifetime prevalence .0157 (1.57%). Generally a point estimate will be lower than a one-year prevalence, which in turn will be lower than a lifetime prevalence (Banks and Kerns 1996).

A number of epidemiologic investigations on the prevalence of various mental disorders have been conducted. Two of the largest have been the ECA study, which involved a probability sample of more than twelve thousand community residents, and the National Comorbidity Study (NCS), which involved a probability sample of more than eight thousand community residents (see Barlow 2002). Recently Reiger, Narrow, and Rae (cited in Barlow 2002:22) used the data from these two epidemiological studies to provide best estimates of the one-year prevalence of a number of disorders. These estimates suggested, for example, that .049 (4.9%) of the overall U.S. population suffer from agoraphobia; 5.3% from major depressive disorder;

and 3.6% from post-traumatic stress disorder at some point over a one-year period. Other studies have suggested that a liberal estimate of the point prevalence of MPD (or DID) is about .01, or 1% (Garb 1998), and that a point estimate of the prevalence of major depression among adolescents is 3.4%, and a lifetime prevalence 24.8% (Lewinsohn et al. 1993).

As noted earlier, numerous writers have argued that practitioners need to take into account prevalence rates when making assessment and diagnostic inferences. The use of general population prevalence rates when making inferences from assessment results assumes that these rates are the same as those in the population of persons actually seeking services. However, the prevalence of some disorders and problems appears to be greater within specific subpopulations than in the general population. For example, within the population of persons with certain physical diseases the prevalence of major depression may be higher than in the general population. For example, studies have led to estimates of the prevalence of major depressive disorder (MDD) as high as 54% among chronic pain patients (Banks and Kerns 1996).

Other lines of research have suggested that prevalence rates among persons seeking services will differ from general population rates. For example, it has been estimated that only 10% of those who experience depression actually seek services (NIH 2001). Some epidemiologic research has suggested that only about 13% of those persons with a single diagnosable disorder actually seek treatment (Blazer et al. 1994). As suggested by these results, as well as the prevalence estimates above for specific groups of people with chronic pain, the prevalence rate of those suffering from a particular disorder in the general population may not be the same as that among those who seek services. The prevalence rate among those seeking services could be either higher or lower than that in the general population, and in many cases may not be known.

A caveat is in order concerning these (as well as all other) prevalence estimates: they are only as accurate as the methodology upon which they are based. While the ECA and NCS prevalence estimates were based upon probability samples, and therefore may be reasonably accurate, the other prevalence estimates reported above may be less sound; the reader is referred to the original studies for details of the methodologies upon which the estimates are based. Another concern is that prevalence estimates are themselves based upon fallible assessment procedures. Thus, all prevalence estimates are vulnerable to measurement error inherent in the results of the assessment procedures. The implications of these uncertainties are considered later.

The Sensitivity and Specificity of Commonly Used Assessment Methods

For illustrative purposes, let's consider the sensitivity and specificity of various assessment procedures for determining whether a person has a major depressive disorder (or MDD). Recently Williams et al. (2002) synthesized the results of thirty-eight studies, involving thirty-two thousand participants, on the sensitivity and specificity of sixteen different measures of depression used in primary care settings to identify people with MDD. The median sensitivity was .85, and the median specificity was .74, and the results suggested that there were no significant differences among any of the sixteen instruments. These sensitivity and specificity values were used to compute the probability that a client actually has MDD given that he or she has been diagnosed as having MDD [i.e., $p(X|dX)$]—and the probability that the client does, in fact, *not* have MDD, given that he or she has been inferred as *not* having MDD [i.e., $p(\sim X|\sim dX)$]—for five different prevalence rates: .05, .15, .25, .54, and .70. The results of these computations are shown in table 6.1. The prevalence value of .05 is approximately equal to the one-year prevalence of MDD in the general population; the .54 value represents an upper bound for the relatively high rates of MDD that have been estimated for chronic pain patients; while the .70 value represents a prevalence exceeding any found in the literature for special populations and is used to illustrate $p(X|dX)$ and $p(\sim X|\sim dX)$ values in this highest of prevalence contexts. The range .05 to .70 likely captures the range of prevalence rates of MDD among many populations seeking services in health and mental health settings. Also shown in table 6.1 are estimates of the type A error rate (in parentheses), and the type B error rate (*italicized in parentheses*).

The uppermost entries in table 6.1 show the values of $p(X|dX)$ and $p(\sim X|\sim dX)$ computed from the Williams et al. (2002) sensitivity and specificity estimates for the five prevalence rates. For example, given the sensitivity of .85 and the specificity of .74, and a prevalence of .05, then $p(X|dX)$ = .15, and the type A error rate is .85; and $p(\sim X|\sim dX)$ = .99 and the type B error rate is .01. As this table shows, $p(X|dX)$ ranges from .15 to .88 (and type A error rates from .12 to .85), and $p(\sim X|\sim dX)$ values range from .67 to .99 (and type B error rates from .01 to .33).

In another recent study Bech et al. (2001) investigated the sensitivity and specificity of the Major Depression Inventory (MDI) for detecting MDD. Bech et al. (2001) reported an upper value for the sensitivity of the MDI of .92, and an upper value for the specificity of .86, for detecting MDD. The second set of entries in table 6.1 shows the $p(X|dX)$, $p(\sim X|\sim dX)$, and error rate values for the MDI within the context of each of the prevalence rates. The $p(X|dX)$ values range from .26 to .94 (and type A error rates from .06

Table 6.1

$p(X|dX)$ and $p(\sim X|\sim dX)$ Values for the Diagnosis of Major Depressive Disorder for Five Prevalence Rates and Three Assessment Procedures: Sixteen Measurement Scales (Williams et al. 2002); the MDI (Bech et al. 2001); and the DIS (Murphy et al. 2000; Eaton et al. 2000).

Williams et al. (2002) results						
	prevalence =	.05	.15	.25	.54	.70
Sensitivity = .85;	$p(X\|dX) =$	.15 (.85)	.37 (.63)	.52 (.48)	.79 (.21)	.88 (.12)
Specificity = .74;	$p(\sim X\|\sim dX) =$	.99 (.01)	.97 (.03)	.94 (.06)	.81 (.19)	.67 (.33)
Bech et al. (2001) results						
Sensitivity = .92;	$p(X\|dX) =$	26 (.74)	.54 (.46)	.69 (.31)	.88 (.12)	.94 (.06)
Specificity = .86;	$p(\sim X\|\sim dX) =$	.99 (.01)	.98 (.02)	.97 (.03)	.90 (.10)	.82 (.18)
Murphy et al. (2000) results						
Sensitivity = .55;	$p(X\|dX) =$	.22 (.78)	.54 (.46)	.65 (.35)	.87 (.13)	.93 (.07)
Specificity = .90;	$p(\sim X\|\sim dX) =$	.97 (.03)	.92 (.08)	.86 (.14)	.63 (.37)	.46 (.54)
Eaton et al. (2000) results						
Sensitivity = .25;	$p(X\|dX) =$	.40 (.60)	.69 (.31)	.81 (.19)	.94 (.06)	.97 (.03)
Specificity = .98;	$p(\sim X\|\sim dX) =$	.96 (.04)	.88 (.12)	.80 (.20)	.65 (.35)	.36 (.64)

to .74), and the $p(\sim X|\sim dX)$ values range from .82 to .99 (and type B error rates from .01 to .18). The $p(X|dX)$ and $p(\sim X|\sim dX)$ values are somewhat higher, and the diagnostic error rate values somewhat lower, than those for the depression measures in the first example because the sensitivity and specificity estimates are higher for the MDI.

The Diagnostic Interview Schedule (DIS) is a highly structured interview for use in identifying mental health problems, such as depression, and for making *DSM*-type diagnoses (Robins et al. 1981). A recent study conducted by Murphy et al. (2000) reported a sensitivity for the DIS of .55, and a specificity of .90, for identifying MDD. The third set of entries in table 6.1 shows $p(X|dX)$, $p(\sim X|\sim dX)$, and the diagnostic error rate values for the DIS under the five different prevalence rates. In a second recent study, conducted by Eaton et al. (2000), the sensitivity of the DIS was estimated at .25, while the specificity was estimated to be .98. Note that in this study the estimated sensitivity was lower, .25 versus .55, than that estimated by Murphy et al. (2000), while the specificity was a bit higher, .98 versus .90. The fourth set of entries in table 6.1 shows the $p(X|dX)$, $p(\sim X|\sim dX)$, and the diagnostic error rate values based on the Eaton et al. (2000) sensitivity and specificity estimates. It is important to note here that even though the estimated sensitivity of the DIS is lower in this second study, .25, versus .55 in the previous study, the probabilities that a client diagnosed as having MDD actually has MDD are uniformly higher across the range of prevalence values.

This illustrates the importance of attempts to gather evidence that is inconsistent with a particular diagnosis or assessment result, thereby increasing the specificity, a topic discussed in detail below. Note also that as the prevalence of the disorder increases, the prevalence of *not* having the disorder decreases, so as $p(X|dX)$ values increase, $p(\sim X|\sim dX)$ values decrease. This again illustrates the important role that prevalence plays in interpreting what the results of an assessment tell the practitioner.

In summary, these results should be quite sobering. Even in the context of a prevalence rate as high as .70, the sensitivity and specificity values shown in table 6.1 imply diagnostic error rates as high as .64 for making diagnostic inferences concerning major depressive disorder. These results imply that even in this exceedingly high-prevalence-rate context, as many as 64% of clients may be misdiagnosed. The actual rates of misdiagnosis are likely higher, for two reasons. First, in all but the most unusual of circumstances the prevalence rates of disorders in populations of people seeking services are most likely less than .70. This means that the values in table 6.1 for the prevalence rates less than .70 are most likely representative of the probabilities and diagnostic error rates found in actual clinical practice. Second, the most common assessment approaches used in actual practice are most likely unstructured approaches (Garb 1998; see discussion immediately below). Since the sensitivity and specificity values for unstructured approaches are almost certainly lower than for structured approaches (Garb 1998; Nugent 2003), this second consideration implies that the actual diagnostic error rates found in clinical practice are almost certainly higher than those shown in table 6.1 at each prevalence rate. This is not a happy outcome for either practitioner or client.

Research on Unstructured Assessments by Practitioners

Unstructured assessment methods, within the context of the free-style interview, may be the most common form of assessment conducted by practitioners (Garb 1998). The assessment inferences made by practitioners who use such methods are, therefore, an important research topic. Research has suggested that clinicians make assessment decisions, such as diagnoses, very quickly, frequently after gathering very little information (see Ambady and Rosenthal 1992; Gambrill 1997; Garb 1998; Houts and Galante 1985). Further, practitioners frequently do not attend to diagnostic criteria when they are conducting assessments (e.g., Jampala, Spears, and Neubauer 1988; Rubinson, Asnis, and Friedman 1988; see also discussion in Garb 1998). For example, in one study, replicated by Blashfield and Herkov (1996), Morey and Ochoa (1989) compared the criteria used by clinicians to make *DSM-III* diagnoses with the actual *DSM-III* criteria. The results showed that the agreement, expressed as a kappa coefficient, between the criteria used by clinicians and the actual *DSM-III* criteria ranged from only .05 to .59. Practitioners also engage in a number of cognitive processes that focus on confirming impressions already formed, and they do not appear to explicitly search for information that would contradict initial clinical impressions and diagnostic decisions (Garb 1998). This confirmation bias supports diagnostic error (Garb and Boyle 2003).

What Type of Evidence Increases $p(X \mid dX)$ and $p(\sim X \mid \sim dX)$ the Most?

An important question concerns what types of information can help the practitioner to increase either the probability that a client actually has the disorder that he or she has been diagnosed as having, or the probability that he or she does, in fact, *not* have a disorder that he or she has been inferred to *not* have. Nugent (2003) derived equations (3) and (4), which implied that: (1) if a practitioner has made a tentative inference based upon the results of an assessment procedure that a client has disorder X, then subsequent efforts to obtain new information *inconsistent with the diagnosis of disorder* X will lead to greater increases in the probability that the client actually has disorder X, given the diagnosis of disorder X, than will efforts to obtain information consistent with the diagnosis; and (2) if a practitioner has made a tentative inference that a client does *not* have disorder X based upon the results of an assessment procedure, then subsequent efforts to obtain new information *inconsistent with the inference—that is, consistent with the client HAVING disorder* X—will lead to greater increases in the probability that the client actually does *not* have disorder X given the inference that he or she does *not* have the disorder. Equations (3) and (4) are consistent with the conclusions of many writers (e.g., Garb 1998; Gibbs and Gambrill 1999; Gilovich 1993) that one of the most important activities that a practitioner can engage in is the search for information that contradicts a belief, inference, or conclusion.

These results also imply that practitioners, contrary to what appears to be common practice (see Garb 1998), should view assessment as an ongoing process that ends only when the services being provided to the client have ended. Research suggests that practitioners make diagnoses very quickly, based upon limited information, and then tend not to seek information that would contradict their initial impressions. In many cases, once a diagnosis has been made, no subsequent efforts are made to obtain new information that might lead to reconsideration of the validity of the diagnosis. This approach to assessment, in which assessment is actualized as a brief, time-limited process that essentially ends with the making of a diagnosis and the initiation of some treatment or intervention, is fraught with the risk of erroneous inferences about clients' problems and disorders (Garb and Boyle 2003). However, if assessment is operationalized as an ongoing process throughout the provision of services, the assessment inferences made from the constantly accruing information can be constantly updated and altered as necessary. This ongoing assessment process may thereby lead to increases in specificity and sensitivity and attendant increases in the probabilities represented by the symbols $p(X \mid dX)$ and $p(\sim X \mid \sim dX)$.

Discussion and Conclusion

The above lines of discussion converge to strongly suggest that categorical inferences from assessment procedures, such as *DSM*-type diagnoses, should be avoided if at all possible in social work practice. It should be clear from the foregoing that diagnostic inferences are a form of probability game, no different in kind than roulette or blackjack, and that a "positive" or a "negative" diagnostic result, leading to a diagnosis of "disorder X" or an inference of the absence of disorder X, cannot be meaningfully interpreted without careful consideration of prevalence rates and sensitivity and specificity values. As table 6.1 shows, even in exceedingly high-prevalence contexts, the probability of a diagnostic error can be quite high. Given that there is almost certainly more error in diagnostic inferences made from the results of unstructured assessment approaches, the probability of misdiagnosis when unstructured methods are used is most likely higher, in some cases perhaps much higher, than the illustrative probabilities shown in table 6.1. Since the overwhelming majority of such diagnostic inferences made in practice are based upon results from unstructured assessment approaches, it would appear that misdiagnosis may be far too common an occurrence. The tendency for practitioners to use diagnoses within a confirmatory bias context, and to not look for disconfirmatory evidence that could lead to abandoning the diagnosis, raises the serious possibility of harmful outcomes for clients (Garb 1998; Garb and Boyle 2003).

Another concern with categorical assessment inferences is that in many cases the prevalence rates of the disorder among the population of people seeking health or mental health services either will contain significant error or will not be known at all. In these cases practitioners will not be able to use prevalence rates to help them interpret what a positive or negative diagnostic inference is likely to mean. A similar line of reasoning will suggest that in many cases the estimates of the sensitivity and specificity of the assessment procedure either will contain substantial error or will not exist at all. These considerations suggest that practitioners will, perhaps most of the time, be completely in the dark as to how to properly interpret the meaning of a diagnosis of disorder X, or the absence of disorder X. In these circumstances practitioners are playing a game of chance without any idea of the probabilities involved. Therefore their interpretations of the meaning of a positive or negative assessment outcome are essentially acts of faith. These considerations further suggest that categorical diagnostic inferences should be avoided in practice because of the risk of diagnostic error.

Misdiagnosis may lead to a number of negative outcomes for clients, depending upon the context in which the diagnosis is made. For example, if the diagnosis is of the form "This child has been abused," the negative outcomes can include the child's unnecessary removal from the home; possible criminal charges being filed against one or more family members who are, in fact, innocent; the loss of employment and reputation of the accused family member; and the breakup of the family (Baker 1998; Campell 1998; Lynn et al. 2003; Pendergrast and Gavigan 1996; Wordinsky, Vizcorrondo, and Cruz 1995). Misdiagnosis in mental health settings can lead to inappropriate treatment, such as the unnecessary use of psychotropic medication, and the failure to recognize serious medical conditions because they are misinterpreted as mental disorders (e.g., Gold 1996; Hayes, Butler, and Martin 1986). These and other consequences of diagnostic error can lead to a range of negative outcomes.

The above also suggests that social work educators should deemphasize the use of assessment procedures that lead to *DSM*-type diagnoses or other types of categorical inference. Given the extent to which *DSM*-type diagnoses have been institutionalized in health and mental health settings, the use of these types of diagnoses should still be taught, but with an emphasis on the serious problems associated with such assessment inferences and a clear understanding that the primary utility of such diagnostic decisions is the funding of services. Student social workers should be taught that if they must make such diagnoses they should be made and interpreted, if possible, within the context of sensitivity and specificity estimates for the assessment procedure and the local prevalence rates for the disorders being considered. The assessment process should be viewed as ongoing throughout the provision of services, with new evidence being constantly accumulated and diagnostic decisions altered as necessary as new information is obtained. Assessment approaches in which the assessment process concludes with the making of a diagnosis should be viewed as unethical and in violation of an adequate standard of care. Whatever diagnosis is tentatively made should be used with extreme caution and an appreciation for the reliability and validity problems associated with such inferences. The practitioner must keep in mind that all assessment decisions are provisional and could, in fact, be in error.

Student social workers should also be taught that when categorical assessment inferences must be made, structured assessment approaches should be used to make them. The use of structured approaches, such as standardized measurement scales and structured clinical interview methods, will most likely lead to inferences with greater validity. The use of the free-style, unstructured interview for conducting assessments should be strongly discouraged and, perhaps, considered to be unethical because of the serious reliability and validity problems associated with inferences made from such assessment approaches. Further, once the social worker has made an inference that a client has, or does not have, a given disorder or syndrome, then subsequent efforts should be focused on obtaining evidence inconsistent with the assessment inference that has been made. Efforts to obtain evidence inconsistent with the assessment decision can lead to new information that can increase either $p(X \mid dX)$ or $p(\sim X \mid \sim dX)$, depending upon the nature of the inference made, and thereby decrease the likelihood of diagnostic error.

The foregoing results also strongly suggest that assessments of client problems be used that provide magnitude, severity, or frequency counts as opposed to decisions about categorical membership. For example, the use of a standardized scale such as the Beck Depression Inventory (Beck 1978) or Hudson's Generalized Contentment Scale (Hudson 1982) to measure the magnitude of a client's problem with depression will most likely have less measurement error, and result in inferences with greater validity, than will attempts to make a categorical diagnosis such as dysthymia. This speculation is consistent with recent research on the reliability and validity of *DSM*-type diagnoses and the growing use of measures of symptom magnitude within structured interviews whose aim is to produce *DSM*-type diagnoses (Barlow 2002; Brown et al. 2001; Costello 1992). It can also be shown that the norm-referenced inferences made from such assessment approaches will almost always contain less measurement error than the criterion-referenced inferences made when categorical assessment inferences are made. This is because relative error variance is of concern in the former types of inferences, and this error variance will be smaller than the absolute error variance, which is of concern when criterion-referenced inferences are made, in all but the most unusual of circumstances (Brennan 2001).

Given the extent to which the *DSM* system of diagnoses has been institutionalized, these types of diagnoses will almost certainly continue to be made by social workers and other professionals. Because of this near certainty, and because of the prevalence of other forms of categorical assessment inferences, special social work advocates need to be trained whose primary duty is to protect clients from those who make "diagnoses." These advocates should be highly trained in assessment and measurement methods and the forms of inference made from each. They should be well aware of the serious problems associated with categorical inferences, such as the presence or absence of some "mental disorder" or type of behavioral occurrence, such as "abuse." The primary duties for these special advocates would be to empower clients to be informed service recipients—and to ensure that practitioners be cautious in the use of diagnostic decisions of any type and that they look for evidence inconsistent with any diagnostic decision that they make. In this manner clients, who are in a low-power context, can have greater protection from the potential diagnostic errors made by practitioners.

Appendix 6.1.   Technical Appendix

The Probability That a Client Has Disorder X, Given a Diagnosis of Disorder X

Let the symbol $p(X|dX)$ represent the probability that a person actually has disorder X given that he or she has been diagnosed as having it. This *backward conditional probability* can be computed from figure 6.2 by an equation expressing Bayes theorem (Ash 1993):

$$p(X|dX) = \frac{A \times C}{(A \times C) + (B \times E)} = \frac{p \times s_e}{(p \times s_e) + [(1 - p)(1 - s_p)]}$$

(Equation 1)

In this equation, p represents the prevalence of disorder X; s_e represents the sensitivity of the assessment procedure for detecting the presence of disorder X; and s_p represents the specificity of the assessment procedure for ruling out disorder X. Equation (1) gives the probability that a client actually has disorder X, given that he or she has been inferred to have disorder X on the basis of the assessment results. The equation

$$\Omega_1 = 1 - \frac{ps_e}{ps_e + (1 - p)(1 - s_p)} = \frac{(1 - p)(1 - s_p)}{ps_e + (1 - p)(1 - s_p)}$$
$$= \frac{(1 - p)\text{FPR}}{ps_e + (1 - p)\text{FPR}}$$

gives the probability that the client does *not* have disorder X, given that he or she has been diagnosed as having disorder X on the basis of the results of the assessment procedure. In this equation, Ω_1 represents this type of diagnostic error, referred to as a type A error in the above text, and FPR represents the false-positive rate of the assessment procedure.

It can be shown by way of some simple algebra that

$$\text{FPR} = \frac{\Omega_1 ps_e}{(1 - \Omega_1)(1 - p)} = \frac{\Omega_1 ps_e}{p(X|dX)(1 - p)}.$$

Thus, the false-positive rate FPR will not be the same as the type A error rate Ω_1 except in the most unusual of circumstances, when $ps_e = p(X|dX)(1 - p)$.

The Probability That a Client Does Not Have Disorder X, Given Such an Inference

Let the symbol $p(\sim X|\sim dX)$ represent the probability that a person actually does *not* have disorder X, given that he or she has been inferred to not have the disorder from the results of some assessment procedure. The probability that a client does *not* have disorder X, given that he or she has been inferred as not having the disorder based upon the results of the assessment procedure, can similarly be computed from figure 6.2 by the equation

$$p(\sim X|\sim dX) = \frac{(1 - p)s_p}{(1 - p)s_p + p(1 - s_e)} = \frac{(1 - p)s_p}{(1 - p)s_p + p\text{FNR}}$$

(Equation 2)

The equation

$$\Omega_2 = 1 - \frac{(1 - p)s_p}{(1 - p)s_p + p\text{FNR}} = \frac{p\text{FNR}}{(1 - p)s_p + p\text{FNR}}$$

gives the probability that a client *does* have disorder X, given that he or she has been inferred to *not* have the disorder based upon the results of the assessment procedure. This diagnostic error, referred to as a type B error in the text, is symbolized by Ω_2.

Again, it can be shown by simple algebra that

$$\text{FNR} = \frac{\Omega_2(1 - p)s_p}{(1 - \Omega_2)p} = \frac{\Omega_2(1 - p)s_p}{p(\sim X | \sim dX)p}.$$

Thus, the false-negative rate (FNR) will not be the same as the type B error rate, Ω_2, except in the most unusual of circumstances, specifically when $(1 - p)s_p = p(\sim X | \sim dX)p$.

What Information Increases $p(X | dX)$ *and* $p(\sim X | \sim dX)$ *the Most?*

An important question concerns what type of information will increase $p(X | dX)$ the most, information that increases the sensitivity of the assessment procedure or information that increases the specificity. The partial derivative of $p(X | dX)$ with respect to the sensitivity, s_e, gives the rate of change in $p(X | dX)$ per unit increase in s_e, holding the prevalence, p, and the specificity, s_p, constant (Simon 1982). Similarly, the partial derivative of $p(X | dX)$ with respect to the specificity, s_p, gives the rate of change in $p(X | dX)$ per unit increase in s_p, holding the prevalence and sensitivity constant. Nugent (2003) showed that the following relationship exists between these two partial derivatives:

$$\frac{\partial}{\partial s_p} p(X | dX) = \frac{s_e}{\text{FPR}} \frac{\partial}{\partial s_e} p(X | dX)$$

(Equation 3)

This relationship shows that as long as the ratio $(s_e/\text{FPR}) > 1$ holds, there will be a greater increase in $p(X | dX)$ per unit increase in the specificity than per unit increase in the sensitivity. This implies that once the practitioner has arrived at a tentative conclusion that a client has disorder X, then efforts to increase the specificity of the assessment procedure by obtaining new evidence *inconsistent with the diagnosis that the client has disorder X will lead to greater increases in the probability that the client actually has disorder X than will efforts to obtain new evidence consistent with the diagnosis.*

Nugent (2003) also showed that

$$\frac{\partial}{\partial s_e} p(\sim X | \sim dX) = \frac{s_p}{\text{FNR}} \frac{\partial}{\partial s_p} p(\sim X | \sim dX),$$

(Equation 4)

which indicates that as long as the inequality $(s_p/\text{FNR}) > 1$ holds, there will be a greater increase in $p(\sim X | \sim dX)$ per unit increase in the sensitivity than per unit increase in the specificity. This implies that, once the practitioner has arrived at a tentative conclusion that a client does *not* have disorder X, efforts to increase the sensitivity of the assessment procedure by obtaining new evidence *inconsistent with the inference that the client does not have disorder* X *will lead to greater increases in the probability that the client actually does not have disorder* X *than will efforts to obtain new evidence consistent with the inference.*

References

Ambady, N. and R. Rosenthal. 1992. Thin slices of expressive behavior as predictors of interpersonal consequences: A meta-analysis. *Psychological Bulletin* 111 (2): 256–274.

Arkes, H. 1991. Costs and benefits of judgement errors: Implications for debiasing. *Psychological Bulletin* 110 (3): 486–498.

Ash, C. 1993. *The Probability Tutoring Book*. New York: John Wiley—IEEE Press.

Baker, R., ed. 1998. *Child Sexual Abuse and False Memory Syndrome*. New York: Prometheus.

Banks, S. and R. Kerns. 1996. Explaining high rates of depression in chronic pain: A diathesis-stress framework. *Psychological Bulletin* 119 (1): 95–110.

Barlow, D. 2002. *Anxiety and Its Disorders*. 2d ed. New York: Guilford.

Bech, P., N. Rasmussen, R. Olsen, V. Noerholm, and W. Abildgaard. 2001. The sensitivity and specificity of the Major Depression Inventory, using the present state examination as the index of diagnostic validity. *Journal of Affective Disorders* 66 (2–3): 159–164.

Beck, A. T. 1978. *Beck Depression Inventory*. San Antonio: Psychological Corporation.

Blashfield, R. and M. Herkov. 1996. Investigating clinician adherence to diagnosis by criteria: A replication of Morey and Ochoa 1989. *Journal of Personality Disorders* 10:219–228.

Blazer, D., R. Kessler, K. McGonagle, and M. Swartz. 1994. The prevalence and distribution of major depression in a national community sample: The National Comorbidity Survey. *American Journal of Psychiatry* 151 (7): 979–986.

Boisvert, C. and D. Faust. 2002. Iatrogenic symptoms in psychotherapy: A theoretical exploration of the potential impact of labels, language, and belief systems. *American Journal of Psychotherapy* 56 (2): 244–259.

Brennan, R. 2001. *Generalizability Theory*. New York: Springer Verlag.

Brown, T., P. Di Nardo, C. Lehman and L. Campbell. 2001. Reliability of *DSM-IV* anxiety and mood disorders: Implications for classification of emotional disorders. *Journal of Abnormal Psychology* 110:49–58.

Campbell, P. 1996. The diagnosis of multiple personality disorder: The debate among professionals. *Der Zeitgeist: The Student Journal of Psychology*. Available online at http://www.ac.wwu.edu/~n9140024/CampbellPM.html.

Campbell, T. 1998. *Smoke and Mirrors: The Devastating Effects of False Sexual Abuse Claims*. New York: Perseus.

Caplan, R. and G. Caplan. 2001. *Helping Helpers Not to Harm: Iatrogenic Damage and Community Mental Health*. New York: Brunner-Routledge.

Dawes, R. 1986. Representative thinking in clinical judgment. *Clinical Psychology Review* 6 (5): 425–441.

———. 1996. *House of Cards: Psychology and Psychotherapy Built on Myth*. New York: Free Press.

Eaton, W., A. Dryman and M. Weissman. 1991. Panic and Phobia. In L. Robins and D. Regier, eds., *Psychiatric Disorders in America: The Epidemiological Catchment Area Study*. New York: Free Press.

Eaton, W., K. Neufeld, L. Chen, and G. Cai. 2000. A comparison of self-report and clinical diagnostic interviews for depression: Diagnostic Interview Schedule and Schedules for Clinical Assessment in Neuropsychiatry in the Baltimore Epidemiologic Catchment Area follow-up. *Archives of General Psychiatry* 57 (3): 217–222.

Finn, S. 1982. Base rates, utilities, and *DSM-III*: Shortcomings of fixed rule systems of psychodiagnosis. *Journal of Abnormal Psychology* 91 (4): 294–302.

Gambrill, E. 1997. *Social Work Practice: A Critical Thinker's Guide*. New York: Oxford University Press.

Garb, H. 1998. *Studying the Clinician: Judgment Research and Psychological Assessment*. Washington, D.C.: American Psychological Association.

Garb, H. and P. Boyle. 2003. Understanding Why Some Clinicians Use Pseudoscientific Methods: Findings from Research on Clinical Judgment. In S. Lilienfeld, J. Lohr, and S. Lynn, eds., *Science and Pseudoscience in Clinical Psychology*, 17–38. New York: Guilford.

Gibbs, L. and E. Gambrill. 1999. *Critical Thinking for Social Workers: Exercises for the Helping Professions*. Thousand Oaks, Calif.: Pine Forge Press.

Gilovich, T. 1993. *How We Know What Isn't So*. New York: Free Press.

Gold, M. 1996. The Risk of Misdiagnosing Physical Illness as Depression. In F. Flach, ed., *The Hatherleigh Guide to Managing Depression*, 93–112. New York: Hatherleigh.

Hayes, J., N. Butler, and C. Martin. 1986. Misunderstood somatopsychic concomitants of medical disorders. *Psychosomatics* 27 (2): 128–133.

Houts, A. and M. Galante. 1985. The impact of evaluative disposition and subsequent information on clinical impressions. *Journal of Social and Clinical Psychology* 3:201–212.

Hudson, W. 1982. *The Clinical Measurement Package*. Homewood, Ill.: Doresy.

Jampala, V., S. Spears, and D. Neubauer. 1988. The use of *DSM-III* in the United States: A case of not going by the book. *Comprehensive Psychiatry* 29:39–47.

Kohn, L., J. Corrigan, and M. Donaldson, eds. 2000. *To Err Is Human: Building a Safer Health System*. Washington, D.C.: National Academy Press.

Lewisohn, P., H. Hops, R. Roberts, J. Seeley, and J. Andrews. 1993. Adolescent psychopathology: I. Prevalence and incidence of depression and other *DSM-R* disorders in high school students. *Journal of Abnormal Psychology* 102 (1): 133–144.

Lilienfeld, S. and S. Lynn. 2003. Dissociative Identity Disorder: Multiple Personalities, Multiple Controversies. In S. Lilienfeld, J. Lohr, and S. Lynn, eds., *Science and Pseudoscience in Clinical Psychology*, 109–144. New York: Guilford.

Lynn, S., T. Lock, E. Loftus, E. Krackow, and S. Lilienfeld. 2003. The Remembrance of Things Past: Problematic Memory Recovery Techniques in Psychotherapy. In S. Lilienfeld, J. Lohr, and S. Lynn, eds., *Science and Pseudoscience in Clinical Psychology*, 205–242. New York: Guilford.

Mendenhall, W. 1975. *Introduction to Probability and Statistics*. 4th ed. Belmont, Calif.: Wadsworth.

Morey, L. and E. Ochoa. 1989. An investigation of adherence to diagnostic criteria: Clinical diagnosis of the *DSM-III* personality disorders. *Journal of Personality Disorders* 3 (3): 180–192.

Murphy, J., R. Monson, N. Laird, A. Sobol, and A. Leighton. 2000. A comparison of diagnostic interviews for depression in the Stirling county study. *Archives of General Psychiatry* 57 (3): 230–236.

NIH. 2001. Depression can differ in men and women. *The NIH Record* 53 (10). Available online at http://www.nih.gov/news/NIH-Record/05_15_2001/story08.htm#top.

Nugent, W. R. Forthcoming. The role prevalence rates, sensitivity, and specificity on assessment accuracy: Rolling the dice in social work process. *Journal of Social Service Research*.

Pendergrast, M. and M. Gavigan. 1996. *Victims of Memory: Sex Abuse Accusations and Shattered Lives*. New York: Upper Access Books.

Poulin, F., T. Dishion, and B. Burraston. 2001. Three-year iatrogenic effects associated with aggregating high-risk adolescents in cognitive-behavioral preventive interventions. *Applied Developmental Science* 5 (4): 214–224.

Robins, L. N., J. E. Helzer, J. Croughan, and K. S. Ratcliff. 1981. National Institute of Mental Health Diagnostic Interview Schedule: Its history, characteristics, and validity. *Archives of General Psychiatry* 38:381–389.

Rubinson, E., G. Asnis, and J. Friedman. 1988. Knowledge of diagnostic criteria for major depression: A survey of mental health professionals. *Journal of Nervous and Mental Disease* 176:480–484.

Simon, A. 1982. *Calculus with analytic geometry*. Glenview, Ill.: Scott, Foresman.

Wexler, R. 1990. *Wounded Innocents: The Real Victims of the War Against Child Abuse*. Buffalo, N.Y: Prometheus.

Williams, J., M. Pignone, G. Ramirez, and C. Stellato. 2002. Identifying depression in primary care: A literature synthesis of case-finding instruments. *General Hospital Psychiatry* 24 (4): 225–237.

Witztum, E., J. Margolin, R. Bar-On, and A. Levy. 1995. Stigma, labelling, and psychiatric misdiagnosis: Origins and outcomes. *Medicine and Law* 14 (7–8): 659–669.

Wordinsky, T., F. Vizcarrondo, and B. Cruz. 1995. The mistaken diagnosis of child abuse. *Military Medicine* 160 (1): 15–20.

Chapter 7

Assessing the Scientific Status of "Schizophrenia"

John R. Bola and Deborah B. Pitts

Introduction

In 1856 Benedict Morel introduced the term "demence precoce" to describe the progression of a healthy adolescent into a withdrawn and disaffected state. In 1896 Emil Kraepelin Latinized the expression to "dementia praecox" and applied it to a group of psychoses with a deteriorating course. In 1908 Eugen Bleuler coined the term "schizophrenia" to represent a "splitting of psychic functions" (1987 [1908]:59), reflecting his belief that it was the lack of integration of cognition, affect, and volition rather than a deteriorating course that characterized the disorder, thereby expanding the proportion of the population diagnosable with schizophrenia.

"Schizophrenia," in its short history, has become the subject of many thousands of books and articles, the focus of manifold research endeavors, and the locus of substantial ongoing controversy within the field of mental health. At the same time, schizophrenia has remained essentially enigmatic, failing to yield its secrets to several generations of researchers. Karno and Norquist (1989) call it "the classical refractory mental disorder—refractory to consensual conceptualization, definition, and identification of etiology, and tragically refractory to treatment" (699).

As Van Praag (1976) pointed out a quarter century ago, the crucial questions regarding schizophrenia, then as now, are (1) does schizophrenia exist as a classical disease entity with a distinct pathologic process or is it a collective term covering a range of conditions or "subtypes," and (2) if it is a collective term, do the various conditions have commonalities that justify their aggregation? Scientifically based answers to these questions have been slow in coming. The protracted, and in some views unproductive, investigations of schizophrenia have provided additional fuel for the controversy. Those who view the term as a social construct (Sarbin 1991) used to legitimate psychiatry (Szasz 1976) have been particularly vocal critics. In assessing the scientific status of schizophrenia we consider the concept from the related perspectives of construct development in psychopathology and the medical approach for establishing clinical validity. One caveat is in order: limitations in the scientific knowledge of schizophrenia do not circumvent or postpone the need to address the problems presented by individuals diagnosed with schizophrenia.

The Science of Construct Development

The development of a scientific construct is a rigorous process that advances through a series of stages. Evaluating the scientific status of schizophrenia involves assessing it for reliability and various types of validity.

Reliability

Reliability refers to a measure's ability to produce consistent results each time it is used. There are several types of reliability: interrater, test-retest, parallel forms, and internal consistency. Interrater (also called interobserver) reliability represents the agreement among two or more observers on whether the condition being evaluated is present or not. This is the most important form of reliability in psychopathology, because it measures the extent of diagnostic agreement. The kappa statistic is the current measure of choice for this purpose, as it corrects the observed proportion of agreement for agreement expected by chance alone. Ranging from zero to one, a "satisfactory" range for kappa is equal to or greater than .70 (Spitzer and Fleiss 1974). Establishing interrater reliability serves as a starting point for investigating validity.

Over the past few decades, efforts have been made to operationalize diagnostic criteria as a way to increase objectivity and interrater agreement (Feighner et al. 1972; APA 1980). However, given the many sets of criteria for diagnosing schizophrenia, as well as the variability in training by diagnosticians and interviewers (Warner and deGirolamo 1995), interrater reliability remains a fundamental concern. An additional concern arises from the reported manipulation of standards for interpreting reliability for political purposes (Kirk and Kutchins 1992).

Interrater reliability is of special concern in clinical settings. A recent investigation of the reliability of a *DSM-III-R* clinical diagnosis in comparison with a Structured Clinical Interview for *DSM-III-R* found a kappa = .55 for schizophrenia (Steiner et al. 1995). This was the highest value for kappa among the eight categories investigated. This means that the same diagnosis of schizophrenia or not schizophrenia was reached only 55 percent of the time over and above that proportion that could be explained as chance agreement. A recent Finnish study found that diagnostic agreement between clinicians and researchers using the *DSM-IV* diagnostic criteria on the first admission of persons labeled with schizophrenia was the lowest among all diagnostic categories investigated, with a kappa value of .44 (Taiminen et al. 2001).

However, through the use of structured diagnostic instruments, reliability is improving in research settings. For example, Stieglitz and colleagues (1996) conducted a field trial of the ICD-10 Diagnostic Criteria for Research in German-speaking countries and found a kappa value for schizophrenia of .89. On the whole, this result suggests that while reliability is fair to poor in clinical settings, it can be quite good in research settings. This provides a beginning basis, in research settings, for investigating the types of validity necessary to establish schizophrenia as a scientific construct.

Validity

The development of validity proceeds through a series of stages. "Face validity" refers to agreement among experts that items used to measure a concept are appropriate. In schizophrenia, this would include agreement that hallucinations, delusions, inappropriate affect, and so forth are parts of what is indicated by the concept. In face validity, criteria would appear to a panel of experts to discriminate schizophrenia from non-schizophrenia. "Content validity" reflects how well an instrument represents a domain of content (Carmines and Zeller 1979). This implies that the content of the domain is known or agreed upon. In order to have content validity, criteria used for the diagnosis should be representative of the various aspects of schizophrenia.

The proliferation of diagnostic criteria for schizophrenia calls into question both content and face validity. Karno and Norquist (1989) report that "at least 15 sets of diagnostic criteria for schizophrenia are in use somewhere in Western psychiatry" (699). *Diagnostic Criteria for Functional Psychoses* (Berner et al. 1992), published under the auspices of the World Psychiatric Organization, delineates seventeen sets of criteria for schizophrenic psychoses. Numerous sets of diagnostic criteria impede the evaluation of validity (Cloninger 1989) and confound the comparison of results across studies.

Criterion validity has two forms, concurrent and predictive. "Concurrent validity" refers to whether a measure is empirically correlated with another measure of the concept at the same point in time. "Predictive validity" refers to whether the measure is correlated with another measure of the same concept taken at a future time. Care should be taken not to confuse the predictive form of criterion validity with predictive construct validity. In predictive criterion validity one measure of a concept is correlated with another measure of the same concept at a later point in time. For example, in measuring academic potential, the extent to which high school Scholastic Aptitude Test (SAT) scores correlate with later college grade-point averages is an indication of predictive criterion validity, since both the SAT and the GPA are viewed as measures of academic potential. By contrast, the predictive form of construct validity requires the future occurrence of predictions derived from theory. For example, if theory indicates that individuals with schizophrenia have diminished functioning over time, correlating a measure of schizophrenia with diminished future functioning might indicate predictive construct validity (more on this below).

In contrast with earlier studies (e.g., Kendell et al. 1979), recent work has found high levels of concurrent criterion validity when diagnosing schizophrenia using two different instruments (*DSM-III-R* and ICD-10; Mason et al. 1997). This same study also found relatively high levels of predictive criterion validity (of subsequent Global Assessment of Functioning scale scores) for various diagnostic formulations of schizophrenia. However, the predictive validity of *DSM-III-R* was largely a result of incorporating a six-month duration criterion, thus opening the question of whether the diagnosis of schizophrenia (including duration and functional impairment) was predicting another measure of schizophrenia or merely a part of the same measure (i.e., functional deterioration) at a different point in time. Later in this chapter we will address the logical and theoretical issues arising from predicting similar outcomes on the same measure.

Construct validity evaluates a measure of the concept in relation to other concepts in the theoretical framework formed around it. The measure should correlate with measures of other concepts that are theoretically related (convergent validity) and not be correlated with unrelated concepts (discriminant validity). Thus the development of construct validity requires the articulation of a theoretical framework.

THE ROLE OF THEORY IN CONSTRUCT VALIDATION

Theory is a set of interrelated statements designed to explain a phenomenon. More formally, it is a set of interrelated laws and postulates making explicit a set of expected relationships (Cronbach and Meehl 1955). Theory indicates which constructs are likely to be linked (associated) with the construct being developed and which constructs are not likely to be related. It is used to develop testable predictions.

However, the current descriptive approach to diagnosis pursued since *DSM-III* endeavors to be theory-neutral (APA 1994). Thus the lack of theory makes evaluating predictions impossible, since without theory there can be no theoretically derived predictions. As Maj (1998) points out, "what emerges from . . . analysis of the *DSM-IV* diagnostic criteria for schizophrenia is that they lack an underlying paradigm. There are residua of the classical Kraepelinian, Bleulerian and Schneiderian paradigms. . . . However, none of those paradigms is actually endorsed" (459). A more formal approach to employing theory in construct validation is known as the deductive-nomological method.

THE DEDUCTIVE–NOMOLOGICAL METHOD
OF SCIENTIFIC EXPLANATION

The deductive-nomological (D-N) method of scientific explanation (Hempel 1965; referred to by Cloninger [1989] as a hypothetico-deductive model) involves the use of a logical argument to show that an observed outcome was logically deducible, and hence predictable, from specified antecedent (prior) conditions and postulated general laws (Gorenstein 1992). The evaluation of whether a given "explanation meets the dual criterion of logical entailment and accurate representation amounts to an evaluation of the explanation's predictive credibility" (Gorenstein 1992:38). Further, "it is a basic tenet of science that an explanation's validity cannot be established post hoc" (Gorenstein 1992:37), that is, after the event to be explained has already occurred. Thus, the two main ingredients in a D-N explanation are the specification of antecedent conditions and the postulation of general laws or lawful relations among events.

The presence of a hypothetical construct is inferred through its criterion of application. The *DSM* diagnostic checklists are an example of operationalized criteria of application ("when A, and B, and five (or more) of nine in C are present then the person receives the diagnosis"). Psychiatric diagnoses are typically of this polythetic form in which a subset from a list of inclusionary criteria forms the criterion of application. This contrasts with monothetic diagnosis in which all criteria are necessary, with only one way to meet the criterion of application. As might be expected, "polythetic criteria can result in considerable heterogeneity within a category" (Widiger and Frances 1987:286). For example, to acquire a *DSM-IV* (APA 1994) diagnosis of schizophrenia, an individual must have two (or more) of five characteristic symptoms and meet several inclusionary and exclusionary criteria. In addition, there are three special circumstances in which one of the symptoms meets the criterion for the diagnosis. This yields a total of twenty-nine distinct ways to receive a diagnosis of schizophrenia.

Construct validation requires reliability of the criterion of application (diagnosis). In the D-N model of scientific explanation, the diagnosis does not define the mental disorder but provides an indicator of its existence (Gorenstein 1992). A hypothetical construct cannot be directly observed, and without an objective marker for the mental disorder (e.g., a laboratory test), the validation of the criterion of application cannot be established independently. It is investigated in tandem with the validity of the construct through the formulation of testable predictions, in a method referred to as "bootstrapping" (Corning 1986).

In formulating predictions for testing, it is important to avoid the circularity of predicting outcomes based "on the content of the criteria of application itself" (Gorenstein 1992:76). Gorenstein (1992) illustrates this point in relation to the diminished functioning criteria added to the *DSM-III* (APA 1980) and *DSM-III-R* (APA 1987) diagnoses for schizophrenia: "It would show nothing of the predictive import of the construct of schizophrenia if we were to establish that schizophrenics exhibit deterioration from some previous level of functioning if, in fact, deterioration is part of the criteria used to identify schizophrenia in the first place" (76). The continuation of motion unless acted upon from outside is, in fact, Newton's first law of motion. In the case of schizophrenia (or any other mental disorder, for that matter), continuing to have characteristics that were part of the diagnosis does not demonstrate the prediction of anything derived from theory. This is analogous to predicting that a ball now rolling down a hill will continue to roll down the hill.

Circular (tautological) reasoning continues as a method to establish the predictive validity of schizophrenia (Maj 1998). For example, in a recent study the existence of a diagnosis of schizophrenia was used to predict future positive symptoms, deterioration of functioning, and a diagnosis of schizophrenia (Mason et al. 1997). This tautological reasoning yields a reification of the concept and contributes to the widespread delusion (unfounded belief) of having established the predictive validity of schizophrenia.

Appraising the accuracy of predictions simultaneously evaluates both the criterion of application (diagnosis) and the theory from which the predictions were derived. In the event of inaccurate predictions it is not readily apparent whether the theory is in error or the diagnosis is incorrectly defined. "Blaming the criterion of application" (Gorenstein 1992:79) is a much easier task than rethinking the formulation of the construct. Often it is assumed that the criterion of application identified the "wrong people," and if it were changed to identify the "right people," the ones to whom the theory really applies, correct predictions will ensue. This desire to identify the "right people" may partially explain the many sets of diagnostic criteria for schizophrenia, as well as the more recent inclusion of length of symptoms and deterioration of functioning criteria in the *DSM*.

In sum, polythetic diagnostic criteria allow considerable heterogeneity within the category of schizophrenia, making prediction based upon theory difficult. The lack of clearly articulated theory makes evaluating predictions impossible, since without theory there can be no theoretically informed predictions. The approach of predicting functional deterioration due to schizophrenia is logically faulty when functional deterioration is used to establish the diagnosis in the first place.

Establishing Clinical Validity

In medicine, an approach to establishing the clinical validity of a diagnostic entity has developed, with methods that partially overlap the process of establishing construct validity. We begin with some central definitions.

Definitions

Signs are observable events (e.g., tears, sweating, incomprehensible behavior). Symptoms are reports of subjective experiences (e.g., pain, confusion, nonordinary perceptions). Syndromes are patterns of signs and symptoms that group together in characteristic ways and have "a more or less distinctive temporal evolution" (Kendell 1989:308). A mental disorder involves the presence of a "recognizable syndrome which leads to distress, disability or both" (Hovarith et al. 1989:604).

The mental disorders catalogued in the *DSM* are considered to be either descriptive classifications (Millon 1991), a collection of hypothetical constructs (Morey 1991), or both (Widiger and Frances 1987).

SCHIZOPHRENIA AS SYNDROME

Bentall (1990) cites poor correlations between symptoms of schizophrenia as evidence against symptomatic clustering in schizophrenia. A clustering of signs and symptoms is one of the criteria for a syndrome, and meeting syndrome criteria is required in the definition of mental disorder. Boyle, in *Schizophrenia: A Scientific Delusion?* (2002), points to the lack of evidence for symptom clustering in schizophrenia. Maj elaborates:

> The main problem with the symptomological criterion is that it does not characterize schizophrenia as a syndrome. It may well be true that the definition of schizophrenia must be polythetic rather than monothetic . . . but at least the clustering of symptoms should be characteristic. Unfortunately, the DSM-IV symptomological criterion does not identify such a characteristic clustering. In fact, that criterion can be fulfilled by several cases of mania (disorganized speech plus grossly disorganized behaviour), manic depression with psychotic features (al-

ogia plus delusions), dementia (grossly disorganized behaviour plus hallucinations) and delirium (disorganized speech plus hallucinations). (1998:458).

In relation to the second criterion for syndrome, long-term studies of schizophrenia suggest that no distinct temporal evolution exists. Several long-term (twenty to thirty years) follow-up studies conducted in Europe indicate complete recovery in 22% to 26% of subjects and functional recovery in about one third (Bleuler 1978; Ciompi 1980; Huber et al. 1980). An American long-term follow-up study of *DSM-III* schizophrenia (incorporating length of illness and diminished functioning criteria; Harding et al. 1987) found that "outcome varied widely, but one-half to two-thirds of the sample had achieved considerable improvement or recovered" (727). Ciompi (1980) characterized eight course types by mode of onset, recurrence, and end state. This prompted him to later raise the central validity question: "Is there really a schizophrenia?" (Ciompi 1984:636).

Clinical Validity of Schizophrenia

More than thirty years ago Robins and Guze (1970) proposed an atheoretical method designed to facilitate "the development of a valid classification in psychiatry" (983). Their method has been termed the five-phase approach, consisting of (1) Clinical description, (2) laboratory studies, (3) delimitation from other disorders, (4) follow-up study, and (5) family study. They emphasize the importance of "the index group. [being] as homogenous as possible" (984). In their view, the process of developing a valid diagnostic system is "one of continuing self-rectification and increasing refinement leading to more homogeneous diagnostic grouping . . . [that] provides the soundest base for studies of etiology, pathogenesis, and treatment" (984).

Kendell (1989) added a sixth criterion to the Robins and Guze approach, that of treatment response. Different treatment response has, in medicine, assisted in discriminating different clinical entities and thus contributed to their validation. It may also assist in the discrimination of similar but distinct mental disorders.

Robins and Guze's method, with its emphasis on atheoretical description, has been extremely influential, forming the basis of both the Feighner diagnostic criteria for research (Feighner et al. 1972) and the *DSM-III* (APA 1980; Cloninger 1989). Subsequent editions of the *DSM* (APA 1987, 1994) have maintained this descriptive approach. Cloninger (1989) points out that this is "an extension of the work of Thomas Sydenham (1624–1689) . . . [whose] method for studying the natural history of disorders became the basis for classification in medicine in the absence of information about specific etiologic agents" (10–11). An important limitation is that the approach is atheoretical. Reiterating a point from our earlier discussion, Cloninger notes, "Scientific progress requires a hypothetico-deductive approach which can be postponed, but not satisfied, by an atheoretical model" (1989:14).

Assessing the clinical validity of schizophrenia follows the five-phase approach of Robins and Guze (1970), adding Kendell's (1989) criterion of treatment response.

LABORATORY STUDIES

Laboratory studies have not yet demonstrated consistent findings associated with a diagnosis of schizophrenia (Robins and Guze 1970; Karno and Norquist 1989; Copolov and Crook 2000). Sponheim and colleagues (2001) investigated whether psychotic patients could be classified with multiple laboratory procedures, including ocular motor functioning, encephalogram frequency characteristics, nailfold plexus visibility, and electrodermal activation. Three clusters of test results discriminated psychotic and nonpsychiatric groups, but none aligned with clinical diagnoses. Efforts to discriminate schizophrenia patients from controls using brain magnetic resonance imaging (MRI) have so far produced only modest interrater reliability (Sachdev et al. 1999). These results suggest that a definitive test for schizophrenia may not be available anytime in the near future.

DELIMITATION FROM OTHER DISORDERS

Delimitation from other disorders involves homogenizing the diagnostic category so that members are similar to each other and also different from members of other diagnostic categories. In the United States, some progress has been made toward a more careful ruling out of bipolar affective disorder in the diagnosis of schizophrenia. However, the unreliability of diagnosing schizoaffective disorder and the recognized heterogeneity in schizophrenia continue to make further delimitation and/or subtyping central to the progress of science in this area (Heinrichs 1993; Bola and Mosher 2003).

FOLLOW-UP STUDY

Long-term follow-up studies of individuals diagnosed with schizophrenia have yielded results that are similar across studies. As summarized above, the clear pattern is one of heterogeneity, rather than homogeneity of outcomes. Robins and Guze (1970) have noted that "marked differences in outcome should be regarded as a challenge to the validity of the original diagnosis" (984).

FAMILY STUDY

Family study involves investigating the prevalence of disorder in relatives of diagnosed individuals. Whether the investigations study environmental or genetic influences, "an increased prevalence of the same disorder among the close relatives of the original patients strongly indicates that one is dealing with a valid entity" (Robins and Guze 1970:984). Family studies indicate that "first-degree relatives have approximately a five to 10-fold greater chance of developing schizophrenia than nonrelatives" (Karno and Norquist 1989:702). Twin and adoption studies attempt to segregate the genetic from the environmental component in heritability by examining concordance rates for schizophrenia among individuals with known genetic similarities raised in different environments. Plomin (1990) summarizes this literature: "A risk of 30% for an identical co-twin of a schizophrenic far exceeds the population risk of 1%, but is a long way from the 100% concordance expected if schizophrenia were an entirely transmissible genetic disorder" (186).

TREATMENT RESPONSE

Differential treatment response would suggest that if a particular treatment exerted an effect only on a specific disorder, or if it exerted different effects in different disorders, there would be some evidence for the validity of the disorders treated. However, Kendell (1989) points out that

> Treatment response has contributed little so far to the validation of psychiatric syndromes. This is because most of our effective therapies—psychological treatments like cognitive therapy and response prevention as well as physical treatments like neuroleptics, antidepressants, and ECT—are not syndrome specific; they are partially effective across a range of related syndromes. Moreover, none of them is invariably effective in the treatment of any syndrome no matter how narrowly that syndrome is defined.
> (312)

In sum, available evidence does not clearly establish the clinical validity of schizophrenia. Only in the area of family studies does the literature unequivocally suggest the presence of a valid clinical entity.

From Clinical Validity to Etiology

Etiology involves "the *sine qua non*—the causal condition which is necessary, but not sufficient, for the disorder to occur" (Meehl 1962:828, italics in original). As an applied science, medicine is often concerned with the removal of specific conditions necessary to the maintenance of an illness. Causality, in its more restricted formulation, involves conditions that are "*both* necessary and sufficient for an effect" (Haynes 1992:28, italics in original). As Kendell (1989) points out: "There is a longstanding and now deeply rooted assumption in medicine that the most valid diagnoses are those whose etiology is known; a corollary is that the most effective way of establishing the validity of a clinical syndrome is to elucidate its etiology" (306).

The two primary competing causal models in schizophrenia research are the biological (Andreasen 1984) and the biopsychosocial (Engel 1977). Adaptations of the biopsychosocial model in schizophrenia are also referred to as stress–diathesis or stress–vulnerability models (Fowles 1992). In addition to differences in the types of explanatory factors within these two explanatory models, a central point of contrast is that in the biological model causality is unidirectional (from biology to behavior), whereas in the biopsychosocial models causality can be multidirectional (e.g., environment can influence both biology and behavior). While available space does not permit a fuller explanation of these differences, below we note some common "biological thinking" errors to be avoided in the development of causal models.

Schizophrenia as a Disease

The identification of etiology (cause) and pathophysiological processes is required for a mental disorder to be considered a disease. In a more formal structure, Heinrichs (1993) delineated three criteria necessary for schizophrenia to be considered a brain disease: existence as a clinical entity distinct from other disorders; linkage with an identifiable neuropathology; and implicated (pathological) brain systems that have behavioral functions that fit the characteristics of schizophrenia. In assessing schizophrenia, he concludes: "In each case, the evidence is weak or equivocal" (Heinrichs 1993:221). Carpenter and colleagues (1990) offer a similar assessment: "Age and rate at onset, premorbid features, symptoms and signs, severity of interepisode impairments, treatment response, laboratory assessments, and brain imaging characteristics all vary so much as to bring into question the hypothesis that schizophrenia is a single disease entity" (98).

Claridge (1990) argued that what complicates identifying schizophrenia as a disease is that psychiatry has applied infectious disease and major gene disorder models and that these have been of limited utility in understanding schizophrenia. Consistent with a biopsychosocial approach, he proposes a "systemic disease" model with three important features: (1) it originates in bodily mechanisms that normally perform perfectly healthy adaptive functions but are capable of becoming dysfunctional, (2) in early stages or mild forms identification of the illness is not always clear, and (3) causality is multiply dimensional and interactive, incorporating underlying disposition and "developmental, accumulating life-load, and short-term triggering factors" (164). Clearly, additional work elucidating causal mechanisms is necessary to establish schizophrenia as a disease entity.

Avoiding "Biological Thinking" Errors

The "biological revolution" in psychiatry (Andreasen 1984) has engendered waves of research into the structure, function, and development of the human brain. Advances in genetics, molecular biology, and neuroscience have fueled the long-standing hope of finding the cause(s) and hence a cure for "schizophrenia." The mapping of brain circuitry, the imaging of brain functioning, and the active development of medications targeting negative symptoms and cognitive functioning appear as signposts on the road of discovery. Yet, while it is likely that brain research will yield new knowledge on risk factors for and biological processes underlying various manifestations of schizophrenia, scientific progress would be furthered through the avoidance of several common "biological thinking" errors.

In the final chapter of his masterful work *The Science of Mental Illness,* Gorenstein (1992) delineates three conceptual errors that are commonly made in biological approaches to psychopathology:

BIOLOGY IS A MEANS OF ESTABLISHING ILLNESS

Since every form of behavior is mediated by the central nervous system, it has a biological substrate. Identifying the substrate corresponding to a particular behavior does not establish that behavior as an illness any more than identifying the biological substrate of having green eyes would make having green eyes an illness. In Gorenstein's words, "A biological determination of mental illness or brain disease rests entirely upon someone's subjective opinion as to the propriety of the behavior associated with a given biological or brain attribute" (1992:120). He critiques the claims that "psychiatric disorders *must* be organic diseases because of the numerous findings that many psychiatric disorders have biological substrates" (121, italics in original). In his view, "the use of biology to substantiate disease in this fashion amounts to the tail wagging the dog" (121).

BIOLOGY IS A MEANS OF ESTABLISHING CAUSE

Since all thinking and behavior arise from biological events in the central nervous system, it is tempting to attribute causal stature to recognized biological events. This, however, confuses biology with causation. Since environmental events conveyed along sensory pathways can induce biological changes and subsequent behavioral effects, identifying a biological substrate to a particular behavior does not distinguish whether the cause of the behavior is biological, environmental, or both. It merely reinforces what is already known: behavior is mediated by biology (Gorenstein 1992).

ANY BIOLOGICAL EVENT CAN EXPLAIN ANY
BEHAVIORAL EVENT

The current biological approach to psychopathology, according to Gorenstein
(1992), correlates brain events with behaviors. This amounts to identifying
"actuarial associations, but it does not explain anything" (127). He goes on to
state: "What is completely missing from this formulation, and all actuarial
formulations like it, is the functional mechanism linking the cause to the
effect" (129). In other words, what is necessary is the conceptualization of
"brain variables at a level of abstraction that explains how they actually produce
behavior" (131). By way of example, Gorenstein links Beck's (1967) cognitive
theory of depression with Hebb's (1949) concept of the cell assembly. In this
way a relationship is forged between learned "psychological mechanisms for
apprehending and interpreting external events" (138) and a concept of brain
functioning. The subsequent functional-material model helps explain the
clinical characteristics of depression and the evidence on treatment effectiveness, including how early experiences create the potential for depression (via
creation of a neural cell assembly); how an individual is stimulated into depression by similar events; how minor social events are interpreted negatively;
how a depressed person could experience almost total normality in between
depressive episodes (the circuits are not activated); how a purely somatic intervention such as electroconvulsive treatment (ECT) could change those
symptoms (interrupting vibrating circuits); the typical immediate side effect
of ECT (retrograde amnesia, via disrupting the electrical activity of reverber-
ating circuits); why ECT does not provide lasting protection against future
depressive episodes (the circuits are disrupted but potentially arousable); why
antidepressants work (by selective influence on neural circuitry). In addition
to explaining depression, this neuropsychological model yields clues to the
method of permanently curing an individual's vulnerability to depression.
"The best (and safest) means of accomplishing this, no doubt, is to employ
methods of verbal and experiential persuasion to create new cell assemblies
that suppress, override, or divert the activity of the problematic one. In this
case, then, the correction of a *structural defect* is accomplished by *psychological*
means" (Gorenstein 1992:141). Therefore, biological correlates do not necessarily dictate biological treatments.

The Scientific Status of Schizophrenia

Van Praag's (1976) questions (above) regarding the status of schizophrenia
recur. In relation to his first question, the evidence weighs against schizophrenia as a classical disease entity and toward its usage as a collective term
covering a range of conditions. Second, whether the range of conditions has

commonalities that justify their aggregation is not yet answerable. Two approaches to this situation suggest themselves. One is the classical approach of subtyping. If coherent subgroups are identified, at that point the question of whether they remain linked diagnostically (and causally) may be answerable. Many working within the construct of "schizophrenia as a syndrome" suggest a need to "parse schizophrenia and reduce heterogeneity" (Heinrichs 1992:221). This is, in essence, a way of subtyping the "group of disorders" into smaller and more homogeneous groups. Approaches to reduce heterogeneity in schizophrenia have included grouping by description, course, prognosis, mathematical algorithms, biological characteristics, and genetic markers. Carpenter and colleagues suggested subtyping through differential treatment response. This is an important and practical suggestion that involves "the development of treatment-relevant subtypes based upon differences in symptom, personality, and family characteristics . . . and associated features . . . [that may be] explored for treatment relevance" (Carpenter et al. 1990:98).

The second approach might be to pursue Bentall's suggestion to abandon the concept of schizophrenia in favor of studying signs and symptoms in an effort to discover natural regularities unclouded by expectations of clustering or temporal course. This line of investigation may yield observations of regularities obscured by the current composite approach. However, this approach appears unlikely to be pursued, given the international popularity of the concept of schizophrenia and its central role in psychiatric nosology.

In any case, available evidence is currently inadequate to establish schizophrenia as a valid hypothetical construct, a valid clinical entity, or a disease entity. The lack of clustering of signs and symptoms and the absence of a distinct temporal pattern argue against schizophrenia as a syndrome, and therefore, since meeting syndrome criteria are required in the definition of mental disorder, against its being considered a mental disorder. Yet the obvious suffering of those afflicted with "the group of illnesses" referred to as schizophrenia urge the scientific community to revisit the conceptual foundations of schizophrenia and the requirements for establishing scientific constructs in an effort to develop knowledge to alleviate this suffering.

References

American Psychiatric Association (APA). 1980. *Diagnostic and Statistical Manual of Mental Disorders*. 3d ed. Washington, D.C.: APA.

———. 1987. *Diagnostic and Statistical Manual of Mental Disorders (DSM-III-R)*. 3d ed. rev. Washington, D.C.: APA.

———. 1994. *Diagnostic and Statistical Manual of Mental Disorders. (DSM-IV).* 4th ed. Washington, D.C.: APA.

Andreasen, N. C. 1984. *The Broken Brain: The Biological Revolution in Psychiatry.* New York: Harper and Row.

Beck, A. T. 1967. *Depression: Clinical, Experimental, and Theoretical Aspects.* New York: Harper and Row.

Bentall, R. P. 1990. The Syndromes and Symptoms of Psychosis: Or Why You Can't Play "Twenty Questions" with the Concept of Schizophrenia and Hope to Win. In R. P. Bentall, ed., *Reconstructing Schizophrenia,* 307. New York: Routledge.

Berner, P., E. Gabriel, H. Katsching, W. Kieffer, K. Koehler, and G. Lenz. 1992. *Diagnostic Criteria for Functional Psychoses.* 2d ed. Cambridge: Cambridge University Press.

Bleuler, E. 1987 (1908). The Prognosis of Dementia Praecox: The Group of Schizophrenias. In J. Cutting and M. Sheperd, eds., *The Clinical Roots of the Schizophrenia Concept: Translations of Seminal European Contributions on Schizophrenia,* 59–74. New York: Cambridge University Press.

Bleuler, M. E. 1978. The Long-Term Course of Schizophrenic Psychosis. In L. C. Wynne, R. L. Cromwell, and S. Matthysse, eds., *The Nature of Schizophrenia: New Approaches to Research and Treatment,* 631–636. New York: John Wiley.

Bola, J. R. and L. R. Mosher. 2003. Clashing ideologies or scientific discourse? *Schizophrenia Bulletin* 28 (4): 583–588.

Boyle, M. 2002. *Schizophrenia: A Scientific Delusion?* 2d ed. London: Routledge.

Carmines, E. G. and R. A. Zeller. 1979. *Reliability and Validity Assessment.* Beverly Hills: Sage.

Carpenter, W. T., B. Kirkpatrick, and R. W. Buchanan. 1990. Conceptual Approaches to the Study of Schizophrenia. In A. Kales, C. N. Stefanis, and J. A. Talbot, eds., *Recent Advances in Schizophrenia,* 95–113. New York: Springer-Verlag.

Ciompi, L. 1980. The natural history of schizophrenia in the long term. *British Journal of Psychiatry* 136:413–420.

———. 1984. Is there really a schizophrenia? The long-term course of psychotic phenomena. *British Journal of Psychiatry* 145:636–640.

Claridge, G. 1990. Can a Disease Model of Schizophrenia Survive? In R. P. Bental, eds., *Reconstructing Schizophrenia,* 157–183. London: Routledge.

Cloninger, C. R. 1989. Establishment of Diagnostic Validity in Psychiatric Illness: Robins and Guze's Method Revisited. In L. N. Robins and J. E. Barrett, eds., *The Validity of Psychiatric Diagnosis,* 9–18. New York: Raven Press.

Cronbach, L. J. and P. E. Meehl. 1955. Construct validity in psychological tests. *Psychological Bulletin* 55 (4): 281–302.

Copolov, D. and J. Crook. 2000. Biological markers and schizophrenia. *Australia and New Zealand Journal of Psychiatry* 34S:108–112.

Corning, W. C. 1986. Bootstrapping Toward a Classification System. In T. Millon and G. L. Klerman, eds., *Contemporary Directions in Psychopathology: Toward the DSM-IV.* New York: Guilford Press.

Engel, G. L. 1977. The need for a new medical model: A challenge for biomedicine. *Science* 196 (4286): 129–136.

Feighner, J. P., E. Robins, S. B. Guze, R. A. Woodruff, G. Winokur, and R. Muñoz. 1972. Diagnostic criteria for use in psychiatric research. *Archives of General Psychiatry* 26:57–63.

Fowles, D. C. 1992. Schizophrenia: Diathesis-stress revisited. *Annual Review of Psychology* 43:303–336.

Gorenstein, E. E. 1992. *The Science of Mental Illness*. San Diego: Academic Press.

Harding, C. M., G. W. Brooks, T. Ashikaga, J. S. Strauss, and A. Breier. 1987. The Vermont longitudinal study of persons with severe mental illness, II: Long-term outcome of subjects who retrospectively met DSM-III criteria for schizophrenia. *American Journal of Psychiatry* 144 (6): 727–735.

Haynes, S. N. 1992. *Models of Causality in Psychopathology: Toward Dynamic, Synthetic, and Nonlinear Models of Behavior Disorders*. New York: Macmillan.

Hebb, D. O. 1949. *Organization of Behavior*. New York: Wiley.

Heinrichs, R. W. 1993. Schizophrenia and the brain: Conditions for a neuropsychology of madness. *American Psychologist* 48 (3): 221–233.

Hempel, C. G. 1965. *Aspects of Scientific Explanation*. New York: Free Press.

Hovarith, T. B., L. J. Siever, R. C. Mohs, and K. Davis. 1989. Organic Mental Syndromes and Disorders. In H. I. Kaplan and B. J. Sadock, eds., *Comprehensive Textbook of Psychiatry*, 1:599–641. 5th ed. Baltimore: Williams and Wilkins.

Huber, G., G. Gross, R. Schuttler, and M. Linz. 1980. Longitudinal studies of schizophrenic patients. *Schizophrenia Bulletin* 6 (4): 592–605.

Karno, M. and G. S. Norquist. 1989. Schizophrenia: Epidemiology. In H. I. Kaplan and B. J. Sadock, eds., *Comprehensive Textbook of Psychiatry*, 1:699–705. 5th ed. Baltimore: Williams and Wilkins.

Kendell, R. E. 1989. *Clinical Validity: The Validity of Psychiatric Diagnosis*. Edited by L. W. Robins and J. E. Barnett. New York: Raven Press.

Kendell, R. E., I. F. Brockington, and J. P. Leff. 1979. Prognostic implications of six alternative definitions of schizophrenia. *Archives of General Psychiatry* 36:25–31.

Kirk, S. A. and H. Kutchins. 1992. *The Selling of DSM: The Rhetoric of Science in Psychiatry*. New York: Aldine De Gruyter.

Maj, M. 1998. Critique of the DSM-IV operational criteria for schizophrenia. *British Journal of Psychiatry* 172:458–460.

Mason, P., G. Harrison, T. Crodace, C. Glazebrook, and I. Medley. 1997. The predictive validity of a diagnosis of schizophrenia: A report from the International Study of Schizophrenia. *British Journal of Psychiatry* 170 (4): 321–327.

Meehl, P. E. 1962. Schizotaxia, schizotypy, schizophrenia. *American Psychologist* 17:827–838.

Millon, T. 1991. Classification in psychopathology: Rationale, alternatives, and standards. *Journal of Abnormal Psychology* 100 (3): 245–261.

Morey, L. C. 1991. Classification of mental disorder as a collection of hypothetical constructs. *Journal of Abnormal Psychology* 100 (3): 289–293.

Plomin, R. 1990. The role of inheritance in behavior. *Science* 248:183–188.

Robins, E. and S. B. Guze. 1970. Establishment of diagnostic validity in psychiatric illness: Its application to schizophrenia. *American Journal of Psychiatry* 126 (7): 107–111.

Sachdev, P., S. Cathcart, R. Shnier, W. Wen, and H. Brodaty. 1999. Reliability and validity ratings of signal hypertensities on MRI by visual inspection and computerized measurement. *Psychiatry Research* 92 (2–3): 103–115.

Sarbin, T. R. 1991. The Social Construction of Schizophrenia. In W. F. Flack, Jr., D. R. Miller, and M. Weiner, eds., *What Is Schizophrenia?* 173–197. New York: Springer-Verlag.

Spitzer, R. L. and J. L. Fleiss. 1974. A re-analysis of the reliability of psychiatric diagnosis. *British Journal of Psychiatry* 125:341–347.

Sponheim, S. R., P. D. Iacono, P. D. Thuras, and M. Beiser. 2001. Using biological indices to classify schizophrenia and other psychotic patients. *Schizophrenia Research* 50 (3): 139–150.

Steiner, J. L., J. K. Tebes, W. H. Sledge, and M. L. Walker. 1995. A comparison of the structured clinical interview for DSM-III-R and clinical diagnosis. *Journal of Nervous and Mental Disease* 183 (6): 365–369.

Stieglitz, R. D., M. Albus, J. Zimmermann, and R. T. Schaub. 1996. Schizophrenia, schizotypal, and delusional disorders. F2. Results from the ICD-10 field trial of the Diagnostic Criteria for Research in German-speaking countries. *Psychopathology* 29 (5): 280–284.

Szasz, T. S. 1976. Schizophrenia: The sacred symbol of psychiatry. *British Journal of Psychiatry* 129: 308–316.

Taiminen, T., K. Ranta, H. Karlsson et al. 2001. Comparison of clinical and best-estimate research: DSM-IV diagnoses in a Finnish sample of first-admission psychosis and severe affective disorder. *Nordic Journal of Psychiatry* 55 (2): 107–111.

Van Praag, H. M. 1976. About the impossible concept of schizophrenia. *Comprehensive Psychiatry* 17 (4): 481–497.

Warner, R. and G. deGirolamo. 1995. *Schizophrenia*. Geneva: World Health Organization.

Widiger, T. A. and A. Frances. 1987. Definitions and diagnoses: A brief response to Morey and McNamara. *Journal of Abnormal Psychology* 96 (3): 286–287.

PART II

THE SOCIAL CONTEXT
OF INTERVENTION

Chapter 8

"To Stem the Tide of Degeneracy": The Eugenic Impulse in Social Work

Amy LaPan and Tony Platt

> They should go to sleep at night without any intimation of what was coming and never awake.
>
> —*John Randolph Haynes, 1918*

Introduction

"In order not to repeat past mistakes," observed state senator Patricia S. Ticer, "it is necessary and important to acknowledge them and to express regret" (*New York Times* 2001). Such was the sentiment expressed by several political leaders in Virginia when Governor Mark Warner issued a formal apology in May 2002 to the more than eight thousand women and men who had undergone forced sterilization between 1927 and 1979. The governor referred to the state's 1924 eugenics legislation as "a shameful effort in which state government never should have been involved" (*Washington Post* 2002).

Virginia was the first state to officially acknowledge the government's role in eugenics policies.[1] Other states quickly followed: Oregon and North Carolina in December 2002, South Carolina in January 2003, and California in March 2003. Similarly, North Carolina established a panel of experts to review the state's use of forced sterilization and to consider reparations to victims (Zitner 2003). Oregon's governor, John Kitzhaber, apologizing for "misdeeds that resulted from widespread misconceptions, ignorance, and bigotry," proclaimed December 10 as Human Rights Day in the state, in memory of those who had been forcibly sterilized (Reynolds 2002). "Our hearts are heavy for the pain caused by eugenics," noted California governor

Gray Davis in a statement marking "a sad and regrettable chapter" in his state's history (Ingram 2003).

This moment of public acknowledgment of past tragedies offers social work an opportunity to come to terms with its own role in eugenics policies and practices. Eugenics found wide support in Europe and the United States from the last of the nineteenth century through the first third of the twentieth. It was based, according to its founder, English scientist Francis Galton, on a desire to improve the human stock by giving "the more suitable races or strains of blood a better chance of prevailing speedily over the less suitable" (quoted in Kevles 1997:xiii). Its earliest proponents in the United States, including the best and brightest academics and reformers, used eugenics to promote their beliefs in the genetic superiority of "Nordic" civilizations over uncivilized peoples. Eugenics was also a cultural vehicle for expressing anxiety about the degeneration of middle-class "Aryans" through a declining birthrate and the "evil of crossbreeding" (Popenoe and Johnson 1926:301)

Under the banner of "national regeneration" (Popenoe 1934:257), tens of thousands of women and men, mostly poor, were subjected to involuntary sterilization in the United States between 1907 and 1940 (Carlson 2001:215). And untold thousands of women were sterilized without their informed consent after World War II.[2] For eugenicists, sterilization was not so much a technical procedure to enhance physical and mental health as it was a way to cleanse the body politic of racial and sexual impurities.

Eugenics is rooted in assumptions about the existence of distinct biological races—notably, the messianic role of "Anglo-Saxon" societies as the bedrock of modernity—and the need for policies of segregation and apartheid in order to preserve genetic purity. The leading advocates of eugenics believed that a variety of social successes (wealth, political leadership, intellectual discoveries) and social problems (poverty, illegitimacy, crime, mental illness, and unemployment) could be traced to inherited, biological attributes associated with "racial temperament." Is there any other conclusion, asked a popular 1926 textbook, than that "the Negro lacks in his germ plasm excellence of some qualities which the white race possess, and which are essential for success in competition with the civilizations of the white races at the present day" (Popenoe and Johnson 1926:285). Though the movement to improve the human species through the scientific use of heredity ebbed in the wake of Nazism, it has been revived in current debates about the racial basis of intelligence, sociobiology, and human genetic engineering. "A new wave of neo-eugenic scholarship flourishes," notes historian Michael Katz (1996:192), "and for much the same reasons, and with much the same dangers, as the old."

In the last decade there has been a flurry of revisionist interest in the influence of eugenics in the United States. The canon under challenge was established by historian Mark Haller in his 1963 book, *Eugenics,* and in Daniel Kevles's authoritative study, which appeared first as an essay in the *New Yorker,* then as a 1985 book, *In the Name of Eugenics.* Kevles suggests that by the mid-1930s the right-wing version of eugenics "had generally been recognized as a farrago of flawed science." After World War II, he argues, biologists managed to repudiate Nazi pseudoscience and reestablish human genetics as a "solid field of science that would explain the complexities of human heredity and assist medicine by illuminating the relationship of genetics to disease" (Kevles 1997:164, vii).

Recent studies, building upon the pioneering work of Linda Gordon,[3] take issue with the view that eugenics was a short-run fad or that its influence was limited to the right-wing fringe (Carlson 2001; Kline 2001; Kühl 1994; Ordover 2003). "The 'golden age' of eugenics," proposes Wendy Kline, "occurred long after most historians claim the movement had vanished" (156) and enjoyed broad appeal among reformers, feminists, and professionals. Eugenics reinvented itself in post–World War II initiatives to promote "marriage and motherhood as the central goal of motherhood" (Kline 2001:127), to justify the systematic sterilization of poor women of color in the 1950s and 1960s, and to search for the biological roots of sexual orientation in the 1990s (Ordover 2003).

For the most part, these historians do not focus on social work's relationship with eugenics.[4] The prevailing view, reflected in the social work literature, is that the profession began to break away from eugenics after World War I, because of its generally pessimistic assumptions about human malleability, and completed the break in the 1930s, with the adoption of a paradigm based on the redemptive possibilities of environmental interventions.[5] In brief, that casework replaced social Darwinism. If the profession in any way collaborated with eugenics, it is a challenge to find this information in social work histories or textbooks, which remain silent and amnesiac on the topic.[6] Walter Trattner (1984:190–191) locates social workers only in the pre–World War II opposition to sterilization policies, concluding that "infatuation with heredity proved to be relatively short-lived; by the 1920s, it was fading rapidly."[7]

In this chapter we build upon Michael Katz's (1996:188) insight that "from its inception, eugenics had close ties to welfare." We argue that social workers were actively involved in the eugenics movement in the first part of the twentieth century; that eugenics played an important ideological and practical role in the formative years of the profession; that biologically informed views about social problems retained a respectable role within social work beyond the 1920s; and that the class, racial, and gender biases permeating eugenics left an enduring legacy in the profession.

Eugenics and Social Work, 1910s–1920s

In the period before and after World War I, social workers actively embraced eugenics: they created one of its foundational methodologies, helped to legitimate its scientific pretensions through fund-raising and research, developed professional relationships with eugenics proponents, and advocated in favor of sterilization and segregation of the "unfit."

The year 1904, when Andrew Carnegie funded Charles Davenport's initiative to establish a laboratory to study heredity at Cold Spring Harbor, Long Island, is typically identified as the starting point of the eugenics movement in the United States (Kevles 1997:45). But long before Davenport began his eugenics research, social workers already had established through pedigree studies the hereditary dimensions of social problems.[8] Richard Dugdale, who inspected prisons for the New York Prison Association, delivered the essay "Hereditary Pauperism" to the National Conference of Charities and Corrections (NCCC) in 1877. He chronicled the troubling social conduct of multiple generations of the Jukes family and ascribed their pauperism in part to hereditary factors. A few years later, C. R. Henderson of the University of Chicago, in his presidential address to the NCCC's annual meeting, outlined the problems of "those who cannot compete" and called for the "extermination" and "closing out the stock of a hopelessly degenerate line" (NCCC 1899:4, 9). Although pedigree studies pointed to the biological roots of poverty, their early proponents failed to offer any practical recommendations for intervention.

Josephine Lowell, a leading figure in the early social work movement, however, undertook this responsibility.[9] Appointed in 1876 by New York's Governor Samuel J. Tilden as the first woman commissioner of the New York State Board of Charities and Corrections, she was later a founder of New York City's Charity Organization Society (COS) in 1882. She was active in the child-saving movement and campaigns to protect delinquent and vagrant girls from crime and immorality, and her lobbying efforts were rewarded in 1878 when New York appropriated money for a reformatory in Newark for the custodial care of "fallen women" (Haller 1963:28; Trent 1994). The reformatory set a precedent, according to historian Mark Haller, because it was the "first important recognition of eugenic principles by a state" (1963:28).

In her 1879 address to the NCCC, "One Means of Preventing Pauperism," Lowell argued that vagrant and degraded girls and their "unrestrained liberty" were the "links in the direful chain of hereditary pauperism" (NCCC 1879:189, 195). As Dugdale's study had asserted, hereditary pauperism was inseparable from "sexual passion" and idiocy (NCCC 1877:86–87). "Idiot," "simpleton," "moron," and "defective" were often synonyms for "feeblemindedness." In post-Revolutionary America, feeblemindedness referred to conditions that today would be classified under the rubric of "mental retardation" (Trent 1994). The question of who was considered feebleminded, however, was elastic and shaped by cultural constructions of abnormality. Lowell reflected the belief of her time that women with unrestrained sexual passion were necessarily intellectually subnormal (NCCC 1877; Trent 1994). After the turn of the century, the term referred not only to the mentally retarded and prostitutes but also to those who displayed socially transgressive behavior, such as juvenile delinquency or single parenthood.

In the 1910s social workers interpreted illegitimacy per se as evidence of women's mental defects. "The connection was clear," observes Regina Kunzel (1993:52): feebleminded women were in constant danger of becoming pregnant because of their unregulated sexual appetite, and therefore most unmarried mothers were feebleminded. To social workers, who recognized the circular link between feeblemindedness, promiscuity, pregnancy, illegitimacy, and the reproduction of feeblemindedness, the solutions were to be found in early diagnosis, segregation and surveillance—preferably in locked institutions—and later through sterilization, birth control, and population control (Kunzel 1993:54).

To stop the further proliferation of feebleminded children, Josephine Lowell wanted predatory women securely segregated in reformatories where they would no longer engage in sexual relations and risk birthing such children (NCCC 1879; Haller 1963; Trent 1994). Aside from campaigning for new prisons, social reformers of the late nineteenth century lacked a eugenics program. Social workers and their colleagues in related disciplines, however, continued pedigree research, further documenting the hereditarian nature of social problems. Such research became the foundation of the Eugenics Record Office.

Mary Harriman, a friend of Eleanor Roosevelt's who would later head Franklin D. Roosevelt's Consumer Advisory Board, was one of the first social workers to become involved with Charles Davenport's Eugenics Record Office (ERO) at Cold Spring Harbor. Intrigued by the idea that "the laws of heredity might be used for the amelioration of man," she worked with Davenport in 1905 and introduced him to her mother, the philanthropist Mrs. E. M. Harriman (Kevles 1997:54). With support from Harriman, Rockefeller, and others, Davenport used the ERO to train a new kind of social worker, the field-worker, by offering training scholarships to university graduates. Field-workers received lectures in anatomy, sterilization, inheritance, classification of crime, and insanity, among other subjects (Document 1106, "Syllabus of lectures given to field workers," Image Archive on the Eugenics Movement). The tools Davenport created for collecting field data on mental defects rested on recording the presence or absence of traits; in effect, he assumed the Mendelian pattern of transmission, which ERO workers were supposed to verify (Haller 1963:70).[10] The insistence on a particular defect's being linked to a specific gene allowed eugenicists to assert that all defective traits might be "eliminated with proper strictures upon breeding" (Gould 1996: 192).

With their training completed, field-workers set out across the country to conduct pedigree studies on inmates in institutions for the insane and feebleminded. Workers spent a minimum of fifteen days per month in the field. They documented the family distribution of personal traits by conducting door-to-door surveys and by scrutinizing prison, hospital, almshouse, asylum, and feebleminded institutional records (Kevles 1997). They spent the balance of the month examining institutional inmates, writing up field notes, and analyzing their data ("Basis for the Joint Employment of Field Workers by the Eugenics Record Office and Institutions for the Socially Inadequate," hereafter referred to as "BJEFW/ERO"; John Randolph Haynes Papers, box 193, Sterilization folder). After the first year many workers remained at the host institution, assisting in after-care work. By 1916 the ERO estimated that there were more than a hundred well-trained eugenics field-workers across the country ("BJEFW/ERO," Haynes Papers, box 193, Sterilization folder). Amy Eaton, a field-worker who moved on to conduct social science research at the University of Utah, welcomed the "close relationships existing between social workers and biologists" (COS 1911:352).

The ERO was more than a mere research center. As Kühl (1994) points out, from the beginning eugenics was an applied science in the service of social action. Armed with research data, field-workers actively lobbied state commissions and legislatures for eugenics measures. In the first decade of the new century, sterilization and intelligence testing were added to their repertoire. Dr. Henry Sharp introduced the vasectomy around 1900 and Dr. M. Madlener the salpingectomy around 1910 (Reilly 1991). Virginia was the first state to legislate compulsory sterilization policies, in 1907; California was the first, in 1909, to include as candidates for sterilization "moral degenerates" and "sexual perverts showing hereditary degeneracy." By 1932 thirty states had passed sterilization statutes (Ordover 2003:79, 134).

For some policymakers, eugenics was preferable to the provision of social services to "undesirable types," with its tendency to encourage dependency and the cycle of social pathologies (COS 1911–1912; Survey Associates 1921–1922:573). Sociologist John Lewis Gillin asserted that in-home relief resulted in nothing more than a "burden" on society by enabling "defective" parents to reproduce and pass on their mental abnormalities to another generation (Gillin 1926:118–119). As Mary Richmond pointed out, some eugenicists called for the "abolition of social work activities and the turning over of moneys thus saved for the prosecution of further eugenic research" (1922:148–149). The assumptions of eugenics may be "gloomy," she conceded, but its "fundamental message . . . is not to be ignored" (1922:149). Richmond acknowledged in 1917 that although the "far-reaching inquiry of eugenic studies" was beyond most practitioners, the caseworker still had to "get at the facts of heredity" when she suspected the presence of mental disease, in order to facilitate the diagnostic and treatment process (Richmond 1917:187).[11] Even Jane Addams, who campaigned for social solutions to personal problems, welcomed eugenics insights into "the inheritance of well-born children" and the "evil heritage" that prostitutes transmitted to their children (Addams 1913:130–131).

With sterilization now technically and easily possible for men and women, ERO field-workers lobbied state commissions and legislatures to authorize sterilization of the "unfit." According to Daniel Kevles (1997), if so much of eugenics legislation was written into law in the United States, it was "probably not least because American eugenics activists could draw upon the publications or allies of the Eugenics Record Office" (104). In 1915, social workers and other professionals—with assistance from Charles Davenport and Alexander Johnstone, the superintendent of the Vineland School for feebleminded persons in New Jersey, and funds from Mrs. Harriman—organized themselves into the Committee on the Provision for Feeble-Minded Persons (CPFP). Board members included Davenport, David Starr Jordan of Stanford University, and several members of state boards of charities and corrections (Haller 1963). "No other one measure means so much to those who are struggling with the problem of the mental defective," observed the California State Board of Charities and Corrections in its 1917 defense of sterilization policies (CSBCC 1917:33).

Alexander Johnson, who served as a board member on the NCCC and eventually headed the Red Cross, served as CPFP's field secretary. He and Elizabeth Kite, a field-worker at the Vineland School, crisscrossed the country delivering warnings about the feebleminded "menace" to legislative assemblies, schools of social work, national and state conferences of charities and corrections, and anyone who would invite them (Johnson 1923). The dangerousness of the feebleminded resided in their unchecked sexuality, their lack of self-control, and their capacity to pass on their defects to their children. As a prominent member of California's State Board of Charities and Corrections explained, "Owing to their lack of intellectual 'normalcy' the feeble-minded person is unable to properly weigh the reasons for the desirability or practicability of a suggestion" (letter dated December 5, 1923, from J. R. Haynes to Ross Stephens, Haynes Papers, box 84, Insanity folder). In Riverside, California, the superintendent of the County Bureau of Welfare and Relief, believed that sterilization and other birth control measures were necessary in order to stem the increase of the "menace to the race at large" (letter dated July 26, 1926, from J. H. Dodge to E. S. Gosney, E. S. Gosney Papers, box 16.5).

The CPFP achieved its goal of raising awareness and persuading legislatures to increase support for institutionalization of the feebleminded (Johnson 1923). While Johnson enthusiastically supported segregation, he was ambivalent about sterilization because he shared the view widely held among social workers that eliminating the risk of reproduction likely promoted immoral behavior, namely sex without risk of pregnancy. Once he realized the "enormous" number of mental defectives in the country, however, he could see "no other practical way to stem the tide of degeneracy" (Survey Associates 1912–1913:173). After all, legislatures were not willing to fund a massive increase in institutionalization when cheaper ways to limit reproduction were available (Gillin 1921; Johnson 1923). Most social workers ultimately agreed with John Reily, medical superintendent of Southern California State Hospital (Patton) that "being robbed of their reproductive powers I do not feel that the harmless Moron is particularly unfit to live in the average community. After they are sterilized their burden on society has been reduced to a minimum" (letter dated September 16, 1916, from Reily to John Randolph, Haynes Papers, box 84, Insanity folder).

In addition to promoting eugenics laws, field-workers had a direct influence on treatment in institutions, where the information they collected was central to decision making about sterilization and parole. By 1908 social workers had access to the Simon and Binet test, a supposedly objective measure of innate intelligence that had been used on army recruits with funding provided by the CPFP (Survey Associates 1917–1918:657). Eugenicists widely supported Henry Goddard's version of the test because it offered a seemingly scientific demonstration that crime and deviance were the result of feeblemindedness (Aldrich 1975). Social workers and other professionals introduced intelligence testing into reformatories, prisons, and asylums where, "expecting to find feeblemindedness among these populations, they found it with a vengeance, linking almost every variety of antisocial behavior to inherited mental defects and reporting alarming rates of feeblemindedness among prostitutes, tramps, criminals, and paupers" (Kunzel 1993:53).

Some social work organizations, such as the Council on Jewish Women, Department of Immigrant Aid in New York, raised their concerns about the impartiality of testing after it was reported that an alarmingly large number of immigrants were feebleminded. Goddard, they pointed out, had developed his test for use on U.S.-born schoolchildren, not the foreign-born with poor English skills (Survey Associates 1917–1918:152). Despite these objections, most social workers regarded the test as adding credence to their a priori knowledge that "unimprovable" cases of illegitimacy and sexual immorality had their basis in low intelligence and would require a "plan for state control" (NCMH 1918a:435). The tests and pedigree studies ultimately branded large groups of people as having defective "germ plasm" and as being incapable of rising to the level of civilization achieved by social workers and other educated professionals (Gould 1996; Kevles 1997; Trent 1994).[12]

Social workers also faced a problem of how to categorize and treat the many clients who tested "normal" but whom they were convinced suffered from mental deficiency. The solution was to supplement testing with the observational expertise of trained field-workers. A book on poverty relief in the 1920s stated that the "high-grade defective" (someone whose intellectual impairment was not overtly apparent) might be detected only through the use of "social tests of conduct" (Gillin 1921:317). As Charles Davenport had observed in a 1915 talk to the NCCC, "Perhaps that most important and indispensable service that the field worker performs is . . . [what] we cannot at present properly measure at the institution, and that is the emotional control that the person has . . . his capacity for reacting according to the *mores*—his *morality*" ("BJEFW/ERO," Haynes Papers, box 193, Sterilization folder).

At the Sonoma State Home for feebleminded persons in California, staff used social intelligence tests to detect depravity among working-class women who were found intellectually normal by intelligence tests. Sexual immorality in particular was perceived as a sign of mental defect that intelligence tests failed to detect (Kline 2001:42–43). Ethel Thayer, a field-worker for the ERO, similarly used family histories to elicit critical information not detected by intelligence tests. "I spoke to Dr. Hatch about the investigation of the family histories of cases proposed for sterilization," she wrote in 1915. "A history that I am getting at present seems to be increasing the desire and efforts of Dr. Stocking [medical superintendent of Agnews State Hospital] . . . to secure the sterilization of two unfit individuals who are now at large and raising a family only to become county charges" (Gottshall 1995:6). ERO fieldwork in other states provided similar kinds of data that would prove "essential" in "restricting the propagation of the unfit" ("BJEFW/ERO," Haynes Papers, box 193, Sterilization folder).

Sterilization was also intertwined with aftercare work or what would eventually fall under the rubric of "psychiatric social work." Parole was used to reduce inmate populations by allowing them to live and work in the community. In 1913 New York hospitals paroled only 861 patients. In 1914 this number increased to 1,300 after social workers were employed. By 1920 the number reached 2,283 (NCMH 1920:648).[13] Soon after F. O. Butler, described as a "self appointed social worker" (Wardell 1944:31), took over as superintendent of the Sonoma State Home in 1918, he established his own social work department and boosted institutional paroles (Turner 1964).

Social workers proposed all paroles, monitored parolees in the community, found jobs for parolees, and interviewed patients, relatives, and employers to gather information on cases (Chan and Bary 1936; Department of Institutions 1930; Gosney and Popenoe 1929). Under Butler's program, inmates typically were not paroled unless they were sterilized before their release from the institution. One social worker reported in 1926 that the sterilization of prostitutes held at Sonoma tended to "minimize their former sexual irregularities" (Louise Keaton Bray questionnaire, Gosney Papers, box 16.5, 1926). Another social worker from Santa Barbara remarked that "sterilization is the only cure for adults" (M. O. Winters questionnaire, Gosney Papers, box 16.5, 1926).[14]

Many families consented to sterilization because they felt it was the only way to control their child's sexuality in a time of drastically changing sexual mores. However, whether or not families authorized sterilization, they had little choice but to consent to it if they wanted their family member back. As Paul Popenoe of the Human Betterment Foundation wrote in 1930, "Dr. Butler has always had a strong weapon to use in getting consents for sterilization by telling the relatives that the patient could not leave without sterilization" (letter dated March 14, 1930, to John R. Haynes; Haynes Papers, box 77, Human Betterment Foundation folder).[15] Butler in particular targeted women for sterilization because "the male is not the aggressor and does not have sufficient intelligence to have sex relations" (Butler 1945:2).[16] As Butler pointed out, if women with children in Sonoma had been sterilized in the first place, "they could probably have been kept out of the institution, and we would surely not have the children with us" (Butler 1925:4).

Social service organizations in California working in conjunction with state institutions also lent their support to sterilization. The Jewish Committee for Personal Service (JCPS) was founded as an agency of the San Francisco Federation of Jewish Charities in 1921. The organization's initial director was Rabbi Martin Meyer, who served as a member of the State Board of Charities and Corrections (1911–1920). He was replaced by Rabbi Rudolph Coffee, who held a Ph.D. from the University of Pittsburgh (1908). Coffee served as president of the Travelers' Aid Society from 1921 to 1926, as a lecturer for the American Eugenics Society, as a founding member of the Human Betterment Foundation, and as a member of the California State Board of Charities and Corrections from 1924 to 1931 ("A List of Eugenics Lecturers," 1927, Haynes Papers, box 65, AES folder; Gosney and Popenoe 1929; *National Cyclopedia of American Biography* 1958).

At the forefront of psychiatric social work, JCPS workers counseled clients on adjustment issues, prepared case histories for developing "proper corrective treatment," and, most important, helped locate housing and employment for potential parolees ("What Is the JCPS?" Samuel Holcenberg

Papers, JCPS folder). JCPS executive secretary William Blumenthal kept statistics on siblings who were paroled from state institutions to the agency "to show statistically what a factor heredity plays" (letter dated October 17, 1922, from Blumenthal to Haynes, Haynes Papers, box 193, Sterilization folder). Coffee believed in the ability of sterilization to "build a better race" and made a point when visiting institutions to "encourage the superintendents to continue their magnificent efforts toward improving the generation of tomorrow" (letter dated August 30, 1929, from Coffee to E. S. Gosney, Gosney Papers, box 18.2).

Blumenthal helped John Randolph Haynes, a member of the California State Board of Charities and Corrections (1912–1923), to raise a $100,000 guarantee fund to protect institutional physicians from prosecution in the event that the California sterilization statute was declared unconstitutional (letter from Blumenthal to Haynes, dated May 16, 1922; Haynes Papers, box 193, Sterilization folder). Haynes, a leading Progressive reformer with an M.D. and a Ph.D. from the University of Pennsylvania who had made his fortune in real estate and banking (Starr 1985; Stadtman 1967) was a strong advocate of eugenics: "The whole stream of human life is being constantly polluted by the admixture of the tainted blood of the extremely defective," he wrote in a 1918 report. "If this source of contamination could be cut off, the beneficial effects would begin to show in a single generation and in a very few generations the average level of human society would be very materially lifted" ("Report on the Care of the Insane and the Care of Adult Offenders: October, 1918," Haynes Papers, box 84, Insanity folder). Even after the decision in the 1927 case of *Buck v. Bell,* which upheld the constitutionality of involuntary sterilization, Haynes believed superintendents of institutions for the insane and feebleminded needed assurances that financial aid would be provided if someone threatened a damage suit, thus avoiding any reduction in the number of sterilizations performed.

Social workers' adoption of eugenics measures can in part be explained by the emerging profession's search for professional respectability and a distinct body of knowledge (Walkowitz 1990; Kunzel 1993). Between 1904 and 1907, the first training schools for social work were established at Columbia University, Simmons College in Boston, and the University of Chicago. By 1910 Jane Addams had published *Twenty Years at Hull House,* and the first White House conference on dependent children had been convened. In 1921 the American Association of Social Workers was established (Platt and Cooreman 2001). Throughout the 1920s, according to one historian, "social workers battled the public's association of social work with nineteenth-century benevolence and voiced frustration over the disparity between the public image of social work as sentimental charity and their self-image of a profession offering skilled service." Professionalization generated a much more conservative perspective, with those who emphasized social justice over individual adjustment increasingly marginalized within the profession. Social work now emphasized the "talismans of professionalization—objectivity, efficiency, rationality" (Kunzel 1993:43, 44).

With increasing importance placed on "scientifically" grounded interventions, social work entered an identity crisis in the early twentieth century as competing middle-class occupations questioned whether or not it engaged in "professional" practice. If the new social worker was to distinguish herself from her predecessor, the unpaid female volunteer, she would need a "language of professionalism" (Walkowitz 1990:1060). Eugenics offered a "rational" foundation in which to anchor professional activity and a clearly articulated, organizing goal (the improvement of human welfare by thwarting "degeneration of the race"), which leaders such as Abraham Flexner asserted was necessary for professional status (Kirk and Reid 2002:3–6).

Other conceptual bases, such as Freudian psychology, offered social work a theoretical foundation, but its principles were difficult to operationalize and it specified no rational interventions derived from its theories (Kirk and Reid 2002). Eugenics, in contrast, offered a theoretical explanation of human behavior and an intervention plan for resolving socially deviant behavior. It established the hereditarian foundations of social problems through "scientific" inquiry, using technical tools, such as pedigree studies and intelligence tests. Now social workers could do what they had been called upon to do at the turn of the century: "rationally" and "deliberately" ensure the welfare of the community and future race by using "sound practices" that would halt "deterioration" and "corruption of the blood" and "protect future society" (NCCC 1899:6–9). As a commentator in the *Survey* suggested, eugenics "constitutes the link between the social reform of the past, painfully struggling to improve the conditions of life, and the social hygiene of the future which is authorized to deal adequately with the conditions of life because it has its hands on the sources of life" (Survey Associates 1912–1913:243).

Across the country, social work schools in Chicago, Richmond, Philadelphia, and Houston provided course content that "made plain" the "relations between feeble-mindedness and all other forms of social defect" (Johnson 1923:412). As Laura Briggs has noted, eugenics was very much a part of the Progressive agenda to improve the state of the family through reduction of children, encouragement of two-parent families, and lowering of maternal and infant mortality rates (Briggs 2002:75, 99). In an era when increasing emphasis was placed on scientifically verified education, psychiatric social work training at Smith College included "a sound knowledge of the biological backgrounds of modern community problems [that] impress[es] upon social workers the tremendous importance of the hereditary equipment of the individual . . . and guards her against sentimental and un-scientific methods which might tolerate the marriage and hence the multiplication of a type of person innately incapable of conformity to prevailing social standards" (NCMH 1918b:592).

The powerful appeal of eugenics to the emerging field of social work, however, went beyond the quest for scientific respectability and practical panaceas. Behind the language of technocratic expertise also lurked deeply held cultural fears of the dangerous and combustible mix of poverty, insanity, and sexuality (Noakes 1984). In his personal notes John Randolph Haynes expressed what many professional policymakers believed:

> Millions of human beings live under conditions that prevent them from attaining full mental, moral and physical efficiency. In order to prevent this waste of human endeavor, society should rid itself of degenerates and preverts [sic] who commit terrible crimes . . . and by the sterilization of the unfit stop the propagation of this type even if they have not committed crimes. . . . There are thousands of hopelessly insane in California, the condition of those minds is such that death would be a merciful release. How long will it be before society will see the criminality of using its efforts to keep alive these idiots, hopelessly insane, and murderous degenerates. . . . Of course the passing of these people should be painless and without warning. They should go to sleep at night without any intimation of what was coming and never awake.
> (Haynes Papers, box 84, Insanity folder, c. 1918)[17]

Nature and Nurture

Some historians have argued that as Freudian theories rose in prominence among the helping professions, hereditarian explanations for human behavior declined in influence (Haller 1963). They suggest that by the 1920s, the fascination with "adjustment" psychology, embodied in the mental hygiene movement, supplanted the earlier decade's "short-lived fascination with eugenics" (Trent 1994:205).[18] Kevles (1997) notes that during World War I, a number of genetics researchers were concerned that eugenics was "tarnishing the genetics enterprise" and sought to separate themselves from eugenics by opposing conferences or scientific publications that presented eugenics and genetic material synonymously (121–122). They called into question the scientific credibility of mainline eugenics (represented by men like Charles Davenport, Roswell Johnson, and Henry Laughlin). In a state of increasing disrepute between the two world wars, eugenics received a severe blow when the Third Reich fell, exposing the extent to which Nazi eugenics policies had been carried out in the name of racial purity (Haller 1963; Kevles 1997). Within social work, critics increasingly challenged the limitations of eugenics: inadequate attention to environmental factors in the generation of social problems, overstated allegations about the inherited roots of social problems, and exaggerated claims that eugenics interventions could "save the race."

A close examination of debates within social work, however, suggests that eugenics concepts retained a dynamic, albeit changed, role within the profession. In the 1930s, despite widespread criticism of eugenics, hundreds of surgeons performed almost two thousand sterilizations a year "on retarded persons in the name of social welfare" (Reilly 1991:125). Eugenics and social work "did not conflict," suggested one commentator, because they were working for a "common objective, the improvement of the human race" (American Eugenics Society 1929:22). As John Morrow Ford, a member of the National Conference of Social Work and a professor of social service administration at Harvard, noted in 1937, eugenics was a "rapidly evolving science." Old theories were discarded as new theories were added to its "mass of accepted principles" (Ford and Ford 1937:58; *National Cyclopedia of American Biography* 1958). Some key eugenics assumptions not only persisted into the 1930s but also influenced foundational concepts within social work and welfare policy throughout the twentieth century.

Within social work there were conflicts and debate about the value of eugenics. Six years after Sigmund Freud delivered his lectures on psychoanalysis in the United States and five years after the establishment of the ERO, Adolf Meyer of the Phipps Psychiatric Clinic at Johns Hopkins Hospital asserted that, although heredity played a role in a large percentage of mental cases, there simply was not a "sufficiently decisive body of facts established" to justify enacting eugenics measures, such as marriage restriction (Survey Associates 1915:558). In 1917 Dr. Abraham Myerson, who would eventually head an investigation on sterilization for the American Neurological Association, challenged the methodology of eugenics researchers Charles Davenport and Aaron Rosanoff, the future director of California's Department of Institutions. Their "efforts seem to me," wrote Myerson, "to be directed not so much to discover the laws of the transmission of insanity as to fit the facts to Mendelian theory" (1917:359). By the early 1920s commentators in the *Survey* were arguing that "the transmission of social heritage is conditioned largely by social factors" (Survey Associates 1922–1923:799).

If eugenicists had to rely on measures, such as social intelligence tests, to uncover mental defects, argued critics, then it was plausible that environmental factors, rather than any innate biological quality, were the genesis of social pathologies. Some social workers, such as Maurice Karpf, director of the Training School for Jewish Social Work, observed that the biological point of view left "little room for programs of social adjustment through the means of social control and social reform" (Karpf 1931:87). He believed that "changes in the environment . . . and organization of society" would do much more to improve society than changing the "genetic constitution of the population" (Karpf 1931:91). If eugenics prevailed, then a large portion of what was being codified as "social work" would convince no "self-respecting" and "forward looking person" to aspire to be a social worker (Karpf 1931:90).

At the same time, however, a reformed eugenics retained a respectable, racialized role within social work. Until the United States declared war against Germany, American eugenicists exchanged ideas and proposals with their Nazi counterparts. The relationship was mostly cordial and collaborative, with California's sterilization program serving as a model for Germany's 1934 Law for the Prevention of Hereditarily Diseased Offspring (Kühl 1994). It was widely known in the United States, long before the collapse of the Nazi regime, that Germany's eugenics policies were guided by racial politics. In August 1934 readers of the *New York Times* learned that the Reich Commission of National Health was advising Germans to "choose only a wife of the same or of Nordic blood [and] keep away from aliens of non-European racial origin" (*New York Times* 1934:15). The following year, the *Los Angeles Times* published a long defense of Germany's sterilization policies. The Nazis "had to resort to the teachings of eugenic science," argued Dr. Burchardi, because Germany, "deprived of her colonies, [is] blessed with many hundreds of defective racial hybrids as a lasting memory of the colored army of occupation, and dismembered all around" (Burchardi 1935).

Many social workers tried to meld eugenics and environmental policies. The argument that John Randolph Haynes had made in the 1920s resonated with practitioners in the 1930s: "to hold, as do certain classes of reformers, that environment is everything, and that the question of heredity may be disregarded . . . is to shut one's eyes to all the realities of life" ("Sterilization of the Unfit," 1922, Haynes Papers, box 193, Sterilization folder). There was value in "social adjustment," claimed a typical textbook, but it "should not blind the eyes of the social worker to the eugenic measures necessary to prevent reproduction, in cases where there is good evidence of hereditary defect" (Gillian 1926:387). In its mental hygiene survey, published in 1930, the California Department of Social Welfare recommended the "continuation of the sterilization program . . . particularly for the [feebleminded] girls" (State Department of Social Welfare 1930:136). Anne Saylor, chairman of the survey committee, "heartily" endorsed the eugenics ideas of the Human Betterment Foundation (letter dated September 24, 1929, to E. S. Gosney, Gosney Papers, box 18.2).

While sociologist John Lewis Gillin warned against overly optimistic claims for sterilization, he recognized that the procedure "will prevent the propagation of the feeble-minded by those who patently have defective genes. Every case prevented is a gain" (Gillin 1937:339). Criminologist Maurice Parmelle suggested that while there was not "sufficient biological knowledge" to justify eugenics measures for a "number of abnormal or pathological traits," intervention was permissible in cases where "reliable evidence" proved that feeblemindedness was "unquestionably due to hereditary traits" (1926:303–304). Social scientists held firm to this line of thinking through the 1930s. In *The Abolition of Poverty*, Ford and Ford wrote: "The simpler [Mendelian] theories of the inheritance of mental deficiency are . . . now pretty generally discarded. Nevertheless, the conviction remains justified that much of feeble-mindedness—at least a third and perhaps much more—is, in some manner not yet fully determined, hereditary in origin" (Ford and Ford 1937:53).

After World War I, supporters of sterilization policies also turned to birth control, which, as Linda Gordon first observed, became increasingly "saturated with eugenics ideas" (1974:63). Originally, the campaign for women's access to information about contraception was organized by grassroots feminists, committed to reproductive and sexual self-determination (Gordon 2002). Feminists and leftists used eugenics to campaign for "programs which could lessen suffering through the prevention of hereditary birth defects and the improvement of pre-natal care for women" (Gordon 1974:72). But during the 1920s the birth control movement reproduced the same kind of ethnocentric, racist, and anti–working class attitudes that permeated eugenics.

John Randolph Haynes, for example, served as treasurer for the Los Angeles Mothers' Clinic, founded by a social worker, Cora Tasker, to provide birth control information to women ("The Mother's Clinic," Frances Noel Papers, box 2, folder 11). Haynes could support an agency that wanted to limit the breeding of "weakened human organisms" and believed that "unless well born, the child has an inalienable right not to be born" (pamphlet, Haynes Papers, box 8, Birth Control folder). "Children of defective parents are exposed to environmental influences that predispose them to crime, sex, delinquency, alcoholism, drug addiction, and the gamut of social ills," noted the clinic in 1930. "Rather than treat social maladjustment as an end result, it is better to treat it at its source. . . . Prevention is better than cure" ("5th Annual Report, 1930," Noel Papers, box 2, folder 11).

During the 1930s the birth control movement, later reformulated as "population control," had replaced its earlier radical feminism with a defense of traditional sex roles and the nuclear family, and a moral crusade against working-class degeneracy (Gordon 1974:79). By 1933 the formerly socialist

Margaret Sanger and the deeply conservative Haynes were sharing ideas about how birth control could be used to stop the reproduction of "less desirable social types" and "safeguard" and "benefit the home, and the family" ("Executive Power—Health Department—Free and Sovereign State of Veracruz-Llave" and letter from Sanger to Haynes, dated January 4, 1933, Haynes Papers, box 8, Birth Control folder).

A reformed eugenics sought out alliances with social work. For example, Frank Lorimer, who would go on to conduct family planning research for UNESCO, argued for "eugenical social work" (American Eugenics Society 1930:95). Since community-based social workers were in "close touch" with families "not well fitted to bear and rear children," they could use their connections with these families to promote birth control. "Visionary and dogmatic eugenics, divorced from economic and social consequences, is futile," argued Lorimer, "but it is not more so than short-sighted and unscientific social work, divorced from considerations of size of family and hereditary factors" (American Eugenics Society 1930:95). And in Los Angeles, the head of the Children's Protective Association and a leading eugenicist collaborated on a study demonstrating that the longer a family is dependent on welfare, the more children it will produce. Paul Popenoe and Ellen Williams argued that charitable aid to poor families should be accompanied by contraceptive instructions and materials or sterilization at public expense if the family could not be relied upon to effectively use contraception (Popenoe and Williams 1934:220).[19] As the authors wrote, failing to so do would promote a "vicious circle" of dependency and relief for which "efficient, self-supporting taxpayers" would have to "foot" the bill, consequently forcing them to "reduce the number of [their] own children still further" (Popenoe and Williams 1934:219). More than sixty years later, this policy would occupy a central place in the "welfare reform" movement of the 1990s.

Legacies

After World War II the language of eugenics gradually disappeared from social work, but its basic assumptions continued to shape the social work canon and welfare policies. An influential social work book, published in 1950, defended "selective sterilization as one approach to a happier world where all people will be truly 'well born' " (Woodside 1950:163). Its author, Moya Woodside, criticized the German sterilization law for the "authoritarian manner" of its application and the "misuse of eugenic principle" (24), without any discussion of how it was a precursor to the killing of 100,000 mentally ill patients and then the mass-produced butchery of millions. Nor is there any mention of the racial uses of eugenics in the United States prior to World War II. Instead, Woodside calls for targeting African Americans in North Carolina for sterilization, given their tendency to "perpetuate former ways of behaving" and to be "less responsive to new ideas" (xiv) She urged caseworkers to persuade their clients that sterilization is "one way of bringing about greater stability in the family" (153). And her suggestions were apparently followed. Between 1929 and 1940, 78 percent of candidates approved for sterilization in North Carolina were women, and of these, 21 percent were African American. By 1964 black women constituted 65 percent of all women sterilized in the state (Ordover 2003:165). "Contrary to common belief," concludes a recent study by the *Winston-Salem Journal,* "many of the thousands marked for sterilization were ordinary citizens, many of them young women guilty of nothing worse than engaging in premarital sex" (Begos 2002; Special Report 2002).

Before World War II, advocates of sterilization in the United States focused primarily on poor women and men in penal institutions and mental hospitals. After the war, government authorities targeted poor women of color in their communities and increasingly used public health and welfare incentives to induce, trick, and coerce patient consent. In Puerto Rico, social workers were "enthusiastic supporters of eugenics," which throughout the 1920s was rooted in feminist ideas about birth control. But by the mid-1930s, this approach was replaced by policies closely aligned with "conservative eugenics and the colonial impulse to protect the United States from too many of 'them' " (Briggs 2002:98, 102). In Puerto Rico, between the 1930s and 1970s, one third of Puerto Rican women of childbearing age were sterilized (Gordon 2002:343; Briggs 2002:143). During the 1970s, according to Sally Torpy, the Department of Health, Education, and Welfare funded 90 percent of the cost of sterilization of poor women. It is estimated that between 1970 and 1975, approximately one million women were sterilized annually (Torpy 2000), primarily African American women and poor whites (especially in the South), Puerto Rican women in New York, and Chicanas and Native American women in the Southwest (Davis 1981; Ordover 2003:161–178).

Not surprisingly, political opposition to government-sponsored sterilization emerged initially from communities of color during the activist 1970s, led by Puerto Rican organizations in New York, the Committee to End Sterilization Abuse, the National Women's Health Network, and many other grassroots organizations (Gordon 2002:342–347). The Black Panther Party— following in the tradition of W. E. B. Du Bois, who had warned African Americans in 1936 to keep a sharp eye on "so-called eugenic sterilization" (quoted in Ordover 2003:153)—educated Black communities about the abuses of sterilization policies and campaigned to de-link sterilization from welfare rights (*The Black Panther* 1971).

Our motivation for writing this chapter is not only to set straight the historical record and encourage social work to take responsibility for its past practices, but also to draw attention to how old concepts continue to shape welfare policies and political attitudes toward inequality. We share Nancy Ordover's conclusion, in her study *American Eugenics,* that "whenever biologism and public policy have intersected, they have extracted a terrible price from the poor, physically and politically" (xv). Today, we can recognize the influence of eugenics on the search for racial differences in intelligence (Herrnstein and Murray 1994) and biological determinants of sexuality (Ordover 2003); on the imposition by government of sexual and reproductive restrictions on women on welfare (Solinger 1998; Boris 1998; Mink 2001); and on the ideas of leading welfare policymakers and executives who, in Simon Schama's words (2003:35), have adopted "the habit of dressing the business of power in the garb of piety."[20] Arguing against what they perceive as the dangerous "ideology of equality," two modern-day eugenicists—whose work has had a profound impact on recent changes in federal welfare—say, "It is time for America once again to try living with inequality, as life is lived" (Herrnstein and Murray 1994:533, 551). Today, with muscular conservatives throwing their weight around in Washington, D.C., and economic inequality returning to levels reminiscent of the Gilded Age, it is not surprising that restricting the birthrate of the poor and promoting marriage have become the mainstay of welfare policy.

Our critique of social work's involvement with eugenics in the United States does not imply repudiation of biological and genetic interpretations of human behavior, or of specific measures to limit reproduction through birth control and sterilization. Clearly, heredity plays a part, along with environment, in determining people's capabilities and limitations; and sterilization is an acceptable way for people to control reproduction if they so choose. Our concern is the use of scientific paradigms to legitimate white supremacy and the division of humanity into racial categories; to limit reproductive rights on the basis of class and ethnic prejudices; and to reduce complex social inequalities to one-dimensional panaceas.

Notes

1. In 1999, the provincial government of Alberta, Canada, apologized for the forced sterilization of more than 2,800 people and compensated 246 victims with payments totaling $82 million. Another $140 million was paid in settlements with 900 other victims (*Washington Post* 2002).

2. The number typically used is 60,000 to 65,000 (see, for example, Zitner 2003), but this is based largely on anecdotal evidence and does not include the many Puerto

Rican, American Indian, and African American women whose sterilization was effectively coerced as a condition of welfare from the 1950s through the 1970s. Ordover (2003:134) estimates that 70,000 people "are known to have been sterilized" between 1907 and 1945.

3. Linda Gordon (1974, 1976, 2002) was the first historian to draw attention to the class, gender, and racial biases within the eugenics movement and their enduring influences on social policy. Gordon's insights framed Angela Davis's popular essay "Racism, Birth Control, and Reproductive Rights," first published in 1981. Gordon's 1976 book has been updated and substantially revised in a 2002 edition.

4. Linda Gordon (1976) refers to social workers' role in the birth control movement, but in rather one-dimensional terms; Nancy Ordover (2003) documents the ties between welfare policy and sterilization practices after World War II; Regina Kunzel's (1993) study of how social workers regulated the lives of unmarried mothers between the World Wars offers perceptive insights into the profession's formative years.

5. See, for example, Nakashima (1984) and Gilbert and Specht (1981). See also Haller (1963:170–171) and Trent (1994:205).

6. "Eugenics" and "sterilization" are not listed in the index to Bruce Jansson's *The Reluctant Welfare State* (2001). Popple and Leighninger (1996:201–203, 382–383) briefly discuss the "eugenics movement," but not social work's involvement. An important exception to the trend is historian Michael Katz (1996), whose social history of welfare in the United States suggests that eugenic ideas and policies persisted well into the twentieth century.

7. Mimi Abramovitz (1996:148–149, 152, 167) similarly limits eugenics to its nineteenth-century association with social Darwinism. There is no discussion in her book—nor in Jill Quadagno's (1994) critique of race and welfare—of the misuses of sterilization policy against poor women in the twentieth century.

8. The term "pedigree study" is a modern term used in genetic counseling to refer to the documenting of an extended family's medical history so as to ascertain the pattern of disease occurrence in the family line. While we use this term in the essay, it is not necessarily a term that would have been familiar to Dugdale. At the 1877 conference, Richard Dugdale referred to the Jukes family as an illustration of "hereditary pauperism" (NCCC 1877:81). The Eugenics Record Office at Cold Spring Harbor referred to pedigree studies as "family history studies" ("Basis for the Joint Employment of Field Workers by the Eugenics Record Office and Institutions for the Socially Inadequate"; Haynes Papers, box 193, Sterilization folder). Some referred to them as "studies in heredity" (COS 1911:353).

9. Although we use the term "social worker," it was not systematically used in the late 1800s and early 1900s to refer to friendly home visitors or settlement workers. By 1917 "social work" as a term that referred to professional activity began to take shape. In *Social Diagnosis,* Mary Richmond used "social case work" and "social workers" to refer to those activities she was attempting to systematize into formal practice. Walkowitz (1990) points out that the debates over professionalization, which intensified in the 1920s, led to the formation of a gendered "social worker" identity.

10. The terms "mental defect" or "hereditary defect" were broad categories that referred to children and adults with conditions like feeblemindedness, insanity, epilepsy, licentiousness, and criminal behavior.

11. Although there is an understanding today that biological conditions are not necessarily genetically inherited ones, we use the terms "biology" and "heredity" interchangeably in this chapter.

12. "Germ plasm" referred to what we know today as genes. It implied that there was an innate source of "fitness" or "degeneracy" in the body. "Fitness" was heavily tied to notions of human worth, and "worthwhile" human beings were identified as having those qualities many eugenicists and social workers "presumed themselves to possess—the sort that facilitated passage through schools, universities, and professional training" (Kevles 1997:77). "Appropriate social conduct" was thus imbued with notions of intellectualism and morality, both of which the "degenerate" lacked.

13. The cost savings provided by parole were significant. F. O. Butler, superintendent of the Sonoma State Home, estimated that for 198 cases on parole in 1928, the state paid $5,626.85 for community supervision but saved $27,153.24 on inpatient care costs (Department of Institutions 1929:10).

14. The questionnaires cited in the paper are the responses received from a survey on sterilization the Human Betterment Foundation sent out in 1926.

15. The Human Betterment Foundation was founded in 1929 by E. S. Gosney. With Paul Popenoe as its executive director, the foundation published copious studies aimed at demonstrating the scientific soundness of sterilization for the mentally and socially unfit.

16. 2,445 women and 1,865 men underwent the procedure from 1910 to 1945 at the Sonoma State Home. The California sterilization statute was initially adopted in 1909 (Chapter 720, California Statute 1093) and later revised in 1913 (Chapter 363, California Statute 775) and 1917 (Chapter 489, California Statute 571). The number sterilized includes the 12 sterilizations performed at the Sonoma State Home before Butler's arrival in 1918. For the figures cited, see Butler's 1943 paper.

17. While the document referenced ("Millions of human beings . . . ") has no date or name on it, it is clear from its contents and style that it was written by Haynes around 1918.

18. Mental hygiene, or the "new psychiatry," as Trent (1994) calls it, was formally founded in 1909 when the National Committee for Mental Hygiene was established. It emphasized amelioration and prevention of mental problems. One key aspect of the movement was its concern with child mental health. Influenced by Freudian ideas of personality development, hygienists focused on the importance of proper parenting and environment in promoting healthy emotional development and adjustment to society.

19. Their report was based on a study of 504 families listed with the county welfare department in Los Angeles.

20. With respect to welfare policy, the Bush administration has relied on the perspective and advice of Marvin Olasky, a right-wing, born-again historian; John DiIulio, a conservative, born-again political scientist; Attorney General John Ashcroft, who, as Senator Ashcroft, lobbied to broaden the role of religious organizations in the provision of welfare services; and James Towey, a former legal counsel to

Mother Teresa, who heads the White House Office of Faith-Based and Community Initiatives.

References

MANUSCRIPT AND ARCHIVAL COLLECTIONS

California Institute of Technology, Pasadena, California. Register of the E. S. Gosney Papers and Records of the Human Betterment Foundation, 1880–1945.

California State Library. Government Publications Division.

Image Archive on the Eugenics Movement. Dolan DNA Learning Center, Cold Spring Harbor Laboratory. http://www.eugenicsarchive.org.

Magnes Museum Archives, Berkeley, California. Samuel Holcenberg Papers, Collection 81/6.

University of California, Los Angeles, California. John Randolph Haynes Papers, Collection 1241.

———. Frances Noel Papers, Collection 814.

GOVERNMENT PUBLICATIONS

California State Board of Charities and Corrections (CSBCC). 1917. *Seventh Biennial Report of the State Board of Charities and Corrections of California from July 1, 1914, to June 30, 1916.* Sacramento: California State Printing Office.

Department of Institutions. 1929. *Fourth Biennial Report of the Department of Institutions of the State of California for the Two Years Ending June 30, 1928.* Sacramento: California State Printing Office.

———. 1930. *Fifth Biennial Report of the Department of Institutions of the State of California for the Two Years Ending June 30, 1930.* Sacramento: California State Printing Office.

State Department of Social Welfare. 1930. *Mental Hygiene Survey of the State of California.* Sacramento: California State Printing Office.

ARTICLES, BOOKS, PERIODICALS, AND UNPUBLISHED STUDIES

Abramovitz, M. 1996. *Regulating the Lives of Women: Social Welfare Policy from Colonial Times to the Present.* Boston: South End Press.

Addams, J. 1913. *A New Conscience and an Ancient Evil.* New York: Macmillan.

Aldrich, M. 1975. Capital theory and racism: From laissez-faire to the eugenics movement in the career of Irving Fisher. *Review of Radical Political Economics* 7 (3): 33–42.

American Eugenics Society. 1929. *Eugenics* 2 (12). Connecticut: Galton Publishing.

———. 1930. *Eugenics* 3 (3). Connecticut: Galton Publishing.

Begos, K. 2002. "Thousands Were Sentenced to Sterilization." *Winston-Salem Journal.* December 8.

Black Panther Intercommunal News Service. 1971. Sterilization: Another part of the plan of black genocide. *Black Panther* 6 (15, May 8).

Boris, E. 1998. When work is slavery. *Social Justice* 25 (1): 28–46.

Briggs, L. 2002. *Reproducing Empire: Race, Sex, Science, and U.S. Imperialism in Puerto Rico.* Berkeley: University of California Press.

Burchardi, K. 1935. Why Hitler says sterilize the unfit! *Los Angeles Times.* August 11.

Butler, F. O. 1925. Sterilization procedure and its success in California institution. Publisher unknown. Located in the California State Library, Government Publications Division.

———. 1945. A quarter of a century's experience in sterilization of mental defectives in California. *American Journal of Mental Deficiency* 49 (4): 1–6.

Carlson, E. A. 200. *The Unfit: A History of a Bad Idea.* Cold Spring Harbor: Cold Spring Harbor Laboratory Press.

Chan, F. and V. Bary. 1936. *Welfare Activities of Federal, State, and Local Governments in California, 1850–1934.* Berkeley: University of California Press.

Charity Organization Society (COS). 1911. *The Survey* 26. New York: COS.

———. 1911–1912. *The Survey* 27. New York: COS.

Davis, A. Y. 1981. Racism, Birth Control, and Reproductive Rights. In *Women, Race, and Class,* 202–221. New York: Random House. Reprint, New York: Vintage Books, 1983.

Ford, J. and K. M. Ford. 1937. *The Abolition of Poverty.* New York: Macmillan.

Gilbert, N. and H. Specht. 1981. *The Emergence of Social Welfare and Social Work.* 2d ed. Illinois: Peacock.

Gillin, J. L. 1921. *Poverty and Dependency: Their Relief and Prevention.* New York: Century.

———. 1926. *Poverty and Dependency: Their Relief and Prevention.* 2d ed. New York: D. Appleton-Century.

———. 1937. *Poverty and Dependency: Their Relief and Prevention.* 3d ed. New York: D. Appleton-Century.

Gordon, L. 1974. The politics of population: Birth control and the eugenics movement. *Radical America* 8:61–97.

———. 1976. *Woman's Body, Woman's Right: A Social History of Birth Control in America.* New York: Grossman.

———. 2002. *The Moral Property of Women: A History of Birth Control Politics in America.* Urbana: University of Illinois Press.

Gosney, E. S. and P. Popenoe. 1929. *Sterilization for Human Betterment: A Summary of Results of 6,000 Operations in California, 1909–1929.* New York: Macmillan.

Gottshall, Jon. 1995. The cutting edge: Sterilization and eugenics in California, 1909–1945. Retrieved September 26, 2000, from http://www.gotthsall.com/thesis/article.htm.

Gould, S. J. 1996. *The Mismeasure of Man: The Definitive Refutation to the Argument of the Bell Curve.* New York: Norton

Haller, M. 1963. *Eugenics: Hereditarian Attitudes in American Thought.* New Brunswick, N.J.: Rutgers University Press.

Herrnstein, R. J. and C. Murray. 1994. *The Bell Curve: Intelligence and Class Structure in American Life.* New York: Free Press.

Ingram, C. 2003. State issues apology for policy of sterilization. *Los Angeles Times.* March 12.

Jansson, B. S. 2001. *The Reluctant Welfare State: American Social Welfare Policies—Past, Present, and Future.* Belmont: Brooks/Cole.

Johnson, A. 1923. *Adventures in Social Welfare.* Fort Wayne: Alexander Johnson.

Karpf, M. 1931. *The Scientific Basis of Social Work: A Study in Family Case Work.* New York: Columbia University Press.

Katz, M. B. 1996. *In the Shadow of the Poorhouse: A Social History of Welfare in America.* New York: Basic Books.

Kevles, D. 1997. *In the Name of Eugenics: Genetics and the Uses of Human Heredity.* Cambridge, Mass.: Harvard University Press, 1997. (Orig. pub. 1985, New York: Alfred A. Knopf.)

Kirk, S. and W. J. Reid. 2002. *Science and Social Work.* New York: Columbia University Press.

Kline, W. 2001. *Building a Better Race: Gender, Sexuality, and Eugenics from the Turn of the Century to the Baby Boom.* Berkeley: University of California Press.

Kühl, S. 1994. *The Nazi Connection: Eugenics, American Racism, and German National Socialism.* New York: Oxford University Press.

Kunzel, R. G. 1993. *Fallen Women, Problem Girls: Unmarried Mothers and the Professionalization of Social Work, 1890–1945.* New Haven: Yale University Press.

Mink, G. 2001. Faith in government? *Social Justice* 28 (1): 5–10.

Myerson, A. 1917. Psychiatric family studies. *American Journal of Insanity* 73 (3): 355–486.

Nakashima, T. 1984. Social work and eugenics. Master's thesis, School of Social Work, California State University, Sacramento.

National Committee for Mental Hygiene. 1918a. *Mental Hygiene* 2 (3). New York: National Committee for Mental Hygiene.

———. 1918b. *Mental Hygiene* 2 (4). New York: National Committee for Mental Hygiene.

———. 1920. *Mental Hygiene* 4 (3). New York: National Committee for Mental Hygiene.

National Conference of Charities and Corrections (NCCC). 1877. *Proceedings on the Fourth Annual Conference of Charities and Corrections.* Boston: George H. Ellis Press.

———. 1879. *Proceedings on the Sixth Annual Conference of Charities and Corrections.* Boston: George H. Ellis Press.

———. 1899. *Proceedings on the Sixteenth Annual Conference of Charities and Corrections.* Boston: George H. Ellis Press. *National Cyclopedia of American Biography.* 1958. New York: James T. White. *New York Times.* 1934. Nazis issue rules of choices of wife. August 25. *New York Times on the Web.* 2001. National News Briefs: Virginia expresses regret for past sterilizations. Retrieved October 5, 2002, from nytimes.com.

Noakes, J. 1984. Nazism and Eugenics: The Background to the Nazi Sterilization Law of 14 July 1933. In R. J. Bullen, H. Pogge von Strandmann, and A. B. Polonsky, eds., *Ideas Into Politics: Aspects of European History, 1880–1950,* 75–94. Totowa, N.J.: Barnes and Noble Books.

Ordover, N. 2003. *American Eugenics: Race, Queer Anatomy, and the Science of Nationalism.* Minneapolis: University of Minnesota Press.

Platt, A .M. and J. L. Cooreman. 2001. A multicultural chronology of welfare policy and social work in the U.S. *Social Justice* 28 (1): 91–155.

Popenoe, P. 1934. The German sterilization law. *Journal of Heredity* 25 (7): 257–260.

Popenoe, P. and R. H. Johnson. 1926. *Applied Eugenics.* New York: Macmillan.

Popenoe, P. and E. M. Williams. 1934. Fecundity of families dependent on public charity. *American Journal of Sociology* 40 (2): 214–220.

Popple, P. R. and L. Leighninger. 1996. *Social Work, Social Welfare, and American Society.* Boston: Allyn and Bacon.

Quadagno, J. 1994. *The Color of Welfare: How Racism Undermined the War on Poverty.* New York: Oxford University Press.

Reilly, P. R. 1991. *The Surgical Solution.* Baltimore: Johns Hopkins University Press.

Reynolds, D. 2002. Oregon governor apologizes for eugenics "misdeeds." *Inclusion Daily Express.* December 2. Retrieved June 1, 2003, from http://www.inclusiondaily.com.

Richmond, M. 1917. *Social Diagnosis.* New York: Russell Sage Foundation.

———. 1922. *What Is Social Case Work? An Introductory Description.* New York: Russell Sage Foundation.

Schama, S. 2003. The unloved American. *New Yorker.* March 10.

Solinger, R. 1998. Dependency and choice: The two faces of Eve. *Social Justice* 25 (1): 1–27.

Special Report. 2002. Against their will: North Carolina's sterilization program. *Winston-Salem Journal.* December 8–12. Retrieved June 1, 2003, from http://www.against theirwill.journalnow.com.

Stadtman, V. 1967. *The Centennial Record of the University of California.* Berkeley: University of California Press.

Starr, K. 1985. *Inventing the Dream: California Through the Progressive Era.* New York: Oxford University Press.

Survey Associates. 1912–1913. *The Survey* 29. New York: Survey Associates.

———. 1915. *The Survey* 34. New York: Survey Associates.

———. 1917–1918. *The Survey* 38. New York: Survey Associates.

———. 1921–1922. *The Survey* 46. New York: Survey Associates.

———. 1922–1923. *The Survey* 49. New York: Survey Associates.

Torpy, S. J. 2000. Native American women and coerced sterilization: On the Trail of Tears in the 1970's. *American Indian Culture and Research Journal* 24 (2): 1–22.

Trattner, W. I. 1984. *From Poor Law to Welfare State: A History of Social Welfare in America.* New York: Free Press.

Trent, J. 1994. *Inventing the Feeble Mind: A History of Mental Retardation in the United States.* Berkeley: University of California Press.

Turner, H. B. 1964. The Waiting List and Dr. Butler. In J. Leiby, ed., Social Welfare Services in California 1925–1927: Historical Essays. Master's thesis, School of Social Welfare, University of California, Berkeley.

Walkowitz, D. J. 1990. The making of a feminine professional identity: Social workers in the 1920's. *American Historical Review* 95 (4): 1051–1075.

Wardell, W. R. 1944. Care of the feebleminded in California: Illustrated by the care given in three generations in a single family. Master's thesis, School of Social Welfare, University of California, Berkeley. *Washington Post.* 2002. Virginia apologizes for forced sterilizations. May 5.

Woodside, M. 1950. *Sterilization in North Carolina: A Sociological and Psychological Study.* Chapel Hill: University of North Carolina Press.

Zitner, A. 2003. The Nation: Davis' apology sheds no light on sterilizations in California. *Los Angeles Times.* March 16.

Chapter 9

Assertive Community Treatment (ACT): The Case Against the "Best Tested" Evidence-Based Community Treatment for Severe Mental Illness

Tomi Gomory

> We have now sunk to a depth where the restatement of the obvious is the first duty of intelligent men.
>
> —*George Orwell*

Introduction

The Shifting Psychiatric Landscape

The decades following World War II heralded a dramatic refocusing of psychiatric treatment for those who were severely emotionally disordered. The provision of care that had been offered to this very troubled and troubling population for most of America's earlier history was the community-based decision to confine them to suburban or rural asylums (later government-funded state hospitals) to avoid the toxic stress of community living (Grob 1994b; Rothman 1990). The approach was to "alienate" the patient, usually *forcibly,* from the "hubbub" of community life, which was deemed to be primarily responsible for their mental health problems in the first place, and allow respite and healing before reintegration: "Having caused the pain, it was incumbent on the community to help relieve it. . . . Here was an opportunity to meet the pressing needs of the insane, by isolating them from the dangers at loose in the community. . . . The product of this effort was the insane asylum" (Rothman 1990:129).

By the early decades of the twentieth century, however, various exposés of harmful and coercive institutional psychiatric practices were highlighting the problems of institutional care and undermining its optimistic early promise. Here is how one influential writer, the journalist Albert Deutsch, described a visit to a psychiatric ward in the late 1940s:

> Cots and beds were strewn all over the place to accommodate the 289 mental patients packed into wards intended for 126. Cots lined the corridors, with restless patients often strapped to them. (It appeared that about one-third of all patients . . . were under mechanical restraint that night—tied down to their beds by leather thongs, muffs or handcuffs linked to chains).
> (as quoted in Grob 1994b:204)

Although the actual condition of the nation's various state mental hospital systems was apparently improving by the 1950s, this improvement was ignored for the most part, and more attention was paid to expanding community focused care:

> Faith in the effectiveness of community programs and institutions was characteristic of the postwar years. Psychological and environmental explanations of normal and abnormal behavior strengthened the belief that early intervention could prevent the onset of serious mental illnesses and thus prevent hospitalization. . . . During the 1950s the rhetoric and enthusiasm for community-oriented programs far exceeded any specific achievements. . . . The concept of prevention and the belief in the superiority of community care and treatment found a receptive audience among political, professional, and lay audiences.
> (Grob 1994b:234–236)

These political, philosophical, and practical developments encouraged the increasing involvement of the federal government in mental health policy and supported the notion that fragmented state services could be mended only by comprehensive federal planning and funding. In addition to the evolving mental health conceptual landscape, the introduction in the 1950s of psychotropic drugs with great "scientific" promise of psychiatric symptom reduction (functionally understood as increasing socially appropriate behavior without the need for obvious coercive physical restraint) provided the justification for the idea of successful rapid community reintegration with the help of appropriate "community-based" treatment of thousands of institutionalized psychiatric patients. Not only was this seen as an attainable reality but, and more important, as a very significant moral and social good (Grob 1994b).

Deinstitutionalization, as this approach was named, for better or worse became the focus and the political agenda of those making mental health policy from the 1950s onward. As the historian Gerald Grob (1994a), noting this sea change, states:

> An enhanced social welfare role for the federal government not only began to diminish the authority of state governments, but also hastened the transition from an institution-based to a community-oriented policy. Throughout the postwar decades the rhetoric of community care and treatment . . . and, by implication, the obsolescence of mental hospitals shaped public debates and agendas. That many of the rhetorical claims had little basis in fact was all but ignored by professionals, public officials, and especially the larger public.
> (273)

The passage of the Mental Health Act of 1963 provided further impetus for the development and testing of community mental health treatment alternatives to hospital care. The act's hoped-for effect according to Dr. Robert Felix, the influential director of the National Institute of Mental Health (NIMH) at the time (Connery 1968), as stated in his U.S. Senate testimony in support of its passage, was to facilitate "the day when the State mental hospitals as we know them today would no longer exist" (51).

Assertive Community Treatment (ACT), originally called Training in Community Living (TCL), the community mental health intervention program for the severely mentally ill (SMI), was developed along with other community-based efforts during the late 1960s and early 1970s specifically to address the new federal mandate for shifting the locus of care to the community (for the "smorgasbord" of community services that were available at the time, see Mosher and Burti 1989). Psychiatrist Leonard Stein and social work professor Mary Ann Test (1985), two of the inventors of ACT (psychiatrist Arnold Marx was the other) acknowledge that this agenda was the explicit rationale for creating ACT when they ask and answer the question:

> Can chronically mentally ill persons be treated in the community? . . .
> This question has plagued policy makers, planners and clinicians since the deinstitutionalization movement began in the mid 1950s. . . . The late 1960s and the 1970s witnessed the birth of a number of model programs that provided community care and treatment. . . . These carefully researched programs demonstrated . . . that chronic patients

can be treated in the community . . . [and] community treatment is often more effective than hospital-based models of care. . . . Training in Community Living was designed . . . as an alternate to hospital treatment.
(1)

Their very first article reported treatment success:

The effectiveness of a new model, "total in-community treatment" [TCL] was evaluated on a group of patients considered still in need of hospital care. . . . Experimental patients, regardless of symptomatology, were discharged and treated "on the spot" in their neighborhoods. Results indicated that . . . these patients had attained more autonomous living and employment situations. . . . These results point to a successful alternative to institutional treatment.
(Marx, Test, and Stein 1973:505)

ACT's Current Status in Community Mental Health

As of June 2003 more than 360 scholarly articles in the PsycINFO database dealt with ACT. Thirty-four states were using ACT or an adaptation of it and consuming well in excess of $160 million in public tax dollars annually. The National Alliance for the Mentally Ill (NAMI), an organization made up of family members of psychiatric patients who believe that mental disorders are "brain diseases" and the inventors of ACT (both originating in Madison, Wisconsin), established a national nonprofit agency in 1996 (Allness and Knoedler 1998) with the following agenda:

Design and implement a means of rapid and effective replication of the PACT model of ACT;
    Promote a consensus among public mental health authorities, advocates, and service providers for adoption of national standards to set minimum criteria for ACT programs; and
    Influence state and local mental health authorities that have not already done so to adopt ACT as a core program within their service delivery system.
    To carry out the work of the NAMI/ACT Initiative, a new organization will be established, Programs of Assertive Community Treatment Incorporated (ACT, Inc.). ACT Inc. will be a private, nonprofit corporation with national focus and representation of consumers, family members, clinicians, administrators and *researchers dedicated to the dissemination of the ACT model as the gold standard of ACT.*
(*Community Support Network News* 1997:10, emphasis added)

ACT has been acclaimed as "a gold award program" (Test and Stein 1976:193), with "the strongest empirical support" of all community mental health treatments for the SMI population (Essock, Drake, and Burns 1998:176), on the basis of its "repeated and unequaled success in twenty-five years of confirming research" (Allness and Knoedler 1998:foreword). The Madison ACT model's "success" is well documented through the originators' published research (summarized in Stein and Test 1985). In addition, there is a rapidly expanding literature by ACT replicators and others who are attempting to formally institutionalize this treatment as a model of "evidence-based mental health treatment" (Phillips et al. 2001). The influential American Psychiatric Association journal *Psychiatric Services* dedicated itself in 2001 to promoting "evidence-based practice" in psychiatric treatment and published several articles arguing that ACT's effectiveness has been well established by the experimental evidence and should be deemed an "evidence-based" treatment. Most recently, this effort appears to be under federal auspices and supported by America's largest health care foundation:

> Despite . . . limitations, assertive community treatment has many proven benefits. . . . The purpose of this article is to familiarize mental health care providers with the principles of the [ACT] model and its implementation. The article is a prelude to the detailed guidelines and strategies that are being developed as an implementation "toolkit" in the Evidenced-Based Practices Project, an initiative funded by the Robert Wood Foundation and the Substance Abuse and Mental Health Services Administration.
> (Phillips et al. 2001:772)

ACT has been subjected to at least twenty-five randomized controlled trials (RCTs), which have been presented in numerous articles and literature reviews (e.g., Mueser et al. 1998), all agreeing with the claim reported in a special section focusing on ACT in the April 1998 issue of the *American Journal of Orthopsychiatry* that "since the deinstitutionalization era began nearly 50 years ago, several models of community-based care for persons with severe mental illnesses have been developed. Of these models, the assertive community treatment (ACT) program has by far the strongest empirical support" (Essock, Drake, and Burns 1998:176). Phillips et al. further argue:

> Research has shown that assertive community treatment is no more expensive than other types of community-based care and that it is more satisfactory to consumers. . . . Compared with other treatments under controlled conditions . . . assertive community treatment results in a

greater reduction in psychiatric hospitalization and higher level of housing stability.
(Phillips et al. 2001:778)

Researcher Robert Rosenheck and his team (Rosenheck et al. 1995; Rosenheck and Neale 1998) claim that their ten-site RCT, the largest ever done on ACT, "showed reduced hospital use, cost savings, greater consumer satisfaction, and, in the long term, less severe symptoms and better community functioning" (Rosenheck and Neale 2001:1395–1396).

The balance of this chapter will examine whether ACT does causally reduce hospitalization, or improve symptomatology, or provide other treatment benefits, when compared with alternate treatment, without any possible adverse effects, as claimed. First a brief description will be offered of the falsificationist analytic approach employed in the chapter to review the ACT research, then eight major claims concerning ACT research methodology and successful treatment outcomes will be examined. Each ACT claim will be stated and an analysis/discussion of the available scientific evidence will follow. The concluding section will sum up the analytic findings of the case against ACT effectiveness.

Analytic Approach Used in This Chapter

Two methods have generally been used in scientific inquiry and evaluation. One approach, used by ACT researchers, accumulates confirmatory scientific data about theories or interventions through "objective" observations. The more such confirmations are found, the better a theory or intervention is thought to be. The more "support" found, the higher the "reliability," providing more assurance about the efficacy of the theory or intervention in the future. The methodological effort in science to accumulate discrete data for the purpose of theory building or for seeking empirical proof or confirmation is called "induction." The "inductive method" has been rigorously critiqued by the evolutionary epistemology and accompanying methodology of "Critical Rationalism" (Popper 1962, 1979; Campbell 1987). Critical Rationalists (fallibilists) assert that induction is a false scientific method and recommend using another method, based on deductive logic. The criticism of the inductive method, put somewhat crudely but succinctly, argues three key points: (1) no "objective" observation is possible (all observations are filtered through fallible biological cognitive systems and are always socially contextual); (2) similar past events cannot logically predict similar future ones (the unknown future is underdetermined by the known past and may not resemble it); and (3) the summing of such past discrete events cannot be reliably and validly used for universal generalizations in the future (one future negative event logically destroys such generalization's "evidence-based" reliable universal standing, whether theoretical or pragmatic) (Munz 1993). Since it is logically impossible to provide absolute proof but logically possible to provide potential falsifying instances, the preferred approach involves the stringent testing of ideas and empirical solutions by means of a reiterative trial-and-error feedback process. It consists of rigorous efforts at falsification and subsequent elimination of falsified theories or interventions using critical debate, empirical testing, or skeptical reanalysis of research "findings," as done in the present chapter (for its application to clinical practice and research, see the four-article debate between Thyer and me and commentary by other social work academics [Gomory 2001a, 2001b, 2001c, 2002; Thyer 2001a, 2001b; Munro 2002; Drisko 2001]).

One further comment needs to be added about looking for and finding support in research. It is always very easy to find supportive evidence when using a preferred theory. Our psychological predisposition is to look for agreeable evidence about our theoretical favorites while ignoring evidence that undermines our preferences. This inclination is called *confirmatory bias* (Nickerson 1998). It behooves us, as rigorous researchers, to guard against confirmatory bias by making the methodological commitment to be constantly vigilant and to actively search for negative data—that is, experimental *dis*confirmation.

Analysis of ACT Claims

Claim 1

ACT research uses the very best measures and research methods for its evaluation studies:

> Research . . . has been a hallmark of ACT program development. . . . This body of research provides strong evidence of overall effectiveness for the service system. The . . . Madison-based ACT . . . set the gold standard. . . . to be used in subsequent studies; [including] the research instrument's measurement domains . . . and the research design–randomized clinical trials.
> (Stein and Santos 1998:30)

EVIDENCE
Instead of a rigorous "gold standard," we often find that highly problematic methodology is employed, which is then downplayed and censored in the

published literature contributing to ACT's "success." Olfson (1990b) in a draft report prepared for NIMH, identified several problems with ACT research methodology and the resultant findings:

> The clinical significance of the observed decrease in inpatient service utilization is difficult to assess. Restricting the clinical criteria for hospitalization is an explicit tenet of assertive community treatment. Under such conditions, reducing hospitalization becomes more of an independent . . . variable than an outcome variable. . . . Even when there are not systematic efforts to change admitting practices, hospitalization may not be a robust measure of clinical outcome. . . . Although several [ACT] studies have included rates of . . . medication compliance, no studies have provided quantitative evaluations of antipsychotic dosing. If higher doses of antipsychotic medication are required to maintain patients in community programs, then the added risk of tardive dyskinesia would become an important negative consequence of community care. . . . The validity of clinical ratings is highest when measurements are taken by well-trained raters who are blind to the treatment condition. Of the reviewed studies [only] Marx and colleagues used blind ratings. More commonly, researchers use independent but unblinded raters. Although logistical problems complicate preserving rater blindness . . . this goal has been accomplished in psychosocial research and should be strived for in future investigations of assertive community treatment. Occasionally clinical staff . . . has been used to conduct research interviews. . . . This practice opens bias favoring clinicians who are enthusiastic about . . . their work[;] it should be avoided in future studies.
> (C74–C80)

The article published by Olfson (1990a) on the basis of this internal report, however, avoids mentioning any of these critical problems, referring to them merely as "methodological issues of interest mostly to researchers" (640) and providing a very positive impression of ACT effectiveness in the scholarly literature despite the contradictory empirical evidence.

NIMH and all subsequent ACT research have uniformly ignored the original recommendations of Olfson. The well-known adverse effects of antipsychotic medications (Gelman 1999) are not addressed in any of the studies, although almost 50% of ACT client-contact time is spent dispensing and managing psychotropic medication.[1] No ACT studies have used blinded evaluators since the Marx, Test, and Stein (1973) study mentioned by Olfson (Gomory 1998). Additionally, only one ACT study has included a no-treatment control group (Solomon and Draine 1995a, 1995b). Findings from comparison group studies indicate only if one treatment is superior to another. A no-treatment control group is required to evaluate whether the experimental treatment is better than no treatment at all, which is an important question in evaluation research. The usual rationale for excluding a no-treatment group in psychosocial experimental research is the assumed unethical nature of withholding "effective" treatments from ill clients. But this ethical problem arises only if the treatment withheld is known to be "effective." A trial is conducted precisely because we do not know if the experimental treatment is effective. No experimental treatment can be assumed to be effective a priori; it could turn out to be helpful, ineffective, or even harmful. In fact, placebo (pharmaceutical no-treatment) controlled research for the Federal Drug Administration is mandatory for gaining federal approval of all drugs, even those for mental disorders (antidepressants for depression, for example) (see Kirsch et al. 2002).

Another serious methodological issue is the frequent use of unreliable or poorly validated research measures in ACT research. For instance, I (Gomory 1998) reviewed the use of the Short Clinical Rating Scale in the single Madison ACT study (Stein and Test 1980) that claimed symptom improvement for the intervention and found the overall average "intraclass" correlations of that thirteen-item scale to be a troubling .59, ranging from .34 for hallucinations to .76 for thought disorder (Gomory 1998:135–140). Additionally, the Cochrane Collaboration's comprehensive ACT review noted:

> A striking and unexpected finding . . . was the extent to which inadequately validated instruments were used to measure outcome. Of particular interest was the fact that data that failed to meet quality criteria was four times more likely to show a significant difference between treatment and control. This finding suggests that there may be as yet some uncharted bias related to the use of outcome scales in psychiatry. (Marshall and Lockwood 1998:14)

Finally, outcome variables, some statistically significant and others nonsignificant, appear to be inappropriately combined to give erroneous impressions of ACT effectiveness where none was actually achieved. In a fourteen-year longitudinal study, the longest study ever implemented on ACT (Test et al. 1991), the researchers state: "Analysis of data from the first seven years of this investigation has been completed. To date the ACT intervention group demonstrated relative to the control group . . . less time in a *combination* of hospitals, skilled nursing facilities, penal settings, and conditions of homelessness" (Allness and Knoedler 1998:5, emphasis added). The authors assert that the patients in the experimental group did significantly better in a "combined" category (time spent in hospitals/skilled nursing homes plus penal settings plus homelessness) than the control group over the whole experimental period (Allness and Knoedler 1998:5). This "combined" variable suggests that the experimental program not only reduces time spent hospitalized and in skilled nursing homes (these settings are considered to be the same by the researchers [Test et al. 1991:243]) but also significantly reduces, independent of this result, the amount of time spent in homelessness and, independent of either of the other components, time spent in penal settings. These are exactly the outcomes we would want such programs to impact.

The Madison ACT inventors reported this combined variable for the first time in 1994, some sixteen years after the inception of the long-term study in 1978. They introduced it in a paper presented at the 1994 annual meeting of the American Psychiatric Association (Test et al. 1994). Their previously published articles on this long-term study analyzed each of these variables separately, as was also done in their earlier studies (i.e., Stein, Test, and Marx 1975). The "summing" of the three independent variables yielded statistically significant measurements favoring the experimental group at certain measurement periods. What this combining of previously discretely measured variables camouflages is that the only significant difference between the experimental and control groups among these "component variables" was on the variable "time hospitalized/time in skilled nursing homes." Neither the "homelessness" nor the "penal settings" variable was statistically significant between experimental and control treatment for the first two years of the study, so any claimed statistical significance for the combined variable had to have been driven by the statistically significant difference found for the "time in hospital/nursing home" component. The only way one could have known this was by reviewing an earlier article (Test et al. 1991), which gave the two-year results of the long-term study but did not mention any "combined" variable. Subjects in the experimental group spent significantly ($p =$ .001) less mean time, from study entry through twenty-four months, in hospital/skilled nursing home settings than did those in the control group (Test et al. 1991:243). But when it came to the two-year findings on homelessness and penal settings, which constitute two thirds of the currently "combined" variable, the researchers state: "We also studied time spent in jail or other penal settings and in homelessness or homeless shelters. Throughout the first 2 years the time that patients in both groups spent in these settings was small and did *not differ significantly between the groups*" (Test et al. 1991:244, emphasis added). Although the unpublished paper introducing this new "combined" variable is cited in the publication *The ACT Model of Community-Based Treatment for Persons with Severe and Persistent Mental Illness: A Manual for ACT Start-up* (Allness and Knoedler 1998) and elsewhere to support the claim that ACT is an effective long-term treatment, I was refused permission by

Dr. Test, the principal investigator of the long-term ACT study, to quote or use the seven-year data directly from the 1994 paper. It is clear, however, from my unpublished review of that paper that neither homeless conditions nor penal settings differ significantly between the two groups, not only for the first two years but for the balance of the seven years as well. It is difficult to see why this combined variable was created so late in the analysis of the long-term study other than to suggest that there was a program effect, in reducing homelessness and jail time, when none in fact existed. Because I was denied permission to quote the unpublished text directly, we will have to await the ACT inventors' long-promised data and results on clinical and psychosocial outcomes for full clarification. Drs. Test and Stein admitted in a recent response to my published criticism of the lack of published data available for critical review twenty-four years after beginning the long-term ACT study (Gomory 2001b) that

> Dr. Gomory . . . accurately notes that we have not yet published data on psychosocial outcomes from a long-term study of assertive community treatment whose early (two-year) findings on hospitalization were reported in 1991. . . . Data analyses and writing are now our primary focus, and readers can be assured that all dimensions of the findings will be published as soon as this work is completed.
> (Test and Stein 2001:1396)

Three years later we are still waiting for these published results.

Claim 2

The assertive community treatment approach never was, and is not now, based on coercion (Test and Stein 2001:1396).

EVIDENCE

One of the primary rationales for shifting from psychiatric institutional care to community care was the recognition that better social functioning required less coercion and more autonomous behavior (Marx, Test, and Stein 1973). Another was the desire to reduce the harmful effects of institutional living. Coercion as "treatment" is rarely used in physiological medicine (to prevent the spread of highly infectious disease, for example) but is routinely used in psychiatric medicine (to force highly toxic antipsychotics on resistant schizophrenics, for example). To be considered ethically justified, such coercive treatment must benefit the recipient, and even those psychiatric professionals who believe it useful see it as the treatment of last resort (Dennis and Monahan 1996). Does ACT offer autonomy and coercion-free treatment to its clients? What does the ACT program look like in practice? Stein (1990) explains:

> The ACCT [the team] serves as a fixed point of responsibility . . . and is concerned with *all* aspects of . . . the patients' lives that influence their functioning, including psychological health, physical health, living situation, finances, socialization, vocational activities, and recreational activities. The team sets no time limits for their involvement with patients, is assertive in keeping patients involved. . . . In addition to the day to day work . . . the team is available 24 hours a day, seven days a week.
> (650, emphasis added)

This methodology appears to be highly intrusive. ACT activities may include such coercive moves as becoming the representative "financial payee" of the client, providing opportunities to blackmail the clients by enforcing medication compliance or threatening to withhold monies that belong to the client (Stein and Test 1985:88–89). Forcing treatment on ACT clients who do not want it is also routinely done (91–92). Even bribery may be appropriate ACT treatment: "It might be necessary to pay a socially withdrawn patient for going to the movies in addition to buying his ticket" (Test and Stein 1976:78).

To validate the use of assertive[2] outreach and treatment, the original ACT researchers rely on two studies, one of which is their own (Test 1981:80). The other is by Beard, Malamud, and Rossman (1978), who describe their Fountain House outreach program as follows: "Phone calls, letters, and home and hospital visits made by both staff and members. Through such contacts, subjects who dropped out were provided with further information. . . . *In those . . . instances when an individual requested that no further contacts be made, his wishes, of course, were respected*" (624, emphasis added). Respect for the wishes of people who choose not to be involved in the Fountain House program contrasts with the coercive methods used by Test and Stein (1976):

> A staff person attempting to assist an ambivalent patient to a sheltered workshop in the morning is likely to receive a verbal and behavioral "no." . . . If . . . the staff member approaches the patient with a firm, "It's time for you to go to work; I'll wait here while you get dressed," the likelihood of compliance increases. The latter method allows less room for the patient to "choose" passivity.
> (77)

Two questions come to mind. First, why is the patient described as ambivalent, when the patient's reported behavior indicates a resolute opposition to going to work? Second, why is the patient's active refusal redefined as "passivity"? The disregard of patients' expressed wishes and the reinterpretation of their behavior to justify programmatic interventions appear to be the outstanding characteristics of ACT. The Fountain House model, by contrast, immediately discontinues client outreach efforts if asked to do so. This difference leaves the ACT experts with nothing except their own self-validating research to support the particular assertive approach that they advocate.

Coercion appears to be a vital part of the ACT model, according to the candid admission of Diamond (1996), a close associate of the original ACT group in Madison:

> Paternalism has been a part of assertive community treatment from its very beginning. . . . In the early stages of ACT, consumer empowerment was not a serious consideration. . . . It was designed to "do" for the client what the client could not do for himself or herself. Staff were assumed to know what the client "needed." Even the goal of getting clients paid employment was a staff-driven value that was at times at odds with the client's own preferences. Current assertive treatment programs continue to be influenced by traditions . . . from this . . . history. Paternalism continues to be reinforced by mandates from the community to "control" the behavior of otherwise disruptive clients. . . . A significant number of clients in community support programs . . . have been assigned a financial payee. . . . This kind of coercion can be extremely effective. . . . Obtaining spending money can be made . . . dependent on participating in other parts of treatment. A client can then be pressured by staff to take prescribed medication. . . . The pressure to take medication . . . can be enormous. . . . While control of housing and control of money are the most common . . . methods of coercion in the community other kinds of control are also possible. This pressure can be almost as coercive as the hospital but with fewer safeguards.
> (53–58)

Finally, I (Gomory 2002) have reviewed the early professional history of the ACT inventors that helps conceptualize the program's present deep ethical and scientific difficulties. Using their published works, I analyzed and documented both their condescending, paternalistic attitude toward mental health clients and their use of highly coercive methods to conduct "scientific" research that they claimed was based on behavioral principles but that actually contradicted the explicit findings of the then current behavioral research literature. To be considered ethically justified, coercive treatment should be seen as benefiting the recipient of that treatment. Let's review the outcome claims of ACT next.

Claim 3

ACT significantly reduces hospitalization when compared to standard treatment. (This claim has been primarily responsible for the enthusiastic response to ACT, and it is the only consistent outcome found across all studies.)

EVIDENCE

ACT methods have no direct bearing on the reduced hospital stays found in the studies. This result is obtained because of a fairly strict administrative rule not to admit or readmit any ACT clients for hospitalization, regardless of the psychiatric symptoms, and to carry out all treatment in the community, while at the same time freely readmitting any troubled client in the comparison group. The ACT originators make this explicit in their first experimental trial, where they list "virtual abstention from rehospitalizing any patients being managed in the community" (Marx, Test, and Stein 1973:506) as their second treatment guideline. Similarly, in one of the acclaimed Australian ACT replications, "the project group patients were not admitted if this could be avoided: instead they were seen by members of the project team . . . who took them back to the community" (Hoult et al. 1983:161). No effort was made to keep the control group from readmission, and 96% were readmitted (160). In sum, any decrease in hospitalization is not intervention-dependent; it results from an administrative rule.

The ACT inventors realized, even in 1978, that time spent in inpatient settings was not a persuasive measure of outcome success for a mental health intervention: "[ACT] treatment results in less time spent in the hospital. This finding is certainly not surprising since experimental patients were usually not admitted . . . initially and there were subsequent concentrated efforts to keep them out" (Test and Stein 1978:353–354)

Claim 4

ACT is more cost-effective than standard interventions.

EVIDENCE

Since hospitalization is by far the more costly treatment, the cost savings are dependent not on specific ACT interventions but on keeping people away from hospitals. Cost reduction occurs as a by-product of the ACT approach; it could occur with any other treatment that rigorously pursued the same objective of not admitting patients to hospitals.

Claim 5

ACT provides significantly greater client satisfaction.

EVIDENCE

Client satisfaction appears to be independent of distinct ACT activity. For example, in the Australian study previously mentioned, the claim of client satisfaction favoring the ACT methods is contradicted by the data. It appears that the greater autonomy provided by any community treatment is what causes this increased satisfaction, not the particular interventions of ACT. In the Australian study the patients were surveyed at a twelve-month follow-up: "The majority (80%) of experimental group patients who were not ad-mitted to the hospital were pleased and grateful about it; only 30% of control group patients were pleased and grateful about being admitted to hospital, whereas 39% were upset and angry" (Hoult 1986:142). Stated differently, "Treatment preference was explored by asking *all* patients whether they pre-fer admission to Macquarie Hospital or treatment at home by a community team. The majority of the project (87%) and control (61%) patients preferred community treatment" (Hoult et al. 1983:163, emphasis added). A majority (61%) of the group that did not experience the ACT treatment still preferred community treatment rather than admittance to an institution. In fact, the experimental group reported that the most important elements of the ACT treatment were the availability of staff for frequent caring; supportive, per-sonal contact; and the enhanced freedom—therapeutic elements that were not specific to ACT (Hoult et al. 1983:163).

Lending further support, a survey of "client perspectives" on ACT "in-gredients" (McGrew, Wilson, and Bond 1996) identified, in order of pref-erence, "helping relationship, attributes of therapist, availability of staff, and non-specific assistance" as what clients liked most (16, table 1). Again, these attributes are not specific to ACT but are applicable to all forms of "helping." The least liked of the twenty-five elements associated with ACT treatment was "intensity of service," the component that was most representative of ACT's philosophy. The survey's authors, themselves longtime ACT experts, admit, "Somewhat surprisingly, non-specific features of the helping rela-tionship emerged as the aspects of [ACT] most frequently mentioned as helpful" (McGrew, Wilson, and Bond 1996:190).

Claim 6

ACT significantly improves symptomatology and client functioning. "Our study showed . . . in the long term, less severe symptoms and better com-munity functioning" (Rosenheck and Neale 2001:1395–1396).

EVIDENCE

ACT specific treatment does not achieve significantly superior client functional or symptomatological improvement over an alternate treatment. This can best be explained by briefly reviewing the largest controlled trial ($N = 873$) done on ACT (Rosenheck and Neale 1997, 1998). Rosenheck and Neale's quote is misleading. The study actually claimed to find this outcome at only one of the two types of settings where ACT was tested. Only "at the 6 General Medical and Surgical Hospital sites (GMS) ($n = 528$) [was] ACT associated with greater improvement in long-term (2-year) clinical outcomes." At the four neuropsychiatric hospital sites ($N = 345$) ACT did not differ from the standard treatment on clinical outcomes (Rosenheck and Neale 1998:459).

One problem here is that the claim of clinical effectiveness at the GMS sites suffers from methodological difficulties. It rests in part on finding significantly higher community living skills favoring ACT patients in the four follow-up periods, while finding only at "the final interview" significantly lower symptoms, higher functioning, and increased satisfaction with services (459). The "finding" of significantly higher community living skills across treatment periods favoring the ACT group is belied by the data. At six and twelve months the "community living skills competence" scores favor the control treatment. The control group outperformed the experimental group for well over twelve months, but an impressive difference favors the experimental treatment at the exit interview (Rosenheck and Neale 1998:463, table 2, and Rosenheck and Neale 1997, figure 3). The seemingly positive result in the exit interview could have been caused by many factors, including (1) relief at being free of a coercive program, (2) fear of offending a potentially dangerous authority in a coercive program, or (3) a desire to please the interviewer. An expensive, long-term, and potentially abusive program should not be justified on the basis of an exit interview that contradicts data gathered during the treatment period.

Another issue has to do with unintended research results. The researchers identified, post facto, two GMS study sites (nos. 2 and 5) that did not fully implement the ACT treatment: site 2 provided substantially fewer community-based services and underperformed in most ACT categories when evaluated for program fidelity (Rosenheck and Neale 1997:11), and site 5 "developed a low-intensity patient tracking program rather than [ACT] services" (Rosenheck 1995:134). Attempting to show that the increased costs of ACT were the result of these two sites' *ineffective* ACT implementation, the researchers decided to reanalyze the data with these two sites excluded. They thus eliminated 34% of the original sample. This decision proved fruitful because the statistically significant difference found during the original analysis of costs was reduced to a non-significant difference (Rosenheck and

Neale 1998:463). More to the point, eliminating these two sites created an unintended experimental situation to reanalyze clinical outcomes.

If the dropped programs were less or completely *ineffective,* the reanalyzed clinical outcome measures of those sites *effectively* implementing ACT should have increased the statistically significant impact of ACT originally found. However, after "excluding the 2 general medical and surgical sites that did not . . . implement the [ACT] program . . . clinical outcome results did not change" (Rosenheck and Neale 1998:463). In other words, with more than a third of the original sample removed, about half of whom were essentially in a no-treatment group, no change occurred in "the clinical outcome data." Being or not being in ACT made no difference to clinical outcome. Dr. Rosenheck confirmed that in the original analysis the clinical results of the two excluded sites were in the same direction and with similar significance as the results found at the other sites (personal communication, October 1997).

Claim 7

Occasionally, positive significant vocational effects are observed as a result of ACT (Marx, Test, and Stein 1973; Stein and Test 1980).

EVIDENCE
There are three ACT studies that report positive effects on vocational outcomes and five that do not. Two of the ones that found a positive effect were conducted by the Madison group (Marx, Test, and Stein 1973; Stein and Test 1980). However, their long-term RCT building on these earlier suggestive studies found that ACT needs an "intensive vocational component" (Mueser et al. 1998:56) to show any effect. The only other study with positive findings (Chandler et al. 1996) corroborated the need for intense additional vocational efforts in such programs if they are to achieve positive vocational effects. ACT, like other mental health interventions, cannot significantly affect employment alone.

Claim 8

ACT has no negative effects. "The ACT literature has been very consistent in suggesting the absence of negative outcomes" (Bond et al. 2001:149).

EVIDENCE
Solomon and Draine found one of two key negative effects. The study, part of a larger randomized controlled trial of two hundred homeless SMIs leaving an urban jail system (Solomon and Draine 1995b), aimed to test the effec-

tiveness of ACT as compared to individual case management and to a no-intervention control group. Solomon and Draine (1995a) noticed a high recidivism rate (56%) among the ACT group, compared to 22% among case-managed individuals and 36% among the controls (168). The researchers subsequently compared twenty-two clients in the ACT to twenty-nine clients in individual case management in order to explain this unexpected finding. The significant findings of this second study were that clients of case managers who sought legal stipulations were more likely to return to jail, case managers were more likely to initiate a violation of probation process as an intervention strategy with clients for whom they sought legal stipulations, and these clients returned to jail faster (170). ACT case managers primarily pursued these activities. Because of ACT's highly intrusive methods, ACT clients were more likely to have their activities observed than clients in the other two control alternatives, resulting in their return to penal institutions more frequently (172). Solomon and Draine (1995a) note: "These findings raise provocative questions regarding the possibility of deleterious consequences of intensive case management services for seriously mentally ill people" (171). They also note the difficulties inherent in using coercion as treatment, as is done in ACT: "Coercive case management may defeat the goal of increased independence and is antithetical to the general principle of client self-determination . . . [and] is antithetical to both social work and community support system values of self-determination and client choice" (171–172).

In addition, Solomon and Draine (1995b) found no differences among the three treatment groups in any domain. This result argues strongly for the use of no-treatment control groups in every ACT trial to determine whether ACT is even superior to minimum or no treatment.

A second negative effect, possibly related to the coercive elements of ACT, is the increased incidence of suicide in ACT settings. Cohen, Test, and Brown (1990:603) report one possible and eight clear-cut suicides among the subjects of the long-term study conducted by the Madison ACT team of Test, Knoedler, Allness, and Burke (Test et al. 1985). There may have been one additional suicide in this study. Test et al. (1985) report that after three months of participation, the subjects in the study were given the structured interview from which the baseline data were obtained. Reporting on clients who were excluded from this interview, they state: "It was not possible to interview five subjects: one committed suicide during the first three months" (854). Since Cohen, Test, and Brown (1990) reported only the data collected on those suicides that were given at least one structured interview; they may have left out the one suicide that occurred in the first three months.

Another study, by Hoult et al. (1983), reports that "during the eight months after presenting at Macquire Hospital 10% of the project but none of the control patients were reported by relatives as having attempted suicide. These were . . . project patients, who prior to and during the study period made repeated suicide attempts" (165).

Another replication study (Marks et al. 1994) reports: "In the cohort of 189 patients, five died of self-harm in the 20 month study (three [ACT], two control). As with SMI suicides in Madison [Test and Stein's study] such deaths were unexpected and occurred despite recent contact with staff" (187). While the result does not directly implicate ACT as a cause of suicidal behavior, it suggests that ACT was unable to prevent these suicides. The study's authors spend considerable article space attempting to demonstrate that the ACT treatment was carefully and comprehensively provided to these patients. The ACT experts judged several ACT patients to have been improved immediately before they committed suicide. This account illustrates the problems with psychiatric evaluations. Psychiatry cannot reliably identify who will commit suicide, nor can it prevent suicides (Gomory 1997).

Research is needed to explore the possible harmful coercive elements in assertive treatment that may contribute to both suicidal behavior and completed suicides. We should question the scientific validity and professional ethics of using any coercive methods in working with such vulnerable patients (Gomory 1997). Marks et al. report that the ACT patients had very close attention paid to them by the assertive treatment team: "The . . . three [ACT] suicidal patients had had unusually persistent care" (Marks et al. 1994:187). Can such coercive scrutiny be countertherapeutic?

Conclusion

Although ACT is packaged by institutional psychiatry and its various promoters as a discrete, well-tested, "evidence-based" modality of effective treatment, after examining some of its developmental history and the controlled experimental research, I found little support for that claim, finding instead that ACT is extremely paternalistic and has possible harmful effects. Why ACT remains aggressively marketed may be explained by the failure of institutional and biopsychiatric treatment efforts in general (Breggin 1997; Fisher and Greenberg 1997; Valenstein 1998). It is also consistent with current trends to resort to increasingly coercive approaches. As Mosher and Burti (1989) note in their comprehensive review of community mental health programs, "the major problem [with ACT is] the level of paternalism, the 'doing to' activity it generates. . . . Medication is . . . the mainstay of the treatment. . . . In this system you can be cased managed to death, but no one is likely to sit down and spend . . . time discussing your experiences, thoughts, feelings and reactions" (344–345).

The paradigm of mental illness as medical/brain disease organizes and restricts the vast majority of potential research into helping interventions for seriously troubled persons to the biomedical model, the one model asserted to be "scientific" by institutional psychiatry and its powerful political lobbies (i.e., the American Psychiatric Association, NAMI, the pharmaceutical industry), despite the scarcity of well-tested evidence for this explanation of "mental disorderliness." The surgeon general's recent mental health report (U.S. Department of Health and Human Services 1999) confirms the conjectural nature of claims about the biological basis of "mental disorderliness": "There is no definitive lesion, laboratory test, or abnormality in brain tissue that can identify [mental] illness" (44).

NIMH's annual budget of more than one billion dollars sends a powerful signal. Researchers must attempt to find solutions that support and justify mental illness as medical/brain disorder if they expect to be funded. The ACT model, paradoxically, fully embraces this paradigm. As one ACT originator, Leonard Stein, along with his coauthor, freely admits: "Congruent with our conceptual model, we tell our patients that indeed we believe they are [medically] ill, otherwise we would not be prescribing medication for them" (Stein and Diamond 1985). ACT's misinterpreted early results appeared to demonstrate treatment success (Gomory 1998). By not examining critically the outcome claims of these early studies, which often used unreliable psychiatric measures and instruments, but instead accepting the tautological arguments of the Madison ACT group (for example, for reduced hospital stays) and relying on them for "support," the newer research "replications," not unexpectedly, confirmed ACT's "success." Once research careers are established around specific, well-entrenched treatment paradigms supported by politically savvy constituencies and are anointed as "evidence-based," the need for self-justification rarely allows self-critical admissions of error. Instead, contradictory evidence is ignored, leading to ever more problematic results (Popper 1962). ACT—a long-term, expensive, coercive, and potentially unethical program—continues to be promoted as "evidence-based" despite research results that negate ACT claims of effectiveness.

Notes

1. Descriptions of PACT (Programs of Assertive Community Treatment) technology are vague. The voluminous writings of the PACT inventors do not include a single detailed case example of the methodology at work. In a "case example," Stein and Test describe the first meeting with a client thus: "It was soon evident that John was in the midst of a schizophrenic episode, but was not immediately suicidal"

(1978:50). How this was assessed or what interventions helped in John's dramatic clinical improvement "within a week" is not provided (51). Test (1992) offers the following methodological description for "Direct Assistance with Symptom Management": "Specific interventions employed . . . include medication . . . 24-hour crisis availability, and occasional brief hospitalization. Additionally, we provide each patient with a long-term one-to-one relationship aimed at problem solving, at assisting them to learn about their illness, and at enhancing their own coping strategies for dealing with serious symptoms" (157). PACT spends 21.4% of its contacts medicating patients, the second-highest percentage of worker contacts. One-to-one support, largely spent convincing the clients that they are mentally ill and in need of psychotropic medication, is the highest (24.9%). Taking these two figures together, it appears that PACT is spending 46.3% of total client contacts dispensing psychotropic medications and related management, compared with 10.9% on vocational issues, 2.5% on their living situation, 0.2% on physical health, 12.1% on social recreation, 11.3% on psychotherapy/case monitoring, and 9.2% on activities of daily living (Brekke and Test 1992:240).

2. Behavior described as "assertive," as normatively used in the behavioral assertion training literature, is defined as "effective social influence skills that are acquired through learning" (Gambrill 1995). And, as opposed to the coercive PACT approach, "fundamental to the concept of assertion is a concern with basic human rights" (82). Assertive and aggressive behaviors are carefully distinguished by both their form and their effect (85). PACT theorists do not differentiate "assertive" behavior from "aggressive" behavior, which appear to be interchangeable in PACT (Dennis and Monahan 1996:3).

References

Allness, D. J. and W. H. Knoedler. 1998. *The ACT Model of Community-Based Treatment for Persons with Severe and Persistent Mental Illness: A Manual for ACT Startup*. Arlington, Va.: National Alliance for the Mentally Ill.

Beard, J. H., T. J. Malamud, and E. Rossman. 1978. Psychiatric rehabilitation and long-term rehospitalization rates: The findings of two research studies. *Schizophrenia Bulletin* 4 (4): 622–635.

Bond, G. R., R. E. Drake, K. T. Mueser, and E. Latimer. 2001. Assertive community treatment for people with severe mental illness: Critical ingredients and impact on consumers. *Disease Management and Health Outcomes* 9:141–159.

Breggin, P. R. 1997. *Brain-Disabling Treatments in Psychiatry: Drugs, Electroshock, and the Role of the FDA*. New York: Springer.

Brekke, J. S. and M. A. Test. 1992. A model for measuring the implementation of community support programs: Results from three sites. *Community Mental Health Journal* 28:227–247.

Campbell, D. T. 1987. Evolutionary Epistemology. In G. Radnitzky and W. W. Bartley III, eds., *Evolutionary Epistemology, Rationality, and the Sociology of Knowledge*, 47–89. LaSalle, Ill.: Open Court.

Chandler, D., J. Meisler, N. McGowen, and J. Minz. 1996. Client outcomes in two model capitated integrated service agencies. *Psychiatric Services* 47:175–180.

Cohen, L. J., M. A. Test, and R. L. Brown. 1990. Suicide and schizophrenia: Data from a prospective community treatment study. *American Journal of Psychiatry* 147:602–607. *Community Support Network News (CSNN)*. 1997. 11 (4).

Connery, R. H. 1968. *The Politics of Mental Health*. New York: Columbia University Press.

Dennis, D. L. and J. Monahan. 1996. Introduction to D. L. Dennis and J. Monahan, eds., *Coercion and Aggressive Community Treatment*, 1–9. New York: Plenum.

———, eds. 1996. *Coercion and Aggressive Community Treatment*. New York: Plenum.

Diamond, R. J. 1996. Coercion and tenacious treatment in the community. In D. L. Dennis and J. Monahan, eds., *Coercion and Aggressive Community Treatment*, 51–72. New York: Plenum.

Drisko, J. W. 2001. The role of theory in social work research. *Journal of Social Work Education* 37 (3): 585–586.

Essock, S. M., R. E. Drake, and B. J. Burns. 1998 A research network to evaluate assertive community treatment: Introduction. *American Journal of Orthopsychiatry* 68 (2): 176–178.

Fisher, S. and R. P. Greenberg, eds. 1997. *From Placebo to Panacea: Putting Psychiatric Drugs to the Test*. New York: John Wiley.

Gambrill, E. 1995. Assertion Skills Training. In W. O'Donohue and L. Krasner, eds., *Handbook of Psychological Skills Training: Clinical Techniques and Applications*, 81–118. Boston: Allyn and Bacon.

Gelman, S. 1999. *Medicating Schizophrenia: A History*. New Brunswick, N.J.: Rutgers University Press.

Gomory, T. 1997. Does the goal of preventing suicide justify placing suicidal clients in care? No. In E. Gambrill and R. Pruger, eds., *Controversial Issues in Social Work Ethics, Values, and Obligations*, 63–75. Boston: Allyn and Bacon.

———. 1998. Coercion justified? Evaluating the training in community living model: A conceptual and empirical critique. Ph.D. diss., University of California, Berkeley.

———. 2001a. Critical rationalism (Gomory's blurry theory) or positivism (Thyer's theoretical myopia): Which is the prescription for social work research? *Journal of Social Work Education* 37 (1): 67–78.

———. 2001b. A critique of the effectiveness of assertive community treatment. *Psychiatric Services* 52 (10): 1394.

———. 2001c. A fallibilistic response to Thyer's theory of theory-free empirical research in social work practice. *Journal of Social Work Education* 37 (1): 26–50.

———. 2002. The origins of coercion in assertive community treatment: A review of early publications from the special treatment unit of Mendota State Hospital. *Ethical Human Sciences and Services* 4 (1): 3–16.

Grob, G. N. 1994a. The History of the Asylum Revisited: Personal Reflections. In M. S. Micale and R. Porter, eds., *Discovering the History of Psychiatry*, 260–281. New York: Oxford University Press.

———. 1994b. *The Mad Among Us: A History of the Care of America's Mentally Ill*. New York: Free Press.

Hoult, J. 1986. Community care of the acutely mentally ill. *British Journal of Psychiatry* 149:137–144.

Hoult, J., I. Reynolds, M. Charbonneau-Powis, P. Weekes, and J. Briggs. 1983. Psychiatric hospital versus community treatment: The result of a randomized trial. *Australian and New Zealand Journal of Psychiatry* 17:160–167.

Kirsch, I., T. J. Moore, A. Scoboria, and S. S. Nicholls. 2002. The emperor's new drugs: An analysis of antidepressant medication data submitted to the U.S. Food and Drug Administration. *Prevention and Treatment* 5. Retrieved January 12, 2003, from http://journals.apa.org/prevention/volume5/pre0050023a.html.

Marks, I. M., J. Connolly, M. Muijen, B. Audini, G. McNamee, and R. E. Lawrence. 1994. Home-based versus hospital-based care for people with serious mental illness. *British Journal of Psychiatry* 165:179–194.

Marshall, M. and A. Lockwood. 1998. Assertive community treatment for people with severe mental disorders. *Cochrane Library* 2:1–30.

Marx, A. J., M. A. Test, and L. I. Stein. 1973. Extrohospital management of severe mental illness. *Archives of General Psychiatry* 29:505–511.

McGrew, J. H., R. G. Wilson, and G. R. Bond. 1996. Client perspectives on helpful ingredients of assertive community treatment. *Psychiatric Rehabilitation Journal* 19:13–21.

Mosher, L. R. and L. Burti. 1989. *Community Mental Health.* New York: Norton.

Mueser, K. T., G. R. Bond, R. E. Drake, and S. G. Resnick. 1998. Models of community care for severe mental illness: A review of research on case management. *Schizophrenia Bulletin* 24:37–74.

Munro, E. 2002. The role of theory in social work research: A further contribution to the debate. *Journal of Social Work Education* 38 (3): 461–470.

Munz, P. 1993. *Philosophical Darwinism: On the Origin of Knowledge by Means of Natural Selection.* London: Routledge.

Nickerson, R. S. 1998. Confirmation bias: A ubiquitous phenomenon in many guises. *Review of General Psychology* 2 (2): 175–220.

Olfson, M. 1990a. Assertive community treatment: An evaluation of the experimental evidence. *Hospital and Community Psychiatry* 41 (6): 634–647.

———. 1990b. "The Efficacy of Assertive Community Treatment for the Severely Mentally Ill." Draft paper prepared for the Research Resources Panel National Plan of Research to Improve Care for Severe Mental Disorders, National Institute of Mental Health, appendix 2.

Phillips, S. D., B. J. Burns, E. R. Edgar et al. 2001. Moving assertive community treatment into standard practice. *Psychiatric Services* 52:771–779.

Popper, K. R. 1962. *Conjectures and Refutations: The Growth of Scientific Knowledge.* New York: Basic Books.

———. 1979. *Objective Knowledge.* London: Oxford University Press.

Rosenheck, R. A. and M. S. Neale. 1997. "A Multi-Site Cost-Effectiveness Study of Intensive Psychiatric Community Care." Manuscript submitted for publication.

———. 1998. Cost-effectiveness of intensive psychiatric community care for high users of inpatient services. *Archives of General Psychiatry* 55:459–466.

———. 2001. A critique of the effectiveness of assertive community treatment: In reply. *Psychiatric Services* 52 (10): 1395–1396.

Rosenheck, R. A., M. S. Neale, P. Leaf, R. Milstein, and L. Frisman. 1995. Multisite experimental cost study of intensive psychiatric community care. *Schizophrenia Bulletin* 21:129–140.

Rothman, D. J. 1990. *The Discovery of the Asylum: Social Order and Disorder in the New Republic*. Boston: Little, Brown.

Solomon, P. and J. Draine. 1995a. Jail recidivism in a forensic case management program. *Health and Social Work* 20: 167–172.

———. 1995b. One-year outcomes of a randomized trial of case management with seriously mentally ill clients leaving jail. *Evaluation Review* 19: 256–273.

Stein, L. I. 1990. Comments by Leonard Stein. *Hospital and Community Psychiatry* 41:649–651.

Stein, L. I. and R. J. Diamond. 1985. The chronic mentally ill and the criminal justice system: When to call the police. *Hospital and Community Psychiatry* 36: 271–274.

Stein, L. I. and A. B. Santos. 1998. *Assertive Community Treatment of Persons with Severe Mental Illness*. New York: Norton.

Stein, L. I. and M. A. Test. 1980. Alternative to mental hospital treatment. Part 1. Conceptual model, treatment program, and clinical evaluation. *Archives of General Psychiatry* 37:392–397.

———. 1985. *The Training in Community Living Model: A Decade of Inexperience*. San Francisco: Jossey-Bass.

———, eds. 1978. *Alternatives to Mental Hospital Treatment*. New York: Plenum.

Stein, L. I., M. A. Test, and A. J. Marx. 1975. Alternative to the hospital: A controlled study. *American Journal of Psychiatry* 132 (5): 517–522.

Test, M. A. 1981. Effective community treatment of the chronically mentally ill: What is necessary? *Journal of Social Issues* 37 (3): 71–86.

———. 1992. Training in Community Living. In R. P. Liberman, ed., *Handbook of Psychiatric Rehabilitation*, 153–170. New York: Macmillan.

Test, M. A., W. H. Knoedler, D. J. Allness, and S. S. Burke. 1985. Characteristics of young adults with schizophrenic disorders treated in the community. *Hospital and Community Psychiatry* 36:853–858.

Test, M. A., W. H. Knoedler, D. J. Allness, S. S. Burke, R. L. Brown, and L. S. Wallisch. 1991. Long-term community care through an assertive continuous treatment team. In C. A. Tamminga and S. C. Schulz, eds., *Advances in Neuropsychiatry and Psychopharmacology*. Vol. 1, *Schizophrenia Research*, 239–246. New York: Raven Press.

Test, M. A., W. H. Knoedler, D. J. Allness, S. Kameshima, S. S. Burke, and L. Rounds. 1994. "Long-Term Care of Schizophrenia: Seven Year Results." Paper presented at the annual meeting of the American Psychiatric Association, Philadelphia, May.

Test, M. A. and L. I. Stein. 1976. Practical guidelines for the community treatment of markedly impaired patients. *Community Mental Health Journal* 12:72–82.

———. 2001. A critique of the effectiveness of assertive community treatment. In reply. *Psychiatric Services* 52 (10): 1396.

————, eds. 1978. Community treatment of the chronic patient: Research overview. *Schizophrenia Bulletin* 4 (3): 350–364.

Thyer, B. A. 2001a. Research on social work practice does not benefit from blurry theory: A response to Tomi Gomory. *Journal of Social Work Education* 37 (1): 51–66.

————. 2001b. The role of theory in social work research—Reply. *Journal of Social Work Education* 37 (3): 588–591.

U.S. Department of Health and Human Services. 1999. *Mental Health: A Report of the Surgeon General.* Rockville, Md.: U.S. Department of Health and Human Services, Substance Abuse and Mental Health Services Administration

Valenstein, E. S. 1998. *Blaming the Brain: The Truth About Drugs and Mental Health.* New York: Free Press.

Chapter 10

Empowerment: The Foundation for Social Work Practice in Mental Health

Stephen M. Rose

Introduction

The very existence of the concept of empowerment within social work and mental health practice reflects the struggle of people committed to human dignity, cultural diversity, self-determination, and social justice to *name* (Lorde 1984) oppression and identify the framework for formulating a response.

Naming the bases for individual and collective rage or suffering, making the causes visible, provides us with the possibility of identifying the targets for change and acting to transform them (Lorde 1984). Naming depends upon shared or collective consciousness. Shared consciousness is a prerequisite to *understanding* our situation and its causes, a principle that applies to both micro- and macro-level practice. So as we begin to consider the meaning of "empowerment" in the context of this discussion, my task will primarily involve creating clarity about its meaning, then using this definition to reflect on social work practice in mental health and sketching a concept of empowering practice for social work in mental health case management.

Value-Based Practice: The Basis for Meaning

When we cannot name or construct the meaning of our own authentic struggles for understanding, liberation, or validity, significant power is extracted from us. We are unable to understand ourselves and our relation to the social context that is embodied in us (see Krieger 2001, for a discussion of "embodiment"). Without this understanding, we cannot identify the targets for or the need for change. This paper will attempt to reclaim that power and the authenticity of the struggle for it by linking the concept of empowerment to a systematic value framework rooted in human dignity, social justice, self-determination, and cultural diversity, and by critically examining this framework and its implications.

To accomplish this task, we first have to distinguish between value-based practice and practice grounded in service providers' interests or domains. Value-based practice articulates a statement of fundamental beliefs that define practice principles and against which practice activities and outcomes can be measured. When we address "empowerment," for example, we have to ask which values inform our operational use, which fundamental assumptions define our meaning. How do we know when practice is "empowering" beyond simply making this claim?

Provider-based practice is enmeshed with its sources and structure of funding. Funding can both permit or enable *and* obstruct empowering practice. When funding streams are permitted to define meaning in social work practice, the intended outcomes occur only within their parameters; choices are contained and named for clients and workers, who then operationalize them—for example, in filling out pre-cast "individual treatment plans" or individual service plans constructed around reimbursement formulas. When reimbursement or other funding-stream constraints depend upon disease-based diagnosis and treatment options are reviewed for fidelity to a disease-based model of mental illness, the social workers and clients are both confined to that universe of meaning. Both become domesticated "Objects" that are known and acted upon, reduced from being "Subjects" who know and act (Freire 1968).

Value-based practice begins with explicit basic or orienting beliefs or values that establish the parameters for a person's perception of reality. These beliefs act as premises or fundamental assumptions about oneself, about people, and about our connection to our social context (Janoff-Bulman 1992). These fundamental assumptions structure the theories for practice and the practice principles within which we operationalize our work.

Empowerment, for example, is a practice principle that derives its meaning from the assumptions we hold about the value and meaning of human dignity and social justice. It contains an implied critical stance; the very notion of "empowerment" could not be imagined in a socially, economically, and politically just society. Its meaning derives from an acknowledged absence of social and economic justice—the prerequisite for equally distributed human dignity and valid cultural diversity—as well as from a recognition of the salience of these building blocks for living. Empowerment, in this construction, attempts to redress the absence of equality and its impact on human beings and our relationships. The following example illustrates this point.

Informed consent can begin with the *right* of a person to be a fully knowledgeable, active participant in decisions about his or her life—about what the problem is that must be addressed, about what is to be done, about the merit and plausibility of different options, and about the potential repercussions from each option for the client, for his or her family, and so on. Informed consent can also be a *rite:* a person with little power passively assents to information exchange or actions taken by professionals or their employing institutions with little knowledge about what is actually being done or why, and authorizes these actions with a signature. Both kinds of situations are used as illustrations of empowerment by people with contradictory assumptions. These assumptions differ with respect to their view and valuing of human dignity.

The concept of human dignity, therefore, requires elaboration. Ironically, this fundamental belief rarely gets defined or operationalized even though most human service workers and social work educators would claim that it is part of what we do—perhaps even part of who we are.

On Human Dignity

My perception of human dignity begins with assumptions about what distinguishes us from other species. Let's refer to these inherent, universal human attributes as our "species character" (Fromm 1969). As we think through what makes us uniquely human, we can identify several factors. First is the capacity for consciousness that grows out of mutuality or connection (Berger and Luckmann 1967; Miller 1986)—or a cognitive capacity to recognize, name, and understand our social context and our experience in it.

We naturally use all of our functioning sensory capacity to gather impressions about our world, and we are unable to stop trying to process and integrate this information. This represents an active process of *knowing* with the intent to apply knowing to acting in our environment.

Knowing about our world is inseparable from our relationship to it and our relationships in it. Cognitive understanding, in this sense, is inevitably social and embodies our social context (Krieger 2001). We use whatever we know to inform and assess our actions in the world. Knowing, therefore, always interacts with *knowledge,* and knowledge, in this meaning, is socially derived and maintained in a societal context. Knowledge, therefore, must be politically understood as moving toward or away from social justice and human dignity, reflecting its contextual situation.

As creators of knowing, we are inherently *productive* (producing knowing) and able to be proactive. As a species, we are not confined to being reactive. On the basis of sharing our knowing with others, we produce *understanding*. Because we can *understand* our context, or elements of it, we can create purposeful change. We are not confined to simple, permanent reaction and adaptation. This species characteristic is central to the belief in *human* dignity. Human beings are capable of creative intervention when permitted or encouraged to apply their knowing to knowledge about their life situations—mediated by the content that we are able to use and its degree of embeddedness in existing power relations. When we are reduced to being only reactive, to being consumers or recipients of our context, as repetitive participants in an oppressive structure for human relationships, we are dehumanized or coerced into behaviors appropriate to species that are other than human.

Human dignity, in this meaning, is intertwined with social justice and requires that we produce knowing and use it to challenge knowledge. Knowing is not confined to legitimated cognitive or socially accepted meaning. That level of meaning embodies existing power inequalities and replicates them. Knowledge can be challenged through an ongoing interactive dialogue among equally valid people (Freire 1968; Miller 1986). But, as Freire has shown, people must first believe in themselves as sources of knowing and producers of knowledge. Freire considers people with this confidence to be *Subjects* (who know and act), in contrast to *Objects* (who are known and acted upon).

Berger and Luckmann (1967) describe the process of knowledge accumulation by identifying a process of people socially producing and then *naming* the reality of their shared experience. This serves as the basis for emerging purposeful or consciously directed action. Thus we create or produce history. We connect with others in a social context, interact to *name* our shared experience, and grow through acting on, producing, and reflecting on our lives in interaction with others.

Freire (1968) applies this understanding to practice in *Pedagogy of the Oppressed*. People are encouraged to make visible their prevailing perceptions of their social situations, then guided to discuss how they *understand* the situation, its foundation structurally and conceptually, and its potential for change. In this dialogue among themselves, with leadership from professionals, people reflect on their views of their situation as static and impermeable. As they come to create or produce enlightened understanding, through mutual exploration and the development of an emerging collective knowing, their understanding becomes transformed, moving from a *circle of certainty* to a *limit situation*. Shared knowing produces trust; trust permits authentic dialogue; dialogue creates collective consciousness that makes new understanding possible. This collective consciousness creates opportunities for action strategies that were previously impossible for isolated, impoverished people to see. Ruth Parsons (1991) describes a very similar process drawn from empowering social work practice.

A Note on Diversity

When we perceive one another and interact in a context of mutual validity or social justice, diversity becomes the species' vehicle for human enrichment. Differentiation resulting from diversity among equally valid beings inherently produces enrichment. A context characterized by social justice accords authenticity and validity to all people; this condition creates the basis for dialogue, the open (versus circle of certainty) potential for learning and changing the world. Openness to learning necessarily implies that people who are different from who we perceive ourselves to be have the greatest potential for extending our knowledge because they are different. When our context is based on domination or power over and competition among the exploited, diversity becomes the vehicle for internecine warfare.

These characteristics form the basis for human dignity: individual and shared knowing, creating, producing, dialoging, naming, acting, and reflecting in a context of mutuality and diversity. When we live in a historical context permeated by inequality, our species character is mediated, modified, or distorted, perhaps even subverted by inequality and its inherent characteristics of domination and exploitation. Each aspect of our species character interacts with the character of the oppressive context. Jean Baker Miller's comments highlight this point; she says: "All forms of oppression encourage people to enlist in their own enslavement. . . . In this sense, psychological problems are not so much caused by the unconscious as by deprivations of full consciousness. . . . Lacking full consciousness, we create out of what is available" (1986).

Humanizing and Dehumanizing Action

In table 10.1 species characteristics are seen as humanizing and empowering; oppressive contextual characteristics are seen as dehumanizing and objectifying. Humanizing actions thus comprise species characteristics; dehumanizing actions co-opt, undermine, or subvert these characteristics. In this way, historical context mediates species characteristics. Empowerment embodies humanizing action, dynamic, alive and interactive within relationships of mutuality. Stagnation permeates conscious action imbued with oppression,

Table 10.1
Consciousness >< Action >< History

Species Character	Context Character
Knowing	Knowledge
Creating	Reacting
Producing	Consuming
Naming	Labeling
Connecting	Mastering
Dialoging	Diagnosing
Authenticity	Functioning

embodied in relationships that are coercively contained by extant roles and the institutional structures and the ideologies in which they are embedded.

Knowing and Knowledge Building

We are inherently knowing and knowledge building. We observe and assess our context in the process of relationships with others, to produce what we need to survive. This necessity creates action that reproduces, sustains, or improves our situation—which creates, produces, or reproduces history. We are, or can become Subjects who know and act, according to Paolo Freire (1968). This capacity guides empowering practice and establishes the empowering perspective of strengths-based practice (Saleebey 2002)—to identify, elicit, support, and encourage clients to become Subjects. Dialogue, respecting clients' immersion in circles of certainty, directs discussion toward quality-of-life wishes or needs as a shared framework for action and assessment of needs. Cowger and Snively (2002) amplify this process through evoking clients' strengths in an assessment process focused on the client's "situation"—an example of creating a "limit situation" from the "circle of certainty," confining the problem to the client himself/herself. In this framework the "situation" becomes the problem to be assessed and the focus of action strategy development as shared activity by social workers and their clients.

To put it more simply, we are always in the process of knowing. We use our knowing to create actions. This means that potentially we can recognize and *name* aspects of reality and produce, reproduce, or refine positives or avoid negatives. *Naming* becomes a contextual or collective practice that expresses and reflects our consciousness. As such, it can be a source of authentic power or mutual empowerment. This fundamental notion is the basis for empowering practice and its commitment to clients' being full partners in the process and outcome of their involvement in any service; clients are supported to empower themselves. They are the experts in their own lives, certainly in describing how they would like to be living, what they value and want to see happen, and what they are able to contribute to producing the action steps necessary to produce their stated goals. Our task is to develop their knowing and enhance its validity in the face of "knowledge" that has been assembled about them. We act to separate the person from containment within a "circle of certainty" (Freire 1968) composed of knowledge accumulated about him or her. When we can bring people together to do this reflective action in groups, the potential for emerging collective consciousness and shared empowerment increases. Creating groups for mutual aid and assessment of shared problem situations should be a constant objective within this practice framework.

When what we can know is contained by "what is available," and availability reflects domination and inequality—for example, as manifest in the *DSM-IV* and disease-based funding streams—available *knowledge* leads us away from authentic communication or knowledge-building or knowledge-challenging interaction. Many provider-driven treatment plans capture this process. Rather than being Subjects who know and act to define their view of how they would like to be living, people often are reduced to Objects that are known and acted upon (Freire 1968) and to revenue-generating objects coerced into compliance with a treatment plan. Goal framing, rather than reflecting an authentic expression of a desired quality of life, often becomes reduced to behavioral measures of compliance with regimented service requirements.

Human agency, through mutuality and its thrust toward consciousness, drives history or, under conditions of oppression, reproduces its contradictions. Repetitive action, without conscious direction and shared production of the meaning of our lives, heightens our distance from the authentic action based on understanding ("naming") that constitutes growth. Adherence to or compliance with treatment plans in most instances reflects this process of objectification—of being known and acted upon by ritual participation in rigidly constructed service programs designed to improve or maintain behavioral functioning within contained mental-patient identities (Rose and Black 1985).

Knowledge, when embedded in hierarchical power relationships and granted an aura of approval by hierarchy or legitimation, replaces knowing and its experience of validation or mutual connection. When domination permeates relationships or a larger social context, cognitive, knowledge-bearing, function-oriented, role-based relationships and their legitimation will dominate and undermine connection, mutuality, experiential and collective aspects of being.

Knowledge is knowing, codified by existing social relationships. Knowledge reflects power relations as it reproduces them. Knowledge, therefore, contains a dual utility: it informs us about its subject and legitimates perceptions of that subject that are permitted by dominating power relations. In contexts characterized by mutuality and social justice, knowledge and knowledge producers are fluid, generative (Saleebey 2002), heuristic. Its vitality is embodied in dialogue, critical reflection, and action (Freire 1968).

Provider-driven practice, in contrast, is structured by "Experts" in designated roles located within legitimated institutions. They preside over the fundamentally human effort to be knowing, and they struggle to confine ideas to the known. The application of the already known (sometimes called the "professional use of self") contains both experts and the "objects" of their attention within circles of certainty. As such, experts are inherently domesticating. An example would be diagnosis, using a classification scheme: experts, who own static knowledge, apply it to people who are prevented from producing knowing about themselves. Dignity, defined by the expert, reaffirms experts; it legitimates existing power. Its most common expression is the offer to the client to approve the template-based, diagnosis-dependent treatment plan—without which access to housing, some income, and some relative privilege within the confines of allotted identities may not be available.

Creative and Connecting Interaction

Parallel to the undermining of the mutual process of knowing, we see the subversion of creative interaction and discovery. Repetitive reacting reflects the reduction of our capacity for conscious knowing, naming, connecting, and acting to adaptive positioning, repeating, disconnecting, and reproducing extant power relations. A considerable amount of social work practice in mental health, following pathology-based knowledge and its derived contained interventions, reflects these concerns.

Our species character requires us, through mutuality, connecting, and naming experience, to be producing our lives. In Jean-Paul Steiner's (1967) incredible book, *Treblinka,* the individual ego structures of the concentration camp inmates he describes disintegrate through collective synthesis and the realization of common interests, resulting in a mutual process of producing a revolution in the camp and creating its place in history. Before that, the inmates, disconnected and isolated in their allotted roles and their embodied identities yet longing for one another, were consumed by slave labor, its attendant identity, and genocidal murder. People produced collective consciousness to understand their situation differently from what their individual cumulative knowledge(s) would permit or their oppressors could contemplate. This knowing altered their knowledge and made different pathways of action imaginable. Franz Fanon (1967), Lillian Rubin (1976), and Audre Lorde (1984) describe parallel processes related to internalizing domination across class, race, ethnicity, gender, and sexual orientation.

Striving to be fully human, but prevented from knowing and naming by externally coercive power, people see what is made cognitively possible or "available" to them within the roles modeled by their oppressors. These roles, seen by the oppressors as universally appropriate for human life, and for the dominated contexts within which they are envisioned, create services for unequal or marginalized people. Naming reality occurs within the services provided and reproduces knowledge about the world and the roles of the providers and clients.

Ruth Parsons (1991:12–13) offers the alternative possibility:

> The process of empowerment involves the development of attitudes and beliefs about one's efficacy to take action; the development of critical thinking about one's world; the acquisition of knowledge and skills needed to take action; the support and mutual aid of one's peers in any given situation; and the taking of action to make change in the face of impinging problems. It is both a process and an outcome.

To create this process/outcome, social workers must have the capacity to engage their clients as Subjects in dialogue (Freire 1968). To engage clients in authentic dialogue, an activating purposeful discourse about being in the world and acting to change it (locally, in this meaning), social workers must know it themselves. Without being seen and engaged as Subjects who know and act, social workers cannot communicate this principle to their clients. Unfortunately, most social workers are not participating in settings where these characteristics routinely, if ever, occur. That makes the bringing together of clients for mutual problem defining, problem solving, and action very difficult to accomplish.

Empowerment, based upon the value of human dignity and reflective of the factors described above, is a relationship among people, based upon mutual connection, designed to produce knowing, creative, connecting persons who experience themselves as SUBJECTS and who work together to create a world (at the micro and/or macro levels) where subjects are welcome.

The Meaning for Social Work

Empowerment involves social work with clients who are always seen as developing "Subjects." This principle requires that we work collaboratively, in partnership with each other and with clients to create client-defined goals and move toward their implementation (Rose 1992). Assessment never is done on another person, but collaboratively, with the other person, to examine the person's social situation and the problems as well as assets that it offers. Provider-driven social work replaces clients' active involvement with service or treatment plan construction that perceives and treats clients as Objects. We can see this in table 10.1, which compares different case-management models. Case management, from the client-driven or empowering perspective, constitutes an optimal social work intervention in mental health, responsible for both interpersonal practice and systemic advocacy.

Clearly, the potential for creating empowering models is mediated by organizational structures and funding streams. While that is not our focus here, we can observe that capitated forms of funding substantially increase the potential for creative interventions when compared with retrospective, fee-for-service interventions tied to medicalized or pathology-driven models. This form of funding, with its demands for aggregate outcomes and cost accountability, has the capacity to view populations; fee-for-service, diagnosis-based funding can only perceive aggregates of disconnected individuals. Data from population-based evaluations can be used to advocate for policy change because of the capacity of such evaluations to identify structural assets and barriers to social justice. Equally obvious is the fact that community-controlled nonprofit or public sector organizations independent from service providers constitute the optimum administrative auspice for client-driven case management; the foundation of such organizations would be within community constituencies whose relationship to client populations is inclusive. This approach would produce an emphasis on recovery, strengths, and contribution to community life.

Whatever the organizational entity, what is paramount is to build empowering relationships guided by dialogue. Authenticity in these relationships, and with each other, comes from turning over our knowledge to knowing, converting our hierarchical isolation to building partnerships, to creating what Jean Baker Miller (1986) and the other Stone Center people (Jordan et al. 1991) so articulately and positively define as "connection." The almost universal failure of our practice models and their defect-based paradigms to prevent or even recognize human despair and its structural bases, or to alleviate its universal suffering, creates the opportunity to transform—and to be transformed. Empowerment is that process—one that we participate in, not hand down; one that we create, not co-opt; one that we share, not own.

Social work, as fully capable of identifying oppressive structures as it is of connecting with survivors of them, can use empowerment to advance the prospects for transformation—or it can stagnate in provider-driven castles.

My deepest hope is that we can create relationships with each other and with our clients that demand that we know the difference and act on it.

References

Berger, P. and T. Luckmann. 1967. *The Social Construction of Reality: A Treatise on the Sociology of Knowledge*. New York: Doubleday Anchor.

Cowger, C. D. and C. A. Snively. 2002. Assessing Client Strengths: Individual, Family, and Community Empowerment. In D. Saleebey, ed., *The Strengths Perspective in Social Work Practice*, 106–123. 3d ed. Boston: Allyn and Bacon.

Fanon, F. 1967. *Black Skin, White Masks*. New York: Grove Press.

Freire, P. 1968. *Pedagogy of the Oppressed*. New York: Continuum.

Fromm, E. 1969. *Marx's Concept of Man*. New York: Frederick Ungar Publishing.

Janoff-Bulman, R. 1992. *Shattered Assumptions: Towards a New Psychology of Trauma*. New York: Free Press.

Jordan, J. V., A. G. Kaplan, J. B. Miller, I. P. Stiver, and I. L. Surrey. 1991. *Women's Growth in Connection*. New York: Guilford Press.

Krieger, N. 2001. A glossary for social epidemiology. *Journal of Epidemiology and Community Health* 55:693–700.

Lorde, A. 1984. *Sister Outsider*. Freedom, Calif.: Crossing Press.

Marx, K. 1967. *The Economic and Philosophic Manuscripts of 1844*. Moscow: Progress Publishers.

Miller, J. B. 1986. *Toward a New Psychology of Women*. Boston: Beacon.

Parsons, R. J. 1991. Empowerment: Purpose and practice principle in social work. *Social Work with Groups* 14 (2): 7–21.

Rose, S. M., ed. 1992. *Case Management and Social Work Practice*. White Plains, N.Y.: Longman.

Rose, S. M. and B. L. Black. 1985. *Advocacy and Empowerment: Mental Health Care in the Community*. London: Routledge and Kegan Paul.

Rubin, L. B. 1976. *Worlds of Pain*. New York: Basic Books.

Saleebey, D., ed. *The Strengths Perspective in Social Work Practice*. Boston: Allyn and Bacon, 2002.

Steiner, J. P. 1967. *Treblinka*. New York: Simon and Schuster.

Warren, R. L., S. M. Rose, and A. F. Burgunder. 1974. *The Structure of Urban Reform*. Lexington, Mass.: D. C. Heath.

Chapter 11
Self-help Mental Health Agencies

Steven P. Segal

The mental health client self-help movement is one of the most significant new mental health service efforts (USDHHS 1999). The Center for Self-Help Research's collaborative study with the National Association of State Mental Health Program Directors (NASMHPD) shows that forty-six states are funding 567 self-help programs for persons with severe mental disabilities (NASMHPD 1993). Self-help is an attempt by people with a mutual problem to take control over the circumstances of their lives. Formal self-help efforts involve participation in organized groups for individuals with similar problems or in more differentiated and structured multiservice agencies. Self-help agencies include independent-living programs that help members access material resources and gain practical skills, as well as drop-in community centers that provide a place for members to socialize, build a supportive community, and get advocacy and a gamut of independent-living services (Zinman 1987). Self-help agencies are distinguished from self-help groups that work to help individuals gain control over or acceptance of their problems in that they are formal organizations providing services and often have a parallel focus on efforts directed toward changing social conditions (Emerick 1989). For example, many self-help agencies set up to assist poverty-stricken ex-patients reflect the belief that members' problems result from social and economic inequities, but that members must take individual responsibility for making changes in their own lives and for reforming social structures. These agencies may offer mutual support groups as well as material resources to members. They also promote the involvement of members in policy-making structures

This research is supported by grants from the National Institute of Mental Health (#MH47487), the Zellerbach Family Fund, and the San Francisco Foundation.

that affect their lives: boards of directors of nonprofit social service agencies, local mental health advisory commissions, state mental health planning agencies, and so forth. Their goal is to empower their members to take responsibility for their lives.

Self-help View of Empowerment

As Rappaport (1985) noted, the absence of empowerment is easy to notice, but its presence is difficult to define, as it takes various forms in different contexts (see, for example, Kahn and Bender 1985; Pinderhughes 1983; Rappaport, Swift, and Hess 1981). In describing how self-help agencies empower their clients Zinman (1986) notes:

> First, people who use the services run them, making all the decisions; service providers and recipients are one and the same. Second, these groups strive to share power, responsibility, and skills and seek a non-hierarchical structure in which people reach across to each other, rather than up and down. Third, client-run programs are based on choice; they are totally voluntary. . . . And finally, they are based on a non-medical approach to disturbing behavior and therefore see and address the real economic, social, and cultural needs of suffering people. (213)

The issue of empowerment, then, underlies self-helpers' understanding of the nature of the problems with which they contend and under whose control such problems should be addressed, the goal of efforts to deal with them, and appropriate strategies for doing so.

Self-help Agency Practice and Empowerment

The mental health client self-help movement promotes the role of mentally disabled people as active consumers who determine which services will best meet their needs (Budd 1987; Center for Rehabilitation Research and Training in Mental Health 1984). The desired outcomes are the same as those of the independent-living movement—personal independence in accordance with one's self-defined goals, as long as these goals do not infringe on the rights of others. Empowerment, for self-help, is both a systems and an individual phenomenon. Self-help agency efforts, geared toward forcing the larger environment to accommodate disabilities, are designed to work in tandem with efforts directed at and with the individual consumer. Hasenfeld

(1987), in discussing empowerment in social work practice, made a distinction that is also relevant to self-help agencies. He talked about how empowerment must occur on at least three levels: (1) on the individual level, through resource improvement; (2) at the organizational level, through actions directed toward "harnessing the agency's power advantage to increasingly serve the needs of the client" (479); and (3) at the policy level, where people become involved in the formation and enactment of policy that affects them. Similarly, the self-help agency's goal is to empower its clients through the following related activities at the three levels:

1. Individuals are directly provided or helped to gain access to resources and skills necessary to reach desired goals, and alternative models are provided to counter stigma.
2. Organizations are structured to give clients access to roles that permit them to take responsibility for and exercise discretion over policies that affect them collectively within the agencies.
3. Changes are sought in the larger society that both better the condition of people with disabilities as a class and empower them to participate in making decisions concerning policies that affect them.

Self-help Activities

Overcoming Barriers to Resources and Skill Development

Any discussion of empowerment and self-concept runs the risk of blaming the victim and of ignoring the very large disempowering structures faced by the person with the disability. As a master status, a mental disability creates a real barrier to a person's ability to marshal necessary and desired resources. A mentally disabled person's control of life circumstances is often limited by decisions that view his or her competence as more limited than the actual disability would make it, by general societal and specific organizational structures unwilling to accommodate the disability, and by political decisions limiting the resources that are available.

For many self-helpers the disabling aspects of their disability cannot be separated from their poverty. Self-help agencies seem to be offering the social and psychological package of services that are unfunded and missing in mainstream mental health programs. Results of our 2002 study of 226 new users of eleven such organizations in the greater San Francisco Bay Area indicate that during a six-month assessment period, basic resources from the self-help agency were received by the following percentage of those in the sample: food (71%), bus pass (31%), place to shower (35%), clothing (33%), mailing address (29%), personal items (28%), housing (23%), storage (16%), employment (10%), help in finding a job (10%), help with rent (10%,), and service information (20%).

Self-help agencies also attempt to provide their clients with necessary skills. For example, many such agencies employ clients on either a paid or a volunteer basis, thus giving them a work history and references. Many offer independent-living classes taught from the perspective of someone who has experienced disability and poverty.

Altering Self-concepts and the Meaning of Disability

For empowerment to occur, the person with the disability must command the necessary skills and resources to secure desired outcomes. However, even commanding the necessary skills and resources is insufficient when the environment is unresponsive or the individual does not believe in the possibility of success and therefore does not exercise power. A person with a mental disability is given an overriding basis for self-identification, and he or she is largely defined by that status; it organizes others' expectations about a large range of behaviors unrelated to the disability and leads to negative evaluations made on the basis of these expectations. For self-help agencies one of the aspects of empowerment is to alter the meaning of the disability for the member-clients. Of particular importance is altering all the negative stereotypes that attack the person's identity and create an expectation of rejection.

To alter the meaning of the disability, the self-help agency first provides the individual with concrete proof that he or she is not alone and that there are others who share and effectively cope with the same problems. The agency then provides a community that accepts and values the person.

Rosenberg (1979) discussed how self-concept is formed by social comparison with others. This idea, with a slight revision, can be applied to the work of self-help groups. By presenting the client with evidence that a group defined by a mental disability is capable of creating an agency, staffing its services, and governing its own behavior, the self-help community redefines the implications of the disability. In effect, the group rather than the individual serves as the basis of comparison with other groups. In particular, to the extent that the agency expands the work of social services agencies, it shows that people with disabilities can be as competent, if not more so, than the professionals who serve them (Katz and Maida 1990; Mowbray, Wellwood, and Chamberlain 1988; Segal, Silverman, and Temkin 1996).

The self-help agency can also serve as a local frame of reference (Gecas 1982). Some member-clients are given controlling power in the organization as well as the possibility of filling positions of importance and trust. By directly empowering its members in this manner, the agency provides them with direct evidence of competence and worth to the group. Following Bem's (1972) notion of self-attribution, individuals are able to observe their own behavior and make positive inferences about themselves.

Self-help agencies also deal directly with issues of stigma and self-worth. All strive to provide a setting in which individuals are accepted for who they are and for their contributions to the organization, rather than for their disability. All run some form of discussion group and provide peer counseling. Furthermore, the self-help community has worked to develop understandings of mental illness that avoid the stigmatizing implications of the term, and these writings and concepts are available to clients through written sources as well as discussion.

Organizational Empowerment

Perhaps the single most important factor shown to be empirically associated with enhancing member-client outcomes in self-help agencies is organizational empowerment (Segal and Silverman 2002). Member-clients are given an active role in the running of the agencies. All agencies are controlled by member-clients. At community meetings, the entire membership is given authority over important policy decisions, including such items as staffing, services offered, and center rules. Governing boards are elected by members and contain a majority of member seats. Staff positions, both paid and unpaid, are largely or totally filled by members. When members break center rules, decisions about what should be done are made either by elected committees or by the entire center membership. Furthermore, the membership attempts to minimize hierarchy within the organization, despite the exigencies of maintaining corporate structures (Zinman 1987). As result, members are empowered within the organization through exercising control over their collective experiences. Experience with responsible decision making within the organization seems to carry over to more-effective decision making in their personal lives and a sense of personal empowerment.

Empowerment Efforts Directed at the Larger Society and Systems Change

As noted earlier, empowerment in the social services context must occur at the policy level as well as in the spheres of the organization and worker-client interaction. Such power in policy formation translates, in turn, into increased influence at the local, state, and national levels. In general, consumer–self-helpers have worked to attain legitimate power, the normative assumption being that former patients should be involved in policy roles (French and Raven 1960). Strategies to attain power include advocacy work to influence policy development; input into systems planning, including needs assessments, program design, program management, and evaluation; allocation of existing resources; development of new resources; governance of other agencies; research direction; and community education. Member-client involvement is intended to create conditions in which members can gain greater control over their environments and realize their aspirations.

Consumer–self-helpers have influenced legislative and regulatory policy decisions at the national, state, and local levels; in turn, these reforms have led to greater consumer involvement in other spheres of systems change. Mentally disabled self-helpers have been an increasingly visible presence on local and state systems planning boards. The Anti-Drug Abuse Act of 1988 (P.L. 100-690) and the ADAMHA [Alcohol, Drug Abuse, and Mental Health Administration] Reorganization Act of 1992 (P.L. 102-321) mandated the inclusion of mental health clients and family members on planning councils.

Self-helpers are increasing their representation on the governing boards of nonprofit agencies whose client base may include mental health clients. As board members, self-helpers can assist these agencies in becoming more responsive to the needs of mental health clients. The impact goes beyond the ability of individual organizations to meet those needs; the aggregate effect is to increase the resources in the community that clients can use to improve their lives.

Consumer-Operated Services

Self-help agencies are run by and for consumers. They may be defined by having a consumer or a former client as a director, having a board membership of at least 50% consumers, and having the right to hire and fire any professionals employed by the organization. Yet consumer control, though it is a necessary condition for a self-help agency, is not a sufficient condition to ensure that the organization's empowerment ideology and, therefore, its major contributions to member-client outcomes will be carried into practice. In a recent conversation with a director of a consumer-operated program outside of California, I was informed that "sharing policy responsibilities with the mentally ill might be dangerous" and was therefore not part of her organization's operations. She focused on "providing services." The mental health field has a long history, dating back to the subversion of moral treatment principles in early psychiatric asylums, of compromising promising psychosocial programming to accommodate either fiscal constraints or vocational ambitions. McLean (1995) offers a counterpoint to the great potential evidenced by self-help agencies. This qualitative study reports on the unfulfilled promise of a self-help agency drop-in center embedded in a community mental health system and of the potential disempowering effects of pursuing a combined-services approach. McLean's findings associate the combined-services approach with the abandonment of the key self-help agency principles of consumer participation in empowering decision making and with the sacrifice of goals to bureaucratic and funding pressures. A consumer-operated service without its empowering approach may be no more than cheap care at best, not a self-help agency within the conceptual and operational achievement of self-help agency founders.

As consumer-run agencies demonstrate their success in serving mentally disabled people, they become recognized as a source of specialized knowledge; thus, they develop expert power (French and Raven 1960). Providers of mental health services and other social services have invited self-helpers to assist them in making their services more responsive to the needs of their clientele. To the extent that consumer-operated agency directors fail to appreciate the unique contribution of the empowering approach to their organizational successes and fail to protect it within their organizations, the self-help approach may ultimately join the ranks of previously promising but discredited psychosocial treatment efforts.

Eleven Self-help Programs

In order to better illustrate self-help agency objectives, I describe eleven self-help agencies. The observations are drawn from several years of structured and informal observations at these agencies. The programs combine unstructured drop-ins with structured meetings and other activities and services. All call themselves self-help because the entire membership—staff, volunteers, and others—must fit the consumer control criteria specified above and because the programs employ an empowering approach directed toward helping members gain the resources and capacities to better their lives and their self-concept. The programs serve people with a mental disability, and at least two thirds of the member-clients are homeless or marginally housed (see table 11.1).

The programs vary in the services and activities offered. All offer a drop-in space and coffee, and several offer meals. All run support groups and serve as advocates, helping members to obtain shelter and housing referrals and assisting members with securing benefits and negotiating the welfare bureaucracy. All offer peer and job counseling, independent-living skills training, and general discussion sessions. Four programs schedule weekly movies and organized recreational activities such as excursions to baseball games and roller-skating parties for their membership.

Table 11.1 presents the characteristics of 226 new member-clients of these organizations (Segal, Hardiman, and Hodges 2002). Information on the sample was obtained from structured interviews with those who were part of the sample. As shown in table 11.1, more than a third of the participants are African American, though ethnicity tended to be representative of the catchment area population from which the self-help agency drew its clientele.

The programs are funded from a variety of sources, including federal, state, and county monies and foundation grants. They serve anywhere from twenty to well over a hundred people a day. Although there are important differences among the programs, we find fundamental similarities in the way each establishes a viable self-help setting. The following five organizational characteristics seem to be important features of such progams:

Focus on Shared Experience

Self-help or, more descriptively, mutual assistance is defined by the importance of shared experience. The self-help agencies differ from "regular" social service agencies in that all, or the majority of, services are delivered by people who have and continue to struggle with the kinds of disabilities that bring new clients to the agency. Thus, for example, many of the staff and volunteers that we interviewed were literally homeless (living on the street or in shelters) at the time of the interview or had been homeless at some point in their lives.

As a result, services are delivered by people who can draw on their own experiences in living with disabilities, stigma, and racism, and in dealing with the sometimes chaotic and seemingly irrational world of social service agencies. They can offer advice, for example, on how best to secure disability benefits or which shelters are most accommodating. They can offer peer counseling on living with voices that counsel suicide or on trying to stay clean of illegal drugs in an environment where drug use or alcohol use may be the norm. Their advice to clients and their ability to listen resonate, perhaps with greater authority since they have been there themselves.

One pattern often observed was for staff to tell clients that they do not need to play the games that were seen as necessary to secure informal and formal assistance in the larger world. Staff told the clients that they themselves had played such games to get social service personnel to give them a scarce referral to housing or to maintain a benefit after a rule had been broken. In theory, and usually in practice, staff did not divide clients into the deserving and the undeserving poor as a basis for giving assistance. Staff felt further that when clients did not think they had to spin stories to receive help, they were better able to take more responsibility for their actions.

At this point there is no rigorous evidence as to whether staff claims are correct. On the one hand, staff and volunteers do serve as models of what is possible for clients. Yet those who give help continue to struggle with the

Table 11.1
Characteristics of New SHA Clients (*N* = 226)

Demographic Characteristics	%/Mean	Housing and Income Characteristics	%/Mean
Gender		Housing	
Male	58	Stably housed	32
Female	42	Marginally housed	36
Marital Status		Literally homeless	32
Married	4	Income (mean dollars received	
Separated	9	last month)	546
Divorced	26	Income Source★	
Widowed	4	SSI	49
Never Married	57	SSI + SSDI	22
Ethnicity		Subtotal SS	71
African American	36	GA	12
White	49	TANF/AFDC	4
Latino/Black Latino	7	Food stamps	21
Native American	2	Money from family/friends	8
Asian	3	Employment ·	10
Other, No answer	2	Other sources	16
Education★★		Diagnostic Characteristics★★★	
High school	37		
High school	21	Primary Psychiatric Diagnosis	
Technical	4	(Axis I):	
Some college	34	Schizophrenia/shizoaffective	20
Bachelor's or more	8	Major depression	54
Employment		Bipolar disorder/mania	7
Currently working	23	Anxiety/panic/PTST/	
Working for pay	9	dysthymia	12
Looking for work	30	No mental illness diagnosis	8
Ever held paying job	93	Substance Use/Dependence	
Mean hours of paid work		No substance use	33
per week	4.35	Alcohol abuse	6
Mean weeks worked at		Substance abuse	5
paying job in last year	6.68	Alcohol dependence	9
		Substance dependence	46

★SSI = Supplemental Security Income; SSDI = Social Security Disability Insurance; GA = General Assistance; TANF = Temporary Assistance to Needy Families; AFDC = Aid to Families with Dependent Children
★★Adds to 105% because technical school training is counted in addition to standard education.
★★★Established by using Diagnostic Interview Schedule assessments.

problems that brought them to the agencies, and sometimes these problems gain a greater hold over them. Some clients who were interviewed spoke bitterly and skeptically about the issue of how they could be expected to be helped by someone who had their own troubles. Unlike a typical social service agency, where a greater formal separation between client and staff exists, the self-help agency blurs the boundaries. The possible greater identification of the client with staff may lead to a greater set of expectations of how the staff should behave.

Focus on Mutual Assistance

Certainly the staff helped the clients, but member-clients who did not have a formal role helped out as well. The agencies themselves did not have sufficient personnel to perform all duties; therefore, members might volunteer to do certain tasks, maybe to go pick up donated coffee or to answer phones when a staff member was not available. The agencies formalized this informal helping by creating the role of volunteer. Members who performed volunteer duties were often rewarded through the provision of bus passes or an addition to their résumé. Most of them, however, as did the staff, worked far more hours than necessary, since their duties gave them a chance to help and to be valued for that help.

Members also helped each other directly. One member was observed giving another member who was in visible distress the valued and scarce resource of a cigarette. They were not friends—he just knew how it felt to be depressed. Another was observed giving information about the best place to obtain free meals or to secure needed services.

Reevaluation of the Meaning of Having a Disability

Whereas the problems that bring clients to traditional agencies serve as a source of stigma, at these self-help agencies, they define membership, and the agencies work to make that membership have a real positive meaning. It is indicative that only one percent of the long-term users were ashamed of being a member-client at an agency for homeless and mentally disabled individuals, while 51% were proud of being a member-client at the agency. Seventy-eight percent disagreed with the statement "This [the agency] is just a place I come to, it's not that important to me."

The agencies provide direct evidence that people with disabilities can govern their own affairs. Even if any one individual is not capable at that moment of contributing to the agency, he or she can see that others with similar disabilities can help and be trusted to assume important positions. Several vignettes are indicative: A newcomer to one of the agencies was sitting in a community meeting. He questioned the leader of the meeting about a statement. In listening to the leader's answer, the newcomer began to realize that the leader was just like him—struggling with the problems of being homeless and having a mental disability. For a few minutes the newcomer kept questioning the leader, unable to believe that an agency of that size would use people with disabilities in important positions. As he began to understand the agency, he was visibly shaken. In another case an individual talked about truly understanding what it meant to be empowered. Although a relative newcomer to the agency, he had been selected to represent the agency's interests at a city function. He had asked the coordinator what he should say and was told that he would be supported in whatever he proposed. He had been homeless and a client of the mental health system and therefore was an expert on what was really needed.

Accommodation of Disability

While the programs turned what were elsewhere stigmatized attributes into sources of contribution and worth, they also had to deal with the day-to-day realities of members who had mental disabilities, substance abuse problems, and general problems from dealing with the frustrations of being homeless. There were ongoing problems of maintaining order and permitting the programs to continue. The agencies evolved a series of strategies to deal with members' difficulties. People who were severely depressed or lost in conversation with their voices would be treated with respect. One man, for example, sat in a chair working on a painting with a brush that had no paint. He was left to his art but also involved in activities or discussions when he turned outward to the meeting. Another man who lost track of his actions and refilled a coffeepot several times so that its water spilled over was not visibly noticed or ostracized but instead calmly permitted to clean up the resulting mess. A very depressed woman who was also screaming obscenities was asked by a staff member if she would help him. The request—showing that she had value to the organization—was sufficient to cause her to smile and help out. Finally, for a porter's job that the organization was recruiting for, the agency board interviewed, along with all other applicants, a man who was actively hallucinating. The man was responsive to questions and was considered, like all the other applicants, on the merits of his application and interview.

Some behavior went beyond what was permitted if the agencies were to continue to function. Violence and theft were recurring problems. Members who broke agency rules were brought before a rules committee composed of their peers, and they were allowed to defend their own position. When behavior went beyond what the organization could reasonably tolerate, clients might be suspended, but they were permitted to reapply for attendance privileges after a reasonable period of time. Even while banned, these individuals could continue to use the center as a mailing address so that they would not lose a necessary service.

In this manner the agencies recognized that it would be naive to expect anything close to perfection in the behavior of the membership. However, unlike other agencies that permanently banned individuals, the self-help agencies gave people second and third chances.

Participatory Democracy

The formal organizational structure of the self-help agencies supported the above practices by moving much of the important decision making into the hands of the clients. Boards of directors had a mandate, and a large number of clients held seats on the board. As mentioned, staff positions were largely held by clients. Furthermore, all agencies were at least partially run as participatory democracies. At weekly community meetings members discussed and voted on agency policy, staffing, rules, and discipline. Staff were selected by a vote of the membership (membership status usually being achieved after a modest period of attendance) at four agencies and by a committee composed of members and staff at the others. Similarly, members determined agency rules and policies, such as the timing of service availability, location of nonsmoking areas, and agency positions on external issues that affected the organization. Policies toward and case-by-case decisions on those who break the rules were decided either by an open vote of the membership or by an elected committee.

Conclusion

Throughout the United States there is increasing awareness of the importance of actively involving patients/clients/consumers in the decision making of professionally run organizations and of supporting their efforts to add new organizational types to the service spectrum. The future of these efforts must be carefully evaluated, yet their process seems rich for learning about effective helping.

References

Alcohol, Drug Abuse, and Mental Health Administration (ADAMHA). Reorganization Act of 1992, P.L. 102-321, 106 Stat. 383.

Bem, D. J. 1972. Self-Perception Theory. In L. Berkowitz, ed., *Advances in Experimental Social Psychology* 6:1–57. New York: Academic Press.

Budd, S. 1987. Support Groups. In S. Zinman, H. Harp, and S. Budd, eds., *Reaching Across: Mental Health Clients Helping Each Other,* 41–51. Riverside: California Network of Mental Health Clients.

Center for Rehabilitation Research and Training in Mental Health. 1984. *A Network for Caring: The Community Support Program of the National Institute of Mental Health. Proceedings of the Sixth National Conference, 1983.* Boston: Center for Rehabilitation Research and Training in Mental Health.

Emerick, R. 1989. Group demographics in the mental patient movement: Group location, age, size as structural factors. *Community Mental Health Journal* 25 (4): 277–300.

French, J. R. P. and B. Raven. 1960. The Bases of Social Power. In D. Cartwright and A. Zander, eds., *Group Dynamics,* 607–623. 2d ed. New York: Harper and Row.

Gecas, V. 1982. The self-concept. *Annual Review of Sociology* 8:1–33.

Hasenfeld, Y. 1987. Power in social work practice. *Social Service Review* 61:469–483.

Kahn, A. and E. Bender. 1985. Self-help groups as a crucible for people empowerment in the context of social development. *Social Development Issues* 9:4–13.

Katz, A. and C. Maida. 1990. Health and Disability Self-help Organizations. In T. Powell, ed., *Working with Self-help,* 141–155. Silver Spring, Md.: NASW Press.

McLean, A. 1995. Empowerment and the psychiatric consumer/ex-patient movement in the United States: Contradictions, crisis, and change. *Social Science and Medicine* 40 (8): 1053–1071.

Mowbray, C. T., R. Wellwood, and P. Chamberlain. 1988. Project Stay: A consumer-run support service. *Psychological Rehabilitation Journal* 12 (1): 33–42.

National Association of State Mental Health Program Directors. 1993. "NASMHPD Position Paper on Consumer Contributions to Mental Health Service Delivery Systems." Alexandria, Va.: NASMHPD.

Pinderhughes, E. 1983. Empowerment for our clients and for ourselves. *Social Casework* 64:331–338.

Rappaport, J. 1985. The power of empowerment language. *Social Policy* 16 (2): 15–22.

Rappaport, J., C. Swift, and R. Hess, eds. 1981. *Studies in Empowerment: Steps Toward Understanding and Action.* Binghamton, N.Y.: Haworth.

Rosenberg, M. 1979. *Conceiving the Self.* New York: Basic Books.

Segal, S. P., E. Hardiman, and J. Hodges. 2002. Characteristics of new clients at self-help and community mental health agencies in geographic proximity. *Psychiatric Services* 53 (9): 1145–1152.

Segal, S. P. and C. Silverman. 2002. Determinants of outcomes in mental health self-help agencies. *Psychiatric Services* 53 (3): 304–309.

Segal, S. P., C. Silverman, and T. Temkin. 1996. Self-help mental health programs. *Breakthrough* 1 (1): 23–34.

U. S. Department of Health and Human Services (USDHHS). 1999. *U.S. Department of Health and Human Services. Mental Health: A Report of the Surgeon General.* Rockville, Md.: USDHHS, Substance Abuse and Mental Health Services Administration, Center for Mental Health Services.

Zinman, S. 1986. Self-help: The wave of the future. *Hospital and Community Psychiatry* 37 (3): 213.

———. 1987. Definition of Self-help Groups. In S. Zinman, H. Harp, and S. Budd, eds., *Reaching Across: Mental Health Clients Helping Each Other.* Sacramento: California Network of Mental Health Clients.

Chapter 12

Power, Gender, and the Self: Reflections on Improving Mental Health for Males and Females

Sarah Rosenfield and Kathleen J. Pottick

Among the most consistent patterns in the epidemiology of mental health problems are the differences by gender (Nolen-Hoeksema 1990; Rosenfield 1999a, 1999b). Males are more likely than females to externalize problems, including aggression and other types of antisocial behavior. Thus, men more often express problematic feelings in outward behavior and experience related problems in forming close, enduring relationships. Males also exceed females in substance abuse, with greater dependency and more work- and family-related problems because of drugs or alcohol use. Females predominate in internalizing problems, such as depressive symptomatology and anxiety (Miller and Eisenberg 1988), which turn problematic feelings inward against themselves. Thus, women more often experience a sense of loss and hopelessness, with attributions of self-blame and self-reproach. Women also live with more fear, including phobias, panic attacks, and free-floating anxiety.

These gender differences cannot be completely explained by physical differences between the sexes (Brooks-Gunn and Warren 1989; Paikoff, Brooks-Gunn, and Warren 1991). Nor do the differences in norms for expressing emotions between males and females account for the disparities (Ross and Mirowsky 1995). Instead, it appears that males' and females' social positions and experiences predispose them to these different problems (Dohrenwend and Dohrenwend 1976). Most research on gendered positions

This work was supported in part by grants from the National Institute of Mental Health (#RO1 MH 39195-01 and #RO1 MH 42917-02).

and experience focuses on adult social roles. However, recent studies show that gender differences emerge in early adolescence, suggesting that socialization and dimensions of the self are crucial factors (Avison and McAlpine 1992; Compas and Orosan 1993; Kessler et al. 1993; Peterson, Sarigiani, and Kennedy 1991; Sorenson, Rutter, and Aneshensel 1991; Turner and Lloyd 1995).

In this chapter we delineate the social, interpersonal, and individual forces that affect the emotional makeup of males and females in order to identify strategic targets of intervention across the life cycle. First, we briefly provide a historical perspective on some of the conceptions of gender that are now taken for granted. Second, to illuminate how differential conceptions of self and other emerge and are nurtured, we describe how individuals are socialized to their gender roles. We then describe how these "self-other" conceptions translate into different mental health problems for males and females, most notably disruptive behavior disorders among men and depressive disorders among women. Throughout, we support these ideas with existing empirical, quantitative literature from our own work and that of other colleagues. Finally, on the basis of the results of this inquiry, we recommend interventions at the macrosocial, social, and individual levels to modify power inequities, alter the course of mental health disparities among men and women, and improve the mental health conditions of both genders in childhood, adolescence, and adulthood.

A Historical Perspective on Gender and Power

The differences between males and females in psychological problems can be traced to large cultural and structural divisions that have become associated with gender. These divisions, in turn, shape dimensions of the self that have consequences for both externalizing and internalizing disorders.

With the rise of industrial capitalism in the 1800s, the social situations of males and females shifted (Flax 1993). Earlier, both men and women produced goods within the home. In addition to raising children, women had productive responsibilities together with men. With industrialization, the workplace became separate from the home. Men began to leave home to work, and women stayed home to care for the children and the household. Thus the public and private spheres became more sharply divided by gender. The public realm of production and the associated characteristics of independence, self-sufficiency, and self-assertion were separated from the private realm of domesticity and the characteristics associated with it, such as nurturance and caretaking. The public sphere became associated with males and masculinity, while the private sphere became associated with females and femininity.

Regardless of employment status, women today retain primary responsibility for domestic labor, especially caring for the young and the old. Women are also more responsible for emotion work—that is, managing personal and interpersonal emotional life in private relationships and in the jobs they hold (Hochschild 1979).

Gender continues to shape power through men's and women's economic resources and the status or esteem connected with their social positions (Weber 1946). In the labor force, women earn less than men, a wage gap attributable in part to the devaluation of women's skills (Kilbourne et al. 1994). Women's economic vulnerability is represented in the feminization of poverty. Also, income is often divided unequally within the family. Husbands receive more than wives, and wives spend more of their share on the children. Consistent with this, within marriages wives generally have less decision-making power than their husbands do (Rosenfield 1989, 1992, 1999b).

Current social practices reflect these divisions, polarizing the social experiences of males and females. From childhood, parents treat sons and daughters differently. Sons are given more freedom and independence than daughters (Best and Williams 1993). The greater freedom promotes a risk-taking, entrepreneurial spirit among boys that prepares them to enter the adult sphere of production. Greater supervision discourages girls from risk-taking and independence, preparing them for the domestic sphere. A great deal of research has demonstrated that such differential socialization of males and females occurs across a host of settings and situations—in nursery and elementary school and college classrooms (Geis 1993), in play activities and household chores (Lytton and Romney 1991; Tittle 1986), and in peer-group interactions (Meyer et al. 1991).

Gender, Self-conceptions, and Mental Health

The divisions in power and labor between males and females have implications for their self-conceptions, including their schemas about the self and social relationships (Rosenfield 1999b). Men's greater power and responsibility for the public sphere encourage self-conceptions that privilege the self over the collective, including higher esteem for the self in general and relative to others, greater autonomy, and more dominance in relationships. Women's lower power and responsibility for the private sphere promote conceptions of the self that emphasize the collective over the self, including lower self-esteem generally and relative to others, greater connectedness to other people, and a more subordinate stance in relationships.

These arguments draw on schema theories insofar as they propose that individuals develop cognitive generalizations from past experiences (Epstein

1991; Markus 1977). In contrast to most schema theories, however, our perspective emphasizes the role of macrosocial forces such as gender stratification in developing interpretations about the self and the social world. Our view also stresses the role of schemas about the importance of the self versus the collective in mental health. These schemas, referred to as self-salience, include individuals' evaluations of their *worth* (i.e., self-esteem and mastery in general and relative to others), *boundaries* (connectedness versus separateness), and *ranking* of their own needs and interests versus those of others (Rosenfield 1999b, 2002; Rosenfield, Lennon, and White 2003). Self-salience schemas have a strong emotional as well as cognitive valence and, like other schemas, filter our interpretations of experiences in a seemingly automatic way.

Self-salience schemas are transmitted through macrosocial processes, reinforced in socialization experiences and expressed in individual emotional tendencies and behavioral inclinations among boys and girls, as well as men and women. Our own research, together with that of others, leads us to conclude that these schemas play a large role in laying the foundation for the divergence of psychopathology based on gender. Moreover, these assumptions take hold during adolescence, becoming somewhat habitual ways of seeing oneself, interacting with others, and coping with new situations.

Self-salience, Adolescent Development, and Mental Health

While gender socialization begins in childhood, it intensifies in adolescence—the time when the differences in mental health symptoms emerge. In childhood, individuals have a limited developmental capacity to view themselves and others as objects to be judged and evaluated (Harter 1999). During adolescence, youth concretize their schemas about the self in general and in relation to others in large part because they enter the formal operations stage of development. At this stage, individuals acquire an increased capacity for abstraction and generalization (Harter 1999; Piaget 1954). These cognitive abilities are prerequisites for the self-reflection, self-evaluation, and finely tuned social comparison processes necessary for a looking-glass self and a sense of generalized other (Harter 1999; Rosenberg 1989). In addition, establishing a separate identity is one of the primary psychological goals of adolescence. Issues of individuation and autonomy preside at this time (Chodorow 1978; Erikson 1968). For these reasons, the conceptions of gender developed in childhood become personalized in adolescence. That is, in adolescence we begin to apply to ourselves the general stereotypes that we internalized in childhood (Link 1987), and self-salience becomes a highly developed fundamental assumption about the self. With repeated reinforcements from significant others, core schemas about the self in relation to others carry a great deal of weight and have considerable stability (Dodge 1993; Harter 1999; Hoyle et al. 1999; Rosenberg 1989).

Thus, conceptions about one's relative worth, the boundaries between self and others, and the relative ranking of one's needs versus the needs of others emerge in adolescence. Gender-based differences in mental health may arise at this time partly because of the way that boys and girls are socialized to understand, feel, and act on their conceptions of self in relation to others. In the main, boys learn to devalue others in relation to self, and girls to devalue self in relation to others; boys learn the value of distancing themselves from others, and girls learn to connect; boys learn to put their needs before those of others, and girls learn to put the needs of others before their own (Rosenfield 1999b, 2002, 2003; Rosenfield, Vertefuille, and McAlpine 2000). These discrepancies contribute to the divergence of depressive symptoms and antisocial behavior.

Power, Privilege, and Mental Health Outcomes

At the extremes, schemas that privilege the collectivity are connected to internalizing problems (Rosenfield 1999b; Rosenfield, Lennon, and White 2003). The more individuals take on and attend to the feelings and desires of others, the less they can act in their own interest. In its strongest form, taking others' needs too seriously precludes acting on one's own. The inability to act in pursuit of one's own interests predisposes individuals to feelings of helplessness and hopelessness that characterize depressive symptoms. Insofar as individuals feel that there is something fundamentally wrong with them that they cannot change, low self-esteem also contributes to feelings of helplessness. Excessive reliance on others generates uncertainty and anxiety about one's own abilities and self-worth, feelings that also distinguish depressive symptomatology (Turner and Turner 1999).

At the other extreme, assumptions that overemphasize the self are more conducive to externalizing behavior (Rosenfield 1999b; Rosenfield, Lennon, and White 2003). Focusing on one's own interests and feelings to the exclusion of those of others allows one to act against the latter: others are viewed as an interference, something to get out of the way. Conversely, identifying with another's interests or feeling what another might feel (i.e., experiencing empathy) impedes any desire to harm another person (Ohbuchi, Ohno, and Mukai 1992). An act against someone else is experienced as an act against oneself.

There is evidence that low self-salience—including low self-esteem, interpersonal dependency, and perceptions of relationship inequality—is tied to symptoms of depression and anxiety (see, for example, Hirschfield et al. 1976; Lennon and Rosenfield 1995; Mirowsky 1985; Mirowsky and Ross 1996; Pearlin et al. 1981; Rosenberg 1989; Rosenfield, Lennon, and White 2003; Rosenfield, Vertefuille, and McAlpine 2000; Turner and Turner 1999). There is also evidence that high self-salience—such as greater self-esteem relative to others, high autonomy, and dominance in relationships—is linked to antisocial behavior and substance abuse (Baumeister, Smart, and Boden 1999; Beck 1999; Kaplan 1980; Kaplan, Martin, and Johnson 1986; Rosenfield, Lennon, and White 2003; Rosenfield, Vertefuille, and McAlpine 2000).

Application to Gender Differences in Mental Health

The perspective above suggests that internalizing and externalizing mental health problems have common roots in relational schemas about self-salience, which are gendered. Because females tend toward extremes that emphasize the group at the expense of the self, they are pushed more strongly than males toward internalizing symptoms. Because males tend toward extremes that emphasize the individual over the collectivity, they are pushed more strongly than females toward externalizing behaviors. Through this process, the gender divisions in power and labor predispose males and females to opposing problematic extremes.

Ample research shows that males and females differ in aspects of self-salience. In adolescence and adulthood, females are lower in self-esteem and personal control than males (Craighead and Green 1989; Josephs, Markus, and Tafarodi 1992; Nolen-Hoeksema, Girgus, and Seligman 1991; Owens 1994; Pearlin et al. 1981). They also report greater interpersonal dependency and empathy, while males are higher in autonomy (Rosenfield, Lennon, and White 2003; Rosenfield, Vertefuille, and McAlpine 2000). Finally, females perceive fewer options to relationships than males do (Lennon and Rosenfield 1995; Rosenfield, Vertefuille, and McAlpine 2000).

Research also shows that these differences contribute to the gender differences in mental health problems. Females' greater rates of internalizing symptoms and males' higher levels of externalizing problems are partly explained by their tendencies toward low and high self-salience, respectively (Avison and McAlpine 1992; Kessler, McLeod, and Wethington 1984; Rosenfield 2002; Rosenfield, Lennon, and White 2003; Rosenfield, Vertefuille, and McAlpine 2000; Turner and Turner 1999).

The Role of Power and Privilege in Coping

The macrosocial processes that privilege males relative to females lead to different responses to social situations. Such differences in reacting to and coping with stress may also account for some of the sex differentials in mental health problems. For example, men more often actively engage in problem-solving efforts and attempt to control problems than women do (Thoits 1992, 1999). By contrast, women more often solicit social support, express their feelings, and try to distract themselves from problems (Thoits 1992, 1999). Coping strategies that reflect a high sense of mastery are associated with lower depression and may partly explain the lower rates of depression in men relative to women (Folkman and Lazarus 1980; Kessler, McLeod, and Wethington 1984).

Men and women also react to similar social situations differently by using norms for gender-appropriate behaviors and feelings. For example, males are expected to suppress emotions, especially those viewed as feminine and weak (Tavris 1992). Men are discouraged from showing feelings like helplessness, worry, and insecurity—all of which are associated with anxiety and depression. By contrast, emotions such as fear and helplessness are more normative for women (Tavris 1992). Cross-sex emotions are discouraged, sometimes punished, and may even lead to service-delivery disparities between the genders. For example, our own research has shown that men who come into psychiatric emergency rooms with depressive symptoms are hospitalized at much higher rates than women with the same symptoms. Likewise, women who enter with antisocial disorders or substance abuse are more likely to be hospitalized than men with the same problems. These types of cases of "double deviance" are treated much more severely, illustrating that there are norms even in deviating (Rosenfield 1984) and also demonstrating that gender-based normative reactions function to reinforce the divergent mental health problems that are observed in males and females.

Improving Mental Health Among Males and Females

We have presented data to show that males and females tend to have different psychological problems because they (a) encounter different social experiences, (b) develop self-conceptions that encourage these tendencies, and (c) follow gender-based norms based on these self-conceptions in reacting to their social situations. To improve the mental health of both men and women, and to prevent the gendered divergence of mental health problems witnessed across the life cycle, we must develop effective strategies of intervention in these three processes.

Changing Social Experiences

Promoting social structures that support equality of men and women will help to improve the mental health conditions of both men and women. This requires intervening in the macrosocial environment. For example, the changing structure of work and family life, and its meaning to both men and women, is one potential target of intervention. Our own research, based on a national survey, showed that men whose wives worked experienced less job and life satisfaction than men whose wives did not work. Controlling for a number of demographic and workplace factors, we found that this result was attributable to husbands' concerns about their adequacy as breadwinners: men whose wives worked did not think they could support their families comfortably on their incomes alone, while men whose wives did not work thought they could support their families comfortably on their incomes alone. Thus, men's perception of their breadwinner adequacy contributed to the disparities between the dual-earner and single-earner families (Rosenfield 1992; Staines, Pottick, and Fudge 1985).

In general, women who combine roles of work and family—especially when children are involved—are frequently conflicted about being employed and question their family commitment. For women, income is not a central aspect of the parent and spousal role, though it is for men. However, raising a family on one income alone is becoming a great hardship for a vast number of families, so that dual-earner families are now the norm rather than the exception.

The changing character of the public and private spheres for men and women represents a unique opportunity to help both men and women to adjust their responses and to develop new self-conceptions that recognize the financial resourcefulness of both members of the unit. Macro-level interventions that promote income equality in the labor force would help to equalize male and female resourcefulness and would support a resulting change in self-conceptions. Effective community organization and political activity will continue to be necessary to stimulate and maintain the essential conditions for legislative and judicial action. To the extent that power and responsibilities shift for men and women in combining the public and private spheres, it is likely to lead to a shift in self-conceptions that will ultimately improve mental health outcomes for both men and women. This will, however, require interventions to help both men and women develop skills to cope with, and adapt to, the different social experiences inherent in changing power relations.

Changing Self-conceptions

Promoting self-conceptions that encourage a balance of high self-regard and regard for others among both men and women will help to improve mental health for both genders. This requires interventions that target the individual psyche. Helping both males and females to strike a balance between valuing the interests of others and valuing their own interests also may reduce the likelihood that males and females will veer toward externalizing or internalizing disorders and may even ease the severity of these mental health problems. Self-conceptions that place one as neither better nor worse than others, neither overly connected nor detached, and neither dominant nor submissive in relationships should lead to lower levels of internalizing and externalizing problems. We take a preventative stance here and suggest that strategic interventions should start in childhood when conceptions of self are being shaped—long before they bloom and become solidified during adolescence.

Dimensions of the self are only one source of mental health problems, but they are particularly promising for sociological investigation and social work intervention. Schemas about one's worth, the boundaries between self and other, and power in relationships are developed in reaction to social experiences. However, the internal workings of the self are sometimes viewed in isolation, as if they were characteristics of the individual that are relatively unaffected by social processes. This inner colonization of the self is particularly problematic, for it obscures the role of the social by making it appear purely personal (Foucault 1978). We propose that significant others in children's social settings must learn basic skills to improve how they influence children to think about themselves. In addition to macrosocial interventions that alter social experiences, social work interventions should focus on helping adults—parents and other caregivers, teachers, and others in the child's network—to pay attention to and observe children's behaviors, thoughts, and feelings, and to respond to the children in ways that respect them and boost their confidence about themselves.

Practically speaking, social workers should devote considerable effort to modeling behaviors that identify injustices and support appropriate feelings that emerge from experiencing injustice. In this way, children may gain confidence in their ability to evaluate their experiences: girls may be more likely to understand the environmental sources of their feelings, potentially derailing negative self-evaluations that undergird depression; boys may be less likely to embrace their "unearned privilege," potentially suppressing feelings of superiority that underscore aggression (McIntosh 1998). Thus, validating children's feelings that result from unfair social experiences, and training adults who are in the child's network, would help to improve the mental health of both males and females.

Changing Reactions to Social Situations

Promoting a new set of reactions to social situations that weaken the impact of normative, gender-based self-conceptions will improve the mental health of both males and females. This requires interventions that target individuals in their social environments, and demands practicing new behaviors in actual situations so that the gender-based and dominant reaction is replaced by a new, nondominant one that is less normative. Learning new reactions in social situations means learning new social skills. The toughest test is among individuals who have already incorporated gender-based social experiences, corresponding self-conceptions, and mental health problems of aggression (predominantly males) and depression (predominantly females).

Among children, there is growing evidence that cognitive-behavioral interventions for depressive or aggressive disorders are successful in reducing symptoms. Kendall and MacDonald (1993) note that depressed youth suffer from low self-evaluations—lower than their counterparts, even when, in fact, they are not less competent scholastically or lower in social status (Asarnow and Bates 1988, as cited in Kendall and MacDonald 1993). For depressed youth, the goal of treatment is to identify the distorted processing, to aid the child in modifying the distorted thinking, and to teach the child new coping processing styles (Kendall et al. 1992a, 1992b). Intervention focuses on modifying maladaptive cognitions, targeting the assumptions and attitudes that underlie the child's thoughts. One such effective therapeutic technique is to helping children learn to be their own "Thought Detectives," identifying their thoughts, looking for evidence, and examining alternative explanations (Stark, Rouse, and Livingston 1991) in reaction to real situations.

Aggression in children, according to Kendall and MacDonald (1993), results from cognitive deficiencies as well as cognitive distortions. In other words, a child's aggressive reaction to a situation is not based entirely on the factual aspects of the situation. Rather, it is largely affected by a deficiency in assessing the situation and the distorted manner in which the child processes the social information. They demonstrate that the children with aggressive responses have deficiencies in correctly utilizing social cues, interpreting cues as hostile when they are not. Also, these youth have difficulties in problem solving that result in part from tendencies to generate aggressive solutions to social problems relative to their non-aggressive peers (see Kendall and MacDonald 1993 for a review). Treatment recommendations include self-evaluation and social perspective-taking skills to aid in changing aggressive children's hostile distortions. To alter cognitive deficiencies of problem solving, verbal solutions such as negotiation and discussion are encouraged, while direct action is discouraged. Children learn cognitive self-control strategies in which they develop a wide range of coping statements that they practice in increasingly more provocative situations.

The above strategies are effective in altering reactions to social situations by building and practicing skills of behaving and thinking differently. As a consequence, these strategies also may help equalize how males and females see themselves: as people of worth, connected yet independent, and with power in relationships.

Conclusion

This chapter has examined a particular line of investigation for explaining gender differences in mental health problems. We focus on relational schemas about self-salience in producing these differences. In general, self-salience shapes the likelihood of experiencing internalizing or externalizing problems. Those who privilege others over the self experience greater internalizing symptoms, while those who privilege the self exhibit more externalizing behavior. Self-salience varies by gender. While females tend to put others first, males tend to privilege the self more highly. These tendencies toward opposite ends of self-salience contribute to the excess of internalizing problems in females and of externalizing problems in males. On the basis of this evidence, we propose a number of interventions aimed at equalizing self-salience in males and females. Since these differences first arise in adolescence and persist through adulthood, the interventions target different developmental points.

More generally, we suggest, for two reasons, that future research requires theoretically driven experimental interventions with detailed specifications. First, specification allows us to replicate effective interventions in actual natural or service settings. Because we want to design interventions that produce better results, we must identify the effective components of the change strategies. Second, specification enables us to test specific relationships between change strategies and outcomes and to identify which change components work well and which require further development. Specificity produces multiple, competing hypotheses, a basic requirement to generate and test theory about cause and effect. In the end, theory-driven research on gender and mental health problems may lead to significant improvements in the mental health of both males and females.

References

Aneshensel, Carol S., Carolyn M. Rutter, and Peter A. Lachenbruch. 1991. Social structure, stress, and mental health: Competing conceptual and analytic models. *American Sociological Review* 56:166–178.

Avison, William R. and Donna D. McAlpine. 1992. Gender differences in symptoms and depression among adolescents. *Journal of Health and Social Behavior* 33:77–96.

Baumeister, Roy F., Laura Smart, and Joseph Boden. 1999. Relation of Threatened Egotism to Violence and Aggression: The Dark Side of High Self-Esteem. In R. Baumeister, ed., *The Self in Social Psychology*, 240–280. Philadelphia: Psychology Press.

Beck, Aaron T. 1999. *Prisoners of Hate: The Cognitive Basis of Anger, Hostility, and Violence*. New York: Harper Collins.

Best, D. and J. Williams. 1993. A Cross-Cultural Viewpoint. In A. Beal and R. Sternberg, eds., *The Psychology of Gender*, 215–250. New York: Guilford.

Brooks-Gunn, J. and Michelle P. Warren. 1989. Biological and social contributions to negative affect in young adolescent girls. *Child Development* 60:40–55.

Chodorow, Nancy. 1978. *The Reproduction of Mothering*. Berkeley: University of California Press.

Compas, Bruce E. and Pamela G. Orosan. 1993. Adolescent stress and coping: Implications for psychopathology during adolescence. *Journal of Adolescence* 16:331–349.

Craighead, Linda Wilcoxon and Barbara Joan Green. 1989. Relationship between depressed mood and sex-typed personality characteristics in adolescents. *Journal of Youth and Adolescence* 18:467–474.

Dodge, Kenneth A. 1993. Social-cognitive mechanisms in the development of conduct disorder and depression. *Annual Review of Psychology* 44:559–584.

Dohrenwend, Bruce P. and Barbara Dohrenwend. 1976. Sex differences in psychiatric disorders. *American Journal of Sociology* 81:1447–1454.

Epstein, Seymour. 1991. Cognitive-Experiential Self-Theory: An Integrative Theory of Personality. In R. Curtis, ed., *The Relational Self: Convergence in Psychoanalysis and Social Psychology*, 111–137. New York: Guilford Press.

Erikson, Erik H. 1968. *Identity, Youth, and Crisis*. New York: Norton.

Flax, Jane. 1993. *Disputed Subjects: Essays on Psychoanalysis, Politics, and Philosophy*. New York: Routledge.

Folkman, S. and R. S. Lazarus. 1980. An analysis of coping in a middle-aged community sample. *Journal of Health and Social Behavior* 21:219–329.

Foucault, Michel. 1978. *The History of Sexuality*. New York: Vintage Books.

Geis, F. 1993. Self-Fulfilling Prophesies: A Social Psychological View of Gender. In A. Beal and R. Sternberg, eds., *The Psychology of Gender*, 9–54. New York: Guilford Press.

Harter, Susan. 1999. *The Construction of the Self*. New York: Guilford Press.

Hirschfield, Robert M. A., Gerald L. Klerman, Paul Chodoff, Sheldon Korchin, and James Barrett. 1976. Dependency–self-esteem–clinical depression. *Psychoanalysis* 4:373–388.

Hochschild, Arlie Russel. 1979. Emotion work, feeling rules, and social structure. *American Journal of Sociology* 85:551–575.

Hoyle, Rick H., Michael H. Kernis, Mark R. Leary, and Mark W. Baldwin. 1999. *Selfhood: Identity, Esteem, Regulation*. Boulder: Westview.

Josephs, Robert A., Hazel Rose Markus, and Romin W. Tafarodi. 1992. Gender and self-esteem. *Journal of Personality and Social Psychology* 63:391–402

Kaplan, Howard. 1980. *Deviant Behavior in Defense of Self.* New York: Academic Press.

Kaplan, Howard, Steven S. Martin, and Robert J. Johnson. 1986. Self-rejection and the explanation of deviance: Specification of the structure among latent constructs. *American Journal of Sociology* 92:384–411.

Kendall, Philip C., T. E. Chansky, M. T. Kane et al. 1992a. *Anxiety Disorders in Youth: Cognitive-Behavioral Interventions.* Needham, Mass.: Allyn and Bacon.

Kendall, Philip C., E. Kortlander, T. E. Chansky, and E. Brady. 1992b. Comorbidity of anxiety and depression in youth: Implications for treatment. *Journal of Consulting and Clinical Psychology* 60:869–880.

Kendall, Philip C. and Jennifer P. MacDonald. 1993. Cognition in the psychopathology of youth and implications for treatment. In K. S. Dobson and P. C. Kendall, eds., *Psychopathology and Cognition,* 387–416. San Diego: Academic Press.

Kessler, Ronald C., Katherine A. McGonagle, Marvin Schwartz, Dan G. Glazer, and Christopher B. Nelson. 1993. Sex and depression in the National Comorbidity Survey. I. Lifetime prevalence, chronicity, and recurrence. *Journal of Affective Disorders* 25:85–96.

Kessler, Ronald C., Jane D. McLeod, and Elaine Wethington. 1984. The Costs of Caring: A Perspective on the Relationship Between Sex and Psychological Distress. In I. G. Sarason and B. R. Sarason, eds., *Social Support, Theory, Research, and Application,* 491–506. The Hague: Martinus Nijhof.

Kilbourne, Barbara Stanek, Paula England, George Farkas, Kurt Brown, and Dorothea Weir. 1994. Returns to skill, compensating differentials, and gender bias: Effects of occupational characteristics on the wages of white women and men. *American Journal of Sociology* 100:689–719.

Lennon, Mary Clare and Sarah Rosenfield. 1995. Relative fairness and the division of household work. *American Journal of Sociology* 100:506–531.

Link, Bruce G. 1987. Understanding labeling effects in the area of mental disorders: An assessment of the effects of expectations of rejection. *American Sociological Review* 52:96–112.

Lytton, H. and D. M. Romney. 1991. Parents' differential socialization of boys and girls: A meta-analysis. *Psychological Bulletin* 109:267–296.

Markus, Hazel. 1977. Self-schemata and processing information about the self. *Journal of Personality and Social Psychology* 35:63–78.

McIntosh, Peggy. 1998. White Privilege: Unpacking the Invisible Knapsack. In Monica McGoldrick, ed., *Re-visioning Family Therapy: Race, Culture, and Gender in Clinical Practice.* New York: Guilford.

Meyer, S. L., C. Murphy, M. Cascardi, and B. Birns. 1991. Gender and relationships: Beyond the peer group. *American Psychologist* 46:537–549.

Miller, Paul A. and Nancy Eisenberg. 1988. The relation of empathy to aggressive and externalizing/antisocial behavior. *Psychological Bulletin* 103:324–344.

Mirowsky, John. 1985. Depression and marital power: An equity model. *American Journal of Sociology* 91:557–592.

Mirowsky, John and Catherine Ross. 1996. Fundamental analysis in research on well-being: Distress and the sense of control. *Gerontologist* 36:584–594.

Nolen-Hoeksema, Susan. 1990. *Sex Differences in Depression.* Stanford, Calif.: Stanford University Press.

Nolen-Hoeksema, Susan, J. S. Girgus, and M. E. P. Seligman. 1991. Sex differences in depression and explanatory style in children. *Journal of Youth and Adolescence* 20:233–245.

Ohbuchi, Ken-Ichi, Tsutomu Ohno, and Hiroko Mukai. 1992. Empathy and aggression: Effects of self-disclosure and fearful appeal. *Journal of Social Psychology* 133:243–253.

Owens, Timothy J. 1994. Two dimensions of self-esteem: Reciprocal effects of positive self-worth and self-deprecation on adolescent problems. *American Sociological Review* 59:391–407.

Paikoff, Roberta I., Jeanne Brooks-Gunn, and Michelle P. Warren. 1991. Effects of girls' hormonal status on depressive and aggressive symptoms over the course of one year. *Journal of Youth and Adolescence* 20:191–215.

Pearlin, Leonard I., Morton A. Lieberman, Elizabeth G. Menaghan, and Joseph T. Mullan. 1981. The stress process. *Journal of Health and Social Behavior* 22:337–356.

Peterson, Anne C., Pamela A. Sarigiani, and Robert E. Kennedy. 1991. Adolescent depression: Why more girls? *Journal of Youth and Adolescence* 20:247–271.

Piaget, Jean. 1954. *The Construction of Reality in the Child.* New York: Basic Books.

Rosenberg, Morris. 1989. Self-concept research: A historical overview. *Social Forces* 68:34–44.

Rosenfield, Sarah. 1984. Race differences in involuntary hospitalization: Psychiatric vs. labeling perspectives. *Journal of Health and Social Behavior* 25:14–23.

———. 1989. The effects of women's employment: Personal control and sex differences in mental health. *Journal of Health and Social Behavior* 30:77–91.

———. 1992. The costs of sharing: Wives' employment and husbands' mental health. *Journal of Health and Social Behavior* 33:213–225.

———. 1999a. Gender and Mental Health: Do Women Have More Psychopathology, Men More, or Both the Same (and Why)? In A. Horwitz and T. Sheid, eds., *The Sociology of Mental Health and Illness,* 348–360. New York: Cambridge University Press.

———. 1999b. Splitting the Difference: Gender, Psychopathology, and the Self. In C. Aneshensel and J. Phelan, eds., *Handbook of the Sociology of Mental Health,* 209–224. New York: Plenum.

———. 2002. "Gender, Race, and Mental Health." Paper presented at the Society for the Study of Social Problems, Chicago.

Rosenfield, Sarah, Mary Clare Lennon, and Helene Raskin White. 2003. "Mental Health and the Self: Self-Salience and the Emergence of Internalizing and Externalizing Problems." Paper presented at the American Sociological Association meeting, Atlanta.

Rosenfield, Sarah, Jean Vertefuille, and Donna McAlpine. 2000. Gender stratification and mental health: An exploration of dimensions of the self. *Social Psychology Quarterly* 63:208–223.

Ross, Catherine E. and John Mirowsky. 1995. Sex differences in distress: Real or artifact? *American Sociological Review* 60:449–468.

Sorenson, Susan, Carolyn Rutter, and Carol Aneshensel. 1991. Depression in the community: An investigation into age of onset. *Journal of Consulting Clinical Psychology* 59:541–546.

Staines, Graham, Kathleen J. Pottick, and Deborah Fudge. 1985. Wives' employment and husbands' attitudes toward work and life. *Journal of Applied Psychology* 71:118–128.

Stark, Kevin D., Lawrence W. Rouse, and Ronald B. Livingston. 1991. Treatment of Depression During Childhood and Adolescence: Cognitive-Behavioral Procedures for the Family. In P. C. Kendall, ed., *Child and Adolescent Therapy: Cognitive-Behavioral Procedures,* 165–208. New York: Guilford Press.

Tavris, Carol. 1992. *The Mismeasure of Woman.* New York: Simon and Schuster.

Thoits, Peggy A. 1992. Identity structures and psychological well-being: Gender and marital status comparisons. *Social Psychology Quarterly* 55:236–256.

———. 1999. Self, Identity, and Mental Health. In C. Aneshensel and J. Phelan, eds., *Handbook of the Sociology of Mental Health,* 345–368. New York: Plenum.

Tittle, C. K. 1986. Gender research and education. *American Psychologist* 42:1162–1168.

Turner, Heather A. and R. Jay Turner. 1999. Gender, social status, and emotional reliance. *Journal of Health and Social Behavior* 40:360–373.

Turner, R. Jay and Donald Lloyd. 1995. Lifetime traumas and mental health: The significance of cumulative adversity. *Journal of Health and Social Behavior* 36:360–376.

Weber, Max. 1946. *Max Weber: Essays in Sociology.* Oxford: Oxford University Press.

PART III

EVIDENCE–BASED PRACTICE

Chapter 13

Evidence-Based Practice: Breakthrough or Buzzword?

William J. Reid and Julanne Colvin

Evidence-based practice (EBP) is currently receiving considerable attention in mental health. From one point of view it can be seen as a major break-through—the culmination of a long-term movement to place human services on a scientific footing. After decades of effort, enough scientifically validated knowledge and technology have now accumulated to enable practice to be based on evidence as opposed to theory, authority, tradition, or some other source of enlightenment. From another, more cynical point of view, EBP is the latest buzzword, one that will be on people's lips for a while but that will eventually fade into the background, while the world of practice remains pretty much the same. Somewhere between those two extremes, EBP could be seen as one of many recent developments in the human services that will have a noteworthy but limited effect on practice—perhaps comparable to the addition of another model of intervention to the scads that are already in use. Which of these—or other—views prevail is, of course, the fundamental issue in EBP. How much of a difference will it make in services to clients?

How this question is answered hinges on the outcome of a variety of specific issues relating to EBP. Whether they are solvable and how they are solved will determine how much of an impact EBP will have. In this chapter we will review and comment on some of the more salient of these issues. Our focus will be on agency-based mental health services provided by social workers.

What Is EBP?

While general agreement exists that EBP is a form of practice that makes systematic use of scientific evidence, there are quite different notions about how this practice should be defined.

Perhaps the best-articulated vision of EBP is the one derived from the work of Sackett et al. (1996, 2000) and Gray (2001), who have been the principal architects of the EBP movement in medicine. Leading exponents of their views in social work have been Gambrill (1999, 2003) and Gibbs (2003). In this conception EBP consists of a number of steps: needs for knowledge are translated into answerable questions; questions are answered through scientifically based evidence acquired primarily through search of computerized databases; the evidence is critically appraised and applied to the decision at hand; the outcome of the application is recorded. The method emphasizes client concerns and expectations, sharing of evidence with clients, and collaborative decision making about the course of action suggested by the evidence (Gambrill 2003; Gibbs and Gambrill 2002). This vision of EBP amounts to a complex and systematic problem-solving model.

The other major conception of EBP is less well developed. It refers generally to practice that uses knowledge and interventions with research validation, but it leaves open the question of how this practice is to be done. For example, Hoagwood et al. (2001:1179) define EBP in child and adolescent mental health services research as "a body of scientific knowledge about service practices—for example, referral, assessment, and case management—or about the impact of clinical treatments on the mental health problems of children and adolescents." In her *Evidence-Based Social Work Practice with Families,* Corcoran (2000:xi) refers to EBP as "approaches with demonstrated effectiveness" but has little more to say in the way of definition or procedures. Drake et al. (2001) and Torrey et al. (2001) discuss implementation of EBP on the assumption that such practice consists of service practitioners using research-supported treatment guidelines. None of the literature cited in this paragraph mentions the kind of EBP that follows the conception of Sackett et al. (2000) or Gibbs (2003).

Although the Sackett et al./Gibbs conception is the more systematic, there is question about how well social workers might be able to apply it in today's mental health settings with their oversized caseloads and undersized budgets. The approach is labor-intensive, requiring time to formulate questions and do searches. Moreover, practitioners must have access to computers and databases and know how to use them. Finally, the approach may work better in medicine than in mental health, given medicine's more extensive research base. Despite these limitations, the use of EBP should be encouraged. Its stress on finding evidence-based answers to practice questions concerning individual clients and involving clients in evidence-based decisions is a commendable feature that can be used in conjunction with other forms of EBP.

Henceforth we will use the broader (and looser) conception of EBP in our examination of issues, since this conception currently appears to be the dominant one in the mental health services literature. Most of the issues raised, however, will apply to all forms of EBP. The notion of "evidence-based" practice may apply to any form of social work practice, including administrative and policy decisions as well as clinical assessment and intervention. Most attention has been given to its use in clinical intervention, and that will also be our focus.

What Kind of Evidence Is Needed?

Questions inevitably arise about how much and what kind of evidence is needed in order to regard a particular intervention as "evidence-based," or as being more effective than an alternative intervention. A major effort to tackle this problem with respect to interventions in the mental health area has been the work of the Society of Clinical Psychology, which has developed a list of empirically supported interventions that must meet certain evidentiary criteria (Chambless and Hollon 1998; Chambless and Ollendick 2001; Weisz et al. 2000). For example, in order to qualify as "well established" or clearly empirically supported, an intervention must demonstrate superiority to another therapy, including placebo treatment (or equivalence to an already established treatment). Designs must be "good," effects must be demonstrated by two more investigators (or teams), and treatment manuals must be used. A lesser level of empirically supported intervention is referred to as "probably efficacious" and requires less-rigorous standards of proof; for example, an intervention can qualify if it surpasses a waitlist control group in two experiments.

Such "rules of evidence " (Weisz et al. 2000) raise at least three sets of issues. One has to do with the methodological quality of the research used to evaluate the evidence obtained. While there may be general agreement at the extremes—that a randomized trial produces better evidence than an uncontrolled study—there may be differences of opinion about how to weigh the host of design compromises that fall in between. For example, the society's criteria referred to above regard as "probably efficacious" a treatment that surpasses waitlist controls in two experiments. However, it could be argued that waitlist controls may produce the same selection biases from one study to the next. For instance, clients who are more highly motivated, who are likely to do better, may be more likely to end up in the experimental group. Thus replications of waitlist designs may be of questionable value.

Such debates may, of course, also involve types of outcomes selected, measurements used, the length of follow-up periods, if any, and other design elements. Systematic, multidimensional methods of evaluating methodology quality, such as those developed by Miller et al. (1998), offer promise, particular if one such method could be generally accepted as a standard.

Another aspect of methodological quality concerns more or less standard features of intervention research that limit confidence in the results. Here the issue is usually not which experiment is methodologically superior but rather the effect of weaknesses that characterize most studies. One of the more troublesome is investigator allegiance, a form of bias that suggests that the outcome of an intervention experiment might be shaped in the direction of the researcher's expectations, hopes, and other predictions. There is a good deal of evidence to suggest that such effects occur (Gorey 1996; Luborsky et al. 1999; Robinson, Berman, and Neimeyer 1990; Smith, Glass, and Miller 1980). Since most intervention experiments are conducted by adherents who have a stake in the outcome (Reid and Fortune 2003), investigator allegiance can be seen as a standard limitation, even though there is evidence that allegiance does not account for all intervention effects (Gorey 1996) and one can argue that adherence to an intervention may be the consequence of proof of its effectiveness (Weisz et al. 1995).

The classic solution in science to problems of investigator bias has been independent replication, little of which is done. To be sure, repeated trials of an intervention by different investigators may be referred to as "replications"—for example, in the criteria used by the Society for Clinical Psychology. However, such replications are usually carried out by investigators with similar expectations that the intervention will be effective. What is needed are funded replication programs or centers headed by investigators whose interests lie in advancing evaluation or knowledge generally rather than any particular brand of intervention. In addition, when different treatments are compared it may be possible for adherents of each to be represented on the research team.

Another common limitation of methodological quality is the heavy reliance in mental health intervention research on two kinds of potentially misleading measures: client self-report and hospitalization. Interviews, standardized tests, or other kinds of self-report form the measurement backbone of most evaluations of intervention for outpatient disorders. Clients' reports of symptoms or behavior, even on well-validated instruments, may reflect social desirability, expectation, and cognitive dissonance effects (Karoly and Wheeler-Anderson 2000). In addition, clients who have invested time, effort, and often money in therapy with the expectation that it will make things better may be more likely to exaggerate its benefits or to report transient gains than "control" clients who have received placebo or other minimal treatments. Hospitalization or rehospitalization is widely used in intervention programs, such as intensive case management for people with serious mental illness. While they may be valid indicators of program outcome, these status-change measures may also reflect the biases of practitioners or researchers who may have a lot to say about whether hospitalization will occur (Gomory 1999; see also Gomory, chapter 9 of this volume).

Despite their drawbacks, self-report and status measures do convey useful information and, given the lack of alternatives, will continue to be used. However, the use of principles of triangulation and multiplism (Cook 1987) could place more emphasis on measures such as data from collaterals or independent observers, which are less dependent on either clients served or those serving them.

The general limitations reviewed above do not, in our judgment, contravene the assertion that many forms of intervention are demonstrably effective, even though their effects may be somewhat inflated. When these limitations are combined with other methodological shortfalls, however, the result may be low-grade evidence that offers no better guidance than practice wisdom.

A second issue concerns how to deal with the inevitable variation that occurs between treatments. Statements about the evidentiary base of an intervention typically are based on multiple tests of the intervention carried out by different investigators in different settings. Pure replications of an intervention are rare in human services research, as has been noted. Rather a "theme and variations" approach is used. If one examines a number of experiments testing intervention X, one is likely to find a good deal of purposeful variation in the characteristics of the intervention. It may be adapted to a particular disorder, population, or setting, or it may be enhanced by the addition of new components. In addition, unintended variation may result from such factors as differences in training or discipline of practitioners and differing interpretations of the intervention itself. As Weisz et al. (2000:247) suggest, one can try to ascertain "core elements of a treatment most responsible for the effects," but as they point out, it is often difficult to identify which elements are core, given our lack of empirical knowledge about change mechanisms. For example, whether "strength-based" case management with mentally ill people (Macias et al. 1997) should be lumped together with other intensive case-management programs or seen as a different type of intervention would depend on what the "strength-based" component contributed to outcome. Until a better understanding of change processes is developed, we need to rely on judgments about apparent similarities between interventions. However, such judgments can be informed by additive designs in which combined interventions are tested against their components. For example, in their evaluation of exposure therapy for obsessive-compulsive disorder, Emmelkamp, deHaan, and Hoodguin (1990) found that the use of partners to assist with treatment did not change the effectiveness of the method, which had been established in other research. Thus the test of the partner-assisted intervention could be grouped with other tests of the exposure therapy, despite the phenotypical difference, since the added partner-assisted component apparently was not a causal agent in the change process. If the effect size for the intervention with the added component had been considerably greater, then a case could have been made for differentiating between the two interventions.

A third issue concerns what kind of practice qualifies as "evidence-based." The prevailing approach has been to attach the "evidence-based" designation to interventions that meet some specified criteria of scientific validation. This is the strategy adopted by the Society for Clinical Psychology in creating lists of "well-established" and "probably efficacious" interventions. Similarly, designations of interventions as "evidence-based" or "empirically supported" may be based on reviews of intervention research in particular domains such as those found in Corcoran (2000) and in Nathan and Gorman (2002). Inherent in this approach are arbitrary judgments about what is or is not EBP, since there are no accepted criteria that specify how much and what kind of empirical support is enough to identify an intervention as evidence-based. Nor are there criteria that would specify the extent to which practice in a given caseload or facility must make use of empirically supported intervention to be considered evidence-based. Claims that "my [or our] practice is evidence-based" are likely to swell, since EBP is increasingly being viewed as a desirable mode of service delivery. Such claims will be difficult to validate, to put it mildly.

An alternative approach is to use "evidence-based" to refer to a process rather than to an intervention, as is done in the model discussed earlier (Gibbs 2003; Sackett et al. 2000). Practice is evidence-based if it follows systematic procedures for locating and using the interventions with the best evidentiary credentials. This avoids the perplexities of trying to decide if an intervention is "evidence-based" but leaves open the question of how assiduously this process must be followed if a practice is to be so characterized.

Designations of "evidence-based" themselves require evidence if they are to have any real meaning. What interventions are in fact being used, and what is their empirical support? To what extent are empirically supported methods or evidence-based processes being used by given practitioners and facilities?

How Much Guidance Can the Evidence Provide?

Practitioners faced with making decisions about which intervention to use for a particular problem want to know not only which interventions are effective but also which one is the most effective—which is the treatment of choice. They will be given minimal help if they learn that all applicable interventions are equally effective according to whatever empirical testing has been done. According to one school of thought, they will likely find themselves in exactly that quandary if the issue is some form of emotional or interpersonal problem and the intervention they are considering is some form of psychotherapy.

A number of theorists and researchers have asserted that common factors—for example, establishing a relationship with a caring professional, acquiring new learning experiences, and achieving a sense of mastery—are the primary engines of change in psychotherapy, dwarfing whatever effects may be contributed by specific ingredients (Frank and Frank 1991; Luborsky et al. 1999; Wampold 2001). Perhaps the most persuasive evidence advanced for this claim has been based on the negative findings of research reviews and meta-analyses of comparative experiments in which one form of therapy is compared to another (Ahn and Wampold 2001; Luborsky et al. 1999; Smith, Glass, and Miller 1980; Wampold et al. 1997). Lack of outcome differences between therapies in these comparisons has received support from some rigorous individual comparative studies, for example, Sloane et al. (1975) and Elkin et al. (1989).

The evidentiary base for this conclusion has been challenged on a number of grounds by critics who point to various flaws in the evidence, such as overreliance on statistical averages (Howard et al. 1997), lack of attention to the study of interactions between type of therapy, client characteristics, and other factors (Beutler 2002; Chambless 2002), the lack of statistical power in many of the comparisons (Kazdin and Bass 1989), and ignoring evidence of actual differences between treatments (Chambless 2002; Crits-Cristoph 1997). However, the challenge to the "common factors" position has not progressed much beyond criticisms of the evidence on which it is based. Criticisms of this position, well taken as they may be, do not provide the kind of evidence of differential effects that would be helpful for practitioners trying to use EBP. What is in short supply is positive evidence that different forms of psychotherapy have differential effects. Until such evidence is forthcoming, the common-factors argument beclouds the future of EBP.

In an attempt to determine if evidence for differential effects could be found, the authors and a colleague (Reid, Kenaley, and Colvin 2003) examined thirty-one social work experiments (1990–2001) that tested for differential effects between interventions that might involve common factors.

Significant differential effects were found in the great majority and in 84% of the nineteen experiments that dealt with mental health problems. Analysis of the interventions compared offered some clues as to why differential effects appeared in these experiments, as opposed to the psychotherapy experiments that have failed to find between-treatment differences. Comparisons involved greater contrasts in structure (e.g., family versus group treatment), relatively more use of groups (in which the practitioner-client relationship might be less influential), and more work with persons who had schizophrenia (with perhaps less intensity in the therapeutic relationship and more attention to environmental factors). The study suggests that the influence of common factors may become attenuated as one moves away from the intervention model with which they have been traditionally identified—interpersonal treatment of adults for nondisabling emotional and interpersonal problems.

Differences in effectiveness are not the only determinants of decisions about which alternative interventions to select. Evidence on cost-effectiveness may also be relevant (Gould et al. 1995). Two interventions may have similar outcomes, but one might be less expensive. For example, planned short-term intervention may frequently match outcomes of longer forms of treatment at less cost, group therapy may be less expensive than individual therapy without a sacrifice in effectiveness, and so on. Although adequate cost data are often not reported, and it may sometimes be difficult to make informed judgments, one can often make reasonable inferences about the relative expenses of alternative programs. Thus if there were no differences in outcomes, a standard service involving an hour of service contact a month might be preferred over an "intensive" program that called for several times as much contact.

To What Extent Can Research-Tested Interventions Become Part of Ordinary Practice?

The diffusion of experimentally validated interventions into regular service programs involves two distinct but related considerations. One has to do with the transportability of the intervention, which is roughly equivalent to the external validity of an experiment. How well will the intervention work in routine practice? The other concerns dissemination. How can the intervention be communicated to service programs and their line practitioners?

Transportability issues arise from disparities between conditions involved in tests of the intervention and conditions in regular programs. Recognition of these disparities is reflected in the distinction between demonstrating an intervention's efficacy (e.g., positive results from a randomized trial) and its effectiveness ("whether the treatment can be shown to work in actual clinical practice") (Chambless and Hollon 1998:14). Interventions tested in experiments are carried out under more-favorable conditions (small caseloads, detailed treatment manuals, and special training and supervision for practitioners) than their counterparts in ordinary practice. Overburdened practitioners may not have the time to learn complex new procedures, and since most are likely to have an eclectic orientation toward practice (Reid 2002), they may be selective about which parts of the intervention they will use. As Richey and Roffman (1999) ask, "How much [can] the intervention plan be altered before it is no longer viable" (316). Some studies have suggested that the degree of fidelity to prescribed protocols is in fact associated with better outcomes in intensive case-management programs for the seriously mentally ill (Jerrell and Ridgely 1999; McHugo et al. 1999). Such high- versus low-fidelity comparisons, however, do not answer the question of whether the low-fidelity application still retains some measure of effectiveness.

Generalization from research samples raises additional issues. Client samples used in validation studies may differ substantially from the clientele in a typical agency program. The latter may be less well motivated, have a different demographic profile, and be more likely to have multiple diagnoses. Finally, experimental tests of an intervention are conducted in a supportive, or at least tolerant, organizational environment. Their offspring may not be so fortunate, especially if they are forced from the "top down" on units that don't particularly want them.

The transportability of interventions tested through randomized clinical trials (RCTs) can be examined empirically through "benchmarking" studies. In such studies, the treatment protocols used in the RCTs are applied in nonrandomized designs to client samples, with exclusions kept to a minimum. Instruments used in the original RCTs are employed to determine the extent of correspondence between outcome data from the RCTs and those from the benchmarking study. A number of such benchmarking studies have suggested that the results of randomized controlled trials of mental health interventions can be attained when the interventions are implemented in ordinary service settings (Addis 2002). Moreover, in a recent meta-analysis, Shadish et al. (2000) found that experiments carried out under "clinically representative conditions"—for example, heterogeneous samples, lack of special practitioner training, and absence of treatment manuals—showed significantly positive results, comparable to those of previous meta-analyses based on experiments conducted under conditions that were not clinically representative.

Transportability could become less of an issue if circumstances of experimental testing and ordinary practice were more similar or if similarities were recognized. Thus Chambless and Hollon (1998) argue that randomized clinical trials, the main vehicle of efficacy testing, could be made more clinically realistic through such means as accepting clients with comorbid disorders—and that many in fact do. As Shadish et al. (2000) point out, many clinically representative studies meet critical criteria of efficacy studies—random assignment and low attrition. In a similar vein, Reid and Fortune (2003) found that social work experiments in mental health and other areas conducted during the 1990s varied on a continuum of clinical realism, which did not seem to be a significant factor in their outcomes. Also, the extent to which testing has involved different client samples in different settings can be taken into account in assessments of transportability. For example, one might have more confidence in the clinical utility of skills training for persons with schizophrenia, given the number and variety of programs tested (Penn and Meuser 1996) than in an intervention backed by a single experiment.

Finally, concern about transportability could be addressed by case monitoring and evaluation (Woody 2000). This could be seen as a form of benchmarking that would use instruments employed in the original validation studies. Do data from individual case applications in a given program approximate those obtained in previous randomized clinical trials of the intervention?

Dissemination involves issues concerning both what is to be transmitted and how this transmission is to occur. In respect to content, the prevailing trend is to disseminate specific interventions (manualized, if possible) for specific disorders or problems. As the base of empirically supported treatments grows, lists of effective interventions and their related guidelines and theories continue to proliferate. As a result, practitioners would face a considerable and increasing demand to master a variety of different techniques and theories, which they may have neither the time nor the inclination to do. An alternative proposed by Beutler (2000) is to develop and disseminate an integrated model or models that would guide practitioners in the use of empirically based principles for bringing about change, principles that could be adapted to a variety of clinical situations and that could incorporate specific techniques. For example, one of Beutler's research-supported principles posits that "the likelihood of therapeutic change is greatest when the patient's level of emotional stress is moderate, neither being excessively high nor excessively low" (2000:16). Beutler's proposal reflects a long-term effort to develop integrative frameworks for psychotherapy (Beutler and Clarkin 1990; Norcross and Newman 1992). By attempting to identify the core change processes underlying diverse theories and techniques, these frameworks have the potential to offer a more efficient and encompassable way of transmitting scientific knowledge about intervention effectiveness than diverse lists of empirically supported treatments. Although the current usefulness of change principles is limited by their abstract language and lack of knowledge about underlying mechanisms of change, there may be value in disseminating both the principles and more-specific problem-related techniques.

If one opts for a focus on specific treatments, dilemmas still exist concerning what exactly is to be disseminated. Obviously information about the intervention itself needs to be made available, preferably in the form of practice guidelines (Torrey et al. 2001), but there is question about what kind and how much research evidence should be communicated. In the approaches advocated by Sackett et al. (2000) and Gibbs (2003), practitioners access evidence directly and are expected to make judgments about it; however, the prevailing practice seems to emphasize the how-to of the intervention with perhaps only brief summaries or citations of studies supporting it. Although it is certainly desirable that practitioners have knowledge of the evidence and be able to think critically about it, it may be unrealistic to expect them to master both the intricacies of the intervention and its research underpinnings.

Finding the best means of disseminating empirically supported treatment poses an additional set of challenges. Since traditional methods of disseminating scientifically based knowledge to practitioners through journals and books have such an abysmal track record (Kirk and Reid 2002), new ways are being sought. The most promising approach seems to be concerted, systematic efforts to disseminate EBP methods to agency programs. Such efforts may include obtaining administrative support, arranging for financial and other incentives, providing instruction and training materials to staff, ensuring ongoing supervision of practice with the help of practice guidelines, conducting follow-up visits to offer feedback on the implementation, and enlisting the help of consumer organizations to create demand for EBP (Carpinello et al. 2002; Schoenwald and Hoagwood, 2001; Torrey et al. 2001). Dissemination procedures and materials may be packaged in the form of "toolkits" or similar devices (Card 2001; Torrey et al. 2001).

This kind of thoroughgoing, top-to-bottom implementation effort involves both dissemination and transportability concerns—the latter reflected in attempts to secure the support of various stakeholders, such as administrators and consumers. Such implementation models are relatively new in the mental health field, and there has been relatively little evaluation of their success, although the results of some studies have been encouraging. These models also require considerable investment of time and money. It remains to be seen whether mental health agency systems will be able to make that investment.

While direct infusion of EBP into agency systems may be the primary vehicle for dissemination, support from other sources may also be needed. With its capacity for providing and updating unlimited amounts of text concerning intervention protocols and related research, the Internet holds considerable promise as a dissemination medium. For example, the Web site being developed by the Society for Clinical Psychology features descriptions of empirically supported treatments and links to relevant research, thereby offering at least one solution to the problem of how much research information to provide to practitioners. The links in such Web sites could enable practitioners to obtain varying amounts of information about the research base of an intervention, from short summaries to extensive reviews or detailed reports of key studies.

Agency and Internet initiatives will have limited success unless practitioners are imbued with a positive orientation to the value of EBP. The nurturing of this kind of orientation in professional training programs strikes us as fundamental. With respect to social work, most educators might agree that exposure to EBP should be a part of the curriculum. The real question is how far should schools go? Should EBP form the primary basis of curricula in clinical social work? Should an emphasis on EBP be required as a condition of accreditation, as suggested some years ago by the Task Force on Social Work Research (1991)? While it is not feasible to insist that EBP form the sole basis of training in clinical social work, it may not be unreasonable to mandate that schools give priority to empirically supported interventions when such are available. If that were done, then instruction in mental health could stress EBP, since we now have a critical mass of research-validated interventions in that area. Even without such a mandate, it is likely that some schools will develop EBP-oriented curricula. Howard, McMillen, and Pollio (2003) offer an example of how a leading school is trying to do just that. We hope that others will follow suit.

Conclusion

Efforts to create a scientific base for practice in mental health have inched ahead incrementally over the past century. Whether EBP represents another inch of progress or something more substantial remains to be seen. But whatever its contribution, it seems here to stay. It has clearly gone beyond the buzzword phase.

If there has been a breakthrough, it is probably in the accumulation over the past three decades of a critical mass of empirically validated interventions covering a wide range of mental health problems and services. To be sure, many gaps still exist and important issues about the definition and refinement of EBP need to be resolved, but we now know enough about what works to make a difference. Knowledge is not practice, however. We need to find ways to make EBP more of a reality in agency-based services. The energy and funding that have been used to build effective interventions need also to be applied to problems of transportability and dissemination.

References

Addis, M. E. 2002. Methods for disseminating research products and increasing evidence-based practice: Promises, obstacles, and future directions. *Clinical Psychology: Science and Practice* 9:367–378.

Ahn, H.n. and B. E. Wampold. 2001. Where oh where are specific ingredients? A meta-analysis of component studies in counseling and psychotherapy. *Journal of Counseling Psychology* 48 (3): 251–257.

Beutler, L. E. 2000. Empirically based decision making in clinical practice. *Prevention and Treatment* 3:1–16.

———. 2002. The dodo bird is extinct. *Clinical Psychology: Science and Practice* 9 (1): 30–34.

Beutler, L. E. and J. F. Clarkin. 1990. *Systematic Treatment Selection*. New York: Brunner/Mazel.

Card, J. K. 2001. The sociometrics program archives: Promoting the dissemination of evidence-based practices through replication kits. *Research on Social Work Practice* 11 (4): 521–526.

Carpinello, S. E., L. Rosenberg, J. Stone, M. Schwager, and C. J. Felton. 2002. New York State's campaign to implement evidence-based practices for people with serious mental disorders. *Psychiatric Services* 53 (2): 153–155.

Chambless, D. L. 2002. Beware of the dodo bird: The dangers of overgeneralization. *Clinical Psychology: Science and Practice* 9 (1): 13–16.

Chambless, D. L. and S. D. Hollon. 1998. Defining empirically supported theories. *Journal of Consulting and Clinical Psychology* 66 (1): 7–18.

Chambless, D. L. and T. H. Ollendick. 2001. Empirically supported psychological interventions: Controversies and evidence. *Annual Reviews of Psychology* 52:685–716.

Cook, T. D. 1987. Positivist Critical Multiplism. In W. R. Shadish and C. S. Relchardt, eds., *Evaluation Studies: Review Annual*. Vol. 12. Newbury Park, Calif.: Sage.

Corcoran, Jacqueline. 2000. *Evidence-Based Social Work Practice with Families: A Lifespan Approach*. New York: Springer.

Crits-Christoph, P. 1997. Limitations of the dodo bird verdict and the role of clinical trials in psychotherapy research: Comment on Wampold et al. *Psychological Bulletin* 122:216–220.

Drake, R. E., H. H. Goldman, H. S. Leff et al. 2001. Implementing evidence-based practices in routine mental health service settings. *Psychiatric Services* 52 (2): 179–182.

Elkin, I., M. T. Shea, J. T. Watkins, and S. Imber. 1989. National Institute of Mental Health Treatment of Depression Collaborative Research Program: General effectiveness of treatments. *Archives of General Psychiatry* 46:971–982.

Emmelkamp, P. M. G., E. deHaan, and C. A. L. Hoodguin. 1990. Marital adjustments and obsessive-compulsive disorder. *British Journal of Psychiatry* 156:55–60.

Frank, J. D. and J. B. Frank. 1991. *Persuasion and Healing: A Comparative Study of Psychotherapy.* 3d ed. Baltimore: Johns Hopkins University Press.

Gambrill, E. 1999. Evidence-based practice: An alternative to authority-based practice. *Families in Society* 80:341–350.

———. 2003. Evidence-Based Practice: Implications for Knowledge Development and Use in Social Work Empirical Foundations for Practice Guidelines in Current Social Work Knowledge. In A. Rosen and E. Proctor, eds., *Developing Practice Guidelines for Social Work Intervention: Issues, Methods, and Research Agenda.* New York: Columbia University Press.

Gibbs, L. E. 2003. *Evidence-Based Practice for the Helping Professions.* Pacific Grove, Calif.: Brooks/Cole.

Gibbs, L. and E. Gambrill. 2002. Evidence-based practice: Counterarguments to objections. *Research on Social Work Practice* 12 (3): 452–476.

Gomory, T. 1999. Programs of assertive community treatment (PACT): A critical review. *Ethical Human Sciences and Services* 1 (2): 147–163.

Gorey, K. M. 1996. Effectiveness of social work intervention research: Internal versus external evaluations. *Social Work Research* 20 (2): 119–128.

Gould, R. B. et al. 1995. The development, validation, and applicability of "The Program Evaluation Standards: How to Assess Evaluations of Education Programs." Joint Committee on Standards for Educational Evaluation.

Gray, J. A. M. 2001. *Evidence-Based Health Care: How to Make Health Policy and Management Decisions.* 2d ed. New York: Churchill Livingston.

Hoagwood, K., B. J. Burns, L. Kiser, H. Ringeisen, and S. K. Schoenwald. 2001. Evidence-based practice in child and adolescent mental health services. *Psychiatric Services* 5 (9): 1179–1189.

Howard, K. I., M. S. Krause, S. Merton, S. M. Saunders, and M. S. Kopta. 1997. Trials and tribulations in the meta-analysis of treatment differences: Comment on Wampold et al. 1997. *Psychological Bulletin* 122 (3): 221–225.

Howard, M. O., C. J. McMillen, and D. E. Pollio. 2003. Teaching evidence-based practice: Toward a new paradigm for social work education. *Research on Social Work Practice* 13 (2): 234–259.

Jerrell, J. M. and M. S. Ridgely. 1999. Impact of robustness of program implementation on outcomes of clients in dual diagnosis programs. *Psychiatric Services* 50 (1): 109–112.

Karoly, P. and C. Wheeler-Anderson. 2000. The Long and Short of Psychological Change: Toward a Goal-Centered Understanding of Treatment Durability and Adaptive Success. In C. R. Snyder and R. E. Ingram, eds., *Handbook of Psychological Change,* 154–176. New York: John Wiley.

Kazdin, A. E. and D. Bass. 1989. Power to detect differences between alternative treatments in comparative psychotherapy outcome research. *Journal of Consulting and Clinical Psychology* 57:138–147.

Kirk, S. A. and W. J. Reid. 2002. *Science and Social Work: A Critical Appraisal.* New York: Columbia University Press.

Luborsky, L., L. Diguer, D. A. Seligman et al. 1999. The researcher's own therapy allegiances: A "wild card" in comparisons of treatment efficacy. *Clinical Psychology: Science and Practice* 6 (1): 96–106.

Macias, C., O. W. Farley, R. Jackson, and R. Kinney. 1997. Case management in the context of capitation financing: An evaluation of the strengths model. *Administration and Policy in Mental Health* 24 (6): 535–543.

McHugo, G. J., R. E. Drake, G. B. Teague, and H. Xie. 1999. Fidelity to assertive community treatment and client outcomes in the New Hampshire dual disorder study. *Psychiatric Services* 50 (6): 818–824.

Miller, W. R., N. R. Andrews, P. Wilbourne, and M. E. Bennett. 1998. A Wealth of Alternatives: Treating Addictive Behavior. In William R. Miller and Nick Heather, eds., *Treating Addictive Behavior,* 203–216. New York: Plenum.

Nathan, P. E. and J. M. Gorman. 2002. *Treatments That Work.* 2d ed. New York: Oxford University Press.

Norcross, J. D. and C. F. Newman. 1992. Psychotherapy Integration: Setting the Context. In J. C. Norcross and M. R. Goldfried, eds., *Handbook of Psychotherapy Integration,* 3–45. New York: Basic Books.

Penn, D. L. and K. T. Meuser. 1996. Research update on the psychosocial treatment of schizophrenia. *American Journal of Psychiatry* 153:607–617.

Reid, W. J. 2002. Knowledge for direct social work practice: An analysis of trends. *Social Service Review* 76:6–33.

Reid, W. J. and A. E. Fortune. 2003. Empirical Foundations for Practice Guidelines in Current Social Work Knowledge. In A. Rosen and E. Proctor, eds., *Developing Practice Guidelines for Social Work Intervention: Issues, Methods, and Research Agenda.* New York: Columbia University Press.

Reid, W. J., B. Kenaley, and J. Colvin. 2003. "Common Factors Versus Specific Ingredients: A Review of Social Work Experiments." Paper presented at the annual conference of the Society for Social Work and Research, January 17–19.

Richey, C. A. and R. A. Roffman. 1999. On the sidelines of guidelines: Further thoughts on the fit between clinical guidelines and social work practice. *Research on Social Work Practice* 9:311–321.

Robinson, L. A., J. S. Berman, and R. A. Neimeyer. 1990. Psychotherapy for the treatment of depression: A comprehensive review of controlled outcome research. *Psychological Bulletin* 100:30–49.

Sackett, D. L., W. Rosenberg, J. A. M. Gray, R. B. Haynes, and W. S. Richardson. 1996. Evidence-based medicine: What it is and what it isn't. *British Medical Journal* 312:71–72.

Sackett, D. L., S. E. Straus, W. S. Richardson, W. Rosenberg, and R. B. Haynes. 2000. *Evidence-Based Medicine: How to Practice and Teach EBM.* 2d ed. New York: Churchill Livingston.

Schoenwald, S. K. and K. Hoagwood. 2001. Effectiveness, transportability, and dissemination of interventions: What matters when? *Psychiatric Services* 52 (9): 1190–1197.

Shadish, W. R., A. M. Navarro, G. E. Matt, and G. Phillips. 2000. The effects of psychological therapies under clinically representative conditions: A meta-analysis. *Psychological Bulletin* 126 (4): 512–529.

Sloane, R. B. et al. 1975. *Psychotherapy Versus Behavior Therapy*. Cambridge, Mass.: Harvard University Press.

Smith, M. L., G. V. Glass, and T. I. Miller. 1980. *The Benefits of Psychotherapy*. Baltimore: Johns Hopkins University Press.

Task Force on Social Work Research. *Building Social Work Knowledge for Effective Services and Policies: A Plan for Research Development. A Report*. Austin, Tex.: Capital Printing.

Torrey, W. C., R. E. Drake, L. Dixon et al. 2001. Implementing evidence-based practices for persons with severe mental illnesses. *Psychiatric Services* 52 (1): 45–50.

Wampold, B. 2001. *The Great Psychotherapy Debate: Models, Methods, and Findings*. Mahwah, N.J.: Lawrence Erlbaum.

Wampold, B., G. Mondin, M. Moody, F. Stich, K. Benson, and H. Ahn. 1997. A meta-analysis of outcome studies comparing bona fide psychotherapies: Empirically, "All Must Have Prizes." *Psychological Bulletin* 122:203–215.

Weisz, J. R., K. M. Hawley, P. A. Pilkonis, S. R. Woody, and W. C. Follette. 2000. Stressing the (other) three R's in the search for empirically supported treatments: Review procedures, research quality, relevance to practice, and the public interest. *Clinical Psychology: Science and Practice* 7:243–258.

Weisz, J. R., B. Weiss, S. S. Han, D. A. Granger, and T. Morton. 1995. Effects of psychotherapy with children and adolescents revisited: A meta-analysis of treatment outcome studies. *Psychological Bulletin* 117 (3): 450–468.

Woody, S. R. 2000. On babies and bathwater: Commentary on Beutler (2000). *Prevention and Treatment*. 3 vols. Article 30, posted September 1, 2000. Available at http://journals.apa.org/prevention/volume 3/pre0030027a.html.

Chapter 14

Critical Thinking, Evidence-Based Practice, and Mental Health

Eileen Gambrill

The mental health industry is huge. Billions of dollars are consumed by those who try to improve or maintain the mental health of those who voluntarily seek or are coerced into contact with them and by training and educational programs that purport to provide related values, knowledge, and skills. Prozac had sales of $2.699 billion in the twelve months to January 2001 (http://www.imshealth.com). Mental health services expanded during the community mental health movement, and the number of mental health professionals increased greatly. Parity for treatment of mental health problems with treatment of medical problems has been actively pursued. The industry grows ever larger by virtue of the relentless medicalization of behaviors and emotions as mental illnesses in need of expert intervention, and often medication (e.g., Houts 2002; Kutchins and Kirk 1997). Mainstream journals such as the *British Medical Journal* reflect a concern about such medicalization in titles of articles such as "Selling Sickness" (Moynihan, Heath, and Henry 2002).

In this chapter I suggest that values, knowledge, and skills related to critical thinking and their overlap with the philosophy and evolving technology of evidence-based practice (EBP) as described in original sources (Sackett et al. 2000; Gray 2001a; Guyatt and Rennie 2002) should contribute to an informed dialogue regarding controversial issues in the area of mental health and to honoring ethical obligations described in professional codes of ethics—for example, integrating practice and research and informing clients about the risks and benefits of recommended services and alternatives. The need for thinking critically about mental health is illustrated by lapses in use of related values, knowledge, and skills in the mental health industry. Such lapses are reflected in the use of propaganda methods such as question begging (assuming what should be argued), misrepresenting the philosophy of evidence-based practice, and using the rhetoric of science to give an illusion of objectivity.

What Is Critical Thinking?

Critical thinking involves the careful examination and evaluation of beliefs and actions in order to arrive at well-reasoned ones. But who is to say what is well reasoned? Criteria used over the centuries suggest guidelines. We can examine the quality of reasoning related to a claim or position if it is clearly described (e.g., positions and warrants). Thus, one criterion would be a sufficient description of the reasoning process that would allow one to determine if a position or claim were well reasoned. "One cannot tell truth from falsity, one cannot tell an adequate answer to a problem from an irrelevant one, one cannot tell good ideas from trite ones—unless they are presented with sufficient clarity" (Popper 1994:71). We should be only as precise as we have to be to do the best that can be done under given circumstances (Popper 1992). Critical thinking involves clearly describing and taking responsibility for claims and arguments, critically evaluating our views (no matter how cherished), and considering alternative views and related evidence. It involves paying attention to the process of reasoning (how we think), not just the product, and being fair-minded—for example, accurately describing opposing views and critiquing all views using the same rigorous standards. Critical thinking can help us to evaluate claims and arguments. It can help us to recognize informal fallacies such as implied obviousness and circular reasoning (e.g., Dawes 2001; White 1971). Thinking carefully about claims can help us to avoid cognitive biases and to recognize pseudoscience, fraud, and quackery. It requires asking questions about who funds certain kinds of endeavors; disclosure of special interests is now a requirement in journals such as the *British Medical Journal*. Studies of decision making in professional contexts reveal a variety of concerns, such as confirmation biases that result in incorrect definitions of problems (e.g., missing physical causes) and use of ineffective or harmful assessment and intervention methods (e.g., see Gambrill 1990; Garb 2000; Skrabanek and McCormick 1998). Criticism is viewed as essential to forward understanding, including self-criticism. It prompts questions such as "Could I be wrong?" "Have I considered alternative views?" "Do I have sound reasons to believe that this plan will help this client?" Values and attitudes related to critical thinking include open-mindedness, a desire to be well informed, a tendency to think before acting, and curiosity (Paul 1993). Critical thinking involves questioning what others take for granted. It involves thinking for oneself. For example, what is mental health? What does "mental" mean? What does "health" mean, and who is to say what health is? Critical thinkers question what others view as self-evident. They ask:

- How do I know this claim is true?
- Who presented it as accurate? Are vested interests involved? How reliable are these sources?
- Are the facts presented correct?
- Have any facts been omitted?
- Is there any reliable evidence that a claim is true? Have critical tests been performed? If so, were they free of bias? Have results been replicated? How representative were the samples used?
- Are there other promising points of view? Have these been tested?

Thinking critically about a subject requires examining assumptions related to a position—exploring the "subtexts" rather than skimming the surface. It encourages us to think contextually, to consider the big picture, and to connect personal troubles to social issues. Its value is in deepening our understanding of issues and selecting well-reasoned beliefs and actions. It encourages us to examine the perspectives within which we reason and the possible consequences of different beliefs or actions. It requires accurate descriptions of well-argued alternative views on a subject, both preferred and disliked, and a candid discussion of controversies rather than hiding conceptual problems with preferred points of view and hiding empirical data that contradict them. Critical thinking and scientific reasoning are closely related. Both use reasoning for a purpose (to solve a problem), relying on standards such as clarity, relevance, and accuracy. Both regard criticism as essential to forward understanding. Both encourage us to challenge our assumptions, consider opposing views, and check our reasoning for errors. Both encourage asking questions, such as "Are mental health problems mental diseases?" "What is a 'disorder'?" "Are problems such as anxiety and depression biologically based?"

Evidence-Based Practice and Policy

Evidence-based medicine (EBM) arose as an alternative to authority-based medicine, in which decisions are based on criteria such as consensus among experts, anecdotal experience, or tradition. Hallmarks include maximizing knowledge flow by, for example, increasing transparency regarding the evidentiary status of services, attending to ethical obligations of professionals, and addressing application problems, including development of tools to facilitate integration of research and practice, such as the steps involved in EBP (Sackett et al. 2000). For example, on the back cover of *Clinical Evidence,* we find the statement that this book "provides a concise account of the current state of knowledge, ignorance, and uncertainty about the prevention and treatment of a wide range of clinical conditions" (2002). Although its philosophical roots are old, the blooming of EBP as a process attending to evidentiary, ethical, and application issues in all professional venues (education, practice/policy, and research), is fairly recent, facilitated by the Internet revolution. EBP is an evolving process designed to attend to evidentiary, ethical, and implementation concerns. "It is a guide for thinking about how decisions should be made" (Haynes, Devereaux, and Guyatt 2002). EBP involves the "conscientious, explicit and judicious use of best current evidence in making decisions about the care of individual clients" (Sackett et al. 1996). It involves "the integration of best research evidence with clinical expertise and [client] values" (Sackett et al. 2000:1). "Clinical expertise" refers to the use of practice skills and past experience to rapidly identify each client's unique circumstances and characteristics, "their individual risks and benefits of potential interventions, and their personal values and expectations" (1). It is drawn on to integrate information from these varied sources (Haynes, Devereaux, and Guyatt 2002). "Client values" refers to "the unique preferences, concerns and expectations each [client] brings to an . . . encounter and which must be integrated into . . . decisions if they are to serve the [client]" (1).

EBP requires locating and critically reviewing research findings related to important practice/policy decisions and sharing what is found (including nothing) with clients. It draws on the results of systematic, rigorous, critical appraisal of research related to important practice questions such as "Is this assessment measure valid?" and "Does this intervention do more good than harm?" Efforts are made to prepare comprehensive, rigorous reviews of all research related to questions addressed (see, for example, the Cochrane and Campbell Collaboration databases). Different questions require different kinds of research methods to critically appraise proposed assumptions (e.g., see Gray 2001a; Greenhalgh 2001; Guyatt and Rennie 2002; Sackett et al. 2000). EBP describes a series of steps (such as converting information needs related to practice decisions into four-part answerable questions) and takes advantage of technologies such as electronic dissemination of systematic reviews, to forward integration of external evidence with information about a client's unique characteristics and circumstances, and preferences and actions, in a context of limited resources (Haynes, Devereaux, and Guyatt 2002). Many authors define EBP much more narrowly (see Gambrill 2003): "We use evidence-based practice here primarily to denote that practitioners select interventions based on their empirically demonstrated links to the desired outcomes" (Rosen and Proctor 2002). This definition leaves out local implementation concerns, the importance of considering client values and expectations, and involving clients as informed participants.

Reasons that Sackett and his colleagues (2000) suggest for the rapid spread of EBM include: (1) practitioner need for valid information about decisions they make; (2) the inadequacy of traditional sources for acquiring this information because they are out-of-date, ineffective, frequently wrong, overwhelming in volume, and variable in validity); (3) the gap between assessment skills and clinical judgment, "which increase[s] with experience, and our up-to-date knowledge and clinical performance, which decline" (2); and (4) lack of time to locate, appraise, and integrate evidence (2). For example, a variety of biases in published research (submission, publication, methodological, abstracting, and framing biases) compromise the accuracy of available material (e.g., Altman 2002; Gray 2001b). Developments that have allowed improvement in this state of affairs include the design of strategies for efficiently tracking down and appraising evidence for its validity and relevance; the Web revolution, allowing greater access, to both professionals and clients, to related information; the invention of the systematic review; and the development of strategies to encourage lifelong learning. Although misleading in the incorrect assumption that EBP means only that decisions made are based on evidence of their effectiveness, use of the term calls attention to the evidentiary status of claims and the importance of accurately sharing this with clients. This often involves sharing our state of ignorance and uncertainty. Smith (2003) suggests that "the history of medicine is mostly a history of ineffective and often dangerous treatments. . . . Unfortunately there is still no evidence to support most diagnostic methods and treatments. Either the research hasn't been done or it is of too poor a quality to be useful" (1307). (For a more optimistic view, see Gray (2001a.) Smith also notes that implementing research of the required quality to determine effects is very difficult.

> Because the benefit from most medical treatments is small and so hard to detect, you need very many patients in the trial. Although "double blind randomized trials" are the best way of working out whether a treatment works, many of them have not been well done and have given misleading results.
> (1307)

It is hoped that professionals who consider related research findings regarding decisions and inform clients about them will provide more effective and ethical care than those who rely on criteria such as status, anecdotal experience, fads and fashions, available resources, or popularity.

Critical thinking and evidence-based practice are integrally related, if the philosophy and technology of EBP described by its originators are used. Both are antiauthoritarian. Both attend to ethical aspects of decision making. Both encourage transparency in relation to the evidentiary status of claims. Both value clarity over obscurity, accuracy over misinformation, and honesty over deception.

The Mental Health Industry: A History of Lapses in Critical Thinking and Lack of Evidence-Based Practices and Policies

Interrelated characteristics of professions involved with mental health and fellow travelers that highlight the need for critical thinking and reasons for the development of EBP are suggested in the sections that follow. There are many indications that critical thinking and its reflection in evidence-based practice do not thrive in the area of mental health. This can be seen by the prevalence of pseudoscience and propaganda in related venues (e.g., Lilienfeld, Lynn, and Lohr 2003). All involve lack of integration of ethical, evidentiary, and application issues. For example, use of methods of unknown effect, so common in the history of psychiatry, typically occurred without informed consent (e.g., Valenstein 1986). Both omissions (lack of informed consent) and commissions (inflated claims of knowledge) suggest a disregard of critical thinking values and related knowledge and skills and a lack of EBP that forwards honoring ethical obligations to clients such as disclosure concerning the degree of uncertainty associated with important decisions. A key reason why critical thinking and EBP do not thrive is a preference for authority-based practice—for example, basing recommendations on tradition—and related incentives such as status and economic interests (Chalmers 1983; Gambrill 2000). This preference is reflected in the prevalence of propaganda in the helping professions.

The Prevalence of Propaganda

The purpose of propaganda is to encourage beliefs and actions with the least thought possible (Ellul 1965); its purpose is not to inform but to persuade. Propagandists take advantage of informal fallacies. They may misrepresent their position (tell only part of the truth) or rely on slogans and put-downs. Social work and other professions such as psychiatry and clinical psychology have well-organized national and state organizations dedicated to maintenance and expansion of turf. Related efforts reflected in professional publications are often based not on claims of effectiveness that have survived critical tests but on classic propaganda methods such as implied obviousness, appeals based on authority (e.g., consensus), and deliberate omissions (e.g., of contradictory data) and scare tactics (McCormick 1996).

Rather than addressing cogent criticisms of the diagnosis of ADHD (attention-deficit hyperactivity disorder) and related recommended interventions, Barkley, Cook, and Diamond et al. (2002) dismiss criticisms as dangerous myths in the International Consensus Statement on ADHD. (For an example of a critique, see Timimi and Taylor [2004].) Indeed, this two-page statement (most pages contain a series of signers and references) is replete with propaganda strategies such as begging the question and hiding problems in views presented. Methods used by the psychiatric establishment to promote claims fall into Rank's (1984) fourfold description of propaganda methods (figure 14.1). Rank suggests that the essence of propaganda is inflating positive attributes and hiding negative ones of preferred views and exaggerating negative attributes of disliked views and hiding their positive ones. Problematic methodological concerns are hidden, such as the low reliability of diagnostic categories (Kirk and Kutchins 1992; Kutchins and Kirk 1997). Even more damaging concerns, such as failure to address the validity of such categories, are often not even mentioned. A key function of propaganda in the helping professions is to maintain and expand turf by obscuring mismatches between claims and their evidentiary status—for example, by rechristening an ever-increasing variety of behaviors, feelings, and thoughts, including ethical and moral dilemmas, as illnesses in need of expert attention (e.g., Houts 2002; Szasz 1987). Those who produce promotional material for pharmaceutical companies make full use of propaganda and persuasion methods (Mansfield 2003).

Interrelated kinds of propaganda in the helping professions include deep propaganda that obscures political, economic, and social contingencies that influence problem-related behaviors claimed by a profession (e.g., alcohol use, depression) and the questionable accuracy of basic assumptions, for example relabeling problems in living as mental disorders that require the help of experts. It also includes inflated claims of effectiveness regarding assessment, intervention and evaluation methods that woo clients to professionals and professionals to professions perhaps because of profit and/or prophet motives (Jarvis 1994). There are troubling gaps between the obligations of researchers to report limitations of research, prepare systematic reviews, and accurately describe well-argued alternative views and what we find in published literature.

Poor-quality research continues to appear in professional journals (Altman 2002). Related concerns were key in the development of EBP and health

Figure 14.1
Mental Illness Model and Rank's (1984) Fourfold Classification
of Propaganda

Overemphasize the positive aspects of preferred model
  Inflated claims of success in removing complaints (puffery)
  Inflated claims of success in preventing problems (puffery)

Hide and minimize negative aspects of preferred model
  Harmful effects of neuroleptic drugs
  Questionable reliability and validity of psychiatric classification systems

Overemphasize negative aspects of opposing views (e.g., behavior analysis)
  Associate alternative approaches with negative terms (mechanistic,
    dehumanizing)
  Allege that positive effects of alternative approaches are only temporary

Hide and minimize positive aspects of opposing views (e.g., behavior analysis)
  Ignore research showing that nonprofessionals are as effective as
    professionals with many problems (e.g., see Dawes 1994)
  Ignore positive results achieved by alternative approaches

care (e.g., see Gray 2001a and 2001b). We often find little match between questions addressed and use of methods that can critically test them, together with hiding limitations and inflated claims of effectiveness. Given that claims do not match reality, they are a form of propaganda. If harms result from such propaganda (for example, choosing services that harm rather than help clients [Rose, Bisson, and Wessely 2001]), it is important to examine its nature and to develop ways to avoid its effects. Censorship is a key propaganda strategy. As Rosenthal (1994) suggests in his description of hyperclaiming (telling others that proposed research is likely to achieve goals that it will not) and causism (implying a causal relationship when none has been established), "Bad science makes for bad ethics" (128). Chalmers (1990) argues that failure to accurately describe research methods used is a form of scientific misconduct.

Obscuring the Problematic Nature of Basic Assumptions Regarding Mental Illness

Some scholars argue that some state of affairs becomes a social problem when an objective state exists. Others argue that social problems are socially constructed (Gusfield 1996). People have had to deal with troubled, troubling, and dependent behavior throughout the centuries (Conrad and Schneider 1992; Szasz 1994). They have done so in different ways, considering certain behaviors first as sins, then as crimes, and now as mental illnesses in need of treatment by experts. Changing ideas about what is and what is not mental illness illustrate the consensual nature of psychiatric diagnoses. Homosexuality was defined as a mental illness until 1973, when the American Psychiatric Association, under pressure from gay and lesbian advocacy groups and bitter infighting, decided that it was not. "Problem crusaders" (people with a particular interest in a particular view of a problem) forward particular definitions (see Best 2001). Psychiatrists, public health officials, and the pharmaceutical industry have been very successful in forwarding medical definitions of troubled, troubling, and dependent behavior as illustrated by the ever lengthening list of behaviors that are viewed as signs of mental illness requiring the help of experts. The number of listings in the *Diagnostic and Statistical Manual* of the American Psychiatric Association continues to increase (Kutchins and Kirk 1997). The metaphors used to describe problems (e.g., "illness") influence how given problems are viewed and what solutions are proposed and adopted. The word "health" is used to encompass an ever wider range of behaviors (Farrant and Russell 1986; McCormick 1996). Genetic determinism and biological reductionism in which the complexity of causation is ignored is common (Strohman 2003).

The extent to which rhetorical devices, including classic propaganda methods such a begging the question (assuming what should be argued), are used in the mental health area to misrepresent the evidentiary status of basic concepts such as "mental disorder," is aptly described in *Schizophrenia: A Scientific Delusion?* (2002) by Mary Boyle. She describes how language used (such as repeated use of the word "clinical"), kinds of arguments presented, and benefits both touted and actual, intersect to maintain an illusion that a coherent entity called schizophrenia exists and that the methods used to identify it are unproblematic. She illustrates the problematic nature of terms such as "mental illness" and "mental disorder" on both methodological and conceptual grounds. She gives many examples of how the discourse of science is used to create a false impression of objectivity and rigor, for example by using specialized terminology that is often unfamiliar to lay readers as well as to many in the mental health profession. She notes that terms are often misused (e.g., "base rate") in a manner that favors the assumption that schizophrenia exists as a unique entity, that it is a "mental disorder," and that it is biochemical in origin. Appeals to the language of neuroscience are rife. Boyle (2002) suggests that narratives of scientific progress are used to suggest that advances are being made when they are not (see also Houts 2002). For example, even though biochemical correlates have not yet been discovered, claims are made that they soon will be. She points out that the language of medicine is also appealed to and that this combines with the language of science in a potent rhetorical mix to give illusions of objectivity, knowledge, and progress. She notes that medicine is a profession and that professions are given unique rights to address certain problems within a framework of indeterminate (unspecified and special) knowledge, such as intuition and clinical expertise, which is a hallmark of professionals that distinguishes them from technicians (those who make use of clear, routinized knowledge). Thus, professionals are not expected to be able to clearly describe their knowledge; they can appeal to special expertise.

Boyle (2002) argues that our dependence on secondary sources contributes to acceptance of bogus claims about mental illness and related concepts. That is, the detail required to carefully examine claims is usually not provided in such contexts. Ellul (1965) suggested that academics are especially open to the effects of propaganda because they read so much material in secondary sources. Students in professional education programs such as social work often read secondary sources. Inaccuracies in texts contributed to the origin of evidence-based health care. Gray (2001a) suggests that if physicians want to keep up with the literature, they should not read texts (355). LaCasse and Gomory (2003) found that the reliability of diagnostic categories in the *DSM* was misrepresented (inflated) in required texts in psychopathology courses in social work. Scores of books contain the word "schizophrenia" in the title. Thousands of articles contain this word, and we see it daily in the press. As Boyle (2002) notes, it is easy to believe that what is referred to by a word actually exists—particularly if authority figures such as psychiatrists use the term and act as if it is unproblematic. (This is not to say that the behaviors, thoughts, or feelings referred to do not exist.) Our tendency to rely on "experts," and to believe that if there is a word it refers to something in the real world (reification), combines with other factors, such as lack of time or interest in digging deeper, a desire to understand our environments with little effort (e.g., the causes of troubled or troubling behavior), and an interest in escaping from responsibility for our behavior or troubles by attributing them to a mental disorder. This is a powerful mix.

Hiding or Minimizing Social Control and Economic Interests

There is a great deal at stake in how problems are framed, and people with vested interests devote considerable time, money, and effort to influence what others believe. Some argue that the primary function of mental health professionals is to encourage values that are compatible with a capitalistic culture. The coffers of helping professionals grow rich by the medicalization of problems. Problem definition is influenced by professionals' interest in maintaining and gaining power, status, and economic resources, as well as by differences of opinion about what makes one explanation better than another. Profit making is the key aim of for-profit and many (supposedly) not-for-profit service enterprises. Residential psychiatric facilities for youth and nursing homes are multimillion-dollar businesses. The concern for profit rather than service is reflected in the mistreatment of clients (such as unneeded hospitalization) in order to make money (e.g., Schwartz 1989). Margolin (1997) suggests that social workers are mainly involved with judging and evaluating. Critics argue that expansion of mental health services was not in the interests of clients but in the interests of the containment of unproductive deviance (Szasz 1994). Sources of human misery that are related to environmental factors and that create deviant behavior are falsely attributed to individual characteristics ("mental illness") and thus encapsulated. Special service-delivery systems can then be created for these individuals, and these systems become a source of jobs for professionals. The pharmaceutical industry has been very creative and proactive in promoting a psychiatric view of troubled, troubling, and dependent behavior—for example, providing funds to the National Alliance for the Mentally Ill (NAMI) and the American Psychiatric Association. According to the *Ecologist* of March 2002 (32 [2]), the marketing expenditure (in dollars) for the promotion of drugs for anxiety, depression, and related problems in America for January–October 2001 was Zoloft (Pfizer) $45,993,698; Sarafem (Lilly) $42,467,315; Paxil (GSK) $32,363,685; Ambien (Pharmacia) $31,666,217; and Prozac (Lilly) $31,554,601.

Ignoring the Context of Troubled, Troubling, and Dependent Behaviors

Mirowsky and Ross (1989) explored the relationship between psychological distress (depression and anxiety) and social factors and concluded that half of all symptoms of depression are attributable to social factors. They suggest that

> the patterns of distress reflect the patterns of autonomy, opportunity, and achievement in America . . . and that minority status is associated with a reduced sense of control partly because of lower levels of education, income and employment, and partly because for members of minority groups, any given level of achievement requires greater effort and provides fewer opportunities.
> (16)

Breggin suggests that "the mental health professions, led by psychiatry, have rushed into the void left by the default of the family, the schools, the society, and the government" (1991:275). He suggests that by blaming child victims, psychiatry "takes the pressure off the parents, the family, the school, and the society" (275). Lepenies (1992) suggests that in certain historical circumstances, entire groups become melancholy ("fear and sorrow without a cause" [see Burton 1855]).

> They are the necessary expression of a world that is awry in countless different ways. When we consider them, we do not wish that they might have had access to modern psychiatric remedies. For they are not isolated individual sufferers. They belong to a class that has lost its public significance, and they feel as useless as they are.
> (Shklar, foreword to Lepenies 1992:vi)

Hiding Gaps Between Rhetoric Regarding Ethical Obligations and Practices and Policies

There is a gap between obligations described in professional codes of ethics regarding informed consent, competence, and integrating practice and related research findings (NASW Code of Ethics 1996) and what occurs in everyday practice. Most professionals do not keep up-to-date with practice-related research (e.g., Rosen et al. 1995). Related research is a key reason for the development of evidence-based practice (Sackett et al. 1997). Not keeping up with new research findings related to important practice decisions renders our knowledge increasingly out of date. As a result, decisions may be made that harm rather than help clients (see Jacobson, Mulick, and Schwartz 1995). This violates obligations described in professional codes of ethics (NASW Code of Ethics 1996). Most programs in current use have never been critically tested to determine if they do more good than harm. The quality of services in many public agencies is poor. For example, in many states child welfare programs that make use of mental health services have been deemed so deficient that they have been placed under various kinds of conservatorship. Screening programs for depression and anxiety are promoted even though there is no evidence that they do more good than harm. Hiding limitations in practice and policy-related research and failing to accurately describe limitations in research are common (Altman 2002). Critical appraisals of practice-related literature in clinical psychology reveal pseudoscience as well as science (Lilienfeld, Lynn, and Lohr 2003), material with the trappings of science without the substance. Programs that have been critically tested and found to be helpful and cost-effective are often ignored (Olds et al. 1998), as are alternative well-argued views and related evidence that challenge favored views such as applied behavior analysis (Baldwin 1999; Todd and Morris 1992). Most clients are not involved as informed participants in making decisions. Those who prescribe neuroleptic medications often do not inform clients that they may result in irreversible side effects such as tardive dyskinesia (Brown and Funk 1986). Lack of informed consent is also of concern in health care (Braddock et al. 1999). Some would argue that mental health legislation is growing ever more coercive—as reflected, for example, in outpatient commitment laws and legislation designed[1] in the United Kingdom to deal with high-risk patients.

Inflated Claims of Knowledge

Claims of effectiveness are often inflated; they misrepresent the evidentiary status of methods. Consider the claim by Moseley and Deweaver (1995) that programs of assertive community treatment for the "severely and chronically mentally ill" have been shown to be effective. This claim is not accompanied by a critical review of related research. Gomory's rigorous review (1999) suggests that this program is not effective. The source in which the Moseley and Deweaver chapter appears (Wodarski and Thyer 1995) has been referred to by Reid as part of a "critical mass of tested intervention knowledge" (2001:278) that can guide practice. Use of terms such as "well established" and "well validated" convey a certainty that cannot be had. Consider the view that two well-controlled randomized controlled trials "establishes" an intervention as effective. For all we know, the next two trials will find the opposite. There is a continuing attempt to bamboozle the public, and perhaps practitioners themselves, into believing that more is known than is or can ever be (Popper 1972) the case. If professionals are so effective in resolving or preventing problems, as suggested in such titles as *What Works* (Nathan and Gorman 2000), why do related problems remain so prevalent? Reviews of clinical trials funded by pharmaceutical companies compared to those that do not have that source of funding indicate that the former are not as rigorous and are more likely to report positive findings (Bekelman, Mphil, and Gross 2003). Inflated claims regarding knowledge of causality are also common. Consider claims that depression and social anxiety are brain diseases, when this has not been demonstrated. Such views are widely promoted by those who represent federal agencies, such as the U.S. Department of Health and Human Services (1999). Use of lifetime prevalence as a measure conveys inflated estimates of alleged mental disorders. Screening programs based on dubious measures inflate such estimates.

The very origins of the helping professions also reveal inflated claims of effectiveness. Certain occupations became professions not because they had a better track record of solving certain kinds of problems but because they were successful in selling the view that they were most successful and therefore should have a unique right to address them (Abbott 1988; Friedson 1986). These special rights are protected by certificates and licenses that are alleged to protect the public from interlopers. Proposed legislation in California claims that restricting use of the title "social worker" to those with a degree from an accredited program will protect consumers (Assembly Bill No. 949, California). There is no evidence for this claim. Critics of the helping professions call our attention to mismatches between what is claimed (e.g., via certification) and what is offered to clients. For example, Dawes (1994) argues that research shows that those without certain credentials, licenses and experience are as effective in achieving a range of outcomes as those who have such credentials. This suggests that credentials offer an illusion of special competency. Professional organizations play a key role in promoting false claims. Consider the claim by the Royal Society of Psychiatrists that eight out of ten patients who received electroconvulsive therapy responded well and that memory loss is not clinically important. A meta-analysis of related studies showed such claims to be unfounded (Rose et al. 2003). Professional organizations routinely make grandiose claims about the effectiveness of their respective cohorts. It is in the nature of the beast (professional organizations) to make such claims. The purpose of professional organizations is to expand and maintain turf (Abbott 1988). Governmental organizations encourage misleading claims by fielding unrealizable expectations—for example, that no child be harmed in care.

Hiding or Minimizing Harming in the Name of Helping

Exposés of bogus claims, harm in the name of helping, and conceptual mystifications are often brought to our attention not by researchers and academics but by journalists. Consider exposés of conditions in group homes for the mentally ill in the state of New York (e.g., see Levy 2002). Reviews of facilitated communication and recovered memories illustrate harming in the name of helping (Ofshe and Watters 1994; Jacobson, Mulick, and Schwartz 1993). Some argue that institutionalized psychiatry reflects such a history (Szasz 1987, 1994; Valenstein 1986). Six of seven randomized controlled studies regarding brief psychoanalytic debriefing designed to decrease post-traumatic stress disorder showed no effects, and one showed a negative effect (Rose, Bisson, and Wessely 2001). Little attention is given in the mental health area to identifying errors that may result in harm and how to avoid them. Publications of professional organizations such as the *NASW News* routinely ignore harms and problems sometimes revealed in sources concurrently published in newspapers. For example, a front-page article in the *NASW News* titled "Gala Focuses on Child Welfare" (Stoesen 2003) makes no mention of the shocking lapses repeatedly described in our newspapers (e.g., see Purdy 2003). A review of case records in the child welfare system in New Jersey (DePanfilis 2003), released only after a lawsuit was brought against the department, revealed alarming lapses. The Stoesen (2003) article suggested that lapses are caused by those who do not have a social work degree. Is this so? Do individuals involved in such cases lack a social work degree? Blaming problems on not having a social work degree obscures systemic causes that diminish quality of services, no matter what degree one has.

Bogus Use of the Term "Evidence-Based"

Literature on evidence-based practice reflects values, knowledge, and skills related to critical thinking to differing degrees. Definitions of EBP differ greatly in their breadth and attention to ethical issues ranging from the broad, systemic philosophy and related evolving technology envisioned by its originators (Sackett et al. 1997; Gray 2001a) to narrow, fragmented views and total distortions (see Gambrill 2003; Gibbs and Gambrill 2002). The term "evidence-based" is widely used to refer to material that has few if any of the hallmarks of the philosophy and technology of evidence-based practice as EBP originated and continues to evolve. Misrepresentations of the philosophy and technology of EBP suggest an interest in continuation of authority-based practices that hide limitations of research and inflate claims of effectiveness and knowledge. As with pseudoscience, one can claim the name (evidence-based practice) and forgo the substance. This is revealed by ignoring involvement of clients as informed participants, overlooking application problems (such as lack of resources), and inflating claims of knowledge.

Transparency of what is done and to what effect is emphasized in EBP, particularly in relation to the evidentiary status of practices and policies. Transparency (clear description) of basic assumptions and conceptual problems with them has not been as strongly emphasized. Publications such as the journal *Evidence-Based Mental Health* reflect unquestioned use of psychiatric classifications and inflated claims of knowledge. For example, a recent issue noted that more than five thousand new articles had appeared, as if all of these might add to our knowledge. Many descriptions in the social work literature misrepresent the philosophy and technology of EBP as described in original sources—for example, omitting attention to ethical issues and flaws in published research. Many descriptions omit any mention that a primary reason for the development of EBP and related enterprises such as the Cochrane and Campbell Collaborations was flaws in published research, such as hiding methodological limitations. Misrepresenting ideas and views is a hallmark of propaganda, not of critical thinking. Such misrepresentations illustrate that critical-thinking values are not necessarily reflected in content that is described as evidence-based. Many seem to want their cake (to use the term "evidence-based" because it sounds good and is au courant) and eat it too, for example continuing to make inflated claims of knowledge and misrepresenting disliked positions. But aren't we ethically obligated to accurately describe well-argued alternative views and methodological and conceptual limitations?

Trends That Encourage Honest Brokering of Knowledge and Ignorance

Increasing access to information on the Internet, the invention of the systematic review, an interest in involving clients as informed participants (e.g., Coulter 2002; Edwards and Elwyn 2001), and the creation of organizations designed to prepare, maintain, and disseminate them (such as the Cochrane and Campbell Collaborations), the transparency encouraged by EBP and evolving ways to encourage this, including Web sites that help us to critically appraise practice-related research—all of these strategies contribute to thinking critically about issues related to mental health (see also Edwards and Elwyn 2001). Increasing attention is being given to pseudoscience in mental health and to fraud, quackery, and propaganda (Lilienfeld, Lynn, and Lohr 2003; Sarnoff 2001). The increasing concern on the part of professional education programs about the influence of propaganda from pharmaceutical companies is illustrated by inclusion of courses in medical school designed to alert students to such persuasion effects (Wilkes and Hoffman 2001). Porter (2000) suggests that "historians of medicine may find it profitable to examine the careers of quacks and regulars in tandem, rather than, as is traditional, distinctly in separate genres of study" (208). This might provide a means of introducing students in professional education programs to the field of mental health in a way that highlights the distinctions between these two approaches while also illustrating the fuzzy boundaries between them and possible reasons for such fuzziness and thereby perhaps decreasing the percentage of graduates who succumb to pseudoscience and quackery.

In Conclusion

The goal of helping clients sounds straightforward. However, other functions of the helping professions, such as social control and economic self-interest, suggest that problem definition and related proposed remedies are not clear-cut. If indeed the mental health industry is concerned with troubled, troubling, and dependent behaviors, as Thomas Szasz has long suggested, it is not surprising that controversy abounds. Such behaviors often demand attention. As professionals become immersed in the everyday world of practice and planning, it is easy to forget about the economic, political, and social context in which personal and social problems are defined and reacted to. And it is always tempting to have one's cake and eat it too, as reflected in the use of term "evidence-based" without the substance—which is not surprising given the prevalence of pseudoscience throughout history. The common misrepresentation of the original vision and philosophy of evidence-based practice, with its emphasis on honest brokering of knowledge and ignorance (transparency) and involving clients as informed participants, bodes ill for encouraging these characteristics which are highlighted in professional codes of ethics. That is, these characteristics are often ignored in descriptions of EBP. The term "evidence-based" is often used to refer to business-as-usual—inflated claims of success and the hiding of methodological and conceptual problems. Promotion of a medicalized view of troubled and troubling behavior and related treatments such as medication in the absence of conceptual robustness and methodological soundness has been stunningly successful. Such framing has flourished in spite of withering critiques even in professions such as social work, which historically has emphasized the role of environmental variables. Deep problems seem not to be recognized by those who use the language of mental disorder. For example, during a day-long workshop on substance abuse I asked the instructor (a psychologist with a Ph.D.), who repeatedly used the word "disorder," "What is a disorder?" His answer was "a lack of order." He seemed quite satisfied with this reply.

Some barriers to open critical discussion of controversial issues, such as a reluctance to confront uncertainties or assume responsibilities associated with difficult decisions, stem from the clients. There is a symbiotic relationship between the goals of the involved parties: clients' interests in seeking certain and hopeful answers and predictions and professionals' interests in fulfilling their expected role to help clients and make money in the process. The history of both quackery and medicine highlights these symbiotic goals (Porter 2000). Houts (2002) suggests that giving up the narrative of discovery, progress, and science promoted (he argues falsely) by advocates and designers of the *DSM* may be no more popular to society and its expectations of scientists (for example, to have real answers to problems) than to scientists themselves (58) (see also Boyle 2002). He suggests that positive consequences of psychiatric diagnoses include providing solutions to social problems (getting rid of troubling persons); entitlement of clients to services and escape from responsibility for troubled or troublesome behaviors; providing relief for practitioners (minimize confusion, suggest treatment); making it easier to obtain research funding (related to a certain alleged "disorder"); providing ever-expanding marketing opportunities for pharmaceutical companies, and providing profits for the American Psychiatric Association in sales of psychiatric paraphernalia.

The greatest loss in lack of open discussion of controversies involved with mental health (what is health? what is mental health?) is encapsulation in a reductionistic view of troubling, troubled, and dependent behaviors and its consequences. A psychiatrized view of depression, anxiety, fear, and aggression obscures how we are affected by our environments and the shared existential nature of our lives and the challenges this involves as described throughout the ages by deep thinkers (Arendt 1998; Eiseley 1975). Potential negative consequences of premature acceptance of psychiatric constructions of troubled and troubling behaviors are not vivid. For example, the emotional dulling that may result from taking prescribed medication is less vivid than the anxiety that precipitated the request for help and resulted in the prescription. The anxiety may be uncomfortable; however, struggling with this, perhaps with the help of an empathic, wise counselor, may result in acquisition of insights and problem-solving skills that would be forgone by taking a pill. Suggesting to people with social anxiety that they take "Paxil" to resolve their problems decreases the likelihood that they will consider their troubling reactions not only in relation to their unique psychological characteristics, developmental history, and social environment but also in relation to common influences that affect us all, such as social ranking and fear of ostracism (Gilbert 1989). This constricted view hides opportunities to understand how our shared humanness and its circumstances contribute to what we experience as unique miseries and circumstances. It takes away opportunities to connect with each other and the world as we struggle to deal with common problems and to survive, and perhaps grow, in the process and to seek a kind of help that may allow us to do so. It diminishes opportunities to enhance empathic reactions as we realize the shared circumstances in which we live. With increased access to alternative, well-argued views by both clients and professionals on the Internet, there will be greater opportunity to consider alternative views and related evidence.

Many highlight the close relationship between critical thinking and arriving at moral decisions. The gap between obligations described in professional codes of ethics and what is done indicates that this close relationship is not honored. Many reasons have been offered as to why, but do these reasons provide a moral rationale to abandon the relationship? Thinking critically about the mental health industry would reveal that most services used are of unknown effectiveness, that some services do more harm than good, and that nonprofessionals can provide many services with the same degree of success, or more, than can those with specialized training and licenses that are presumed to protect the public. It would reveal bogus claims of effectiveness as well as conceptual mystifications. Such revelations would have implications for funding and require self-examination on the part of policymakers, administrators, practitioners, educators, and researchers. Thinking critically about "mental health" requires practitioners to consider ethical issues related to their decisions, including decisions they make about their degree of ignorance of well-argued theory and related research findings and the ethics of self-deception. If we have been indoctrinated in a professional education program into a psychiatrized view of mental health in which people are labeled with psychiatric diagnoses and medication is the norm, and if such views are not accurate in terms of causes and possible remedies and indeed may harm clients, what is our obligation to "think outside the box"? When are we responsible for avoiding influence by propaganda in the helping professions? When are we responsible for challenging our own self-deceptions, which may be created and maintained by professional propaganda? When is self-deception morally wrong? White (1971) suggests that although no one can be blamed for being biased since we are all biased in some ways, "a person can be blamed if he makes little or no effort to recognize and counteract it" (34). This seems a reasonable position and an appropriate closing suggestion.

References

Abbott, A. 1988. *The System of Professions: An Essay on the Division of Expert Labor.* Chicago: University of Chicago Press.

Altman, D. G. 2002. Poor-quality medical research. What can journals do? *Journal of the American Medical Association* 287:2765–2767.

American Psychiatric Association (APA). 2002. *Diagnostic and Statistical Manual of Mental Disorders (DSM-IV).* 4th ed. Washington, D.C.: APA.

Arendt, H. 1998. *The Human Condition.* 2d ed. Chicago: University of Chicago Press.

Baldwin, S. 1999. Applied behavior analysis in the treatment of ADHD: A review and rapprochement. *Ethical Human Sciences and Services* 1:35–59.

Barkley, R. A., E. H. Cook Jr., A. Diamond et al. 2002. International Consensus Statement on ADHD. *Clinical Child and Family Psychology Review* 5:89–111.

Bekelman, J. E., L. Y. Mphil, and G. P. Gross. 2003. Scope and impact of financial conflicts of interest in biomedical research. *Journal of the American Medical Association* 289 (4): 454–465.

Best, J. 2001. *Damned Lies and Statistics: Untangling Numbers from the Media, Politicians, and Activists.* Berkeley: University of California Press.

Boyle, M. 2002. *Schizophrenia: A Scientific Delusion?* New York: Routledge.

Braddock, C. H., K. A. Edwards, N. M. Hasenberg, T. L. Laidley, and W. Levinson. 1999. Informed decision-making in outpatient practice: Time to get back to basics. *Journal of the American Medical Association* 282 (24): 2313–2320.

Breggin, P. R. 1991. *Toxic Psychiatry: Why Therapy, Empathy, and Love Must Replace the Drugs, Electroshock, and Biochemical Theories of the "New Psychiatry."* New York: St. Martin's.

Brown, P. and S. C. Funk. 1986. Tardive dyskinesia: Barriers to the professional recognition of an iatrogenic disease. *Journal of Health and Social Behavior* 27:116–132.

Burton, R. 1855. *The Anatomy of Melancholy.* Philadelphia: J. W. Moore.

Campbell Collaboration. http://campbell.gse-upenn.edu.

Chalmers, I. 1983. Scientific inquiry and authoritarianism in perinatal care and education. *Birth* 10 (3): 151–166.

———. 1990. Underreporting research limitations is scientific misconduct. *Journal of American Medical Association* 263:1405–1408. *Clinical Evidence.* June 2002. BMJ Publishing Group.

Cochrane Collaboration. UK Cochrane Centre, HNS R and D Program. Summertown Pavilion, Middle Way, Oxford, OX2 7LG. U.K. E-mail address: mailto:general@cochrane.co.uk.

Conrad, P. and J. W. Schneider. 1992. *Deviance and Medicalization: From Badness to Sickness.* Philadelphia: Temple University Press.

Coulter, A. 2002. *The Autonomous Patient: Ending Paternalism in Medical Care.* London: Nuffield. Published by TSO (The Stationers Office), Norwich, U.K.

Dawes, R. M. 1994. *House of Cards: Psychology and Psychotherapy Built on Myth.* New York: Free Press.

———. 2001. *Everyday Irrationality: How Pseudo-Scientists, Lunatics, and the Rest of Us Systematically Fail to Think Rationally.* Boulder: Westview.

DePanfilis, D. 2003. *Review of IAIU Investigations of Suspected Child Abuse and Neglect in DYFS Out-of-Home Care Settings in New Jersey. Final Report.* Baltimore: School of Social Work, University of Maryland.

Edwards, A. and G. Elwyn. 2001. *Evidence-Informed Patient Choice: Inevitable or Impossible?* New York: Oxford University Press.

Eiseley, L. C. 1975. *All the Strange Hours: The Excavation of a Life.* New York: Scribner.

Ellul, J. 1965. *Propaganda: The Formation of Men's Attitudes.* New York: Vintage.

Farrant, W. and J. Russell. 1986. *The Politics of Health Information.* Bedford Way Papers 28. Institute of Education, University of London, distributed by Turnaround Distribution.

Friedson, E. 1986. *Professional Powers: A Study of the Institutionalization of Formal Knowledge.* Chicago: University of Chicago Press.

Gambrill, E. 1990. *Critical Thinking in Clinical Practice: Improving the Accuracy of Judgments and Decisions About Clients.* San Francisco: Jossey-Bass.

———. 2001. Social work: An authority-based profession. *Research on Social Work Practice* 11:166–175.

———. 2003. Evidence-based practice: Sea change or the emperor's new clothes? *Journal of Social Work Education* 39:3–23.

Garb, H. N. 2000. *Studying the Clinician: Judgment, Research, and Psychological Assessment.* Washington, D.C.: American Psychological Association.

Gibbs, L. and E. Gambrill. 2002. Evidence-based practice: Counterarguments to objections. *Research on Social Work Practice* 12:452–476.

Gilbert, P. 1989. *Human Nature and Suffering*. New York: Guilford.

Gomory, T. 1999. Programs of assertive community treatment (PACT): A critical review. *Ethical Human Services and Services* 1:147–163.

Gray, J. A. M. 2001a. *Evidence-Based Health Care: How to Make Health Policy and Management Decisions*. 2d ed. New York: Churchill Livingstone.

———. 2001b. Evidence-based medicine for professionals. In A. Edwards and G. Elywn, eds., *Evidence-Informed Patient Choice*, 19–33. New York: Oxford University Press.

Greenhalgh, T. 2001. *How to Read a Paper*. 2d ed. London: BMJ.

Gusfield, J. R. 1996. *Contested Meanings: The Construction of Alcohol Problems*. Madison: University of Wisconsin Press.

Guyatt, G. and D. Rennie, eds. 2002. *Users' Guide to the Medical Literature: A Manual for Evidence-Based Clinical Practice*. Chicago: American Medical Association Press.

Haynes, R. B., P. J. Devereaux, and G. H. Guyatt. 2002. Clinical expertise in the era of evidence-based medicine and patient choice. [Editorial] *ACP Journal Club* (March/April) 136: A11, pp. 1–7.

Houts, A. 2002. Discovery, Invention, and the Expansion of the Modern Diagnostic and Statistical Manuals of Mental Disorders. In L. E. Beutler and M. L. Malik, eds., *Rethinking the DSM: A Psychological Perspective*, 17–65. Washington, D.C.: American Psychological Association.

Jacobson, J. W., J. A. Mulick, and A. A. Schwartz. 1995. A history of facilitated communication: Science, pseudoscience, and antiscience working group on facilitated communication. *American Psychologist* 51:1031–1039.

Jarvis, W. T. 1990. *Dubious Dentistry: A Dental Continuing Education Course*. Loma Linda University School of Dentistry, Loma Linda, California 92350.

Kirk, S. A. and H. Kutchins. 1992. *The Selling of DSM: The Rhetoric of Science in Psychiatry*. New York: Aldine de Gruyter.

Kutchins, H. and S. A. Kirk. 1997. *Making Us Crazy: DSM—the Psychiatric Bible and the Creation of Mental Disorders*. New York: Free Press.

LaCasse, J. and T. Gomory. 2003. Is graduate social work education promoting a critical approach to mental health practice? *Journal of Social Work Education* 39:383–408.

Lepenies, W. 1992. *Melancholy and Society*. Translated by Jeremy Gaines and Doris Jones. Cambridge, Mass.: Harvard University Press.

Levy, C. J. 2002. Where hope dies. Broken homes. *New York Times*. April 29.

Lilienfeld, S. O., S. J. Lynn, and J. M. Lohr. 2003. *Science and Pseudoscience in Clinical Psychology*. New York: Guilford.

Mansfield, P. R. 2003. How does pharmaceutical company promotion affect prescribing? http://www.who.int/dap-icium/posters/4P7-fintext.html.

Margolin, L. 1997. *Under the Cover of Kindness: The Invention of Social Work*. Charlottesville: University Press of Virginia.

McCormick, J. 1996. Health Scares Are Bad for Your Health. In D. M. Warburton and N. Sherwood, eds., *Pleasure and Quality of Life*, 189–199. New York: John Wiley.

Mirowsky, J. and C. E. Ross. 1989. *Social Causes of Psychological Distress*. New York: Aldine de Gruyter.

Moseley, P. G. and K. L. Deweaver. 1995. Empirical Approaches to Case Management. In J. S. Wodarski and B. A. Thyer, eds., *Handbook of Empirical Social Work*, Vol. 2, *Social Problems and Practice Issues*, 393–412. New York: John Wiley.

Moynihan, R., I. Heath, and D. Henry. 2002. Selling sickness: The pharmaceutical industry and disease mongering. *British Medical Journal* 324:886–891.

Nathan, P. E. and J. M. Gorman, eds. 2002. *A Guide to Treatments That Work*. 2d ed. New York: Oxford University Press.

National Association of Social Workers (NASW). 1996. *Code of Ethics*. Silver Spring, Md.: NASW.

Ofshe, R. and E. Watters. 1994. *Making Monsters: False Memories, Psychotherapy, and Sexual Hysteria*. New York: Charles Scribner's.

Olds, D., C. R. Henderson Jr., R. Cole, J. Eckenrode et al. 1998. Long-term effects of nurse home visitation on children's criminal and antisocial behavior: 15-year follow-up of a randomized controlled trial. *Journal of the American Medical Association* 280:1238–1444.

Paul, R. 1993. *Critical Thinking: What Every Person Needs to Survive in a Rapidly Changing World*. 3d ed. Sonoma, Calif.: Foundation for Critical Thinking.

Popper, K. R. 1972. *Conjectures and Refutations: The Growth of Scientific Knowledge*. 4th ed. London: Routledge and Kegan Paul. Originally published in 1963.

———. 1992. *In Search of a Better World: Lectures and Essays from Thirty Years*. London: Routledge and Kegan Paul.

———. 1994. *The Myth of the Framework: In Defense of Science and Rationality*. Edited by M. A. Notturno. New York: Routledge.

Porter, R. 2000. *Quacks: Fakers and Charlatans in English Medicine*. Charleston, S.C.: Tempus.

Purdy, M. 2003. Our towns: Little boys, already fading in big picture. *New York Times*. January 15.

Rank, H. 1984. *The Pep Talk: How to Analyze Political Language*. Park Forest, Ill.: Counter-Propaganda Press.

Reid, W. J. 2001. The role of science in social work: The perennial debate. *Journal of Social Work* 1:273–293.

———. 2002. Knowledge for direct social work practice: An analysis of trends. *Social Service Review* 76:6–33.

Rose, S., J. Bisson, and S. Wessely. 2001. Psychological debriefing for preventing post-traumatic stress disorder (PTSD). Cochrane Review. In The Cochrane Library, Issue 4, 2001. Oxford: Update Software.

Rose, D., P. Fleischmann, T. Wykes, M. Leese, and J. Bindman. 2003. Patients' perspectives on electroconvulsive therapy: Systematic review. *British Medical Journal* 326:1363–1365.

Rosen, A. and E. K. Proctor. 2002. Standards for Evidence-Based Social Work Practice. In A. R. B. Roberts and G. J. Greene, eds., *The Social Worker's Desk Reference*, 743–747. New York: Oxford University Press.

Rosen, A., E. K. Proctor, N. Morrow-Howell, and M. Staudt. 1995. Rationales for practice decisions: Variations in knowledge use by decision task and social work service. *Research on Social Work Practice* 15:501–523.

Rosenthal, T. 1994. Science and ethics in conducting, analyzing, and reporting psychological research. *Psychological Science* 5:127–134.

Sackett, D. L., W. S. Richardson, W. Rosenberg, and R. B. Haynes. 1997. *Evidence-Based Medicine: How to Practice and Teach EBM.* New York: Churchill Livingstone.

Sackett, D. L., W. M. C. Rosenberg, J. A. M. Gray, R. B. Haynes, and W. S. Richardson. 1996. Evidence-based medicine: What it is and what it isn't. *British Medical Journal* 312:71–72.

Sackett, D. L., S. E. Straus, W. S. Richardson, W. Rosenberg, and R. D. Haynes. 2000. *Evidence-Based Medicine: How to Practice and Teach EBM.* 2d ed. New York: Churchill Livingstone.

Sarnoff, S. K. 2001. *Sanctified Snake Oil: The Effects of Junk Science and Public Policy.* Westport, Conn.: Praeger.

Schwartz, I. M. 1989. *(In)justice for Juveniles: Rethinking the Best Interests of the Child.* Lexington, Mass.: Lexington.

Skrabanek, P. and J. McCormick. 1998. *Follies and Fallacies in Medicine.* 3d ed. Glencaple, Dumfries: Beaufort Press.

Smith, R. 2003. Do patients need to read research? *British Medical Journal* 326:1307.

Stoesen, L. 2003. Gala focuses on child welfare. *NASW News* 48 (5): 7/10.

Strohman, R. C. 2000. Genetic Determination as a Failing Paradigm in Biology and Medicine: Implications for Health and Wellness. Reprinted from M. S. Jamner and D. Stokol, eds., *Promoting Human Wellness,* 99–129, with an epilogue in *Journal of Social Work Education* (2003) 39:169–191.

Szasz, T. S. 1987. *Insanity: The Idea and Its Consequences.* New York: John Wiley.

———. 1994. *Cruel Compassion: Psychiatric Control of Society's Unwanted.* New York: John Wiley.

Timimi, S. and E. Taylor. 2004. ADHD is best understood as a cultural construct. *British Journal of Psychiatry* 184:8–9.

Todd, J. T. and E. K. Morris. 1992. Case histories in the great power of steady misrepresentation. *American Psychologist* 47 (11): 1441–1453.

U.S. Department of Health and Human Services. 1999. *Mental Health: A Report of the Surgeon General.* Rockville, Md.: U.S. Department of Health and Human Services. Substance Abuse and Mental Health Services Administration.

Valenstein, E. S. 1986. *Great and Desperate Cures: The Rise and Decline of Psychosurgery and Other Radical Treatments for Mental Illness.* New York: Basic Books.

White, R. K. 1971. Propaganda: Morally Questionable and Morally Unquestionable Techniques. In R. D. Lambert, ed., and A. W. Heston, assistant ed., *The Annals of the American Academy of Political and Social Science.* Philadelphia: American Academy of Political and Social Science.

Wilkes, M. S. and J. R. Hoffman. 2001. An innovative approach to educating medical students about pharmaceutical promotion. *Academic Medicine* 76:1271–1277.

Wodarski, J. and B. Thyer. 1995. *Handbook of Empirical Social Work Practice.* Vol. 2. New York: John Wiley.

Chapter 15

Mental Health Practice Guidelines: Panacea or Pipe Dream?

Matthew O. Howard, Tonya Edmond, and Michael G. Vaughn

It is easier to produce ten volumes of philosophical writings than to put one principle into practice.

—*Leo Tolstoy*

Mental health practice guidelines have proliferated widely in recent years. Recently published guidelines include those designed to improve the conduct of forensic psychiatric examinations, increase the quality of mental health assessments performed in child custody evaluations and juvenile justice facilities, encourage better management of violence in mental health treatment settings, and promote more effective use of videoconferencing technology in service delivery (Butrej 1998; Herman 1997; Kennedy and Yellowlees 2000; Simon and Wettstein 1997; Wasserman et al. 2003). Population and condition-specific clinical care guidelines for individuals with borderline personality disorder (Oldham 2002), depression (Center et al. 2003; Kurlowicz 1997; Schulberg et al. 1998), attention-deficit-hyperactivity disorder (ADHD) (Pliszka et al. 2000a, 2000b), schizophrenia (Chiles et al. 1999; Smith and Docherty 1998), bipolar disorder (Bauer et al. 1999), nicotine dependence (Friend and Levy 2001), and other mental health problems have also been disseminated. August professional groups, such as the American Psychiatric Association, the American Academy of Child and Adolescent Psychiatry, and the American Psychological Association, and sundry governmental, insurance, and managed-care entities are currently actively engaged in comprehensive programs of guideline development for diverse mental health problems (Howard and Jenson 2003).

By any reckoning, guideline development is a growth industry that will affect mental health practice significantly in the near term and for the foreseeable future. Below, we review relevant definitional issues, reasons for and current methods of guideline development, characteristics of good guidelines, evidence pertaining to guideline quality, research findings relating to guideline dissemination, adherence, and effectiveness, and emerging issues with implications for mental health guidelines. Although guidelines could play a salubrious role in rationalizing mental health policy, few efforts have been made to develop or evaluate mental health policy practice guidelines. Thus, discussion is limited to clinical rather than policy issues pertaining to mental health practice.

Definitions

Practice guidelines are recommendations for care made on the basis of empirical findings and the consensus of experts with substantial experience in a given practice area. The Institute of Medicine (IOM) provided one of the earliest definitions of guidelines, describing them as "systematically developed statements to assist practitioner and patient decisions about appropriate care for specific clinical circumstances" (1990:27). Proctor and Rosen (2003) defined guidelines as sets of "systematically compiled and organized knowledge statements that are designed to enable practitioners to find, select, and use the interventions that are most effective and appropriate" (1). Marsh (2003) suggested that guidelines are "highly developed and tested forms of practice knowledge related to the effectiveness of specific interventions under specific conditions" (1). Other professional bodies have referred to guidelines as "preferred practice patterns" or "practice parameters" in order to emphasize the need for flexibility in guideline application and the perils of rigidly prescriptive practice recommendations (Sommer, Weinter, and Gamble 1990). The terms "practice options," "protocols," "standards," "algorithms," and "critical pathways" are broadly synonymous with the practice guidelines concept, although each possesses some nuanced meanings (see Howard and Jenson 2003).

Although guidelines can take many forms, most definitions emphasize their common objective—improving practitioner decision making by describing appropriate indications for specific interventions. Videka (2003) and Zayas (2003) accurately observed that guidelines have not generally attended to client, provider, service setting, and social factors related to effective service delivery. Most available guidelines also do not address the economic, ethical, or organizational implications of guideline implementation. Thus, it seems prudent that practitioners be accorded considerable flexibility in the use of guidelines.

Thousands of guidelines can be found in the medical and allied health literatures, but until relatively recently, few of them addressed problems, populations, or interventions relevant to mental health practice. At present, mental health guidelines are a heterogeneous group with regard to the methods used in their development, dissemination, and evaluation. Some guidelines represent the efforts of small groups with questionable expertise relying largely on informal consensus-driven approaches, whereas other guideline development efforts are massive and costly undertakings involving the systematic collection, grading, and synthesis of research findings via meta-analysis, in conjunction with explicit consensus-development methods and weighted treatment recommendations.

Rationale

More or less formalized guidelines have been published for more than sixty years (Howard and Jenson 1999a, 1999b). However, the past decade has witnessed an unprecedented growth in guideline development and the application of increasingly sophisticated methods and greater resources to guideline construction, dissemination, and evaluation (Howard and Jenson 2003; Howard et al. 2003).

Three related developments beginning in the 1970s gave rise to the modern guideline movement. Wennberg's investigations documented noteworthy unexplained regional variation in health care practitioners' use of common medical procedures and therapies (Wennberg, Freeman, and Culp 1987; Wennberg and Gittelsohn 1973). Practice variation was believed to reflect inappropriate under- and over-utilization of therapeutic interventions and was attributed, in turn, to practitioners' uncertainties regarding appropriate indications for selected treatments. In addition, informed observers increasingly called into question the effectiveness of popular treatments, leading to a growing awareness of the need for more-comprehensive outcome assessments and explicit statements of preferred practice approaches in different practice contexts (Howard and Jenson 1999b). Studies documenting inappropriate use of health care interventions also supported the need for more systematic recommendations for treatment in relation to specific health problems. Thus, growing recognition of substantial unjustifiable variation in the use of common health care interventions, many of uncertain value, contributed to the growing demand for guidelines. Guideline proponents believed that guidelines could decrease practitioner uncertainty and thereby reduce rates of inappropriate care by codifying knowledge in particular practice areas.

Despite vigorous efforts to encourage more evidence-based practice (Howard et al. 2003, Howard, McMillen, and Pollio 2003), current findings suggest that substandard mental health care remains a significant problem. McGlynn, Asch, and Adams (2003) evaluated 439 quality-of-care indicators for thirty acute and chronic health disorders using a sample of 6,712 respondents residing in twelve U.S. metropolitan areas. Chart reviews and telephone interviews revealed substantial divergence of reported care from practice recommendations based on pertinent available practice guidelines. Across all disorders, participants received only 54.9% of recommended care. Adherence to alcohol-dependence treatment performance standards, one of few psychiatric conditions examined, was poor. Alcohol-dependent clients received only 10.5% of recommended care, the lowest rate for all disorders examined. Patients treated for depression received 57.7% of recommended care, a figure substantially lower than comparable rates for many medical disorders, including prenatal care, breast cancer, and senile cataracts (for which delivered care ranged from 73% to 79% of that recommended). McGlynn et al. (2003) concluded that "the deficits we have identified in adherence to recommended processes for basic care pose serious threats to the health of the American public" (2635). Deficits in mental health care are especially worrisome.

Results of other investigations also suggest widespread inappropriate treatment of common mental health conditions. Young et al. (2001) identified a nationally representative sample of 1,636 adults who had experienced clinical depression or an anxiety disorder within the past year. Although 83% of adults with a probable disorder saw a health care provider, only 30% received medication or counseling consistent with current treatment guidelines. Poorly educated, African American, young, and old persons were significantly less likely than their counterparts to receive appropriate care.

Wang, Berglund, and Kessler (2000) found that only 14.3% of 3,032 study participants meeting *DSM-III-R* criteria for a major depressive disorder or anxiety disorder within the previous twelve months had received guideline-concordant care. Nonwhites, men, the less seriously ill, and the uninsured were least likely to receive acceptable care.

Recent studies indicate that inadequate or inappropriate treatment of mental health disorders is widespread. Socially disenfranchised client populations receive less-adequate care than their less vulnerable counterparts, a state of affairs that increases their susceptibility to adverse health and social outcomes. Current treatment of mental health conditions less prevalent than depression and anxiety disorders may be even less consistent with evidence-based guidelines. These findings also make it clear that merely developing guidelines is not sufficient to ensure adequate mental health care. Adequate dissemination and implementation of guidelines is a key to guideline effectiveness.

Many factors may account for the discrepancy between current mental health care practices in the community and agreed-upon professional guidelines. New clinical research findings often make previous training obsolete, and the brisk pace of intervention research demands that practitioners remain current with practice-relevant research or risk quickly becoming outdated. Low levels of awareness of available sources of evidence-based clinical information also contribute to substandard care (Sigouin and Jadad 2002). Efficient use of guidelines and other evidence-based practice resources requires access to computers and numerous databases and the ability to assess, critique, and apply relevant knowledge (Gosling, Westbrook, and Coiera 2003).

Although the guideline movement has clearly commenced in the mental health arena, many uncertainties remain with regard to the identification of optimal methods for guideline development and dissemination. These areas are addressed below with attention to recent research findings.

Current Guideline Development Activities

At present, more than forty professional and governmental organizations are actively involved in guideline development (Stuart, Rush, and Morris 2002). One recent nationally representative investigation of 417 managed-care organizations offering 752 products in sixty market areas found that 73.8% of products relied on guidelines for behavioral health, alcohol/drug, or mental health services (Levy et al. 2002). Kaiser Permanente, the largest U.S. HMO, recently announced that it would publish on its Web site the guidelines created and applied by its physicians to the care of hundreds of conditions (www.kaiserpermanente.org). Several exemplary efforts are described below.

Guidelines differ substantially in their scope, sophistication, developmental costs, and perceived credibility. For example, guidelines for the treatment of individuals with intellectual disabilities/dementia (Wilkinson, Janicki, and Edinburgh Working Group on Dementia Care Practices 2002), depression and suicide in physicians (Center et al. 2003), and mental health evaluations in juvenile justice settings (Wasserman et al. 2003) were developed after two-to-three-day consensus conferences and offer useful, though limited, guidance to practitioners confronting these issues.

Significantly more-ambitious guideline development efforts have also been undertaken in recent years. The American Psychiatric Association (APA) has published comprehensive guidelines for the treatment of delirium and dementia, Alzheimer's disease, AIDS, major depression, bipolar disorder, schizophrenia, panic attacks, eating disorders, substance use disorders, and borderline personality disorder (APA 2002). APA guidelines are developed by large expert panels through an iterative process that incorporates significant feedback from clinicians, researchers, and affected professional and consumer groups. APA guideline development involves costly and time-consuming analyses explicitly weighing the quality of the evidence supporting individual guideline recommendations, and the resulting guidelines are of high quality and considerable utility.

The Department of Veterans Affairs Office of Performance and Quality has supported the development of VA clinical guidelines for management of persons with psychoses. One such guideline for the treatment of bipolar disorder comprises specific assessment and treatment algorithms with identified decision points complete with supporting annotations from the scientific literature (Bauer et al. 1999). A core guideline module addresses diagnostic issues and assignment of patients to a specific mood state. Other guideline modules address diagnostic and treatment tasks specific to manic/hypomanic/mixed mood episodes, bipolar depressive episodes, rapid cycling, and bipolar disorder with psychotic features. The VA guidelines were developed over a six-month period, subjected to expert review, and then published on the World Wide Web (http://www.psychiatrist.com/bauer).

Another guideline development project of substantial scope is the Texas Children's Medical Algorithm Project/Texas Medical Algorithm Project (TCMAP/TMAP). Participants in the TCMAP were the first to develop guidelines for the treatment of childhood mental disorders (Pliszka et al. 2000a, 2000b). TCMAP guidelines specifically targeted children treated within the public mental health sector, although guideline developers believe they possess utility for children treated in the private sector as well. The first TCMAP guideline addressed the proper pharmacological management of ADHD. TMAP has developed guidelines for adults treated in the public mental health sector in Texas for schizophrenia, major depressive disorder, and bipolar disorder. Guidelines were established through an extensive consensus development, feasibility testing, and clinical trial process (Chiles et al. 1999; Crismon et al. 1999; Rush et al. 2003; Suppes, Swann, and Dennehy 2001; Suppes et al. 2002, 2003). Comprehensive efforts such as those of the APA, VA, or TCMAP/TMAP are relatively unusual. Extant guidelines represent a heterogeneous mix with regard to the nature of the processes used to develop them, their scope, and the evidentiary base.

Qualities of Good Guidelines

Guidelines differ substantially in their usefulness to practitioners. Desirable features of guidelines were identified early in the guideline development movement. Most theorists agree that guidelines should be widely disseminated, based on a transparent developmental process, revised regularly to reflect significant scientific advances, and based on empirical findings of the highest quality (Howard and Jenson 1999b). Guidelines should be *comprehensive,* including all indications for an intervention or procedure; *specific,* clearly describing conditions under which an intervention is recommended; *inclusive,* incorporating all factors that should be considered before recommending a treatment or procedure; and *manageable,* easy to understand and apply in practice (Leape 1990). Social work scholars have also stressed the importance of interdisciplinary and interprofessional collaboration in guideline development (Bailey and Aronoff 2003; Thyer 2003).

Contemporary guideline development protocols often incorporate extensive systematic reviews of published/unpublished research findings; an explicit process for selecting, weighing, and summarizing study findings; an iterative feedback process, including members of relevant professional and consumer groups, by which guidelines are revised in response to professional feedback; and a method whereby scientific findings are melded with expert opinion.

Methods for evaluating and comparing guidelines are currently in development. In 1992 IOM published a provisional instrument for the assessment of guidelines in its *Clinical Practice Guidelines: Directions for a New Program.* Shaneyfelt, Mayo-Smith, and Rothwangl (1999) developed a twenty-five-item instrument to assess guideline adherence with the recommended guideline development standards of twenty-five experts in the field. Evaluations of 279 guidelines published between 1985 and 1997 revealed that an average of fewer than 11 standards (43.1%) were met. Few guidelines included an expiration date or date of scheduled review (10.8%), specified the method of identifying scientific evidence (16.8%) or the method of data extraction (5.0%), described formal methods of combining evidence and expert opinion (7.5%), or attempted to quantify costs (14.3%). Guidelines developed before 1985 met an average of 9.2 of 25 standards, compared to 12.6 for guidelines developed after 1995. Clearly, the need for methodological improvements in guideline development remains. Support for this conclusion is provided by Grilli et al. (2000), who found that only 5% of the 431 guidelines they examined involved a multidisciplinary development process, reported study selection criteria, and provided confidence ratings for guideline recommendations based on the quality of the underlying evidence. Ward and Grieco (1996) examined Australian guidelines developed before the publication of the National Health and Medical Research Council's "guidelines for guidelines" in 1995. Few of the 34 guidelines examined met even a majority of the eighteen criteria across which they were assessed.

Guideline Adherence

Adherence to guidelines is often very poor. For example, Azocar et al. (2003) compared a general mailing of depression guidelines to mental health clinicians ($N = 443$) in a managed behavioral health care organization to a mailing in which guidelines were specifically linked to the care of a patient starting treatment with each clinician and to a no-guideline mailing condition. Guideline adherence was low across conditions.

Disappointing findings were also reported for a physician education intervention that sought to increase adherence to depression guidelines in a primary care setting (Lin et al. 1997). Dobscha et al. (2003) found that depression guidelines were frequently not followed in a VA primary care setting. Similarly, Dickey et al. (2003) found low rates of adherence to the Schizophrenia Patient Treatment Outcomes Team guidelines in Medicaid patients receiving outpatient treatment for schizophrenia.

Several conclusions can be drawn from studies evaluating the effectiveness of guidelines in changing clinicians' behaviors. Merely disseminating guidelines (i.e., passive diffusion approaches such as direct mailings and journal publication of guidelines) is not effective (Howard and Jenson 2003). Instead, incentives such as reduced malpractice insurance premiums or professional recognition for excellence should be offered to practitioners to encourage them to adopt guidelines (Howard and Jenson 2003). Garnering the active participation of practitioners in the guideline development process via small group consensus-building (Borduas et al. 1998) and local adaptation of national guidelines (Puech et al. 1998) are also potentially fruitful approaches. Use of practitioner opinion leaders, practitioner profiling, and feedback and clinical auditing has proved effective in some studies. In general, the more intense and multifaceted the dissemination methods and the greater the practitioner involvement, the more likely it is that clinicians will be aware of guidelines and apply them in practice.

One recent systematic review of guideline adherence studies found highly variable rates of guideline use. Bauer (2002) reviewed twenty-six cross-sectional, six pre-post (with no intervention), and nine controlled trials of specific interventions with respect to guideline adherence. Only 27% of cross-sectional studies found adequate guideline adherence, whereas 67% of controlled trials suggested positive findings. Bauer (2002) noted that effective strategies to promote guideline adherence were often resource-intensive and complex. Further, only six of thirteen (46%) studies in which patient outcomes were examined reported positive effects of guideline adherence. Equally worrisome was the tendency of adherence rates to return to baseline levels over time.

Few studies have sought to identify potential personal and organizational barriers to guideline implementation (Glisson 2002). A British investigation of 3,530 general practitioners in eleven geographic areas revealed that 58% were aware of depression treatment guidelines. Respondents perceived the primary barriers to providing guideline-concordant care to depressed persons to be having too little time to spend with patients and problems with access to appropriate services. Time constraints were also cited by practitioners as a significant barrier to the provision of evidence-based care in a recent study of obstacles to the implementation of evidence-based treatment (Ely et al. 2002). However, Lenfant (2003) described multiple cases in which demonstrably effective, simple, and inexpensive therapies were not routinely used in medical care nationally, despite clear indications supporting their use.

Although a variety of technical efforts have been made to improve guideline adherence, including the use of computerized reminders (Cannon and Allen 2000; Rollman et al. 2001), decision-support aids (Medow et al. 2001), and analyses of state administrative, pharmacy (Finnerty et al. 2002), and federal patient (Chen and Rosenheck 2001) databases, impediments to the use of guidelines continue to limit guideline use. Staff shortages, limited awareness of available guidelines (Sigouin and Jadad 2002), limited access to computerized databases, poor perceived credibility of guidelines, and shortages of time (Gosling, Westbrook, and Coiera 2003; Williams, Lee, and Kerr 2002) negatively influence guideline utilization.

Despite the barriers to guideline implementation and the low rates of adherence often reported, there are some reasons for optimism vis-à-vis guidelines. There are growing indications that practitioners are receptive to guidelines, particularly those developed by independent and respected national bodies (Putnam et al. 2002), and can acquire useful skills for applying guidelines and other evidence-based practice products relatively quickly (Fritsche et al. 2002). Additional studies of cost-effective guideline dissemination and implementation strategies are clearly needed.

Guideline Effectiveness

Relatively few studies have evaluated whether adequately disseminated and implemented guidelines alter the behaviors of practitioners and improve clients' mental health outcomes. Earlier reviews of the general medical literature suggest that properly developed and disseminated guidelines can influence practitioners' behaviors under propitious conditions. Grimshaw and Russell (1993) reviewed fifty-nine rigorous evaluations of the effects of guidelines on the processes and outcomes of health care; only four studies failed to report statistically significant positive findings related to guideline implementation on the processes of care, although the effects were of widely varying magnitude. Nine of eleven studies examining the impact of guidelines on clients' outcomes reported significant positive findings.

Worrall, Chaulk, and Freake (1997) reported that only five of thirteen controlled studies examining the effects of guidelines on patients' outcomes in primary care produced statistically significant findings. The authors noted that "there is relatively little evidence that the use of guidelines improves patients' outcomes in primary medical care," but observed that "most studies published to date have used older guidelines and methods" (many of which were not explicitly evidence-based).

Recent research findings suggest that guidelines may have the potential to improve mental health practice. Miranda et al. (2003) randomly assigned 267 depressed, primarily poor Latina and black women to Agency for Healthcare Research and Quality (AHRQ) guideline-concordant antidepressant ($N = 88$) or cognitive-behavioral ($N = 90$) treatment, or to a standard educational intervention with assisted referral to community-based mental health services. Both conditions of guideline-concordant care produced significant reductions in depression symptoms and significant improvements in functioning relative to the community referral condition. Overall, medication was more effective than cognitive-behavioral treatment with regard to amelioration of depressive symptoms and instrumental role functioning.

Mela et al. (1998) used survival analysis to identify significant predictors of relapse among 4,052 Medicaid patients receiving antidepressant treatment. Adherence to antidepressant treatment guidelines, the presence of comorbid psychiatric conditions, and race were all significantly related to risk for depression relapse over a two-year follow-up period.

Fortney et al. (2001) found that only 29% of the community-based sample of depressed patients they studied received care consistent with AHRQ depression guideline recommendations. Receipt of guideline-concordant care was highly related to resolution of depressive symptoms for participants who met criteria for depression. Other research findings suggest that guidelines and quality improvement programs can increase primary care practitioners' detection of depression and associated symptoms and lead to significantly increased rates of patient adherence to prescribed antidepressant drug regimens (Upton et al. 1999; Unutzer et al. 2001).

Few evaluations of mental health guideline effectiveness in areas other than depression have been published. A recent study of TMAP's algorithm-driven drug treatment for patients with a history of mania found that patients treated in accordance with manualized treatment recommendations and an algorithm for medication management had significantly greater improvements in symptoms of mania and psychosis than did patients who received treatment as usual in public mental health centers (Suppes et al. 2003).

Even accounting for the possibility that publication bias and sample selection bias contribute to current positive findings in relation to guidelines, current research suggests that further study of guidelines is warranted. If guidelines are properly developed, disseminated, and implemented, their use might increase the quality of care provided to mentally ill clients.

Emerging Issues

A host of emerging practices promises to increase the utility of guidelines and improve the quality of mental health care. These advances include more widespread and sophisticated use of economic analyses in guideline evaluation, greater use of health care informatics and Internet resources to increase guideline use, more attention to the incorporation of patient preferences into guideline-based care, and greater sensitivity to the development of guidelines for historically neglected client populations and to ethical issues associated with guidelines.

Economic Issues

Perhaps the chief early concern with guidelines was the perception that they were primarily cost-saving measures rather than instruments intended to increase the quality and value of health care. Insurance companies have been interested in guidelines since their inception, as have employers, who increasingly pay employee health claims directly through self-funded health plans. Parker (1995) noted that reimbursement policies influence which conditions are treated and procedures performed and suggested that "a first role for practice guidelines is helping insurance companies to establish reimbursement policies that reflect the best current opinion on which procedures are appropriate for which patients in which circumstances" (57). Marsh (2003) noted that public and private insurers could help legitimate the use of guidelines within social work by requiring their use, instead of relying solely on professional degrees and licensure for reimbursement eligibility determinations. Guideline adherence can also be used in determining whether or not selected providers will be included or excluded from provider networks. In addition, many insurance industry analysts argue that capitated payments for mental health services could increase incentives to use guidelines. Other issues that have arisen concern the implications of conflicting guidelines for the treatment of clients who are covered by multiple insurance contracts and whether or not the insurance industry should promote guidelines that have not been vetted via a peer review process.

Cost-benefit analyses of guidelines have provided a number of useful insights into the potential economic consequences of guidelines. Questions have been raised regarding the role and weight that should be accorded cost considerations in the development and evaluation of guidelines, the availability of valid and generalizable cost estimates, and the presentation of cost data to clinicians by economists in a manner that is most useful to them (Mason et al. 1999).

Professional groups have called for the inclusion of economic data in guideline discussions of the cost implications of alternative approaches to the prevention, diagnosis, and treatment of psychiatric conditions. Optimal means of incorporating economic data into guidelines have not yet been identified. It is unclear whether economic analyses should be incorporated into organic guideline development processes or serve an adjunctive purpose, with the primary emphasis on indications of clinical effectiveness (Mason et al. 1999). To date, most guidelines do not address health economic issues, although there are indications that economic data can be used fruitfully in guideline development. Mason et al. (1999) described innovative efforts in the United Kingdom to explicitly include economic analyses in the guideline development process and proffered a set of recommendations for the economist involved in guideline development.

An important final consideration regarding the economic impact of guidelines concerns the distinction between individual- and societal-level cost-benefit assessment. Granata and Hillman (1998) demonstrated that guidelines chosen to maximize cost-effectiveness at the individual level might not maximize cost-effectiveness at the population level. They observed that we must guard against the notion that "decisions reached individually will, in fact, be the best decisions for an entire society" (61).

Health-Care Informatics and Internet Resources

Evaluations of computerized decision-support aids (Medow et al. 2001), electronic client records with reminder systems (Rollman et al. 2001), patient administrative databases to assess guideline adherence (Chen and Rosenheck 2001), computer-administered mental health assessments (Finfgeld 1999), and comparative approaches to clinical informaticist service design (Greenhalgh et al. 2002) are increasingly found in the mental health literature. Substantially greater development of computer software designed to promote adherence to mental health practice guidelines is likely to occur in the near term.

Numerous Web sites are available to mental health practitioners interested in accessing clinical guidelines, among them MDConsult (www.mdconsult.com), Medscape (www.medscape.com), and the Ottawa General

Hospital Campus Library Evidence-Based Medicine and Practice Resources (www.ogh.on.ca/library/evidence.htm) Web site. Owens (1998) provides a comprehensive enumeration of the many Web sites currently available to practitioners who are interested in accessing guidelines.

Patient Preferences

Patient preferences are increasingly being taken into account in health care decision making. Several organizations have published client versions of guidelines in an effort to ensure that clients and their advocates understand the potential risks and benefits of the treatment options available to them.

The methods by which patient preferences are assessed range from the highly informal (e.g., discussions with clinicians) to the highly structured (e.g., computerized "utility" assessments providing quantitative assessments of the desirability of given health states) (Owens 1998). Research to date suggests that practitioners often hold invalid views of the utilities their clients attach to different health states and outcomes and that clients with similarly severe symptoms may have very different feelings about their symptoms and the options for treating them (Nease et al. 1995). Guidelines that base treatment recommendations solely on symptom severity may offer less-than-optimal treatment recommendations when they fail to take patient preferences into account.

A number of prototypic multimedia and interactive computerized client preference assessment software packages are currently being evaluated, but such assessments are not routinely incorporated into modern medical practice. Brennan and Strombom (1998) commented that "in order for patient preferences to be effectively used in the delivery of health care, it is important that patients be able to formulate and express preferences, that these judgments be made known to the clinician at the time of care, and that these statements meaningfully inform care activities" (257). At present, it is unclear in which settings, under what conditions, and how patients' preferences should be assessed. Additional research is needed to identify approaches to the assessment of patients' preferences that are valid, efficient, and easily incorporated into the daily routines of mental health practitioners in a manner that best serves the clients' interests.

Vulnerable Populations and Neglected Conditions

Few guidelines have been developed for vulnerable client populations and less-prevalent mental health disorders, although guidelines might be most helpful in these situations. Many practitioners, for example, would find the treatment of intermittent rage disorder or trichotillomania substantially more challenging than that of depression. Guidelines are particularly needed to direct practice in complex emerging areas of importance, such as those at the interface of mental health and genetics (UK Nuffield Council on Bioethics 2001). Whether economic realities will allow for the development of guidelines specifically targeted to the needs of vulnerable populations and for the care of less-prevalent mental health conditions is currently unclear.

Ethical Considerations

Few analyses of the ethical consequences of guideline implementation have been published. Panek (1999) suggested that practitioners and clients who embraced utilitarian philosophical principles would be relatively accepting of guidelines because they value that course of action which produces the greatest good for the largest number of people and not necessarily the individual case at hand. Guidelines are generally constructed with the average case in mind and occasionally recommend suboptimal care for a particular client. Deontologically inclined practitioners repudiate guidelines that have the effect of "violating [their] autonomy and perhaps generating a maleficent result in any individual patient" (270). Social contracts proponents believe that all members of a society should receive equal treatment vis-à-vis access to and distribution of health care and other resources. Guidelines are "designed to foster reasoned use of resources, and in a just system, would be a useful tool to facilitate such a solution" (270). From this perspective, guidelines ration health care in a socially just and equitable manner and thus are desirable.

Other theorists have asked, "Who should be responsible for ensuring that guidelines are ethical in their formulation and implementation?" and "To what extent could guidelines help to avoid or resolve such [ethical] conflicts or, alternatively, cause them to arise?" (Somerville 1993). Informed health care analysts agree that guidelines are likely to raise a plethora of ethical issues for practitioners, but a full accounting of the ethical implications of guidelines has not been undertaken.

Conclusions

Guideline development has proceeded at an exponentially increasing rate over the past decade. Although guidelines have proliferated widely, much of core significance remains unknown about them. How best might they be developed? What are the standards by which they should be judged, and how effective are they and under what conditions? How should patients' preferences, economic considerations, and value judgments be incorporated into guidelines? Although substantially more needs to be learned about guidelines, one conclusion seems unassailable: guidelines are here to stay.

In the near term, additional research is needed to examine organizational, economic, political, and ethical factors relevant to guideline development, adoption, and effectiveness. Videka (2003) and others have also called for more studies examining agency-related and client-specific factors such as ethnicity, gender, and social class that have rarely been systematically addressed in guidelines. Mental health guidelines, in addition to other evidence-based practice products, such as systematic reviews, manualized therapies, and clinical trial registries, promise to change the face of mental health practice in a profound way over the next decade. However, only further experience with and evaluation of guidelines will enable health care policymakers and practitioners to determine whether guidelines are the panacea or pipe dream that some have made them out to be.

References

American Psychiatric Association (APA). 2002. *American Psychiatric Association Practice Guidelines for the Treatment of Psychiatric Disorders: Compendium 2002.* Washington, D.C.: APA.

Aronoff, N. and D. Bailey. 2003. Social Work Practice Guidelines in an Interprofessional World: Honoring New Ties That Bind. In A. Rosen and E. K. Proctor, eds., *Developing Practice Guidelines for Social Work Intervention: Issues, Methods, and Research Agenda,* 253–267. New York: Columbia University Press.

Azocar, F., B. Cuffel, W. Goldman, and L. McCarter. 2003. The impact of evidence-based guideline dissemination for the assessment and treatment of major depression in a managed behavioral health care organization. *Journal of Behavioral Health Services Research* 30 (1): 109–118.

Bauer, M. S. 2002. A review of quantitative studies of adherence to mental health clinical practice guidelines. *Harvard Review of Psychiatry* 10 (3): 138–153.

Bauer, M. S., A. M. Callahan, C. Jampala et al. 1999. Clinical practice guidelines for bipolar disorder from the Department of Veterans Affairs. *Journal of Clinical Psychiatry* 60 (1): 9–21.

Borduas, F., R. Carrier, D. Drouin, D. Deslaurievs, and G. Tremblay. 1998. An interactive workshop: An effective means of integrating the Canadian Cardiovascular Society clinical practice guidelines on congestive heart failure into Canadian family physicians' practice. *Canadian Journal of Cardiology* 14:911–916.

Brennan, P. F. and I. Strombom. 1998. Improving health care by understanding patient preferences: The role of computer technology. *Journal of the American Medical Informatics Association* 5:257–262.

Butrej, T. 1998. Evidence-based guidelines for managing violence in mental health. *Lamp* 55 (2): 22.

Cannon, D. S. and S. N. Allen. 2000. A comparison of the effects of computer and manual reminder on compliance with a mental health clinical practice guideline. *Journal of the American Medical Informatics Association* 7 (2): 196–203.

Center, C., M. Davis, T. Detre et al. 2003. Confronting depression and suicide in physicians: A consensus statement. *Journal of the American Medical Association* 289 (23): 3161–3166.

Chen, R. S. and R. Rosenheck. 2001. Using a computerized patient database to evaluate guideline adherence and measure patterns of care for major depression. *Journal of Behavioral Health Services Research* 28 (4): 466–474.

Chiles, J. A., A. L. Miller, M. I. Crismon, A. O. Rush, A. S. Krasuote, and S. S. Shon. 1999. The Texas Medical Algorithm Project: Development and implementation of the schizophrenia algorithm. *Psychiatric Services* 50 (1): 69–74.

Crismon, M. L., M. Trivedi, T. A. Pigott et al. 1999. The Texas Medication Algorithm Project: Report of the Texas Consensus Conference Panel on Medication Treatment of Major Depressive Disorder. *Journal of Clinical Psychiatry* 60 (3): 142–156.

Dickey, B., S. L. Normand, R. C. Hermann et al. 2003. Guideline recommendations for treatment of schizophrenia: The impact of managed care. *Archives of General Psychiatry* 60 (4): 340–348.

Dobscha, S. K., M. S. Gerrity, K. Corson, A. Balu, and N. M. Luilwik. 2003. Measuring adherence to depression treatment guidelines in a VA primary care clinic. *General Hospital Psychiatry* 25 (4): 230–237.

Ely, J. W., J. A. Osheroff, M. H. Ebell et al. 2002. Obstacles to answering doctors' questions about patient care with evidence: Qualitative study. *British Journal of Medicine* 324:1–7.

Finfgeld, D. L. 1999. Computer-based mental health assessments: Panaceas, pariahs, or partners in research and practice. *Comprehensive Nursing* 17 (5): 215–220.

Finnerty, M., R. Altmansberger, J. Bopp et al. 2002. Using state administrative and pharmacy databases to develop a clinical decision support tool for schizophrenia guidelines. *Schizophrenia Bulletin* 28 (1): 85–94.

Fortney, J., K. Rost, M. Zhang, and J. Pyne. 2001. The relationship between quality and outcomes in routine depression care. *Psychiatric Services* 52 (1): 56–62.

Friend, K. and D. T. Levy. 2001. Smoking treatment interventions and policies to promote their use: A critical review. *Nicotine and Tobacco Research* 3 (4): 299–310.

Fritsche, L., T. Greenhalgh, Y. Falck-Ytter, H. H. Neumayer, and R. Kunz. 2002. Do short courses in evidence-based medicine improve knowledge and skills? Validation of Berlin questionnaire before and after study of courses in evidence-based medicine. *British Medical Journal* 325:1338–1341.

Glisson, C. 2002. The organizational context of children's mental health services. *Clinical Child and Family Psychology Review* 5 (4): 233–253.

Gosling, A. S., J. I. Westbrook, and E. W. Coiera. 2003. Variation in the use of online clinical evidence: A qualitative analysis. *International Journal of Medical Informatics* 69:1–16.

Granata, A. V. and A. L. Hillman. 1998. Competing practice guidelines: Using cost-effectiveness analysis to make optimal decisions. *Annals of Internal Medicine* 128:56–63.

Greenhalgh, T., J. Hughes, C. Humphrey, S. Rogers, D. Swinglehurst, and P. Martin. 2002. A comparative case study of two models of a clinical informaticist service. *British Journal of Medicine* 321:524–529.

Grilli, R., N. Magrini, A. Penna, G. Mura, and A. Liberati. 2000. Practice guidelines developed by specialty societies: The need for critical appraisal. *Lancet* 335:103–106.

Grimshaw, J. M. and I. T. Russell. 1993. Effect of clinical guidelines on medical practice: A systematic review of rigorous evaluations. *Lancet* 242:1317–1322.

Herman, S. P. 1997. Practice parameters for child custody evaluation: American Academy of Child and Adolescent Psychiatry. *Journal of the American Academy of Child and Adolescent Psychiatry* 36 (10): 57S–68S.

Howard, M. O., J. Bricout, T. Edmond, D. Elze, and J. M. Jenson. 2003. Evidence-Based Practice Guidelines. *Encyclopedia of Social Work*. 19th ed. Washington, D.C.: National Association of Social Workers Press.

Howard, M. O. and J. M. Jenson. 1999a. Barriers to development, utilization, and evaluation of social work practice guidelines: Toward an action plan for social work. *Research in Social Work Practice* 9:347–364.

———. 1999b. Clinical practice guidelines: Should social work develop them? *Research on Social Work Practice* 9:283–301.

———. 2003. Clinical Guidelines and Evidence-Based Practice in Medicine, Psychology, and Allied Professions. In A. Rosen and E. K. Proctor, eds., *Developing Practice Guidelines for Social Work Intervention: Issues, Methods, and Research Agenda*, 83–107. New York: Columbia University Press.

Howard, M. O., J. C. McMillen, and D. Pollio. 2003. Teaching evidence-based practice: Toward a new paradigm for social work education. *Research on Social Work Practice* 13:234–259.

Institute of Medicine. 1990. *Clinical Practice Guidelines: Directions for a New Program*. Washington, D.C.: National Academy Press.

Kennedy, C. and P. Yellowlees. 2000. Guidelines for using videoconferencing in mental health services. *Journal of Telemedicine and Telecare* 6 (6): 352–353.

Kurlowicz, L. H. 1997. Nursing standard of practice protocol: Depression in elderly patients. *Geriatric Nursing* 18 (5): 192–199.

Leape, L. 1990. Practice guidelines and standards: An overview. *Quality Review Bulletin* 16:42–49.

Lenfant, C. 2003. Clinical research to clinical practice—lost in translation? *New England Journal of Medicine* 349:868–874.

Levy, M. E., D. W. Garnick, C. M. Horgan, and D. Hodgkin. 2002. Quality measurement and accountability for substance abuse and mental health services in managed care organizations. *Medical Care* 40 (12): 1238–1248.

Lin, E. H., W. J. Katon, G. E. Simon et al. 1997. Achieving guidelines for the treatment of depression in primary care: Is physician education enough? *Medical Care* 35 (8): 831–842.

Marsh, J. C. 2003. Organizational and Institutional Factors in the Development of Practice Knowledge and Practice Guidelines in Social Work. In A. Rosen and E. K. Proctor, eds., *Developing Practice Guidelines for Social Work Intervention: Issues, Methods, and Research Agenda*, 236–252. New York: Columbia University Press.

Mason, J., M. Eccles, N. Freemantle, and M. Drummond. 1999. Incorporating economic analysis in evidence-based guidelines for mental health: The profile approach. *Journal of Mental Health Policy and Economics* 2 (1): 13–19.

McGlynn, E. A., S. M. Asch, J. Adams et al. 2003. The quality of health care delivered to adults in the United States. *New England Journal of Medicine* 348 (26): 2635–2645.

Medow, M. A., T. J. Wilt, S. Dysken, S. D. Hillson, S. Woods, and S. J. Borowsky. 2001. Effect of written and computerized decision support aids for the U.S. Agency for Health Care Policy and Research depression guidelines on the evaluation of hypothetical clinical scenarios. *Medical Decision Making* 21 (5): 344–356.

Mela, C. A., A. J. Chawla, T. W. Croghan et al. 1998. The effects of adherence to antidepressant treatment guidelines on relapse and recurrence of depression. *Archives of General Psychiatry* 55 (12): 1128–1132.

Miranda, J., J. Y. Chung, B. L. Green et al. 2003. Treating depression in predominantly low-income young minority women: A randomized controlled trial. *Journal of the American Medical Association* 290 (1): 57–65.

Nease, R. F., T. Kneeland, G. T. O'Connor et al. for the Ischemic Heart Disease Patient Outcomes Research Team. 1995. Variations in patient utilities for outcomes of the management of chronic stable angina: Implications for clinical practice guidelines. *Journal of the American Medical Association* 273:1185–1190.

Oldham, J. M. 2002. Development of the American Psychiatric Association Practice Guideline for the Treatment of Borderline Personality Disorder. *Journal of Personality Disorders* 16 (2): 109–112.

Owens, D. K. 1998. Use of medical informatics to implement and develop clinical practice guidelines. *Western Journal of Medicine* 168:166–175.

Panek, W. C. 1999. Ethical considerations related to outcome studies-based clinical practice guidelines. *Journal of Glaucoma* 8:267–272.

Parker, C. W. 1995. Practice guidelines and private insurers. *Journal of Law, Medicine, and Ethics* 23:57–61.

Pliszka, S. R., L. L. Greenhill, M. L. Crismon et al. 2000a. The Texas Children's Medication Algorithm Project: Report of the Texas Consensus Conference Panel on Medication Treatment of Childhood Attention-Deficit/Hyperactivity Disorder. Part I. Attention-deficit/hyperactivity disorder. *Journal of the American Academy of Child and Adolescent Psychiatry* 39 (7): 908–919.

Pliszka, S. R., L. L. Greenhill, M. L. Crismon et al. 2000b. The Texas Children's Medication Algorithm Project: Report of the Texas Consensus Conference Panel on Medication Treatment of Childhood Attention-Deficit/Hyperactivity Disorder. Part II. Tactics: Attention-deficit/hyperactivity disorder. *Journal of the American Academy of Child and Adolescent Psychiatry* 39 (7): 920–927.

Proctor, E. K. and A. Rosen. 2003. The Structure and Function of Social Work Practice Guidelines. In A. Rosen and E. K. Proctor, eds., *Developing Practice Guidelines for Social Work Intervention: Issues, Methods, and Research Agenda*, 108–127. New York: Columbia University Press.

Puech, M., J. Ward, G. Hirst, and A. Hughes. 1998. Local implementation of national guidelines on lower urinary tract symptoms: What do general practitioners in

Sydney, Australia, suggest will work? *International Journal for Quality in Healthcare* 10:339–343.

Putnam, W., P. L. Twohig, F. I. Burge, L. A. Jackson, and J. L. Cox. 2002. A qualitative study of evidence in primary care: What the practitioners are saying. *Canadian Medical Association Journal* 166 (12): 1525–1530.

Rollman, B. L., B. H. Hanusa, T. Gilbert, H. J. Lowe, W. N. Kapoor, and H. C. Schulberg. 2001. The electronic medical record: A randomized trial of its impact on primary care physicians' initial management of major depression. *Archives of Internal Medicine* 161 (2): 189–197.

Rush, A. J., M. L. Crismon, T. M. Kashner et al. 2003. Texas Medication Algorithm Project, Phase 3 (TMAP-3): Rationale and study design. *Journal of Clinical Psychiatry* 64 (4): 357–369.

Schulberg, H. C., W. Katon, G. E. Simon, and A. J. Rush. 1998. Treating major depression in primary care practice: An update of the Agency for Health Care Policy and Research Practice Guidelines. *Archives of General Psychiatry* 55 (12): 1121–1127.

Shaneyfelt, T. M., M. F. Mayo-Smith, and J. Rothwangl. 1999. Are guidelines following guidelines? The methodological quality of clinical practice guidelines in the peer-reviewed medical literature. *Journal of the American Medical Association* 281:1900–1905.

Sigouin, C. and A. R. Jadad. 2002. Awareness of sources of peer-reviewed research evidence on the Internet. *Journal of the American Medical Association* 287 (21): 2867–2869.

Simon, R. I. and R. M. Wettstein. 1997. Toward the development of guidelines for the conduct of forensic psychiatric examinations. *Journal of the American Academy of Psychiatry and Law* 25 (1): 17–30.

Smith, T. E. and J. P. Docherty. 1998. Standards of care and clinical algorithms for treating schizophrenia. *Psychiatric Clinics of North America* 21 (1): 203–220.

Somerville, M. A. 1993. Ethics and clinical practice guidelines. *Canadian Medical Association Journal* 148:1133–1137.

Sommer, A., J. P. Weinter, and L. Gamble. 1990. Developing specialty-wide standards of practice: The experience of ophthalmology. *Quality Review Bulletin* 16:65–70.

Stuart, G. W., A. J. Rush, and J. A. Morris. 2002. Practice guidelines in mental health and addiction services: Contributions from the American College of Mental Health Administration. *Administration and Policy in Mental Health* 30 (1): 21–33.

Summerskill, W. S. M. and C. Pope. 2002. "I saw the panic rise in her eyes, and evidence-based medicine went out the door." An exploratory qualitative study of the barriers to secondary prevention in the management of coronary heart disease. *Family Practice* 19 (6): 605–610.

Suppes, T., E. B. Dennehy, A. C. Swan et al. 2002. Report of the Texas Consensus Conference on Medication Treatment of Bipolar Disorder 2000. *Journal of Clinical Psychiatry* 63 (4): 288–299.

Suppes, T., A. J. Rush, E. B. Dennehy et al. 2003. Texas Medication Algorithm Project, Phase 3 (TMAP-3): Clinical results for patients with a history of mania. *Journal of Clinical Psychiatry* 64 (4): 370–382.

Suppes, T., A. C. Swann, and E. B. Dennehy. 2001. Texas Medication Algorithm Project: Development and feasibility testing of a treatment algorithm for patients with bipolar disorder. *Journal of Clinical Psychiatry* 62 (6): 439–447.

Telford, R., A. Hutchinson, R. Jones, S. Rix, and A. Howe. 2002. Obstacles to effective treatment of depression: A general practice perspective. *Family Practice* 19 (1): 45–52.

Thyer, B. A. 2003. Social Work Should Not Develop Practice Guidelines: A Response to Proctor and Rosen. In A. Rosen and E. K. Proctor, eds., *Developing Practice Guidelines for Social Work Intervention: Issues, Methods, and Research Agenda,* 128–139. New York: Columbia University Press.

United Kingdom, Nuffield Council on Bioethics. 2001. Mental disorders and genetics: The ethical context: Conclusions and recommendations. *Journal of International Bioethiques* 12 (2): 89–92.

Unutzer, J., L. Rubenstein, W. J. Katon et al. 2001. Two-year effects of quality improvement programs on medication management for depression. *Archives of General Psychiatry* 58 (10): 935–942.

Upton, M. W., M. Evans, D. P. Goldberg, and D. J. Sharp. 1999. Evaluation of ICD-10 PHC mental health guidelines in detecting and managing depression within primary care. *British Journal of Psychiatry* 175:476–482.

Videka, L. 2003. Accounting for Variability in Client, Population, and Setting Characteristics: Moderators of Intervention Effectiveness. In A. Rosen and E. K. Proctor, eds., *Developing Practice Guidelines for Social Work Intervention: Issues, Methods, and Research Agenda,* 169–192. New York: Columbia University Press.

Wang, P. S., P. Berglund, and R. C. Kessler. 2000. Recent care of common mental disorders in the United States: Prevalence and conformance with evidence-based recommendations. *Journal of General Internal Medicine* 15 (5): 284–292.

Ward, J. E. and V. Grieco. 1996. Why we need guidelines for guidelines: A study of the quality of clinical practice guidelines in Australia. *Medical Journal of Australia* 165:574–576,

Wasserman, G. A., P. S. Jensen, S. J. Ko et al. 2003. Mental health assessments in juvenile justice: Report on the consensus conference. *Journal of the American Academy of Child and Adolescent Psychiatry* 42 (7): 752–761.

Wennberg, J. E., J. L. Freeman, and W. J. Culp. 1987. Are hospital services rationed in New Haven or overutilised in Boston? *Lancet* 1:1185–1189.

Wennberg, J. E. and A. Gittelsohn. 1973. Small-area variation in health care delivery. *Science* 182:1102–1108.

Westphal, J., S. Kumar, J. Rush, and I. S. Sarkar. 1997. Addressing issues of face validity in the application of a clinical guideline. *Evaluation Review* 21 (3): 379–387.

Wilkinson, H., M. P. Janicki, and Edinburgh Working Group on Dementia Care Practices. The Edinburgh Principles with accompanying guidelines and recommendations. *Journal of Intellectual Disability Research* 46 (Pt. 3): 279–284.

Williams, A., P. Lee, and A. Kerr. 2002. Scottish Intercollegiate Guidelines Network (SIGN) guidelines on tonsillectomy: A three cycle audit of clinical record keeping and adherence to national guidelines. *Journal of Laryngology and Otology* 116 (6): 454–454.

Wissow, L., K. Fothergill, and J. Forman. 2002. Confidentiality for mental health concerns in adolescent primary care. *Bioethics Forum* 18 (3–4): 43–54.

Worrall, G., P. Chaulk, and D. Freake. 1997. The effects of clinical practice guidelines on patient outcomes in primary care: A systematic review. *Canadian Medical Association Journal* 156:1705–1712.

Young, A. S., R. Klap, C. D. Sherbourne, and K. B. Wells. 2001. The quality of care for depressive and anxiety disorders in the United States. *Archives of General Psychiatry* 58 (1): 55–61.

Zayas, L. H. 2003. Service-Delivery Factors in the Development of Practice Guidelines. In A. Rosen and E. K. Proctor, eds., *Developing Practice Guidelines for Social Work Intervention: Issues, Methods, and Research Agenda,* 193–206. New York: Columbia University Press.

PART IV

PSYCHOTHERAPY AND SOCIAL WORK

Chapter 16

Putting Humpty Together Again: Treatment of Mental Disorder and Pursuit of Justice as Parts of Social Work's Mission

Jerome C. Wakefield

As the social work profession enters its second century, it remains divided and confused about how to define its essential mission and especially about the relation of its psychotherapeutic activities to its more traditional responsibilities. One common view is that social work is primarily concerned with social justice, particularly with providing for the deprived and oppressed. Another view, reinforced by social work's immense role in mental health care and by state licensing of social workers as mental health clinicians, holds that social work is primarily a mental health profession aimed at treating mental disorders, perhaps distinguished from other mental health professions by a more person-in-environment emphasis. These conflicting views have led to an intellectual fragmentation of the profession about its own foundations. A profession that lacks a clear, consensual understanding of its mission is likely to function less effectively and to have trouble presenting its case to the public. Therefore, attaining an intellectually defensible resolution of the question of how each of these conceptions is in fact related to the profession's mission should be among the profession's highest priorities.

This chapter contains a revised version of material that appeared in J. C. Wakefield, "Psychotherapy, Distributive Justice, and Social Work Revisited," *Smith College Studies in Social Work* 69 (1998): 25–57.

Minimal Distributive Justice as the Essential Mission of Social Work

There is a straightforward sense in which psychiatry, clinical psychology, and psychiatric nursing are mental health professions; the basic mission that they exist to pursue, or what I have called their *organizing value* (Wakefield 1988a), is mental health, in the specific medical sense of treating (including preventing) mental disorder. Just as medicine aims at health, law at legal justice, and teaching at transmission of knowledge as their essential defining goals, so the mental health professions aim to treat mental disorder.

When we say that social work is a mental health profession (or even that clinical social work is a mental health profession—I will return to the subspecialty of clinical social work below), we mean something much more complex than we do in these other cases (Wakefield 1988a, 1988b). It is not that social work is not concerned with mental disorder; of course it is. But the conceptual relationship between the profession and its treatment of mental disorder is different from what it is in the other mental health professions. Unlike the other mental health professions, social work did not originate as and has never primarily been a mental health profession but has rather been concerned with a broad range of interventions addressing human need and deprivation, including economic aid to relieve the effects of poverty, provision of housing for the homeless, child protection and placement, helping broken families to meet their basic needs, guiding wayward youth, helping medical patients to gain access to medical care and to get their nonmedical needs met, guiding immigrants in coping with their new life, helping children to take advantage of the opportunity for schooling, ensuring that the needs of the elderly are met, and many other interventions aimed at problems that are not inherently mental disorders.

While not specifically concerned with mental disorders, all of these interventions potentially involve a psychological component, and thus from the beginning social workers became competent in the methods for encouraging psychological growth and change that evolved into what we now call psychotherapy. These psychological methods are an essential part of our profession's skill base. Clinical social workers may specialize in the application of such methods, but throughout the profession's history these clinical methods have been applied to a broad range of problems. Given the social need for such interventions to treat mental disorder and the lack of adequate personnel trained in them, however, society licenses social workers to perform psychotherapeutic services for those who have mental disorders.

I have argued elsewhere that social work's essential organizing value—the mission that defines it as a profession and encompasses all of its traditional tasks—is not mental health but rather ensuring that all members of society possess at least a minimally acceptable level of a variety of basic economic, social, and psychological goods necessary to live a decent life and participate in social institutions (Wakefield 1988a, 1988b). In putting forward this account of social work's mission as "minimal distributive justice," I rely on John Rawls's (1971) theory of justice, and especially his concept of the "social minimum," a certain level of possession of socially produced economic, social, and psychological goods below which it would be unfair to allow any member of society to fall. Distributive justice demands that no member of society be allowed to fall below the social minimum of such goods. Note that the notion of a social minimum or "safety net" is widely accepted and is not really dependent on Rawls's theory, although Rawls tried to present a systematic theoretical rationale for this wide agreement.

We might think of social work, then, as a "safety net" institution, where the safety net is interpreted broadly to encompass protection against unjust deprivation of needed economic (e.g., money, housing), social (e.g., fair occupational opportunity, fair opportunity for social participation), and psychological (e.g., self-respect) goods. The inclusion of psychological goods is a relatively novel aspect of Rawls's theory that I use to explain certain strands of clinical social work, as I detail below.

The goods subject to considerations of justice are those Rawls calls "primary social goods," that is, goods (in the broad sense of "good things") that are necessary for the effective pursuit of virtually any life plan (i.e., they are "primary" goods that everyone needs) and that are created through social cooperation or distributed in accordance with social rules and structures (i.e., they are "social" goods). Note that this latter sense of "social," referring to the fact that certain primary goods are socially created, shaped, and/or distributed (unlike other goods that are not mainly socially distributed, like beauty or height or health) and thus are subject to considerations of justice, is to be distinguished from the sense of "social" noted above in which certain goods are social as opposed to economic or psychological (e.g., educational opportunity as opposed to money or self-respect) in their content. All these kinds of goods can be "social" in the creation/distribution sense, and if they are social goods in this sense, they are subject to considerations of just distribution.

When people fall below a contextually defined "social minimum" of any one of such goods so that they cannot pursue a life plan at even a minimally effective level, that constitutes deprivation and injustice, according to Rawls. Social work, I argued, is ultimately concerned with ensuring that each individual possesses at least the minimal acceptable level of each of the primary social goods, a goal I labeled *minimal distributive justice*.

The analysis of the essential mission of social work as the pursuit of minimal distributive justice allows for both the profession's involvement in social reform and its concern for individual change in the quest for distributive justice for deprived individuals. At first glance, however, the redistribution of primary social goods to deprived individuals does not seem to involve psychotherapy. The analysis thus leaves us with the question "What is the relation of clinical social work to social work?" That is, why should a justice-oriented profession use psychotherapeutic methods?

Two Questions About Clinical Social Work

The identification of clinical social work with the use of psychotherapy depends on some rough distinctions among categories of social work. First, there is traditional casework, which encompasses all direct social work intervention with individuals and families, whether the intervention is psychotherapeutic (e.g., intervention to alleviate demoralization or to impart new coping skills) or nonpsychotherapeutic (e.g., cash relief, child placement, provision of housing, concrete advice, etc.) in nature. One area of casework is *psychiatric social work,* a form of medical social work, in which the mental patient's basic needs, such as needs for housing, for family support, or for case management in the community, are pursued using nonpsychotherapeutic interventions. However, psychotherapeutic-style interventions may also be used in psychiatric social work to build social skills, reduce symptoms, and accomplish other intervention goals, which may in effect involve treating the mental disorder in the course of trying to help the client to meet basic needs. So, both casework and psychiatric social work can include psychotherapeutic as well as nonpsychotherapeutic methods. *Clinical social work* refers to those aspects or forms of casework intervention that are specifically psychotherapeutic in nature.

However, the above clarifications still leave the term "clinical social work" ambiguous in an important way. Analogously to clinical psychology, clinical social work is often construed as that branch of the social work profession that treats mental disorders. But psychotherapy as a set of methods can be used to change internal mental states and processes even when no disorder exists, and sometimes "clinical" intervention is construed as any intervention that uses such psychological change methods, whether the target is mental disorder or some other kind of psychological problem. It is important here to remember that current diagnostic criteria in *DSM-IV* (APA 1994) are overly inclusive and incorrectly classify many social problems as mental disorders (Wakefield 1993b, 1996, 1997). Many social work problems do not involve a mental disorder, even when they do involve problematic psychological states. Reflecting this distinction between mental disorders and non-disordered problematic psychological states, *clinical social work* sometimes refers to casework in which psychotherapeutic methods are used to change any kind of disordered or non-disordered problematic psychological state. One must distinguish psychotherapy in the sense of psychotherapeutic techniques themselves—which were developed to treat mental disorder but which can be used for other purposes—from psychotherapy aimed specifically at treatment of mental disorder. Each sense of *psychotherapy* gives rise to a corresponding sense of *clinical social work*.

Thus, there are really two different conceptual questions that one can ask about clinical social work: (1) Does psychotherapy have a role in social work's pursuit of justice? (2) Is the treatment of mental disorder part of the profession's essential justice-related defining mission?

Regarding the first question, caseworkers commonly use psychotherapeutic-style methods to help remove the client's internal psychological impediments to better social functioning or to provide the client with basic psychological needs and thus to pursue social work's goal of justice. The fact that justice rather than mental health is the ultimate goal is important because it makes a great difference to which cases one thinks are most appropriate for treatment, to the focus of one's intervention, and to one's criteria for success.

Regarding the second question, although there is a great overlap between psychological problems related to justice and mental disorder, still mental disorder is not, as such, part of social work's essential mission because mental disorder is not generally intrinsically unjust (except perhaps in those cases where unjust social circumstances are directly responsible for the existence and maintenance of the disorder). Mental disorder may make it impossible to effectively pursue a life plan, but in itself it is not generally an injustice committed by society in maldistributing its goods. Thus, alleviating mental disorder is not an essential part of providing minimal distributive justice, although helping people to obtain fair access to mental health treatment is a matter of justice. Moreover, mental disorder will often be treated incidentally as social workers attempt to help people develop the capacity to meet their basic needs. Analogously, physical disorder can deprive a person of primary goods necessary to pursue a life plan and warrant action to make sure that the person has those primary goods that can be redistributed (e.g., food, housing, social support), but physical disorder is not generally an injustice in itself in the literal sense that society is responsible and owes the person a cure (except in some cases where society has failed to provide fair distribution of environments or other conditions necessary for maintaining health). Feelings of benevolence and caring and a desire to alleviate suffering, not a perception of injustice, generally motivate us to try to cure the mentally and physically disordered.

Of course, social work is also ultimately motivated by feelings of benevolence and caring and the desire to alleviate suffering. The difference between social work and other professions lies not in this shared motivation but in the specific causes of suffering that are addressed by each profession. Just as medicine attempts to address suffering resulting from physical disorder, law attempts to address suffering resulting from legal injustice, the clergy attempts to address suffering resulting from spiritual challenges, and educators attempt to prevent suffering resulting from ignorance, so social work as its specific mission attempts to alleviate suffering resulting from deprivation of basic needs, that is, from minimal distributive injustice. Physical disorders in themselves (as opposed to the distributive problems they entail), although they cause suffering that social workers, like all empathic human beings, would like to alleviate, are not generally injustices. The same considerations apply to mental disorders.

Treatment of Mental Disorder as a Derived Task of Social Work

In addition to my denial that treatment of mental disorder is encompassed by social work's traditional organizing value of minimal distributive justice, I also hold that the treatment of mental disorder does have a place in the social work profession's mission as what I called a *derived task*. That is, it is a task that is not part of social work's essential defining mission or organizing value, but because social workers have the appropriate skills, it is a task that society has nonetheless mandated the profession to add to its other, more traditional responsibilities. Thus, social work is indeed a mental health profession, but only in the same conceptually incidental way that, for example, medicine is a profession concerned with beauty by virtue of its performance of cosmetic surgery. Physicians have been socially sanctioned and licensed to relieve suffering by providing cosmetic surgery because they have the necessary skills, but that is not an essential task of medicine, since it does not aim at health. People who are trained as social workers and then practice psychotherapy with the purpose of treating mental disorders just like other mental health professionals are social workers in the legal sense, but they are not doing social work in the essential conceptual sense, any more than doctors who specialize in cosmetic surgery are doing medicine in the strict conceptual sense.

The analogy between social workers treating mental disorders and physicians performing cosmetic surgery is misleading in one important respect. Cosmetic surgery—even though it often relieves considerable suffering—is generally considered less important than essential medical goals. However, treatment of mental disorder is not in my view less important than relief of distributive injustice. As a general principle, there is nothing necessarily more superficial or less important about a derived versus an essential task; it all depends on the particular tasks.

It must be admitted that most psychotherapeutic practices include not only disordered patients but also many people who, partly because of internal psychological impediments that are not disorders, are having difficulty functioning adequately in their social roles (as noted earlier, *DSM* criteria are overinclusive and cannot be used as a guide to mental disorder). So, in day-to-day practice there is only a fuzzy distinction between psychotherapists who treat mental disorders and clinical social workers who use psychotherapeutic methods to pursue social work's goals. But there is an important conceptual distinction nonetheless.

The failure of society to create a separate profession of psychotherapy to treat mental disorders has meant that practitioners from several existing professions, including social work, have been pressed into service in this important area, where their skills are urgently needed. It is hypocritical for the social work profession to ignore this expanded mandate, to continue to pretend that it is inappropriate for students to enter the profession expecting to be psychotherapists, and to resist providing adequate educational opportunities for them to be trained for this option, while accepting the social benefits that come with the profession's involvement in the mental health field. Of course, it is equally undesirable for the profession to become so enamored of these possibilities that its traditional mission becomes obscured. One needs a balance here between respect for the essential mission and acceptance of the derived task.

Note that treatment of mental disorder is not the only possible derived task of clinical social workers using psychotherapy. As Specht (1990) emphasizes, there are many people looking for meaning in their lives who have all the primary goods. Their problem is neither mental disorder nor deprivation but rather that life is intrinsically painful and puzzling as to its meaning. I agree with Specht that treatment of such problems has nothing to do with social work's traditional mission. If clinical social workers are mandated to use their expertise to help such people, this is a derived task, like treatment of mental disorder.

Psychotherapy and the Pursuit of Minimal Distributive Justice

A critical challenge arising out of the above account is to identify some instances where the use of psychotherapeutic methods serves the essential mission of the profession, and thus to show that the justice account can explain the profession's traditional use of psychological change methods. Psychotherapy's place in pursuing social work's essential mission is often questioned because the goods traditionally associated with justice are economic and social goods, not psychological change. However, an adequate understanding of the demands of justice, including Rawls's (1971) point that there are psychological as well as economic and social primary goods, helps to explain why psychotherapy has long been an integral part of social work's interventive approaches. Rawls persuasively argues that the possession of at least a minimal level of certain socially imparted psychological properties is as basic to the pursuit and enjoyment of any life plan as are economic and social goods. Because psychotherapeutic methods can influence such justice-related psychological properties, such methods are directly relevant to a profession pursuing minimal distributive justice.

To the question of exactly how psychotherapy can be used to pursue justice, there are three basic answers. First, there is the traditional answer that internal psychological states are often impediments to acquisition of basic justice-related goods and can curtail adequate social functioning. The classic cases include lack of adequate coping skills to deal either with challenging environments or with transitions to new environments or roles; demoralization or low self-esteem caused by chronic deprivation and failure; reaction to frustration by diversion into substance abuse; and use of antisocial strategies for survival in threatening or opportunity-deprived environments. But the potential forms are endless. Such psychological states usually are not mental disorders but rather problematic but normal responses to difficult environmental conditions. It is normal to be sad over loss, anxious about threat, and to survive as best one can even if that entails breaking the rules. For example, it is not a mental disorder for an adolescent who comes to America after growing up in a war-torn country where he or she is used to violence as a routine way of dealing with conflict to continue to engage in such learned behavior in the new environment (even *DSM-IV* acknowledges this possibility of environmental, non-disordered causation of adolescent antisocial behavior). Working with such an adolescent, perhaps using psychotherapeutic techniques, is a legitimate task of social work as it attempts to enable the youth to function in our society and to meet basic needs in this new environment. Many clinical social work interventions are of this nature; they are interventions aimed not at alleviating mental disorder but at changing psychological properties that do not qualify as disorders but are blocking adequate social functioning or the meeting of basic needs.

In addition to the role of psychological traits in enabling people to meet basic economic and social needs, there is a further sense in which psychological traits can be justice-related. Here I rely heavily on Rawls's theory to make my point. Contrary to the traditional focus exclusively on economic and social goods in theories of justice, Rawls argues that the psychological property of self-respect—or at least the social experiences that are the basis for development of self-respect—is a central social good. That is, self-respect is essential in effectively pursuing almost any life plan, yet the bases for self-respect are largely determined by social rules and opportunities and thus in effect are "distributed" by society. Each individual should thus, as a matter of justice, have at least a minimally adequate opportunity to partake of those activities that form the basis for self-respect.

In earlier publications (Wakefield 1988a, 1988b), I built on Rawls's argument regarding self-respect to suggest that the social bases for other psychological traits as well—such as the experiences that build self-esteem, self-confidence, and self-knowledge—must be an integral part of a theory of minimal distributive justice. These traits are like self-respect in that they are largely socially based (i.e., developed and "distributed" via social rules and interactions) and are as integral to effectively pursuing any life plan as economic relief and social opportunity. Thus these psychological goods are in themselves justice-related, and lack of them, or lack of the social conditions for developing them, is a form of unjust deprivation. Psychotherapy, when aimed at providing the conditions for the development of these justice-related psychological traits, is justice-related psychotherapy and thus an essential task of social work.

There is a third sense in which psychotherapy can be justice-related. The lack of justice-related psychological goods often occurs partly because of deprivation in the family or broader social environment during the individual's maturation and socialization. Thus there is a sense in which clinical social work is often an after-the-fact attempt to redistribute the opportunity to develop justice-related psychological properties when the social system of distribution of environments has failed to give a person a fair allocation of such early facilitating environmental conditions. Clinical intervention cannot of course guarantee that the individual will change for the better, but it can provide some compensating opportunities in response to earlier deprivation.

In sum, aside from the use of psychotherapy to perform the derived task of treating mental disorder, social workers who pursue the traditional professional mission of minimal distributive justice may use psychotherapy in at least three conceptually overlapping ways: (1) to change psychological attributes that are obstacles to the individual's capacity to obtain basic economic or social goods or to function socially; (2) to provide psychologically deprived individuals with missing psychological primary social goods (i.e., psychological attributes that are necessary for the effective pursuit of any life plan and depend for their development on social experiences), such as self-respect, self-esteem, self-confidence, and self-knowledge; and (3) to provide individuals who were deprived of the psychosocial environment where psychological primary goods generally develop with a therapeutic environment that gives the individual a second opportunity to experience the conditions that encourage the development of such psychological goods.

Two Confusions About the Minimal Distributive Justice View

The complexity of my position—specifically, the fact that I reject treatment of mental disorder as part of the traditional essential mission of the profession but accept psychotherapeutic methods as part of the set of techniques useful for pursuing that mission and accept treatment of mental disorder as a derived part of the mission—has made my view a target for both sides in the broader debate between clinically oriented and justice-oriented thinkers. Neither side tends to distinguish the goal of curing mental disorder from the use of psychotherapeutic techniques, or essential (primary) from derived (secondary) tasks. Thus, failing to acknowledge the distinctions on which my analysis is based, both sides see my view as problematic. Those who, like Specht (1990) and Specht and Courtney (1994), want to defend the traditional mission of the profession attack my view because they mistakenly see my defense of the use of psychotherapy in social work as a rejection of social work's traditional mission. Those who, like Dean (1998), want to defend clinical social work attack my view because they mistakenly see my exclusion of mental health from the essential organizing value of social work as a rejection of the use of psychotherapeutic methods by social workers or as a rejection of the treatment of mental disorders by social workers.

In a critique of my views, Harvey Dean (1998) characterizes my position as follows: "Wakefield (1988) defines social justice as the primary mission of social work and thereby relegates mental health as outside of social work's mission" (12). He argues, in opposition to what he thinks I say, that social work's mission does encompass psychotherapy. However, Dean's statement of my views is potentially misleading in several ways. First, note a gap in the logic of his statement; the fact that I define justice as social work's primary mission does not "thereby" relegate mental health to being outside of social work's mission altogether, because the primary mission need not be all of the mission. Nor does it even relegate outside of social work's primary mission those aspects of mental health that are themselves interpretable as aspects of justice. A correct inference would be that my identification of social work's primary mission as justice relegates those aspects of mental health treatment not directly related to justice to at best a secondary or derived role in the mission. And in fact, this is exactly what my view does; it identifies a variety of mental health–related tasks that are aspects of justice, places them squarely within the traditional primary mission of the profession, and holds that treatment of mental disorder per se, to the degree that it is not an aspect of the striving for justice but rather strictly aimed at curing mental disorder, is a secondary (or "derived") part of social work's overall mission. This may not be enough for those who want to feel that the mental health focus is conceptually primary in social work, but it is a lot more than critics like Dean acknowledge in my view.

There are other misleading elements of Dean's statement. In approaching the nature of social work, I do not arbitrarily *define* social work as aimed at social justice but rather *analyze* the concept of social work implicit in common intuitions, trying to explain the judgments we make about what is and what is not social work. I conclude not that the mission is social justice but that it is minimal distributive justice, a narrower and more precise idea than social justice (see below). And, as elaborated above, my view of the relationship of mental disorder, psychotherapy, and social work is much more complex and multifaceted than Dean's summary suggests. My view implies a wide range of essential and derived reasons for social workers to intervene with individuals who have mental disorders.

However, it remains true that I claim that treatment of mental disorders in itself is not an essential function of the social work profession. This is the contention that Dean and many other clinically minded social workers find unacceptable. Yet it seems plainly true. Consider the following thought experiment: Imagine that social workers stopped doing any psychotherapy aimed at cure of mental disorder and pursued strictly minimal distributive justice goals (for which, as noted, psychotherapeutic intervention is sometimes appropriate). In such an eventuality, there would be no doubt that the social work profession would continue. But now imagine that all the justice-related activities of the profession ceased and that social workers strictly treated mental disorder aiming at cure of disorder. In such an eventuality, it seems plain that the social work profession would have ceased to exist in any other than an institutional sense and that social work would in fact have become part of a generic psychotherapy profession. If the reader's intuitions agree here with mine, then the reader implicitly agrees that, although treatment of mental disorder might be part of the mission of social work, it is not part of the essential mission that makes the profession what it is and distinguishes it conceptually from other professions.

A second and opposite kind of confusion appears in Specht and Courtney's (1994) book, *Unfaithful Angels: How Social Work Has Abandoned Its Mission,* in which they critique the psychotherapeutic turn in social work. They assert that my view that psychotherapy can be part of social work's justice-related mission simply comes down to the claim that social workers have the aim of bringing psychotherapy to the deprived who would not otherwise be able to afford it. This is a misreading of my view. Of course social workers should be concerned about fair access to mental health services for the deprived. But that alone would not imply that they should do the treatment themselves. The justice element in the use of psychotherapy that makes psychotherapy a legitimate part of social work is not related to the goal, however noble, of fairly distributing access to psychotherapy. To understand why, just consider that the same argument would justify social workers' actually performing medical services like surgery, legal services such as defending clients in court, and other professional services that are unfairly distributed and that are not as available to the deprived as to the affluent. But no one thinks that social workers should actually provide such services, although they do have the mission of assuring adequate access to such services compatible with the requirements of a just distribution of social resources. My view explains why, in the case of psychotherapy, society mandates that social workers not only help the deprived to gain access to the mental health services they need but also provide the actual services themselves. The answer lies, first, in justice-related non–mental-health goals of the application of psychotherapy as elaborated above, and second, in the derived assignment to use the skills that social workers obtain in their training that can also be used for treatment of mental disorder. Neither rationale applies to the skills of other professions.

The Overinclusiveness and Underinclusiveness Fallacies

There are two fallacies that are very common in conceptual analyses of social work's mission. The first fallacy is to define the profession in terms of a mission that is too broad and overinclusive. Definitions of social work's mission in terms of self-realization, well-being, improvement of social functioning, improvement of the fit between individual and environment, and many other such goals are just too broad to identify social work as distinct from other professions. Even distributive justice is too broad a concept for social work's mission, because many aspects of justice (e.g., should executives earn so much more than the workers they supervise?) concern relative distributive fairness and not issues of minimally acceptable levels of primary goods, and accordingly are not seen as within social work's essential domain. This is why I suggested minimal distributive justice as social work's mission; the focus on deprivation of basic goods seems to be unique to social work.

For example, Harvey Dean (1998; see Wakefield 1998) commits the overinclusiveness fallacy by arguing that the goal of clinical social work is to provide meaningful narratives to people. Narratives, as Dean uses the concept, encompass just about all meaning, and both individual minds and cultures are essentially meaning systems, so basically he is assigning to social work a task that is common to every profession and social institution. Doctors, lawyers, teachers, priests, and journalists all are mandated to create certain interpretations and meanings and to impart those "narratives" to their clients. A narrativist account of clinical social work must begin by defending a view of exactly what kinds of narrative problems are the special domain of social work, and Dean does not adequately confront this problem.

The second fallacy is to define social work in terms of a mission that is preferred by the theoretician but is manifestly too narrow to encompass the essential core activities of the profession. The most common strategy here is to try to define the profession in terms of non-clinical practice—such as social action or case management or interfacing between individuals and institutions—and to conclude that clinical practice is not part of the profession. An example is Specht's (1990; see Wakefield 1992) rejection of the legitimacy of using psychotherapeutic methods in social work, based on his definition of the profession in terms of community development goals, which arbitrarily ignores the strong clinical social work tradition dating from Mary Richmond. These overly narrow, partisan accounts are not really conceptual analyses but rather what philosophers call "stipulative definitions" (i.e., decisions to use a word in a new way) or "persuasive definitions" (i.e., attempts to get others to accept a new definition). Such definitions are attempts to transform the profession to be in one's desired image rather than to analyze the profession's actual nature.

Does my definition of social work in terms of minimal distributive justice also fall prey to the same problem of excessive narrowness because of promoting one segment of the profession's activities? Rather than arguing that social work ideally ought to be about justice, I conclude on the basis of an analysis of social work's varied activities that the profession is in fact aimed at justice. I argue that the history of the field makes it clear that the use of psychotherapeutic methods is integral to the profession and must somehow fit into any acceptable definition, and I use Rawls's theory of justice to explain how the use of psychotherapy can indeed be an essential part of a justice-oriented profession. Rather than being stipulative or persuasive, my analysis is primarily an attempt to provide a "lexical" definition of the profession—that is, a definition that explains how social workers and others actually think about social work and how they judge whether an activity is or is not social work. I mainly attempt to explain people's judgments, not to legislate or change them. Whether my view is adequate or inadequate, it is at least an attempt to directly address the real complexity of the profession's goals.

What about the objection that Rawls's theory provides not an account of overall benevolence but only of justice and that social work is concerned with benevolence generally? The sense of justice and feelings of benevolence are two different things. Benevolence often goes beyond justice (e.g., helping a friend at considerable personal cost), and justice is often not a matter of benevolence (e.g., refusing to give someone something he or she wants but has no right to). On the basis of such examples, I would argue that it is minimal distributive justice, not benevolence more generally, that social work pursues.

Indeed, minimal distributive justice requires impartiality and thus some judgments that may go against what clients or others want, and therefore may at moments seem less than benevolent to some. Does this aspect of the justice account conflict with the traditional nonjudgmental approach of social workers?

The suggestion that social workers traditionally take a nonjudgmental approach is quite true in relation specifically to clinical social work, for that attitude is at the heart of clinical intervention. However, clinical intervention takes place after it has been established that there is a psychological need for such intervention, so such nonjudgmentalness is not in conflict with the justice account. But social work is not just clinical intervention, and with regard to other areas of intervention, it is quite untrue that social workers are entirely nonjudgmental. For example, from the profession's inception in friendly visiting, social workers have been seriously concerned about the legitimacy of clients' claims for material assistance. The reason for such judgments is obvious; in the material domain, to give more to a client than is warranted by minimal justice considerations would be unjust both to others who really need (not just desire) the limited resources and to those who give the resources because they think justice demands it. To take another example, social workers involved in child placement make judgments all the time about the suitability of parents or of proposed foster parents, and these judgments may at times go against the desires of the involved individuals. The issue that provokes such judgments is obvious; each child deserves as a matter of justice at least a minimally adequate psychosocial environment in which to grow. So, looking at the ways that social workers have been judgmental in some areas of their endeavors, it appears that these judgments are entirely consistent with the justice view. It is no doubt true that benevolence (or what I elsewhere consider as "altruism" [Wakefield 1993a]) does play at least a motivating role in social work; as noted earlier, a concern about minimal distributive justice is generally motivated by benevolence. But from a conceptual point of view, justice is the essential concept, and benevolence is overinclusive. Medicine and nursing, for example, are equally motivated by benevolence. Social work has always been concerned with those who are deprived of basic needs, and this suggests a concern specifically with justice.

Again, it is sometimes suggested by psychodynamically oriented practitioners that self-knowledge of the kind imparted in psychotherapy is the general mission of social work. Beyond a certain minimal amount required to pursue most life plans, self-knowledge is not a primary good but rather part of an individual's distinctive vision of the good. Some people believe in a life of action and are determinedly non-psychologically minded, perhaps even averse to looking inward; contrary to the fantasies of mental health professionals, not all such people fall ill, and many lead fulfilling lives. Others, from Socrates to Woody Allen, enshrine the pursuit of self-knowledge as a central part of what makes life worth living, although the precise form that this self-knowledge takes may vary dramatically, reminding us that even fervently held beliefs about the self may not always constitute true "knowledge." It is not a matter of justice, and certainly not social work's concern, whether everyone pursues a life devoted to such concerns. Beyond its limited role in minimal distributive justice, self-knowledge in general is not by any historical or conceptual criterion the distinctive mission or mandate of social work (Socratic philosophy and psychoanalysis might have better claims).

In defending a broad psychotherapeutic mission of social work and specifically a mission of treating mental disorder, the point is often made that clinical social workers are confronted daily with the reality of the relationship between clients' inner psychological realities and the failures of their interpersonal and social worlds. I agree that we are confronted with such manifest links between the psychological and the social. However, this argument is based on a confusion between psychological problems that may form obstacles to social functioning versus mental disorders. Most inner psychological obstacles to social functioning (e.g., demoralization, lack of coping skills) are not disorders. Nor do all mental disorders lead to failed social functioning; certain kinds of depressive or anxiety disorders, for example, may be terribly painful to the individual but may not significantly affect social functioning or access to basic needs. This argument that social work specifically and essentially aims to cure mental disorder is based on a spurious equation between psychological obstacles to social functioning and mental disorders.

Of course, mental disorders would be a form of injustice if they were socially imposed psychological injustices. But mental disorders are not generally just the result of social rules and decisions about the distribution of meanings. There is no evidence for anything like such a thoroughly social account of mental disorder; indeed, there is much evidence against it. Like physical illness, mental disorder transcends the system of social distribution on which the principles of distributive justice are based. And even in those cases where mental disorders do lead to deprivation, it is not the mental disorder itself but its effects on acquisition of other goods that are a matter of injustice. It is clearly the case that deprivation sometimes is a factor in causing mental disorder, but by no means is this a regular feature. For all these reasons, mental disorders do not in themselves generally constitute minimal distributive injustice.

Conclusion

Many social workers insist that mental health must be included within the essential mission of the social work profession by definition, much as thinkers of an earlier generation, reacting against what they saw as social workers' excessive zeal for psychoanalysis, attempted to exclude therapeutic intervention from the profession by definition. The strategy by which treatment of mental disorder is encompassed within the essential mission of social work generally is to inflate the essential mission until it is large enough to encompass mental health as well as justice. The typical result is a portrayal of the profession as having such a vast and nebulous domain that the profession loses its authority as a repository of specialized skills and knowledge aimed at performing a specific, mandated social function.

By contrast, the "minimal distributive justice" account, which conceives of social work as a "safety net" profession concerned with ensuring that no one falls below some acceptable minimum in the possession of basic economic, social, and psychological goods necessary to pursue life plans and participate socially, offers a relatively delimited domain that corresponds to the realities of the profession's historical mandate. Psychotherapy can be seen to have a secure place in the techniques that are useful to such a profession because of the intimate relationship of psychological states to social functioning and, as illuminated by Rawls's theory, to distributive justice. The cost of this understanding of the profession is that we must confront the fact that treatment of mental disorder, while a legitimate function mandated by the public, is not part of the essential mission of social work and has a more indirect, derived conceptual status within the profession's set of responsibilities.

References

American Psychiatric Association (APA). 1994. *Diagnostic and Statistical Manual of Mental Disorders (DSM-IV)*. 4th ed. Washington, D.C.: APA.

Dean, H. E. 1998. The primacy of the ethical aim in clinical social work: Its relationship to social justice and mental health. *Smith College Studies in Social Work* 69:9–25.

Rawls, J. 1971. *A Theory of Justice*. Cambridge, Mass.: Harvard University Press.

Specht, H. 1990. Social work and the popular psychotherapies. *Social Service Review* 64:345–357.

Specht, H. and M. E. Courtney. 1994. *Unfaithful Angels: How Social Work Has Abandoned Its Mission*. New York: Free Press.

Wakefield, J. C. 1988a. Psychotherapy, distributive justice, and social work: I. Distributive justice as a conceptual framework for social work. *Social Service Review* 62:187–210.

———. 1988b. Psychotherapy, distributive justice, and social work: II. Psychotherapy and the pursuit of justice. *Social Service Review* 62:353–382.

———. 1992. Why psychotherapeutic social work don't get no re-Specht. *Social Service Review* 66:141–151.

———. 1993a. Is altruism part of human nature? Toward a theoretical foundation for the helping professions. *Social Service Review* 67:406–458.

———. 1993b. Limits of operationalization: A critique of Spitzer and Endicott's (1978) proposed operational criteria for mental disorder. *Journal of Abnormal Psychology* 102:160–172.

———. 1996. DSM-IV: Are we making diagnostic progress? *Contemporary Psychology* 41:646–652.

———. 1997. Diagnosing DSM-IV, Part 1: DSM-IV and the concept of mental disorder. *Behavior Research and Therapy* 35:633–650.

———. 1998. Psychotherapy, distributive justice, and social work revisited. *Smith College Studies in Social Work* 69:25–57.

Chapter 17

The Problem of Psychotherapy in Social Work

William M. Epstein

In spite of its quick perfusion and enduring popularity, psychotherapy is a problematic foundation for social work practice and an impediment to professional standing. It is a failed enterprise of science but an immensely successful social institution. Unfortunately this insight has little force, since students do not enter social work's educational programs to be discomfited with the ineffectiveness of their chosen occupation or the pointlessness of their motives; patients continue to sign up for treatment or are forced into treatment bereft of any scientifically credible ability to resolve their problems; the society does not demand rigorous tests of psychotherapeutic efficacy or close regulation of its practitioners. Through all of its franchises—clinical psychology, psychiatry, social work, counseling, and a multitude of educational, supportive, vocational, motivational, and community services that target individual change through a process of "rational induction" or behavioral manipulation—psychotherapy in America flourishes in good emotional health with the support of a credulous clientele but without any ability to resolve social problems.

Despite the impressive lineage of psychotherapy's social authority, it lacks a rational justification. This paradox is resolved in the rituals of America's secular religiosity: social work and the personal social services are deeply involved in the social drama of confirming social mores. The symbolic and political role dominates their engagement in prevention, cure, and rehabilitation or in the more mundane chores of assuring greater equality through the creation of surrogates for failed social institutions, notably the family and community. Without a true production function, the longevity of psychotherapy and social work needs to be explained by their symbolic usefulness rather than by any clinical prowess.

The Effectiveness of Psychotherapy

Psychotherapy's effectiveness has been largely considered through summaries of clinical outcomes: intuitive critiques, box-score comparisons, and meta-analyses. Each approach screens the clinical literature for individual studies that are then combined in a variety of ways into general conclusions about the state of the art. Fully cognizant that the quality of research rather than the subject matter separates pseudoscience from the real thing, psychotherapy, just like medicine, has come to accept—at least formally—the definitive power of the classical scientific experiment—prospective, randomized clinical trials with placebo and nontreatment controls, large randomly selected samples, reliable measures, independent judges, follow-up measures, low rates of attrition and censoring, and so forth.

Early criticisms of psychotherapy intuitively summarized perhaps a score of primary studies, deriving their conclusions subjectively without any formal criteria for the selection of research or for clinical success. In fact, the early summaries were as idiosyncratic as the faulty primary clinical evaluations (Eysenck 1952, 1961, 1965; Rachman 1971; Rachman and Wilson 1980; Bergin 1971; and the subsequent editions of the *Handbook of Psychotherapy and Behavior Change*). Luborsky, Singer, and Luborsky (1975) appeared to improve upon the capriciousness of the intuitive analyses by defining objective categories—box scores—for summing up the outcomes of different therapies. However, they also failed to consider the scientific credibility of the separate studies; simply making objective the process of assigning primary research to different categories and then keeping a box score of outcomes lumps together good and bad research while failing to appreciate separate sample sizes, the measurement processes, instruments, representativeness, and so forth.

One prominent criticism of Eysenck's reviews might have been applied with equal force to the entire psychotherapeutic literature: "Within the framework of Eysenck's nonexperimental data base, there are limits to one's certainty about any conclusions" (Office of Technology Assessment 1980:41). The outcome research itself was routinely too imperfect to sustain any endorsement of practice—either the critics' growing affection for behavioral methods or the enchantment with interpersonal therapy and other adaptations of Freudian pscyhoanalysis. Rachman (1971) argued that evaluations of practice require a controlled prospective design to prove that patient recovery proceeded from psychotherapy itself rather than from "spontaneous remission."[1] Rachman was voicing the emerging consensus of therapists and academics: a field that claimed to be scientific should employ scientific methods.

Smith, Glass, and Miller (1980) (hereafter SGM)—a true "citation classic"—attempted to resolve the problems of summary clinical evaluation by conducting a meta-analysis of only the scientifically credible outcome research. Meta-analysis is an objective statistical technique used to compare the outcomes of disparate research. SGM wrote at length and forcefully about the necessity of scientific clinical research for psychotherapy. After screening the entire body of outcome research, they came up with 475 studies that adhered to "the acknowledged canons of experimental science" (8). They concluded that psychotherapy was very effective, producing an average effect size of .86, which means that "the average person who would score at the 50th percentile of the untreated control population could expect to rise to the 80th percentile with respect to that population after receiving psychotherapy." This represents a very large benefit, fully 60% of the maximum possible improvement.

However, their methods, their interpretations, and—most important—their base of studies were too faulty to sustain any judgment except indeterminacy, probable ineffectiveness, and possible routine harm. SGM's base of studies, in addition to measurement reactivity, suffered from an enormous number of researcher biases related to questionable instruments and measurement procedures, patient selection, attrition, censoring, and others. Indeed, if Rosenthal and Rubin (1978) are correct, then "interpersonal expectancy biases," a variation of Orne's (1962) demand characteristics, account for more of the positive effects than even the researchers' report, again suggesting deterioration as a palpable likelihood. After SGM's estimates are corrected, professional treatment emerges as only modestly more effective than time-structured activities—that is, the customary placebo.[2]

Moreover, SGM's base of studies and outcome research generally reflects therapy that was usually conducted in optimal conditions, university settings that closely supervise some of the best therapists. The common conditions of community practice are far different, providing evidence for some of the field's fiercest critics (Pilgrim 1997; Dineen 1996; Epstein 1995; Dawes 1994; Kline 1988; Massoon 1988; Gross 1978; Pope 1974; Stuart 1970). In the end, rather than endorsing psychotherapy, SGM create just the opposite view, in which beholden researchers exaggerate the putative benefits of psychotherapy while ignoring its probable harms.

SGM, and the field generally, insist that the burden to prove harm rests with the critic of psychotherapy, arguing that the research does not *credibly* demonstrate harm. However, the literature fails to credibly demonstrate any outcome. But even on SGM's evidence, harm is a constant companion of positive outcomes. The tight underlying distribution of patient outcomes that SGM estimates converts into a Wild West of unpredictability, with enormous numbers of treated patients falling below the means of the control groups.[3]

Any generalization of outcomes is limited by its own methods, but more importantly by the quality of the primary research that it cites. Psychotherapy's brief period of self-doubt in the 1970s has been subsequently over-whelmed by a self-serving faith in its efficacy. While a number of meta-analyses have improved on SGM's methods, none have been able to identify a credible base of clinical research that justifies their summaries. With rare exceptions, the twenty-five-year parade of meta-analyses blithely repeats SGM's errors of acceptance while conveniently overlooking the many prob-lems of bias. There is little, if any, progress of science in the most recent summary reviews that have appeared in the field's leading journals (e.g., Wampold et al. 2002; Byrd and Nicolosi 2002; Michael and Crowley 2002; Stetter and Kupper 2002; Fedoroff and Taylor 2001; Shadish et al. 2000; Martin, Garske, and Davis 2000; Butz, Bowling, and Bliss 2000). While meta-analytic techniques, as well as the field's methodological narrative, seem to have improved over time, the essential repetition of grievously flawed research belies a growing scientific authority. Current research, while in-creasingly sophisticated, is little improved over earlier attempts.

Even the most selective of the recent meta-analyses are stuck on a weak base of primary research. As one example, Casacalenda, Perry, and Looper (2002) reassessed the six most credible randomized controlled trials for the treatment of mild to moderate depression. Each of the six experiments com-pared psychopharmacology and psychotherapy with a placebo control, usu-ally an inert pill together with clinical management. Outcomes were re-ported for the initially randomized patients rather than simply for those who completed treatment—a prudently conservative method. Both types of treated patients fared equally well, with about twice the recovery of control patients. About 45% of the patients given drug therapy or psychotherapy experienced complete remission at a single point in time (usually at the end of treatment or within about eight months afterward) compared with only about 25% of control patients. Thus, about one in five mild to moderately depressed patients seeking treatment recovered completely at least at a single point in time.

However, this very modest recovery rate is circumscribed by a variety of debilitating methodological pitfalls. As Casacalenda, Perry, and Looper (2002) acknowledge, the findings, such as they are, may not be relevant to severely depressed patients, children, adolescents, or the elderly. Random-ized controlled studies are conducted in unusual settings, which brings Cascalenda, Perry, and Looper (2002) to suggest that recovery rates would have been *higher* for typical clinical practice, where treatment protocols can be changed when patients do not respond. However, they neglect to add that trials are customarily conducted in optimal settings, while the typical clinical setting is probably far more perilous for patients. Moreover, the new treatment may be as ineffective as the initial treatments. But the biggest barrier to scientific credibility, undercutting each of the six studies included in the meta-analysis, is created by their measurement of relevant behaviors.

In each of these cases, patient self-report (the Hamilton Depression Scale) was the source of data to assess depression. Depressed people in treatment, probably grateful for their therapists' attentions, were asked to report on their symptoms, knowing full well that their condition was a measure of their therapists' professional abilities. It is worth speculating that the relationship with therapists was strongest for psychotherapy patients and weakest for patients taking drugs and for controls. If this is so, and if a true control for drug therapy is provided by the placebo, then it is likely that psychotherapy is not as effective as drug treatment within the limited samples of these studies. Many other imperfections mar each of the six studies, most notably Elkin et al. (1989) shrinking to invisibility the reported levels of psychotherapy's ability to handle depression (Epstein 1995).

And so it is with the other meta-analyses of psychotherapy, including those such as Prioleau, Murdoch, and Brody (1983) that analyzed only randomized controlled trials. Their claims fall apart on the poor quality of the underlying research even when it employs randomized controls but ignores the other methodological requirements of scientifically credible clinical research. The following three examples of psychotherapy's primary evaluative research that appear to support its clinical value are chosen from among the best outcome research. They were published in the *Archives of General Psychiatry* and the *Journal of Consulting and Clinical Psychology,* two of the social sciences' most respected journals, with *Journal Citation Report* (2001) impact scores of 12.0 and 3.6, respectively.[4] Each study employs prospective randomized controls, relatively large samples, quantitative and multiple measures, appropriate statistical designs, and sensitivity to other potential methodological pitfalls. Each one claims success in addressing an important personal and social problem with a standard form of psychotherapy. However, each of these three studies, and by implication the entire body of outcome research in psychotherapy, fails to credibly establish its findings.

Psychotherapy for Female Substance-Abusing Patients

Winters et al. (2002) compared behavioral couples therapy (BCT) with individual-based treatment (IBT) in treating alcohol and drug abuse among a sample of married or cohabiting female subjects. BCT and IBT both provided cognitive-behavioral therapy "in developing coping-skills behaviors conducive to abstinence" (347); the females in the BCT condition participated in one-hour individual sessions and ninety-minute group sessions without their "intimate partners" and one-hour sessions with their partners. IBT did not provide any conjoint therapy, only one-hour individual sessions and ninety-minute group sessions without intimate partners. Both treatment conditions covered 24 weeks, with participants scheduled for 56 treatment sessions. In short, "the only difference between the BCT and IBT conditions was that during the 12-week primary treatment phase, the BCT cases received 1 couples therapy session and 1 individual session each week, whereas the female patients in the IBT condition received 2 individual sessions each week" with both conditions receiving one weekly group therapy session (347). BCT was delivered by master's-level therapists; IBT was delivered by state-certified substance abuse counselors trained by a psychologist in cognitive-behavioral therapy. Treatments were manualized, and fidelity was checked by rating videotaped sessions. The 75 research subjects were randomly assigned to the two different conditions and followed for one year after treatment.

The sample was obtained from "277 married and cohabiting women entering treatment for substance abuse" (346). Of the 277, 31 declined to participate, and another 171 were excluded because the partners were abusing drugs or alcohol. Of the 75 patients who participated in the experiment, 26 entered through the coercion of either the courts or the welfare department under threat of incarceration or loss of benefits. On average, women in both groups were about thirty-three years of age, had completed more than twelve years of schooling, had been living with their partners for about six years, and had about two children. They had substantial histories of substance abuse.

Dependence was measured before treatment, at the end of treatment, and every subsequent three months for one year after treatment. Urine tests and breath tests, but not hair tests, were given to the women at each point of data collection after pretreatment. In addition, other outcome measures related to the social impact and severity of addiction were collected from subjects through semi-structured interviews. Abuse was measured by self-reported percentage of days abstinent (PDA). Not surprisingly, patient reports agreed well with urine and breath tests . . . so long as patient reports were paired with the more objective tests.

While there were no significant differences between the outcomes of the two treatment conditions twelve months after treatment, both groups achieved large and clinically significant gains compared with their pretreatment levels of abuse. BCT reported a pretreatment mean PDA of 42.3% and a twelve-month PDA of 74.2%, an improvement of about thirty percentage points. IBT participants moved from 45.2% PDA to 65.4%, a gain of about twenty percentage points. About 60% of the BCT subjects and 40% of the IBT subjects reported continuous abstinence one year after treatment. In addition, both groups reported impressive drops in the indicators of the severity of their addictions.

Unfortunately, these results are neither applicable to the general population of drug addicts, even female drug addicts, nor credible estimates of the

outcomes of the experiment. First, the subjects were among the most amenable and highly motivated for treatment; although about one third were
forced to seek treatment, two thirds sought treatment voluntarily. The
women had also reached the magic age of thirty, at which deviance of all
sorts becomes increasingly burdensome. They were mothers in fairly stable
families that were threatened by their addiction. Their partners were not
addicts and presumably were encouraging their sobriety.

Second, while the experiment randomized subjects to two treatment conditions, it still lacked essential controls. There was neither a nontreatment
condition nor a placebo treatment condition, and thus the motivation of the
clients and the expectations for recovery apart from treatment remain alternative explanations for whatever improvements may have occurred. Yet the
measurement problem is more general. The measures of substance abuse, and
thus the extent of recovery, are uncertain. The patients' self-report of their
pretreatment substance abuse was not checked with any objective test, relying
on recall for the year before treatment. As one of the authors admits, substance abuse immediately before treatment may be greater than in the whole
one-year period.[5] Indeed, in order to obtain treatment patients may inflate
the actual severity of their addictions. The true extent of pretreatment abuse
was probably considerably less than the study's reported levels, and thus the
likely extent of recovery was also proportionately less. Furthermore, urine
tests were scheduled at all follow-up points, with the strong likelihood that
some patients obscured their abuse. The failure to employ hair analyses at
any time is puzzling, since hair tests reliably cover three months (the periods
for follow-up), while the kidneys usually purge drug traces in 72 hours. Thus
the study's estimates of "days of continuous abstinence after treatment" are
speculative.

In addition, the self-reports of addiction severity, referring to substance
abuse, employment, and family and social functioning, may be more reactive
to the patients' relationships with their therapists than indicative of their
actual social circumstances. In fact, self-reported treatment success may itself
be a form of denial.

In the end, then, the creaming of patients, the absence of relevant controls,
and the porous, unreliable quality of the measurements undercut the study's
claims that its interventions were effective in achieving substantial remission
for substance-abusing patients. To a far greater extent than even acknowledged in the field, motivated, older addicts with strong stakes in relationships
that were threatened by their addictions are the most likely to achieve sobriety even without treatment. But taking into consideration the measurement problems of the experiment, even these highly conducive motivations
failed to achieve a substantial amount of recovery.

It is notable that just these sorts of poorly designed experiments have led
to the conclusion that psychotherapy is effective. The false faith in treatment

efficacy in turn justifies standard treatment controls and the absence of non-treatment and placebo controls that allow a community of practice to sidestep the issue of accountability. False science produces false proofs that reinforce the continuation of false science. Still, the underlying permission for porous research is given by the society seeking a myth of social service rather than effective cures or meaningful improvement.

Psychotherapy for Bulimia Nervosa

Wilson et al. (2002) and Agras et al. (2000) compared the effectiveness of cognitive-behavioral therapy with interpersonal psychotherapy in treating bulimia nervosa. Manualized treatments were provided to 220 patients in nineteen sessions of fifty minutes each over twenty weeks. Potential subjects were excluded if they had severe physical or psychiatric conditions, current anorexia nervosa, conditions that did not reach the threshold of severity for bulimia nervosa, and a few other characteristics. Selected subjects were randomized to each of the two treatment conditions at two different sites. Measures were taken before, during, and after treatment, including an eight-month follow-up. All of the behavioral data, notably vomiting and binge eating, were self-reported by patients.

At the end of treatment, CBT was superior to IPT: 32 (29%) of the CBT patients recovered (no bingeing or vomiting for 28 days) and 48% remitted (fewer than two episodes per week of bingeing and vomiting during the previous 28 days), as compared with 7 (6%) recovered and 28% remitted among the IPT patients. There were no significant differences at follow-up (Agras et al. 2000). These analyses compute outcomes by comparing successful patients with the total sample, wisely counting those who dropped out of treatment as failures.

In contrast, for the subjects who completed treatment, CBT was superior to IPT at the end of treatment, but both appeared to be remarkably effective: for CBT vomiting and bingeing were both down 80%; for IPT vomiting was down 52% and bingeing down 44%. At the eight-month follow-up, there was no difference between the two treatments, although both were successful. Some of the measures improved: vomiting was down 61% for CBT patients and 62% for IPT patients; bingeing was reduced by 72% for CBT patients and 70% for IPT patients. Moreover, 66% of the CBT patients and 80% of the IPT patients who improved maintained their improvements at eight-month follow-up (although data are not reported by Wilson et al. for the twelve-month follow-up).

However, the self-selection of motivated patients offers itself as an alternative explanation even for the findings that compute outcomes on the basis of the total sample. Indeed, patients seeking treatment and then pursuing inclusion in research are probably quite different from the general population of those with bulimia nervosa. As in many other studies of psychotherapy, potential subjects were recruited by advertisement and clinical referral. Of the 923 initial calls, 584 were screened out because they did not reach a sufficient frequency of bingeing and purging, were receiving antidepressants or other treatment, or were not motivated to enter the study. The remaining 339 made appointments for a qualification interview. Ninety-five failed to keep their appointments or were unwilling to proceed with the study, and 24 others failed to meet appropriate criteria for inclusion. Of the successful 220 subjects, only 154 lasted through treatment and only 129 reported at follow-up. This effective attrition rate of 41% (much greater than the authors had anticipated) beggars the study's findings for the group who completed treatment, especially in light of the very large number of unmotivated and severely disabled patients who were initially excluded and the patterns of self-referral and clinical referral that probably produced an initial research sample of more amenable subjects.

Furthermore, all of the study's measures except for "the suitability of treatment" (fidelity) that was made of the therapists' videotaped sessions were drawn from patient self-reports, which were at no point objectively corroborated. Moreover, Kelly's (2000) attempt to reconfigure patient misrepresentation as therapeutic self-presentation tortures her acknowledgment throughout that painful personal behavior, perhaps including failure in treatment, is routinely hidden.

As with the previous study of substance abuse treatment, Agras et al. (2000) and Wilson et al. (2002) assumed on the basis of research as flawed as their current studies that standard treatments were effective. In tribute to replication as well as documented re-test effects—the remission of symptoms without intervention (Arrindell 2001 and a similar finding from Carlson and Schmidt 1999)—a rigorous clinical science routinely includes both nontreatment and placebo controls in all subsequent tests of treatment outcome. In short, the methodological imperfections of Agras et al. (2000) and Wilson et al. (2002) plausibly reduce their small reported gains to insubstantiality. If there is a clinical significance for the findings, it concerns the marvel of professional acceptance rather than the benefits to patients.

It is well to emphasize that the burden of proof within a scientific community rests with the researcher and not with the skeptic. A test of clinical worth carries the obligation to prove effectiveness by dispelling reasonable threats to a study's validity. The failure to discredit alternative explanations remains a serious pitfall to the authority of the research. Outside of science and within the society at large, however, the skeptic carries the burden of proof in challenging established social institutions or tradition. The community of psychotherapy operates as a social tradition rather than as a scientific community with a political rather than a rational mandate.

Preventing Depression with Psychotherapy

Clarke et al. (2001) tested whether psychotherapy for the "subsyndromal adolescent offspring of parents treated for depression" would prevent the later onset of depression. Participants were recruited from the membership of a very large HMO. The experimental psychotherapy condition provided "15 one-hour sessions for groups of 6 to 10 adolescents"; the usual-care control was free to utilize any of the HMO's services. Corroborating an earlier experiment (Clarke et al. 1999), the authors concluded that preventive psychotherapy for these youth was very successful:

> We obtained significant preventive effects in this at-risk group of off-spring, across continuous and diagnostic depression outcome variables, suicide symptoms, and functioning. The adjusted risk for development of depression in the control group was more than 5 times that of the prevention group. Preventive effects were clinically significant; that is, large enough to be considered meaningful in the real world. Clarke et al. (2001):1133.

Yet the research itself does not sustain this joyful conclusion. Differences between the experimental and control groups were inconsistent across measures and never very large. Two of the principal outcome measures favored the experimental group at completion of treatment and for the 24-month follow-up period; one did not. Most benefits fell off considerably over time. The report of suicide items was greater for the control than for the experimental group, although the amount is not specified. Major depressive episodes were greater for the control (28.8%) than for the experimental group (9.3%). Of the initial 49 youths in the control group, 12 developed a mood disorder (mean time to onset of 14.0 months) within 24 months, while 9 of the 45 youths who received psychotherapy did so (mean time to onset of 6.3 months). Moreover, youth receiving psychotherapy "reported an average of 33 fewer depressed days in the year after intake than did control subjects (11 vs. 44)."

The authors, however, never considered that their modest findings might be accounted for by biased reporting. The youths in psychotherapy may well have learned to suppress the report of their suicide idealizations, the number of days they actually felt depressed, and even their mood disorders through the vehicle of group support and their positive relations with the therapists.

The opposite motivation, perhaps to exaggerate depressive symptoms in pursuit of treatment among the controls, may have falsely increased their reported differences with the experimental patients. Whether attributed to Kelly's patient hiding, Orne's demand characteristics, or Rosenthal and Rubin's confirmational research bias, the study did not take steps to assure that the therapy rather than the reports of subjects accounted for the positive results, such as they were.

Moreover, the final randomized sample of 94 was a highly screened, tiny fraction of the initial group of 2,995 families of depressed parents who were initially "judged appropriate for the study." Only 65 of the 94 randomized youths provided information at the 24-month follow-up. Apart from the questionable representativeness of the research sample, the enormous amount of lost information at follow-up by itself undercuts claims for treatment effectiveness.

Finally, the reach for greater authority in the fact that one experiment corroborates another may be more the result of symmetrical biases in similarly flawed research than of true scientific replication. The enormous rewards for the discovery of effective cures for emotional disorders create enormous incentives in research for distortion, bias, and error. The consistency of these pitfalls—indeed, their ubiquity—underscores the field's institutional ambitions, notably including its usefulness as a social symbol, and contradicts its scientific authority.

The Persistent Possibility of Harm

These three patently inadequate studies are among the best outcome research ever conducted of psychotherapy. Yet even the most selective of the meta-analyses routinely build their optimism from far less-rigorous research. Most troubling, the research largely ignores the side effects of psychotherapy, tending to report grouped data without consideration of research subjects who may deteriorate *because* of psychotherapy. The possibility that the average deterioration rate for therapy patients is lower than the average deterioration rate among controls does not prove that deterioration in the experimental group is a natural progression of mental illness and is independent of psychotherapy. At the price of helping some, psychotherapy may greatly exacerbate the problems of others.

Even if the etiological baseline could be established for psychiatric disease (and it has not been established), obviating the necessity for nontreatment controls so long as research samples were representative of the underlying population, the fact of an experimental group's general improvement along with the deterioration of some patients still raises serious ethical issues. The percentage of those who deteriorate in the natural state may be greater than those who deteriorate in the experimental condition, but here the deterioration may be more severe for those who would be better off without psychotherapy. That is, psychotherapy may have a morbid effect on some patients.

The research setting is far better supervised than the community setting, where the typical solo practitioner is often an entrepreneur free of restraint. The research setting may also place a greater demand upon the patient to reward her therapist with favorable reports of remission in spite of continuing problems. The practice of psychotherapy as it is commonly conducted outside of the protective research university may well be an open frontier where crackpots, charlatans, and Madame Blavatskys prey on the weak, the insane, and the needy.

Psychotherapy is not sold with a label warning that some patients may be harmed, nor are patients asked to sign an informed-consent form. Yet both the benefits and the risks of psychotherapy still need to be credibly established. To this end, it is disheartening that the field continues to develop fashions of research that supplant a credible science of psychotherapy.

Fashions in Method

Psychotherapy and social work beguile themselves with fictions of their social importance and clinical effectiveness drawn from their illusions of scientific rigor. As one style of truth is worn threadbare, a new suit is stitched together. The faith in the clinician to accurately evaluate the outcomes of her own patients was suppressed as the field sought greater social authority by accepting SGM's famous "canons" of clinical research, that is, clinical trials. But in fact, rigorous trials have been constantly subverted, first by the fancy of "clinical significance" and shortly after by a truly imaginative if not an actually magical series of methodological canards, best at home in the nineteenth century of pseudoscience and absolute idealism.

In social work the subversion of clinical rigor emerged with Heineman's (1981; Heineman-Pieper 1989) celebration of practice wisdom and her disdain for scientific methods. Oblivious to bias, self-deception, and organizational imperatives, Heineman's antagonism toward scientific methods as "obsolete" endorsed the growing popularity of postmodern methods such as hermeneutics and heuristics and the increasing reliance on single-subject designs.

The same disrespect for scientific logic was expressed by the psychotherapeutic community's easy acceptance of an evaluation by Seligman (1995), a recent president of the American Psychological Association. The evaluation endorsed the field's prevailing sense of itself that all forms of psychotherapy are effective. Seligman's data were derived from a small convenience sample that produced a tiny response rate to questions about utilization and satisfaction with psychotherapy, appended to the *Consumer Reports* annual product survey. Both Seligman and Heineman were explicitly opposed to randomized controlled trials. Although they were criticized by some of their peers, their positions are popular, if not actually dominant, in fields that proclaim clinical science as their guiding principle.

Two more-recent attempts to subvert rigor in psychotherapy research continue its hostility to rationality accountability. "Stepped care models" reprise the earlier popularity of appropriate treatment and differential diagnosis, by extension endorsing the taxonomic wisdom of the *DSM* (Haaga 2000; Newman 2000; Otto, Pollack, and Maki 2000; Wilson, Vitousek, and Loeb 2000; Sobell and Sobell 2000; Davison 2000). However, stepped care models, envious of clinical medicine, lack a comparably rigorous base of research. For example, Sobell and Sobell's (2000) advocacy of "a heuristic approach to the treatment of alcohol problems" involving individualized treatment "consistent with the research literature and supported by clinical judgment" ignores the very failure of that literature to sustain the efficacy of any treatment. Indeed, without scientific authority, clinical judgment in the guise of a "heuristic" recalls Merlin's meddlings, not Salk's vaccine.

Patient-focused research is more complex than stepped care models but equally defective. Psychotherapy has insisted on a distinction between efficacy and effectiveness (which is *not* respected in this chapter). Presumably, efficacy studies are rigorous clinical tests that "identify potential differences in treatment outcomes that are due to the systematic effects of specific treatments" (Lambert 2001:147). On the other hand, effectiveness research tests

> the generalizability of experimental findings to some degree by measuring the outcome of patients encountered in routine clinical practice. However, these investigations often lack adequate internal validity and may take the form of post hoc surveys, such as the recent *Consumer Reports* (1995) survey.
> (Lambert 2001:147)

The third subversion of rigor—the patient-focused paradigm—"seeks to identify empirical methods to improve outcome for individual patients in ongoing clinical practice" (Lambert 2001:148; Lueger et al. 2001; Lambert, Hansen, and Finch 2001; Barkham et al. 2001). It embraces single-subject designs that dominate social work education and research. Patient-focused research and single-subject designs are retreats from a commitment to science, not because they employ weak methodologies but because they *sub-*

stitute clinical judgment and weak methods for the authority of rigorous science. After all, a scientific inquiry necessarily begins with uncertain observations and haphazard comparisons, proceeding only gradually to definitive tests. Indeed, the art of medicine is practiced and tolerated because of scientific ignorance but not as a replacement for proven practice. But the success of clinical judgment as a rival to scientific authority undermines the discipline of definitive tests and thwarts the search for effective cure, prevention, and rehabilitation.

These meanders from science are particularly noticeable in light of the poor instrumentation in psychotherapy. Without reliable and valid measures of outcome, evaluative research is premature and unjustified. However, the patient, judicious conduct of scientific inquiry in psychotherapy and social work has been hastily preempted by research methods that are too advanced for its current sophistication, suggesting a preoccupation with social standing at the price of scholarly responsibility.

The Cunning of Fashion

Psychotherapy and, pointedly, social work have taken refuge in their weak research to congratulate themselves for effective practice, ignoring the plausibility of ineffectiveness and pernicious harms. The ineffectiveness of psychotherapy results from the deficiency of its most basic claim to clinical potency: the ability to change embedded behaviors in relatively short periods of time through modulated discussions with a trained psychotherapist but without attention to the patient's social and economic environment. Presumably, behavioral change precedes better circumstances. Yet talking may not compensate for long-standing deprivations of family, peer group, education, employment, and community. Moreover, insisting that the patient take responsibility for herself—the climactic epiphany of therapy—mimics the American religion of individual responsibility in which the acceptance of Christ as a personal savior is the epiphany of grace. Indeed, psychotherapy is better appreciated as a secular form of American pietism than as a serious clinical endeavor.

The telling point lies in the benefit that American society derives from psychotherapy's implicit insistence on character imperfections as the source of social problems and its depreciation of the social situation in creating problems. Deviance as impaired character is far more compatible with American righteousness than deviance reflecting the isolating coldness of American life, its denial of greater equality, its indifference to suffering, and its rigid cruelties toward the less well-off. The culture apparently needs to believe that psychotherapy is effective and therefore a legitimate test of character: those who are virtuous benefit from therapy, choosing to conform with social expectations, but those who are stubborn in their immorality deserve little and get less. The success stories are testimonials to virtue that conserve the national treasury, and the failures justify their own misery and unrelieved poverty.

The psychotherapeutic process, especially in its concentrated potency of sixteen weeks to health and comfort, is far less expensive than repairing the social institutions that may be the essential cause of so many dysfunctional, unhappy, predatory, self-destructive citizens. In just this way, psychotherapy becomes the modern equivalent of auto-da-fé, although the United States has graciously decided not to burn witches. Instead it runs trials of their character in which they either accept the virtues of normality and lately, through compassionate conservatism, of traditional religious practice or reveal themselves as backsliders, incorrigibles, heathen sinners, and subversives, deserving the scorn of a chosen people. Psychotherapy and, by extension, social work become rituals of social accommodation rather than vehicles of greater autonomy, liberation, or fulfillment. Even the so-called reformers have accepted this bizarrely tame idea of help, attuned to the Mission on the Bowery rather than a call toward greater equality of circumstances. The preference for individual blame perfuses social work, a cultural form so old in America that its choice of personal as opposed to social responsibility has lost any semblance of inadvertence or innocence.

Social Work as Ritual

Psychotherapy has never credibly demonstrated an ability to treat mental disease or emotional problems. There is no clinical practice of wisdom or generosity. Consequently, social work's reliance on psychotherapy throughout most of its history cannot be understood as a rational response to need. Instead, social work is best explained politically as a ritual of American values, that is, as a ritual of social efficiency, the notion that services are to be provided at the lowest levels compatible with political tastes rather than with need. Psychotherapy is the apotheosis of the socially efficient intervention, supplanting material assistance with a few hours of uncertain preaching.

With its soul in the psychotherapeutic clinic, social work is not simply unproven but mythic. Clinical outcomes may be beside the point. Psychotherapy's persistence and institutionalization in social work and the personal social services signal its political utility as a ceremony of the culture's longstanding preference to tax the individual with personal responsibility rather than to attend to society's imperfections. Social work's allegiance to core cultural values in denial of a central role as a voice for those in need justifies politically the very meanness of purse and heart that the field repeatedly abjures. Indeed, psychotherapy and social work have become sacraments of social efficiency, the national ethos that actually accounts for American social policy. However, social work pays for its institutional longevity with a permanent professional immaturity. Without either effective interventions or the desire to search for them, the field's vitalities shrivel into Orwellian rituals of political obedience as a liberationist rhetoric obscures the failure to attend to social or individual problems.

Preference is known by choice rather than by stated opinions or intentions. Thus social work's embrace of psychotherapy exposes its actual role and cultural meaning. Its mawkish feelings for the downtrodden mask its attachment to the nation's ferocious individualism. It would not be this way if American politics were polarized on issues of class, poverty, and social causation. Great cleavage in American attitudes would provide a substantial constituency for a more structural ideology and therefore a more concrete form of social work practice. However, the American consensus is satisfied with current social welfare arrangements. It is also deeply optimistic, not just hopeful, that personal change proceeds from a spiritual transformation of motivation attendant upon an epiphany of personal responsibility rather than from social circumstances (DiMaggio, Evans, and Bryson 1996; Epstein unpublished). This widely shared, mystical complacency with welfare policy circumscribes any movement toward greater equality, quickly ascribing sin to those who fail as workers, parents, spouses, or citizens. Unfortunately, the universalism of the American creed also hides a cruelty and an indifference to suffering.

Abraham Flexner, dead for many decades, outlives his critics. An effective profession of helping requires proof of its positive outcomes—the source of autonomous expertise—in order to compete for social and economic standing. Scientific proof confers greater status than nonscientific proof. Science contends with faith, rationality with politics, substance with vanity and delusion, free choice with the strictures of tradition. Social work is not a profession, and so long as psychotherapy is its preferred intervention, it will never mature but will forever remain an occupation of questionable value for service recipients and a ceremony of cultural preferences.

Notes

1. Waitlist control subjects may maintain fictive symptoms in order to stay eligible for treatment. They may also seek alternative therapy during their wait.

2. At times the field has insisted that placebo effects ("nonspecific effects") are legitimate therapeutic effects. If this were true, then placebo effects equate professional training and practice with time-structured activities, grandmothering, and Bert Lahr's signature line, "Be a pal."

3. SGM offered very tight distributions by assuming that their average effect sizes were means of individual patient scores rather than means of mean scores. The problems of SGM are discussed at length in Epstein (1995).

4. Moreover, the journals are rated second and twenty-seventh, respectively, from among the approximately 1,700 journals included in the *Social Sciences Citation Index* (2001).

5. Correspondence with one of the authors.

References

Agras, W. S., B. T. Walsh, C. G. Fairburn, G. T. Wilson, and H. C. Kraemer. 2000. A multicenter comparison of cognitive-behavioral therapy and interpersonal psychotherapy for bulimia nervosa. *Archives of General Psychiatry* 57 (May): 459–466.

Arrindell, W. A. 2001. Changes in waiting-list patients over time: Data on some commonly-used measures. Beware! *Behavior Research and Therapy* 39:1227–1247.

Barkham, M., F. Margison, C. Leach et al. 2001. Service profiling and outcomes benchmarking using the Core-OM: Toward practice-based evidence in the psychological therapies. *Journal of Consulting and Clinical Psychology* 69 (2): 184–196.

Bergin, A. E. 1971. The Evaluation of Therapeutic Outcomes. In S. L. Garfield and A. E. Begin, eds., *Handbook of Psychotherapy and Behavior Change*. New York: John Wiley.

Butz, M. R., J. B. Bowling, and C. A. Bliss. 2000. Psychotherapy with the mentally retarded: A review of the literature and the implications. *Professional Psychology: Research and Practice* 31 (1): 42–47.

Byrd, A. D. and J. Nicolosi. 2002. A meta-analytic review of treatment of homosexuality. *Psychological Reports* 90:1139–1152.

Carlson, K. D. and F. L. Schmidt. 1999. Impact of experimental design on effect size: Findings from the research literature on training. *Journal of Applied Psychology* 84 (6): 851–862.

Casacalenda, N. C., J. C. Perry, and K. Looper. 2002. Remission in major depressive disorder: A comparison of pharmacotherapy, psychotherapy, and control conditions. *American Journal of Psychiatry* 159 (8): 1354–1360.

Clarke, G. N., M. Hornbrook, F. Lynch et al. 2001. A randomized trial of a group cognitive intervention for preventing depression in adolescent offspring of depressed parents. *Archives of General Psychiatry* 58 (December): 1127–1134.

Clarke, G. N., P. Rohde, R. M. Lewinsohn, H. Hops, and J. R. Seeley. 1999. Cognitive-behavioral treatment of adolescent depression: Efficacy of acute group treatment and booster sessions. *Journal of the American Academy of Child and Adolescent Psychiatry* 38:272–279.

Davison, G. C. 2000. Stepped care: Doing more with less? *Journal of Consulting and Clinical Psychology* 68 (4): 580–585.

Dawes, R. M. 1994. *House of Cards.* New York: Free Press.

DiMaggio, P., J. Evans, and B. Bryson. 1996. Have Americans' social attitudes become more polarized? *American Journal of Sociology* 102 (3): 690–755.

Dineen, T. 1996. *Manufacturing Victims.* Montreal: Robert Davies Publishing.

Elkin, I. T., J. T. Shea, S. D. Watkins et al. 1989. National Institute of Mental Health treatment of depression collaborative research program: General effectiveness of treatments. *Archives of General Psychiatry* 46:971–982.

Epstein, W. M. 1995. *The Illusion of Psychotherapy.* New Brunswick, N.J.: Transaction Publishers.

———. 1997. Social science, child welfare, and family preservation: A failure of rationality in public policy. *Children and Youth Services Review* 19 (1/2): 41–60.

———. Unpublished. "Cleavage in American Attitudes Toward Social Welfare."

Eysenck, H. F. 1952. The effects of psychotherapy: An evaluation. *Journal of Consulting Psychology* 16:319.

———. 1961. The Effects of Psychotherapy. In H. F. Eysenck, ed., *Handbook of Abnormal Psychology.* New York: Basic Books.

———. 1965. The effects of psychotherapy. *International Journal of Psychiatry* 1:97.

Fedoroff, I. C. and S. Taylor. 2001. Psychological and pharmacological treatments of social phobia: A meta-analysis. *Journal of Clinical Pharmacology* 21 (3): 311–324.

Gross, M. L. 1978. *The Psychological Society.* New York: Random House.

Haaga, D. A. F. 2000. Introduction to the special section on stepped care models in psychotherapy. *Journal of Consulting and Clinical Psychology* 68 (4): 547–548.

Heineman, M. B. 1981. The obsolete scientific imperative in social work. *Social Service Review* 55 (3): 371–397.

Heineman-Pieper, M. 1989. The heuristic paradigm: A unifying and comprehensive approach to social work research. *Smith College Studies in Social Work* 60 (1): 8–34.

Kelly, A. E. 2000. Helping construct desirable identities: A self-presentational view of psychotherapy. *Psychological Bulletin* 126 (4): 475–494.

Kline, P. 1988. *Psychology Exposed or the Emperor's New Clothes.* London: Routledge.

Lambert, M. J. 2001. Psychotherapy outcome and quality improvement: Introduction to the special section on patient-focused research. *Journal of Consulting and Clinical Psychology* 69 (2): 147–149.

Lambert, M. J., N. B. Hansen, and A. E. Finch. 2001. Patient-focused research: Using patient outcome data to enhance treatment effects. *Journal of Consulting and Clinical Psychology* 69 (2): 159–172.

Luborsky, L., B. Singer, and L. Luborsky. 1975. Comparative studies of psychotherapies: Is it true that "everybody has won and all must have prizes"? *Archives of General Psychiatry* 32 (August): 995–1008.

Lueger, R. J., K. I. Howard, Z. Martinovich, W. Lutz, E. E. Anderson, and H. G. Grissom. 2001. Assessing treatment progress of individual patients using expected treatment response models. *Journal of Consulting and Clinical Psychology* 69 (2): 150–158.

Martin, D. J., J. P. Garske, and M. K. Davis. 2000. Relation of the therapeutic alliance with outcome and other variables: A meta-analytic review. *Journal of Consulting and Clinical Psychology* 68 (3): 438–450.

Masson, J. 1988. *Against Therapy: Emotional Tyranny and the Myth of Psychological Healing.* New York: Atheneum.

Michael, K. D. and S. L. Crowley. 2002. How effective are treatments for child and adolescent depressions? A meta-analytic review. *Clinical Psychology Review* 22:247–269.

Newman, M. G. 2000. Recommendations for a cost-offset model of psychotherapy allocation using generalized anxiety disorder as an example. *Journal of Consulting and Clinical Psychology* 68 (4): 549–555.

Office of Technology Assessment. 1980. *The Implications of Cost-Effectiveness Analysis of Medical Technology. Background Paper #3: The Efficacy and Cost Effectiveness of Psychotherapy.* Washington, D.C.: Government Printing Office.

Orne, M. T. 1962. On the social psychology of the psychological experiment: With particular reference to demand characteristics and their implications. *American Psychologist* 10 (17): 776–783.

Otto, M. W., M. H. Pollack, and K. M. Maki. 2000. Empirically supported treatments for panic disorder: Costs, benefits, and stepped care. *Journal of Consulting and Clinical Psychology* 68 (4): 556–563.

Pilgrim, D. 1997. *Psychotherapy and Society* Thousand Oaks, Calif.: Sage.

Pope, H. 1997. *Psychology Astray.* Boca Raton, Fla.: Upton Books.

Prioleau, L., M. Murdock, and N. Brody. 1983. An analysis of psychotherapy versus placebo studies. *Behavioral and Brain Sciences* 6:275–310.

Rachman, S. 1971 [1980, with G. T. Wilson]. *The Effects of Psychological Treatment.* Oxford: Pergamon.

Rosenthal, R. and D. B. Rubin. 1978. Interpersonal expectancy effects: The first 345 studies. *Behavioral and Brain Sciences* 3:377–415.

Schneider, K. J. 1999. The revival of the romantic means a revival of psychology. *Journal of Humanistic Psychology* 39 (3): 13–29.

Seligman, M. E. P. 1996. Long-term psychotherapy is highly effective: The *Consumer Reports* study. *Harvard Mental Health Letter* 13 (1): 5–9.

Shadish, W. R., G. E. Matt, A. M. Navarro, and G. Phillips. 2000. The effects of psychological therapies under clinically representative conditions: A meta-analysis. *Psychological Bulletin* 126 (4): 512–529.

Smith, M. L., G. V. Glass, and T. I. Miller. 1980. *The Benefits of Psychotherapy.* Baltimore: Johns Hopkins University Press.

Sobell, M. B. and L. C. Sobell. 2000. Stepped care as a heuristic approach to the treatment of alcohol problems. *Journal of Consulting and Clinical Psychology* 68 (4): 573–579.

Stetter, F. and S. Kupper. 2002. Autogenic training: A meta-analysis of clinical outcome studies. *Applied Psychophysiology and Biofeedback* 27 (1): 45–98.

Stuart, R. B. 1970. *Trick or Treatment.* Champaign, Ill.: Research Press.

Wampold, B. E., T. Minami, T. W. Baskin, and S. C. Tierney. 2002. A meta-(re)analysis of the effects of cognitive therapy versus "other therapies" for depression. *Journal of Affective Disorders* 65:159–165.

Wilson, G. T., C. C. Fairburn, W. Stewart Agras, B. Timothy Walsh, and H. Kraemer. 2002. Cognitive-behavioral therapy for bulimia nervosa: Time course and mechanisms of change. *Journal of Consulting and Clinical Psychology* 70 (2): 267–274.

Wilson, G. T., K. M. Vitousek, and K. L. Loeb. 2000. Stepped care treatment for eating disorders. *Journal of Consulting and Clinical Psychology* 68 (4): 564–572.

Winters, J., W. Fals-Stewart, T. J. O'Farrell, G. R. Birchler, and M. L. Kelley. 2002. Behavioral couples therapy for female substance-abusing patients: Effects on substance use and relationship adjustment. *Journal of Consulting and Clinical Psychology* 70 (2): 344–355.

Chapter 18

The Misfortunes of Behavioral Social Work: Misprized, Misread, and Misconstrued

Bruce A. Thyer

Science moves, but slowly slowly, creeping on from point to point

—*Alfred, Lord Tennyson*

More than a decade ago I authored a modest paper titled "Behavioral Social Work: It Is Not What You Think" (Thyer 1991), in which I described a number of common misconceptions of contemporary behavioral theory and practice that could be found in the social work literature. Over the intervening years I have continued to come across further illustrations of inaccurate portrayals of behavioral social work, misrepresentations that have been so pervasive, even dating back to the emergence of the field, that I marvel that the behavioral perspective has made any headway at all. The most common error has been that of simple overstatement, through the use of unqualified assertions that include words such as "all," "never," "none," "always," "every," and similar extreme adjectives. From the point of view of philosophy of logic, extreme assertions are usually fraught with error, since all it takes is one disconfirming instance to disprove the statement. For example, it takes only one example of a black swan to disprove the hypothesis "All swans are white."

In this chapter I describe some common misrepresentations of behavioral social work as it has been depicted for more than thirty years in our profession's literature. This follows up and extends with a new collection of illustrative quotations the proposition that behavioral social work is frequently inaccurately described by social work authors and that such misrepresentations are one possible reason for the malaise with which behavioral social work has in general been received by the members of our profession.

There are several reasons why behavioral social work is misrepresented by authors. One is that the social learning theory foundations upon which behavioral social work is based represent a sophisticated and difficult-to-comprehend conceptual framework, which by virtue of its broad applicability across virtually the entire spectrum of social work practice poses serious intellectual challenges. Behavioral social work encompasses a comprehensive philosophy of science (see Thyer 1999), a far-reaching model of practice that has applications to virtually all areas of social work (see Thyer 1983, 1987; Thyer and Wodarski 1990), and a research methodology (single-system designs) often (also erroneously) viewed as being at odds with the conventional methods of scientific inquiry taught to our students (see Thyer 1998, 2001a, 2001b). A second reason for the misrepresentation of behavioral social work is that leading mainstream theorists and practitioners within our field often hold allegiance to alternative perspectives, some of which, such as the psychodynamic orientation so predominant decades ago, are seriously challenged by behavioral concepts and practices. This can lead to such literary practices as setting up straw-man arguments (presenting a flawed, easy-to-knock-down, oppositional point of view). And a third reason, which I have come to believe to be true on the basis of anecdotal evidence only, is the practice of some writers who deliberately translated behavioral principles into a social work context without accurate attribution of their behavioral origins, even to the point of creating neologisms in order to gain the appearance of creating something new. In the marketplace of the academy, there is more credit to be gained by an author appearing to create a "new" practice theory or model than from simply extrapolating one from another field (e.g., behavioral psychology or behavior analysis) into social work. And perhaps a fourth reason is that the behavioral perspective is viewed as politically and philosophically incorrect. Behaviorists have been construed as wishing to impose Machiavellian systems of control on people, and especially as liable to be employed by evil-minded persons seeking effective ways to manipulate others. Philosophically, behaviorism's positivist roots, and assumptions of determinism, realism, empiricism, materialism, operationism, parsimony, and avoidance of metaphysics, reification, teleology, cognitivism, mentalism, and vitalism, are often seen at odds with the fuzzy concepts that are widely and uncritically embraced (and poorly understood) and litter the social work intellectual landscape—concepts such as self-determination, respect for client autonomy, the ecosystems perspective, the strengths perspective, and the like.

In another effort to provide corrective information, I will enumerate a few of the more common general misconceptions of contemporary behavioral social work and explain why I believe these common views are erroneous.

All Behavior Is Learned

The problem here is the use of the unqualified adjective "all." It is obvious that behavior has multiple causes, some biological and some environmental (which includes psychosocial influences); thus the unqualified assertion that behaviorists believe that all behavior is learned is seen as silly at the outset, just as if one were to similarly claim, "All behavior is genetically governed" or "All behavior is a function of psychodynamic factors." Yet our social work texts dating back for decades and even up to the present, authored by leading intellectuals in our field, frequently made the assertion that behaviorists claim that all behavior is learned. For example:

> "In a behavioristic perspective, acts are stimulated by the environment" (Frederico 1973:70).
> "The child, then, is born as a tabula rasa into an organized environment that becomes the source for all psychological phenomena. . . . Man is a 'mechanical mirror' of his environment and his behavior is the essence of his personality. Behavior is explained by environmental shaping" (Whittaker 1974:75).
> "Since all behavior is malleable, and if the conditions maintaining behavior can be controlled and the proper reinforcers found, then change is possible" (Whittaker 1974:87).
> "Another assumption of social learning theory is that behavior is learned through external reinforcement" (Whittaker 1974:77).
> "All behavior, including social behavior, is considered to be learned" (Brieland, Costin, and Atherton 1975:213).
> "From a learning standpoint, there is no qualitative difference between normal and abnormal behavior, since all behavior is learned" (Brieland, Costin, and Atherton 1975:312).
> "Problematic behavior is seen as resulting from mislearning rather than from illness" (Anderson and Carter 1978:136).
> "Problem behavior develops through miseducation" (Anderson and Carter 1978:138).
> "Overt behavior is thought to be learned behavior" (Gilbert, Miller, and Specht 1980:76).
> "**Behavioral psychology** The branch of psychological theory that asserts that all behavior is learned" (Frederico 1980:391, bold in original).

"Behavior is caused by its antecedents and consequences" (Garvin 1981:88).

"All behavior is learned" (Johnson 1983:377).

"The behaviorist takes the position that all (or nearly all) of people's thoughts, feelings, and behaviors are the result of learning" (Mehr 1986:140).

"In the framework of the behaviorist, abnormal, deviant, or disordered behavior is 'learned,' just as is normal behavior" (Mehr 1986:143).

"**Behavior theory or learning theory** . . . sees human behavior as almost entirely determined through learning that takes place as a result of reinforcement of our behavior by others or as a result of our observation of behaviors modeled by others" (Shriver 2001:131, bold in original).

"The main assumption in this therapy is that maladaptive behaviors are acquired primarily through learning and can be modified through additional learning" (Zastrow 2003:385).

What is the reality? Behaviorists contend that learning influences are often very important in explaining the behavior of people, of everyone—clients, ourselves, children, those with developmental disabilities, people from different parts of the world, and so on. Exactly how important remains to be determined empirically. It is as scientifically incorrect to overemphasize the role that learning experiences play in accounting for a person's present behavior as it is to ignore it. Below are some more-accurate portrayals of the behavioral perspective on this issue:

"Behaviorism contends that many maladaptive behaviors are, at least in part, acquired through learning processes and can potentially be unlearned" (Barker 1999:43)

"The consequences of a given behavior, to a very large extent, influence the future occurrence of that behavior" (Thyer 1987:151).

"It does not appear possible to determine the full extent to which a client/system's behavior is a function of its consequences. Certainly contingency relationships coexist with a multitude of biological factors and physical environments present at all levels of human activity" (Thyer 1987:152).

The qualifiers found in the above three statements render the behavioral position much more tenable and less likely to be rejected out of hand. It is perhaps because of this that individual writers who are not sympathetic to behaviorism have chosen instead to caricature it as an extremist point of view, thereby leading to its being rejected out of hand, before it is given a thorough examination.

Behaviorists Try Only to Explain Observable Behavior

This argument was of course made by the psychologist John Watson in the early part of the twentieth century, but in the 1930s Skinner's radical (in the sense of "complete") behaviorism extended a scientific analysis of behavior into the world beneath the skin. For Skinner, behavior was everything the body does, whether it can be observed or not. Thus the term "behavior" for the past seventy-five years and more, subsumed not only observable comportment but also private events such as thoughts, feelings, dreams, perceptual phenomena, etc. Since many social work clients seek assistance in changing private events (e.g., depressed mood, distressing thoughts) as well as overt behavior, this contention, by portraying behavioral social work as capable only of explaining and intervening with observable behavior, almost by definition was seen as extremely limited and not applicable to a very wide array of the issues that concern our clients. Here are a few examples of the limited perspective:

> "Behavior therapy involves only observable, measurable change goals" (Whittaker 1974:207).
> "The focus is on observable behavior rather than psychological events" (Mehr 1986:139).
> "The focus of the helping person is on observable behavior" (Brieland, Costin, and Atherton 1975:213).

What are the facts of the matter? Consider the views of Skinner: "Radical behaviorism . . . can therefore consider events taking place in the private world within the skin" (Skinner 1974:16), or the definition found in *The Social Work Dictionary*: "**Behavior** Any action or response by an individual, including observable activity, measurable physiological changes, cognitive images, fantasies, and emotions" (Barker 1999:42, bold in original). In fact, Skinner has written extensively on the topics of feelings, emotions, perceptions, and thoughts. One of his very last essays was titled "The Origins of Cognitive Thought" (Skinner 1989), and one of his first books, *Science and Human Behavior* (1953), contained chapters titled "Emotion," "Self-Control," "Thinking," "Private Events in a Natural Science," and "The Self." The treatment of such topics occupied a major portion of Skinner's conceptual writings throughout his lifetime, and ironically, it was the behavior therapies derived in large part from Skinner's framework that proved to be the first psychosocial treatments effective in alleviating pathological anxiety (a feeling!) states (i.e., systematic desensitization), helping depression, and managing psychosis. Where behaviorism differed was its emphasis on including measures of overt behavior as (usually) crucial dependent variables in outcomes research studies. Clearly it is a major misconception to assert that behavioral social work is limited to interventions dealing with publicly observable behavior only, but the persistence of this view undoubtedly causes the approach to be seen as more limited than is the case.

Behaviorism Ignores the Causes of Behavior

From the beginnings of the social survey movement in social work and Mary Richmond's writings, an explicit assumption in our field has been that in order to effectively intervene to alleviate a problematic condition, be it a clinical situation with an individual client or a widespread social issue, one must first "understand" the "causes" of the problem. Despite the pervasiveness of this contention, it is, as an a priori assumption, unsupportable. Rather, the issue is an empirical one—sometimes understanding "causation" is necessary in order to intervene, sometimes it is not. For example, we do not yet have a scientifically rigorous understanding of the causes of dropping out of high school or of domestic violence, but this has not deterred state legislatures from passing laws that mandate the revocation of driver's licenses for high school students who drop out of school or police officers from adhering to pro-arrest policies when they witness domestic violence. The fact is that social workers and related human service professionals intervene all the time, while remaining largely ignorant of the causes of a given problem. But this is a tangential issue. The reality is that it is generally accepted as a given that an understanding of "cause" is a necessary precondition for effective intervention, yet we have been repeatedly told by social work writers that behavioral social work, perhaps unique among all practice perspectives, ignores trying to understand the causes of social problems or of the client's person-in-situation. For example:

> "Undesirable behavior is the real problem that needs eliminating, it is not merely a symptom of some underlying disease, but a problem in itself. Seeking out its historical causes, then, is irrelevant" (Ferguson 1975:201).
> "Skinner holds that the total measure of the man is observed in his actions. He believes strongly that it serves no purpose to 'explain' behavior; what is essential is to learn how to control and modify it" (Anderson and Carter 1978:137).

"The major characteristics of the behavioral approach are: 1. Indifference to the origin of symptoms" (Anderson and Carter 1978:138).

"The operant behaviorist, however, is less concerned with determining the causality of behavior" (Mehr 1986:141).

"The reply of the behaviorist to such criticisms would be simply that they have no impact since they are all predicated on the existence of a concept (underlying cause) that the behaviorist rejects as nonexistent" (Mehr 1986:150).

"Behavior modification practitioners are less interested in the reason for behavior than they are in changing it" (Piccard 1988:71).

"Behavioral approaches seek to change behaviors that are harmful or encourage positive behaviors; understanding the causes or contributing factors of the behavior is less a focus than immediate behavioral change" (Suppes and Wells 1991:138).

If true, these contentions would be damning indeed, but they are false. Completely and unreservedly false. In fact, the essence of behavioral practice is an effort to empirically determine the role of potential psychosocial variables in terms of their influence on target behavior (which includes affect and thought). This process is called undertaking a *functional analysis,* and it involves qualitatively observing clients in their natural or contrived environments, looking for the events preceding and following the occurrence of a target behavior, and developing some hypotheses regarding the role of these antecedent stimuli and consequences. The next step is to intentionally alter suspected controlling antecedent stimuli and/or consequences and see if behavior changes. If it does, then one has come a step closer to identifying the environmental "causes" of a target behavior (see Baer, Wolf, and Risley 1968; Iwata et al. 2000). Much of this is simply common sense, as in the frequent observations that hanging out with unsavory characters is a precursor to drug use and that a child's tantrums seem to be encouraged by parental attention.

The idea that behaviorists are not concerned with the real causes of behavior is perhaps generated by the fact that behaviorists are not interested in so-called mental causes of behavior, or in psychodynamic ones in particular. And this does indeed set us apart from many mainstream perspectives on human behavior that rely on mental or otherwise metaphysical causal agents to attempt to explain human comportment. There are a number of sound reasons for this. Empirical evidence is one, a preference for parsimonious explanatory accounts is another, and the problem that occurs when one attributes causality to some inner, mental state is a third—namely, whence arises this inner state (e.g., superego, neurotic conflict, locus of control, etc.)? The answer almost inevitably takes one back to the person's environment, either the intrauterine environment, the postnatal environment, or the consequences of millions of years of environmental shaping that we call our genetic endowment. It makes little causal sense, in the view of the behaviorist, to say that our client's anxiety is caused by his neurotic conflicts, if indeed the source of the client's neurotic conflicts consists of his treatment at the hands of his caregivers. Behaviorists simply cut out the middleman and are more likely to attribute the causes of so-called neurotic behavior to the person's upbringing, which of course places the causal agency in factors external to the individual. Sound behavioral practice does attempt to complete a functional analysis of a client's problem-in-situation and does attempt to remedy psychosocial factors that have established and/or maintain current dysfunction. Failure to do so sets the stage for relapse, or of incomplete treatment at best. Only poorly trained social workers with a superficial understanding of sound behavioral practice would attempt to induce behavior change without an understanding of the causative environmental factors responsible for a person's condition. Does this sometimes happen? Sadly, yes. Why? Well, perhaps because of erroneous information promulgated in our professional textbooks about the nature of behavioral principles.

Behavioral Principles Are Very Simple and Easy to Understand

Would that the above statement were true! Let's take some fundamental learning principles like the terms "reinforcement" and "punishment." Here are some reasonably accurate definitions:

> "**Reinforcement** In behavior modification, a procedure that strengthens the tendency of a response to recur. If a reinforcer is arranged to follow a behavior, there is increased probability that the behavior will be repeated. Similarly, if performance of a response removes an aversive event, there is increased probability that the behavior will be repeated" (Barker 1999:406, bold in original).
>
> "**Punishment** . . . the presentation of an unpleasant or undesired event following a behavior, the consequence of which is that there is decreased probability that the behavior will be repeated" (Barker 1999:392, bold in original).
>
> "Reinforcement: The procedure of providing consequences for a behavior that increase or maintain the frequency of that behavior" (Chance 1998:462).
>
> "Punishment: The procedure of providing consequences for a behavior that decrease the frequency of that behavior" (Chance 1998:461).

Contrast the above with the definition provided almost thirty years ago by a social work text:

"A reinforcer is any stimulus that alters the strength of the response it follows" (Whittaker, 1974:78).

The error here is that by definition a reinforcer reinforces; that is to say, it strengthens or maintains the behavior that it has followed. Yet according to Whittaker's definition, all that a reinforcer does is simply *alter* future responses. This is incorrect, since the term "alter" subsumes "decrease" or "weaken," whereas by definition reinforcement can only strengthen or maintain, not simply alter. An electric shock administered contingent on a given behavior would certainly alter that behavior, but for the consequence to be labeled reinforcement, it must do more than alter; it must strengthen or maintain.

There is also the common mistake of misrepresenting the behavioral operations of positive and negative reinforcement, and positive and negative punishment (which are four distinct types of consequences). Again, here are some reasonably accurate definitions:

"Positive reinforcer: A reinforcing event in which something is added following a behavior" (Chance 1998:461).
"Negative reinforcer: A reinforcing event in which something is removed following a behavior" (Chance 1998:461).
"Positive punishment is the application of a noxious stimulus and negative punishment is the withdrawal of a pleasant stimulus" (Logan and Wagner 1965:29).

By definition, if a consequence increases the strength of frequency of a behavior it is made contingent upon, the operation is *reinforcement*. Similarly, if a consequence weakens a response, that is *punishment*. The terms "positive" and "negative" refer to the presentation or removal of a stimulus, respectively, not to the presumptively pleasant or unpleasant properties of the stimulus. Turning on a radio and having pleasant music forthcoming strengthens turning on the radio. This is positive reinforcement. Turning the radio off and having obnoxious music be terminated similarly strengthens turning off the radio. This is negative reinforcement, and it is good. People *like* being negatively reinforced. Requiring a misbehaving child to listen to an unpleasant lecture from a parent, resulting in a reduction in misbehavior, is positive punishment. Taking away a child's GameBoy for a limited period of time, contingent on misbehavior and resulting in a reduction in misbehavior, is negative punishment.

Yet these operations are often presented in an erroneous manner. For example:

"Others favor use of negative reinforcement (punishment)" (Ferguson 1975:203).
"*Positive reinforcement* refers to a reward, *negative reinforcement* refers to punishment" (Anderson and Carter 1978:136, italics in original).

Whereas negative reinforcement is clearly *not* punishment. Relatedly, and somewhat more technically,

"*Punishment* is the presentation of an unpleasant or aversive stimulus in order to decrease a particular behavior" (Mehr 1986:141).

Well, sometimes punishment (as in negative punishment) involves the removal of something pleasant, not simply the presentation of an aversive stimulus. If learned scholars authoring social work textbooks misrepresent the most elementary of behavioral principles, what can we expect the undergraduate or graduate student, or practitioner, to make of this approach? Some misrepresentations are simply ignorant, as in (incorrectly):

"Learning and behavior acquisitions follow the stimulus–response model" (Anderson and Carter 1978:138).

The stimulus–response model, elucidated by Pavlov and Watson, is far less influential within behavioral social work than Skinner's operant approach. For example (and accurately):

"**Behaviorism** . . . The school of psychology and related sciences . . . that seeks to explain behavior in terms of events (antecedent stimuli) that occur before a behavior, and consequences (reinforcing and punishing ones) that occur following a behavior" (Barker 1999:43, bold in original).
"**Behavior modification** A method of assessing and altering behavior based on the methods of applied behavior analysis, the principles of operant conditioning, classical conditions, and social learning theory (for example, positive reinforcement, extinction, and modeling)" (Barker 1999:43, bold in original).

Yes, stimulus–response psychology (e.g., classical conditioning) is a part of behaviorism's conceptual framework, but also crucial are operant conditioning principles and learning via imitation. Failure to recognize this, and to portray behavioral practice as being based solely on the ideas of Pavlov or Watson, sets the stage for the rejection of the entire approach as too limited.

Here is another isolated illustration of conceptual confusion:

"Operant conditioning, by and large, attends to behaviors that are more cognitive" (Gilbert, Miller, and Specht 1980:110).

The reality is that operant conditioning focuses on all forms of behavior, observable and private. Claiming that the operant perspective deals with "cognitive" behavior implies that it has little relevance to our understanding of overt actions, which is definitely not the case.

Or take the assertion by social worker Malcolm Payne, that

"Certain behavioural ideas justified locking children up for long periods without day clothes" (Payne 1997:123).

Children have been locked up, beaten, and otherwise abused for millennia, certainly well before the establishment of the behavioral framework. A reading of Skinner and other authorities clearly states that punishment is to be avoided in favor of techniques of positive reinforcement, that client rights must be respected, and that physical, mental, or emotional abuse is never justified by invoking so-called behavioral justifications. I would be willing to place a very large wager indeed that Professor Payne could not find any professional behavioral citation that attempted to justify locking children up for long period of time without clothes. In fact, behavioral social work, like all social work, is guided by the same professional ethical codes and moral values as other practice modalities.

Given the crucial importance in our "Human Behavior in the Social Environment" courses on the concepts of personality development across the life span, what is the contemporary student to make of Zastrow's recent assertion:

"Behavior therapists have devoted little attention to developing a behavioral model of personality" (Zastrow 2003:385).

In reality, considerable work has been accomplished in this regard, extending back over many decades (e.g., Dollard and Miller 1950; Lundin 1974). In Lundin's words: "Since the publication of the first edition of this book in 1969, the amount of experimental data to support a behavioral approach to personality has increased at an almost staggering rate" (Lundin 1974:1). This has encompassed both theoretical (e.g., Lundin 1987) and applied investigations (e.g., Nelson-Gray and Farmer 1999; Waltz and Linehan

1999; Zinbarg and Revelle 1989). While decrying the theory that human beings possess some inner nature labeled a "personality" that causes us to act in certain ways, behaviorists look instead for the psychosocial and environmental influences that cause us to behave in ways that we have labeled as reflective of an underlying personality.

Another tactic is to paint the behavioral perspective as extremist in its claims regarding efficacy, as in:

"Some advocates of behavior therapy, however, have hailed it as the only answer to the behavioral problems of society" (Mehr 1986:75).

Again, I would be most interested if anyone could provide a quotation from a behavioral writer making such a claim. I myself, an unabashed advocate of the behavioral social work perspective, at most have claimed that this conceptual model, research methods, and interventions have much to offer our field in terms of the resolution of interpersonal and societal problems. And I have on more than one occasion in print stated that the behavioral approach is the practice model that presently enjoys the strongest amount of empirical support to be found in the plethora of practice frameworks currently available to social workers. I believe that these are legitimate positions to take. But qualified statements using words like "much" and "best" are not akin to extremist positions invoking words such as "all" and "only," which all too often have characterized how behavioral social work has been portrayed in our professional literature.

On the positive side, it is undeniable that the behavioral perspective is slowly making inroads in mainstream social work education and practice. And as the movement toward evidence-based practice continues, the behavioral perspective will be legitimately advanced, to the extent that its practices are well supported by credible scientific research—as will other, non-behavioral models and interventions whose efficacy and effectiveness become well established. And this is as it should be.

References

Anderson, R. E. and I. Carter. 1978. *Human Behavior in the Social Environment: A Social Systems Approach.* 2d ed. New York: Aldine.

Baer, D. M., M. M. Wolf, and T. R. Risley. 1968. Some current dimensions of applied behavior analysis. *Journal of Applied Behavior Analysis* 1:91–97.

Barker, R. L., ed. 1999. *The Social Work Dictionary.* 4th ed. Washington, D.C.: NASW Press.

Brieland, D., L. B. Costin, and C. R. Atherton. 1975. *Contemporary Social Work*. New York: McGraw-Hill.

Chance, P. 1998. *First Course in Applied Behavior Analysis*. Pacific Grove, Calif.: Brooks/Cole.

Dollard, J. and N. E. Miller. 1950. *Personality and Psychotherapy*. New York: McGraw-Hill.

Ferguson, E. A. 1975. *Social Work: An Introduction*. 3d ed. Philadelphia: Lippincott.

Frederico, R. C. 1973. *The Social Welfare Institution: An Introduction*. Lexington, Mass: D. C. Heath.

———. 1980. *The Social Welfare Institution: An Introduction*. 3d ed. Lexington, Mass.: D. C. Heath.

Garvin, C. D. 1981. *Contemporary Group Work*. Englewood Cliffs, N.J.: Prentice-Hall.

Gilbert, N., H. Miller, and H. Specht. 1980. *An Introduction to Social Work Practice*. Englewood Cliffs, N.J.: Prentice-Hall.

Iwata, B. A., S. Kahng, S., M. D. Wallace, and J. S. Lindberg. 2000. The Functional Analysis Model of Behavioral Assessment. In J. Austin and J. E. Carr, eds., *Handbook of Applied Behavior Analysis*, 61–89. Reno: Context Press.

Johnson, L. C. 1983. *Social Work Practice: A Generalist Approach*. Newton, Mass.: Allyn and Bacon.

Logan, F. A. and A. R. Wagner. 1965. *Reward and Punishment*. Boston: Allyn and Bacon.

Lundin, R. W. 1974. Personality: *A Behavioral Analysis*. 2d ed. New York: Macmillan.

———. 1987. The Interbehavioral Approach to Psychopathology. In D. H. Reben and D. J. Delprato, eds., *New Ideas in Therapy*, 37–51. New York: Greenwood Press.

Mehr, J. 1986. *Human Services: Concepts and Intervention Strategies*. Newton, Mass.: Allyn and Bacon.

Nelson-Gray, R. O. and R. F. Farmer. 1999. Behavioral assessment of personality disorders. *Behaviour Research and Therapy* 37:347–368.

Payne, M. 1997. *Modern Social Work Theory*. 2d ed. Chicago: Lyceum.

Piccard, B. J. 1988. *Introduction to Social Work: A Primer*. 4th ed. Chicago: Dorsey.

Shriver, J. M. 2001. *Human Behavior and the Social Environment*. 3d ed. Needham Heights, Mass.: Allyn and Bacon.

Skinner, B. F. 1953. *Science and Human Behavior*. New York: Macmillan.

———. 1974. *About Behaviorism*. New York: Knopf.

———. 1989. The origins of cognitive thought. *American Psychologist* 44:13–18.

Suppes, M. A. and C. C. Wells. 1991. *The Social Work Experience: An Introduction to the Profession*. New York: McGraw-Hill.

Thyer, B. A. 1983. Behavior Modification and Social Work Practice. In M. Hersen, P. Miller, and R. Eisler, eds., *Progress in Behavior Modification*, 173–226. New York: Plenum.

———. 1987. Contingency analysis: Toward a unified theory for social work practice. *Social Work* 32:150–157.

———. 1991. Behavioral social work: It is not what you think. *Arete* 16 (2): 1–9.

———. 1998. Promoting Research on Community Practice: Using Single System Research Designs. In R. H. MacNair, ed., *Research Strategies for Community Practice*, 47–61. Binghamton, N.Y.: Haworth.

———. 2001a. *Single System Designs*. In R. M. Grinnell, ed., *Social Work Research and Evaluation*, 455–480. 6th ed. Itasca, Ill.: Peacock.

———. 2001b. Single System Designs. In B. A. Thyer, ed., *Handbook of Social Work Research Methods*, 239–255. Thousand Oaks, Calif.: Sage.

———, ed. 1999. *The Philosophical Legacy of Behaviorism*. Dordrecht, The Netherlands: Kluwer.

Thyer, B. A. and J. S. Wodarski. 1990. Social learning theory: Towards a comprehensive conceptual framework for social work education. *Social Service Review* 64:144–152.

Waltz, J. and M. M. Linehan. 1999. Functional Analysis of Borderline Personality Disorder Behavioral Criterion Patterns: Links to Treatment. In J. Derksen and C. Maffei, eds., *Treatment of Personality Disorders*, 183–206. New York: Plenum.

Whittaker, J. K. 1974. *Social Treatment*. Hawthorne, N.Y.: Aldine.

Zastrow, C. H. 2003. *The Practice of Social Work*. 7th ed. Pacific Grove, Calif.: Brooks/Cole.

Zinbarg, R. and W. Revelle. 1989. Personality and conditioning: A test of four models. *Journal of Personality and Social Psychology* 57:301–314.

PART V

QUESTIONING PSYCHIATRIC MEDICATIONS

Chapter 19
Clinical Psychopharmacology Trials: "Gold Standard" or Fool's Gold?

David Cohen

For the past half century, physicians in the West have been prescribing psychotropic drugs to hundreds of millions of people, to alter dozens of emotional and behavioral states. Psychotropic drugs are substances that affect thinking, feeling, and behaving by acting directly on the central nervous system. About eighty-five physician-prescribed psychotropic drugs, often termed "psychiatric medications," are usually classified into five major groups: "antidepressants," "antipsychotics," "tranquilizers" (including anxiolytics and sleeping pills), "stimulants," and "mood stabilizers" (essentially anticonvulsants and lithium). Since the late 1980s—with the advent of Prozac and the consecration of biological psychiatry as the reigning school of thought in mental health—members of all helping professions, leaders of science, opinion, and politics, the media, the military, the justice and the educational systems—all have enthusiastically endorsed the use of these mind- and mood-altering drugs as the first resort when any person faces almost any crisis or distress. Prescribing psychotropics to more people, to younger people, and for longer periods has increased to the point that it has approached utter banality and spread into every nook and cranny of culture and commerce (Critser 2002). Prescribing also generates massive revenues for the pharmaceutical industry, the planet's most profitable business. In 2002 world sales of the single class of antidepressants exceeded $17 billion, and three psychotropics were among the ten top-grossing drugs in global sales (IMS Health 2003).

Despite this phenomenal marketing success, mental health outcomes over the last fifty years, for any condition routinely treated with psychotropic drugs, have not improved. Available data suggest unchanged or increased incidence and prevalence of depression and bipolar disorder, unchanged or worsened outcomes in schizophrenia and bipolar disorder, and so on (Healy 1999; Hegarty et al. 1994; Moncrieff 2001; Research Triangle Institute 2002; Whitaker 2002). Recently, the efficacy of the selective serotonin reuptake inhibitors (SSRIs), one of the most celebrated classes of psychiatric medications since the start of psychopharmacology, was shown to be largely duplicated by placebos. Kirsch and colleagues (2002) obtained the data from all forty-seven randomized, placebo-controlled efficacy clinical trials funded and submitted to the Food and Drug Administration (FDA) by the makers of the six most widely prescribed antidepressants. These "Phase III" trials on several thousand patients in sites around the country were submitted to the FDA to obtain approval for these drugs. The studies can be considered the world's best-controlled studies on antidepressant efficacy. At the same time, they can be assumed to employ every available "legitimate" maneuver to paint the drugs in a positive light. Kirsch and colleagues found that 80% of the response of medicated patients was duplicated by patients on placebo. On the chief outcome measure, the Hamilton Depression Rating Scale, the mean difference between drug and placebo groups was 1.8 points on the 50-point or 62-point versions. Although Kirsch and colleagues found it to be statistically significant when tested over this large data set, this minute advantage for medications has no real clinical significance. Similar findings (nearly four fifths of placebo duplication of antidepressant effects) were reported by Khan, Warner, and Brown (2000) using a less robust FDA database, and by the Agency for Health Care Research and Policy (AHCRP 1999b) reviewing 315 published trials of SSRIs and older antidepressants.

These findings reveal the gap that exists between the strength of scientific evidence about psychotropic medications and the weight of therapeutic practices presumably resting on that evidence. Such a "disconnect" is not unique to biological/pharmaceutical psychiatry. Fancher (1995) argues compellingly that all major schools of thought in mental health this century (biological, psychoanalytic, behavioral, and cognitive) overstated their scientific claims to justify their political and cultural outlook. With hindsight, but also in the eyes of some contemporaneous critics, these paradigms appear contradictory and particularistic, their tests self-serving and riddled with defects. At least, that is how some mental health authorities today dismiss Freudian psychoanalytic "dogma" or the "deinstitutionalization fiasco" of social psychiatry.

The regularity of mental health system-wide "delusions" suggests that the history of mental health care can be viewed as the history of mistakes about mental health care. For ordinary people seeking help, mistakes may mean iatrogenic harm—physical and mental damage caused by approved professionals following approved schools of thought and applying approved therapies (Diekelmann and Kavanagh 2002; Morgan 1983; Illich 1976). This capacity of healers to harm is the reason for the helping professions' best-known ethical precept: "First, do no harm."

When helping professions also claim to be "evidence-based" professions, the duty of practitioners begins with critically assessing the scientific claims supporting their practices (Gambrill 2002). Critical assessment means submitting claims to ethical, logical, historical, and other scrutiny. I sometimes ask students why they think that medications are currently favored as "magic solutions." Insightfully, they cite reasons such as citizens' preferences for "quick fixes" and beliefs in "biochemical imbalances" as causes of distress. Invariably, students (as do practitioners) also state that medications have been "proven" effective, or more effective than other interventions, in controlled trials. This belief—that comparative trials of psychotropic drugs using valid methods have established the effectiveness of these agents to treat people with mental disorders—expresses confidence in one of the crucial scientific claims of biological psychiatry. It is the sort of claim that requires critical examination by those who study, manage, monitor, prescribe, or long to prescribe psychotropic drugs.

The Randomized Controlled Trial in Theory and in Practice

Begg (1996) expresses the widely held positive view of randomized controlled trials (RCTs) in clinical research: "The randomized clinical trial is the gold standard methodology for evaluating treatment interventions . . . the embodiment of the scientific method applied to the clinic" (1307). In an RCT, eligible participants are randomly assigned to either a treatment group or an alternate group. Random assignment is the simplest and strongest way to minimize key threats to the internal validity of a study. RCTs are seen to produce the highest-grade evidence to determine how much observed change in participants is the result of a treatment rather than of confounding variables. In drug treatment studies, a refinement of the RCT involves double-blind placebo-control, wherein neither researchers nor participants are supposed to know who is receiving an active drug and who an inert placebo. This precaution helps to counter the impact of researcher and participant expectations with regard to the outcome.

Not everyone agrees that RCTs provide the indispensable basis to make valid causal inferences about treatment effects. Jacobs and Cohen (1999) argue that the RCT as used in psychopharmacology tells us too little about the key effects of psychotropic drugs in complex biopsychosocial beings. The RCT only evaluates the impact (typically over fewer than six weeks) of a drug on a predetermined, narrow set of target symptoms. This excludes understanding the full range of psychological effects brought about by substances acting directly on the central nervous system. Jacobs and Cohen recommend strategies to aim for such broader understanding, none of which fit into the traditional RCT design. Perhaps the RCT design has been overevaluated and some single-group designs carelessly stigmatized. Benson and Hartz (2000) compared recent RCTs and "observational" studies of nineteen different treatments, but found estimates of treatment effects from the lesser-grade studies to be neither larger nor qualitatively different than those from RCTs.

Healy (2002) believes that the RCT has changed how psychiatrists look at patients, because the RCT:

> favors fitting patients into categorical disease entities. . . . A response of these seemingly discrete entities to a drug then creates an illusion of specificity. . . . [Efforts to reduce inter-rater variability] lead to the use of operational criteria and rating scales, which in turn add to the illusion that the disorder being treated is responding in the same way that cultures of bacilli on a Petri dish shrink when exposed to an antibiotic.
> (284)

Another form of critique of the RCT focuses on how its actual implementation has strayed widely from the ideal RCT design. Systematic reviews of some of the hundreds of thousands of reports of RCTs of all medications published since the 1950s, such as the Cochrane reviews,

> are beginning to make painfully clear that, in most of these studies, inadequate steps were taken to control biases, many questions and outcomes of interest to patients were ignored, and insufficient numbers of participants were studied to yield reliable estimates of treatment effects.
> (Chalmers 1998:1167)

If the main dictates of RCTs have been consistently violated, results of most clinical trials are quite uncertain. Does Chalmers's conclusion apply to trials of psychotropic drugs? Examples from two classes of psychotropics provide an answer. In a review of 2,000 RCTs of schizophrenia drug treatments published between 1948 and 1997, Thornley and Adams (1998) find that a mere 1% can be judged methodologically sound. Two thirds of the studies "barely, if at all" described random allocation of patients to treatments and what happened to those who did not complete the study (a major source of bias). Only 6% evaluated the social functioning of the patients. Only 3%

enrolled enough subjects to detect meaningful differences (e.g., a 20% difference in improvement) between treatment arms. Thornley and Adams conclude that schizophrenia trials "may well have consistently overestimated the effects" (1183) of drug treatments.

The AHCRP (1999a) reaches similar conclusions about trials of treatments for attention-deficit/hyperactivity disorder (ADHD). Among hundreds of treatment studies, researchers applied strict criteria (based on standard expectations of the elements of an RCT) to select 92 RCTs of (mostly stimulant) treatments. The authors found that "most studies did not clearly describe clinically important information such as the primary outcomes of interest. . . . The small sample size of most studies limited their power to detect meaningful clinically important differences among the interventions" (3). In addition, 97% of the studies did not describe how subjects were randomized, 95% did not describe how investigators were kept blind about the patients' treatment status, and 87% gave no details on dropouts and reasons for dropouts in each treatment group. Schachter et al. (2001) also conducted a meta-analysis of 62 carefully selected RCTs of short-acting methylphenidate (Ritalin) as a treatment for ADHD. Their observations practically match those of the AHCRP, with the additional detail that fewer than half of the trials lasted more than ten days. (This extremely short duration would, for example, prevent observers from making valid judgments about longer-term effects of stimulants, drugs that are often prescribed for months and years.)

Why would the simple design of the RCT be applied so dismally in practice? The answer involves at least considering how ideology, economics, and trial methodology interact in our unique drug culture.

Threats to the Integrity of Clinical Trials

Ideology and Allegiance

Most people who conduct clinical drug trials in psychopharmacology are heavily invested in a view of medications as the essential form of mental health care. Most of these individuals are physicians and probably maintain a clinical practice in which they prescribe medications. Some of their patients become enrolled as research subjects, and some of their research subjects continue as their patients. As licensed medical practitioners of psychiatry, some have in all likelihood wielded their state-sanctioned power (or the implicit threat of it) to coerce nonconsenting individuals to take medications. Finally, some consume psychotropic medications and prescribe them to relatives. If these researchers questioned the effectiveness of medications, they would not be in a position to secure the qualifications and especially the funding to conduct a clinical trial (given that most funding now originates from drug companies). It is therefore quasi-axiomatic that those who conduct clinical trials of psychotropics, especially large multimillion-dollar trials, are strong pro-medication advocates who have built their careers on promoting and expanding the influence of biological psychiatry (Breggin 1991).

As will be discussed, only recently have mainstream experts such as editors of medical journals found it impossible to ignore the influence of ideology on the conduct of research (e.g., Smith 2003). Given the poor quality of available studies on stimulants, the AHCRP (1999a) recognizes the need for "different groups of stakeholders" (besides academia, the government, or pharmaceutical companies) to exercise vigilance about research activities (see, for example, the Alliance for Human Research Protection, www.ahrp.org) and even to become involved in funding such activities. Chalmers (1998) also stresses that "consumers" must monitor the clinical trial enterprise. Leading conventional psychopharmacologists Quitkin and colleagues (2000) make a more specific and revealing suggestion. Replying to critics of antidepressant trials, they suggest looking to improve future RCTs rather than debating the merits and flaws of the existing body of RCTs. They acknowledge that the "most convincing results" would come from "multisite studies done by mutually monitored collaborating investigators, some with allegiance to psychotherapy and others to pharmacotherapy" (335). Their statement confirms that researcher "allegiance" probably constitutes a major source of bias in drug treatment research.

Science and Money

The esteem in which the RCT design is held has two weighty consequences. First, before the FDA will consider approving a new drug for marketing (or an old drug for new indications or for children), the manufacturer must present the results of at least one (previously two) RCT of the drug on humans, showing superiority to placebo and/or equivalence to an existing medication (the FDA does not require comparison with nonmedical interventions). Second, a large RCT (many patients, multisite) with favorable results is "a major step in creating the 'blockbuster drug' that all companies want" (Smith 2003:1203). The "atypical" antipsychotic Zyprexa (olanzapine) is one such blockbuster. Only six years after it was approved by the FDA for the treatment of psychosis in adults, it had earned in 2002 more than $13 billion for its manufacturer (a 2,600% return on an initial investment of $500 million) and was the most profitable psychotropic pharmaceutical product in the world (IMS Health 2003).

Obviously, the marketing department of a pharmaceutical company is more interested in a clinical trial than anyone else, including researchers. The potential for astronomical returns if a psychotropic drug manages to pass the RCT hurdle makes sensible observers, such as the editors of the thirteen foremost medical journals of the English-speaking world (Davidoff et al. 2001), conclude that the RCT as a major scientific invention of the last fifty years is being "debased" for commercial reasons. Commercial incentives mean that sponsors become inappropriately involved in the design and execution of studies, that investigators and journals are caught in conflicts of interest, and that results of trials are published to emphasize positive findings and distort or conceal negative findings (Quick 2001).

INAPPROPRIATE INVOLVEMENT OF RESEARCH SPONSORS
In the United States, the industry funds 80% of clinical trials and the National Institutes of Health (NIH) funds the rest. It has been observed in a systematic review that studies financed by industry always found outcomes favorable to the sponsoring company (Bekelman, Li, and Gross 2003). Until a decade ago, 80% of industry money for clinical trials went to academic medical centers. Today about 30% does so (Bodenheimer 2000). The rest has gone to a new worldwide industry of about one thousand contract research organizations (CROs). In the past, clinical trials were conducted on patients at academic centers, directed by faculty members who received grants from the industry or the NIH. Researchers were responsible for designing the trials, selecting patients, collecting data, interpreting and reporting findings. Most investigators had no major financial ties to the sponsor or the drug being tested, though many earned part of their salary from the sponsor's grants.

However, the number, size, and complexity of clinical trials have grown. The pharmaceutical industry wants faster results and access to more patients of different ages and both genders, and changes in federal regulations have eased this trend (see review by Sharav 2003, who cites, for example, that the number of children enrolled in clinical trials in the United States swelled from 16,000 in 1997 to 45,000 in 2001). As a result, ethical and administrative requirements of academically administered studies became too cumbersome for the industry. CROs started taking over the clinical trial enterprise because CROs "can do the job for less money and with fewer hassles than academic investigators" (Davidoff et al. 2001:1233). CROs need not be concerned with testing new hypotheses, nor with satisfying requirements of institutional review boards. Their aim is to produce a clinical trial in order to secure FDA approval of a drug. CROs can recruit patients by using full-page ads in newspapers and by paying physicians in private practice rewards to recruit their own patients. The study results are analyzed and interpreted, and articles for publication are often ghostwritten, by drug company employees. CROs generated more than $7 billion in revenues in 2001 from their contracts with the drug industry (Relman and Angell 2002).

CONFLICTS OF INTEREST

In an effort to regain this share of grant revenues lost to CROs, even the most prestigious universities openly court drug companies and offer them easier access to their faculty, centers, facilities, and patients in university-affiliated centers and teaching hospitals, as well as accord them a large share of control over all phases of clinical trials. As a result, the industry now has full control of clinical trials conducted privately and most of the control of trials conducted in academia. In parallel, the industry depends on numerous academic authorities to promote its products among practitioners and to entice them to form mutually satisfying relationships with the industry. "Almost every academic expert who might be qualified to direct a clinical trial now is paid by one or more firms as a consultant or speaker" (Relman and Angell 2002:33). Experts of high stature can earn $10,000 for making one appearance on behalf of a drug company, and many receive annual payments in the six figures (Torrey 2002).

Trying to guarantee the integrity of a clinical trial while knowing that one will enrich oneself if the trial produces favorable results for the drug being tested fits the classic definition of an inappropriate conflict of interest (Margolis 1979). Since Krimsky et al.'s 1998 study of the extent of authors' financial interests in areas related to their research (and the lack of disclosure of these interests by journals publishing the research), medical editors have regularly announced or strengthened various disclosure rules, but observers agree that such measures are ineffectual. When the editor of the *New England Journal of Medicine* sought a research psychiatrist with no ties to the drug industry to evaluate an antidepressant trial, she could find none (Angell 2000).

Journals themselves, in their dual search for credibility and profitability, are caught in similar conflicts, as the following editorials from the *British Medical Journal* explain:

> Journals are caught between publishing the most relevant and valid research and being used as vehicles for drug company propaganda. (Abbasi and Smith 2003:1155).
>
> Reprints [of journal articles] can be a very powerful selling tool, as they are perceived as being independent and authoritative. (Burton and Rowell 2003:1206).
>
> Companies purchase large numbers of reprints of these trials. Sometimes they will spend more than $1M on reprints of a single study, and

the profit margin to the publisher is huge. These reprints are then used to market the drugs to doctors, and the journal's name on the reprint is a vital part of that sell. . . . In one sense, all journals are bought—or at least cleverly used—by the pharmaceutical industry. The industry dominates health care (Smith 2003:1204–1205).

The American Psychiatric Association, publisher of such journals as *American Journal of Psychiatry* and *Psychiatric Services,* in which about one third of the pages are drug ads, receives about one third of its annual income from drug manufacturers ("Trustees Vote" 1997). In sum, it is difficult today to be confident that the testing of new drugs is unbiased, or that the credibility of scientific journals that publish test results is untainted.

PUBLICATION BIAS

Publication bias is today considered to be a ubiquitous problem in all medical research (Easterbrook et al. 1991). It refers to the tendency whereby only favorable trials are published or reported, or multiple versions of a study under different authorship are published (well documented in the case of the newer antipsychotic Risperdal by Huston and Moher 1996). Publication bias interacts with conflicts of interest. For example, researchers in drug company–sponsored trials may sign secrecy agreements, agreeing not to divulge negative results of drug trials without the sponsor's permission (documented in the case of antidepressant drug trials for children by Harris 2003). At best, these practices are likely to introduce systematic bias in literature reviews and meta-analyses. At worst, they are "a form of scientific misconduct that can lead . . . to inappropriate treatment decisions" (Chalmers 1990:1405).

Recently, Melander and colleagues (2003) cleverly documented the extent of publication bias in industry-sponsored psychopharmacology trials: they compared all 42 RCTs of five SSRIs submitted to the Swedish drug regulatory authority as a basis for marketing approval (and therefore unavailable to clinicians and researchers) with the reports from these RCTs actually published in the literature (between 1983 and 1999). They found clear evidence of multiple publication (21 RCTs contributed at least two publications each), selective publication (studies showing significant drug effects were published as stand-alone publications more often than studies with nonsignificant effects), as well as, and more important, selective reporting (all RCTs submitted to the regulatory agency presented results from two or more alternative analyses, but 76% of resulting publications reported results only from the more favorable analysis). Melander et al. conclude:

For anyone who relies on published data alone to choose a specific drug, our results should be a cause for concern. Without access to all studies (positive as well as negative, published as well as unpublished) and without access to alternative analyses . . . , any attempt to recommend a specific drug is likely to be based on biased evidence. (1174)

This is a most disturbing warning, as almost everyone—except the most dedicated and resourceful researcher—can rely only on published studies! More to the point, most medical practitioners do not even rely on any published studies but are content to glean their information about drugs from digests and summaries of these studies, usually provided by industry representatives.

The Unique Methodology of Clinical Trials

By nature the clinical trial is an artificial procedure. Researchers seek to control as many variables as possible in order to isolate the relationship between an intervention and an outcome. Ethical requirements prohibit deceiving or tricking subjects, who must agree to not knowing whether they are given the latest medication or a placebo. Such compliant, trusting, and motivated people are atypical. Most trials also have age limitations. Pregnant women cannot participate. There are anecdotal indications that being a clinical trial subject constitutes steady employment for some people. Subjects must be fluent in the language of the study, which rules out the poorly educated and most recent immigrants. Few trials exceed eight weeks' duration although in real life medications are taken for months and years. For these and many other reasons, one may question whether results of clinical trials have relevance to actual clinical practice (Seeman 2001).

Other procedures used in clinical trials result from choices made by the investigators/analysts/authors/sponsors. The choices have a single aim: to increase the likelihood that an investigational drug does better, on some measure, than the placebo or other drug it is compared to. These methodological choices threaten the internal validity of a study because they obscure the hypothesized relationship between a drug treatment and selected outcome measures. Nonetheless, these questionable methods are used again and again (and thereby legitimated) because regulatory agencies such as the FDA, medical/scientific journal reviewers and editors, and other experts allow them to be used.

Psychopharmacology trials may be particularly prone to using these questionable methods because pathophysiology for any primary mental disorder is unknown and because psychotropic drugs have multiple and nonspecific effects regardless of the problem being treated (for discussion, see Jacobs and Cohen 1999). These inescapable facts mean that all measures—diagnosis, clinical change, improvement or worsening, unwanted effects, duration of treatment—are necessarily subjective and thus highly variable from study to study and even within the same study. To illustrate only the heterogeneity of outcome measures, the 2,000 RCTs of schizophrenia treatment reviewed by Thornley and Adams (1998) employed more than 640 different rating scales; the 14 extended-treatment studies of ADHD reviewed by Schachar et al. (2002) used 26 different scales.

The following brief annotation provides a *partial* listing of some of these controversial design choices. Readers are referred to Cohen (2002), Safer (2002), Moncrieff (2001), Healy (1999), Seeman (2001), and others for several more examples and discussion of their uses in clinical trials of psychiatric drugs.

1. *Using "placebo-washout" periods.* During screening, those with a history of nonresponse to the study drug or similar drugs are routinely excluded. All prospective subjects are then given placebos for one to two weeks. Those whose condition improves during this time are excluded from the pool of subjects before random assignment. This is done to reduce the number of placebo responders (which can reach 20% in this phase of the trial [Antonuccio et al. 1999]). With these subjects gone, the actual drug response rate is likely to be overestimated.

2. *Not using active placebos as comparators.* In the few studies where subjects are given "active placebos" (substances such as atropine, without significant psychotropic effects but that induce noticeable physical changes), the rate of placebo response tends to be greater than when "inert" placebos are given. This is probably because the sensation of unusual physical effects might trick subjects into believing that they are taking "real" medication. Inert placebos are therefore the rule.

3. *Not testing for penetration of the blind.* Inert placebos, such as yeast or sugar, do not produce the more characteristic physical and mental effects of psychotropic drugs. Therefore, both patients and clinicians easily see through the blind (Antonuccio et al. 1999). Knowing the extent of this violation of the RCT procedure therefore seems crucial. Yet regulators do not require testing for this, and investigators very rarely do so (e.g., by simply asking patients and clinicians to guess which substance they received and estimating how much this differs from a chance guess).

4. *Reporting clinician-rated rather than patient-rated outcome measures.* Although the outcomes of both types of measures converge, patient raters tend to report significantly less improvement than clinician raters. Yet clinician-rated scales (such as the Hamilton Depression Rating Scale) are emphasized, though patient-reported scales (such as the Beck Depression Inventory) are also used.

5. *Using high doses of comparator drugs.* When testing a new drug, investigators compare it to high doses of an existing drug (the comparator). This

increases the dose-dependent adverse effects from the comparator. The new drug appears safer. This strategy was used, for example, in clinical trials of atypical antipsychotics (Geddes et al. 2000).

6. *Altering the dose schedule of the comparator.* A variation of point 5 is to use rapid and substantial dose increases of the comparator early in the trial, or an unusual dosing schedule, both of which bring on increased rates of adverse effects. For example, comparing the new paroxetine with amitriptyline (comparator), Christiansen et al. (1996) gave patients the comparator twice daily (versus once daily for the new drug), thus increasing their daytime sleepiness. The new drug appears less sedative.

7. *Using self-serving side-effect scales.* Some investigators use short, truncated "side-effect" scales (usually unpublished) and may omit frequent and even expected effects from the scales. For example, Preskorn (1997) omits unwanted sexual effects from a twenty-three-item SSRI side-effect table, even though these effects have been reported in as high as 50% of patients.

8. *Eliciting unwanted effects solely from spontaneous patient comments.* Waiting for patients to report an effect, or asking about effects in open-ended questions—rather than systematically eliciting reports on specific effects from patients—can result in rates of unpleasant effects usually appearing to be substantially low (Safer 2002).

9. *Classifying unwanted/adverse effects arbitrarily.* To keep prevalence of certain worrisome effects under 2%, these are "chopped up" into smaller bits. Thus a manic syndrome that might affect a full 7 percent of a sample might be reported as "agitation, 2%," "abnormal thinking, 2%," "stimulation, 1%," and "elevated mood, 2%." Only by carefully analyzing these figures might a researcher (e.g., Breggin 2003) reconstruct a meaningful approximation of the drug's unwanted effects observed during the trial

10. *Failing to mention positive response to placebo even if that response exceeds all expectations.* In a placebo-controlled trial by Trivedi et al. (2001) comparing the effects of two antidepressants with each other to reduce anxiety symptoms, the abstract (most often the only part of the article read at all) "ignores" the fact that the placebo equaled both antidepressants and had far fewer adverse effects.

11. *Prescribing other psychoactive medications to trial subjects.* In 25 of 47 SSRI trials in the FDA database, subjects were also prescribed a sedative or tranquilizing drug, presumably to counteract the SSRI's stimulant effects such as insomnia and agitation (Kirsch et al. 2002). This concurrent use is prohibited by the FDA, as it obviously blurs the outcomes, such as hiding certain unwanted effects. Nonetheless, it seems regularly practiced and even reported to the FDA. Published accounts of such trials do not report this simultaneous prescription.

12. *Not reporting patients' post-treatment ratings.* After patients have ceased taking a psychotropic drug, their retrospective evaluation may differ greatly

from their evaluation while they were on the drug (e.g., Healy and Farquhar 1998). The FDA expects post-treatment ratings to be collected, but they are very rarely reported except by researchers who are specifically investigating the issue.

13. *Using post hoc comparisons.* Researchers collect data on multiple endpoints and periods, then sift through these data until they identify some positive findings, which are the ones reported in the published report. These endpoints are not specified in the primary hypothesis tested by the trial, and the reported length of the trial is not necessarily how long it actually lasted.

14. *Using "last observation carried forward" (LOCF) versus "observed cases" (OC).* When a substantial number of subjects drop out before the end of the trial (e.g., more than 70% of subjects in clinical trials of some atypical antipsychotics; see Whitaker 2002), researchers typically "carry forward" the results of the dropouts' last evaluation visit as if they had not dropped out. In "observed cases" analyses, the results are reported only for those subjects who are still participating at the end of the trial period. In the FDA antidepressant database of SSRI trials, Kirsch et al. (2002) found that LOCF analyses showed greater drug–placebo differences than did OC analyses. Because degrees of freedom are necessarily larger in LOCF analyses, it is more likely that a mean difference will be statistically significant.

Ideology, Economics, and Bias in Action: The Clinical Trials of Prozac for Children

The way in which ideology, commercial incentives, and questionable methodological choices can come together is illustrated by the clinical trials leading to the FDA approval of Prozac for children in 2003. Soon after the drug's approval for adults in 1988, the prescription of Prozac quickly spread to children, as an "off-label" indication since Prozac was not approved for pediatric use. Older antidepressants, the tricyclics (TCAs), had long been prescribed to children despite lack of FDA approval and recognized lack of efficacy. For example, Birmaher and colleagues (1996) published a ten-year review confirming that not one of about fifteen studies showed that TCAs improved outcomes more than placebos or cognitive interventions in depressed children, and one of two studies showed some improvement with an SSRI. Nonetheless, that same year SSRI prescriptions to children had soared to 580,000 from 343,000 two years earlier (Huffington 1997).

In 1997 Emslie and colleagues published a study in *Archives of General Psychiatry,* the most prestigious psychiatric journal in the world. Emslie and his six coauthors were listed as affiliated with academic centers. The study was funded by a grant from the National Institute of Mental Health. Emslie et al. screened 583 patients by telephone and interviewed 256. They excluded 150 and enrolled 106 in the placebo-washout period. Ten improved on placebo and were dropped. The remaining 96 were randomized to fluoxetine ($N = 48$) or placebo ($N = 48$). An inert placebo was used. No testing for the integrity of the blind was reported. The duration of the trial was eight weeks, and 37.5% of the children dropped out before the end. Of the completers, 74% responded to fluoxetine and 58% to placebo. Complete symptom remission occurred in only 15 of the fluoxetine-treated children versus 11 of children on placebo. Five different outcome measures were used, including one self-rated, but the improvement was seen on only one clinician-rated measure. Emslie et al. reported that "side effects, as a reason for discontinuation, were minimal, affecting only 4 patients who were receiving fluoxetine" (1033). However, these 4 children (8.3%) developed "manic symptoms" and "a severe rash." No other information on side effects was provided. In sum, despite several methodological problems that would tend to bias results in favor of fluoxetine, the drug outperformed placebo only slightly and on only *one* of the five measures, and induced mania in a disturbingly high proportion of children. Nevertheless, Emslie et al. concluded that "fluoxetine treatment was superior to placebo in relieving depressive symptoms" (1031), and the study was widely cited in the media and in later articles as a justification for the continued prescription of SSRIs to children despite the lack of FDA approval.

Emslie and colleagues (2002) published a second placebo-controlled RCT of Prozac for depression in children and adolescents. This time, the group of eight investigators included only two academic researchers, but both were also listed as "paid consultants for Eli Lilly and Company for this study." The remaining six authors were listed as employees of Eli Lilly and Company, which also funded the study. Emslie et al. screened 420 patients, excluded 201 (only 8 for placebo response this time), and randomized the remaining 219 to fluoxetine ($N = 109$) or placebo ($N = 110$). Again, an inert placebo was used, and the integrity of the blind was not tested. (Testing would have been much more important in this case: all investigators were paid consultants or direct employees of the drug's manufacturer and could not be expected to remain objective). The trial lasted nine weeks; 28% of the children dropped out before the end. Numerous reasons are now given for dropouts, but the reasons are categorized under terms that are difficult to assess for true distinction: "adverse event," "lack of efficacy," "patient decision," "physician decision" (unclear if "physician" was "researcher"), and so on. A similar pattern of results as in the previous study was observed. The authors acknowledged frankly in the abstract that "more fluoxetine- (65%) than placebo-treated (53%) patients met the prospectively defined response criteria . . . but this difference was not significant" (1205). However, other post

hoc criteria for improvement were produced that were statistically significant. Seven rating scales were used. The one patient-rated scale showed no
significant difference in improvement. Adverse events in the placebo group
seemed more frequent, but children who might have received stimulants,
antidepressants, or neuroleptics more than a week before the start of this
study were not excluded. Indeed, some children on placebo were discontinued for adverse events such as rash, severe hair loss, and dizziness—all of
which indicate drug or drug-withdrawal effects. This possibility (i.e., that
children in the placebo group were still under the effects of previous drugs)
was not discussed in the report. Only one patient in the fluoxetine group
was discontinued for "manic reaction," a term that overlaps with the ambiguous "agitation" and "hyperkinesia" of two other discontinued youths.
The authors/sponsor conclude: Prozac "appears to be well-tolerated and
effective for acute treatment of [major depressive disorder] in child and adolescent outpatients. Fluoxetine is the only antidepressant that has demonstrated efficacy in two placebo-controlled, randomized clinical trials of pediatric depression" (1205). In January 2003 the FDA announced the formal
approval of Prozac for pediatric use to treat depression.

Duncan, Miller, and Sparks (2004), whose own critical analysis of the
Emslie trials largely inspired the above, ask what difference FDA approval
makes if antidepressant prescription in youths is already established and growing. Their answer:

FDA blessing allows the unfettered marketing of these drugs to those
who may be concerned about their impact in a child's life. [It] quells
real fears of parents, clinicians, and clients. . . . This "fact" [of efficacy]
is now repeated in future research articles, mental health websites, promotional materials, workshops, classrooms, popular and professional
books, ads, and more—media saturation reinforces truth.
(189)

The sad irony is that this reassurance is likely to be temporary—only a
phase in the complex life cycle of medications (Cohen et al. 2001). Indeed,
six months after its approval of Prozac for pediatric use, the FDA officially
warned the public that no one under eighteen years of age should be prescribed Paxil (paroxetine), another SRRI, for depression ("U.S. Issues Warning," 2003). The agency was responding to a ban of this drug for minors
issued the previous week in the United Kingdom. There, regulators "redis-
covered" findings in their possession that in clinical trials of Paxil for the
treatment of depression in children and adolescents, three times more suicide
ideation and self-injurious behaviors were observed among drug-treated than
placebo-treated youths. In June 2004, acting on information that the drug's
manufacturer, GlaxoSmithKline, had actively concealed these unfavorable

findings [as had the makers of other antidepressants with other negative findings from their own drug trials (e.g., Vedantam, 2004)], the Attorney General of the State of New York filed a lawsuit against that company for engaging in consumer fraud (Harris, 2004).

Discussion

Limitations of the Critique

The foregoing critical review does not consider possible positive impact of industry sponsorship on the quality of health care interventions. It implies a causal link between industry sponsorship and poor quality of studies, although the evidence so far only suggests an association. For example, a recent meta-analysis of studies analyzing research in numerous treatment areas sponsored by industry does confirm that "systematic bias favors products which are made by the company funding the study" (Lexchin et al. 2003:1167). However, industry-funded studies do not seem to be of poorer quality than those funded by government sources. The authors believe that the systematic bias is best explained by the selection of an inappropriate comparator to the drug being studied and by publication bias. Of course, the choice of an inappropriate comparator can itself be considered an indicator of poor quality. Finally, the complex role of the FDA—as regulator of an industry on which it partially depends financially and as de facto arbiter of legitimate standards in drug research—is not addressed (see, for example, Fried 1998; Sharav 2003).

Conclusion

The use of comparative psychopharmacology trials is considered a major scientific foundation of biological psychiatry, the reigning school of thought in mental health today. Results from such trials are also widely considered to provide substantial support for this school of thought. Biological psychiatry promotes the view that people's emotional problems actually are symptoms of diseases of the body (brain), usually resulting from genetic abnormalities. The number of social, economic, spiritual, psychological, and educational problems considered to be diseases or treated as diseases has, needless to say, increased dramatically over the last quarter century—a trend commonly referred to as medicalization (Conrad and Schneider 1992).

The unchecked medicalization of distress does not merely have positive implications: it also carries its share of intellectual mystification, iatrogenic injury, and sociocultural oppression. Fully a quarter of the population is implied to be genetically deficient because affected with "diagnosable" or "treatable disorders" (Surgeon General 1999). In one of history's strangest social experiments, up to 15% of children in North America are given stimulants to make them conform to schools' expectations (McCubbin and Cohen 1999). The consequences of long-term psychotropic drug use are manifold and detrimental for individual brains and possibly for the species' evolutionary capacity (Nesse and Berridge 1997). In human bodies, families, and groups, drugs only seem to blunt people's responses to stress—they neither banish stress or the sources of stress nor enhance people's capacity to cope with stress (Mirowsky and Ross 2003).

It goes without saying that people suffer, and undoubtedly there are prudent ways for ordinary people whose lives have been disrupted by the slings and arrows of fate to benefit from psychotropic drugs. However, this chapter has suggested that the all too commonly accepted view that medication can solve these problems needs urgently to be reevaluated. In particular, it hardly seems possible to use the findings of psychopharmacology-controlled trials to enlighten us on potential benefits and psychological effects of drugs and to inform us on their potential risks. Randomized controlled trials of psychotropic drugs present a sharply limited view of the effects of drugs. These trials are contrived, through numerous dubious methodological strategies, and through outright concealment of negative data from publication, to present tested drugs in a falsely positive light and to dismiss the formidable power of placebos. These strategies are obvious to many observers, but are countered by the inertia of the entire "drug-testing system" and the huge gains—financial and professional—to be made by numerous participants if the inertia persists.

Reevaluating the value of medicating all manner of troubled and troubling behavior is especially important for nonmedical helping professionals, such as social workers, psychologists, and counselors, who constitute the most numerous professional groups in mental health settings. While such practitioners do not (yet) prescribe medications, their contacts with medicated individuals are more prolonged than patients' contacts with the physicians who write prescriptions. More important, nonmedical professionals play a pivotal role in ensuring clients' "medication compliance" (Cohen 2003), thus helping greatly to perpetuate the influence and consequences of biological psychiatry. Given this weighty role, it is time for more helping professionals to become seriously engaged in the critical assessment of the psychotropic drug treatment enterprise.

References

Abbasi, K. and R. Smith. 2003. No more free lunches (Editorial). *British Medical Journal* 326:1155–1156.

Agency for Health Care Research and Policy (AHCRP). 1999a. *Treatment of Attention-Deficit/Hyperactivity Disorder.* Summary, Evidence Report/Technology Assessment: Number 11, Publication No. 99-E017. Retrieved May 12, 2001, from http://www.ahrq.gov/clinic/epcsums/adhdsum.htm.

———. 1999b. *Treatment of Depression: Newer Pharmacotherapies.* Evidence Report/ Technology Assessment: Number 7, Publication No. 99-E014. Retrieved June 2002 from http://hstat.nlm.nih.gov/hq/Hquest/db/5/screen/DocTitle/odas/1/ s/46631.

Angell, M. 2000. Is academic medicine for sale? *New England Journal of Medicine* 342:1516–1518.

Antonuccio, D. O., W. G. Danton, G. Y. DeNelsky, R. P. Greenberg, and J. S. Gordon. 1999. Raising questions about antidepressants. *Psychotherapy and Psychosomatics* 68:3–14.

Begg, C. B. 1996. The role of meta-analysis in monitoring clinical trials. *Statistical Medicine* 15:1299–1306.

Bekelman, J. E., Y. Li, and C. P. Gross. 2003. Scope and impact of financial conflicts of interest in biomedical research: A systematic review. *Journal of the American Medical Association* 289:454–465.

Benson, K. and A. J. Hartz. 2000. A comparison of observational studies and randomized, controlled trials. *New England Journal of Medicine* 342:1878–1886.

Birmaher, B., N. D. Ryan, D. E. Williamson, D. A. Brent, and J. Kaufman. 1996. Childhood and adolescent depression: A review of the past 10 years. Part 2. *Journal of the American Academy of Child and Adolescent Psychiatry* 35:1575–1583.

Bodenheimer, T. 2000. Uneasy alliance: Clinical investigators and the pharmaceutical industry. *New England Journal of Medicine* 342:1539–1544.

Breggin, P. R. 1991. *Toxic Psychiatry.* New York: St. Martin's.

———. 2003. Fluvoxamine as a cause of stimulation, mania, and aggression: A critical analysis of the FDA-approved label. *Ethical Human Sciences and Services* 4:211–227.

Burton, B. and A. Rowell. 2003. Unhealthy spin. *British Medical Journal* 326:1205–1207.

Chalmers, I. 1990. Underreporting research is scientific misconduct. *Journal of the American Medical Association* 263:1405–1408.

———. 1998. Unbiased, relevant, and reliable assessments in health care. *British Medical Journal* 317:1167–1168.

Christiansen, P. E., K. Behnke, C. H. Black, J. K. Ohstrom, H. Bork-Rasmunssen, and J. Nilson. 1996. Paroxetine and amitriptyline in the treatment of depression in general practice. *Acta Psychiatrica Scandinavica* 93:158–163.

Cohen, D. 2002. Research on the drug treatment of schizophrenia: A critical appraisal and implications for social work education. *Journal of Social Work Education* 38:217–237.

———. 2003. The psychiatric medication history: Context, purpose, and method. *Social Work in Mental Health* 1 (4): 5–28.

Cohen, D., M. McCubbin, J. Collin, and G. Perodeau. 2001. Medications as social phenomena. *Health* 5:441–469.

Conrad, P. and J. Schneider. 1992. *Deviance and Medicalization: From Badness to Sickness*. 2d ed. Philadelphia: Temple University Press.

Critser, G. 2002. One nation, under pills—They can have our meds when they pry them out of our cold, dead hands. *Los Angeles Times*, M-6. December 15.

Davidoff, F., C. D. DeAngelis, J. M. Drazen, M. G. Nicholls, J. Hoey et al. 2001. Sponsorship, authorship and accountability. *Journal of the American Medical Association* 286:1232–1234.

Diekelmann, N. L. and K. H. Kavanagh, eds. 2002. *First, Do No Harm: Power, Oppression, and Violence in Healthcare*. Madison: University of Wisconsin Press.

Duncan, B. L., S. D. Miller, and J. A. Sparks. 2004. *The Heroic Client*. 2d ed. San Francisco: Jossey-Bass.

Easterbrook, P. J., J. A. Berlin, R. Gopalan, and D. R. Mathews. 1991. Publication bias in clinical research. *Lancet* 337:867–872.

Emslie, G. J., J. H. Heiligenstein, K. D. Wagner, S. L. Hood, D. E. Ernest, E. Brown, M. Nilsson, and J. G. Jacobson. 2002. Fluoxetine for acute treatment of depression in children and adolescents: A placebo-controlled, randomized clinical trial. *Journal of the American Academy of Child and Adolescent Psychiatry* 41:1205–1215.

Emslie, G. J., J. Rush, W. A. Weinberg, R. A. Kowatch, C. W. Hughes, T. Carmody, and J. Rintelmann. 1997. A double-blind, randomized, placebo-controlled trial of fluoxetine in children and adolescents with depression. *Archives of General Psychiatry* 54:1031–1037.

Fancher, R. 1995. *Cultures of Healing*. San Francisco: Freeman.

Fried, S. 1998. *Bitter Pills: Inside the Hazardous World of Legal Drugs*. New York: Bantam.

Gambrill, E. 2002. Encouraging transparency. *Journal of Social Work Education* 38:211–214.

Geddes, J., N. Freemantle, P. Harrison, and P. Bebbington. 2000. Atypical antipsychotics in the treatment of schizophrenia: Systematic overview and meta-regression analysis. *British Medical Journal* 32:1371–1376.

Harris, G. 2003. Debate resumes on the safety of depression's wonder drugs. *New York Times*, 1. August 7.

———. 2004. Spitzer sues a drug maker, saying it hid negative data. New York Times, June 3, pp. A1, C4.

Healy, D. 1999. *The Antidepressant Era*. Cambridge, Mass.: Harvard University Press.

———. 2002. *The Creation of Psychopharmacology*. Cambridge, Mass.: Harvard University Press.

Healy, D. and G. Farquhar. 1998. Immediate effects of droperidol. *Human Psychopharmacology* 13:113–120.

Hegarty, J. D., R. J. Baldessarini, M. Tohen, C. Waternaux, and G. Oepen. 1994. One hundred years of schizophrenia: A meta-analysis of the outcome literature. *American Journal of Psychiatry* 151:1409–1416.

Huffington, A. 1997. Exit Joe Camel, enter Joe Prozac. Retrieved June 23, 2003, from http://www.ariannaonline.com/columns/files/071797.html.

Huston, P. and D. Moher. 1996. Redundancy, disaggregation, and the integrity of medical research. *Lancet* 347:1024–1026.

Illich, I. 1976. *Medical Nemesis: The Expropriation of Health.* New York: Pantheon Books.

IMS Health. 2003. 2002 world pharma sales growth: Slower, but still healthy. Retrieved June 16, 2003 from http://www.ims-global.com/insight/news_story/0302/news_story_030228.htm. February 28.

Jacobs, D. and D. Cohen. 1999. What is really known about alterations produced by psychiatric drugs? *International Journal of Risk and Safety in Medicine* 12:37–47.

Khan, A., H. A. Warner, and W. A. Brown. 2000. Symptom reduction and suicide risk in patients treated with placebo in antidepressant clinical trials: An analysis of the Food and Drug Administration database. *Archives of General Psychiatry* 57:311–317.

Kirsch, I., T. J. Moore, A. Scoboria, and S. N. Nicholls. 2002. The emperor's new drugs: An analysis of antidepressant medication data submitted to the U.S. Food and Drug Administration. *Prevention and Treatment* 5, article 23. Available at http://journals.apa.org/prevention/volume5/toc-jul15-02.htm.

Krimsky, S., L. S. Rothenberg, P. Stott, and G. Kyle. 1998. Scientific journals and their authors' financial interests: A pilot study. *Psychotherapy and Psychosomatics* 67:194–201.

Lexchin, J., L. A. Bero, B. Djulbegovic, and O. Clark. 2003. Pharmaceutical industry sponsorship and research outcome and quality: Systematic review. *British Medical Journal* 326:1167–1176.

Margolis, J. 1979. Conflict of Interests and Conflicting Interests. In T. L. Beauchamp and N. E. Bowie, eds., *Ethical Theory and Business,* 361–372. Englewood Cliffs, N.J.: Prentice-Hall.

McCubbin, M. and D. Cohen. 1999. Empirical, ethical, and political perspectives on the use of methylphenidate. *Ethical Human Sciences and Services* 1:81–101.

Melander, H., J. Ahlqvist-Rastad, G. Meijer, and B. Beermann. 2003. Evidence based medicine—Selective reporting from studies sponsored by pharmaceutical industry: Review of studies in new drug applications. *British Medical Journal* 326:1171–1175.

Mirowsky, J. and C. E. Ross. 2003. *Social Causes of Psychological Distress.* 2d ed. Chicago: Aldine de Gruyter.

Moncrieff, J. 2001. Are antidepressants overrated? A review of methodological problems in antidepressant trials. *Journal of Nervous and Mental Disease* 189:288–295.

Morgan, R. F., ed. 1983. *The Iatrogenics Handbook: A Critical Look at Research and Practice in the Helping Professions.* Toronto: IPI Publishing.

Nesse, R. M. and K. C. Berridge. 1997. Psychoactive drug use in evolutionary perspective. *Science* 278 (5335): 63–66.

Preskorn, S. H. 1997. Clinically relevant pharmacology of selective serotonin reuptake inhibitors. *Clinical Pharmacokinetics* 32 (Suppl. 1): 1–21.

Quick, J. 2001. Maintaining the integrity of the clinical evidence base. *Bulletin of the World Health Organization* 79:1093.

Quitkin, F. M., J. G. Rabkin, J. Gerald, J. M. Davis, and D. F. Klein. 2000. Validity of clinical trials of antidepressants. *American Journal of Psychiatry* 157:327–337.

Relman, A. S. and M. Angell. 2002. America's other drug problem: How the drug industry distorts medicine and politics. *New Republic,* 27–41. December 16.

Research Triangle Institute. 2002. *Screening for Depression: Systematic Evidence Review.* Rockville, Md.: Agency for Health Care Quality and Research.

Safer, D. J. 2002. Design and reporting modifications in industry-sponsored comparative psychopharmacology trials. *Journal of Nervous and Mental Disease* 190:583–592.

Schachar, R., A. R. Jadad, M. Gauld, M. Boyle, L. Booker, A. Snider, M. Kim, and C. Cunningham. 2002. Attention-deficit hyperactivity disorder: Critical appraisal of extended treatment studies. *Canadian Journal of Psychiatry* 47:337–348.

Schachter, H. M., B. Pham, J. King, S. Langford, and D. Moher. 2001. How efficacious and safe is short-acting methylphenidate for the treatment of attention-deficit disorder in children and adolescents? A meta-analysis. *Canadian Medical Association Journal* 165:1475–1488.

Seeman, M. V. 2001. Clinical trials in psychiatry: Do results apply to practice? *Canadian Journal of Psychiatry* 46:352–355.

Sharav, V. H. 2003. Children in clinical research: A conflict of moral values. *American Journal of Bioethics,* InFocus, 1–81. Retrieved May 7, 2003, from http://bioethics.net.

Smith, R. 2003. Medical journals and pharmaceutical companies: Uneasy bedfellows. *British Medical Journal* 326:1202–1205.

Surgeon General. *Mental Health: A Report from the Surgeon General.* 1999. Available at http://www.surgeongeneral.gov/library/mentalhealth/home.html.

Thornley, B. and C. Adams. 1998. Content and quality of 2000 controlled trials in schizophrenia over 50 years. *British Medical Journal* 317:1181–1184.

Torrey, E. F. 2002. The going rate on shrinks. *American Prospect.* Retrieved July 15 from http://www.prospect.org/print-friendly/print/V13/13/torrey-e.html.

Trivedi, M. H., A. J. Rush, T. J. Carmody, R. M. Donahue, C. Bolden-Watson, T. L. Houser, and A. Metz. 2001. Do bupropion and sertraline differ in their effects on anxiety in depressed patients? *Journal of Clinical Psychiatry* 62:776–781.

Trustees vote to maintain freeze on member dues. 1997. *Psychiatric News,* 4. October 3.

U.S. issues warning on child use of Paxil. 2003. Associated Press news release. Retrieved June 29 from http://www.nytimes.com.

Vedantam, S. 2004. Antidepressant makers withhold data on children. *Washington Post,* A01. January 29.

Whitaker, R. 2002. *Mad in America.* Cambridge, Mass.: Perseus.

Chapter 20

Treatment of Newly Diagnosed Psychosis Without Antipsychotic Drugs: The Soteria Project

John R. Bola, Loren R. Mosher, and David Cohen

Introduction

The revolution in the treatment of schizophrenia wrought by antipsychotic medications brings with it issues of special concern to the profession of social work. The "person-in-environment" perspective, traditionally espoused by social work, has been largely superseded by a biological model of mental illness (Andreasen 1984). Interventions derived from the biomedical model are primarily pharmacologic in nature and are intended to treat an underlying putative "biochemical imbalance." Interventions based on clients' wishes and strengths, with attention to environmental supports—the traditional social work approach—are considered less important than medication compliance.

Historically, the role of social work in the field of mental health has been subordinate to that of psychiatry. The hierarchical nature of this relationship was established long ago: "The psychiatrist retains full responsibility for the activities of the psychiatric social worker and yet delegates to her . . . part of the casework" (AAPSW 1934:7). Bertha Reynolds (1934) makes a humorous analogy of the relationship as that of a young female social worker having an affair with an older professional man. Social workers have been viewed as "handmaidens of the psychiatrist" (Ivker and Sze 1987:139), their role built upon the presupposition of psychiatric authority.

Domination of the field by psychopharmacology and a biomedical perspective has further reified the hierarchical relationship between psychiatry and social work (Cohen 2002). This is particularly true for the treatment of schizophrenia, for which clinical practice guidelines consistently recommend antipsychotic medications as the primary treatment (American Psychiatric Association 1997; Canadian Psychiatric Association 1998), with psychosocial treatments relegated to a supportive or ancillary role. However, a small but important (and frequently overlooked) body of evidence indicates that a "primary" psychosocial intervention combined with limited medication use may result in better long-term outcomes in newly diagnosed psychoses (e.g., brief reactive psychosis, schizophreniform disorder, schizophrenia, psychotic disorder NOS).

A seminal study providing evidence that contradicts current practice guidelines is the Soteria project. Conducted from 1971 until 1983, Soteria was designed as a two-year follow-up of persons newly diagnosed with "schizophrenia" who were treated on psychiatric wards of general hospitals (usual care) or in a specially designed environment in a house in the community (Soteria care). Soteria differed from usual care in four important ways: it was not offered in a hospital, it eschewed the medical model of "schizophrenia," it was staffed by nonprofessionals, and antipsychotic drugs were normally withheld for at least the initial six weeks. The primary research question was, "Do Soteria-treated individuals have outcomes that are as good or better than individuals receiving traditional hospital care?"

Background

The Soteria project owed much of its clinical methodology to phenomenological/existential thinkers (Mosher 1999) and incorporated ideas from a number of diverse and radical perspectives: moral treatment in American psychiatry (Bockhoven 1963), Sullivan's (1962) interpersonal theory and his special milieu for persons with schizophrenia at Shepard-Pratt Hospital in the 1920s, labeling theory (Scheff 1966), intensive individual Jungian therapy (Perry 1974), Freudian psychoanalysis (Fromm-Reichman 1948; Searles 1965), the notion that growth was possible from psychosis (Menninger 1959; Laing 1967), as well as earlier community-based treatment such as Fairweather Lodges (Fairweather et al. 1969). Soteria combined insights from these approaches that aspired to improve client outcomes, minimize antipsychotic drug dependence, and contribute to individuals' integration of their psychotic experience into the continuity of their lives.

On the basis of his clinical experience, it seemed evident (to Mosher) that dealing with psychotic persons in an open community residential (nonmedical) setting required some contextual constraints: do no harm; treat everyone, and expect to be treated, with dignity and respect; and guarantee asylum (quiet, safety, support, protection, containment, interpersonal validation), food, and shelter. Perhaps most important, the atmosphere must also be imbued with the notion that recovery from psychosis is to be expected—hence a major reason for using nonprofessionals as primary staff. This contrasts diametrically with the medical view of schizophrenia as having a life-long deteriorating course requiring medication indefinitely, in spite of medication-induced functional and structural brain changes (Cohen 1997; Harrison 1999).

Within this social environment, interpersonal phenomenology could be practiced. Its most basic tenet is "being with"—an attentive but nonintrusive, gradual way of getting oneself "into the other person's shoes" such that shared meaningfulness of the subjective aspects of the psychotic experience can be established within a confiding relationship. Residents were encouraged to acknowledge precipitating events and emotions, to discuss and eventually place them into perspective within the continuity of their life and social network. This requires unconditional acceptance of the psychotic experience as valid and understandable within the historical context of each person's life—even when it cannot be consensually validated. Soteria also paid thoughtful attention to the caregiver's experience (not unlike the psychoanalytic concept of transference). Compared to traditional phenomenology, this represented a new emphasis on the interpersonal, aligning the method with modern concepts of systems and the requirements of interactive fields without sacrificing its basic open-minded, immediate, accepting, nonjudgmental, noncategorizing, "what you see is what you get" core principles. The method aimed to keep in focus the whole "being" ("*Dasein*") in relation to others.

Methods

The Soteria project collected data in two cohorts that used nearly identical study designs: a quasi-experimental treatment comparison using consecutive admission, space-available treatment assignment (1971–1976, N = 79) and an experimental design with random assignment (1976–1979, N = 100). Data were collected for two years after admission. Subjects were recruited from two county hospital psychiatric emergency facilities in the San Francisco Bay area. All persons with an initial diagnosis of schizophrenia by three independent clinicians (*DSM-II* [APA 1968]), judged in need of hospitalization, with no more than one previous hospitalization, between the ages of fifteen and thirty-two, and not currently married were asked to participate. These criteria were intended to produce a relatively-poor-prognosis group by excluding older and married individuals (Strauss and Carpenter 1978). Requirements for participation were explained, and informed consent was obtained from patients and their families, if available.

Emergency room staff psychiatrists made initial diagnoses. Subsequent assessments were made by an independent research team trained to maintain good inter-rater reliability (kappa of 0.80 or better). This team conducted diagnostic assessments before entry into Soteria or hospitalization, and again at 72 hours. The 72-hour reassessment was intended to exclude drug-induced psychoses. If both reassessments confirmed a *DSM-II* diagnosis of schizophrenia, and if at least four of the seven cardinal symptoms of schizophrenia were observed, patients were included.

Subjects

In all, 179 subjects met inclusion criteria (82 were assigned to experimental and 97 to control facilities). The mean age was 21.7 years (SD = 3.4, range = 15–32); 64% were men and 36% were women. Data on 171 subjects indicated that 80% were European American, 9% African American, and 11% from other ethnic groups. The average subject was in the lower portion of Hollingshead's (1957) third social class.

Treatment

As mentioned, treatment involved a small, homelike, intensive, interpersonally focused therapeutic milieu with a nonprofessional staff that related with clients "in ways that do not result in the invalidation of the experience of madness" (Mosher and Menn 1978a:716). Experimental treatment was provided at the original Soteria House and at a replication facility, Emanon. In these experimental facilities, 76% of subjects received no antipsychotic medications during the first 45 days of treatment. However, there were explicit criteria for short-term medication use. After six weeks, medication decisions were made at a treatment conference that included the client, facility staff, and the consulting psychiatrist. A manual describing Soteria treatment in greater detail has been published in German (Mosher et al. 1994; English version available at cost from Mosher).

Control facilities were well-staffed inpatient psychiatric services organized around a medical model and geared toward "rapid evaluation and placement in other parts of the county's treatment network" (Mosher and Menn 1978a:717). Virtually all control subjects (94%) were treated continuously with in-hospital courses of antipsychotic medication (average 700 mg chlorpromazine equivalents per day), and nearly all were prescribed post-discharge medications. In the present study, this is regarded as "usual treatment." In both groups, post-discharge treatment was uncontrolled.

372 • *Questioning Psychiatric Medications*

Measures

Eight outcome measures (representing the five domains of rehospitalization, psychopathology, independent living, working, and social functioning) were used: (1) readmission to 24-hour care (yes or no), (2) number of readmissions, (3) days in readmission(s), (4) a global psychopathology scale (Mosher, Pollin, and Stabenau 1971; 1–7, 1 = normal, 7 = most extremely ill), (5) a global improvement in psychopathology scale (Mosher, Pollin, and Stabenau 1971; coded 1–7, 1 = much improvement, 4 = no change, 7 = much worse), (6) living independently or with peers (yes or no), (7) working or attending school (none, part-time, full-time), and (8) the social functioning subscale of the Brief Follow-up Rating scale (BFR) (Sokis 1970). Each measure was collected at 45 days, one year, and two years after admission. Readmission measures were summed across the two-year follow-up period. A composite outcome scale was created in standard deviation units from these eight outcome measures (see Bola and Mosher 2003 for details).

All *DSM-II* schizophrenia subjects with symptoms for six months were rediagnosed with schizophrenia (71 of 169, or 42%), since the addition of the six-month symptom criterion was the primary change from *DSM-II* to *DSM-III* (APA 1983) and has been carried forward into *DSM-IV* (APA 1994). Subjects with symptoms for less than six months were rediagnosed with schizophreniform disorder (98 of 169, or 58%).

Analysis

Separate but related data analyses address three questions: (1) Do Soteria-treated subjects have comparable or better six-week psychopathology outcomes? (2) Do Soteria subjects have two-year outcomes that are, on the whole and separately by schizophrenia and schizophreniform subgroups, comparable to or better than those treated in the hospital with medications? and (3) Is it possible to retrospectively identify, using baseline client characteristics, those individuals initially treated in Soteria facilities who do not require antipsychotic medication during the follow-up period (a "drug-free responder" subgroup)? Additional detail on these analyses has previously been reported (Mosher and Menn 1978b; Mosher, Vallone, and Menn 1995; Bola and Mosher 2002a, 2003).

The first analysis conducts two-group t-tests comparing psychopathology change in Soteria and hospital groups as well as the six-week mean scores across groups.

Second, multivariate analyses compare outcomes for all subjects completing the two-year follow-up period for Soteria versus hospital groups (completers $N = 129$), and are repeated separately for schizophrenia and schizophreniform groups (Bola and Mosher 2003). Because of between-group differences on three important variables related to outcome, these variables were employed as statistical controls. They were as follows: a higher proportion of insidious-onset subjects in the Soteria group at two-year follow-up (but not at admission); a shorter post-discharge follow-up period for the Soteria-treated subjects because of longer index stays; and a higher rate of attrition in the hospital-treated group.

Third, a retrospective subgroup analysis was conducted in an effort to identify baseline characteristics of individuals treated in Soteria who did not receive antipsychotic medications during the follow-up period. The existence of a "drug-free responder" subgroup in schizophrenia-spectrum psychosis has long been suggested (Buckley 1982; Liberman, Falloon, and Wallace 1984; Marder et al. 1979; Warner 1985; Vaillant 1962). If this subgroup can be identified, these individuals might be spared exposure to drug toxicities. In this sample, 43% of Soteria-treated individuals used no antipsychotic medications during the follow-up period (from the end of the period in which medications were experimentally controlled at day 45 until the two-year follow-up) and had quite good outcomes. We also estimate whether using this model to assign treatment would likely result in improved outcomes (Bola and Mosher 2002a; 2002b, 2003).

Results

Six-Week Outcomes

Because measures of community adjustment were not relevant at six weeks after admission (since many subjects were still inpatients) only changes on the seven-point global psychopathology scale were reported (Mosher and Menn 1978b; Mosher, Vallone, and Menn 1995). Results for both groups were similar: significant and comparable improvement (experimental admission mean = 5.2, control = 5.3 (N = 154), six-weeks experimental mean = 3.5, control = 3.5. Change over six weeks, significant in both groups, p = .01).

This meant that Soteria-treated subjects, only 24% of whom received any neuroleptic drug treatment during the initial six weeks (16% of the Soteria subjects received "substantial" drug treatment, i.e., > seven days), improved as much and as quickly as the neuroleptic-treated controls. Hence, the Soteria environment proved to be as powerful as antipsychotic drugs for acute symptom reduction.

Two-Year Outcomes

Overall, Soteria subjects had nearly one half of a standard deviation better composite outcomes ($+0.47$ SD, $t = 2.20$, $p = .03$) than individuals receiving usual treatment. They also had significantly better outcomes on two of eight outcome measures: a 20% higher probability of being in the lowest two psychopathology categories ($+0.20$, $z = -2.17$, $p = .03$) and nearly one fewer readmissions (-0.98, $z = -2.37$, $p = .02$) than hospital-treated subjects (see table 20.1, column 2).

SCHIZOPHRENIA SUBJECTS
Completing individuals with schizophrenia ($N = 49$; table 1, column 3) had eight tenths of a standard deviation better composite outcomes when treated at Soteria ($+0.81$ SD, $t = 2.42$, $p = .02$). These individuals had significantly better outcomes on four of the eight outcome measures: a 44% higher likelihood of having no or nearly no psychopathology ($+0.44$, $z = -2.11$, $p = .04$), a 48% higher likelihood of having excellent or very good improvement in psychopathology ($+0.48$, $z = -2.67$, $p = .01$), and a 40% higher probability of working ($+0.40$, $z = 2.30$, $p = .02$; which includes a 29% higher likelihood of full-time work).

SCHIZOPHRENIFORM SUBJECTS
Completing individuals diagnosed with schizophreniform disorder ($N = 80$; table 20.1, column 4) had one third of a standard deviation better outcomes when treated at Soteria (not statistically significant) on the composite outcome scale ($+0.34$ SD, $t = 1.22$, n.s.). These individuals had significantly better outcomes on one of the eight outcome measures, with an average of one and one quarter fewer readmissions to 24-hour care (-1.24 readmissions, $z = -2.36$, $p = .02$) than similar individuals receiving hospital treatment.

Drug-free Responders

Using baseline prognostic and diagnostic information, a retrospective model was developed to identify the 43% of Soteria-treated individuals who were not receiving antipsychotic medications during the follow-up period, when medication decisions were made by clinical judgment (the "drug-free responders"). At the two-year follow-up, this group was performing well above the overall group mean (at $+.82$ of a standard deviation) on the composite outcome scale. The model to identify this group incorporates three baseline variables (age, the Goldstein Adolescent Social Competence [GASC; Rodnick and Goldstein 1974] scale score, and number of schizo-

Table 20.1

Effects of Soteria Treatment on Two-Year Outcomes for Completing Subjects: All Subjects ($N = 129$), Subjects with Schizophrenia ($N = 49$), and Subjects with Schizophreniform Disorder ($N = 80$)

Outcome Variable	All Subjects[a]	Schizophrenia[b]	Schizophreniform[b]
Composite Outcome[c]	.47	.81**	.34
Global Psychopathology[d]	.20**	.44**	.07
Improvement in Psychopathology[e]	.17*	.48**	.06
Readmission[f]	−.16*	−.21*	−.20*
Number of Readmissions[g]	−.98	−.92	−1.24**
Days in Readmission[h]	−23.60	−3.83	−41.5
Living Alone or with Peers[i]	.17	.28	.12
Working[j]			
Any	.08	.40**	−.09
Full-time	.07	.29**	−.08
Social Functioning[k]	.08	.59	−.22

*$p < .10$.
**$p < .05$.

[a]Estimates control for schizophrenia/schizophreniform disorder, number of days between initial discharge and two-year follow-up, and likelihood of nonattrition.

[b]Estimates control for number of days between initial discharge and two-year follow-up, and likelihood of nonattrition.

[c]Difference in the composite outcome for Soteria subjects (in standard deviation units).

[d]Difference in the probability of membership in the two best categories (having little or no psychopathology).

[e]Difference in the probability of membership in the two best categories (having excellent or very good improvement in psychopathology).

[f]Difference in the probability of the event occurring (readmission).

[g]Difference in the expected value (number of readmissions).

[h]Difference in the expected value (days in readmission).

[i]Difference in the probability of the event occurring (living alone or with peers).

[j]Difference in the probability of the events occurring (any work, full-time work).

[k]Difference in social functioning (on a three-point scale).

phrenia symptoms) and correctly identifies this subgroup 79% of the time (95% confidence interval, 65%–90%). The influences of the individual variables on the probability of being a "drug-free responder" (the marginal effects) are: age 0.05 ($p = .03$), GASC 0.03 ($p = .06$), and number of schizophrenia symptoms −0.14 ($p = .06$). This means that each one-unit increase in these variables will change the probability of being a "drug-free responder" by the indicated amount. Predicted drug-free responders had moderately better outcomes (effect size range: 0.38 to 0.64 of a SD) when treated in Soteria (Bola and Mosher 2002a).

Discussion

These striking findings from Soteria, if replicated and widely implemented, would produce a major shift in thinking about and treating "schizophrenia." Key findings are:

1. For all subjects, Soteria had a medium-effect size advantage ($+0.47$ SD).
2. For schizophrenia subjects, Soteria had a large-effect size advantage ($+0.81$ SD).
3. The 43% of subjects who went through the Soteria program and did not receive antipsychotic drugs during follow-up had strikingly good outcomes ($+0.82$ SD).
4. "Drug-free responders" are preliminarily identified with nearly 80% accuracy and appear to have moderately better outcomes when treated in Soteria.

These findings demonstrate a striking advantage for early-episode subjects treated at Soteria. As with all psychosocial treatment "black boxes," the importance of Soteria components varied across individuals. Milieu characteristics, relationships, staff qualities, attitudes, and social processes all appear to have been important.

Treatment Components

MILIEU CHARACTERISTICS
Differences between treatment milieus were assessed with the Moos Ward Atmosphere Scale (WAS) and the Community Oriented Program Environment Scale (COPES) (Moos 1974). Significant differences were found on eight of ten subscales, notably favoring Soteria on involvement, support, and spontaneity (Wendt et al. 1983).

RELATIONSHIPS AND STAFF CHARACTERISTICS
An important therapeutic ingredient in Soteria emerged from the quality of relationships that formed, partly because of the additional treatment time allowed. Staff in both interventions were characterized as psychologically strong, independent, mature, warm, and empathic. However, Soteria staff was significantly more intuitive, introverted, flexible, and tolerant of altered states of consciousness (Hirschfeld et al. 1977). Soteria interactions are best described in the treatment manual (Mosher et al. 1994). Since Soteria staff worked 24- or 48-hour shifts, they had the opportunity to "be with" residents for more extended time periods than did psychiatric facility staff. Thus they were able to experience, firsthand, complete "disordered" biological/

psychological cycles. Although standard staffing at Soteria was two staff to six clients, over time it became clear that within this overall ratio, having about 50% disorganized and 50% relatively "organized" persons (including recovering clients and volunteers) worked best. In this context it is important to remember that the average length of stay at Soteria was four to five months. For the most part, at least partial recovery took place in about six to eight weeks. Hence, many clients were able to act as "helpers" during the latter part of their stays, a role that may also have facilitated their recovery.

SOCIAL PROCESSES

Viewed from an ethnographic/anthropologic perspective, basic social processes differed greatly between Soteria and the hospital psychiatric wards. Five areas of contrast are as follows: at Soteria (1) approaches to social control avoided codified rules, regulations, and policies; (2) basic administrative time was kept to a minimum to allow a great deal of undifferentiated interpersonal contact time; (3) limited intrusion by unknown outsiders into the settings supported the critical contextual constraints; (4) social order worked out on an emergent face-to-face basis resulted in rapid problem resolution; (5) a commitment to a nonmedical model that did not require symptom suppression allowed the development of validating relationships. In contrast, the hospital wards were characterized as utilizing a "dispatching process" that involved patching, medical screening, piecing together a story, labeling and sorting, and distributing patients to various other facilities and programs (Wilson 1983). Over time, an understanding of therapeutic components of Soteria has emerged from a variety of overlapping perspectives that are presented in table 20.2 (adapted from Mosher and Burti 1994).

Other Soteria-like Initiatives

To date, approximately fifteen residential treatment programs or crisis intervention programs inspired by the Soteria project have been established in Germany, Sweden, and Switzerland. Several more are in the planning stages, notably in the United Kingdom. Three early-episode psychosocial treatments have been compared to more-standard treatments. Soteria Berne, a twelve-room house accommodating six to eight patients and two staff founded in 1984 by Luc Ciompi in Switzerland (Ciompi et al. 1992) demonstrated comparable two-year outcomes with substantially less use of medications than hospital treatment. A recent two-year outcome of Finnish Need-Adapted psychosocial treatment with limited use of antipsychotic medications compared to similar psychosocial treatment with standard medication doses reported more-favorable results for the limited-medication-use

Table 20.2
Soteria: Critical Ingredients

1. Small, homelike quarters sleep no more than ten persons, including two staff (one man, one woman) on duty, twenty-four- to forty-eight-hour shifts to allow prolonged intensive 1:1 contact as needed
2. Staff convey positive expectations of recovery, validate the psychotic person's subjective experience of psychosis as real—even if not amenable to consensual validation.
3. Staff put themselves in the shoes of the other by "being with" the clients, use everyday concepts and language to reframe the experience of psychosis.
4. Personal power is preserved to maintain autonomy and prevent the development of unnecessary dependency.
5. Daily running of house is shared to the extent possible. "Usual" activities, shopping, cooking, cleaning, gardening, exercise, etc. are promoted.
6. Minimal role differentiation encourages flexibility of roles, relationships, and responses.
7. Minimal hierarchy mutes authority, encourages reciprocal relationships, and allows relatively structureless functioning—with meetings scheduled quickly to solve problems as they emerge.
8. Clients spend sufficient time in program for relationships to develop that allow precipitating events to be acknowledged, usually disavowed painful emotions to be experienced and expressed, and such emotions put into perspective by fitting them into the continuity of the person's life.
9. Clients are integrated into the local community to avoid prejudice, exclusion, and discrimination.
10. Post-discharge relationships are encouraged (with staff and peers) to allow easy return (if necessary) and foster development of peer-based problem solving and community-based social networks.

group, along with a 43% subgroup of experimental subjects not using antipsychotic medications (Lehtinen et al. 2000). The ongoing Swedish Parachute project has reported one-year results in which the psychosocial-treated group with limited medications had favorable outcomes that were comparable to the hospital-treated group (also treated with limited use of antipsychotic medications) (Cullberg et al. 2002). Thus, rigorously evaluated alternatives to the North American clinical practice of medicating all early episodes exist and have demonstrated more-favorable long-term outcomes.

Questioning the Clinical Practice Guidelines

In an enormously popular reanalysis of mostly first-episode schizophrenia spectrum studies comparing antipsychotic medications versus psychosocial and/or milieu treatment, Wyatt (1991) concluded: "Early intervention with neuroleptics in first-break schizophrenic patients increases the likelihood of an improved long-term course" (325). This conclusion has contributed to the medication requirement in clinical practice guidelines for early-episode schizophrenia and to enthusiasm for pharmaceutical industry-sponsored efforts to prevent psychosis through "early intervention" in the prepsychotic prodrome (Gosden 1999), often with atypical antipsychotic medications. However, most of the studies reviewed by Wyatt (1991) were of a pre-experimental (mirror-image) design that does not control many threats to internal validity (Carpenter 1997). In fact, a preponderance of the few available quasi-experimental or experimentally designed early-episode studies in which one group was initially not medicated (Schooler et al. 1967; Carpenter, McGlashan, and Strauss, 1977; Rappaport et al. 1978; Ciompi et al. 1992, 1993; Lehtinen et al. 2000; Bola and Mosher, 2003) show better long-term outcomes for the initially unmedicated subjects (exceptions are Wirt and Simon 1959; May et al. 1981). The more-favorable long-term outcomes from these studies suggest a more central role for psychosocial treatments combined with limited medication use in newly diagnosed psychotic disorders (see Bola 2002).

Application of Soteria Principles to Advancing Community-Based Care

Soteria-type facilities can provide a temporary artificial social network when a natural one is absent or dysfunctional. However, common sense tells us that immediate family and social network intervention at the crisis site is preferable, when possible, because it avoids medicalization (i.e., locating "the problem" inside one person by labeling, sorting, and disempowering him/her) of what is really a social system problem (Weick 1983). The special contextual conditions of Soteria-type programs can be created in a family home, a nonfamily residence, or a network meeting held nearly anywhere. Such care has been pioneered in Finland (Alanen et al. 1994) and is now also being studied in Sweden (Cullberg et al. 2002). As the impressive data from Scandinavian studies inform us, the preferable modus operandi is immediate response to a crisis site by a team dedicated to long-term involvement. Such programs typically withhold neuroleptics for at least two weeks, using benzodiazepines as necessary during this time. Antipsychotic medication is used only in about 50% of cases, but in very low doses and for as short a time as possible, resulting in better outcomes than when traditional doses are used in similar in-home crisis intervention clinical programs (Lehtinen et al. 2000).

Soteria's clinical methods are applicable across contexts once the necessary constraints described earlier have been established. The most relevant Soteria components incorporated into emerging Scandinavian system of care are:

1. *"Being with" and "doing with,"* as described earlier in this chapter.
2. *Contextualization.* Every person/family has a unique history that must be understood. "Being with" the family and individuals allows this to happen. Such understanding also promotes continuity of relationships and flexible responsivity by the team.
3. *Normalization.* All interventions should focus on the establishment or restoration of culturally sensitive, "normal" styles of person/family/network functioning. Working in family residences in the community facilitates this process and encourages a concrete problem-solving focus.
4. *Preservation of power.* The family unit must make, and take responsibility for, decisions. The aim of intervention teams must be partnerships based on equality. Because the team operates in communal territory, it must recognize that it will eventually disappear but the person/network will have to live with whatever changes are brought about by the intervention(s). The team's task is to help people and networks involved develop needed self-help and coping skills.

Conclusion

The Soteria project demonstrated that a community-based, non-drug residential psychosocial program for acutely psychotic individuals, staffed by nonprofessionals, can do as well or better than the best available hospital-based drug treatment program manned by psychiatric personnel. Owing to Soteria's comparable six-week outcomes without drugs and strikingly favorable two-year outcomes, in conjunction with comparable recent results in Europe, research efforts to replicate these findings might be expected. Yet, despite fifty years of widespread use of neuroleptic drugs and the recognition that the prognosis for medication-treated individuals with schizophrenia may be bleaker today than ever before (Hegarty et al. 1994), there have been no attempts to replicate Soteria's findings in the United States. In fact, current schizophrenia practice guidelines appear to preclude these replication efforts, out of ostensible concern for denying human subjects access to "proven" drug treatments. As can be seen from this report, however, a small but important body of research is developing that suggests that clinical practice guidelines for early-episode psychosis should be revisited, encouraging replication of these important findings. Should that be done and this type of intervention more widely adopted, considerable additional opportunities for leadership in shaping and adapting psychosocial interventions in psychosis would become available. This would allow social workers to take a more equal role in the provision of psychosocial treatment to individuals in early-epsiode psychotic disorders and might actually improve long-term outcomes of psychotic disorders.

References

Alanen, Y. O., B. Rosenbaum, E. Ugelstad, B. Armelius, K. Lehtinen, and R. Sjostrom. 1994. *Early Treatment of Schizophrenic Patients: Scandinavian Psychotherapeutic Approaches*. Oslo: Scandinavian University Press.

American Association of Psychiatric Social Workers (AAPSW). 1934. The psychiatric social worker from the standpoint of the American Psychiatric Association. *News-Letter of the American Association of Psychiatric Social Workers* 3 (5): 7.

American Psychiatric Association (APA). 1968. *Diagnostic and Statistical Manual of Mental Disorders (DSM-II)*. 2d ed. Washington, D.C.: APA.

―――. 1983. *Diagnostic and Statistical Manual of Mental Disorders (DSM-III)*. 3d ed. Washington, D.C.: APA.

―――. 1994. *Diagnostic and Statistical Manual of Mental Disorders (DSM-IV)*. 4th ed. Washington, D.C.: APA.

―――. 1997. Practice guidelines for the treatment of patients with schizophrenia. *American Journal of Psychiatry* 154 (4 Suppl.): 1–63.

Andreasen, N. C. 1984. *The Broken Brain: The Biological Revolution in Psychiatry*. New York: Harper and Row.

Bockhoven, J. S. 1963. *Moral Treatment in American Psychiatry*. New York: Springer.

Bola, J. R. 2002. "Long-Term Effect of Antipsychotics in First-Episode Schizophrenia." Paper presented at the Third International Conference on Early Psychosis, Copenhagen, Denmark. *Acta Psychiatrica Scandinavica* 413 (106s): 47.

Bola, J. R. and Mosher, L. R. 2002a. Predicting drug-free treatment response in acute psychosis from the Soteria project. *Schizophrenia Bulletin* 28 (4): 559–575.

―――. 2002b. Clashing ideologies or scientific discourse? *Schizophrenia Bulletin* 28 (4): 583–588.

―――. 2003. The treatment of acute psychosis without neuroleptics: Two-year outcomes from the Soteria project. *Journal of Nervous and Mental Disease* 191 (4): 219–229.

Buckley, P. 1982. Identifying schizophrenic patients who should not receive medication. *Schizophrenia Bulletin* 8 (3): 429–432.

Canadian Psychiatric Association. 1998. Canadian clinical practice guidelines for the treatment of schizophrenia. *Canadian Journal of Psychiatry* 43 (Suppl. 2 rev.): 21–40.

Carpenter, W. T. J. 1997. The risk of medication-free research. *Schizophrenia Bulletin* 23 (1): 11–18.

Carpenter, W. T., T. H. McGlashan, and J. S. Strauss. 1977. The treatment of acute schizophrenia without drugs: An investigation of some current assumptions. *American Journal of Psychiatry* 134 (1): 14–20.

Ciompi, L., H.-P. Dauwalder, C. Maier, E. Aebi, K. Trütsch, Z. Kupper, and C. Rutishauser. 1992. The pilot project "Soteria Berne": Clinical experiences and results. *British Journal of Psychiatry* 161 (Supp. 18): 145–153.

Ciompi, L., Z. Kupper, E. Aebi, H.-P. Dauwalder, T. Hubschmidt, K. Trütsch, and C. Rutishauser. 1993. Da pilot-projekt "Soteria Bern" zur behandlung akut schizophener. II. Ergebnisse der vergleichenden prospektiven verlaufsstudie uber 2 jahre [The pilot project "Soteria Bern" for the treatment of acute schizophrenics. II. Results of a comparative prospective study over 2 years]. *Der Nervenartz* 64: 440–450.

Cohen, D. 1997. A Critique of the Use of Neuroleptic Drugs in Psychiatry. In L. Fisher and R. G. Greenberg, eds., *From Placebo to Panacea: Putting Psychiatric Drugs to the Test,* 173–228. New York: John Wiley.

———. 2002. Research on the drug treatment of schizophrenia: A critical appraisal and implications for social work education. *Journal of Social Work Education* 38: 217–239.

Cullberg, J., S. Levander, R. Holmquist, M. Mattsson, and I.-M. Weiselgren. 2002. One-year outcome in first episode psychosis patients in the Swedish Parachute project. *Acta Psychiatrica Scandinavica* 106 (4): 276–285.

Fairweather, G. W., D. Sanders, D. Cressler, and H. Maynard. 1969. *Community Life for the Mentally Ill: An Alternative to Institutional Care.* Chicago: Aldine.

Fromm-Reichmann, F. 1948. Notes on the development of treatment of schizophrenics by psychoanalytic psychotherapy. *Psychiatry* 11:263–273.

Gosden, R. 1999. Prepsychotic treatment for schizophrenia: Preventive medicine, social control, or drug marketing strategy? *Ethical Human Sciences and Services* 1:165–177.

Harrison, P. 1999. The neuropathological effects of antipsychotic drugs. *Schizophrenia Research* 40 (2): 87–99.

Hegarty, J. D., R. J. Baldessarini, M. Tohen, C. Waternaux, and G. Oepen. 1994. One hundred years of schizophrenia: A meta-analysis of the outcome literature. *American Journal of Psychiatry* 151:1409–1416.

Hirschfeld, R. M., S. M. Matthews, L. R. Mosher, and A. Z. Menn. 1977. Being with madness: Personality characteristics of three treatment staffs. *Hospital and Community Psychiatry* 28:267–273.

Hollingshead, A. B. 1957. *Two Factor Index of Social Position.* New Haven, Conn.: August Hollingshead.

Ivker, B. and W. C. Sze. 1987. Social work and the psychiatric nosology of schizophrenia. *Social Casework* 68:131–139.

Laing, R. D. 1967. *The Politics of Experience.* New York: Ballantine

Lehtinen, V., J. Aaltonen, T. Koffert, V. Rakkolainen, and E. Syvalahti. 2000. Two-year outcome in first-episode schizophrenia treated according to an integrated model: Is immediate neuroleptisation always needed? *European Psychiatry* 15 (5): 312–320.

Liberman, R. P., I. R. H. Falloon, and C. J. Wallace. 1984. Drug-Psychosocial Interactions in the Treatment of Schizophrenia. In M. Mirabi, ed., *The Chronically Mentally Ill: Research and Services,* 175–212. New York: Spectrum.

Marder, S. R., D. P. van Kammen, J. P. Docherty, J. Rayner, and W. E. Bunney. 1979. Predicting drug-free improvement in schizophrenic psychosis. *Archives of General Psychiatry* 36:1080–1085.

May, P. R. A., A. H. Tuma, W. J. Dixon, C. Yale, D. A. Theile, and W. H. Kraude. 1981. Schizophrenia: A follow-up study of the results of five forms of treatment. *Archives of General Psychiatry* 38:776–784.

McKelvey, R. D. and W. Zavoina. 1975. A statistical model for the analysis of ordinal level dependent variables. *Journal of Mathematical Sociology* 4:103–120.

Menninger, K. 1959. *Psychiatrist's World: The Selected Papers of Karl Menninger.* New York: Viking.

Moos, R. H. 1974. *Evaluating Treatment Environments: A Social Ecological Approach.* New York: John Wiley.

Mosher, L. R. 1999. Soteria and other alternatives to acute hospitalization: A personal and professional review. *Journal of Nervous and Mental Disease* 187:142–149.

Mosher , L. R. and L. Burti. 1994. *Community Mental Health: A Practical Guide.* New York: Norton.

Mosher, L. R. and A. Z. Menn. 1978a. Community residential treatment for schizophrenia: Two-year follow-up. *Hospital and Community Psychiatry* 29 (11): 715–723.

———. 1978b. Enhancing Psychosocial Competence in Schizophrenia: Preliminary Results of the Soteria Project. In W. C. Fann, A. D. Karacan, R. L. Pokorny, and R. L. Williams, eds., *Phenomenology and Treatment of Schizophrenia*, 371–386. New York: Spectrum.

Mosher, L. R., V. Hendricks, and Participants. 1994. Dabeisein: Das Manual zur Praxis in der Soteria [Treatment at Soteria House: A manual for the practice of interpersonal phenomenology]. In D. Ford, ed., *Psychosoziale Arbeitshilfen.* No. 7. Berlin: Psychiatrie-Verlag.

Mosher, L. R., W. Pollin, and R. Stabenau. 1971. Identical twins discordant for schizophrenia: Neurologic findings. *Archives of General Psychiatry* 24 (5): 422–430.

Mosher, L. R., R. Vallone, and A. Menn. 1995. The treatment of acute psychosis without neuroleptics: Six-week psychopathology outcome data from the Soteria project. *International Journal of Social Psychiatry* 41 (3): 157–173.

Perry, J. W. 1974. *The Far Side of Madness.* Englewood Cliffs, N.J.: Prentice-Hall.

Rappaport, M., H. K. Hopkins, K. Hall, T. Belleza, and J. Silverman. 1978. Are there schizophrenics for whom drugs may be unnecessary or contraindicated? *International Pharmacopsychiatry* 13 (2): 100–111.

Reynolds, B. C. 1934. The relationship between psychiatry and psychiatric social work. *News-letter of the American Association of Social Workers* 3 (6): 1–4.

Rodnick, E. H. and M. J. Goldstein. 1974. Premorbid adjustment and recovery of mothering function in acute schizophrenic women. *Journal of Abnormal Psychology* 83: 623–628.

Scheff, T. 1966. *Being Mentally Ill.* Chicago: Aldine.

Schooler, N. R., S. C. Goldberg, H. Boothe, and J. O. Cole. 1967. One year after discharge: Community adjustment of schizophrenic patients. *American Journal of Psychiatry* 123 (8): 986–995.

Searles, H. F. 1965. *Collected Papers on Schizophrenia and Related Subjects.* New York: International Universities Press.

Sokis, D. A. 1970. A brief follow-up rating. *Comprehensive Psychiatry* 11 (5): 445–459.

Strauss, J. S. and W. T. Carpenter. 1978. The prognosis of schizophrenia: Rationale for a multidimensional concept. *Schizophrenia Bulletin* 4 (1): 56–67.

Sullivan, H. S. 1962. *Schizophrenia as a Human Process.* New York: Norton

Tobin, J. 1958. Estimation of relationships for limited dependent variables. *Econometrica* 26:24–36.

Vaillant, G. E. 1962. The prediction of recovery in schizophrenia. *Journal of Nervous and Mental Disease* 135:534–543.

Warner, R. 1985. *Recovery from Schizophrenia: Psychiatry and Political Economy.* London: Routledge and Kegan Paul.

Weick, A. 1983. Issues in overturning a medical model of social work practice. *Social Work* 28 (6): 467–471.

Wendt, R. J., L. R. Mosher, S. M. Matthews, and A. Z. Menn. 1983. A Comparison of Two Treatment Environments for Schizophrenia. In J. G. Gunderson, O. A. Will, and L. R. Mosher, eds., *The Principles and Practices of Milieu Therapy,* 17–33. New York: Jason Aronson.

Wilson, H. S. 1983. Usual hospital treatment in the USA's community mental health system. *International Journal of Nursing Studies* 20: 176–189.

Wirt, R. D. and W. Simon. 1959. *Differential Treatment and Prognosis in Schizophrenia.* Springfield, Ill.: Charles C. Thomas.

Wyatt, R. J. 1991. Neuroleptics and the natural course of schizophrenia. *Schizophrenia Bulletin* 17 (2): 325–351.

Chapter 21

Psychosocial Side Effects of Drug Treatment of Youth

Tally Moses and Stuart A. Kirk

Drugging our children is now commonplace. Millions of prescriptions for stimulants, antidepressants, and antipsychotics for children and youth are written each year, a dramatic increase in the last several decades (Rushton and Whitmire 2001; Zito et al. 2000; Jensen et al. 1999a; Safer, Zito, and Fine 1996). Psychotropic drugs are dispensed for depression, mania, anxiety, phobias, obsessive-compulsiveness, and hyperactivity, as well as for a myriad of behaviors, such as aggressiveness, school failure, antisocial behavior, eating and sleeping difficulties, and so on (Shuchman 1991; Fisher and Fisher 1997). There has also been a major rise in the use of combined psychotropic medications with youngsters, primarily to treat a "complex" of symptoms that overlap diagnostic categories or to augment a medication judged to be ineffective (Martin et al. 2003; Safer, Zito, and dosReis 2003; Rushton and Whitmire 2001). Drug treatment of youth has become so accepted that it is now the "first line of treatment," with psychotherapy referred to as the backup intervention. This is even suggested by a 1999 report from the surgeon general: "Psychotherapies are especially important alternatives for those children who are unable to tolerate, or whose parents prefer them not to take, medications. They are also important for conditions for which there are no medications with well-documented efficacy" (U.S. Public Health Service 1999:140).

Many researchers, mental health professionals, parents, child advocates, and others question the appropriateness and consequences of this explosion in prescriptions (Vitiello and Jensen 1995; Breggin 1999; Breggin and Breggin 1994; Diller 1999; Pear 2000; Kalb 2000; Armstrong 1993). They are concerned with the physical and biological safety of using psychopharmacological interventions with children and adolescents. Because youth absorb, metabolize, and respond to drugs differently than adults do, mental health professionals are concerned about dose-response schedules, potency, tolerance, possible drug interactions, and other "pharmaco-dynamics," as well as the unknown long-term effects on maturational development (Gadow 1992). Even what is known about these effects can be troubling. Most drugs produce side effects, which can range from relatively mild (dryness of mouth, dizziness, headaches, asthenia, vomiting, weight gain, excessive sedation) to severe (e.g., tardive and withdrawal dyskinesias, cardiac side effects such as dysrhythmia or heart blockage). Even stimulant treatment, which some consider to have "a good safety profile" (Greenhill, Halperin, and Abikof 1999), produces both side effects that are mild, short-lived, and responsive to dose and timing adjustments, and also some that are serious, including tics, psychotic symptoms, long-term effects on growth/height suppression, and small, sustained increases in blood pressure (Whalen and Henker 1997).

Over and above concerns with side effects, some experts question whether there actually are positive main effects of some psychotropic drugs for children and adolescents, because many of these drugs have *not* received FDA approval for use with juveniles (Jensen et al. 1994; Jensen et al. 1999a). Existing clinical studies on the effectiveness of psychotropics for children and adolescents generally yield inconsistent findings, although stimulant drugs for ADHD appear to have positive short-term effects that include reduced distractibility and increased compliance (Greenhill, Halperin, and Abikof 1999; Whalen and Henker 1997; Walkup 1995; also see *Journal of the American Academy of Child and Adolescent Psychiatry* 1999, issue 38, number 5). As with adults, the efficacy of psychotropic drugs with child and adolescent populations is usually addressed with randomized clinical trials (RCTs). Although RCTs are powerful methods of investigating whether psychoactive medications, alone or in combinations, yield distinct acute effects, they often are marred by methodological deficiencies, such as very brief follow-up periods, the possibility of experimenter bias (even when "double blind"), very limited and simplified clinical problems treated, and research settings that are unlike circumstances faced by clinicians in the community (Parker, Anderson, and Haddad 2003; Jacobs 1999; Fisher and Greenberg 1997; Cohen, chapter 19). Beyond these methodological deficiencies, the validity of the RCT data is seriously called into question because of the precipitous increase in financial backing of university biomedical research by the pharmaceutical industry in recent decades, which sets up a strong potential for conflicts of interest that are not always considered or disclosed to the public. Actually, there is strong and consistent evidence that industry-sponsored research is far more likely to yield findings that favor the industry's product (drug) (Bekelman, Li, and Gross 2003:463; Kirsch, Scoboria, and Moore 2002). This fact, coupled with the well-known academic publication bias favoring the dissemination of "positive results" (Parker, Anderson, and Haddad 2003; Antonuccio, Burns, and Danton 2002), demand extreme caution in interpreting the efficacy results of even rigorous scientific inquiry.

In addition, there are serious accusations that kids are overmedicated. Some critics (Breggin and Breggin 1994; Diller 1999; Pear 2000) believe that parents and teachers are too eager to use psychiatric drugs to mute youths' misbehavior or nonmedical problems that are a normal part of childhood experience. These critics suggest that drugs are prescribed when nonmedical treatment or no treatment at all is preferable, in combinations or dosages that are excessive, or in ways that are incompatible with the child's diagnosis or genuine problem.

Some investigators argue, by contrast, that the problem is undermedication, that youth who need medications do not get them. For example, these observers point to community studies that show that many youth who meet the criteria for a mental disorder (such as ADHD/ADD) do not get drugs (e.g., Lewinsohn, Rohde, and Seeley 1998; Jensen et al. 1999a; Zima et al. 1999a; Keller et al. 1991). This inconsistency in findings in whether youth are over- or undermedicated could be an artifact of the validity problems that arise with the diagnostic criteria of *DSM* (see Hsieh and Kirk, chapter 3; Nugent, chapter 6). If the *DSM* criteria for childhood mental disorders are too broad and identify children as disordered when they are not, then both those who point to overmedication and those who point to undermedication could be correct. On the one hand, if the *DSM* criteria are too broad, kids who do not have disorders are given drugs that they don't need (overmedication). On the other hand, if the *DSM* criteria are valid and don't have a tendency to identify false positives, then many children in the community who do have disorders are not identified and therefore are "undermedicated." The dispute may be partly over differences in views of the validity of the *DSM* definitions of children's mental disorders, but the main point here is that there are many important open questions about the use, effectiveness, and consequences of medicating youth.

The Neglect of Psychosocial Side Effects

While research is now addressing some of the concerns about the safety, efficacy, and necessity of psychotropic drug treatment for youth, other equally important questions have been neglected. We know comparatively little about the overall experience of being treated with psychotropic drugs. In addition to symptomatic physical changes produced by medications, what is the subjective experience for youth of taking psychotropic drugs? Are there direct or indirect social and psychological effects on esteem, identity, and other views of the self? At times, clinicians have noted the more subtle and covert long-term effects of medication on attitudes, beliefs, and feelings and on the client's relationships with the physician, friends, and family (e.g., Nevins 1990). But these questions are seldom asked by the research community or discussed in the mental health literature. Many studies, including randomized clinical trials, simply don't bother to evaluate the subjective experience of youth in treatment or to worry about the arguably harder-to-measure alterations to self-image or sense of personal mastery (Jacobs 1999). Clearly, because RCTs are usually undertaken by investigators who have some financial or professional ties with the pharmaceutical industry or simply have a narrow biomedical orientation, assumptions regarding the necessity of using drugs or the broader human consequences are never questioned (Jacobs and Cohen 1999). Nevertheless, while overt symptom changes and short-term physical side effects resulting from medication garner more attention, there is preliminary evidence to suggest that psychosocial effects are a different class of consequences that should also be considered in the risk-benefit equation that is applied to medication decisions.

For several reasons, the psychosocial effects of medication could be profoundly important. Long-term psychiatric treatment can be invasive and potentially stigmatizing. It can undermine one's sense of efficacy and magnify one's sense of personal deficits. These effects may be exaggerated or distorted with adolescents because at their stage of development they have a propensity to deny vulnerability, challenge authority, act out internal conflicts, or be particularly self-conscious in relation to peers. Such drug/developmental interactions might undermine important developmental tasks such as forming a more cohesive and enduring identity and more-sophisticated coping skills. Unfortunately, these concerns about potential problems are largely speculative, because most studies fail to focus on such subjective experiences. More common is for research to focus on youths' attitudes toward medication in relation to noncompliance, which is a significant clinical and economic preoccupation in psychiatry (e.g., Brown et al. 1987; Lloyd et al. 1998; Ghaziuddin et al. 1999; Sirey et al. 2001; Bernstein et al. 2000). Some of what little we know about youth and medication comes from these studies of noncompliance.

Studies with children and adolescents who are taking medication find that they are often knowledgeable about the purpose of medication and why they are taking it but still feel ambivalent about it. Even when they realize that it helps them, many dislike taking it (Baxley et al. 1978; Bowen, Fenton, and Rappaport 1991; Clarke 1998). A study by Bowen, Fenton, and Rappaport (1991) of 58 children (average age twelve) who were taking stimulant treatment for ADHD and receiving psychotherapy found that while

88.9% reported feeling that the drugs were helpful to them, more than a third of them expressed profound worries about stigma, control, and long-term effects. Other studies of adolescents' attitudes toward their psychotropic medication find a sense of stigma and shame (Scott et al. 1992), a strong belief that "people should solve problems on their own," and fears that medication might hurt or create physical discomfort (Williams et al. 1998). One study of 115 psychiatric inpatient adolescents with affective or psychotic diagnoses reported that 58% disagreed with the need to take prescribed medication and 61% reported a lack of positive expectation that medication would help them (Scott, Lore, and Owen 1992). In another survey, of 651 middle and high school students using stimulant treatment for ADHD (average age fifteen), Moline and Frankenberger (2001) found that even though students were aware of positive effects, nearly 50% wanted to discontinue medication or were uncertain about whether to continue it. The last study found that more students reported taking medication because others (primarily parents) wanted them to (20%) rather than because they wanted to (11%).

Studies of adults taking psychotropic medication—mainly case studies and qualitative research—suggest that psychiatric treatment affects people's views of themselves and the attitudes of others toward them (Conrad and Schneider 1992). Although many clients eventually come to terms with their need for long-term medication to control their symptoms, the internal psychological process of acceptance of new definitions of self and illness is often long and fraught with ambiguity, ambivalence, doubt, and shame (Venarde 1999; Melamed and Szor 1999; Karp 1996; Hoencamp, Stevens, and Haffmans 2002). Taking medication serves as a reminder that something is wrong with oneself, a constant sign of "differentness" from others (Conrad 1985). Even when medication effectively reduces burdensome symptoms, the client's personal autonomy and control can be undermined. Common to almost all clients, including the chronically mentally ill, is the desire to retain control over their lives and discretion over taking medication to the extent possible (Lucksted and Coursey 1995).

The studies discussed above suggest that a medication prescription is a social transaction that transcends the bounds of the doctor's office and the confines of medical terminology. To a youth, a prescription becomes an event that generates fantasies, wishes, concerns, and meaning. It structures one's own expectations and those of others in ways that are not necessarily intended or foreseen.

This chapter will search for a better understanding of (or at least grounded speculation about) the psychosocial effects of psychopharmacological treatment of youth. The literature suggests that issues of identity, control, self-reliance, shame, and stigma are central concerns among both adults and youth who take psychotropic medication. Each of these issues will be addressed, drawing on whatever studies are available. The chapter will then call attention to a particularly vulnerable group of children—abused and neglected youth—and the potential consequences of psychopharmacologic treatment for them. Last, we will address the need for social workers to be more mindful in considering the uses of medication in the treatment of youth.

Identity

All people have a basic need for a sense of self-identity, the experience of self-continuity, unity, and purpose. This profound need may be either thwarted or facilitated by psychotropic medication (Gara, Rosenberg, and Cohen 1987). Even when medications lessen troublesome symptoms, thereby allowing some individuals to achieve a newly clarified sense of self, others may experience a threat to their identity (Venarde 1999). In Peter Kramer's *Listening to Prozac* (1993), adults who were taking Prozac (a new-generation SSRI antidepressant) experienced not only relief from symptoms of depression but also a personal transformation in how social or outgoing, confident, sensitive, and risk-taking they were. These alterations are central to one's identity.

In a qualitative study of 50 individuals diagnosed and treated for depression—not all of whom were significantly helped by the drugs—Karp (1996) found that they engaged in a continuous process of trying to make sense of their experience. While living with psychotropic drugs, they were grappling with questions of what was wrong with them, what caused them to suffer, and what treatment meant to them. Karp concluded: "The experience of taking antidepressant medications involves a complex and emotionally charged interpretive process in which nothing less that one's view of self is at stake" (102).

Other studies have also found that medications affect self-identity. Venarde (1999) studied the subjective experiences of 12 individuals who were taking SSRIs (ages 19 to 41). He found that taking antidepressants, which provided symptom relief in all cases, led to major improvements in self-esteem and profoundly changed individuals' basic view of self: "For many, the old depressed identity felt more alien and the new and less depressed identity felt familiar" (62). All of his participants, who had been taking medications for shorter lengths of time than Karp's study participants, experienced more self-confidence, less self-criticism, more forgiveness toward self and others, more "peace," and more competence. They also reported improvements in relationships with family, friends, or romantic partners, and in accomplishments in school and work. One of the participants, a man in his late thirties, commented, "It's been sort of strange that it [Prozac] could have so many effects that feel more like you than less like you" (63). For others, medication effects created confusion as they struggled to figure out which "self" was the real self. This was articulated by one woman in her early thirties: "It's kind of more when I go off the medication when I say, who is the real me? And is the real me depressed? But then when I'm on the medication, I guess I hope that that's the way it's supposed to be. I have a hard time saying it is, but I sort of wonder if this is who I am and I really do have stuff to work with" (65).

Individuals who begin taking medication in adulthood have developed a fairly stable sense of who they are before drug treatment. Adolescents, by contrast, cannot rely on such a mature perspective. Although identity formation is an ongoing process throughout life, the challenge of developing a stable sense of self is particularly intense during adolescence (Cromer and Tarnowski 1989; Schowalter 1989; Rappaport and Chubinsky 2000). Youth are struggling with concerns about personality, body image, sexuality, relationships with family and friends, and occupational goals. If, as we have seen above, identity transformation often occurs in adults who are taking medication, for youth, drug treatment may be even more complex and confusing. For example, young clients in the turbulence of identity development may fear losing a sense of themselves to medication and worry that they will not be able to distinguish between the effects of the drug and the expression of their own personality. Such fears were expressed by a young patient who wanted to discontinue medication treatment: "I need to know what is my personality and what is caused by the pill. I don't know whether my feelings are what I feel or what the pill causes me to feel" (Goldstein 1992:238). Williams, Hollis, and Benoit (1998), studying the attitudes of 214 incarcerated adolescent females toward psychiatric medications, found that even girls who had firsthand experience with psychotropic medications (mostly antidepressants) continued to express resistance and concerns: "Medicines are a crutch," and "Medicine might change my personality and not let me be me" (1304).

For adolescents, medication can symbolize their own imperfections at precisely the age of heightened bodily awareness and the quest for self-perfection. At this developmental moment, the physical and sexual side effects of drugs can be very frightening, heightening their fears of performing sexually or gaining weight, making them feel that they lack energy, or raising their anxiety about drinking alcohol while taking medications. Especially if the youth doesn't believe that she is ill and therefore views the medication as needless, she will be disinclined to tolerate the side effects or to abide by the restrictions that taking medication necessitates (Clarke 1998; Melamed and Szor 1999). Even positive effects of medication—which can be dramatic and immediate—may frighten the adolescent, if that result is interpreted as confirming unambiguously that she or he is indeed disordered (Rappaport and Chubinksy 2000; Melamed and Szor 1999). Conversely, if medication fails to alleviate symptoms, the youth may view the situation as especially ominous, indicating that he or she is "beyond help." Adolescence identity formation and medication treatment are a potent combination.

Autonomy and Control

People of all ages express concerns about being dependent on medications, even when the drugs bring dramatic symptom relief (Goldstein 1992). In Venarde's study (1999), adults taking SSRIs felt weak because of having to rely on medication, worried about overreliance on the drug, feared that the drug might become ineffective or unavailable, and wished that they could cope without having to rely on "artificial" chemical intervention to feel well. Reluctance to be dependent creates both a hope and a fear of discontinuing the drug in the future. The threat of dependency produces a significant and ongoing ambivalence about taking the medication and anxiety about what it means.

In one of the only empirical studies of the meaning that children attribute to psychotropic medication (Clarke 1998), these concerns about psychological dependence on psychotropic medication were echoed by 20 children (ages 8 to 14) who had been diagnosed with ADHD and were receiving stimulant treatment (mostly Ritalin). While the majority of participants (17 of the 20) experienced better academic performance, better general and classroom behavior, and improved social relations with peers, teachers, and family, almost all the children also reported growing anxiety over perceived dependency on medication for adequate functioning. These worries and shame about dependency over time attenuated the positive effects of the medication. As with adults, these children expressed a strong desire for self-reliance. As one 12-year-old who had been on Ritalin for six years said:

> I'm just wondering if I'm going to have to take it for my whole life, or if it's going to set me straight or whatever. I think what the doctors need to do is keep lowering the dosages little by little as they get older. Like from their teenage years, just keep lowering it, because as they're on the Ritalin, they're dependent on it, and they're not doing that much themselves, so they're pretty much depending on the Ritalin to calm them down.
> (Clarke 1998:79)

Both children and adults often feel anxious about having to taking medication but also apprehensive about not taking it. Clarke's study suggests that children who had seen their dosages increase over time (because of tolerance to the drug) were especially frustrated and worried because this undermined their sense of self-reliance. The older children, as well as the children who had been taking the medication for longer periods, seemed less accepting of the medication. Several children commented that they would be very concerned if they didn't get their "act together" and still needed the medication when they were older.

For adolescents in particular, reliance on a long-term treatment regimen can be at odds with the growing need for autonomy and privacy (Rappaport and Chubinsky 2000). Adolescents' resistance to being medicated can increase conflicts with authority figures (Clarke 1998). This conflict is not unique to psychiatric treatment; it also occurs in the treatment of adolescents with chronic physical disorders such as asthma, diabetes, epilepsy, and even cancer (e.g., Boice 1998; Williams 1999; van Es et al. 1998; Woodgate 1998; Tebbi et al. 1988). Teens often strongly resent the intrusiveness that accompanies medical scrutiny and the familial overprotection that sometimes ensues (Boice 1998). Whereas adults most often have the discretion to start and stop medication treatment at will (though they too are subject to social pressure), adolescents and younger children are usually not autonomous, and their parents/caretakers are likely to have significant control over treatment-related decisions (King et al. 1997). In some families, psychotropic treatment may become a source of conflict in the dependence/independence dynamics between youth and parents in which the psychoactive agent is experienced as a form of rejection or control by the parents (Masi, Marcheschi, and Luccherino 1996). Even in the best of familial circumstances, adolescents need to exert influence over their environment, and so when they are not well informed about the psychotropic medication process and their consent is often not secured, conflicts can easily emerge (Batten 1996).

Stigma

Stigma frequently accompanies the diagnosis of mental disorder (U.S. Public Health Service 1999). The diagnostic label may set the person apart from the "normal," making him feel ashamed and devalued and worried about rejection by others if the status is publicly known. Such worries are particularly strong during adolescence, a time when "the peer group looms large as a source of values, directives, feedback and social comparison" (Harter 1990:353). The question is whether youth who are prescribed psychotropic medication will experience long-term negative consequences associated with a stigma of being labeled and treated. On the one hand, psychopharmacologic intervention can reduce disturbing symptoms, thereby enabling youth to feel more like their peers and increasing the capacity to pass for "normal." Assuming that medication provides relief from symptoms, it can empower and optimize the youngster's ability to have positive interactions with others and receive positive feedback (Clarke 1998). On the other hand, taking psychotropic medication and the implication of having a psychological disorder can also heighten feelings of being different and defective, undercutting the adolescent's need to experience a sense of similarity, commonality, and kinship with others.

Children, youth, and adults alike report feeling stigmatized by taking psychotropic medication. In Venarde's study (1999) of adults, despite symptom reduction, some of those taking medications were preoccupied with stereotypes of people who take psychotropic medications (e.g., "weird") and the associated shame about how they might be perceived by others. Children's and adolescents' accounts of stigma are not much different. In Clarke's study (1998) of preadolescent children diagnosed with ADHD, 14 of the 20 perceived stigma associated with being medicated and strong feelings of being "different" from peers. One child commented, "I kind of feel weird, because you need like a pill to control yourself" (90). Only 4 of 20 felt comfortable with peers knowing about their medication (unless peers were also on medication, which brought comfort), because they were afraid of being rejected or considered "stupid, weak or weird" (68). For some, medication negatively affected peer relations over time; some blamed the medication for actual or imagined rejection by peers. In Scott et al.'s study (1992) of adolescents with affective or psychotic diagnoses, 56% of the sample sensed stigma and shame to such an extent that they felt the need to hide their conditions from peers (best friend) to avoid negative appraisals. Bowen, Fenton, and Rappaport's study (1991) of 58 preadolescent children who were receiving stimulant treatment found that 49% reported worries about feeling different, 44% worried that "something must be wrong with me," and 27% reported embarrassment about medication. This last study found that the discontinuance of drugs was more likely to occur if the medication made youth feel as if something was wrong with them or if they felt embarrassed about taking the meds.

Learned Helplessness

Children develop a sense of self-competence and self-efficacy as they successfully cope with their environment. Does taking psychotropic medication interfere with a youth's opportunity to develop natural coping skills?

Clinical observations of adult psychiatric patients have suggested that individuals in treatment may be more prone to develop an identity based on a sense of pathology and to adopt a sick role, characterized by passivity, futility, and dependence. For example, Sarwer-Foner (1960) and Amarasingham (1980) found that patients interpret getting medication as a message that they are sick and need external substances in order to function. Adult inpatients who perceived their psychiatric disorder as a physical illness were significantly more apt to assume a sick role than patients who interpreted their problems in nonmedical, psychosocial terms (Augoustinos 1986). Another study also found a strong correlation between a "medical model orientation" and attitudes of dependence on the part of adult psychiatric patients (Morrison et al. 1977).

A substantial amount of research on youngsters' personal reactions to treatment focuses on the extent to which medication creates passivity or "learned helplessness" (Maier and Seligman 1976). The issue is whether children who receive medication to curb problematic behavior or emotions come to believe that they have an internal dysfunction over which they have no control and are, therefore, helpless. If kids attribute successes and failures to the medication and underestimate their own efforts, they may come to see themselves as ineffectual without chemical intervention. To address this concern, researchers have examined whether children attribute both positive and negative changes in functioning to medication rather than to their own efforts. Research findings on this question are inconsistent.

On the one hand, there is some empirical support to suggest that medication, whether clinically effective or not, is associated with an external locus of control whereby youngsters perceive that the means to resolve personal problems are external to the self or beyond their control (Borden and Brown 1989; Whalen and Henker 1997). For instance, a positive drug response to stimulant treatment is often interpreted by youngsters, caretakers, teachers, and doctors as a confirmation of a biochemical or genetic dysfunction that is not subject to personal or environmental control. Children and adolescents often attribute their positive behavior to medication and their negative behavior to their failure to take medication. At times they may even act out more severely when falsely believing that they are not medicated (Rosen et al. 1985; Johnston et al. 2000; Ohan and Johnston 1999; Allen and Drabman 1991; Alston and Romney 1992; Amirkhan 1982). In her study, Clarke (1998) found that her young respondents exhibited some "learned helplessness" because they attributed their success to medication and expected that their functioning would be impaired if medication was withdrawn. They also blamed the pill for their failures. Clarke noted that only a few of the sample attributed success and failure in a balanced way to both their own effort and the medication.

On the other hand, others did not find negative self-attributions as a result of taking medications, but rather improvement in self-confidence and self-acceptance and an alleviation of guilt, effects that are probably mediated by behavioral improvements (Cohen and Thompson 1982; Pelham et al. 1997; Ialongo et al. 1994; Frankel et al. 1999; Milich et al. 1991; Whalen and

Henker 1997). In short, medication treatment with youth probably results in both positive and negative effects on their sense of self-efficacy and on others' response to them. Certainly the messages we give youngsters when prescribing medication for them may affect their own ability to resolve problems and cope with their environment. If adolescents are encouraged to adopt a purely biological viewpoint, to perceive their problems in purely somatic terms, and to expect success when medicated, they may come to expect a quick, comprehensive fix with medication and fail to take ownership of their behaviors (Masi, Marcheschi, and Luccherino 1996). Worse, they may adopt an impaired sense of self-efficacy and helplessness.

Especially Vulnerable Youth

There are some groups of children and youth who may be particularly vulnerable to unintended negative psychosocial side effects of medication or the misuse of psychotropics. These are abused and neglected youngsters who suffer from such calamitous family circumstances that they have become wards of the state and have landed on the caseloads of overburdened social workers. With these troubled youth, it is likely that their reactions to medication are complicated by the family trauma they have already experienced (Rappaport and Chubinsky 2000; Masi, Marcheschi, and Luccherino 1996), their dependency status as wards of the state, and their experiences in out-of-home care.

There are no reliable estimates of the prevalence of abused or neglected children in either the community or institutional care who are receiving psychotropic medication, but anecdotal reports suggest it is high (Weber 1998a; Kaplan and Busner 1997; Gadow 1997). Several surveys found that three to five times as many children and adolescents who are wards of the state are prescribed psychotropic medication relative to their age peers who are not in the state's custody (Zima et al. 1999a; dosReis et al. 2001; Martin et al. 2003). Part of this discrepancy, undoubtedly, is attributable to the association of child abuse and neglect with a high rate of developmental, mental, emotional, educational, and social problems, as well as higher rates of substance abuse (Stein et al. 1996; Zima et al. 1999a; Flisher et al. 1997; Pilowsky 1995; Trupin et al. 1993; Klee and Halfon 1987).

Psychotropic medication is not inherently incompatible with the psychosocial treatment needs of this population, especially if medication enhances the effectiveness of interpersonal therapy. The uses of drugs in this context, however, require comprehensive assessment and clinical sensitivity. Psychiatrists and other medical providers often lack training in treating abused and neglected youth and are generally insensitive to their special needs (Klee and Halfon 1987). The problems of these youths are usually associated with traumatic events that have led to placement in a foster care system, problems that defy simple solutions. In medical and foster care systems, which emphasize rapid clinical response and the control of disruptive symptoms, medication may too often be used without consideration for the process or its subjective meaning to youth. This is even more likely given the general trend for psychiatrists to spend less time with each patient, provide less psychotherapy, and prescribe medication more often (Olfson et al. 1999). Some critics have argued, in fact, that drugs may be unhelpful and even deleterious and that psychopharmacology has simply put a new face on social control (Cohen 1993; Murphy et al. 1994).

At the very least, the treatment of abused and neglected youth requires a long-term, multifaceted, team approach and a therapeutic style that is open, intimate, direct, and yet extraordinarily delicate. A primary aim of treatment is to help these youth integrate and transcend the realities of the painful events they have endured and develop a positive sense of self (James 1989). Traumatized youth need to come to terms with what has happened to them and perhaps experience their anger or pain in a way that enables them to avoid depression, aggression, withdrawal, failure to achieve, acting out, and so on. Their lack of consistent nurturance and positive parental involvement leaves many abused and neglected youth extremely vulnerable to a sense of worthlessness and helplessness. Even more than for most adolescents, for them, issues of identity, self-worth, self-reliance, interpersonal trust, self-control, self-determination, and intimate or close relationships are of paramount importance (Penzerro and Lein 1995; Yancey 1992; Rest and Watson 1984; Zimmerman 1988).

Like everyone else, abused and neglected youth have a need for a sense of continuity and cohesion, achieved through the ongoing construction of a personal narrative (one's life story), which essentially constitutes the basis of identity (Saari 1991). As part of their "story," youth are likely to try to make sense of the meaning of their treatment by figuring out if their "problems" are biochemical/genetic or social/environmental in nature. One would assume that many youth who grew up in an abusive home or were shuffled around among caregivers would attribute their problems to their family environment. If so, these youth could be easily perplexed by being labeled with a psychiatric diagnosis and prescribed medication, as if the origin or cause of their "symptoms" resided within them. Helping professionals who view the youth's behavioral or emotional problems as *biogenetic,* rather than as *social* responses to unsatisfactory and harmful conditions or a form of social learning, may be unwittingly conveying to the youth that their troubles are of their own making. In reaction, these adolescents' mistrust of others may heighten; they may resist the treatment process, fail to comply with medication, and view themselves as bad, shameful, rejected, and misunderstood. Especially when youth have suffered physical harm or sexual abuse, the act of being given medication, unless handled with considerable skill and sensitivity, can undermine the youngster's sense of physical and psychological integrity (Masi, Marcheschi, and Luccherino 1996; Rappaport and Chubinsky 2000).

Youth in congregate out-of-home care facilities (i.e., group homes, residential treatment centers, and hospitals) are among those abused youth who are most likely to receive insensitive or coercive treatment. There are two possible reasons for this risk. First, congregate care agencies focus on maintaining order and organization. In settings where child care staff are outnumbered by residents, the inherent problems of managing difficult behavior and ensuring safety often necessitate measures designed to minimize disruption (Moses 2000). To achieve order, staff often advocate for medical measures to suppress disruptive behavior (Weber 1998a; Stein 1995). Sometimes this results in overly aggressive medication treatment to combat the disturbing symptoms. Connor et al. (1998), for example, found that among 83 youths in a residential treatment facility, more than half of the residents who were receiving neuroleptics were prescribed this potentially highly toxic treatment in the absence of the appropriate diagnostic indications. The authors concluded that "[neuroleptics] are over-prescribed for non-specific and non-indicated behavioral reasons" (35).

The second reason for medication misuse is that these youth lack advocates, committed parents, guardians, or other caretakers who can protect their best interests. Treatment in a group setting may be less carefully monitored and individualized than care received by youth in regular or kinship foster care placements or at home with parents. A *Los Angeles Times* investigation of medication practices for youth in group care settings found many worrisome practices. It reported the use of high dosages of drugs or drug combinations whose safety and effectiveness for children were not validated, employment of psychiatrists who are untrained to work with this population, and poor documentation of prescription drug records (Weber 1998a). The investigation also found poor oversight of psychotropic medication practices by the child welfare and juvenile court authorities. Since this report was published, state legislative reform has been under way to develop a better monitoring system for dispensing psychotropic medication to children who are wards of the juvenile court. Currently in California, child welfare workers must obtain a juvenile court judge's approval for the treatment before they can start a child on psychotropic medication, and children's medical records must accompany them to each placement (Weber 1998b). Although these efforts signify a growing recognition of the problems associated with psychiatric treatment in out-of-home care, they also point out the serious need for a systematic and comprehensive evaluation of psychiatric practices and their effects on traumatized youth.

Implications for Social Work Practice

Social workers represent the majority of mental health treatment providers in the United States in medical and mental health settings and in schools, residential treatment, and juvenile detention centers (Knowlton 1995). Their central role in the delivery of mental health services places them in a strategic position to encourage more-informed and -sensitive practices that recognize the emotional and cognitive effects of medication treatment.

An important component of such practices involves engaging youth more fully in the treatment process. The "person-in-environment" framework suggests that it would be ill advised to ignore either the subjective experience of the medicated youth or the youth's social environment, which includes interactions with family, peers, teachers, employers, romantic partners, and others. Too often, children and youth are not fully informed or consulted about taking medication, or if their opinions are solicited, their views are discounted in decision making. It is small wonder that many adolescents exert their power by not complying with medication. This does not mean that medication treatment should never be prescribed for resistant clients; rather it means that social workers need to be mindful of the process by which psychopharmacologic treatment is initiated, negotiated, and monitored. This process should be more client-centered, especially with abused and neglected children, and attuned to the insidious effects of medication on their sense of self, autonomy, stigma, self-efficacy, sociability, and expectations for the future. Young clients should be engaged in an ongoing discourse about what medication means for them, and they should be allowed the maximum opportunity to influence treatment decisions.

Such an approach places new demands on social workers. First, they need to become better informed about the subtle dynamics of psychopharmacotherapy so that they can provide better advice to youth, parents, and other professionals. Second, they need to communicate better with troubled adolescents, particularly in assessing the meanings of medication to them. One barrier is the difficulty youth may have in communicating their reactions to others, because their cognitive and emotional skills develop unevenly and they have difficulty recognizing and articulating their feelings about medication. To overcome these barriers, social workers need to ask the right questions: questions about what expectations, fantasies, myths, symbols, and realistic hopes are attributed to the medication and to the self; questions about how treatment and information about one's treatment are managed in daily life; questions about the perceived overt and covert responses of significant others.

The meaning of medication in the lives of youth is undoubtedly complex and can lead them both to request drug treatment and to be resistant to it.

They may request medication out of a desire to avoid the intrapsychic or interpersonal dimension of problems or to be dependent on a parent/ authority figure. Refusal of medication, on the other hand, may signify a rejection of the notion that they are ill or a deep distrust of caretakers. Or such refusal could represent a fear of losing the symptoms, getting better, giving up the secondary benefits of the sick role, and facing the prospect of "health" and the changes in lifestyle that it would signify (Melamed and Szor 1999). Attitudes that clients develop toward their medication may have direct implications for the outcome of treatment. The scant empirical literature addressing this question of the association between attitudes toward medication (mostly conducted with psychotic adults receiving neuroleptic medication) invariably finds an association between favorable versus unfavorable responses to medication and reduction in symptom severity (e.g., Hellewell 2002; Awad et al. 1996; Van Putten and May 1978). We don't know whether such findings would hold for nonpsychotic youth receiving medications for diverse diagnoses. But in any case, attitudes and meanings attributed to treatment are likely to have bearing on issues of medication acceptability and compliance.

Many of the concerns raised in this chapter are based on reasoned speculation, interpolation from only a few studies, and research that is methodological flawed. It is not just unfortunate but nearly scandalous that the vast expansion of the use of psychotropic medication for children and youth has advanced without adequate knowledge about its short-term and long-term psychosocial side effects. Research efforts are sorely needed on these topics. Many of the studies cited in this chapter are based on fairly weak research designs, involve small study samples, and lack control or comparison groups to study the differential effects of medication on different types of youth. There are few, if any, larger-scale studies using longitudinal designs. Research is especially needed with regard to abused and neglected youth and those in institutional care. Using larger study samples could enable us to identify factors that predict psychosocial effects of medication and could allow the assessment of outcomes such as treatment satisfaction, treatment adherence, and such indicators of well-being as self-esteem, autonomy, self-efficacy, and stigma. In addition, longitudinal studies of children who are medicated as they age into adolescence and adulthood are critically needed to enable us to examine whether changes in relationship to medications occur over time, what sort of changes they are, and whether certain predictable "medication career" paths, as proposed by Karp (1996), who studied adults taking antidepressants for depression, also hold true for youth. In short, the mental health field's current knowledge is very limited and its ignorance vast. Drugging so many of our children should compel us to learn much more about the hidden and unintended psychosocial side effects on them.

References

Allen, S. and R. Drabman. 1991. Attributions of children with learning disabilities who are treated with psychostimulants. *Learning Disability Quarterly* 14 (1): 75–79.

Alston, C. and D. Romney. 1992. A comparison of medicated and nonmedicated attention-deficit disordered hyperactive boys. *Acta Paedopsychiatrica: International Journal of Child and Adolescent Psychiatry* 55 (2): 65–70.

Amarasingham, L. 1980. Social and cultural perspectives on medication refusal. *American Journal of Psychiatry* 137 (3): 353–358.

Amirkhan, J. 1982. Expectancies and attributions for hyperactive and medicated hyperactive students. *Journal of Abnormal Child Psychology* 10 (2): 265–276.

Antonuccio, D., D. Burns, and W. Danton. 2002. Antidepressants: A triumph of marketing over science? *Prevention and Treatment* 5:N.p.

Armstrong, L. 1993. *And They Call It Help: The Psychiatric Policing of America's Children.* Reading Mass.: Addison-Wesley.

Augoustinos, M. 1986. Psychiatric inpatients' attitudes toward mental disorder and the tendency to adopt a sick-role. *Psychological Reports* 58 (2): 495–498.

Awad, A. G., L. N. Voruganti, R. J. Heslegrave, and T. P. Hogan. 1996. Assessment of patient's subjective experience in acute neuroleptic treatment: Implications for compliance and outcome. *International Clinical Psychopharmacology* 11:55–59.

Batten, D. 1996. Informed consent by children and adolescents to psychiatric treatment. *Australian and New Zealand Journal of Psychiatry* 30 (5): 623–632.

Baxley, G., P. Turner, and W. Greenwold. 1978. Hyperactive children's knowledge and attitudes concerning drug treatment. *Journal of Pediatric Psychology* 8:172–176.

Bekelman, J., Y. Li, and C. Gross. 2003. Scope and impact of financial conflicts of interest in biomedical research. *Journal of the American Medical Association* 289 (4): 454–465.

Bernstein, G. A., L. K. Anderson, J. M. Hektner, and G. M. Realmuto. 2000. Imipramine compliance in adolescents. *Journal of the American Academy of Child and Adolescent Psychiatry* 39 (3): 284–291.

Boice, M. M. 1998. Chronic illness in adolescence. *Adolescence* 33 (132): 927–939.

Borden, K. A. and R. T. Brown. 1989. Attributional outcomes: The subtle messages of treatments for attention deficit disorder. *Cognitive Therapy and Research* 13 (2): 147–160.

Bowen, J., T. Fenton, and L. Rappaport. 1991. Stimulant medication and attention deficit–hyperactivity disorder. *American Journal of Diseases of Children* 145:291–295.

Breggin, P. 1983. Iatrogenic Helplessness in Authoritarian Psychiatry. In R. Morgan, ed., *The Iatrogenics Handbook: A Critical Look at Research and Practice in the Helping Professions.* Fair Oaks, Calif: Morgan Foundation Publishers.

———. 1999. Psychostimulants in the treatment of children diagnosed with ADHD. Part II. Adverse effects on brain and behavior. *Ethical Human Sciences and Services* 1 (3): 213–242.

Breggin, P. and G. Breggin. 1994. *The War Against Children.* New York: St. Martin's.

Brown, R. T., K. A. Borden, M. E. Wynne et al. 1987. Compliance with pharmacological and cognitive treatments for attention deficit disorder. *Journal of the American Academy of Child and Adolescent Psychiatry* 26 (4): 521–526.

Clarke, C. H. 1998. An exploratory study of the meaning of prescription medication to children diagnosed with attention deficit hyperactivity disorder. *Dissertation Abstracts International Section A: Humanities and Social Sciences* 58 (9–A): 3722.

Cohen, C. I. 1993. The biomedicalization of psychiatry: A critical overview. *Community Mental Health Journal* 29 (6): 509–521.

Cohen, N. J. and L. Thompson. 1982. Perceptions and attitudes of hyperactive children and their mothers regarding treatment with methylphenidate. *Canadian Journal of Psychiatry* 27 (1): 40–42.

Connor, D., K. Ozbayrak, R. Harrison, and R. Melloni. 1998. Prevalence and patterns of psychotropic and anticonvulsant medication use in children and adolescents referred to residential treatment. *Journal of Child and Adolescent Psychopharmacology* 8 (1): 27–38.

Conrad, P. 1985. The meaning of medications: Another look at compliance. *Social Science and Medicine* 20 (1): 29–37.

Conrad, P. and J. Schneider. 1992. *Deviance and Medicalization: From Badness to Sickness.* Philadelphia: Temple University Press.

Cromer, B. and K. Tarnowski. 1989. Noncompliance in adolescents: A review. *Journal of Developmental and Behavioral Pediatrics* 10 (4): 207–215.

Diller, L. 1999. More and more, families seem eager to take the Ritalin step (commentary). *Los Angeles Times.* December 27.

dosReis, S., J. Zito, D. Safer, and K. Soeken. 2001. Mental health services for youths in foster care and disabled youths. *American Journal of Public Health* 91 (7): 1094–1099.

Fisher, R. and S. Fisher. 1997. Are We Justified in Treating Children with Psychotropic Drugs? In E. Seymour Fisher and E. Roger Greenberg, eds., *From Placebo to Panacea: Putting Psychiatric Drugs to the Test,* 307–322. New York: John Wiley.

Fisher, S. and R. Greenberg. 1997. The Curse of the Placebo: Fanciful Pursuit of a Pure Biological Therapy. In E. Seymour Fisher and E. Roger Greenberg, eds., *From Placebo to Panacea: Putting Psychiatric Drugs to the Test,* xii, 404. New York: John Wiley.

Flisher, A., R. Kramer, C. Hoven, and S. Greenwald. 1997. Psychosocial characteristics of physically abused children and adolescents. *Journal of the American Academy of Child and Adolescent Psychiatry* 36 (1): 123–131.

Frankel, F., D. Cantwell, R. Myatt, and D. Feinberg. 1999. Do stimulants improve self-esteem in children with ADHD and peer problems? *Journal of Child and Adolescent Psychopharmacology* 9 (3): 185–194.

Gadow, K. D. 1992. Pediatric psychopharmacotherapy: A review of recent research. *Journal of Child Psychology and Psychiatry* 33:153–195.

———. 1997. An overview of three decades of research in pediatric psychopharmacoepidemiology. *Journal of Child and Adolescent Psychopharmacology* 7 (4): 219–236.

Gara, M., S. Rosenberg, and B. Cohen. 1987. Personal identity and the schizophrenic process: An integration. *Psychiatry: Journal for the Study of Interpersonal Processes* 50 (3): 267–279.

Ghaziuddin, N., C. A. King, J. D. Hovey, J. Zaccagnini, and M. Ghaziuddin. 1999. Medication noncompliance in adolescents with psychiatric disorders. *Child Psychiatry and Human Development* 30 (2): 103–110.

Goldstein, M. 1992. Psychosocial strategies for maximizing the effects of psychotropic medications for schizophrenia and mood disorder. *Psychopharmacology Bulletin* 28 (3): 237–240.

Greenhill, L., J. Halperin, and H. Abikof. 1999. Stimulant medications. *Journal of the American Academy of Child and Adolescent Psychiatry* 38 (5): 503–512.

Harter, S. 1990. Self and Identity Development. In S. Feldman and G. Elliott, eds., *At the Threshold: The Developing Adolescent.* Cambridge, Mass.: Harvard University Press.

Hellewell, J. 2002. Patients' subjective experiences of antipsychotics: Clinical relevance. *CNS Drugs* 16 (7): 457–471.

Hoencamp, E., A. Stevens, and J. Haffmans. 2002. Patients' attitudes toward antidepressants. *Psychiatric Services* 53 (9): 1180–1181.

Ialongo, N., M. Lopez, W. Horn et al. 1994. Effects of psychostimulant medication on self-perceptions of competence, control, and mood in children with attention deficit disorder. *Journal of Clinical Child Psychology* 23 (2): 161–173.

Jacobs, D. 1999. A close and critical examination of how psychopharmacotherapy research is conducted. *Journal of Mind and Behavior* 20 (3): 311–350.

Jacobs, D. and D. Cohen. 1999. What is really known about psychological alterations produced by psychiatric drugs? *International Journal of Risk and Safety in Medicine* 12 (1): 37–47.

James, B. 1989. *Treating Traumatized Children: New Insights and Creative Interventions.* New York: Free Press.

Jensen, P., B. Vitiello, H. Leonard, and T. Laughren. 1994. Design and methodology issues for clinical treatment trials in children and adolescents. *Psychopharmacology Bulletin* 30 (1): 3–8.

Jensen, S., V. S. Bhatara, B. Vitiello, K. Hoagwood, M. Feil, and L. B. Burke. 1999a. Psychoactive medication prescribing practices for U. S. children: Gaps between research and clinical practice. *Journal of the American Academy of Child and Adolescent Psychiatry* 38 (5): 557–565.

Jensen, S., L. Kettle, M. T. Roper et al. 1999b. Are stimulants overprescribed? Treatment of ADHD in four U.S. communities. *Journal of the American Academy of Child and Adolescent Psychiatry* 38 (7): 797–804.

Johnston, C., S. Fine, M. Weiss, J. Weiss, G. Weiss, and W. S. Freeman. 2000. Effects of stimulant medication treatment on mother's and children's attributions for the behavior of children with attention deficit hyperactivity disorder. *Journal of Abnormal Child Psychology* 28 (4): 371–382.

Kalb, C. 2000. Drugged-out toddlers. *Newsweek,* March 6, 53.

Kaplan, S. and J. Busner. 1997. Prescribing practices of inpatient child psychiatrists under three auspices of care. *Journal of Child and Adolescent Psychopharmacology* 7 (4): 275–286.

Karp, D. 1996. *Speaking of Sadness.* New York: Oxford University Press.

Keller, M. B., W. Lavori, W. R. Beardslee et al. 1991. Depression in children and adolescents: New data on "undertreatment" and a literature review on the efficacy of available treatments. *Journal of Affective Disorders* 21 (3): 163–171.

King, C. A,. J. D. Hovey, E. Brand, R. Wilson, and N. Ghaziuddin. 1997. Suicidal adolescents after hospitalization: Parent and family impacts on treatment follow-through. *Journal of the American Academy of Child and adolescent Psychiatry* 36 (1): 85–93.

Kirsch, I., A. Scoboria, and T. Moore. 2002. Antidepressants and placebos: Secrets, revelations, and unanswered questions. *Prevention and Treatment* 5:N.p.

Klee, L. and N. Halfon. 1987. Mental health care for foster children in California. *Child Abuse and Neglect* 11:63–74.

Knowlton, L. 1995. Licensed to heal. *Los Angeles Times.* August 29.

Kramer, P. 1993. *Listening to Prozac.* New York: Penguin.

Lewinsohn, P., P. Rohde, and J. Seeley. 1998. Treatment of adolescent depression: Frequency of services and impact on functioning in young adulthood. *Depression and Anxiety* 7:47–52.

Lloyd, A., W. Horan, S. R. Borgaro, J. M. Stokes, D. L. Pogge, and D. Harvey. 1998. Predictors of medication compliance after hospital discharge in adolescent psychiatric patients. *Journal of Child and Adolescent Psychopharmacology* 8 (2): 133–141.

Lucksted, A. and R. Coursey. 1995. Consumer perceptions of pressure and force in psychiatric treatments. *Psychiatric Services* 46 (2): 146–152.

Maier, S. and M. Seligman. 1976. Learned helplessness: Theory and evidence. *Journal of Experimental Psychology* 105:3–46.

Martin, A., T. Van Hoof, D. Stubbe, T. Sherwin, and L. Scahill. 2003. Multiple psychotropic pharmacotherapy among child and adolescent enrollees in Connecticut Medicaid managed care. *Psychiatric Services* 54 (1): 72–77.

Masi, G., M. Marcheschi, and L. Luccherino. 1996. Psychotropic medication in adolescence: Psychodynamic and clinical considerations. *Adolescence* 31 (124): 925–933.

Melamed, Y. and H. Szor. 1999. The therapist and the patient: Coping with non-compliance. *Comprehensive Psychiatry* 40 (5): 391–395.

Milich, R., C. Carlson, W. Pelham, and B. Licht. 1991. Effects of methylphenidate on the persistence of ADHD boys following failure experiences. *Journal of Abnormal Child Psychology* 19 (5): 519–536.

Moline, S. and W. Frankenberger. 2001. Use of stimulant medication for treatment of attention-deficit/hyperactivity disorder: A survey of middle and high school students' attitudes. *Psychology in the Schools* 38 (6): 569–584.

Morrison, J. et al. 1977. Relationship between psychiatric patients' attitudes toward mental illness and attitudes of dependence. *Psychological Reports* 41 (3, Pt 2): 1194.

Moses, T. 2000. Attachment theory and residential treatment: A study of staff-client relationships. *American Journal of Orthopsychiatry* 70 (4): 474–490.

Murphy, J., J. Pardeck, W. Chung, and J. Choi. 1994. Symbolic violence and social control in the post–Total Institution era. *Journal of Sociology and Social Welfare* 21 (4): 115–132.

Nevins, D. B. 1990. Psychoanalytic perspectives on the use of medication for mental illness. *Bulletin of the Menninger Clinic* 54:323–339.

Ohan, J. L. and C. Johnston. 1999. Attributions in adolescents medicated for attention-deficit/hyperactivity disorder. *Journal of Attention Disorders* 3 (1): 49–60.

Olfson, M., S. Marcus, and H. Pincus. 1999. Trends in office-based practice. *American Journal of Psychology* 156 (3): 451–457.

Parker, G., I. Anderson, and P. Haddad. 2003. Clinical trials of antidepressant medications are producing meaningless results. *British Journal of Psychiatry* 183:102–104.

Pear, R. 2000. Effort on mood drugs for young is backed. *New York Times.* March 21.

Pelham, W., H. Kipp, E. Gnagy et al. 1997. Effects of methylphenidate and expectancy on ADHD children's performance, self-evaluations, persistence, and attributions on a cognitive task. *Experimental and Clinical Psychopharmacology* 5 (1): 3–13.

Penzerro, R. and L. Lein. 1995. Burning their bridges: Disordered attachment and foster care discharge. *Child Welfare* 74 (2): 351–366.

Pilowsky, D. 1995. Psychopathology among children placed in family foster care. *Psychiatric Services* 46:906–910.

Rappaport, N. and P. Chubinsky. 2000. The meaning of psychotropic medications for children, adolescents, and their families. *Journal of the American Academy of Child and Adolescent Psychiatry* 39 (9): 1198–1200.

Rest, E. and K. Watson. 1984. Growing up in foster care. *Child Welfare* 63 (4): 291–305.

Rosen, L., S. O'Leary, and G. Conway. 1985. The withdrawal of stimulant medication for hyperactivity: Overcoming detrimental attributions. *Behavior Therapy* 16 (5): 538–544.

Rushton, J. and T. Whitmire. 2001. Pediatric stimulant and selective serotonin reuptake inhibitor treatment trends. *Archives of Pediatric Adolescent Medicine* 155:560–565.

Saari, C. 1991. *The Creation of Meaning in Clinical Social Work.* New York: Guilford Press.

Safer, D., J. Zito, and S. dosReis. 2003. Concomitant psychotropic medication for youths. *American Journal of Psychiatry* 160 (3): 438–449.

Safer, D., J. Zito, and E. Fine. 1996. Increased methylphenidate usage for attention deficit disorder in the 1990s. *Pediatrics* 94:462–464.

Sarwer-Foner, G. 1960. The role of neuroleptic medication in psychotherapeutic interaction. *Comprehensive Psychiatry* 1:291–300.

Schowalter, J. 1989. Psychodynamics and medication. *Journal of the American Academy of Child and Adolescent Psychiatry* 28 (5): 681–684.

Scott, C., C. Lore, and R. Owen. 1992. Increasing medication compliance and peer support among psychiatrically diagnosed students. *Journal of School Health* 62 (10): 478–480.

Shuchman, M. 1991. Psychiatric drugs used to treat children. *Washington Post.* August 13.

Sirey, J. A., M. L. Bruce, G. S. Alexopoulos, D. A. Perlick, S. J. Friedman, and B. S. Meyers. 2001. Stigma as a barrier to recovery: Perceived stigma and patient-rated severity of illness as predictors of antidepressant drug adherence. *Psychiatric Services* 52 (12): 1615–1620.

Stein, E., B. Evans, R. Mazumdar, and N. Rae-Grant. 1996. The mental health of children in foster care: A comparison with community and clinical samples. *Canadian Journal of Psychiatry* 41 (6): 385–391.

Stein, J. 1995. *Residential Treatment of Adolescents and Children: Issues, Principles, and Techniques.* Chicago: Nelson-Hall Publishers.

Tebbi, C., M. Richards, M. Cummings, and M. Zevon. 1988. The role of parent-adolescent concordance in compliance with cancer chemotherapy. *Adolescence* 23 (91): 599–611.

Trupin, E., V. Tarico, B. Low, and R. Jemelka. 1993. Children on child protective service caseloads: Prevalence and nature of serious emotional disturbance. *Child Abuse and Neglect* 17 (3): 345–355.

U.S. Public Health Service. 1999. http://www.surgeongeneral.gov/library/mental-health/home.html. *Mental Health: A Report of the Surgeon General.*

van Es, S., E. le Coq, A. Brouwer, I. Mesters, A. Nagelkerke, and V. Colland. 1998. Adherence-related behavior in adolescents with asthma: Results from focus group interviews. *Journal of Asthma* 35 (8): 637–646.

Van Putten, T. and P. May. 1978. Subjective response as a predictor of outcome in pharmacotherapy: The consumer has a point. *Archives of General Psychiatry* 35 (4): 477–480.

Venarde, D. F. 1999. Medication and meaning: Psychotherapy patients' subjective experiences of taking selective serotonin reuptake inhibitors (SSRIs). *Dissertation Abstracts International: Section B: The Sciences and Engineering* 60 (4–B): 1874.

Vitiello, B. and P. Jensen. 1995. Developmental perspectives in pediatric psycho-pharmacology. *Psychopharmacology Bulletin* 31:75–81.

Walkup, J. T. 1995. Clinical decision making in child and adolescent psychopharmacology. *Child and Adolescent Psychiatric Clinics of North America* 4 (1): 23–40.

Weber, T. 1998a. Caretakers Routinely Drug Foster Children. *Los Angeles Times.* May 17.

———. 1998b. Foster care drug policy is focus of reform plan. *Los Angeles Times.* December 31.

Whalen, C. and B. Henker. 1997. Stimulant pharmacotherapy for attention-deficit/hyperactivity disorders: An analysis of progress, problems, and prospects. In E. Seymour Fisher and E. Roger Greenberg, eds., *From Placebo to Panacea: Putting Psychiatric Drugs to the Test,* xii, 404. New York: John Wiley.

Williams, C. 1999. Doing health, doing gender: Teenagers, diabetes, and asthma. *Social Science and Medicine* 50:387–396.

Williams, R., H. Hollis, and K. Benoit. 1998. Attitudes toward psychiatric medications among incarcerated female adolescents. *Journal of the American Academy of Child and Adolescent Psychiatry* 37 (12): 1301–1307.

Woodgate, R. 1998. Health professionals caring for chronically ill adolescents: Adolescents' perspectives. *Journal of the Society of Pediatric Nurses* 3 (2): 57–68.

Yancey, A. 1992. Identity formation and social maladaptation in foster adolescents. *Adolescence* 27 (108): 819–831.

Zima, B. T., R. Bussing, G. M. Crecelius, A. Kaufman, and T. R. Belin. 1999a. Psychotropic medication treatment patterns among school-aged children in foster care. *Journal of Child and Adolescent Psychopharmacology* 9 (3): 135–147.

———. 1999b. Psychotropic medication use among children in foster care: Relationship to severe psychiatric disorders. *American Journal of Public Health* 89 (11): 1732–1735.

Zimmerman, R. 1988. Childhood depression: New theoretical formulations and implications for foster care services. *Child Welfare* 67 (1): 37–47.

Zito, J. M., D. J. Safer, S. dosReis, J. F. Gardner, M. Boles, and F. Lynch. 2000. Trends in the prescribing of psychotropic medications to preschoolers. *Journal of the American Medical Association* 283 (8): 1025–1030.

PART VI

ETHICS, LAWS,
AND REGULATIONS

Chapter 22

Social Work, Mental Health, and Mental Disorders: The Ethical Dimensions

Frederic G. Reamer

There is little doubt that most contemporary social workers identify mental health as their primary interest in the profession. Although many social workers point to other areas of practice—child welfare, criminal justice, elderly affairs, poverty, health care, affordable housing, teenage pregnancy, and so on—mental health issues have been the largest draw in the profession for some time (Gibelman 1995).

Social workers' grasp of clinical and policy issues related to mental health has become much firmer over time. Along with members of allied professions—such as counseling, psychology, psychiatry, and psychiatric nursing—social workers have developed a greatly more mature understanding of clinical phenomena such as affective disorders, anxiety disorders, psychoses, personality disorders, interpersonal conflict, suicide, co-occurring disorders, and substance abuse. Through accumulated research evidence and anecdotal experience we have far greater understanding of pertinent etiological factors and the effectiveness of diverse clinical interventions. In the policy realm, social workers have learned a great deal about wide-ranging issues related to the consequences of deinstitutionalization; the costs and benefits of various models of community-based care; the relevance of race, ethnicity, socioeconomic status, and gender in the diagnosis of mental illness and the delivery of services; the effectiveness of various prevention models; and the impact of managed care on the availability of mental health services. What social workers knew about mental health practice and policy during its early years, following the profession's formal inauguration in the late nineteenth century, pales in comparison with our contemporary fund of knowledge (Kerson 2002; Mattaini 1997).

As a profession, however, social work has done less well with respect to the ethical dimensions of mental health practice and policy. Only recently have social workers begun to pay more than superficial attention to a number of compelling ethical issues related to mental health and the treatment of mental disorders. This is more of an observation than a criticism. To be sure, social workers' fairly recent acknowledgment of serious ethical issues related to mental health parallels the trend in nearly every other corner of the profession, with the possible exception of social work in traditional medical settings (hospitals, nursing homes, rehabilitation facilities). Social workers in these settings generally have been more cognizant of ethical issues because of the prominence of the bioethical challenges that pervade medical care (Foster 1995; Reamer 1995). In fact, developments in the bioethics field have paved the way for social workers' more recent concern about ethical issues generally and, in particular, with respect to mental health.

My principal purpose in this chapter is to survey current thinking and scholarship about professional ethics, social work ethics, and mental health, and highlight three key, overarching issues that warrant social workers' attention. More specifically, I will provide a brief overview of the nature of professional ethics generally, discuss their relevance to social work, and provide a blueprint that outlines essential ethics-related knowledge and agenda items for contemporary social workers active in the mental health field. On the basis of my assessment of the current knowledge base and cutting-edge issues, I will construct three main arguments concerning the need for social workers to (1) invigorate their embrace of traditional social work values, (2) enhance their understanding of, and ability to respond to, ethical dilemmas, and (3) develop comprehensive ethics-related risk-management agendas.

The Historical Context

The applied and professional ethics movement began primarily with the development of the bioethics field in the early 1970s, when a small group of scholars and practitioners began to investigate moral and ethical issues in health care. A key feature of this movement was the deliberate, systematic, and explicit application of moral philosophy and ethical theory to the practical ethical problems faced by various groups of practitioners (for example, doctors, lawyers, engineers, journalists, military officers, police officers, accountants, clergy, social workers). Before this period, moral philosophers had been occupied with rather abstract discussions about the meaning of ethical terminology and the derivation of abstract ethical principles and theory—what is known commonly as meta-ethics (Frankena 1973; Hancock 1974).

For several reasons, in the late 1960s and early 1970s a number of moral philosophers and professionals began to turn their attention to the practical and compelling ethical issues that professionals encounter (Callahan and Bok 1980; Reamer and Abramson 1982). First, in the context of the turbulent 1960s, the general public in the United States, and eventually many professionals, struggled with various "rights" issues, such as civil rights, patients' rights, consumers' rights, prisoners' rights, and welfare rights. In addition, a series of technological developments, especially related to health care (for example, genetic engineering, infertility treatments, organ transplantation, end-of-life interventions), triggered a diverse array of complex ethical issues and debates. Further, widespread media publicity about ethical misconduct on the part of various prominent public officials and professionals (politicians, doctors, clergy, lawyers, and so on)—particularly following the Watergate scandal in the early 1970s involving U.S. president Richard Nixon—led many professions to examine more closely the adequacy of prevailing ethical conduct and standards. Also, the various professions had begun to question the extent to which empirical science and positivism would be able to solve a diverse array of challenging social questions (Sloan 1980).

The proliferation of bioethics and professional ethics "think tanks" in the United States during this period—beginning especially with the Hastings Center in New York and the Kennedy Institute of Ethics at Georgetown University—is a major indicator of the rapid growth of interest in this subject. Today, in fact, the number of such centers is so large that there is a national Association for Practical and Professional Ethics, which includes nearly one hundred organizations as members. This relatively new field has also produced two prominent and influential encyclopedias: the *Encyclopedia of Bioethics* and the *Encyclopedia of Applied Ethics*.

Clearly, the emergence of the applied and professional ethics field influenced the development of social work ethics. Before this period, social work literature on ethics was relatively sparse and focused primarily on the nature of the profession's core values and mission. A number of prominent and influential commentaries appeared in U.S. literature during this time in which authors defined, explored, and critiqued the profession's core values and mission (for a comprehensive overview, see Reamer 2001a). Several authors developed frameworks for examining social work values (Pumphrey 1959; Gordon 1965; Levy 1973, 1976).

In the late 1970s and early 1980s, a small number of social work scholars began writing about ethical issues and dilemmas, drawing in part on literature, concepts, and theories from moral philosophy in general and the newer field of applied and professional ethics (Loewenberg and Dolgoff 1982; Reamer 1982; Rhodes 1986). Since then, the social work literature has explored a range of ethical issues pertaining to ethical dilemmas in practice, ethical decision making, and, most recently, ethics-related risk management. The profession is now at a point where it needs to refine its understanding and analysis of ethical issues germane to its specialty areas, mental health being among the most compelling and relevant.

Social Work Values and Mental Health

One of the defining features of social work has been its earnest concern about values. One of the most significant developments in the profession's history was the addition, for the first time, of a core set of values in the version of the National Association of Social Workers (NASW) Code of Ethics that was ratified in 1996. The NASW Code of Ethics Revision Committee (which I chaired) decided that it was time for the profession to make a formal commitment to a set of core values, which would be derived from an exhaustive review of relevant literature and commentary in the field. The current code, only the third since the inception of the NASW, highlights the profession's core values of service, social justice, dignity and worth of the person, importance of human relationships, integrity, and competence (Reamer 1997).

Despite their lofty and rather idealistic sound, these values have profound implications for social workers' involvement in the mental health field. In fact, ideally these core values should move social workers to challenge several common practices in the field. As several social work scholars have demonstrated (Kutchins and Kirk 1997; Saleebey 1997), mental health professionals' narrow view of mental illness through the lens of the medical model, mainly via their reliance on the American Psychiatric Association's *Diagnostic and Statistical Manual,* has tended to "pathologize" clients and lead to preoccupation with clients' deficits. Many, although certainly not all, social workers have been captivated by the mystique of diagnostic criteria and labels that were popularized by the psychiatric and psychology fields. Although there have been recent loud and clamoring calls for social workers to embrace a "strengths perspective" in their approach to clients' mental health issues, the profession continues to be dominated by a medical-model perspective, a perspective that clashes with several of social work's core values related to client dignity and worth and the need to appreciate the social context and relationships in which clients actually live their lives.

A second unfortunate values-related tendency in the mental health field has been the almost exclusive focus of many practitioners on clients' narrow mental health symptoms. In social work we have struggled with a trend, which began primarily in the late 1970s, characterized by practitioners who obtained an M.S.W. primarily as a fast-track way to become a psychotherapist and eligible for third-party reimbursement. Certainly there are many exceptions, in the form of clinical social workers who care deeply about broader social justice issues—such as poverty, discrimination, and oppression—and who understand the ways in which these phenomena affect mental health. For too many clinical social workers, however, social justice is a politically correct topic to be discussed fleetingly in social work school and then cast aside upon graduation. Many would have chosen to earn a degree in another, more clinically focused profession (such as counseling) if that credential had qualified practitioners for third-party payment. Upon becoming independent clinicians, many practitioners with social work degrees choose to identify themselves professionally as "therapists" rather than as "social workers," the implication being that the mission and values of the profession are less compelling than the allure of whatever status and connotation are attached to the therapist label (Billups 1992; Specht and Courtney 1994). What this has meant is that a significant number of individuals who were trained as social workers and who are actively involved in the mental health field are not paying significant, if any, attention to broader public policy and social justice issues that constitute the heart of social work's mission and have such profound ramifications for individuals' mental health.

To complicate matters, some social workers are engaged in proprietary, profit-making pursuits that have turned into breeding grounds for conflicts of interest. These practitioners depend to a considerable extent on financial reimbursement from third-party payers (primarily insurance companies, managed-care organizations, and government agencies). Incentives abound for practitioners to manipulate data on clinical diagnoses, lengths of stay, and services provided (Kirk and Kutchins 1988). Social workers' motives in these instances are not always exclusively self-serving, of course. Some deceptive practice may be motivated largely or partly by social workers' genuine concern for client well-being; practitioners may view "creative" billing and documentation as the questionable means that are justified by the virtuous ends of serving people in need—a form of renegade social work. While some unscrupulous social workers bill and document fraudulently for self-serving purposes, others may resemble more closely the profession's version of Robin Hood.

I believe it is useful for social workers to sharpen their thinking about the ways in which their involvement in the mental health arena is consistent with the profession's long-standing values and its earnest efforts to enhance "the public good." At times throughout social work's history, practitioners have taken an *enlightened view* of what it means to enhance the public good and commonweal (Reamer 1992b), which in my opinion entails spending at least a portion of one's time serving especially vulnerable citizens. This service can be clinical in nature, or it can take the form of community organizing, social action, or advocacy (for example, organizing community-based groups to lobby public officials about the mental health needs of uninsured individuals, testifying at legislative hearings concerning funding for community mental health programs, and protesting discriminatory managed-care regulations). A key element is that these efforts focus on the needs of people who are, in the words of the *NASW Code of Ethics,* "vulnerable, oppressed, and living in poverty" (NASW 1996). Within this view, professional self-interest is secondary (although, realistically, not irrelevant).

In contrast, a *narrow view* of social workers' efforts to enhance the public good and commonweal is characterized by activities that serve primarily to advance the interests of practitioners, with only secondary concern about the implications for the public in general and, more specifically, its most vulnerable and least advantaged members (Rawls 1971). Social workers' efforts to enhance reimbursement rates, strengthen license protections, and market their services—all of which are legitimate activities on their face—reflect a narrow view of the profession's mission and efforts to enhance the public good when they are motivated primarily by self-interest (which can be camouflaged by the use of baroque rhetoric that suggests more altruistic motives). Too often, these advocacy efforts enhance the delivery of services to more-, rather than less-, affluent and privileged individuals. Although the public may benefit from stricter licensing regulations and greater access to services, and while many social workers pursue these goals quite earnestly and sincerely, a portion of the profession seems motivated primarily by self-serving interests that are largely independent of social work's moral mission—a practice that can be described, at best, as "enlightened self-interest." As Siporin (1982) has observed,

> In the history of social work as a profession, social workers clearly and consistently had a public image and public position as moral agents of society. They were seen as such because of their role in helping people to find and choose ways of individual and social functioning that they themselves and the general society could consider "right" and "good." Social workers stood and fought for certain values, some of which were not generally accepted or implemented by the larger society. They took the traditional values of charity and justice, inspirited them, and gave them secular and expanded definitions. These were then used to establish a new set of moral and ethical principles as well as social institutional provisions for the "social welfare." Welfare, as Frankel said, is a "moral ideal." The welfare to be protected and enhanced was that of all the people in society—the poor, minorities, and the disadvantaged, as well as the rich and privileged. . . . In recent years, however,

this social work value system and its moral vision have been fragmented and weakened. (518–519)

To reclaim its enlightened view of the public good that is consistent with the profession's values, social work's involvement in the mental health field would resemble more closely a secular calling, where one serves primarily because one cares deeply about the most vulnerable and least advantaged, and about social justice. Professional satisfaction is derived primarily from knowing that one has served well, as opposed to enhancing the monetary and status-related fruit of one's labor. This is not to suggest, naively or self-righteously, that social workers should live ascetic lives devoid of status and creature comforts. Certainly, reasonable compensation and job-related perquisites do not necessarily corrupt. Social work is full of remarkably talented, dedicated, and earnest professionals who are amply rewarded for their hard work.

What matters in the end, however, is one's principal motive. A truly enlightened approach to social work in mental health elevates moral mission above self-interest. As Gustafson (1982), a theologian who addressed a social work audience, notes:

> I suppose that studies have been made of the motives of persons going into the learned service professions. I have not attempted to search for such. My impression is that for many persons, especially those going into relatively low-salaried service professions, the incentive is a deeply moral one. The presence of poverty, social disorganization, disease, personal anguish, injustice in the distribution of human services, ignorance, and similar factors move persons to seek the education and training to relieve these impediments to human fulfillment. Incentive might well go beyond relief from suffering and avoidance of evil; persons see unfulfilled possibilities in the lives of individuals, groups, and communities which might be better realized by conscientious and competent professional activity. Such motives and incentives are not primarily self-interested; persons of great ability could certainly receive greater financial remuneration and status in other occupations. These moral motives are part of a "calling."
> (511)

Ethical Dilemmas

The second core challenge for social workers concerned about mental health is to strengthen their ability to identify and address ethical dilemmas in practice. First, it is important to distinguish between ethical issues and dilemmas. There are many ethical issues in social work that do not rise to the level of an ethical dilemma. For example, social workers in mental health settings should be concerned about ethical issues such as protecting clients' confidential information from curious relatives, complying with mandatory reporting laws pertaining to neglect or abuse of children or the elderly, and submitting accurate, as opposed to fraudulent, invoices to managed-care organizations. These are rather straightforward issues. In contrast, ethical dilemmas occur when relatively straightforward ethical duties clash or conflict with other ethical duties. To use the helpful terminology introduced decades ago by the philosopher W. D. Ross (1930), ethical dilemmas—the "hard" cases—occur when two or more prima facie duties clash or conflict. Conflicting prima facie duties force us to make difficult choices—what Ross refers to as our *actual* duty. Prototypical examples include social workers' decisions about whether to comply with a law or regulation that seems to be unjust (for instance, a regulation that requires an Axis I or Axis II diagnosis from the *Diagnostic and Statistical Manual* in order for mental health services to be covered); whether to interfere with a client's fundamental right to self-determination when the client is engaging in a form of self-destructive behavior (for instance, when a psychiatric client, who is legally competent, contemplates suicide to escape the readily apparent anguish in his or her life); and whether to terminate services to a noncompliant client who clearly needs mental health services.

Social workers in mental health settings face three types of ethical dilemmas. The first involves the delivery of clinical services to individuals, couples, families, and small groups (Congress 1998; Linzer 1999; Reamer 1999). Typically these dilemmas involve conflicting duties pertaining to client confidentiality, privacy, privileged communication, the tension between client self-determination and practitioner paternalism, dual relationships and boundary issues, and conflicts of interest.

The second group of dilemmas involves social workers' involvement in social work administration, planning, research and evaluation, social policy, and community practice (so-called "macro" practice). Examples of such dilemmas are social workers' decisions about whether it is morally justifiable to "fudge" certain administratively relevant statistics to save a critically important but financially troubled agency; displace vulnerable community residents to make way for a valuable, job-producing economic development project; cut important social services to vulnerable groups in order to ensure an agency's fiscal health; and engage in illegal, radical protest against government-sponsored, draconian welfare regulations.

The final group of ethical dilemmas involves social workers' relationships with colleagues. This category primarily includes ethical decisions about colleagues who appear to be involved in some form of unethical conduct or who are impaired in a way that compromises that quality of their work. In my experience, these "whistle-blowing" dilemmas are among the most challenging.

In addition to cultivating their ability to identify and grasp ethical dilemmas—which often surface wrapped in various shades of gray rather than in stark black-and-white choices—social workers must learn about constructive strategies designed to help them make sound ethical decisions. Comprehensive ethics education in schools and departments of social work is just beginning to emerge (Reamer 2001a). Thus, most practicing social workers in mental health settings concluded their formal education at a time when conceptually oriented decision-making protocols were not included in the curriculum. Although some social workers have encountered ethical decision-making frameworks in the context of continuing-education offerings, most have not. Social workers would do well to acquaint themselves with the handful of decision-making outlines, frameworks, and protocols now available in the social work literature (Congress 1998; Loewenberg and Dolgoff 1996; Reamer 1999). Typically these frameworks provide practitioners with an outline of steps they can follow to enhance the likelihood that they are approaching ethical dilemmas systematically and thoroughly. In this regard, some of social work's most impressive developments in recent years are based on our enhanced understanding of the ways in which knowledge of ethical theory (what moral philosophers refer to as theories of meta-ethics and normative ethics), codes of ethics, ethics consultation, institutional ethics committees, institutional review boards, legal considerations (statutes, regulations), and cultural and ethnic diversity (variation among cultural and ethnic groups with respect to moral norms and ethical rights and duties) can strengthen ethical decisions.

Some of these elements require specialized knowledge to which most contemporary social workers have not been exposed. For example, many health and mental health settings now have formal institutional ethics committees (IECs). The concept of IECs emerged most prominently in 1976, when the New Jersey Supreme Court ruled that Karen Ann Quinlan's family and physicians should consult an ethics committee in deciding whether to remove her from life-support systems (although a number of hospitals have had something resembling ethics committees since at least the 1920s). The New Jersey court based its ruling in part on a seminal article that appeared in the *Baylor Law Review* in 1975, in which a pediatrician advocated the use of ethics committees in cases when health care professionals face difficult ethical choices (Teel 1975). Social workers in mental health settings need to become familiar with the purposes and modus operandi of ethics committees and the ways in which they can be constructive participants in these committees' efforts to provide colleagues and clients with case consultation, shape ethics-related policies and procedures, and sponsor ethics education and training (Reamer 1987).

Social workers in mental health settings must also become familiar with the growing popularity of ethics consultation. Ethics consultation, as a discrete specialty, began in the late 1960s and early 1970s at Pennsylvania State University, the New Jersey College of Medicine, and the University of Wisconsin, primarily in hospital settings (Fletcher, Quist, and Jonsen 1989; La Puma and Schiedermayer 1991). By the late 1970s "clinical ethics" became a field in and of itself (Pellegrino 1978, 1979; Siegler 1978, 1979). Ethics consultants are individuals who are trained to identify, analyze, and assist colleagues who encounter ethical dilemmas. The relatively few ethics consultants who have social work degrees usually obtain formal education in ethical theory (moral philosophy), applied ethics, and professional ethics to supplement their formal social work education (some ethics consultants are trained primarily in the philosophy and ethics fields and then learn about social work by osmosis or in a more formal way).

Social workers in mental health settings also need to take assertive steps to learn about relevant statutes and regulations that have ethical implications, and about relevant provisions in the *NASW Code of Ethics*. There are a number of federal and state laws and regulations that contain very explicit ethics-related provisions, and social workers who are unfamiliar with them practice at their own peril. Examples of issues addressed in such statutes and regulations concern the nature of clients' right to confidentiality and relevant limitations (for example, laws and regulations concerned with child or elder abuse and neglect, minors who receive social services, individuals who obtain substance abuse counseling, clients who pose a threat to third parties, clients who are HIV +, sharing of confidential information among service providers), clients' right to refuse treatment, involuntary psychiatric commitment, protection of participants in research and evaluation projects, conflicts of interest, boundaries and dual relationships, record retention, and continuing education.

It is also imperative that social workers master the content of the *NASW Code of Ethics* (and any other relevant codes). Most practicing social workers concluded their formal education before the 1996 ratification of the current NASW code. The current code is not a modest revision of the predecessor (1979) code; rather, it is a new document, one with considerable content and novel features not included in the code that was in force when most current practitioners were formally educated. In addition to a statement setting forth social work's central mission and an outline of core values for the profession (both of which are new features), the code contains 155 specific ethical standards to guide social workers' conduct and provide a basis for adjudication of ethics complaints filed against NASW members. Key sections concern social workers' ethical responsibilities to clients (e.g., client self-determination, confidentiality, informed consent, conflicts of interest, dual relationships), to colleagues (e.g., collegial disputes, consultation, impairment), in practice settings (e.g., supervision, consultation, client records, administration, education and training, performance evaluation), as professionals (e.g., competence, discrimination, misrepresentation, private conduct), to the social work profession (e.g., professional integrity, evaluation and research), and to the broader society (e.g., involvement in social and political action). In addition to clarifying standards on a number of issues addressed in the 1979 code (for example, guidelines concerning the disclosure of confidential information to protect third parties, informed consent, and termination of services), the current code addresses a number of issues that the profession simply did not face in the 1970s because the relevant technology did not exist—for example, protecting the confidentiality of e-mail, cellular telephone, and facsimile communications.

Social workers in mental health arenas should also be aware that the implications of the *NASW Code of Ethics* extend far beyond its use as a decision-making guide. Courts of law and state licensing boards frequently cite and draw on the code when issues concerning social workers' ethical conduct arise (Austin, Moline, and Williams 1990; Reamer 1994; Woody 1997). These bodies typically recognize the NASW code as the most visible, comprehensive set of guidelines in the United States and thus invoke it as the principal measuring rod in their assessment of practitioner conduct.

Ethics Risk Management

Beyond enhancing their ability to make sound ethical judgments to protect clients—which should always be social workers' first priority—social workers in mental health settings should draw on the burgeoning knowledge base to minimize risk to themselves by comprehensively assessing the adequacy of their ethics-related policies, practices, and procedures. A significant percentage of litigation filed against social workers in mental health settings and their agencies claims that practitioners violated ethical standards in the profession (Bernstein and Hartsell 1998; Houston-Vega, Nuehring, and Daguio 1997; Reamer 1994). These lawsuits often allege that social workers committed some form of malpractice in the way that they handled confidential information, delivered services (especially with respect to social workers' competence and involvement in dual relationships), and terminated services.

Most social workers have had little education or training on ethics-related risk management, and few have conducted comprehensive assessments of the risks in their own practice settings. Ideally, social workers should conduct an "ethics audit" to enhance quality assurance and prevent ethics-related complaints and lawsuits (Reamer 2001b). The primary purposes of an ethics audit in mental health settings are to: (1) identify pertinent ethical issues, (2) review and assess the adequacy of current practices, policies, and procedures, (3) design a practical strategy to modify current practices, policies, and procedures, as needed, and (4) monitor the implementation of this quality assurance strategy. In addition to being beneficial for clinicians, a social work ethics audit can be useful to social work administrators and supervisors who are concerned about ethical and risk-management issues and whose agencies seek accreditation.

On the basis of data from the insurance industry (reflecting the pattern of ethics-related lawsuits filed against social workers who provide mental health services), state licensing boards (which adjudicate ethics complaints filed against licensed social workers), NASW (which adjudicates ethics complaints filed against members), and criminal courts (concerning a relatively small, but not insignificant, number of criminal cases involving indicted social workers), an ethics audit should focus on a number of key risk areas.

1. *Client rights.* Social workers should assess whether they have developed comprehensive, clearly worded, and comprehensible summaries of clients' rights related to confidentiality and privacy (for example, the extent of clients' rights and relevant limitations), release of information and informed consent, access to services, access to records, participation in the formulation of service plans, options for alternative services and referrals, right to refuse services, termination of services, grievance procedures (when clients want to challenge or appeal adverse decisions or actions), and participation in research and evaluation activities.

2. *Confidentiality and privacy.* The audit should pay considerable attention to a wide range of confidentiality and privacy issues. Key issues include social workers' solicitation of private information from clients; disclosure of confidential information to protect clients from self-harm and to protect third parties from harm inflicted by clients; release of confidential information pertaining to alcohol and substance abuse treatment; disclosure of information about deceased clients; release of information to parents and guardians; sharing of confidential information among participants in family, couples, marital, and group counseling; disclosure of confidential information to media representatives, law enforcement officials, protective service agencies, other social service organizations, and collection agencies; protection of confidential written and electronic records, information transmitted to other parties through the use of computers, electronic mail, facsimile machines, telephones and telephone answering machines, and other electronic or computer technology; transfer or disposal of clients' records; protection of client

confidentiality in the event of the social worker's death, disability, or employment termination; precautions to prevent social workers' discussion of confidential information in public or semipublic areas such as hallways, waiting rooms, elevators, and restaurants; disclosure of confidential information to third-party payers; disclosure of confidential information to consultants; disclosure of confidential information for teaching or training purposes; and protection of confidentiality during legal proceedings (for example, malpractice, divorce, and custody proceedings). Social workers should ensure that they and their staff have a clear and accurate understanding of their obligations to protect confidentiality when served with a subpoena (for example, when and how to resist and challenge a subpoena for written records or oral testimony).

3. *Informed consent.* The ethics audit should closely examine social workers' informed consent documents and procedures to ensure that they comply with current standards. Informed consent procedures should be examined related to social workers' release of confidential information, program admission, service delivery, videotaping, audiotaping, and client participation in research and evaluation activities.

4. *Service delivery.* The ethics audit should assess the extent to which social workers provide services and represent themselves as competent only within the boundaries of their education, training, license, certification, consultation received, supervised experience, or other relevant professional experience. The audit should also examine social workers' use of innovative and nontraditional treatment approaches for which there are no generally recognized standards.

5. *Boundary issues and conflicts of interest.* Boundary issues—where social workers relate to clients or colleagues (including supervisees, trainees, and students) in more than one relationship, whether sexual, social, or business—are among the greatest risks in mental health settings (Berliner 1989; Bullis 1995; Jayaratne, Croxton, and Mattison 1997; Kagle and Giebelhausen 1994; Reamer 1994, 2001c; Strom-Gottfried 1999). Boundary issues occur when social workers face possible or actual conflicts of interest, in the form of "dual" or "multiple" relationships. The ethics audit should assess the extent to which social workers have established clear criteria to help them maintain proper boundaries. Boundary issues that can be especially challenging and problematic include: sexual relationships with current and former clients; counseling of former sexual partners; sexual relationships with clients' relatives or acquaintances; sexual relationships with supervisees, trainees, students, and colleagues; physical contact with clients; friendships with current and former clients; encounters with clients in public settings; attendance at clients' social, religious, or life cycle events; gifts to and from clients; favors for clients; the delivery of services in clients' homes; financial conflicts of

424 • *Ethics, Laws, and Regulations*

interest (for example, borrowing money from or lending money to a client); delivery of services to two or more people who have a relationship with each other (such as couples or family members); barter with clients for goods or services; management of relationships with clients in small or rural communities; self-disclosure to clients; collegial relationships with former clients (for example, when former clients obtain a social work degree and become colleagues); and hiring former clients in one's agency (for example, as case aides).

6. *Documentation.* The ethics audit should pay particular attention to documentation practices and procedures, especially considering their relevance to the delivery of quality services and as evidence in the adjudication of ethics complaints and lawsuits.

7. *Defamation of character.* The ethics audit should examine the extent to which social workers take steps to avoid the use of oral or written language that is harmful to clients and rises to the level of defamation of character. Defamation of character occurs when a social worker says or writes something about a client (or another party) that is untrue, the social worker knew or should have known that the information was untrue, and the communication caused some kind of injury or harm. Defamation can take two forms: libel (when the communication is written) and slander (when the communication is oral).

8. *Client records.* Social workers in mental health settings should assess their polices and procedures for record storage (to ensure confidentiality), retention (to comply with state statutes or relevant contracts with insurers or managed-care organizations), and transfer in the event of the practitioner's disability, incapacitation, termination of practice, or death.

9. *Supervision.* Because of their oversight responsibilities, social work supervisors can be named in lawsuits and ethics complaints. Under the legal doctrines of *vicarious liability* and *respondeat superior* (Latin for "let the master respond"), supervisors may be held partly responsible for the actions or inactions of supervisees (Besharov 1985; NASW 1994; Reamer 1989). The ethics audit should scrutinize supervision procedures—especially their frequency, duration, and content—to ensure their compliance with prevailing standards.

10. *Consultation and referral.* Social workers should examine the criteria they use to determine when consultation with colleagues is required in order to provide competent service, and when client referral is necessary to meet clients' needs. Social workers can be held responsible if they fail to obtain proper consultation, consult with unqualified colleagues, fail to refer clients to colleagues when necessary, or refer clients to unqualified or unethical colleagues.

11. *Fraud.* Social workers should ensure that policies and procedures are in place to prevent fraudulent or falsified invoices (for example, to enhance reimbursement), case notes, and other agency documents.

12. *Termination of services.* Termination of services is a high-risk area, particularly in light of current managed-care policies and procedures (Reamer 1997; Schamess and Lightburn 1998; Strom-Gottfried 1998). To avoid allegations of client abandonment, social workers should assess the adequacy of termination criteria and procedures.

13. *Practitioner impairment.* Relatively recent research has documented the incidence of, and challenges associated with, impaired practitioners in the mental health field (Barker and Branson 2000; Berliner 1989; Bullis 1995; Guy, Poelstra, and Stark 1989; Thoreson, Miller, and Krauskopf 1989; Reamer 1992a). The ethics audit should assess practitioners' and agencies' protocols for identifying, responding to, and preventing impairment among professionals, especially as related to substance abuse and mental illness (Fausel 1988; Schoener and Gonsiorek 1988; Sonnenstuhl 1989; VandenBos and Duthie 1986).

14. *Evaluation and research.* With the increase in research and evaluation efforts in social work and mental health, social workers must ensure that proper policies and procedures are in place to protect client participants, focusing especially on standard "protection of human subjects" guidelines (Grinnell 1997; Reamer 1998; Rubin and Babbie 1997).

15. *Staff development and training.* Perhaps the most effective mechanism to enhance mental health professionals' understanding of and ability to respond to ethical issues and dilemmas is to provide proper training and education. The ethics audit should assess the breadth and depth of social workers' efforts to provide comprehensive ethics education, emphasizing ethical dilemmas in practice and ethics-related risk-management issues.

Social workers' maturing grasp of ethical issues, especially as they pertain to the design and delivery of mental health services, is one of the most significant developments in the profession. Today's social workers have access to an impressive, and expanding, body of knowledge concerning ethical dilemmas and ethics-related risks that were virtually unknown to the profession's earliest practitioners.

What began in the late nineteenth century as social workers' relatively simplistic, and sometimes patronizing, preoccupation with clients' (paupers') morality has evolved into a much more thoughtful, principled, and astute understanding of ethical issues and dilemmas facing contemporary practitioners who are concerned about mental health. For social workers to fulfill the profession's noble purposes, they must critically examine the goodness of fit between the profession's long-standing values—especially its earnest commitment to meeting the needs of the most vulnerable and oppressed citizens—and the attributes of modern-day clinical practice. Above all else, social workers must rededicate themselves to the kind of secular calling that places the common good above self-interest.

References

Austin, K. M., M. E. Moline, and G. T. Williams. 1990. *Confronting Malpractice: Legal and Ethical Dilemmas in Psychotherapy*. Newbury Park, Calif.: Sage.

Barker, R. L. and D. M. Branson. 2000. *Forensic Social Work*. 2d ed. New York: Haworth.

Berliner, A. K. 1989. Misconduct in social work practice. *Social Work* 34:69–72.

Bernstein, B. and T. Hartsell. 1998. *The Portable Lawyer for Mental Health Professionals*. New York: John Wiley.

Besharov, D. 1985. *The Vulnerable Social Worker*. Silver Spring, Md.: NASW.

Billups, J. O. 1992. The Moral Basis for a Radical Reconstruction of Social Work. In P. N. Reid and P. R. Popple, eds., *The Moral Purposes of Social Work,* 100–119. Chicago: Nelson-Hall.

Bullis, R. K. 1995. *Clinical Social Worker Misconduct*. Chicago: Nelson-Hall.

Callahan, D. and S. Bok. 1980. *Ethics Teaching in Higher Education*. New York: Plenum.

Congress, E. P. 1998. *Social Work Values and Ethics*. Chicago: Nelson-Hall.

Fausel, D. E. 1988. Helping the helper heal: Co-dependency in helping professionals. *Journal of Independent Social Work* 3:35–45.

Fletcher, J. C., N. Quist, and A. R. Jonsen. 1989. *Ethics Consultation in Health Care*. Ann Arbor: Health Administration Press.

Foster, L. W. 1995. Bioethical Issues. In R. L. Edwards, ed.-in-chief, *Encyclopedia of Social Work,* 1:292–298. 19th ed. Washington, D.C.: NASW Press.

Frankena, W. K. 1973. *Ethics*. 2d ed. Englewood Cliffs, N.J.: Prentice-Hall.

Gibelman, M. 1995. *What Social Workers Do*. Washington, D.C.: NASW Press.

Gordon, W. E. 1962. Critique of the working definition. *Social Work* 7:3–13.

———. 1965. Knowledge and value: Their distinction and relationship in clarifying social work practice. *Social Work* 10:32–39.

Grinnell, R. M., Jr., ed. 1997. *Social Work Research and Evaluation*. 5th ed. Itasca, Ill.: F. E. Peacock.

Gustafson, J. F. 1982. Professions as "callings." *Social Service Review* 56:501–515.

Guy, J. D., P. L. Poelstra, and M. Stark. 1989. Personal distress and therapeutic effectiveness: National survey of psychologists practicing psychotherapy. *Professional Psychology: Research and Practice* 20:48–50.

Hancock, R. N. 1974. *Twentieth-Century Ethics*. New York: Columbia University Press.

Houston-Vega, M. K., E. M. Nuehring, and E. R. Daguio. 1997. *Prudent Practice: A Guide for Managing Malpractice Risk*. Washington, D.C.: NASW Press.

Jayaratne, S., T. Croxton, and D. Mattison. 1997. Social work professional standards: An exploratory study. *Social Work* 42:187–198.

Kagle, J. D. and P. N. Giebelhausen. 1994. Dual relationships and professional boundaries. *Social Work* 39:213–220.

Kerson, T. S. 2002. *Boundary Spanning: An Ecological Reinterpretation of Social Work Practice in Health and Mental Health Systems.* New York: Columbia University Press.

Kirk, K. and H. Kutchins. 1988. Deliberate misdiagnosis in mental health. *Social Service Review* 62:225–237.

Kutchins, H. and S. A. Kirk 1997. *Making Us Crazy: DSM—the Psychiatric Bible and the Creation of Mental Disorders.* New York: Free Press.

La Puma, J. and D. L. Schiedermayer. 1991. Ethics consultation: Skills, roles, and training. *Annals of Internal Medicine* 114:155–160.

Levy, C. S. 1973. The value base of social work. *Journal of Education for Social Work* 9:34–42.

———. 1976. *Social Work Ethics.* New York: Human Sciences Press.

Linzer, N. 1999. *Resolving Ethical Dilemmas in Social Work Practice.* Boston: Allyn and Bacon.

Loewenberg, F. and R. Dolgoff. 1982. *Ethical Decisions for Social Work Practice.* Itasca, Ill: F. E. Peacock.

———. 1996. *Ethical Decisions for Social Work Practice.* 5th ed. Itasca, Ill.: F. E. Peacock.

Mattaini, M. 1997. *Clinical Practice with Individuals.* Washington, D.C.: NASW Press.

National Association of Social Workers (NASW). 1994. *Guidelines for Social Work Supervision.* Washington, D.C.: NASW.

———. 1996. *NASW Code of Ethics.* Washington, D.C.: NASW.

Pellegrino, E. 1978. Ethics and the moment of clinical truth. *Journal of the American Medical Association* 239:960–961.

———. 1979. Toward a reconstruction of medical morality: The primacy of the act of profession and the fact of illness. *Journal of Medical Philosophy* 4:32–56.

Pumphrey, M. 1959. *The Teaching of Values and Ethics in Social Work.* Vol. 13. New York: Council on Social Work Education.

Rawls, J. 1971. *A Theory of Justice.* Cambridge, Mass.: Harvard University Press.

Reamer, F. G. 1982. *Ethical Dilemmas in Social Service.* New York: Columbia University Press.

———. 1987. Ethics committees in social work. *Social Work* 32:188–192.

———. 1989. Liability issues in social work supervision. *Social Work* 34:445–448.

———. 1992a. The impaired social worker. *Social Work* 37:165–170.

———. 1992b. Social Work and the Public Good: Calling or Career? In P. N. Reid and P. R. Popple, eds., *The Moral Purposes of Social Work,* 11–33. Chicago: Nelson-Hall.

———. 1994. *Social Work Malpractice and Liability.* New York: Columbia University Press.

———. 1995. Social Work in Health Care. In W. T. Reich, ed.-in-chief, *Encyclopedia of Bioethics,* 2405–2407. 2d ed. New York: Macmillan.

———. 1997. Ethical Standards in Social Work: The NASW Code of Ethics. In R. L. Edwards, ed.-in-chief, *Encyclopedia of Social Work,* Suppl., 113–123. 19th ed. Washington, D.C.: NASW Press.

———. 1998. *Social Work Research and Evaluation Skills: A User-Friendly Approach.* New York: Columbia University Press.

———. 1999. *Social Work Values and Ethics.* 2d ed. New York: Columbia University Press.

———. 2001a. *Ethics Education In Social Work.* Alexandria, Va.: Council on Social Work Education.

———. 2001b. *The Social Work Ethics Audit: A Risk Management Tool.* Washington, D.C.: NASW Press.

———. 2001c. *Tangled Relationships: Managing Boundary Issues in the Human Services.* New York: Columbia University Press.

Reamer, F. G. and Abramson, M. 1982. *The Teaching of Social Work Ethics.* Hastings-on-Hudson, N.Y.: Hastings Center.

Rhodes, M. L. 1986. *Ethical Dilemmas in Social Work Practice.* London: Routledge and Kegan Paul.

Ross, W. D. 1930. *The Right and the Good.* Oxford: Clarendon Press.

Rubin, A. and E. Babbie. 1997. *Research Methods for Social Work.* 3d ed. Pacific Grove, Calif.: Brooks/Cole.

Saleebey, D., ed. 1997. *The Strengths Perspective in Social Work Practice.* 2d ed. New York: Longman.

Schamess, G. and A. Lightburn, eds. 1998. *Humane Managed Care?* Washington, D.C.: NASW Press.

Schoener, G. R. and J. Gonsiorek. 1988. Assessment and development of rehabilitation plans for counselors who have sexually exploited their clients. *Journal of Counseling and Development* 67: 227–232.

Siegler, M. 1978. A legacy of Osler: Teaching ethics at the bedside. *Journal of the American Medical Association* 239:951–956.

———. 1979. Clinical ethics and clinical medicine. *Archives of Internal Medicine* 139:914–915.

Siporin, M. 1982. Moral philosophy in social work today. *Social Service Review* 56:516–538.

Sloan, D. 1980. The Teaching of Ethics in the American Undergraduate Curriculum, 1876–1976. In D. Callahan and S. Bok, eds., *Ethics Teaching in Higher Education,* 1–57. New York: Plenum.

Sonnenstuhl, W. J. 1989. Reaching the impaired professional: Applying findings from organizational and occupational research. *Journal of Drug Issues* 19:533–539.

Specht, H. and M. Courtney. 1994. *Unfaithful Angels: How Social Work Has Abandoned Its Mission.* New York: Free Press.

Strom-Gottfried, K. 1998. Is "ethical managed care" an oxymoron? *Families in Society* 79:297–307.

———. 1999. Professional boundaries: An analysis of violations by social workers. *Families in Society* 80:439–449.

Teel, K. 1975. The physician's dilemma: A doctor's view. What the law should be. *Baylor Law Review* 27:6–9.

Thoreson, R. W., M. Miller, and C. J. Krauskopf. 1989. The distressed psychologist: Prevalence and treatment considerations. *Professional Psychology: Research and Practice* 20:153–158.
VandenBos, G. R. and R. F. Duthie. 1986. Confronting and Supporting Colleagues in Distress. In R. R. Kilburg, P. E. Nathan, and R. W. Thoreson, eds., *Professionals in Distress: Issues, Syndromes, and Solutions in Psychology,* 211–231. Washington, D.C.: American Psychological Association.
Woody, R. H. 1997. *Legally Safe Mental Health Practice.* Madison, Conn.: Psychosocial Press.

Chapter 23
Managed Care and Mental Health

Kevin Corcoran, Stephen Gorin, and Cynthia Moniz

Introduction

Managed care is a mess. What was once a promising and simple notion of cost containment and quality assurance has mutated to a complex, confusing, and—some believe—inefficient and ineffective system of care. Some people believe that "bean counters with M.B.A.'s" interfere with the autonomy of the patient and providers' beneficent professional decision making, while concomitantly encouraging managed-care organizations (MCOs) to enroll healthy people who need few services. Others are "true believers" and swear that managed care has saved money. In spite of these differences, few could argue that in an entrepreneurial society like the United States, if government does not provide a good or service, private industry will. Such is the case for managed health and mental health care. The result, in part, is that we no longer have patients, clients, and consumers but rather "covered-lives" and "enrolled members." Currently, however, managed care is facing dramatic new challenges, primarily because of recent efforts to implement the Health Insurance Portability and Accountability Act of 1996 (HIPAA; PL 104-191) and legal challenges to the practices of managed-care organizations (*Cicio v. Vytra Healthcare*, 2003 and *Kentucky Association of Health Plans v. Miller*, 2003).

This chapter examines managed mental health care in its current, though rapidly changing, structure and function. It provides an overview of the origins of managed care and presents concerns about parity between physical and mental health. It also provides new information about the potential impact of recent federal actions and federal court cases on managed care, and it concludes with a discussion of managed care's ability to contain costs and assure quality in the delivery of services.

The Development of Managed Care

During the first third of the twentieth century, health care in the United States underwent fundamental change (Patel and Rushefsky 1999). Inspired by developments in Europe and considerably influenced by Abraham Flexner, medical schools introduced more scientifically based and standardized curricula. In response to the inability of many people to afford medical care and the threats of insolvency during the Great Depression, hospital and medical societies developed Blue Cross and Blue Shield, which offered indemnity insurance and encouraged "commercial carriers" to enter the market (Starr 1982). Consequently, physicians succeeded in consolidating their authority and control over the health care system.

The result was what Dranove (2000) calls "Marcus Welby medicine." In this system, general practitioners worked in individual offices, and patients selected their own practitioner, who diagnosed problems and prescribed treatment. Physicians billed patients or insurers for services. The American Medical Association went to great lengths to defend this system against encroachment from "private corporations" or "agencies of government" (Starr 1982:200), including the earliest forms of health maintenance organizations. In 1938 the federal government indicted the AMA and its affiliates for violating antitrust laws. Although the Supreme Court upheld these charges, the AMA succeeded in persuading state legislatures to enact laws that hindered the development of prepaid group practices (Starr 1982).

There were exceptions to "Marcus Welby medicine." During the 1930s and 1940s, industrialist Henry J. Kaiser built clinics offering prepaid care to his employees; he did so partly because of the wage and price controls that were in place in the wartime economy. Kaiser reasoned that if he could not lure workers with higher salaries, he could offer them benefits. After the war, Kaiser opened this plan to the public under the name Kaiser-Permanente. Other prepaid systems, such as the Group Health Cooperative of Puget Sound and the Health Insurance Plan of New York, also emerged during the postwar era (see Moniz and Gorin 2003).

Perhaps the most serious challenge to "Marcus Welby medicine" came during the early 1970s, when health care costs accelerated rapidly (Kotelchuck 1976). In 1969 Richard Nixon warned that health care inflation threatened "a breakdown in our medical system" (cited in Starr 1982:381). For advice in dealing with this issue, Nixon turned to Paul Ellwood, a Minnesota physician and longtime critic of the fee-for-service system, which Ellwood believed led doctors to provide too much care (Starr 1982). Ellwood argued that the government should provide new incentives by encouraging the development of prepaid group practices, which, in exchange for an annual fee, would offer preventive and comprehensive health care services

(Ellwood et al. 1976). These prepaid group practices, or Health Maintenance Organizations (HMOs), would reward physicians for preventing illness and disease.

In 1973 Congress enacted the HMO Act (PL 93-222), which nullified state laws that had restricted the development of prepaid group practices, provided loans and grants for the development of HMOs, and required businesses that insured their workers to offer an HMO option (Robinson 1999). The law also stipulated that HMOs needed to offer comprehensive benefits, include consumers in governance, and charge no more than "traditional forms of health insurance" (Patel and Rushefsky 1999:173).

The HMO Act changed the definition of prepaid health care. In prepaid plans like Kaiser's, physicians worked exclusively for the organization, as either salaried employees or part of a group of providers (Dranove 2000). HMOs included not only the prepaid plans but also independent practice associations, which reimbursed independent physicians on a fee-for-service basis (Starr 1982). Moreover, while the original prepaid plans were non-profits, the Nixon administration encouraged for-profit entities to enter the emerging HMO industry (Rothfeld 1976). Despite this, HMOs grew slowly and by the end of the decade, they still existed primarily on the West Coast and in Minnesota, which was Ellwood's home state (Dranove 2000).

Additionally, the federal government attempted to control costs with the introduction of a prospective payment system of a particular amount per procedure, known as Diagnostic Related Groups (DRGs). The federal government essentially said to providers, "Take it or leave it," which was possible since Medicare represented 25 percent of all hospital costs. Payments were determined in advance, on the basis of the primary and secondary diagnosis and comorbidity conditions. Payments were predicated on the hospital and conditions as a whole and not on all the other possible services that might be part of patient care (Moniz and Gorin 2003).

Managed care continued to change during the 1980s, when continuing inflation and the election of Ronald Reagan helped fuel the development of market-based efforts. Much of the impetus for this reform came from corporations, which found it increasingly expensive to provide health care coverage (Patel and Rushefsky 1999). Thus the concept of managed care was born. In addition to DRGs, managed care referred to a range of techniques, including selective contracting, capitation, and utilization review, aimed at promoting competition among providers and controlling patients' access to care (Dranove 2000). By 1988 managed care had assumed a dominant role in the nation's health care system.

The Emergence of Managed Behavioral Health Care

For several reasons, DRGs did not initially apply to mental health care in psychiatric hospitals or psychiatric units in general hospitals. First, of the 468 diagnostic groups, only 15 related to psychiatric conditions, and 9 of those were different classifications of substance abuse. This was hardly comprehensive. Second, the major psychiatric diagnostic group in use was psychosis, which lumped together several specific psychiatric conditions that were distinguishable by severity and required different lengths of hospitalization (Namerow and Gibson 1988). Third, the psychiatric DRGs inadequately predicted the use of services, which contributed to random underpayment and overpayment (Namerow and Gibson 1988). Mental health conditions were not, however, exempt from government efforts to control costs. Chief among the efforts was prospective payment authorized through the Tax Equity and Fiscal Responsibility Act of 1982, which allowed the enrollment of Medicare patients in HMOs (see Moniz and Gorin 2003).

Not surprisingly, with the federal government as a role model, business soon followed suit. As managed care grew, insurers began to apply its techniques to mental health and substance abuse treatment, or behavioral health care. This resulted largely from the development of effective psychotropic medications in the early 1950s, since the prescription of medications traditionally had been a covered benefit of insurance. In 1999 around 78% of individuals with health insurance belonged to a managed behavioral health care plan (MBHC) (Findlay 1999). This, however, requires further clarification, since MBHC plans include different types of managed care. The Institute of Medicine (Callahan 2001) identified ten types of managed care, including five types of HMOs (staff model, group model, network model, individual or independent practice association model, and some combination of those four), Preferred Provider Organizations (PPOs), Point of Service (POS) plans, Management Service Organizations (MSO), Employee Assistance Programs (EAPs), and the general term, managed behavioral health care organizations. With these overlapping distinctions in mind, it is understandable why Mechanic argues that managed care is "simply a framework" (1999).

Wernet (1999) notes that managed care has five essential elements of implementation, regardless of structural or organizational differences. These elements are (1) contracts on performance and capitation of costs, (2) policy of directing members to less-expensive services, such as clinical social work rather than psychiatry, (3) preauthorization of services to determine medical necessity for treatment, (4) utilization reviews to assess quality of care and the need for continuing care, and (5) case management or care management for high-volume and high-cost users of services. Of the 78 percent of individuals enrolled in a MBHC plan, Findlay (1999) found, almost 20 percent belonged to plans with case management and utilization review services, while 24 percent belonged to plans with EAPs. Twenty-eight percent belonged to plans in which insurers assume "risk," or financial responsibility for treatment, and 21 percent to non-"risk" plans, in which employers contract out administrative services only.

Insurers often separate mental health and substance abuse treatment from other services and contract them out to specialized providers, thus creating "carve-out" programs. Carve-out plans rely on many of the same techniques as other MCOs to control costs, especially capitation and utilization reviews (Freeman and Trabin 1994). Carve-outs also limit the availability of services, often impose copayments, and determine payments to providers prospectively. By 2002, 164 million individuals belonged to managed behavioral health carve-out plans (Open Minds 2002).

State governments have also used MBHC plans, including carve-outs, to reduce Medicaid costs (Holahan et al. 1998). Massachusetts developed the first mental health and substance abuse carve-out in 1992 and in its first year succeeded in lowering costs by about 20 percent without lowering quality (Callahan et al. 1995). By 1998 fifteen states had introduced MBHC carve-outs for Medicaid recipients (U.S. Department of Health and Human Services 1999). According to Mechanic and McAlpine (1999), managed care seems able to reduce Medicaid costs without having an adverse impact on quality.

Mental Health Parity and Quality of Services

The spread of MBHC has important implications for the debate over mental health parity. In 1996 Congress enacted legislation requiring insurers to provide the same coverage for mental health treatment as they do for other forms of care (U.S. General Accounting Office 2000). However, as Mechanic and McAlpine (1999) point out, by lowering costs, managed care allows insurers to expand behavioral health care benefits. At the same time, by promoting uniformity of care across patient populations, managed care can reduce the intensity of care for individuals with severe mental illnesses (Mechanic and McAlpine 1999).

Burnam and Escarce (1999) argue that under managed care, parity in itself is insufficient, because it does not guarantee "equity" in relation to other medical services. Accordingly, the larger issue is not ensuring parity but "equal health value for dollars spent" (Burnam and Escarce 1999:28). One way of achieving this would be for policymakers to stipulate that a treatment costing, say, $500 would have to "provide at least $700 worth of health benefits, whether it is a mental health or a general medical service" (Burnam and Escarce 1999:29). Gitterman, Sturm, and Scheffler (2000), however, believe that such a position could undermine steps toward parity. They believe that equity is more important to providers, who view it as a way to thwart carve-outs and preserve psychiatrists' incomes.

Besides the cost-containment framework of managed care, the other defining feature is quality assurance. Utilization reviews and case management are particularly notable examples in MBHC. Managed care strives for quality assurance in principle because no one—policy analyst, politician, provider, or consumer—would tolerate the idea of containing costs without an assurance of maintaining quality. After all, what better way to contain costs than to let most enrolled members suffer and die, and then share the profits with the stockholders or the savings with taxpayers? Thus, the idea of concomitantly assuring quality has always been the teaspoon of sugar that helps the medicine of managed care go down.

The primary means of assuring quality in managed mental health care has been the use of more-efficacious treatments. These interventions are based on data from controlled studies where the results are summarized using meta-analysis or the consensus of experts (Vandiver 2002). Such interventions, if implemented correctly, should result in change in the problem. More often than not, these are short-term treatments with observable goals and are often delineated in manuals and protocols.

Recent Developments in Managed Care

Managed care has undergone dramatic change since the implementation of the Health Insurance Portability and Accountability Act of 1996 (HIPAA; PL 104-191) and two federal court cases from 2003. HIPAA addresses privacy interests of consumers in both private and public settings, while the court cases concern consumer choice of providers and the liability of MCOs.

Privacy, or the lack thereof, has been a concern in a system like managed care for more than a decade (Corcoran and Winslade 1994). In almost all types of managed care, information once considered confidential between a patient and provider is now accessible to other personnel. While this practice may be common in insurance law, where the payer has a right to know what most Americans believe to be confidential, in managed care the organization may not actually pay the bill but may simply control the cost. In the mental health arena this practice allows MCOs to eavesdrop on the fifty-minute hour (Corcoran and Winslade 1994) and breach the sine qua non of clinical practice—confidentiality. Confidentiality is an important ethical issue for every professional mental health organization (Winslade and Ross 1985); it fosters trust and disclosure, and encourages those in need of mental health services to actually seek them. MCOs undermine this by soliciting confidential information about mental health conditions, treatment procedures, progress, and outcomes.

Confidentiality emerges from the privacy rights guaranteed by the U.S. Constitution. It emerges from the combination of five enumerated rights, as follows: the First Amendment right to associate, the Third Amendment prohibition against quartering soldiers "in any house" during times of peace without consent, the Fourth Amendment "right of the people to be secure in their persons, houses, paper and effects, against unreasonable searches and seizures," the Fifth Amendment right against self-incrimination, and the Ninth Amendment protection that certain rights shall not be construed to deny or disparage other rights. This combination of rights is known as a penumbra, which is the right to privacy. It is itself a fundamental right and the basis of reproductive rights (e.g., *Roe v. Wade,* 1973). Confidential information, however, is not private information, since it has been disclosed to another. Thus, confidentiality is not a fundamental right and allows for easier intrusion if a state has a rationale for gaining access to confidential information that outweighs the individual's right to keeping the information private (*Whalen v. Roe,* 1977). Confidential information, then, may be disclosed in a number of circumstances, such as the well-known duty to protect (*Tarasoff v. Regents of the University of California,* 1976). In the case of managed care, the exception is information that is related to health payments.

Clearly, the easily stated "right to privacy" is complicated—and even more so when it comes to confidential information. This is more complex yet when it comes to medical records, especially electronic medical records and information disclosed across different state jurisdictions (Winslade 1982). In essence, confidentiality of the content of mental health services is not as protected as most people think it is, and the context of services is even less so. The federal enactment of HIPAA changed all that.

Much of the intent of HIPAA was to assure the portability of insurance policies, allow for coverage even with preexisting conditions and for all health conditions, and encourage medical savings accounts. It also addressed the need to simplify the filing of insurance claims with a single form, which MCOs are likely to support since there are nearly four hundred different forms currently in use (Seifert 2003). However, HIPAA also addresses privacy, establishing a minimum floor for protecting medical information, physical and mental alike. It allows patients access to their records and prohibits the release of information unless the individual from whom the information is sought authorizes it.

HIPAA is the first federal standard that includes medical records, regardless of whether that information is written, electronic, or even orally available.

There are, of course, exceptions, such as—but not limited to—public health, national security, terrorist concerns, and some issues of law enforcement. Just about all medical information is protected from wrongful disclosure under HIPAA, even demographic information, or any information about a health or mental health condition from the past, present, or future. The information is protected if the person can be identified. HIPAA has far-reaching effects, and every single American who seeks provider services after April 14, 2003, will receive written notice of HIPAA.

The Impact of HIPAA on Managed Care

HIPAA, unquestionably, affects managed care, as enumerated in the law. It prohibits the unauthorized release of information for commercial purposes, such as releasing information to pharmaceutical companies, insurance providers, or marketing firms. In general, the release of information authorized under HIPAA is restricted to disclosure for purposes of bettering treatment, thus allowing communication between providers and specialists, although only the minimum information necessary for treatment is to be disclosed. The impact of HIPAA also includes rather routine aspects of practice. For example, information must be protected and access restricted. This means that playing back an audio answering machine at a volume within earshot of other patients in a waiting room would be unlawful. Similarly, something as simple as a receptionist saying loudly to a provider, "Captain Kirk will be a little late picking up his Viagra prescription," or even the routine use of a cellular telephone on public airwaves, is likely a violation of HIPAA.

Much of health and mental health care practice will change because of HIPAA. This is especially so since the law imposes civil and criminal penalties. The civil penalties are rather lenient, only $100 fine per violation. This is far less than most traffic citations, but has a maximum of $25,000 fine per year. For knowingly obtaining individually identifiable information, however, the fines can range up to $50,000 and one year imprisonment, $100,000 and five years imprisonment for obtaining information under false pretenses, and $250,000 and ten years imprisonment for selling, transferring, or using information for commercial advantages, personal gain, or malicious harm. Many of these practices, such as selling mailing lists and recruiting clients, have been routine in managed care.

It is conclusive, then, that much of managed care has already changed because of HIPAA, and yet it is a newly implemented law, and much remains unknown about its impact. The Office of Civil Rights (www.hhs.gov/ocr/hipaa), the agency charged with enforcing HIPAA, will play an important role in the implementation of these regulations and our understanding of these changes. However, it will be critical for all in managed care to monitor the development of HIPAA as the regulations are clarified and the thin light of the penumbra is brightened.

Autonomy and Beneficence: Case Law

A second major change in managed care also has occurred on the federal level in the form of two dramatic court cases. One concerns who determines what provider a client sees, and the other concerns the liability of a managed-care company when a requested treatment is unauthorized. The first issue is one of individual autonomy in selection of a provider, which social work ethics calls self-determination. Beneficence, in contrast, refers to providing the best care possible and is part of the legal basis for malpractice or negligent care.

Autonomy in selecting a provider may be restricted in managed care, since available providers are those who agree to a reduced rate of payment. Many states, about half, have passed "any willing provider" laws, which allow a client to select his or her own provider under the conditions that the provider accepts the reduced payment and holds the patient harmless for the difference in cost between the reduced rate and the regular fee. This last condition is important because it means "any willing provider" cannot use managed care to subsidize the higher fee by having the patient pay the balance.

Kentucky is a state with two "any willing provider" laws, one for chiropractic benefits and the other prohibiting discrimination against "any willing provider who is . . . willing to meet the terms and conditions for participation established by the . . . insurer" (*Kentucky Association of Health Plans, Inc. v. Miller, Commissioner, Kentucky Department of Insurance*, 2003:1). The Kentucky Association of Health Plans filed suit, claiming the law was preempted by the Employee Retirement Income Security Act of 1974. Known as ERISA, this complicated federal law protects workers' insurance coverage. ERISA preempts state laws "insofar as they . . . relate to any employee benefit plan" (29 U.S.C. 8, section 1144[b][2][A]). While it may sound like splitting hairs, the lower courts and the Supreme Court reasoned that the law "regulates insurance" and not insurance plans. The justices averred that this was saved from preemption because the laws were specific to the insurance industry and that the laws that have some general application to insurers do not necessarily fall under ERISA. The Court also reasoned that the "any willing provider" laws do not prohibit or regulate providers. Boring as this may sound, the impact is dramatic in that it allows for states to require "any willing provider" to see clients even if they are not part of an MCO's "chosen few." This simply means a state can enact laws to force HMOs—and thus all managed-care organizations—to open up their networks, and by so doing significantly broaden the scope of choices of providers (i.e., autonomy).

The insurance industry and most MCOs screamed that this ruling would drive up costs and erode quality, while providers, and the health care industry in general, praised the ruling as a victory for patient choice. The eventual impact will take years to determine, but one result is not in dispute. Consumer choice is expanded, and the debate turns to the balance of cost and access.

Beneficence in managed care is addressed in *Cicio v. Vytra Healthcare* (2003), heard by the Second U.S. Circuit Court of Appeals in New York. This case dealt with utilization reviews and the practice of medicine, or possibly the malpractice of medicine, by an MCO. Utilization reviews occur when preauthorization for services is required to determine if the condition is "medically necessary" and if the procedure is covered under the managed-care plan. The facts of *Cicio* are tragic. Bonnie Cicio sued Vytra Healthcare, the physician doing the utilization review, and others for the wrongful death of her husband, Carmine. The case avers that Vytra denied the needed and necessary treatment for Carmine's melanoma, and because Vytra did so, he died. The chief issue in *Cicio* was whether conducting a utilization review determines whether there are benefits covered under the plan or whether a utilization review is the practice of medicine. As is imaginable, some argue that utilization reviews are interfering with the practice of physical and mental health care by determining what is appropriate for intervention in a particular case, while others assert that it avails a wider range of services. The court reached a well-reasoned decision that at times a utilization review is merely to determine if a requested procedure is within the purview of the health benefits plan. At other times the denial of a procedure and recommendation of another intervention may be "a patient-specific prescription . . . and, ultimately, a medical decision" (14), and at still other times it may be both. Only the first option is preempted from state courts by ERISA; the other two are not. While this simply means that Bonnie Cicio may have her case heard in state court, it has dramatic effects on a major structure of managed care. *Cicio* means that MCOs are not protected from utilization review decisions, that such decisions may be "quasi-medical in nature and necessarily involve evaluations," and therefore may be malpractice.

The full impact of *Cicio* will take time to assess. It is certain, though, that the decision in this case will affect utilization reviews across the country and not just in the jurisdiction of the Second Court of Appeals. Some argue that it puts the decision making back in the able hands of the provider. Others argue that it undermines managed care, restricts the right to control cost, and will spell a return to the high costs of the "fee-for-services" approach. Whether or not the case will be appealed to the Supreme Court remains to be seen, and whether they would hear it or overturn it is unknown. In the meantime, *Cicio* speaks loudly and serves as a wake-up call to all MCOs by establishing that they are legally responsible for some of the decisions made with utilization reviews. MCOs are now firmly tied into the liability loop of physical and mental health care malpractice, such that cost containment may prove quite costly.

Conclusions: Prospects for Cost Containment and Quality Assurance

With the above discussion in mind, it seems only predictable to turn to the question of managed care and its impact on health and mental health care. In particular, does it contain costs and assure quality? The answers depend almost exclusively on who responds to the questions. "True believers" in managed care swear, "Oh, my, yes!" Providers tend to scream "No!" The truth is likely some combination of both.

Several studies have shown that MBHC can control costs (e.g., Frank, McGuire, and Newhouse 1995; Ma and McGuire 1998). Other studies suggest that cost savings are available only during a robust economy and that health care inflation has returned (see Moniz and Gorin 2003). Equally important, however, others say it impedes access and quality (Galambos 1999; Davidson, Davidson, and Keigher 1999). Here the evidence is less than clear-cut. The surgeon general's report on mental health found few studies of MBHC's impact on access, making generalization difficult (U.S. Department of Health and Human Services 1999). The question of quality is also unclear, with some studies finding that MBHC has a positive impact on quality of care and others showing a negative impact (U.S. Department of Health and Human Services 1999; Mechanic and McAlpine 1999; Burnam and Escarce 1999).

The debate over efficiency of managed care in containing cost and the effectiveness of assuring quality is like a stick: there are two sides to it, no matter how long or short the stick is. In all likelihood, there have been savings, and these saving may be in the short term. The available data simply are not persuasive—except to those whose minds are already made up, regardless of the facts. It is equally as probable that in some circumstances, quality is assured and in others quality is adversely affected. This is part of the reason we believe that managed care is a mess. To be sure, the old days when "complete care" was defined by the pecuniary limits of the insurance coverage are gone. Similarly, the old days when there was no motivation for mental health providers to use anything but "one size fits all" interventions relying on long-term and insight-oriented therapy are also gone. Therefore, while managed care is a mess, as this chapter evidences, it is an ever-changing mess and, it is to be hoped, a mess that is improving. Although it is probably less messy than unmanaged care, it is still, at times, mismanaged care.

References

Burnam, M. A. and J. J. Escarce. 1999. Equity in managed care for mental disorders. *Health Affairs* 18 (5): 22–31.

Callahan, J. J. 2001. Foreword to N. W. Veeder and W. Peebles-Wilkins, eds., *Managed Care Services: Policy, Programs, and Research.* New York: Oxford University Press.

Callahan, J. J., D. S. Shepard, R. H. Beinecke, M. J. Larson, and D. Cavanaugh. 1995. Mental health/substance abuse treatment in managed care: The Massachusetts Medicaid experience. *Health Affairs* 14 (3): 173–184. *Cicio v. Vytra Healthcare* (Second Court of Appeals, 2003).

Corcoran, K. and W. J. Winslade. 1994. Eavesdropping on the 50-minute hour: Managed mental health care and confidentiality. *Behavioral Sciences and the Law* 12:351–365.

Davidson, T., J. R. Davidson, and S. M. Keigher. 1999. Managed care: Satisfaction guaranteed . . . not! *Health and Social Work* 24 (3): 163–168.

Dranove, D. 2000. *The Economic Evolution of American Health Care.* Princeton, N.J.: Princeton University Press.

Ellwood, P. M., Jr., N. N. Anderson, J. E. Billings, R. J. Carlson, E. J. Hoagberg, and W. McClure. 1976. Health Maintenance Strategy. In D. Kotelchuck, *Prognosis Negative: Crisis in the Health Care System.* New York: Vintage Books.

Findlay, S. 1999. Managed behavioral health care in 1999: An industry at a crossroads. *Health Affairs* 18:116–225.

Frank, R. G., T. G. McGuire, and J. P. Newhouse. 1995. Risk contracts in managed mental health care. *Health Affairs* 14:50–64.

Freeman, M. A. and T. Trabin. 1994. Managed behavioral healthcare: History, models, key issues, and future course. Washington, D.C.: U.S. DHHS, Center for Mental Health Services. October 5.

Galambos, C. 1999. Resolving ethical conflicts in a managed care environment. *Health and Social Work* 24 (3): 191–197.

Gitterman, D. P., R. Sturm, and R. M. Scheffler. 2000. Toward full mental health parity and beyond. *Health Affairs* 20:68–75.

Goldman, W., J. McCulloch, and R. Sturm. 1998. Costs and use of mental health services before and after managed care. *Health Affairs* 17 (2): 40–52.

Holahan, J., S. Zuckerman, A. Evans, and S. Rangarajan. 1998. Medicaid managed care in thirteen states. *Health Affairs* 17:43–63.

Kentucky Association of Health Plans, Inc. v. Janie A. Miller, Commissioner, Kentucky Department of Insurance, 538 U.S. __ (2003).

Kotelchuck, D., ed. 1976. *Prognosis Negative: Crisis in the Health Care System.* New York: Vintage Books.

Ma, C. A. and T. G. McGuire. 1998. Costs and incentives in a behavioral health carve-out. *Health Affairs* 17 (2): 53–69.

Mechanic, D. 1999. *Mental Health and Social Policy: The Emergence of Managed Care.* Boston: Allyn and Bacon.

Mechanic, D. and D. D. McAlpine. 1999. Mission unfulfilled: Potholes on the road to mental health parity. *Health Affairs* 18 (5): 7–21.

Moniz, C. and S. Gorin. 2003. *Health and Health Care Policy: A Social Work Perspective.* Boston: Allyn and Bacon.

Namerow, M. J. and R. W. Gibson. 1988. Prospective Payment for Private Psychiatric Specialty Hospitals: The National Association of Private Psychiatric Hospitals' Prospective Payment Study. In Scherl, D. J., English, J. T., and Sharfstein, S. S., eds., *Prospective Payment and Psychiatric Care,* 41–53. Washington, D.C.: American Psychiatric Press.

Open Minds. 2002. Managed behavioral health and employee assistance program enrollment reaches 227 million in 2002. October 30. Retrieved February 21, 2004, from http://www.openminds.com/pressroom/mbhoyearbook02.htm.

Patel, K. and M. E. Rushefsky. 1999. *Health Care Politics and Policy in America.* Armonk, N.Y.: Sharpe. *Roe v. Wade,* 410 U.S. 113 (1973).

Rothfeld, M. 1976. Sensible Surgery for Swelling Medical Costs. In D. Kotelchuck, ed., *Prognosis Negative: Crisis in the Health Care System,* 352–358. New York: Vintage Books.

Seifert, P. 2003. What is HIPAA? *PSR Connection* 2:1, 3.

Starr, P. 1982. *The Social Transformation of American Medicine.* New York: Basic Books. *Tarasoff v. Regents of the University of California,* 551 P 2nd 334 (1976).

U.S. Department of Health and Human Services. 1999. *Mental Health: A Report of the Surgeon General.* Rockville, Md.: U.S. DHHS, Center for Mental Health Services. December.

U.S. General Accounting Office. 2000. *Mental Health Parity Act: Despite New Federal Standards, Mental Health Benefits Remain Limited.* Washington, D.C.: U.S. General Accounting Office. May.

Vandiver, V. L. 2002. Step-by-Step Practice Guidelines for Using Evidence-Based Practice and Expert Consensus in Mental Health Settings. In A. R. Roberts and G. J. Greene, eds., *Social Work Desk Reference,* 731–738. New York: Oxford University Press.

Wernet, S. P. 1999. *Managed Care in Human Services.* Chicago: Lyceum. *Whalen v. Roe,* 410 U.S. 113 (1977).

Winslade, W. J. 1982. Confidentiality and medical records. *Journal of Legal Medicine* 3:497–525.

Winslade, W. J. and J. W. Ross. 1985. Privacy, confidentiality, and autonomy in psychotherapy. *Nebraska Law Review* 43:118–131.

Chapter 24

Involuntary Medication of the Mentally Ill: Continuing Controversy, Changing Scene

Donald T. Dickson

Setting the Stage: Law and Mental Illness

Law, psychiatry, and mental illness have a long, complex, and uneasy relationship. Legal definitions of mental illness differ from clinical ones. In all states individuals who are mentally ill under a legal definition and dangerous to self or others may be involuntarily committed to institutional settings by means of civil commitment proceedings. Such proceedings are substantially different from trials in the criminal justice system. For example, there is no constitutional requirement that those appearing in civil commitment hearings be provided with counsel, although a number of states through state statutes have elected to do so. The degree of proof in these hearings, clear and convincing evidence, required by the U.S. Supreme Court's *Addington,* 1978, ruling, is a lower standard than the beyond-a-reasonable-doubt standard required for criminal trials. States by statute may impose a higher standard of proof—and some do, but this is not a constitutional requirement. In civil commitments, rules of evidence are more relaxed, jury trials usually are not available, and the individual facing commitment may or may not be present at the hearing. All of this is because the confinement of the mentally ill is a civil, as opposed to a criminal, proceeding. The grounds for commitment are often that the individual meets a legal definition of mental illness and is a danger to self or society, and the rationale for commitment is treatment, not punishment. While incarceration in a correctional facility is time bound, for the most part limited by the sentence imposed, length of confinement to a mental institution depends on when—or if—the patient becomes legally sane or is no longer a danger to self or others.

Mentally Ill Who Commit Crimes: Not Guilty by Reason of Insanity; Not Competent to Stand Trial

In all states, some mentally ill individuals who commit a criminal act may avoid criminal prosecution if they are found not guilty by reason of insanity. While states have different formulations, the general policy is the same. To be tried for a criminal act, the individual must have committed the act and have the criminal intent (*mens rea*). Without the *mens rea,* there can be no criminal offense. Many states still use the *M'Naghten* rule, formulated in England in 1843. Typical of these is the insanity defense statute of New Jersey, which states: "A person is not criminally responsible for conduct if at the time of such conduct he was laboring under such a defect of reason, from disease of the mind as not to know the nature and quality of the act he was doing, or if he did know it, that he did not know what he was doing was wrong" (N.J.S.A. §2C:4-1).

In short, if the individual through a defect of reason does not know right from wrong or does not know the nature and quality of his or her action, he or she cannot be tried in a criminal proceeding

A somewhat different situation occurs if an individual, although legally sane at the time of the commission of the allegedly criminal act, becomes mentally incapacitated sometime after arrest but before trial. In the American legal system, an individual must be competent to aid in his or her own defense in criminal proceedings. If the individual cannot, then he or she may be judged not competent to stand trial and cannot be tried in a criminal proceeding until competence is regained.[1]

Medication of the Mentally Ill

Most competent mentally ill adults, as is the case with any competent adult, may choose to use or not to use medication.[2] This has been held by some courts to be a constitutional right and has at times been codified into state statutory law. The right to refuse medication falls within the larger privacy right of adults to accept or refuse treatment. Some courts have found this to be part of a privacy right in the Fourteenth Amendment protection of liberty; others have found it in state constitutions. The U.S. Supreme Court in the *Cruzan* decision found the right to refuse treatment in the common law right of informed consent:

> At common law, even the touching of one person by another without consent and without legal justification was a battery. Before the turn of the century, this Court observed that "[n]o right is held more sacred,

or is more carefully guarded, by the common law, than the right of every individual to the possession and control of his own person, free from all restraint or interference of others, unless by clear and unquestionable authority of law." This notion of bodily integrity has been embodied in the requirement that informed consent is generally required for medical treatment. . . . The logical corollary of the doctrine of informed consent is that the patient generally possesses the right not to consent, that is, to refuse treatment. . . . The Fourteenth Amendment provides that no State shall "deprive any person of life, liberty, or property, without due process of law." The principle that a competent person has a constitutionally protected liberty interest in refusing unwanted medical treatment may be inferred from our prior decisions.
(*Cruzan*, 1990, at 278)

Medication of the Mentally Ill Against Their Will: The Mental Health System

In 1978 a federal district court in New Jersey held that a patient at a state mental hospital, who had been involuntarily committed, had a constitutional right to refuse treatment, specifically a right to refuse medication. The right was a qualified one, with four factors to be considered when applying it: "(1) the patient's physical threat to other patients and staff at the institution, (2) the patient's capacity to decide on his particular treatment, (3) the existence of any less restrictive treatments, and (4) the risk of permanent side effects from the proposed treatment" (*Rennie*, 1978, at 1144). The patient's lawsuit was later expanded to a class action on behalf of all involuntarily committed and voluntarily admitted mental hospital patients at five large state mental hospitals in New Jersey. In a lengthy opinion, the federal district court judge reaffirmed this right when psychotropic medications were used and set forth a number of conditions, including informed consent requirements, patient advocates, and a procedural process by which patients could appeal medication decisions. Judge Brotman wrote:

Ancora Psychiatric Hospital is a state facility for the mentally ill. . . . It houses about 1000 patients at any one time. . . . Marlboro Psychiatric Hospital is a state facility . . . with a patient population of approximately 800. Greystone Park Psychiatric Hospital . . . has a population of 1100. Trenton Psychiatric Hospital . . . has about 1000 patients. The hospitals are understaffed and patients have trouble seeing psychiatrists. . . . One expert testified that drugs are the "be all and end all" at the hospitals. The medical director of Marlboro states in an office memorandum that the hospital "uses medication as a form of control and as a substitute for treatment." A 1975 study of these institutions found overuse of drugs and inadequate record-keeping. The pattern of drug usage appears to be no different than that of other large state institutions, which was described in an article by Dr. George Crane, a psychiatrist who testified at the hearings: Many physicians, nurses, guardians, and family members who resent the patient's behavior and are threatened by potential acts of violence fail to distinguish between manifestations of illness and reactions to frustrations. Hence, drugs are prescribed to solve all types of management problems, and failure to achieve the desired results causes an escalation of dosage, changes of drugs, and polypharmacy. . . . Neuroleptics are often used for solving psychological, social, administrative, and other nonmedical problems. (*Rennie,* 1979, at 1299)

The decision was appealed to the U.S. court of appeals for the third circuit, part of the second tier of federal courts, where the decision was modified but upheld. That court ruled:

We hold that mental patients who are committed involuntarily to state institutions nevertheless retain a constitutional right to refuse antipsychotic drugs that may have permanently disabling side effects. The state may override that right when the patient is a danger to himself or others, but in non-emergency situations must first provide procedural due process. We further determine that the informal administrative procedures established by New Jersey meet constitutional standards, and accordingly, modify a district court injunction that required a formal adversary hearing and other measures before a patient's refusal can be overridden.
(*Rennie,* 1981, at 838)

The *Rennie* decision was appealed to the U.S. Supreme Court, but was remanded to the circuit court for reconsideration in light of an intervening Supreme Court decision. The third circuit court affirmed the qualified constitutional right of involuntarily committed mental hospital patients to refuse pyschotropic medications and the procedures developed by the state (*Rennie,* 1983). Since then, the right of involuntarily committed patients in the mental health system to refuse psychotropic medication under certain conditions has remained the law in many of the states: under non-emergent conditions, involuntarily committed patients have a right to refuse medication, although that right can be overridden in some circumstances, and the controversy has abated.

Involuntary Medication of the Mentally Ill in the Criminal Justice System

Almost a decade after *Rennie,* the U.S. Supreme Court faced a similar issue in the criminal justice system: whether the State of Washington could medicate a prisoner against his will. The Court held in *Washington v. Harper,* 1990, that "given the requirements of the prison environment, the Due Process Clause permits the State to treat a prison inmate who has a serious mental illness with antipsychotic drugs against his will, if the inmate is dangerous to himself or others and the treatment is in the inmate's medical interest" (*Washington,* 1990, at 227).

The inmate, Walter Harper, had been involuntarily medicated with antipsychotic drugs for what was first diagnosed as a manic-depressive disorder and later as schizophrenia, for a period of almost four years.[3] The involuntary medication took place under the prison's policy:

> First, if a psychiatrist determines that an inmate should be treated with antipsychotic drugs but the inmate does not consent, the inmate may be subjected to involuntary treatment with the drugs only if he (1) suffers from a "mental disorder" and (2) is "gravely disabled" or poses a "likelihood of serious harm" to himself, others, or their property.
> (*Washington,* 1990, at 243)

The Court found:

> The extent of a prisoner's right . . . to avoid the unwanted administration of antipsychotic drugs must be defined in the context of the inmate's confinement. The Policy under review requires the State to establish, by a medical finding, that a mental disorder exists which is likely to cause harm if not treated. Moreover, the fact that the medication must first be prescribed by a psychiatrist, and then approved by a reviewing psychiatrist, ensures that the treatment in question will be ordered only if it is in the prisoner's medical interests, given the legitimate needs of his institutional confinement. These standards, which recognize both the prisoner's medical interests and the State's interests, meet the demands of the Due Process Clause.
> (*Washington,* 1990, at 222)

On the basis of briefs filed and oral argument, the Court was satisfied that the medication would be used only for treatment:

We therefore agree with the State's representations at oral argument that, under the Policy, antipsychotic medications can be administered only for treatment purposes, with the hearing committee reviewing the doctor's decision to ensure that what has been prescribed is appropriate. The legitimacy, and the necessity, of considering the State's interests in prison safety and security are well established by our cases. In *Turner v. Safley* . . . we held that the proper standard for determining the validity of a prison regulation claimed to infringe on an inmate's constitutional rights is to ask whether the regulation is "reasonably related to legitimate penological interests." This is true even when the constitutional right claimed to have been infringed is fundamental, and the State under other circumstances would have been required to satisfy a more rigorous standard of review.
(*Washington*, 1990, at 224)

While treatment was emphasized, prison safety was not ignored by the Court:

The State has undertaken the obligation to provide prisoners with medical treatment consistent not only with their own medical interests, but also with the needs of the institution. Prison administrators have not only an interest in ensuring the safety of prison staffs and administrative personnel, but the duty to take reasonable measures for the prisoners' own safety. . . . Where an inmate's mental disability is the root cause of the threat he poses to the inmate population, the State's interest in decreasing the danger to others necessarily encompasses an interest in providing him with medical treatment for his illness. Special Offender Center Policy 600.30 is a rational means of furthering the State's legitimate objectives. Its exclusive application is to inmates who are mentally ill and who, as a result of their illness, are gravely disabled or represent a significant danger to themselves or others. The drugs may be administered for no purpose other than treatment, and only under the direction of a licensed psychiatrist. There is considerable debate over the potential side effects of antipsychotic medications, but there is little dispute in the psychiatric profession that proper use of the drugs is one of the most effective means of treating and controlling a mental illness likely to cause violent behavior.
(*Washington*, 1990, at 226)

In his dissent, Justice Stevens wrote:

> The record of one of Walter Harper's involuntary medication hearings
> . . . notes: "Inmate Harper stated he would rather die than take med-
> ication." That Harper would be so opposed to taking psychotropic
> drugs is not surprising: as the Court acknowledges, these drugs both
> "alter the chemical balance in a patient's brain" and can cause irre-
> versible and fatal side effects. The prolixin injections that Harper was
> receiving at the time of his statement exemplify the intrusiveness of
> psychotropic drugs on a person's body and mind. Prolixin acts "at all
> levels of the central nervous system as well as on multiple organ sys-
> tems." It can induce catatonic-like states, alter electroencephalographic
> tracings, and cause swelling of the brain. Adverse reactions include
> drowsiness, excitement, restlessness, bizarre dreams, hypertension,
> nausea, vomiting, loss of appetite, salivation, dry mouth, perspiration,
> headache, constipation, blurred vision, impotency, eczema, jaundice,
> tremors, and muscle spasms. As with all psychotropic drugs, prolixin
> may cause tardive dyskinesia, an often irreversible syndrome of un-
> controllable movements that can prevent a person from exercising basic
> functions such as driving an automobile, and neuroleptic malignant
> syndrome, which is 30% fatal for those who suffer from it. The risk of
> side effects increases over time.
> (*Washington,* 1990, at 240)

One concern of Justice Stevens was that medication could be used for
control rather than treatment:

> Policy 600.30 permits forced administration of psychotropic drugs on
> a mentally ill inmate based purely on the impact that his disorder has
> on the security of the prison environment. The provisions of the Policy
> make no reference to any expected benefit to the inmate's medical
> condition. Use of psychotropic drugs, the State readily admits, serves
> to ease the institutional and administrative burdens of maintaining
> prison security and provides a means of managing an unruly prison
> population and preventing property damage.
> (*Washington,* 1990, at 245)

Involuntary Medication to Produce Competence

In *Washington v. Harper,* the Court established that while a prisoner retained
a constitutional liberty interest to avoid involuntary medication, this right

could be overridden for treatment purposes, and perhaps as Justice Stevens indicated, inmate control purposes as defined as protection of the prisoner, others, or property.

A somewhat different issue is raised in litigation around involuntary medication of individuals in the criminal justice system at the pretrial stage. Can these individuals be forced to take antipsychotic medication to achieve competence and allow a criminal trial to proceed?

In *Riggins v. Nevada,* 1992, the accused, while in custody but before trial, voluntarily undertook a course of treatment with Mellaril, an antipsychotic drug. At a subsequent competency hearing, he was determined to be competent to stand trial. He later asked to be taken off the drug, but his request was denied. He appealed his conviction, arguing "that forced administration of Mellaril denied him the ability to assist in his own defense and prejudicially affected his attitude, appearance, and demeanor at trial." Relying on *Washington v. Harper,* the Supreme Court reversed the appellate court, which had upheld Riggins's conviction for murder, stating:

> Under *Harper,* forcing antipsychotic drugs on a convicted prisoner is impermissible absent a finding of overriding justification and a determination of medical appropriateness. The Fourteenth Amendment affords at least as much protection to persons the State detains for trial. ... Thus, once Riggins moved to terminate administration of antipsychotic medication, the State became obligated to establish the need for Mellaril and the medical appropriateness of the drug.
> (*Riggins,* 1992, at 135)

The court indicated that forced medication could be appropriate under certain conditions:

> Although we have not had occasion to develop substantive standards for judging forced administration of such drugs in the trial or pretrial settings, Nevada certainly would have satisfied due process if the prosecution had demonstrated, and the District Court had found, that treatment with antipsychotic medication was medically appropriate and, considering less intrusive alternatives, essential for the sake of Riggins' own safety or the safety of others.
> (*Riggins,* 1992, at 135)

The court also indicated that medication could be permissible to allow the trial: "Similarly, the State might have been able to justify medically appropriate, involuntary treatment with the drug by establishing that it could not obtain an adjudication of Riggins' guilt or innocence by using less intrusive means." But the court noted: "The question whether a competent criminal defendant may refuse antipsychotic medication if cessation of medication would render him incompetent at trial is not before us (*Riggins*, 1992, at 136).

The issue of involuntary medication of a mentally ill individual for the purpose of making the person competent to stand trial was the question in *Sell v. U.S.*, 2003, decided by the U.S. Supreme Court. Sell was charged with a range of counts including Medicaid fraud, mail fraud, and money laundering. Subsequently there were charges of witness intimidation and conspiring to kill a witness. Both Sell's psychologist and the government psychologist diagnosed Sell with delusional disorder, persecutory type. A federal district court judge held a competency hearing and found that Sell was suffering from a mental disease or defect rendering him incompetent to assist properly in his defense, and thus incompetent to stand trial. He was committed to a federal hospital, where two psychiatrists determined that he was in need of antipsychotic medication and that this was the only way to restore his competence. Sell refused the medication and was overruled by the hospital hearing officer, who determined that the medication was the treatment of choice for his delusional symptoms. At a later hearing, a district court judge determined that there was insufficient evidence to show that Sell was a danger to himself, but that involuntary medication could proceed to restore his competence. Sell appealed to the U.S. court of appeals for the eighth circuit. That court agreed that there was insufficient evidence that Sell posed a danger to himself. However, the court held that forced medication could be appropriate for the purpose of restoring competence if there was an essential governmental interest at stake that outweighed Sell's interest in remaining free of medication, if there was no less intrusive means to accomplish this purpose and if the medication was medically appropriate (*U.S. v. Sell*, 2002, at 567).

In a brief filed to the U.S. Supreme Court by the American Psychiatric Association, it was noted that there are now injectable forms of some of the antipsychotic medications with fewer side effects (Am. Psychiatric Assoc. Brief, 2003, at 5). The association supported the position that medication was in Sell's interest and that side effects could be controlled.

A somewhat different perspective was presented by the American Psychological Association in its amicus brief:

When a trial court concludes that non-drug therapy would not be effective in restoring a particular defendant to competency, the court should not simply assume, however, that coercive administration of drugs would be appropriate for that defendant. Antipsychotic drugs can indeed be highly effective and in many cases are medically appro-

priate. On the other hand, there is a highly significant difference between the government's purpose in a case like this—coercively restoring a defendant to competence—and the usual situation in which a health-care professional treats a willing patient. Because the individual has a strong interest in avoiding unwanted medications, the trial court should order coercive administration of antipsychotic drugs only if it is persuaded that the specific medications that the government proposes to administer have a substantial likelihood of success in restoring the defendant to competence, and that that likelihood of success clearly outweighs the possible side effects.
(Am. Psychological Assoc. Brief, 2002, at 3)

Another concern was the potential effect of the medications on Sell's demeanor in a subsequent trial:

There are at least three different ways in which these medications may impair a defendant's fair trial rights. First, antipsychotic drugs can appear to "flatten or deaden [the recipient's] emotional responses," making the defendant look "so calm or sedated as to appear bored, cold, unfeeling, and unresponsive." Such alterations in the defendant's demeanor—whether he is testifying on his own behalf or simply sitting next to counsel—can cause "serious prejudice . . . if [the] medication inhibits the defendant's capacity to react and respond to the proceedings and to demonstrate remorse or compassion." Second, the well documented side effects of restlessness, Parkinsonian tremors, muscle spasms, and slurred speech can adversely affect the jury's opinion of a defendant. Third, antipsychotic drugs may undermine the defendant's ability to participate effectively in his own defense by dulling his cognition, and thus compromising his "interaction with counsel, or his comprehension at trial."
(Am. Psychological Assoc. Brief, 2002, at 25)

The U.S. Supreme Court vacated the appellate court decision and remanded the case for further hearing on whether Sell was a danger to himself or others, whether the side effects of the medication would hinder his defense and whether the government's interest in his prosecution had diminished in that Sell has remained in custody for an extensive period of time. Justice Breyer, writing for the majority, declared:

[T]he Constitution permits the Government involuntarily to administer antipsychotic drugs to a mentally ill defendant facing serious criminal charges in order to render that defendant competent to stand trial,

but only if the treatment is medically appropriate, is substantially unlikely to have side effects that may undermine the fairness of the trial,
and, taking account of less intrusive alternatives, is necessary significantly to further important governmental trial-related interests.
(*Sell,* 2003, at 25)

He noted: "This standard will permit involuntary administration of drugs
solely for trial competence purposes in certain instances. But those instances
may be rare" (*Sell,* 2003, at 25).

Among the factors to be considered are (1) There must be an important
governmental interest at stake, particularly that the crime must be of a serious
nature. However, the Court noted that special circumstances should be considered, such as the length of time the individual has and will be confined,
which might lessen the risks of release, might make a subsequent trial more
difficult, and could be credited against any future sentence. (2) The court
must find that the forced medication is "substantially likely" to make the
defendant competent to stand trial and "substantially unlikely" to have side
effects that will "interfere significantly" with the defendant's ability to assist
counsel in conducting a defense. (3) The court must find that the forced
medication is "necessary" and that "alternative, less intrusive treatments are
unlikely to produce substantially the same results." (4) The court must find
that the drugs are "medically appropriate," and in the patient's best interests
(*Sell,* 2003, at 26–29).

The Court emphasized that forced medication could be appropriate on
other grounds, such as dangerousness to self or others, and in these situations,
the criteria are clearer and more objective, and experts can balance risks of
side effects and benefits of treatment, as is often the case in civil proceedings.
The Court concluded:

When a court must nonetheless reach the trial competence question,
the factors discussed above . . . should help it make the ultimate constitutionally required judgment. Has the Government, in light of the
efficacy, the side effects, the possible alternatives, and the medical appropriateness of a particular course of antipsychotic drug treatment,
shown a need for that treatment sufficiently important to overcome
the individual's protected interest in refusing it? . . . The Government
may pursue its request for forced medication on the grounds discussed
in this opinion, including grounds related to the danger Sell poses to
himself or others. Since Sell's medical condition may have changed
over time, the Government should do so on the basis of current
circumstances.
(*Sell,* 2003, at 32, 37)

In his decision, Justice Breyer suggests that involuntary medication for the purpose of competence, while not prohibited, may be uncommon, but the decision permits the state to resort to involuntary medication when it is medically indicated or when the individual poses a danger. However, it appears that the state may, using the one of these rationales, nonetheless employ forced medication, which also may result in competence for the purpose of a criminal trial. In these situations, the issues raised by the American Psychological Association remain.

Involuntary Medication of the Mentally Ill and Capital Punishment

In the eighth circuit's decision on *Sell,* the court was careful to emphasize that the decision applied only to restoring competence for the purposes of standing trial. The appellate court observed: "Furthermore, we note that an entirely different case is presented when the government wishes to medicate a prisoner in order to render him competent for execution. . . . Therefore, our holding must be read narrowly" (*U.S. v. Sell,* 2002, at 571).

In an earlier decision, *Ford v. Wainwright,* 1986, the U.S. Supreme Court held that the execution of an insane prisoner was an unconstitutional violation of the Eighth Amendment prohibition of cruel and unusual punishment:

> [T]his Court is compelled to conclude that the Eighth Amendment prohibits a State from carrying out a sentence of death upon a prisoner who is insane. Whether its aim be to protect the condemned from fear and pain without comfort of understanding, or to protect the dignity of society itself from the barbarity of exacting mindless vengeance, the restriction finds enforcement in the Eighth Amendment.
> (*Ford,* 1986, at 409).

Ford had been sentenced to death in 1974 for committing murder. However, by 1982, he had become delusional, believing that he was a target of conspiracies, that his relatives were being taken hostage and tortured, that prominent political leaders were being taken hostage, and that as the pope only he could help them. Two psychiatrists found Ford to be insane. Following this, state-appointed psychiatrists found Ford competent to stand trial, and he appealed. The U.S. Supreme Court held that there should be an evidentiary hearing to determine Ford's sanity and that it was unconstitutional to execute an insane person. In this, the Court, drawing upon English common law as well as a review of state statutes, concluded:

> Today, no State in the Union permits the execution of the insane. It is clear that the ancient and humane limitation upon the State's ability to execute its sentences has as firm a hold upon the jurisprudence of today as it had centuries ago in England. The various reasons put forth in support of the common-law restriction have no less logical, moral, and practical force than they did when first voiced. For today, no less than before, we may seriously question the retributive value of executing a person who has no comprehension of why he has been singled out and stripped of his fundamental right to life. Similarly, the natural abhorrence civilized societies feel at killing one who has no capacity to come to grips with his own conscience or deity is still vivid today. And the intuition that such an execution simply offends humanity is evidently shared across this Nation. Faced with such widespread evidence of a restriction upon sovereign power, this Court is compelled to conclude that the Eighth Amendment prohibits a State from carrying out a sentence of death upon a prisoner who is insane. Whether its aim be to protect the condemned from fear and pain without comfort of understanding, or to protect the dignity of society itself from the barbarity of exacting mindless vengeance, the restriction finds enforcement in the Eighth Amendment
> (*Ford,* 1986, at 408)

While holding that it was unconstitutional to execute an insane person, the Court in *Ford* never clarified what constituted sanity or the insanity that would prohibit an execution. This is a critical issue, for if the state is constitutionally prohibited from executing an insane inmate, then, on the basis of the previous discussion, can the state rely on involuntary medication to make the person competent to be executed? That question is raised in *Singleton v. Norris,* 2003.[4] Charles Singleton was sentenced to death in 1979. Subsequently he was first voluntarily and then involuntarily medicated for a psychosis. In the federal court of appeals case, Singleton argued that while he could be involuntarily medicated during a stay of execution under *Washington v. Harper,* when that stay ended, he could not be medicated for the purpose of making him sane, and under *Ford v. Wainwright* he could not be executed if insane. Relying upon its previous decision in *Sell,* the court of appeals for the eighth circuit held that involuntary medication of Singleton was permissible:

> In *Sell,* we held that the government had an "essential interest" in bringing Sell to trial that outweighed his liberty interest in refusing medica-

456 • *Ethics, Laws, and Regulations*

tion. . . . Society's interest in punishing offenders is at its greatest in the narrow class of capital murder cases in which aggravating factors justify imposition of the death penalty. This societal interest must be weighed against Singleton's interest in being free of unwanted antipsychotic medication. The record before us indicates that Singleton prefers to take the medication rather than be in an unmedicated and psychotic state. In addition, Singleton has suffered no substantial side effects. On these facts, the State's interest in carrying out its lawfully imposed sentence is the superior one. . . . The Eighth Amendment forbids the execution of an incompetent person, thus the State may achieve its essential interest in carrying out Singleton's sentence of execution only if Singleton is competent. In its report, the district court concluded that without medication Singleton would revert to a delusional psychotic state, but it is uncertain whether he would also become *Ford*-incompetent. On this record, treatment with antipsychotic drugs is necessary to alleviate Singleton's psychosis, and there is no less intrusive medical treatment by which the government can ensure Singleton's competence. . . . The factor that Singleton contends takes him outside the scope of *Harper* is not the existence of serious harmful side effects or an insufficient medical need, but the very psychosis–reducing effect of the medicine. By focusing on his "ultimate best medical interest," Singleton presents the court with a choice between involuntary medication followed by execution and no medication followed by psychosis and imprisonment. Faced with these two unpleasant alternatives, he offers a third solution: a stay of execution until involuntary medication is no longer needed to maintain his competence.

Singleton's argument regarding his long-term medical interest boils down to an assertion that execution is not in his medical interest. . . . In the circumstances presented in this case, the best medical interests of the prisoner must be determined without regard to whether there is a pending date of execution. Thus we hold that the mandatory medication regime, valid under the pendency of a stay of execution, does not become unconstitutional under *Harper* when an execution date is set. . . . A State does not violate the Eighth Amendment as interpreted by *Ford* when it executes a prisoner who became incompetent during his long stay on death row but who subsequently regained competency through appropriate medical care.
(*Singleton*, 2003, at 1024)

Justice Heaney dissented, arguing that medication and then execution was a violation of *Ford* and questioning whether drug–induced sanity is really sanity:

I believe that to execute a man who is severely deranged without treatment, and arguably incompetent when treated, is the pinnacle of what Justice Marshall called "the barbarity of exacting mindless vengeance." Singleton has been forced to take antipsychotic medication, the stated goal of which is to stabilize his mental condition. However, receiving treatment is not synonymous with being cured. Antipsychotic drugs "merely calm and mask the psychotic symptoms which usually return to debilitate the patient when the medication is discontinued." Thus, when antipsychotic medication results in an improved mental state, the patient is merely displaying what has been termed "artificial" or "synthetic" sanity. One of the pitfalls of equating true sanity with its medically-coerced cousin is that drug-induced sanity is temporary and unpredictable: "the effect of psychoactive drugs on a particular recipient is uncertain; the drugs may affect the same individual differently each time they are administered." Based on the medical history in this case, I am left with no alternative but to conclude that drug-induced sanity is not the same as true sanity. Singleton is not "cured;" his insanity is merely muted, at times, by the powerful drugs he is forced to take. Underneath this mask of stability, he remains insane. *Ford*'s prohibition on executing the insane should apply with no less force to Singleton than to untreated prisoners.
(*Singleton,* 2003, at 1030)

Justice Heaney also questioned whether the motives of the state, medication for treatment, and medication for execution could be distinguished:

The problem with pinning the constitutionality of a prisoner's execution to the State's intent in forcibly medicating him is that it will often be difficult to determine whether the State is medicating a prisoner to protect him from harming himself or others, or whether the State is medicating the inmate to render him competent for execution. Moreover, such an inquiry rests on the faulty assumption that the State maintains one exclusive motive for its actions. Here, even the majority recognizes two competing State interests: the safety of the prison guards and inmates (including Singleton), and its interest in exacting punishment. In light of the record, it is simply illusory for our court to conclude that it can discern the State's single, directed motivation for forcibly medicating.
(*Singleton,* 2003, at 1036)

As for the medical ethics involved in involuntary medication for the purposes of execution, Justice Heaney observed:

Lastly, I am compelled to note that the majority holding will inevitably result in forcing the medical community to practice in a manner contrary to its ethical standards. Physicians are duty bound to act in the best interest of their patients. ("Under the Hippocratic Oath, the physician pledges to do no harm and to act only in the best medical interests of his patients.") Consequently, the ethical standards of both the American Medical Association and the American Psychiatric Association prohibit members from assisting in the execution of a condemned prisoner. Needless to say, this leaves those doctors who are treating psychotic, condemned prisoners in an untenable position: treating the prisoner may provide short-term relief but ultimately result in his execution, whereas leaving him untreated will condemn him to a world such as Singleton's, filled with disturbing delusions and hallucinations.

(*Singleton,* 2003, at 1036)

Continuing Controversy, Changing Scene

In *Sell v. U.S.,* the U.S. Supreme Court has limited the use of forced medication to produce competence for a criminal trial, although involuntary medication is still permissible if it is in the individual's best interests or necessary for protection of self or others, and this may result in restoring competence for a criminal trial. In these situations, the myriad questions around demeanor, ability to assist in a defense, and artificial competence remain. *Singleton's* petition for a hearing before the U.S. Supreme Court was denied in *Singleton v. Norris,* 124 S. Ct. 74 (2003).

Over the two decades since the *Rennie* decision, the range of psychotropic medications has expanded, and their side effects have been reduced but not eliminated. Involuntary medication has been used for management and control purposes, as well as for patient/inmate safety and treatment. More recently, involuntary medication has been used to produce actual competence or the appearance of competence, and perhaps actual sanity or the appearance of sanity. While the scene has changed, from the state mental hospital to the criminal justice system, many of the controversial issues remain, among them: How is the purpose of the involuntary medication to be determined— is it being used in the patient/inmate's best interests for treatment or for the institutional/justice system's interest in control, trials and executions? If the purpose is solely patient treatment or safety, there is no problem. If the purpose is solely to produce competence for trials for less serious offenses or to produce competence to execute prisoners, it is questionable and, according to some courts, illegal. Can medication used for medically appropriate purposes be used if it results in the more questionable outcomes? If the state argues that it is using the medications for both treatment/safety and management/competence to stand trial or be executed, is the existence of a medically appropriate purpose sufficient, no matter what other purposes may be involved? Finally, as Justice Heaney argues, how can it be determined whether the state really has a medically acceptable purpose, such as treatment, rather than simply the desire for trials or executions?

One other issue needs to be addressed. Psychiatrists have a role in prescribing medications for those with mental illnesses, including prescribing antipsychotic drugs for the treatment of certain forms of mental illness. In institutional settings, psychiatrists, among others, have had a role in prescribing medications for treatment but also in prescribing medications that have resulted in patient/inmate management and control. More recently, the role has included medication to restore competence for criminal trials or for executions. The ethical issues that existed two decades ago in the forced medication for nonmedical purposes such as patient management have re-emerged in the forced medication of individuals for nonmedical purposes of legal competency to be tried or executed. The controversy continues.

Notes

1. States employ different standards of mental competence and incompetence. For example, the New Jersey statutes provide:

a. No person who lacks capacity to understand the proceedings against him or to assist in his own defense shall be tried, convicted or sentenced for the commission of an offense so long as such incapacity endures. b. A person shall be considered mentally competent to stand trial on criminal charges if the proofs shall establish: (1) That the defendant has the mental capacity to appreciate his presence in relation to time, place and things; and (2) That his elementary mental processes are such that he comprehends: (a) That he is in a court of justice charged with a criminal offense; (b) That there is a judge on the bench; (c) That there is a prosecutor present who will try to convict him of a criminal charge; (d) That he has a lawyer who will undertake to defend him against that charge; (e) That he will be expected to tell to the best of his mental ability the facts surrounding him at the time and place where the alleged violation was committed if he chooses to testify and understands the right not to testify; (f) That there is or may be a jury present to pass upon evidence adduced as to guilt or innocence of such charge or, that if he should choose to enter into plea negotiations or to plead guilty, that he comprehend

the consequences of a guilty plea and that he be able to knowingly, intelligently, and voluntarily waive those rights which are waived upon such entry of a guilty plea; and (g) That he has the ability to participate in an adequate presentation of his defense.
(N.J.S.A. §2C:4-4)

2. Minors who are legally incompetent may be treated differently.

3. According to the Court, the drugs administered to Harper included Trialafon, Haldol, Prolixin, Taractan, Loxitane, Mellaril, and Navane.

4. The issue has been raised in other cases as well. See, for example, *State of Louisiana v. Perry*, 610 S. 2d. 746 (1992), where the Louisiana Supreme Court found it unconstitutional under the state constitution to medicate an insane prison inmate against his will in order to restore sanity and execute him. The court imposed a stay of execution until Perry regained sanity without the use of psychotropic drugs.

References

Addington v. Texas, 441 U.S. 418 (1978).
American Psychiatric Association et al. "Amicus Curiae Brief in Support of the Respondent, Sell v. U.S." *2002 U.S. Briefs* 5664 (January 22, 2003).
American Psychological Association. "Amicus Curiae Brief Sell v. U.S." *2002 U.S. Briefs* 5664 (December 19, 2002).
Cruzan v. Director, Mo. Health Dept., 497 U.S. 261 (1990).
Ford v. Wainwright, 477 U.S. 399 (1986).
The M'Naghten Case, 8 Eng. Rep. 718 (1843).
New Jersey Statutes Annotated (N.J.S.A.) Title 2.
Rennie v. Klein, 462 F. Supp. 1131 (1978).
Rennie v. Klein, 476 F. Supp. 1294 (1979).
Rennie v. Klein, 653 F. 2d 836 (1981).
Rennie v. Klein, 720 F. 2d 266 (1983).
Riggins v. Nevada, 504 U.S. 127 (1992).
Sell v. U.S., 2003 U.S. LEXIS 4594 (2003).
Singleton v. Norris, 124 S. Ct. 74 (2003).
Singleton v. Norris, 319 F. 3d 1018 (2003).
U.S. v. Sell, 282 F. 3d 560 (2002).
Washington v. Harper, 494 U.S. 210 (1990).

Author Index

Subject Index

Conflicts of interest, considerations for ethics audit, 351–52, 354–55, 423–24

Construct development: reliability of measurements, 121–22; role of theory in, 123–24; science of, 121; validity, 122–23

Consultation and referrals, considerations for ethics audit, 424

Consumer-operated self-help services, 206–7

Content validity, 122

Context, social. *See* Social context in mental disorders

Contextual systems for assessment. *See* Assessment, contextual systems for; Social context in mental disorders

Continuing education, obligations of mental health industry/system, 258, 274

Contraception, 154

Control groups, requirement for, 173

Cost issues. *See* Economic issues

Court cases involving mentally ill persons: *Addington v. Texas,* 443; *Cicio v. Hydra Healthcare,* 439–40; *Cruzan v. Director, Missouri Health Department,* 444–45; *Ford v. Wainwright,* 454–55; *Kentucky Association of Health Plans, Inc. v. Miller, Commissioner, Kentucky Department of Insurance,* 438; *N'Naghten Case,* 444; *Rennie v. Klein,* 445–46; *Riggins v. Nevada,* 450–51; *Sell v. U.S.,* 451–54, 458; *Singleton v. Norris,* 455–58; *Washington v. Harper,* 447–49; *see also* Legal issues

Credentialing and licensing of mental health professionals, 260, 416

Criterion validity, 122

Critical thinking: contributions to ethical practice, 247–48, 251–52, 264–65; description of, 248–49; history of lapses in, 252; honest brokering of knowledge and ignorance, 262; propaganda, prevalence of, 252–62; relationship to EBP, 252; *see also* EBP (evidence-based practice)

CROs (contract research organizations), 353

Cruzan v. Director, Missouri Health Department, 444–45

Cultural colonialism: categorical systems supporting, 66; contextual systems tending to avoid, 74; dimensional systems addressing needs, 78

Database searches. *See* EBP (evidence-based practice)

Deductive-nomological method, 124–26

Defamation of character, considerations for ethics audit, 424

Deficits perspective. *See* Discourse of deficit

Depression: clinical trials of Prozac for children, 359–62; as culturally normative among Flathead people, 68; effect of drugs on self-identity, 390–91; efficacy of guideline-concordant care, 279; evaluation of psychotherapy's effectiveness, 319–20; evidence for substandard care, 273; explaining clinical characteristics, 132; medication versus psychotherapy, 279; meta-analysis of randomized trials, 313–14; TMAP guidelines for treatment, 275; unchanged or increased incidence, 347–48

Diagnosis: client protection from, 112; gnosis and, 37–40; knowledge of DSM as prerequisite, 36; legitimizing existing power, 197; misdiagnosis, results of, 110; as narrowing of concept of assessment, 14; overall error rates, 107; polythetic and monothetic, 124; probability of error, 109; signs, symptoms, syndromes defined, 126; theory-neutrality, 123–24; *see also* Assessment; Social context in mental disorders; Strengths perspective

Diagnostic strengths manual, 36–37

Diagnostic value, 58

Dignity, 192–94

Dimensional systems for assessment, 64, 71–73, 78

Disciplinary matrices, 62

Discourse of deficit: clients as carriers of personal pathology, 65; deviance as impaired character, 323–24; DSM as definer, 23–26; effects of, 26–29; psychiatric treatment/medication as stigmatizing, 388, 389; *see also* Strengths perspective

medicalized view of mental illness, 414; strengths perspective's clash with, 414; *see also* Biological psychiatry; Psychotropic drugs

Medication, involuntary, of mentally ill persons: coercive treatments, 175–78, 180, 182, 183; continuing controversy and change, 458–59; in criminal justice system, 447–49; individuals facing capital punishment, 454–58; individuals who commit crimes, 444; in mental health system, 445–47; to produce competence, 449–54; refusal through privacy or informed consent rights, 444–45; relationship between law and mental illness, 443

Medications/drugs. *See* Psychotropic drugs

Men and mental health. *See* Gender differences in mental health

Mental health industry/system: bureaucratization of care reimbursement, 8–9; credentialing and licensing, 260, 416; hugeness, 247; inflated claims of effectiveness, 259–60; maintenance and expansion of turf, 253; provider-driven practice, 191, 196, 197, 199; psychotherapy and, 299–302; reimbursement pressure, 89–90; *see also* Economic issues; Managed care/managed behavioral health care (MBHC)

Mental health practice guidelines. *See* Practice guidelines, mental health

Mental hygiene, 159n18

Mental illness: as "deficit" defined by DSM, 23–26; biological, biomedical model and approaches, conceptual errors, 131–32, 184; as commodity and opportunity for profit, 78; conduct disorder (CD), 45–46; as dysfunction, 84; DSM's definition of, 84–85; first- and second-generation, 65–66; government efforts to control costs of care, 433; grounds for commitment, 443; ignorance of causes and cure, 9; individuals who commit crimes, guilt and incompetence issues, 444; percent of persons seeking treatment for, 104; practices, policies, and controversies of 1960s, 1–3; prevalence rates and esti-

mates, 96–97, 103–4, 107, 109–10; probability of correct diagnosis, 96–102; psychiatricization of everyday troubles, 6–9; reductionist view of, 264; right to refuse medication, 444–47; signs, symptoms, syndromes defined, 126; social work and, 3–6; tolerance and acceptance, 8; treatment as goal of mental health professions, 294; treatment through social work, 293, 307; *see also* Biological psychiatry

Meta-analysis of psychotherapeutic outcome research, 312–15

Meta-ethics, 412

Minimal distributive justice: compared to benevolence, 305–6; confusions and refutations, 302–4; limited to "basic" good, 304; relationship to alleviation of mental disorder, 297–98; self-respect as integral, 301

Monothetic diagnosis, 124

Mood stabilizers. *See* Psychotropic drugs

MPSI (Multi-Problem Screening Inventory), 73

Mutual assistance. *See* Self-help programs

Naming of oppression, reality, and experience, 190, 193, 195–96

Narratives, social work providing, 304

NASW Code of Ethics, 420–21

Nazi racial politics, 153

NCS (National Comorbidity Survey), 56, 103, 104

Negative diagnosis, true and false, 96–102, 105–7

Nguzo Saba (Seven Pillars) principles, 74

N'Naghten Case, 444

Objectification of clients in provider-driven practice, 196, 197, 199

Office of Civil Rights, 437

Parole of inmates, 147–48

Passivity, 394–96

Paternalism of ACT, 177, 183

Patience as quality in strengths perspective, 37

Patient preferences, 282

Paxil (paroxetine), 361–62

Pedigree study, 158n7